COMPUTER

CONCEPTS & MICROSOFT® OFFICE 2013

COMPUTER
CONCEPTS & MICROSOFT® OFFICE 2013

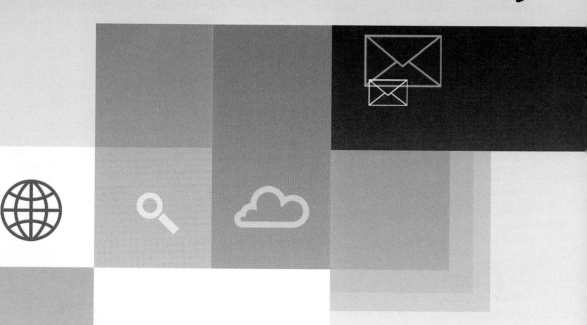

Denise Seguin
Fanshawe College, London, Ontario

PARADIGM
EDUCATION SOLUTIONS

St. Paul

Director of Editorial:	Christine Hurney
Developmental Editor:	Spencer Cotkin
Production Editor:	Lori Michelle Ryan
Cover and Text Designer:	Leslie Anderson
Senior Design and Production Specialists:	Jaana Bykonich, Jack Ross
Copy Editor:	Susan Capecchi
Indexer:	Schroeder Indexing Services

We have made every effort to trace the ownership of all copyrighted material and to secure permission from copyright holders. In the event of any question arising as to the use of any material, we will be pleased to make the necessary corrections in future printings. Thanks are due to the aforementioned authors, publishers, and agents for permission to use the materials indicated.

ISBN 978-0-76385-187-3 (Text + Disc)
ISBN 978-0-76385-183-5 (Text)
ISBN 978-0-76385-483-6 (eBook)

Brief Contents

Contents

Chapter 5
Communicating and Scheduling Using Outlook.....................**127**

Chapter 6
Creating, Editing, and Formatting Documents Using Word.....................**157**

Chapter 7
Enhancing a Document with Special Features **187**

Preface

Today's students arrive in the classroom with more confidence in using technology than any generation before them. Students have grown up with technology as a part of their lives and the Internet as a source of information, entertainment, and communication. Chances are students have used a word processor and a presentation program for several years to prepare materials for school projects and some students may be breaking in their second or third smartphones.

To be successful in any career, students need an understanding of computer hardware, software, and terminology. Furthermore, students need to learn how to use software applications in a way that saves time and makes the best use of the available feature set. To that end, students are looking for a textbook that provides them with the tools they need to succeed immediately in their academic and personal lives as well as prepare them for success in their future careers. In this book, students will learn computer concepts and software skills they can apply immediately to accomplishing projects and assignments for school and to organizing, scheduling, recording, planning, and budgeting for their personal needs. Students will find the work done in this course to be relevant and useful with the content presented in a straightforward approach.

Overview of Course and Textbook

Computer Concepts & Microsoft Office 2013 is divided into two parts: Part I, *Computer Concepts*, and Part II, *Computer Applications with Microsoft Office 2013*. Part I provides a general introduction to hardware, software, the Internet, social media, security, and ethics. Part II offers instruction in the use of the Microsoft Windows operating system, Internet Explorer web browser, and applications within Microsoft Office. The instructional text is designed as two- and four-page topics. Many screen shots illustrate software features so that students can check their work. Reading time is minimized; students will learn just what they need to know to succeed within these programs. Students will complete an activity related to a concept or practice software features with step-by-step instruction interspersed with text that explains why a feature is used or how the feature can be beneficial to them. Students should work through each chapter at a PC or with their tablet or other mobile device so that they can complete the activities or steps as they learn.

At the end of each chapter, students will have a chance to review a summary of the presented features, to complete several objective summary tasks, and then to apply the concept information or software skills in projects that will reinforce and expand the knowledge they have gained. Instructors should assign projects based on their goals for the course and the skill level of their students. A variety of projects that include recall, application, synthesis, research, and composition is included. Each chapter in Part I includes a project on green computing and a project that involves computer-related ethics. These projects are intended to facilitate meaningful student discussion with classmates about issues that everyone faces in the digital world. Also, in Part II, printing of solutions to application activities is limited to when indicated by the instructor.

For courses that emphasize either computer concepts or computer applications, Part I, *Computer Concepts*, and Part II, *Computer Applications with Microsoft Office 2013*, are available as separate textbooks.

Although well-designed textbook pedagogy is important, students learn technology skills through practice and problem solving. Technology provides opportunities for interactive learning as well as excellent ways to quickly and accurately assess student performance. To this end, this textbook is supported with SNAP, Paradigm Publishing's web-based training and assessment learning management system. Details about SNAP as well as additional student and instructor resources appear on pages xxii-xxiii.

Which Applications Are Included?

Computer Concepts & Microsoft Office 2013 provides instruction in achieving entry-level competence with the latest editions of Microsoft Windows, web browsers, and the Microsoft Office productivity suite, including OneNote, Outlook, Word, Excel, PowerPoint, and Access. Students will also be introduced to cloud computing alternatives to the traditional desktop suite. No prior experience with these software programs is required. Even those with some technological savvy can benefit from completing the course by learning new ways to complete tasks or skills. After completing a course that uses this textbook, students will be able to:

- Navigate the Windows operating system and manage files and folders.
- Use web browsers such as Internet Explorer, Google Chrome, or Mozilla Firefox to navigate and search the Web, as well as download content to a PC or mobile device.
- Use navigation, file management, and commands within the Microsoft Office suite that are standard across all applications.
- Organize and manage class notes in OneNote.
- Communicate and schedule items in Outlook.
- Create, edit, format, and enhance documents in Word.
- Create, edit, analyze, format, and enhance workbooks in Excel.
- Create, edit, format, and enhance slides and set up a slideshow in PowerPoint.
- Create and edit tables, forms, queries, and reports in Access.
- Integrate information among the applications within the Microsoft Office suite.
- Use cloud computing technologies to create, edit, store, and share documents.

Are You Using Microsoft Office 2013 with Windows 7?

A version of Part II Chapter 1, written for Windows 7 users, is available for purchase. Students who use a computer with the Windows 7 operating system can use this supplement in place of Chapter 1. In Chapters 2 through 15, instructions for Windows 7 users are included for those steps in which Windows 7 and Windows 8 procedures differ. Therefore, students using Microsoft Office 2013 with a Windows 7 computer can learn with confidence using this textbook.

What Makes This Textbook Different from Others?

Many textbooks that teach computer concepts and computer applications were designed and organized for software that was in effect one or two decades ago. As software evolves and becomes more flexible and streamlined, so too should software textbooks. With this mandate, this textbook has been designed and organized with a fresh look at the skills a student should know to be successful in today's world. The freedom to create a new book from scratch allowed the author to choose and place in a logical sequence those skills that are considered essential for today's student. Consider this book a "software survival kit for school and life." Nothing more, nothing less!

Each topic is presented in two or four pages so that reading time is minimized. Each computer concept topic ends with a hands-on activity so that students can dig deeper into the topic. Some activities involve discussion with classmates, friends, or family members, whereas other activities ask students to try the technology or complete further investigative research.

Many of the student data files used in topic and project activities in Part II are based on files created by students for projects or assignments in courses similar to those students may be enrolled in now. Students will open and manipulate real work completed by someone just like them. Other files include practical examples of documents that students can readily relate to their school and personal experiences.

Because more students are acquiring and using tablets for school work, this textbook was written with touch gestures included. Tablet users can learn with confidence knowing that the book has been written and tested with them in mind!

Chapter Features

Part I, *Computer Concepts*, is divided into seven chapters, which can be undertaken in any order. Some instructors will follow the chapter sequence as written; however, other instructors may choose to assign the chapters in a different order. For example, social media content may be studied before hardware. Regardless of the order, each chapter begins with a brief introduction to the chapter content along with a list of chapter objectives. A typical topic in Part I is shown below.

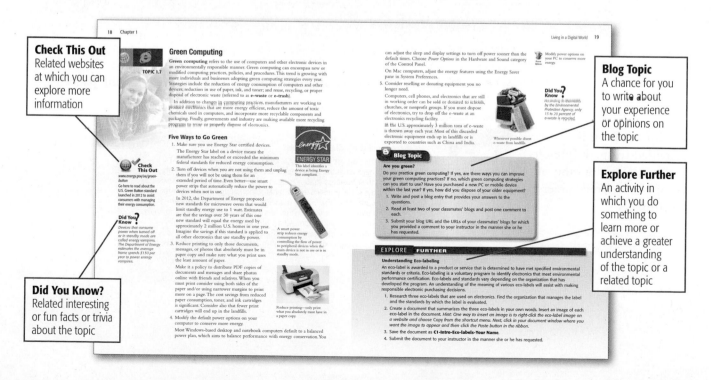

Check This Out
Related websites at which you can explore more information

Did You Know?
Related interesting or fun facts or trivia about the topic

Blog Topic
A chance for you to write about your experience or opinions on the topic

Explore Further
An activity in which you do something to learn more or achieve a greater understanding of the topic or a related topic

Part II, *Computer Applications with Microsoft Office 2013*, is divided into 15 chapters that are best completed in sequence; however, after completing the essential skills learned in Chapters 1 through 5, instructors may opt to complete Word, Excel, PowerPoint, Access, integration, and cloud computing technologies in the order of their choice.

Each chapter in Part II begins with a brief introduction to the chapter content along with a list of chapter objectives. Following each chapter opener, chapter topics are presented in two or four pages. A variety of marginal notes and other features expands or clarifies the content. Students will gain experience with topic features by working through hands-on exercises, which consist of step-by-step instructions and illustrative screen shots. Finally, the end-of-chapter materials include a summary, objective assessments, and projects. A typical topic in Part II is shown below.

SKILLS
Lists of skills that will be learned by completing the steps

App Tip
Useful tips that extend or add to your knowledge about a feature

Quick Steps
Brief summaries of steps to complete major tasks. Use for quick reference or review.

Screen captures with step numbers provide visual confirmation.

Beyond Basics
Provide additional information about the feature that extends the skills described in the topic.

Additional chapter features are described below and on the following pages.

Job information is provided to spark interest and invite exploration of computer-related careers by students.

Career Connection

Social Media Managers
Businesses are increasingly aware of the need for a person to manage all of the social media feeds that can have a huge effect on their business strategies. A social media manager coordinates all of the social media networking and marketing for an organization. Typically, the social media manager is someone who enjoys spending a lot of time online, has excellent writing skills, and enjoys communicating and connecting with all types of people. Jobs in social media management or strategy typically ask for individuals with degrees or diplomas in communications, public relations, or marketing.

Be Aware of Shoulder Surfers!

If you are viewing sensitive information on a mobile device, protect your screen from shoulder surfers. Privacy screens for notebooks, tablets, and smartphones prevent shoulder surfers from seeing personal or confidential information.

Tips for security and privacy help students learn safe computing practices.

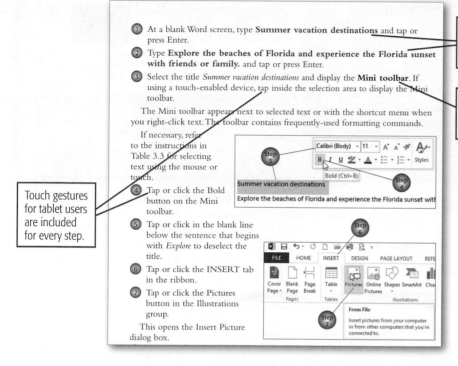

Text to be typed stands out from the instructional text.

Key words included in the glossary are in bold.

Touch gestures for tablet users are included for every step.

Instructions for completing exercises are presented in simple, easy-to-follow steps.

All instructions include steps for touch-enabled devices. Students with a tablet or other mobile device learn with touch gestures, which are the first instruction for each task.

Windows provides multiple other methods for copying files:

- Select files, choose the Copy to button in the Organize group, choose the destination folder;
- Select files, display the shortcut menu, choose Copy, navigate to the destination folder, display the shortcut menu and choose Paste; or
- Drag and drop folders/files in the File Explorer window.

Whenever possible, an Alternative Method feature box provides different ways to accomplish the task learned in the topic.

oops! margin hints anticipate common challenges and provide solutions so that students succeed with the topic.

Check This Out

google.com/chrome

Go here to download and install Google Chrome on your PC or mobile device.

Related websites that students can explore or that include useful downloads are provided where appropriate.

Did You Know?

In Office 2013, ScreenTips have been enhanced to provide more information about the button's feature and use, and in some cases the ScreenTip even provides step-by-step instructions. Point to a button with the mouse to display a ScreenTip.

Did You Know? features provide facts or trivia of interest about the topic.

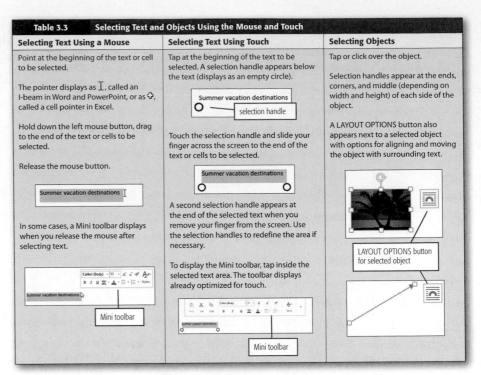

Information that can be presented in a table format is included whenever possible to minimize reading load.

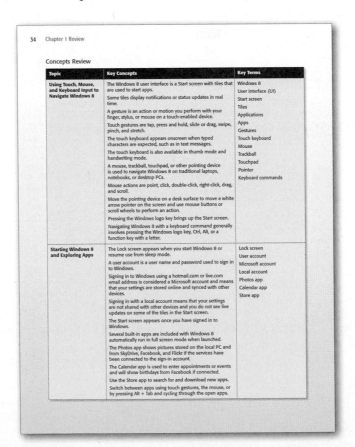

A chapter summary provides a review of the main chapter content and key words in table format, allowing students to easily return to the content if more review is necessary.

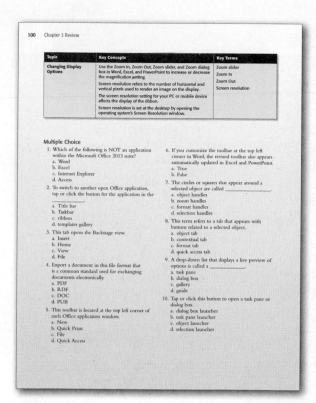

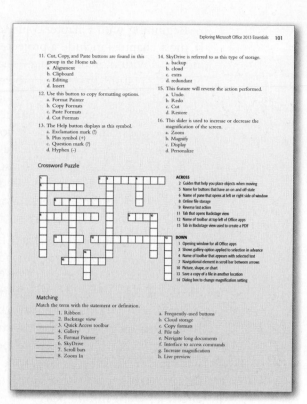

Multiple-choice questions, a crossword puzzle, and a matching exercise provide an opportunity to practice and review understanding of the concepts.

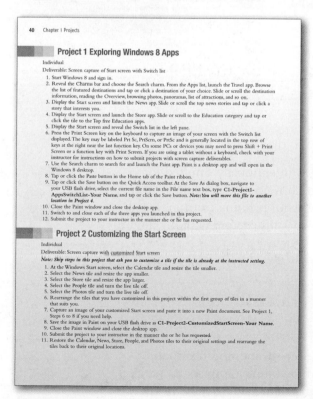

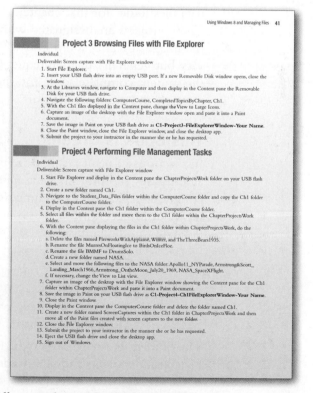

Three to nine projects at the end of each chapter allow students to apply and demonstrate comprehension of the major skills learned in the chapter. In general, projects increase in complexity from the first to the last. Most projects are intended to be completed individually; however, instructors may opt to assign some to pairs or teams of students.

Beginning with Chapter 3 in Part II, most chapters include a project—indicated with a green banner—that presents a culminating visual project in which the student is to create a document similar to the examples shown. The visual project requires that the student notice details and problem solve to create a deliverable with less direction. In some cases, students will be required to do some Internet research and composition to complete the visual project.

Starting in Chapter 4 in Part II, the last project in each chapter instructs students to send output to a OneNote notebook. The OneNote notebook is a repository for all student work. Instructors may opt to have the student share his or her OneNote notebook with the instructor in a SkyDrive folder. Instructors then have the option to check all work in one place.

Starting in Chapter 6 in Part II, some projects instruct students to listen to an audio file in the student data files folder for that chapter. These projects are designated with the image at right. Audio instructions vary but generally include requesting the student complete some Internet research and compose a report.

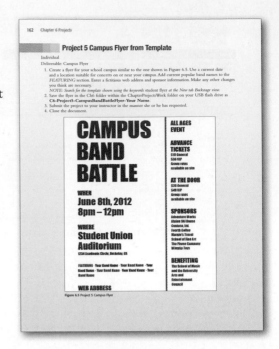

This Book Is Green!

Instructions to print results have been intentionally omitted for all exercises and projects. This approach is consistent with a green computing initiative to minimize wasteful printing for nongraded topics or project work and also provides instructors with maximum flexibility in designing their course structure.

Student and Instructor Resources

Student Resources Disc

The Student Resources disc, which accompanies this textbook, contains documents and files needed to complete topics and projects in Part II. By completing all Chapter 1 topics and projects in Part II, students set up a folder structure and copy all of the student data files from the Student Resources disc to a USB flash drive. As an alternative, instructors may choose to load student data files on a network, in which case alternative instructions may need to be provided.

SNAP Web-Based Training and Assessment

Available at snap2013.emcp.com, SNAP is a web-based program that offers an interactive venue for learning Microsoft Office 2013, Windows 8, and Internet Explorer 10. Along with a web-based learning management system, SNAP provides multimedia tutorials, performance skill items, matching activities, Grade It projects, comprehensive performance evaluations, a concepts test bank, an online grade book, and a set of course planning tools.

Instructor Resources Disc

Instructor support is available on the Instructor Resources disc and includes syllabus and course planning suggestions, chapter teaching hints, model answers, PowerPoint® presentations for student study or classroom instruction for each chapter, and the ExamView® Assessment Suite and test banks.

Internet Resource Center

All content on the Student Resources disc and most content on the Instructor Resources disc is also available at the book-specific Internet Resource Center at www. paradigmcollege.net/conceptsapplications2013. Instructor materials, such as model answers, are password-protected.

Blackboard Course Files

Blackboard files provide course content, self quizzes, and study aids, and facilitate communication among students and instructors via email and e-discussion.

eBook

For students who prefer studying with an eBook, *Computer Concepts & Microsoft Office 2013* is available in an electronic form. The web-based, password-protected eBook features dynamic navigation tools, including bookmarking, a linked table of contents, and the ability to jump to a specific page. The eBook format also supports helpful study tools, such as highlighting and note taking. Part I, *Computer Concepts*, and Part II, *Computer Applications with Microsoft Office 2013*, are available as separate eBooks.

Acknowledgments

The author and editors thank the following individuals for their involvement in this project: Denise Gauthier, Lakehead University, Thunder Bay, Ontario; Lenny E. Andrews, Montgomery Community College, Troy, North Carolina; Lorraine Mastracchio, The College of Westchester, White Plains, New York; Scott Cline, Southwestern Community College, Sylva, North Carolina; Karen J. Allen, Assistant Professor, Community College of Rhode Island, Warwick, Rhode Island; and Janet Blum, Fanshawe College, London, Ontario. Also, we thank the following students for their contributions to and feedback on preliminary versions of the textbook: Patti Ann Reynolds, Toni McBride, and Nicole Oke, Fanshawe College; and Michael Seguin, University of Windsor, Windsor, Ontario. Furthermore, we thank the following for developing supplements for this project: Janet Blum, Fanshawe College; Jeff Johnson, Minneapolis, Minnesota; Judy Peterson, Two Harbors, Minnesota; and Janine Violini, Calgary, Alberta.

About the Author

Denise Seguin has served on the Faculty of Business at Fanshawe College of Applied Arts and Technology in London, Ontario, since 1986. She has developed curriculum and taught a variety of office technology, software applications, and accounting courses to students in postsecondary Information Technology diploma programs and Continuing Education courses. Seguin has served as Program Coordinator for Computer Systems Technician, Computer Systems Technology, Office Administration, and Law Clerk programs and was acting Chair of the School of Information Technology in 2001. Along with authoring *Computer Concepts* and *Computer Applications with Microsoft Office 2013*, she has also authored Paradigm Publishing's *Microsoft Outlook* 2000 to 2013 editions and co-authored *Our Digital World* first and second editions; *Benchmark Series Microsoft Excel* 2007, 2010, and 2013; *Benchmark Series Microsoft Access* 2007, 2010, and 2013; *Marquee Series Microsoft Office* 2000 to 2013; and *Using Computers in the Medical Office* 2003 to 2010 editions.

PART I

Computer Concepts

Chapter 1

Living in a Digital World

After successfully completing this chapter, you will be able to:

- Define *Computer* and identify the various types of computers

- Give an example of technological convergence and ubiquitous computing

- Define *Information Technology* and describe the four processes of a computer: input, output, processing, and storage

- Explain cloud computing and list advantages to individuals and businesses

- Describe the goals of green computing and identify green computing practices

- Recognize ways to use computing devices that conform to good ergonomic design

Individuals and businesses interact with computers in numerous ways every day. Some of these interactions occur while you are at home, at work, or at school using a laptop, smartphone, or tablet. Many times you are interacting with a computing device while shopping, dining, or traveling. Consider the number of times you withdraw money from an ATM, gas up your car, swipe a debit or credit card to complete a purchase, use a self-checkout at the grocery store, or program your alarm clock or coffee maker. Many times throughout the day you are interacting with a computer without thinking about it.

To be successful in today's world requires some understanding of computers and how they work. In this chapter, you will begin your introduction to the digital world by learning to distinguish the various types of computers, recognize the impact of computer innovation and convergence in our lives, explain how data is transformed into useful information, and identify trends and issues such as cloud computing, green computing, and ergonomics.

This chapter is an introduction to the terminology and concepts you will explore in more detail in the chapters that follow.

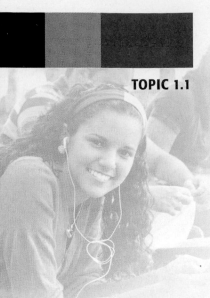

TOPIC 1.1

Personal Computers

A **computer** is an electronic device that has been programmed to process, store, and output data that has been accepted as input. Computers come in many sizes and shapes to meet a variety of computing needs. Most people are familiar with a desktop, laptop, or tablet and recognize it as a computer. Other electronic devices that contain a programmed chip such as a digital camera, game console, GPS, or even some children's toys also have computer capabilities designed to perform limited functions.

A computer needs both **hardware** (all of the physical components and devices) and **software** (instructions that tell the computer what to do) in order to be useful. You will learn about hardware in Chapter 3, operating system programs in Chapter 4, and productivity software applications in Chapter 5.

Personal Computers

A **personal computer (PC)** is a computer in which the input, processing, storage, and output are self-contained. A PC is generally used by one person at a time, although PCs can be connected to a network where other people can access a PC's resources such as a file on a storage medium. A PC is sometimes referred to as a microcomputer.

Figure 1.1 A desktop computer with a vertical system unit (called a tower)

Figure 1.2 Apple's iMac sports an all-in-one case where the monitor, processor, memory, and storage mediums are housed in one unit.

A **desktop computer** is a PC in which the computer's processing, memory, and main storage device are housed within a horizontal or vertical case called the **system unit**. A vertical case is sometimes referred to as a tower. A separate monitor, keyboard, and mouse sit alongside or near the system unit as shown in Figure 1.1. An all-in-one case integrates the system unit and monitor into one device as shown in Figure 1.2.

Mobile Computers

A **mobile computer** is a PC that can be moved from place to place. Mobile computers are also referred to as portable computers and come in a number of configurations that vary in size, shape, and weight. A **laptop computer** fits comfortably on a person's lap and is also referred to as a **notebook**. These PCs often replaced desktops as monitor sizes grew and processors, memory, and storage equaled what previously had been available only in desktops. A typical notebook has a clamshell-style design that when opened has the monitor swivel up to reveal a keyboard with the processor, memory, storage media, and battery housed below the keyboard as shown in Figure 1.3.

Figure 1.3 Laptops, also referred to as notebooks, have a clamshell design where the monitor opens up to reveal the system unit.

A **netbook** (Figure 1.4) is a smaller version of a notebook designed for people who primarily only need access to web-based applications such as email and the Internet. These notebooks contain some productivity software applications but do not have DVD drives. Netbooks offer a lower cost alternative to a traditional notebook.

A type of notebook that is thinner, lighter in weight, but just as powerful as a traditional notebook is called an **ultrabook**. Ultrabooks were originally named by Intel (a company that manufactures computer chips) to differentiate the newer notebook design that aims to achieve faster processing and storage while extending battery life in a slim (most are 0.6 to 0.7 inches thick), lightweight (average 2.5 pounds) notebook. Apple's MacBook Air shown in Figure 1.5 is a popular ultrabook; however, all of

Figure 1.4 Netbooks are popular with people who primarily only use email and the Internet.

the other major hardware manufacturers such as Lenovo, Acer, Toshiba, HP, Dell, and Samsung have also released ultrabooks.

Tablet PCs are lightweight notebooks with smaller screens that you interact with using a touch screen or special pen called a stylus. Slate tablets have an onscreen keyboard only while other tablets come with a keyboard that pivots or plugs into the tablet so that the tablet acts more like a traditional notebook. The popularity of Apple's iPad tablet has led other manufacturers to produce tablets, giving consumers a variety of models to choose from. Figure 1.6 shows Apple's iPad.

Figure 1.5 Ultrabooks such as Apple's MacBook Air are slim, lightweight, yet as powerful as a notebook.

Protect Your Mobile Device

Notebook theft is on the rise. In some areas, organized criminals use people to distract you while another steals your device. Use anti-theft software or devices to track your notebook and protect your data in case of theft. Always have backups just in case!

Blog Topic

Figure 1.6 Apple's iPad is a popular tablet.

Is the personal computer dead?

Smartphones and tablets are increasingly powerful with all of the tools offered on a notebook. Desktop sales have been steadily decreasing. Some people argue that mobile devices are simply supplementing the traditional desktop and notebook and that sales data are misleading since desktops and notebooks are lasting longer.

1. Write and post a blog entry with a paragraph that describes the number of computing devices you own and how you use them. State your opinion to the blog topic *Is the personal computer dead?* and provide your rationale.

2. Read at least two of your classmates' blog entries and post one comment to each.

3. Submit your blog URL and the URLs of the two classmates' blogs to your instructor in the manner she or he has requested.

EXPLORE FURTHER

Compare Ultrabooks with Tablet PCs

Assume the manager at the office where you intern is interested in buying a new mobile computer. The manager is not sure whether an ultrabook or a tablet PC is the better choice.

1. Research the similarities and differences between ultrabooks and tablet PCs. Choose one model of each for your comparison. Specifically, find out the physical characteristics of each (weight and screen size), connectivity options (ports, wireless, Bluetooth options), input options (keyboard, touchscreen), storage options, and processor speeds.

2. Create a table in a document or spreadsheet to present the comparison of an ultrabook to a tablet PC by each criterion. Clearly identify the model of each device you are presenting and include the URLs of the websites from which you obtained the specifications.

3. Save the document or spreadsheet as **C1-Intro-UltrabookvsTablet-Your Name**.

4. Submit the document or spreadsheet to your instructor in the manner she or he has requested.

Mobile Devices, Wearable Computers, and Embedded Computers

TOPIC 1.2

Handheld computing devices smaller than notebooks are referred to as **mobile devices**. These devices have smaller screens and store programs and data within the unit or on a memory card. Some devices rely entirely on touch-based input while others have a built-in or slide-out keyboard. Wearable computers are devices that can be worn on the body by attaching to an arm, belt, helmet, eyeglasses, or clothing. These computers are used to perform special functions such as health monitoring or assist with other hands-free work. Embedded computers reside within an electronic device that is designed to perform a specific task such as the programs found in many household appliances and electronic gadgets.

Mobile Devices

Increasingly, mobile devices are expanding computer use outside our homes and offices. Examples of mobile devices shown in Figure 1.7 include:

- **Smartphones** are cell phones with built-in cameras that offer software applications (called apps), Web-browsing, and messaging capabilities.
- **Ultra–Mobile PC (UMPC)** is a small handheld computer that supports touch, digital pen input, or includes a compact keyboard depending on the design.
- **Portable Media Players** are devices used to play music, watch videos, view photos, play games, and/or read electronic books.

Figure 1.7 A smartphone, handheld computer, and portable media player are popular mobile devices.

Wearable Computers

A computing device that can be worn on the body and functions while the individual is walking or otherwise moving around is called a **wearable computer**. These devices are usually always-on, include sensors for various purposes, and provide for hands-free use with communications capability. Devices may provide for input with voice commands, hand movements, joysticks, buttons, or touch. Wearable computers are used to assist or monitor individuals with health conditions, track items, provide real-time information, access documentation, or engage in virtual reality simulations. For example, the Department of Defense helped develop wearable computers for soldiers that monitor the battlefield environment.

Google's Project Glass eyeglasses (Figure 1.8) use a heads–up virtual display that interacts with the wearer to provide information and communication technologies without the wearer having to use his or her smartphone. Google's eyeglasses could bring wearable computers to the mainstream consumer electronics market.

Embedded Computers

Numerous household appliances and consumer electronics incorporate **embedded computers** that have processors programmed to perform a particular task (Figure 1.9). Examples include: a microwave oven calculates defrost time depending on weight, a refrigerator sounds an alarm when the inside temperature becomes problematic, and a car's navigation console displays a map of your current location.

Digital cameras, game consoles, electronic thermostats, electronic vending machines, ATMs, digital alarms, and digital thermometers are just a few other examples of devices with an embedded system. Digital devices are everywhere and so prevalent that many times you may not be aware you are using a computer!

Figure 1.8 Google's Project Glass eyeglasses use voice commands to display in front of your eyes up-to-date information, take photos, and communicate.

Figure 1.9 Electronic devices with embedded systems are designed to perform a specific task such as this navigation system, digital camera, and handheld game console.

EXPLORE FURTHER

Favorite Computing Devices

1. Conduct a survey with at least 10 relatives, friends, neighbors, or classmates to find out each person's favorite computing device.
2. Compile the results and create a table or chart in a document, spreadsheet, or presentation that presents the results of your informal survey.
3. Save the document, spreadsheet, or presentation as **C1-PCs-DeviceSurvey-Your Name**.
4. Submit the table or chart to your instructor in the manner she or he has requested.

Computers for Connecting Multiple Users and Specialized Processing

TOPIC 1.3

Larger, more powerful computers are used by organizations that need to connect many people to resources and store and process large amounts of data. Individuals use PCs to connect via a network to these larger computers for access to programs, processing, and storage resources. A high-end computer with multiple processors, large amounts of memory and storage capacity can function as a server in a small network; however, larger organizations purchase midrange servers and mainframes when hundreds or thousands of users need to process transactions simultaneously. Supercomputers are used when massive computing power is needed to perform advanced calculations.

Servers

A **server** is a computer with hardware and software that allows it to link together other computers in order to provide services such as Internet access and share resources such as programs, data, printers, and storage. The computers that connect to a server are called **clients**. Servers are high-performance computers often stacked in racks (Figure 1.10) and stored in a room called a **server room** that is maintained to avoid heat, humidity, and dust.

A **midrange server** is used in small and medium-sized organizations that need to connect hundreds of client computers at the same time. Midrange servers are more powerful than a PC but not as powerful as a mainframe.

A computer connected to a network that does not store any data or software on the local PC is called a **thin client**. Some companies use thin clients to reduce costs and/or maintain tighter security on software licensing and data.

Did You Know?
Midrange servers used to be known as minicomputers.

Figure 1.10 Servers mounted in racks are stored in a separate room protected from excessive heat, humidity, and dust.

Mainframes

A large, powerful, and expensive computer used by government and large organizations such as banks, insurance companies, and other corporations to connect hundreds or thousands of users simultaneously is known as a **mainframe** (Figure 1.11). These computers have specialized hardware and software capable of processing millions of transactions and retaining massive volumes of data.

Figure 1.11 Mainframe computers connect thousands of computers simultaneously and process and store millions of transactions.

Supercomputers

The most powerful of all computers is a **supercomputer**. A supercomputer is the fastest, most expensive, and most powerful computer, capable of performing trillions of calculations per second. These massive computers are usually designed for a specific task such as the complex mathematical calculations needed for weather forecasting, nuclear research, oil exploration, or to conduct scientific research analysis.

Supercomputing speed is expressed in **petaflops**. A petaflop (a measurement used in scientific calculations) represents a quadrillion floating point operations per second. In June 2012, a supercomputer named Sequoia (Figure 1.12), installed at the Department of Energy's Lawrence Livermore National Laboratory, achieved 16.32 petaflops per second and was named the top supercomputer in the Top 500 list of most powerful computers.

Check This Out

www.top500.org
Go here to read about the location of supercomputers around the world. A list of the top 500 sites for the most powerful computers is released twice per year.

Figure 1.12 In June 2012, Sequoia, installed at the Department of Energy's Lawrence Livermore National Laboratory, was named the top supercomputer in the Top 500 list of most powerful computers in the world.

EXPLORE FURTHER

History of Computing Time Line

The Computer History Museum located in Mountain View, California, offers information about the most influential people, technology, and events in computing history. An online exhibit *Timeline of Computer History* offers an interactive exploration into the origins of computers.

1. Go to www.computerhistory.org/timeline to view the online Timeline exhibit.
2. Pick five consecutive years in the time line that are of interest to you, click the year, and read the information presented in the online exhibit. *Note: Your instructor may instead choose to assign you a time period for this activity in order to have a complete time line presented to the class.*
3. Create a presentation with one slide per year and provide a brief summary in your own words that describes the significant people, technology, or event that was shown in the time line.
4. Save the presentation as **C1-PCs-ComputerTimeline-Your Name**.
5. Submit the presentation to your instructor in the manner she or he has requested.

Computer Innovations and Converging Technologies

At home you use a computer to communicate with others via email or social media websites; track and pay bills; play games; watch videos, television shows, and movies; listen to music or radio stations; do homework; and more. Computers are put to work in every type of business in a variety of ways. Technology is constantly evolving, meaning there will always be change in the devices and methods that we use for completing tasks at home, at work, and at school. Technologies are also converging, meaning that a device that originally was designed for one purpose, such as a cell phone designed only to make voice calls, is now capable of performing multiple functions such as browsing the Web, taking photos, sending and receiving email, and creating documents.

Ubiquitous Computing

Dictonary.com defines *ubiquitous* as an adjective that means "*existing or being everywhere, especially at the same time; omnipresent.*" **Ubiquitous computing** means that computing technology is everywhere within our environment and used all of the time. Effectively, the technology mostly fades into the background and the user becomes unaware of the technology as the person focuses on the task at hand. With the rapid pace of technology innovation, ubiquitous computing will become even more prevalent to all of us. Consider these five examples of recent computer innovations in various industries:

Retail Macy's is using a new handheld computer at some of its stores that will inform the retail clerk if the store has stock in the customer's shoe size and send a message to a stock person indicating which two doors of the stockroom are closest to the customer. The clerk uses the device, which is about the size of a remote control, to scan the bar code on a shoe, enter the customer's shoe size, and receive instant notification of stock status.

At Macy's, store clerks can get instant stock status by scanning a bar code and entering a customer's shoe size.

Restaurant A digital noise-cancelling technology designed by Meyer Sound and the owner of a restaurant in California uses speakers, microphones, iPads, and sound-dampening materials disguised as art hanging on the walls to make the restaurant as loud or as quiet as the owner sees fit. The system monitors sound levels picked up by microphones that are processed by the computer and used to control sound reverberation levels. If the owner thinks the restaurant is too loud, the system dampens the noise so that diners can easily converse with their guests.

New technology for restaurants lets the owner dampen sound when the noise level becomes too loud for comfortable conversation among guests.

Manufacturing High-end 3-D printers use materials such as hard and flexible plastics, glass, metal powders, and even chocolate to make objects layer by layer, using an array of heat- or light-activated materials sold in cartridges. These printers have led to the emergence of on-demand manufacturing, meaning companies will no longer have to maintain inventories of spare parts. Items can be saved in a database and printed on demand when needed.

3-D printing is leading to manufacturing on demand.

Police officers can use their iPhone or iPod touch to take fingerprints.

Law Enforcement A low-cost sleeve that snaps onto an iPhone or iPod touch is being used by law enforcement agencies in the field to collect fingerprints of suspects, detainees, or even deceased individuals for rapid identification. The device for the mobile phone avoids the costs associated with providing laptops and fingerprint scanners to all officers in a police force.

Sony's Playstation 4 concept image (new console under development at time of writing)

Medicine A new knee brace allows doctors to monitor remotely a patient's healing progress after discharge from the hospital for knee surgery. The brace is embedded with motion sensors. When the patient is moving, the motion is simulated by a 3-D avatar on a remote computer and transmitted to the patient's doctor for viewing on a PC or smartphone.

Convergence

Technological convergence, where innovation merges several technologies into a single device, is not just about cell phones becoming multipurpose smartphones. Game consoles used to just play video games, but today's multipurpose consoles are also used to play movies from Blu-ray, DVD, or the Web. You can also surf the Web, browse through photos, and play music on newer systems.

Doctors can remotely monitor a patient's healing progress.

EXPLORE FURTHER

What new technology innovation is occurring in your field of study?

Technological innovation occurs every day, and a computer innovation will likely occur in your field of study while you are still in school.

1. Either by searching the Web or by interviewing someone who works in your field of study, investigate a technology innovation that is occurring in your field or is to occur by the time you graduate.

2. Create a document with a brief description of the innovation you learned about and the impact the innovation is expected to have within the industry. At the end of the document, include the URLs of websites you used or a reference for the person you interviewed.

3. Save the document as **C1-Intro-ComputerInnovation-Your Name**.

4. Submit the document to your instructor in the manner she or he has requested.

Information Technology and the Information Processing Cycle

TOPIC 1.5

Information technology (IT) refers to the use of computers, software, networks, and other communication systems and processes to store, retrieve, send, process, and protect information. The IT department in an organization is tasked with managing the hardware, software, networks, and other systems that form the information infrastructure. IT specialists are involved with designing, developing, implementing, and maintaining information systems.

Characters that are typed or otherwise entered into a computer are called **raw data**. At the entry stage the data is not meaningful as it is just a string of characters. Software programs provide the instructions for the computer to process and organize the data into meaningful and useful **information**. The **Information Processing Cycle** includes the operations involved in transforming *data* into *information* and includes: input, processing, output, and storage as shown in Figure 1.13.

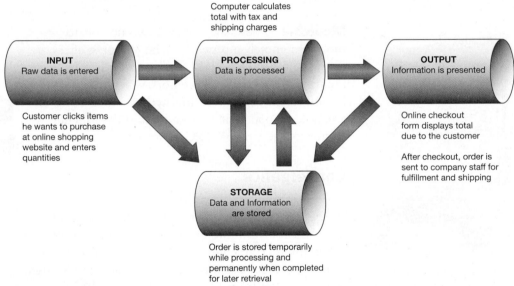

Computer calculates
total with tax and
shipping charges

| INPUT | PROCESSING | OUTPUT |
| Raw data is entered | Data is processed | Information is presented |

Customer clicks items
he wants to purchase
at online shopping
website and enters
quantities

STORAGE
Data and Information
are stored

Order is stored temporarily
while processing and
permanently when completed
for later retrieval

Online checkout
form displays total
due to the customer

After checkout, order is
sent to company staff for
fulfillment and shipping

Figure 1.13 The Information Processing Cycle includes four operations to transform raw data into useful information.

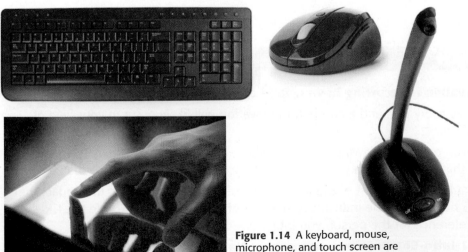

Figure 1.14 A keyboard, mouse, microphone, and touch screen are common devices used to enter input.

Input

Any device used to enter raw data or communicate instructions to the computer is an **input device**. Commonly used devices include a keyboard, mouse, and microphone similar to the ones shown in Figure 1.14. A scanner, bar code reader, digital camera, digital pen, webcam, or touch-screen device can also be used to enter input.

Processing

A computer chip called the **central processing unit (CPU)** carries out the instructions given by the software to perform the **processing** cycle. Think of the CPU as the brain of the computer. A CPU is a silicon chip referred to as the **microprocessor** and is housed on the computer's motherboard (printed circuit board that contains the main computer components). Microprocessors today are typically manufactured with multiple cores, which are independent units on the same chip that can process data simultaneously. These **multi-core processors** significantly increase speed and performance. Intel is a leading designer and manufacturer of microprocessors (Figure 1.15).

Figure 1.15 Intel's popular Core series of microprocessors is available in several variations to suit individual and business users.

Output

Anything used to view the information processed and organized by the computer is an **output device**. Typically, you view information on a monitor and/or print it on a printer similar to the ones shown in Figure 1.16. Other output devices include speakers and screens such as those on mobile devices and televisions.

Figure 1.16 A monitor and printer are commonly used to view information processed by the computer; however, mobile devices such as a tablet or smartphone can also be considered output devices.

Storage

While processing, instructions and data are temporarily stored in a holding area called **random access memory (RAM)**. RAM is also housed on the computer's motherboard. RAM is temporary storage that is emptied when power to the computer is lost.

Cache memory is located either on the CPU chip or on a separate chip between the CPU and RAM and is used to store frequently used data. Speed and performance are increased with cache memory since the CPU checks cache memory first before checking RAM. The faster retrieval of frequently used data saves the processor time.

Permanent storage (Figure 1.17) is any device where data and information are saved for later use; these devices are referred to as **storage media**. Several storage media, some portable and some housed inside the system unit, are available in various capacities. An internal hard disk drive is housed inside the system unit while portable storage media such as USB flash drives (also

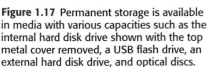

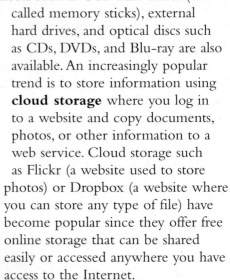

called memory sticks), external hard drives, and optical discs such as CDs, DVDs, and Blu-ray are also available. An increasingly popular trend is to store information using **cloud storage** where you log in to a website and copy documents, photos, or other information to a web service. Cloud storage such as Flickr (a website used to store photos) or Dropbox (a website where you can store any type of file) have become popular since they offer free online storage that can be shared easily or accessed anywhere you have access to the Internet.

In today's highly connected world, a fifth operation called communications is often added to the information processing cycle. Computers accept input and send output to/from other computers via various wired and wireless communication channels such as

Figure 1.17 Permanent storage is available in media with various capacities such as the internal hard disk drive shown with the top metal cover removed, a USB flash drive, an external hard disk drive, and optical discs.

cables, telephone lines, satellite, cellular, microwave, and Bluetooth transmission media. A **communications device** is any component used to facilitate the transmission of data such as a cable modem, DSL modem, or router (Figure 1.18).

In this topic, you have been introduced to terminology and hardware in the information processing cycle that will be explored in more detail in Chapter 3.

Integrated modem and wireless router used to connect the computer devices on the home network to the Internet

Figure 1.18 Computers connect to other computers to receive input and send output using communications devices such as the integrated modem and wireless router shown.

Career Connection

IT Jobs in Demand

If you enjoy working with computers you may want to consider an IT career. *Computerworld* magazine surveyed more than 300 IT executives for its 2012 forecast and included the following in its top IT jobs in demand: programming and application development with emphasis on mobile application developers, project management, help desk and technical support, networking, business intelligence, data center operations and systems integration, security, and telecommunications. If any of these careers are of interest to you, look at courses offered in postsecondary programs in computer engineering, computer science, information systems, information technology, and software engineering.

EXPLORE   FURTHER

IT Job Profile

You have read in Career Connection that IT jobs are in demand. You are interested in working with computers but want to learn more about specific job openings to find out what employers are looking for in new employees.

1. Using a job search website such as Monster.com, locate a current job ad for an IT job that interests you within your area. *Hint: Use titles from the Career Connection section*.

2. Create a document that describes in your own words the job opportunity including the job title, the company offering the job, the duties involved in the job, and the qualifications required. Include information on compensation if the ad lists a salary range. At the end of the document include the URL for the job ad.

3. Save the document as **C1-Intro-ITJobAd-Your Name**.

4. Submit the document to your instructor in the manner she or he has requested.

Cloud Computing

Individuals and businesses are increasingly turning to providers of software and computing services that are accessed entirely on the Internet. This delivery model of software and services is called **cloud computing**. With cloud computing, all you need is a computer with a web browser in order to get your work done since all of the software and the documents you need to access are stored online.

Cloud computing got its name because the Internet has always been identified with a cloud in technology documentation. Cloud computing places the processing and storage operations of the Information Processing cycle at an online service provider's server and/or data center rather than using the hardware and software on your own PC or mobile device (Figure 1.19). In some cases you can use cloud computing services for free. For example, at Google Drive you can use up to 5 GB of cloud storage for free (with an option to pay a fee for more storage space).

The delivery of software applications using the Internet is referred to as **software-as-a-service (SaaS)**. Advantages and disadvantages of cloud computing are listed in Table 1.1.

Figure 1.19 Using cloud computing services means that your software applications and/or data are accessed from your web browser and stored on the service provider's equipment.

Table 1.1	Advantages and Disadvantages of Cloud Computing
Advantages	**Disadvantages**
Applications and data are available at any time from any place since all you need is an Internet connection	You are totally dependent on your Internet connection; if the service goes down, you cannot access your programs or files
Updates to software are automatic and immediately available	You do not have control over changes made to software—upgrading is not at your discretion
The service provider makes continual investment in hardware and software. Pay only the subscription fees after you have purchased your computer and Internet connectivity	Over a long period of time, monthly subscription fees could end up costing more than the initial outlay of cash for hardware and software and ongoing Internet connectivity
Web applications are generally easy to use and navigate	Web applications may be too limiting to meet your needs
Web-based applications are generally compatible with PCs, Macs, and mobile devices—you can use any device	Some businesses may have compatibility issues with exchanging data with legacy systems or infrastructure
Documents, photos, music, videos, and other files are stored offsite. If you experience equipment malfunction, theft, or some other disaster, all that is lost is the physical equipment, which is easily replaced	Large cloud computing vendors have reliable and secure storage; however, there is a risk that personal and/or sensitive data could be accessed by unauthorized users. Also be mindful of who actually owns the data you are storing online—is it you or the provider?

If you open your web browser to check email, create documents, or upload photos, music, videos, or other files to store and share with others, then you are already using SaaS services. A few popular cloud computing services include Google Drive (formerly Google Docs), Dropbox, iCloud, and SkyDrive. Many more cloud computing service providers exist to meet the growing demands and needs of many individuals and businesses.

Figure 1.20 illustrates Google Presentations. If you are familiar with presentation software, creating a presentation in Google Presentations web-based application will be easy for you since the program contains tools similar to what you would find in other presentation programs. As more people become aware of and convert to using web-based applications, traditional office productivity suites may no longer be the mainstream choice.

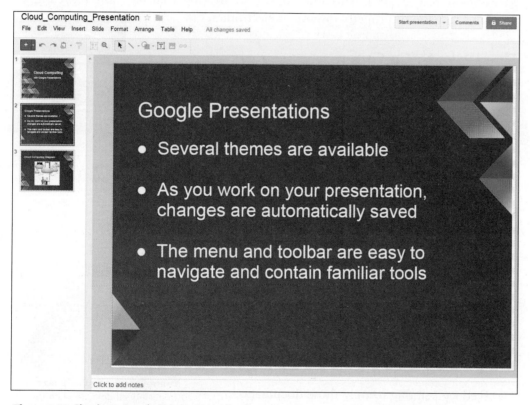

Figure 1.20 Sign in to Google Drive using a Gmail account to access Google Presentations and create a presentation similar to the one shown.

EXPLORE FURTHER

What are IaaS and PaaS?

In this topic you learned about one type of cloud computing known as software-as-a-service (SaaS). Two other types of cloud computing are infrastructure-as-a-service (IaaS) and platform-as-a-service (PaaS).

1. Look up the definitions of IaaS and PaaS.
2. Create a document that explains in your own words what these two types of cloud computing services are and the advantages offered to businesses for these services.
3. Save the document as **C1-Intro-CloudComputing-Your Name**.
4. Submit the document to your instructor in the manner she or he has requested.

TOPIC 1.7

Green Computing

Green computing refers to the use of computers and other electronic devices in an environmentally responsible manner. Green computing can encompass new or modified computing practices, policies, and procedures. This trend is growing with more individuals and businesses adopting green computing strategies every year. Strategies include the reduction of energy consumption of computers and other devices; reduction in use of paper, ink, and toner; and reuse, recycling, or proper disposal of electronic waste (referred to as **e-waste** or **e-trash**).

In addition to changes in computing practices, manufacturers are working to produce electronics that are more energy efficient, reduce the amount of toxic chemicals used in computers, and incorporate more recyclable components and packaging. Finally, governments and industry are making available more recycling programs to reuse or properly dispose of electronics.

Five Ways to Go Green

1. Make sure you use Energy Star certified devices.

   The Energy Star label on a device means the manufacturer has reached or exceeded the minimum federal standards for reduced energy consumption.

This label identifies a device as being Energy Star compliant.

2. Turn off devices when you are not using them and unplug them if you will not be using them for an extended period of time. Even better—use smart power strips that automatically reduce the power to devices when not in use.

   In 2012, the Department of Energy proposed new standards for microwave ovens that would limit standby energy use to 1 watt. Estimates are that the savings over 30 years of this one new standard will equal the energy used by approximately 2 million U.S. homes in one year. Imagine the savings if this standard is applied to all other electronics that use standby power.

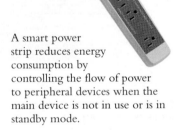

A smart power strip reduces energy consumption by controlling the flow of power to peripheral devices when the main device is not in use or is in standby mode.

3. Reduce printing to only those documents, messages, or photos that absolutely must be in paper copy and make sure what you print uses the least amount of paper.

   Make it a policy to distribute PDF copies of documents and messages and share photos online with friends and relatives. When you must print consider using both sides of the paper and/or using narrower margins to print more on a page. The cost savings from reduced paper consumption, toner, and ink cartridges is significant. Consider also that fewer print cartridges will end up in the landfills.

Reduce printing—only print what you absolutely must have in a paper copy.

4. Modify the default power options on your computer to conserve more energy.

   Most Windows-based desktop and notebook computers default to a balanced power plan, which aims to balance performance with energy conservation. You

Check This Out

www.energy.gov/oe/green-button

Go here to read about the U.S. Green Button standard launched in 2012 to assist consumers with managing their energy consumption.

Did You Know?

Devices that consume power when turned off or in standby mode are called energy vampires. The Department of Energy estimates the average home spends $130 per year to power energy vampires.

can adjust the sleep and display settings to turn off power sooner than the default times. Choose *Power Options* in the Hardware and Sound category of the Control Panel.

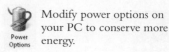

Modify power options on your PC to conserve more energy.

On Mac computers, adjust the energy features using the Energy Saver pane in System Preferences.

5. Consider reselling or donating equipment you no longer need.

Computers, cell phones, and electronics that are still in working order can be sold or donated to schools, churches, or nonprofit groups. If you must dispose of electronics, try to drop off the e-waste at an electronics recycling facility.

In the U.S. approximately 3 million tons of e-waste is thrown away each year. Most of this discarded electronic equipment ends up in landfills or is exported to countries such as China and India.

Whenever possible divert e-waste from landfills.

Did You Know?

According to estimates by the Environmental Protection Agency, only 15 to 20 percent of e-waste is recycled.

Blog Topic

Are you green?

Do you practice green computing? If yes, are there ways you can improve your green computing practices? If no, which green computing strategies can you start to use? Have you purchased a new PC or mobile device within the last year? If yes, how did you dispose of your older equipment?

1. Write and post a blog entry that provides your answers to the questions.

2. Read at least two of your classmates' blogs and post one comment to each.

3. Submit your blog URL and the URLs of your classmates' blogs for which you provided a comment to your instructor in the manner she or he has requested.

EXPLORE FURTHER

Understanding Eco-labeling

An eco-label is awarded to a product or service that is determined to have met specified environmental standards or criteria. Eco-labeling is a voluntary program to identify electronics that meet environmental performance certification. Eco-labels and standards vary depending on the organization that has developed the program. An understanding of the meaning of various eco-labels will assist with making responsible electronic purchasing decisions.

1. Research three eco-labels that are used on electronics. Find the organization that manages the label and the standards by which the label is evaluated.

2. Create a document that summarizes the three eco-labels in your own words. Insert an image of each eco-label in the document. *Hint: One way to insert an image is to right-click the eco-label image on a website and choose* Copy *from the shortcut menu. Next, click in your document window where you want the image to appear and then click the Paste button in the ribbon.*

3. Save the document as **C1-Intro-Eco-labels-Your Name**.

4. Submit the document to your instructor in the manner she or he has requested.

TOPIC 1.8

Computers and Your Health

Frequent use of computing devices can adversely affect your health if proper care and preventive strategies are not used. Physical ailments that can occur include fatigue, eyestrain, blurred vision, backaches, wrist and forearm pain, finger numbness or pain, and neck and shoulder pain. A leading job-related illness and injury in North America is **repetitive-strain injury (RSI)**. RSI is an injury or disorder of the joints, nerves, muscles, ligaments, or tendons.

Two common computer-related RSI injuries are **tendonitis** and **carpal tunnel syndrome (CTS)**. Tendonitis occurs when a tendon in your wrist becomes inflamed. CTS occurs when the nerve that connects the forearm to the palm of the hand becomes inflamed. Both of these conditions are caused by excessive typing, mouse scrolling, mouse clicking, and thumb typing/movements on mobile devices. Symptoms of tendonitis and CTS are listed in Table 1.2.

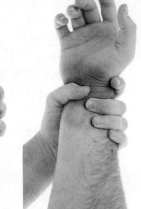

Tendonitis and carpal tunnel syndrome are two common RSI injuries from computer use that cause pain in the wrist and hand.

Table 1.2	Symptoms Associated with RSI Injuries from Computer Use
Symptoms of Tendonitis	**Symptoms of Carpal Tunnel Syndrome (CTS)**
Tingling or numbness in the fingers	Numbness and tingling in the thumb and the first two fingers especially at night (can cause you to awaken from sleep)
Pain in the forearm and wrist	Burning sensation when the nerve is compressed
Decreased mobility of your wrist or fingers	Decreased grip strength leading you to drop objects
Loss of strength in your hand	Loss of strength in your hand

Computer vision syndrome affects 50 to 90 percent of computer users.

Computer Vision Syndrome

Computer vision syndrome (CVS) is a temporary condition caused by prolonged computer use that involves eye strain; weak, itchy, burning, or dry eyes; blurred or double vision; difficulty with focus; sensitivity to light; headaches; and neck pain. According to the American Optometric Association, 50 to 90 percent of computer workers will experience some CVS symptoms.

Posture-Related Injuries

Pain in the lower back, neck, shoulders, and arms are common complaints from computer workers. Sitting for long periods of time in the same position causes fatigue and reduces circulation to muscles and tendons, which can lead to stiffness and soreness.

Neck pain is a common complaint among computer workers.

Prevention Strategies to Reduce Risk of RSI, CVS, and Muscular Pain

Knowing the three primary risk factors for developing health issues when using a computer is key to identifying strategies to reduce risk of injury: poor posture, poor technique, and excessive use. Prevention strategies are listed in Table 1.3. Many of these strategies involve the use of **ergonomics** to improve the computer workspace design. Ergonomics involves the design of equipment and a person's workspace to promote safe and comfortable operation of the equipment by the individual. In other words, good ergonomic design fits the computer equipment to the worker by adjusting components to the optimal height, distance, and angles.

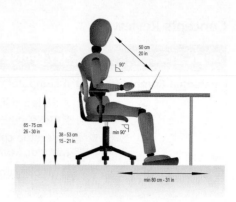

An ergonomically correct computer workspace helps prevent RSI injuries.

Table 1.3	Preventive Strategies for Avoiding Computer-Related Illness
Take frequent breaks. Get up out of the chair and walk around, stretch, and do another activity for a few moments.
Maintain good posture by sitting up straight with feet flat on the floor, shoulders relaxed, head and neck balanced and in line with torso, and your lower back supported by your chair or a rolled towel. If the desk height is not adjustable, use a foot rest.
Sit in a chair that has five legs for stability and allows adjustments to height and angle of backrest, seat, and arm rests.
When typing, the keyboard should be at elbow level with the elbows close to your body and supported by your chair. Wrists and hands should be positioned in line with forearms. If using a notebook computer, consider plugging in an external keyboard so that you can adjust the height and position.
The top of the computer screen should be at or slightly below your eye level. If using a notebook computer, consider using an external monitor that you can adjust to the correct height. Optimal viewing distance is 20 to 40 inches. Increase font size in documents and browsers if necessary to avoid eye strain.
Remember to blink—studies have shown computer users tend to blink about five times less than normal. Also minimize glare and use ambient lighting rather than overhead fluorescents if possible.
Look away from the computer screen once in a while and spend a few moments focusing on something that is off in the distance. For example, look out the window at something outside.

Check This Out

www.osha.gov/SLTC/etools/computerworkstations

Go here for an interactive eTool to learn more about proper workstation setup or view setup checklists.

EXPLORE FURTHER

Notebook, Texting, and Smartphone Ergonomics

Good ergonomic workspace design for a notebook PC involves some factors not discussed in Table 1.3. Increased smartphone use can become a risk for some people. For example, the term **BlackBerry thumb** was devised to describe pain that developed in BlackBerry users in the thumb or wrist from excessive texting.

1. Research ergonomics for laptops and smartphones. Specifically, find at least two articles that address the unique needs of mobile computing device users.
2. Develop a checklist or table with ergonomically correct usage of mobile devices. Include the URLs of the articles you used at the end of the document.
3. Save the document as **C1-Intro-MobileErgonomics-Your Name**.
4. Submit the document to your instructor in the manner she or he has requested.

Concepts Review

Topic	Key Concepts	Key Terms
Personal Computers	A computer needs both hardware and software to work.	Computer
	A PC is a self-contained computer with input, processing, storage, and output.	Hardware
		Software
	A desktop computer includes a system unit and a separate monitor, keyboard, and mouse.	Personal computer (PC)
		Desktop computer
	A mobile computer is a computer that can be moved around.	System unit
		Mobile computer
	A typical laptop (notebook) has a monitor that when swiveled up reveals a keyboard with the remaining components housed below.	Laptop computer
		Notebook
	A netbook is a small notebook designed primarily for email and Internet access.	Netbook
		Ultrabook
	Ultrabooks are thinner, lighter, and more powerful notebooks.	Tablet PCs
	A tablet PC is a lightweight notebook with a smaller screen that you interact with using touch or a digital pen.	
Mobile Devices, Wearable Computers, and Embedded Computers	Mobile devices are handheld computing devices with small screens and with programs and data stored within the unit.	Mobile devices
		Smartphones
	Smartphones, ultra-mobile PCs, and portable media players are popular mobile devices.	Ultra-mobile PC (UMPC)
		Portable media players
	A computer connected to a network that does not store any data or software on the local PC is called a thin client.	Wearable computer
		Embedded computers
	Wearable computers contain sensors that are always on and provide for hands-free interaction and communications.	
Computers for Connecting Multiple Users and Specialized Processing	A server is a high-end computer that connects other computers and is stored in a specially maintained server room.	Server
		Clients
	Computers that connect to a server are called clients.	Server room
	A computer that relies on the server for all programs and data is called a thin client.	Midrange server
		Thin client
	Midrange servers are used to connect hundreds of clients at the same time.	Mainframe
		Supercomputer
	Mainframes are large, powerful, and expensive computers that are capable of handling hundreds or thousands of users.	Petaflops
	A supercomputer is the fastest, most expensive computer capable of processing trillions of calculations per second.	
	Supercomputing speed is measured in petaflops where one petaflop is a quadrillion floating point operations per second.	

continued....

Computer Innovations and Converging Technologies	Ubiquitous computing means that computing technology is everywhere within our environment and used all of the time.	Ubiquitous computing Technological convergence
	Macy's is using a handheld computer to provide instant stock status based on a customer's shoe size.	
	A restaurant owner helped design a noise-dampening technology system that reduces noise when the restaurant gets too loud.	
	3D printers have led to the emergence of on-demand manufacturing.	
	Law enforcement officers can now use a sleeve that attaches to an iPhone or iPod touch that scans fingerprints for rapid identification.	
	A knee brace embedded with motion sensors allows a surgeon to monitor remotely a patient's healing progress.	
	Technological convergence involves the blending or merging of multiple technologies into a single device such as a smartphone or game console.	
Information Technology and the Information Processing Cycle	Information technology involves the use of technology to store, retrieve, send, process, and protect information.	Information technology (IT) Raw data Information Information Processing Cycle Input device Central processing unit (CPU) Processing Microprocessor Multi-core processors Output device Random access memory (RAM) Cache memory Storage media Cloud storage Communications device
	IT specialists are involved with designing, developing, implementing, and maintaining information systems.	
	Raw data are characters entered into a computer that software transforms into meaningful information.	
	The Information Processing Cycle includes four operations: input, processing, output, and storage.	
	Devices used to enter raw data are input devices.	
	Processing is carried out by the central processing unit (CPU), also called a microprocessor.	
	Multi-core processors have independent units on the same silicon chip that allow multiple processes to run simultaneously.	
	Devices used to view information on the computer are output devices.	
	Random access memory (RAM) is temporary storage used to hold data while processing.	
	Cache memory is where frequently used data is stored.	
	Permanent storage media such as hard disk drives, USB flash drives, optical discs, and cloud storage are where data is stored for later use.	
	Communications devices such as a cable modem or router transmit data to/from computers.	

continued....

Topic	Key Concepts	Key Terms
Cloud Computing	Cloud computing is a delivery model where software and computing services are accessed entirely from the Web. Cloud computing places the processing and storage operations in the Web. Some cloud services, such as Google Drive, are free. Several advantages and disadvantages of cloud computing must be considered before signing up for a cloud service. A few popular cloud computing services are Google Drive, Dropbox, iCloud, and SkyDrive.	Cloud computing Software-as-a-Service (SaaS)
Green Computing	Using computers and other electronic devices in an environmentally responsible manner is known as green computing. Green computing practices, policies, and procedures strive to reduce energy consumption; reduce use of paper and paper supplies; and reuse, recycle, or properly dispose of electronics. Five ways to practice green computing include: use Energy Star rated devices, turn off or unplug devices when not in use, reduce printing of documents, modify power options on your computers, and resell or donate old equipment.	Green computing e-waste e-trash
Computers and Your Health	Repetitive-strain injury (RSI) is the leading cause of job-related injury in North America and involves a disorder of the joints, nerves, muscles, ligaments, or tendons. Tendonitis occurs when a tendon in your wrist becomes inflamed. Carpal tunnel syndrome (CTS) occurs when the nerve that connects the forearm to the palm becomes inflamed. Both tendonitis and CTS are caused by computer overuse. Symptoms of tendonitis and CTS include pain, numbness, tingling, decreased mobility and decreased strength in the hand. Computer vision syndrome (CVS) is temporary problems with your eyes caused by prolonged computer use. Ergonomic design involves adjusting components to optimal height, distance, and angles to prevent computer-related injury.	Repetitive-strain injury (RSI) Tendonitis Carpal tunnel syndrome (CTS) Computer vision syndrome (CVS) Ergonomics BlackBerry thumb

Multiple Choice

1. Apple's MacBook Air is an example of this type of notebook computer.
   a. Netbook
   b. Laptop
   c. Tablet PC
   d. Ultrabook

2. Which of the following computers is *not* a personal computer (PC)?
   a. Mainframe
   b. Laptop
   c. Netbook
   d. Desktop computer

3. Google's Project Glass eyeglasses fit into this category of computers.
   a. Supercomputer
   b. Wearable
   c. Server
   d. Desktop PC

4. These computers have a processor that is programmed to perform a particular task.
   a. Multi-core processors
   b. Embedded computers
   c. Servers
   d. Thin clients

5. This type of computer is used to link together other computers in order to share resources.
   a. Ultra-mobile PC (UMPC)
   b. Ultrabook
   c. Netbook
   d. Server

6. Supercomputing speed is measured in
   _____.
   a. Megabytes
   b. Gigabytes
   c. Petaflops
   d. Gigahertz

7. This term is used to describe computing that is everywhere at the same time.
   a. Technological convergence
   b. 24/7 access
   c. Supercomputing
   d. Ubiquitous computing

8. This term describes the merging of multiple technologies into a single device such as a game console being used to play movies and surf the Web.
   a. Ubiquitous computing
   b. Supercomputing
   c. Technological convergence
   d. Embedded computing

9. Which of the following operations is *not* in the Information Processing Cycle?
   a. Printing
   b. Processing
   c. Input
   d. Output

10. A scanner is an example of this type of device used in the Information Processing Cycle.
    a. Input
    b. Processing
    c. Output
    d. Storage

11. The computer chip that carries out the instructions given by software is called the
    _____.
    a. Random Access Memory (RAM)
    b. Central Processing Unit (CPU)
    c. Cache memory
    d. Storage media

12. This term describes a delivery method where software applications are accessed from the Web.
    a. Software-as-a-Service (SaaS)
    b. Infrastructure-as-a-Service (IaaS)
    c. Cloud-as-a-Service (CaaS)
    d. Subscriptions-as-a-Service (SaaS)

13. Cloud computing places the processing and _____ operations in the Information Processing Cycle at the service provider's server.
    a. Output
    b. Storage
    c. Input
    d. Communications

14. This label on a device indicates the manufacturer has met or exceeded minimum federal standards for energy consumption.
    a. Green Star
    b. Star Plus
    c. Energy Star
    d. Eco Star

15. A leading cause of job-related illness in North America is _____.
    a. Computer vision syndrome
    b. Repetitive-strain injury
    c. Computer fatigue
    d. Repetitive-work injury

16. This term describes the design of equipment and workspace for the individual's safety and comfort.
    a. Healthy computing
    b. Work smart
    c. E-computing
    d. Ergonomics

Crossword Puzzle

ACROSS

4 Computer that can be moved around

7 Small notebook for e-mail and the Web

9 Use of technology to manage information

10 Environmentally responsible

12 Fastest, most expensive computer

14 Internet

15 Characters entered into computer

16 Connects thousands, processes millions of transactions

DOWN

1 Blending multiple functions into one unit

2 Inflamed tendon in wrist

3 Eye strain

5 Everywhere, all of the time

6 Thin, light notebook

8 Discarded electronics

11 Hard disk drive

13 Self-contained computer

Matching

Match the term with the statement or definition.

_____ 1. Desktop PC

_____ 2. Multipurpose cell phone

_____ 3. Microwave oven

_____ 4. Midrange server

_____ 5. Multi-core processor

_____ 6. Web-based applications

_____ 7. E-trash

_____ 8. Carpal tunnel syndrome

a. Independent units on the same CPU

b. Connects hundreds of clients

c. Mobile device

d. Repetitive-strain injury

e. Obsolete electronics

f. Apple iMac

g. Embedded computer

h. Cloud computing

Project 1 Technology at Your School

Individual, Pairs, or Team
Deliverable: Presentation

Your school uses technology to meet a variety of needs by different users and perform many different types of tasks. Consider the different uses of technology at your school that would be needed by students, faculty, and administrators. Pick one of the three user groups and list all of the technology that the group would access and the types of tasks for which the technology would be used. You may want to interview someone from faculty or administration to help you complete this task. ***Note: Your instructor may instead assign a user group to you for this project.***

1. Create a presentation with one slide for each use of technology by the user group. Describe the hardware or software that is used and how it is used to complete a task. If you have access to a digital video camera and permission to shoot video from participants, include short videos of the technology being used.
2. Save the presentation as **C1-Project1-SchoolTech-Your Name**.
3. Submit the presentation to your instructor in the manner she or he has requested.

Project 2 Mobile Device Usage

Pairs or Team
Deliverable: Table or Chart

Conduct an informal survey of 20 to 30 friends, relatives, neighbors, or students in another class asking them to estimate the time they spend using technology on a mobile device for the following activities: Talking or Video Calling, Texting, Surfing, Taking Pictures, Playing Games, Other. Ask each person to list activities rated as Other.

1. Compile your results and create a table or a chart in a word processor, spreadsheet, or presentation program to show the results. Include below the chart a list of the activities rated as Other.
2. Save the table or chart as **C1-Project2-MobileUsage-Your Name**.
3. Submit the table or chart to your instructor in the manner she or he has requested.

Project 3 Information Processing Cycle

Individual
Deliverable: Flowchart or Table in a Document or Presentation

Take a task that you completed today using technology and break the task down into each of the four operations in the Information Processing Cycle. Consider the hardware and software that would be used at each operation. Review Figure 1.13 for assistance.

1. Create a flowchart similar to Figure 1.13 or list the operation and place the description in a table in a document or presentation. Include at the beginning of the document or presentation a brief description of the task you analyzed including a list of the hardware and software you determined was used.
2. Save the document or presentation as **C1-Project3-IPCycle-Your Name**.
3. Submit the document or presentation to your instructor in the manner she or he has requested.

Project 4 Comparison of Two Cloud Computing Service Providers

Pairs or Team
Deliverable: Document

Assume you work as interns at a local business magazine. You have been asked to write an article about cloud computing. The editor has asked you to write the article geared toward a small business owner that explains cloud computing and compares two of the leading cloud computing service providers.

1. Research top cloud computing service providers and pick two providers for your article.
2. Create a document written as a magazine article for small business owners that explains cloud computing and describes the services offered by the two providers you selected.
3. Save the document as **C1-Project4-CloudComputing-Your Name**.
4. Submit the document to your instructor in the manner she or he has requested.

Project 5 RSI Costs and Benefits of Ergonomics

Individual, Pairs, or Team
Deliverable: Presentation

You intern at the membership office of the professional association for your industry. At next month's association dinner meeting the president would like to show a presentation that informs the members of current statistics and cost of RSI illness in the workplace. The president would also like to provide information about ergonomics.

1. Research current statistics and costs for RSI in the workplace and the benefits of investing in ergonomics.
2. Create a presentation that could be used by the president at the next association dinner meeting to show statistics, costs, and information about ergonomics as a benefit to reducing RSI injuries.
3. Save the presentation as **C1-Project5-RSIandErgonomics-Your Name**.
4. Submit the presentation to your instructor in the manner she or he has requested.

Project 6 Greener Computing

Individual, Pairs, or Team
Deliverable: Blog Entry

Your workplace does not have a green computing initiative in place. You decide to convince management that the company should embrace green computing practices and policies.

1. Write and post a blog entry that will convince management to adopt green computing in the workplace.
2. Submit your blog URL to your instructor in the manner she or he has requested.

Optional

Read the blog entry for this project of at least two other classmates and post a comment to each. Submit the URLs of your classmates' blogs with Step 2.

Project 7 Technology Innovation

Individual, Pairs, or Team
Deliverable: Blog Entry

How could a technology innovation improve your life? Consider the answer to this question and brainstorm a hardware or software technology that could solve the problem.

1. Write and post a blog entry that describes the problem and how a new technology could improve the situation.
2. Submit your blog URL to your instructor in the manner she or he has requested.

Optional

Read the blog entry for this project of at least two other classmates and post a comment to each. Submit the URLs of your classmates' blogs with Step 2.

Project 8 Discussion—Is Technology Good or Bad?

Team
Deliverable: Document, Blog Entry, or Presentation

Technology has allowed people to live better, more safely, and to access a wealth of resources for personal and work enjoyment and efficiency. Some would argue that technology has made us an "always-on" society where workers have no free time, people are vulnerable to abuse through cyber bullying, and people experience technology burnout from the rapid pace of change.

1. Within your team discuss whether technology innovation is good or bad for society.
2. Prepare a summary of your team's discussion in a document, blog entry, or presentation.
3. Save the document or presentation as **C1-Project8-TechDiscussion-Your Name**.
4. Submit the document, presentation, or blog entry to your instructor in the manner she or he has requested.

Project 9 Ethics Discussion on Personal Use of Technology at Work

Team
Deliverable: Document, Blog Entry, or Presentation

A friend at your workplace who sits near you uses her computer for personal reasons several times throughout the day when she should be working. You have observed her updating her Facebook page, watching YouTube videos, shopping online, and looking at online travel websites. One time at lunch you casually mentioned that you noticed she uses the Web a lot for personal reasons and she told you she prefers the high speed access at work over her home setup.

1. Within your team discuss how you should handle this situation. Should you ignore the situation since you are not her manager? If you answer yes, would your answer be different if the employee was not your friend? In what instances, if any, is it OK to use employer equipment for personal use? How could you convince your friend to stop using the employer's computer for personal use? How should management deal with employees' use of company-provided technology for personal reasons?
2. Prepare a summary of your team's discussion in a document, blog entry, or presentation.
3. Save the document or presentation as **C1-Project9-PersonalUseDiscussion-Your Name**.
4. Submit the document, presentation, or blog entry to your instructor in the manner she or he has requested.

Chapter 2

Exploring the World Using the Internet

After successfully completing this chapter, you will be able to:

- Describe the Internet and the World Wide Web

- Identify the hardware, software, and service you need to connect to the Internet

- List and explain the various types of Internet connectivity options

- Recognize four popular web browsers used to view content

- Distinguish parts of a URL and search, browse, and evaluate online content

- Recognize plug-ins and players used on web pages to enrich content

- Explain online services such as e-commerce, email, and VoIP

C hances are you have used the Internet today at home, at school, or at work to search for information, access study notes, play games, watch videos or movies, update your status, upload photos, or post a comment on a social media site. For many people reading this book, the Internet has always been available to accomplish these tasks, and the ability to connect and share information online with anyone in the world is taken for granted. Society has been shaped in many ways by the proliferation of the Internet over the last 20 years, and the increased use of the Internet on mobile devices is promising to bring even more innovation to the future.

Today's consumers and workers need to be Internet savvy. Knowing how to find the right information quickly, connect with others, and communicate professionally are essential skills for personal and professional success. In this chapter you will learn the difference between the Internet and the World Wide Web, study the equipment options used for Internet connectivity, review the most popular web browsers, search and evaluate web content, understand how multimedia pages access plug-ins and players, and identify the various services available to you in the online world.

Following this introduction to the Internet you will learn to communicate and connect with others using social media and Web publishing options in Chapter 6.

Networks, the Internet, and the World Wide Web

A **network** is two or more computers or other devices (such as a printer) that are linked together to share resources and communicate with each other. Computers are linked by a communications medium such as a wireless signal or a cable that physically connects each device. You may have a small home network set up to share Internet access among a desktop and a laptop, tablet, or other mobile device. Often, home networks also share a printer.

Networks exist in business, government, and other organizations in a variety of sizes and types to facilitate sharing and communicating among workers. These larger networks share software, storage space, printers, copiers, and other devices in addition to Internet access.

The Internet

The **Internet (Net)** is a global network that links together other networks such as government departments, businesses, nonprofit organizations, educational and research institutions, and individuals. Think of the Internet as the physical structure that connects thousands of other networks together to make a worldwide network. In order for this network to transmit data around the world, special high-speed communications and networking equipment is needed to provide the pathway on which the data travels. For example, an email message you send to someone in another state, province, or country would travel through several networks including telephone, cable, or satellite networks to reach its destination. This collection of networks (Figure 2.1) that provides the pathway for data to travel is the Internet.

Did You Know ?

The term information superhighway *was made popular in the '90s by former Vice President Al Gore, who recognized early the importance of building the Internet infrastructure and making it available to everyone. In recognition of his work the Internet Society inducted him into the Internet Hall of Fame in April of 2012.*

Figure 2.1 The Internet is a global network connecting thousands of other networks providing the pathway for data to travel the world.

 **Check This Out**

www.internetworldstats.com
Go here for up-to-date Internet usage statistics for more than 233 countries and world regions. Check the latest world stats or view Internet usage and population by country or region.

You connect your PC or mobile device to the Internet by subscribing to Internet service through an **Internet Service Provider (ISP)**, a company that provides access to the Internet's infrastructure for a fee. You will learn about connecting to the Internet in the next topic.

The World Wide Web

The global collection of electronic documents circulated on the Internet in the form of **web pages** make up the **World Wide Web (Web** or **WWW)**. A web page is a document that contains text and multimedia content such as images, video, sound, and animation. Web pages are usually linked to other pages so that one can start at one page and click links to several other related pages. Web pages are stored in a format that is read and interpreted for display within a **web browser** (a software program used to view web pages). A **website** is a collection of related web pages for one organization or individual. For example, all of the web pages about your school that are available for viewing on the Internet make up your school's website. All of the web pages and resources such as photos, videos, sounds, and animations that make the website work are stored on a special server called a **web server**. Web servers are connected to the Internet continuously so that anyone can access them at any time from any place.

While the Internet provides the path on which a web page is transmitted, web pages are just one type of data that uses the Internet. Other services that use the same network include email messages, instant messages, voice-over-IP services (telephone service via the Internet), and file transfer services. Figure 2.2 illustrates how the Internet delivers the Web content to you at your PC or mobile device while Figure 2.3 provides an example of web pages with multimedia.

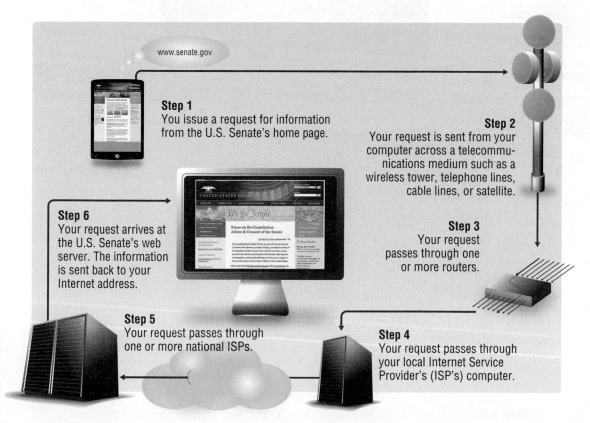

www.senate.gov

Step 1
You issue a request for information from the U.S. Senate's home page.

Step 2
Your request is sent from your computer across a telecommunications medium such as a wireless tower, telephone lines, cable lines, or satellite.

Step 3
Your request passes through one or more routers.

Step 4
Your request passes through your local Internet Service Provider's (ISP's) computer.

Step 5
Your request passes through one or more national ISPs.

Step 6
Your request arrives at the U.S. Senate's web server. The information is sent back to your Internet address.

Figure 2.2 A web page travels along the Internet's collection of networking equipment and telecommunications systems to your PC or mobile device.

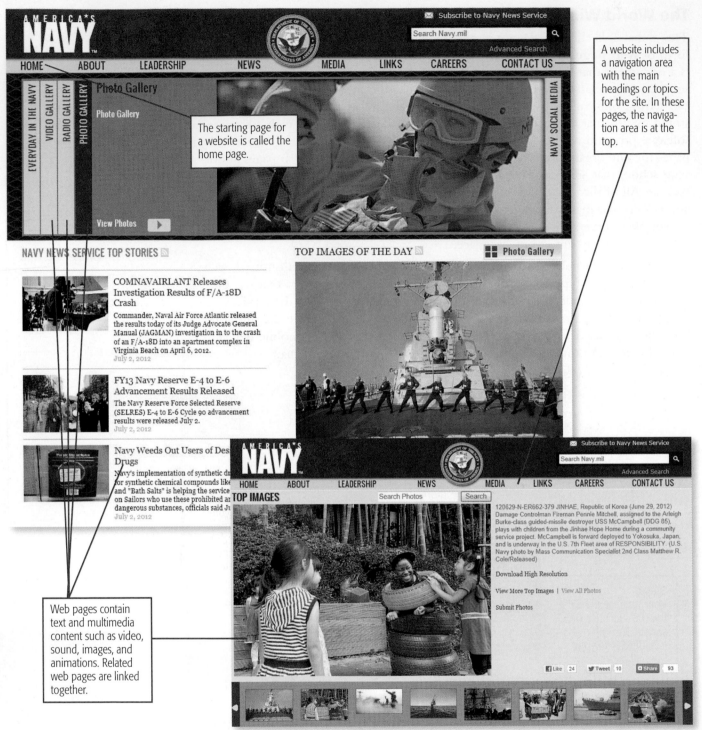

A website includes a navigation area with the main headings or topics for the site. In these pages, the navigation area is at the top.

The starting page for a website is called the home page.

Web pages contain text and multimedia content such as video, sound, images, and animations. Related web pages are linked together.

Figure 2.3 Web pages can contain text, images, video, sound, and animation. A website is a collection of related web pages such as these from the U.S. Navy.

Web 2.0 Initially, web pages mostly were a one-way communication medium where the organization or individual controlled the content and used the Web simply as a means to provide information. Over time, a second generation of two-way communication web pages became available that allowed people to interact with the organization or with each other by sharing ideas, feedback, content, and multimedia. These websites that encourage and facilitate collaboration and sharing and allow users to add or edit content became known as **Web 2.0**.

Web 3.0 The next generation of the Web under development is known as **Web 3.0** or the **Semantic Web**. In this generation of the Web, meaningful connections between data and Web pages will exist, allowing you to find more complex information more easily and quickly. For example, you might type a question such as *Where is the nearest Blue Flag rated beach and a campground?* and the browser will automatically check your geographic location to respond with the closest locations. Web 3.0 will use automated agents or intelligent agents, machines that will adapt and learn the type of content to show you based on previous searches and browsing that you have done. Imagine in the future typing *Where is a good place to eat out tonight?* and the browser responds with a list of restaurants for the type of food you have searched for in the past within a few miles of your current location.

Career Connection

Careers for the Web

Every business needs to have a well-designed, functional website that appeals to its target consumer. Consumers typically turn first to the Web when looking for information to make a purchase. The increase in the use of the Internet on mobile devices means demand for people who can develop websites that display well in mobile web browsers is growing. Web designers design the look, feel, and function of a website, while Web developers specialize in programming the website. Both specialists work together to create a dynamic and interactive site that enhances an organization's brand. If either of these professions interests you, look at online ads for Web designers and Web developers to see what training and experience you will need.

EXPLORE FURTHER

What is Internet2?

If the Internet is the world's largest network of networks, what is Internet2? What is the purpose of Internet2, how is it managed, and what benefits will be gained?

1. Search the Web to locate answers to the above questions.
2. Create a document with a summary of your findings in your own words. Include the URLs of the web pages you used to create your summary.
3. Save the document as **C2-Web-Internet2-Your Name**.
4. Submit the document to your instructor in the manner she or he requested.

Connecting to the Internet

At work or school you connect to the Internet using the high-speed service installed on the organization's network. After logging in by providing your user name and password, you can immediately launch a web browser and start searching the Web. The networks you use in these settings are designed to handle more functions beyond sharing Internet access. In this topic, you will learn about Internet connectivity options for a small home network.

Components Needed for Internet Access

Computers and mobile devices sold today are already equipped with the hardware that is needed to connect to a network. For example, a notebook may be sold equipped with a **network interface card (NIC)**, often referred to in computer ads as an **Ethernet port**. With this type of hardware you plug one end of an Ethernet cable (a twisted-pair cable similar to a telephone cable but larger) into the notebook and the other end into a device that connects to the Internet. Most PCs and all mobile devices also come equipped with a built-in **wireless interface card** that allows you to connect to a network using wireless technology. Newer notebooks and mobile devices may also integrate **Bluetooth** connectivity, which offers the ability to connect to another Bluetooth-enabled device such as your smartphone.

In addition to your network-enabled PC, notebook, or mobile device, you will also need the following account service, hardware, and software to connect to the Internet and browse the Web:

- An account with an Internet Service Provider (ISP)
- Networking equipment (usually provided by your ISP) such as a cable modem, DSL modem, wireless modem, or satellite modem
- A router may be needed if you will be connecting multiple devices (newer modems integrate a wireless router within the same equipment)
- A web browser such as Internet Explorer, Firefox, Chrome, or Safari (you will learn about these software programs in the next topic)

Internet Service Providers (ISPs)

ISPs are companies that sell Internet access by providing the equipment and servers that allow your PC or mobile device to connect to the Internet backbone. Typically, you contract with a telephone or cellular provider, cable company, satellite company, or dedicated Internet access company such as EarthLink.

Fees for Internet access vary and usually are based on the connection speed that you want. High-speed access costs more than a slower connection and is usually priced at various speed levels. Also be aware of download limits (called data caps) in your contract. Some ISPs attach a data cap to a service and if you exceed the cap additional fees may be charged.

Deciding on the connection speed you should sign up for is generally based on your anticipated usage of the Internet. If you primarily only use email and browse web pages, you can get by with a slower speed than someone who wants to participate in online games, watch movies, or stream live music or radio programs.

Conduct a search for ISPs that operate in your area at your school or library to find the best deal and compare services. Generally, along with Internet access you also receive multiple email accounts and security tools to keep your PC or mobile device virus- and spam-free.

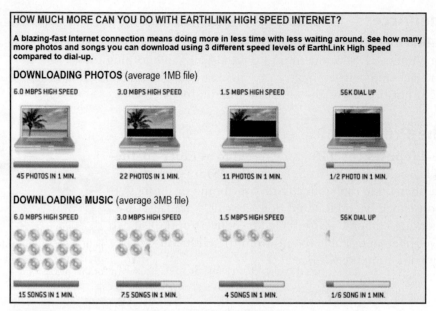

HOW MUCH MORE CAN YOU DO WITH EARTHLINK HIGH SPEED INTERNET?

A blazing-fast Internet connection means doing more in less time with less waiting around. See how many more photos and songs you can download using 3 different speed levels of EarthLink High Speed compared to dial-up.

DOWNLOADING PHOTOS (average 1MB file)

6.0 MBPS HIGH SPEED	3.0 MBPS HIGH SPEED	1.5 MBPS HIGH SPEED	56K DIAL UP
45 PHOTOS IN 1 MIN.	22 PHOTOS IN 1 MIN.	11 PHOTOS IN 1 MIN.	1/2 PHOTO IN 1 MIN.

DOWNLOADING MUSIC (average 3MB file)

6.0 MBPS HIGH SPEED	3.0 MBPS HIGH SPEED	1.5 MBPS HIGH SPEED	56K DIAL UP
15 SONGS IN 1 MIN.	7.5 SONGS IN 1 MIN.	4 SONGS IN 1 MIN.	1/6 SONG IN 1 MIN.

Figure 2.4 ISP EarthLink provides this chart at its website that compares the number of photos and songs that can be downloaded at various connection speeds.

High-Speed Internet Connectivity

High-speed Internet access is called **broadband**, which is a term used to refer to any always-on connection capable of carrying a large amount of data at a fast speed. Speed for broadband connectivity is expressed as **megabits per second (Mbps)**, meaning data transfers at the rate of 1 million bits per second. See Table 2.1 for a list of typical connection speeds by type of connection. When you evaluate ISP contracts, a higher Mbps value means a higher subscription fee. The chart shown in Figure 2.4 puts meaningful context to connection speed by comparing the number of photos and songs that can be downloaded at four speed levels. Various options for broadband access are described below.

Table 2.1	Internet Connectivity Average Connection Speeds
Type of Internet Connectivity	**Average Speed**
Cable	5 to 20 Mbps More expensive plans offer 50 to 75 Mbps access
DSL	1 to 10 Mbps
Fiber-Optic	50 Mbps Some plans available at 75, 150, and 300 Mbps
Satellite	1 Mbps

Cable Internet Access

Cable Internet access is provided by the same cable company with which you subscribe for television service. A cable modem connects to your cable network outlet using a coaxial cable. From the cable modem, you use a twisted-pair cable to plug into your computer or wireless router to enable Internet access. Cable connections are very fast; however, you share the connection with others in your neighborhood so performance can vary.

Did You Know?

Actual connection speed will vary due to numerous factors such as distance from ISP, time of day (congestion slows down networks), and the Web activities of others sharing the connection.

Check This Out

www.speedtest.net

Go here to perform a speed test from your PC or mobile device. Compare speed results at different times of the day until you find when speed is fastest.

A cable modem is connected to the cable company network using coaxial cable.

A DSL modem is connected to the telephone company network using twisted-pair cable.

Check This Out

www.broadbandmap.gov

Go here, type in your city and state, and click <u>Find Broadband</u> to view statistics about broadband providers in your area.

DSL Internet Access

A **Digital Subscriber Line (DSL)** provided by your telephone company connects using telephone lines. A DSL modem uses twisted-pair cable to plug into your telephone jack and your computer or wireless router. With DSL, your telephone line is not tied up while you are using the Internet.

Fiber-to-the-Premises

Fiber-to-the-Premises (FTTP) also referred to as **Fiber-to-the-Home (FTTH)** or **Fiber-Optic-Service (FiOS)** involves the ISP running a fiber-optic cable directly to your home or business. This is the most expensive option and not yet widely available. A piece of networking equipment is installed to convert optical signals transmitted over fiber-optic cable to and from the electrical signals transmitted by your computer devices.

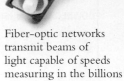

Fiber-optic networks transmit beams of light capable of speeds measuring in the billions of bits per second.

Satellite

Satellite Internet access is an option in rural areas where cable or DSL is not available. Satellite requires the installation of a satellite dish and satellite modem. Access is slower and more expensive.

Satellite Internet is used in rural areas where cable and DSL are not available.

Fixed Wireless Internet Access

Fixed wireless Internet access involves installing an antenna outside your home to send and receive radio signals. A wireless modem is used to connect to your computer or router.

Wi-Fi Hotspots

A wireless access point is used in a Wi-Fi network to provide access to wireless users.

In a **Wi-Fi** network, wireless access points and radio signals are used to transmit data. Wi-Fi is commonly used in public spaces for free Internet access. An area where a Wi-Fi network is within range is called a **hotspot**. Wi-Fi is also commonly used in homes, schools, and workplaces to provide connectivity to notebooks, tablets, and smartphones. A Wi-Fi hotspot encompasses a short distance, which makes it attractive for home users to connect a mobile device via a wireless router connected to their cable or DSL modem, or temporarily access the Internet in an airport, café, library, or other public space.

Depending on the Wi-Fi equipment being used, connection speeds fall within the range of 5 to 6 Mbps for older equipment, 25 to 30 Mbps for mid-range equipment, and 150 to 160 Mbps for newer devices.

Mobile Broadband Sticks

Mobile broadband sticks are portable modems that plug into a USB port on your mobile device and connect via a cellular network. The advantage to a mobile broadband stick is that you can carry your Internet connection with you.

3G and 4G Cellular Communications

Most smartphones used today will be either **3G** (third generation) or **4G** (fourth generation) devices that provide Internet access through cell towers. Average speed for a 3G connection is around 1 Mbps; however, performance varies depending on location. Average speed for 4G devices is often advertised as 10 times faster than 3G and is often described as a 4G **LTE network**, which is the fastest network for mobile devices. These networks use the 4G technology standard with advanced design to improve speed. Devices have to be able to send and receive using 4G technology to take advantage of the higher speed.

A mobile broadband stick is a portable modem that you plug into a USB port.

In some communities, broadband Internet access may not be available, or the cost may be too high for some people. A low-cost way of connecting to the Internet is to use **dial-up**, in which you connect your PC to your telephone system via a modem built into your PC. The ISP provides you with a local telephone number that the computer dials to get on the Internet. The main disadvantages to dial-up are the slow speed and that you cannot use your telephone to make voice calls while the computer is online.

The ISP will provide you with instructions to install and connect to the ISP's network. Generally, the installation requires you to plug in the modem and run a software program from a CD, DVD, or USB flash drive. Appendix B provides instructions for setting up a wireless network in your home.

Once you've established a physical network connection, you are ready to explore the Web using a web browser.

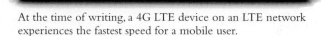

At the time of writing, a 4G LTE device on an LTE network experiences the fastest speed for a mobile user.

EXPLORE FURTHER

What is tethering?

Assume you are planning a vacation in a remote cabin where there is no Internet access. You are bringing your smartphone and notebook with you to the cabin. Your smartphone plan includes Internet access. You decide to investigate tethering as a means to get Internet access on your notebook.

1. Search for information on tethering. Specifically, find out how a cell phone can be used as a modem for another device such as a notebook or tablet. How does it work? What do you need to do to connect the two devices? Are there any issues with tethering that you should be aware of before going to the cabin?

2. Create a document that summarizes your answers to the questions in your own words. At the end of the document, include the URLs of the main articles you used for this topic.

3. Save the document as **C2-Web-tethering-Your Name**.

4. Submit the document to your instructor in the manner she or he has requested.

Popular Web Browsers

Once you have established an Internet connection, you are ready to start browsing, shopping, watching videos, playing games, or checking out what your friends and family are posting at social media websites. Web pages are viewed using browser software. A web browser is a program that locates a web page on the Internet and interprets the code in which the web page has been stored to compose the page as text and multimedia. Many web pages are created using a markup language called **HTML**, which stands for **Hypertext Markup Language**. A markup language uses tags to describe page content. In this topic you will review four popular web browsers for PCs: Internet Explorer, Firefox, Chrome, and Safari. You will also be introduced to the unique needs of mobile web browsers.

Internet Explorer

Internet Explorer (IE) is the web browser included with Microsoft Windows. In Figure 2.5, Internet Explorer is displayed with version 9 (included with Windows 7) on the left and version 10 (included with Windows 8) on the right. Notice the browser in Windows 8 provides more page viewing area. IE 10 is designed to provide more web page viewing with a simpler design. Tools, multiple page tabs, and customization options are only revealed when needed.

Since Windows has such a large market share, IE enjoyed the status as the most popular web browser for many years. People did not look for alternatives when IE was already on one's desktop; however, recently IE has been losing ground to Google's Chrome browser.

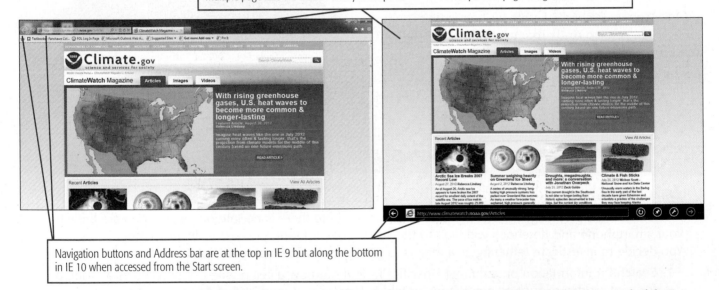

Tabs allow you to open multiple web pages and switch back and forth between them. In IE 10, multiple page tabs are hidden until you swipe down from the top of the page or right-click the mouse.

Navigation buttons and Address bar are at the top in IE 9 but along the bottom in IE 10 when accessed from the Start screen.

Figure 2.5 Internet Explorer (IE) is the web browser included with Microsoft Windows. At the left, IE version 9 in Windows 7 is shown, while the same web page in IE version 10 in shown at the right. IE 10 has a larger page viewing area and simpler design than earlier versions.

Chrome

Google's **Chrome** is a free web browser that runs on Windows-compatible PCs. The browser was initially released in 2008 with features that included fast page loading and the ability to search directly in the Address bar. In Figure 2.6, Chrome is shown with the web page for Grand Canyon National Park.

As of June 2012, Chrome and Internet Explorer were both hovering near the 30 percent market share statistic according to two popular web usage statistic counters, StatCounter and W3Counter. With future trends indicating mobile browsers will be favored over PC browsers, these market share statistics could vary widely going forward.

Navigation buttons and Address bar

In Chrome you can type a web page address here or type a search phrase to search using Google.

Figure 2.6 Google's Chrome browser delivers fast page loading and the ability to search from the address bar.

Firefox

Firefox is a free web browser available at mozilla.org by the Mozilla Foundation. The browser will run on a Windows-compatible PC, a Mac, or a Linux computer. Since the initial release of Firefox version 1 in 2004, the browser's use has been steadily rising. At the time of writing, Firefox was the third most popular browser. Figure 2.7 shows Firefox version 13 with the web page for the Library of Congress. You will notice similarities to IE version 9 with the placement of the navigation buttons, Address bar, and tabs for browsing multiple pages. Fans of Firefox indicate they favor the browser's speed in loading web pages.

Tabs for opening multiple pages

Navigation buttons and Address bar

Type search requests here.

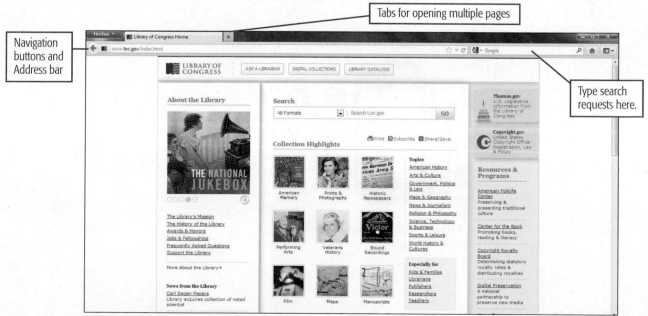

Figure 2.7 Mozilla's Firefox is the third most popular browser.

Type search requests here.

Navigation buttons and Address bar

You can add pages you want to read later to the Reading List. Safari keeps the list up-to-date for all devices such as your iPhone or iPad via iCloud.

Figure 2.8 Safari is the browser supplied on Macs, iPads, and iPhones. Safari also works on Windows-compatible PCs and is available to download for free at Apple.com.

Safari

Apple's **Safari** browser is used on Mac and Apple mobile devices such as iPads and iPhones. The browser is also available as a free download for a PC. Safari 5 includes new features such as the Reading List shown in Figure 2.8 and full-screen browsing.

All of the top four web browsers share similar features and navigation options designed to assist with finding and viewing web pages. Regardless of the browser you use, web addressing and search techniques discussed in the next topic are universal.

Figure 2.9 Opera Mobile is a popular browser for mobile devices.

Mobile Browsers

Mobile web browsers are designed to quickly display web pages optimized for the smaller screens on devices such as tablets and smartphones. The challenge for mobile browsers is that web pages designed for larger screens have to be readable in a smaller viewing area. Mobile browsers incorporate text wrapping and try to avoid the user having to scroll sideways. Mobile versions of IE, Chrome, Firefox, and Safari are available in addition to numerous other browser apps for Android and Apple devices.

In Figure 2.9, Opera Mobile is shown on a smartphone. Opera also provides a browser for Windows-compatible, Mac, and Linux computers.

 Blog Topic

Which browser(s) do you favor?

Which browser do you use? Have you tried one of the other browsers mentioned in this topic? Do you use multiple browsers? If yes, why? If you could develop your dream browser, what would it do differently than what you use now?

1. Write and post a blog entry that provides the answers to the above questions.
2. Read at least two of your classmates' blogs and post one comment to each.
3. Submit your blog URL and the URLs of your classmates' blogs for which you provided a comment to your instructor in the manner she or he requested.

EXPLORE FURTHER

What other web browsers are available?

Other web browsers are available for PCs and Macs in addition to the four mentioned in this topic. Each of these other web browsers is designed to be different in various ways from IE, Chrome, Firefox, and Safari.

1. Research other web browsers that are available for a PC or a Mac. Pick one alternative web browser and learn more about what it does and why people use it.
2. Create a document that describes the alternative web browser in your own words. At the end of the document include the URLs of the articles you used.
3. Save the document as **C2-Web-AlternativeBrowsers-Your Name**.
4. Submit the document to your instructor in the manner she or he has requested.

Understanding Internet and Web Addresses and Navigating Web Pages

If you are invited to visit a friend at his house, you need to know the address so you know where to go to find his home. Similarly, on the Internet, you locate a computer by using an address. When a computing device is connected to the Internet, it is assigned a unique address called an **Internet Protocol (IP) address** so that the device can communicate with other computers. An IP address is a series of four numbers from 0 to 255 separated by periods. For example, in Figure 2.10, the IP address is 209.46.18.200. **ICANN (Internet Corporation for Assigned Names and Numbers)** is a nonprofit organization that is in charge of keeping track of the Internet addresses and names all around the world.

The system of addressing that uses four groups of numbers is referred to as IPv4. A new system called IPv6 was launched because the number of unique IPv4 addresses was running out. IPv6 uses eight groups of characters separated by colons, where a character can be a number 0 through 9 or a letter a through f. With IPv6 there will be enough IP addresses for years to come. For now, both IPv4 and IPv6 will coexist since some equipment and software connected to the Internet cannot handle IPv6 addressing.

Did You Know?

On June 6, 2012, World IPv6 Launch Day was held during which hundreds of websites including heavyweights Google, Microsoft, and YouTube permanently enabled IPv6 addressing.

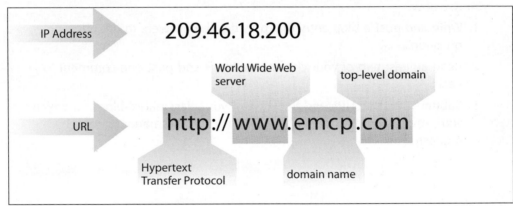

Figure 2.10 A URL contains a domain name that allows you to locate a website using a text-based name rather than the numeric IP address.

Web Addresses

If you know the numeric address for a computer on the Internet, you can navigate to the site by typing it in the browser's Address bar. For example, typing 209.46.18.200 in the Address bar of your browser will bring you to the EMC Corporation website (the publishing company for this textbook). However, most people do not know or could not remember a numeric address. Instead, we use a **web address**, which is a text-based address, to navigate to a website. A web address is also called a **uniform resource locator (URL)**. In Figure 2.10, the URL for the EMC Corporation website is *http://www.emcp.com*. The four parts of this URL are explained in Table 2.2. Each part of a URL is separated by punctuation consisting of a colon (:), one (/) or two slashes (//), and periods (.) referred to as "dots." For example, when telling someone the URL for EMC Corporation you would say "*emcp dot com*."

When you type a URL in the Address bar of a browser, a server has to locate the IP address for the domain name so that data can be transmitted to the correct computer. A server that holds this directory is known as a **Domain Name System (DNS) server** and is owned by a business or ISP.

Table 2.2	The Parts of a URL	
Part of URL	**What It Represents**	**Examples**
http	The protocol for the page. A protocol is a set of rules for transmitting data. Since http is used most of the time, you can omit it when typing the URL.	http Hypertext transfer protocol ftp File transfer protocol https Hypertext transfer protocol secure
www	World Wide Web server Since most servers are World Wide Web servers, you can omit www when typing the URL.	
emcp	The organization's **domain name**, also referred to as a second-level domain name. Domain names are the text-based version of the IP address and are usually the name or an abbreviation of a company or organization.	emcp EMC Corporation domain name nytimes New York Times domain name google Google Inc.'s domain name navy U.S. Navy's domain name loc Library of Congress domain name
com	The part of the domain name that identifies the **top-level domain (TLD)**. TLDs identify the type of organization associated with the domain name. Several TLDs with three or more characters are known as **generic top-level domains (gTLDs)**. ICANN is expanding the number of approved gTLDs. Watch for websites in the future with domain names such as myroadsideinn.*hotel* or mylawfirm.*legal*. Two-character TLDs are country codes called **ccTLDs**.	com Commercial organizations edu Educational institution gov Government website mil Military site net Network providers such as ISPs org Nonprofit organizations biz Business ca Canada

Navigating Web Pages

Most people browse the Web in one of two ways: by typing the web address of a company or organization to go directly to a website (Figure 2.11), or, by typing a search phrase into a search engine website such as Google or Bing to search for information (Figure 2.12). In the next topic you will learn more about using search engines to find information.

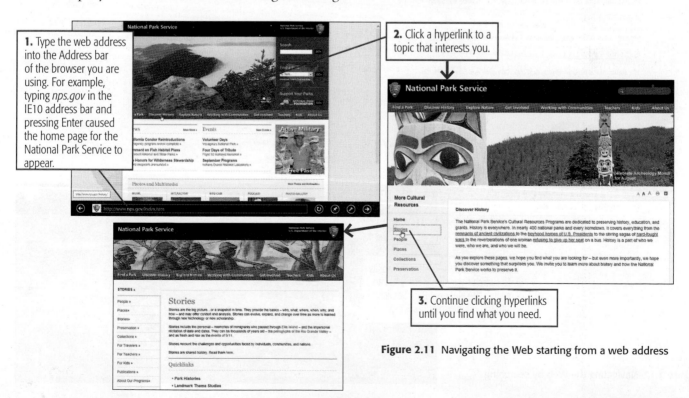

1. Type the web address into the Address bar of the browser you are using. For example, typing *nps.gov* in the IE10 address bar and pressing Enter caused the home page for the National Park Service to appear.

2. Click a hyperlink to a topic that interests you.

3. Continue clicking hyperlinks until you find what you need.

Figure 2.11 Navigating the Web starting from a web address

1. Type the web address for the search engine you like to use such as Google.com or Bing.com (shown here in IE10).

2. Type a search phrase and press Enter or click the Search button.

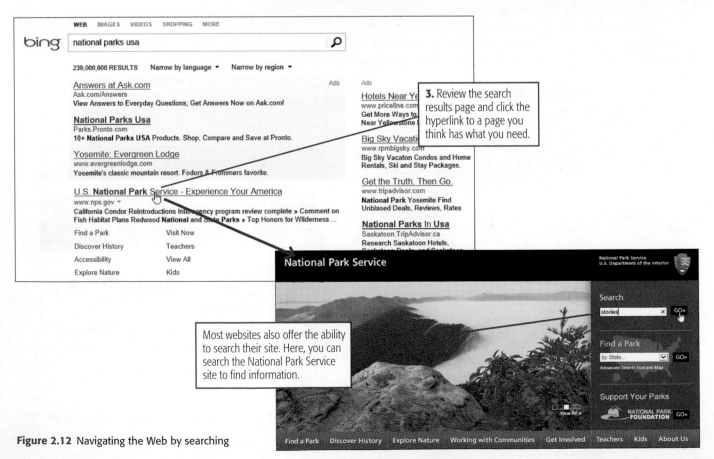

3. Review the search results page and click the hyperlink to a page you think has what you need.

Most websites also offer the ability to search their site. Here, you can search the National Park Service site to find information.

Figure 2.12 Navigating the Web by searching

The first page of a website that displays when the web address is requested is called the **home page**. Main headings appear along the top or edges and are organized by topic to guide you to subpages within the site. Web pages contain **hyperlinks** (**links** for short) that when clicked or tapped on a touchscreen take you to a related web page. Any item on a web page can be hyperlinked to another page. For example, a title, word, phrase, photo, video, graphical icon such as a button, or audio object may be a hyperlink. As you move the mouse around a page, the white arrow pointer will change to a white hand with the index finger pointing upward when you are pointing at text or an object that is a hyperlink. Hyperlinked text is usually a different color, in bold, or underlined. Click when you see the icon change or tap the text or object to move to the related web page.

You can also type the web address of a linked web page directly into the Address bar. For example, typing *nytimes.com/pages/todayspaper/index.html* takes you directly to Today's Paper at The New York Times website.

 Blog Topic

What type of Web activity do you do most often?

Most people do a variety of tasks on the Internet, but one or two types of activities generally predominate. In what activity do you spend most of your time on the Web? Is it reading news or reading or writing blogs? Is it online shopping? Is it connecting with friends and family? Is it sharing photos, videos, or music? Is it looking for information for work, school, or personal interest? How many hours per week on average do you estimate you spend on each of these activities?

1. Write and post a blog entry that provides the answers to the above questions.

2. Read at least two of your classmates' blogs and post one comment to each.

3. Submit your blog URL and the URLs of your classmates' blogs for which you provided a comment to your instructor in the manner she or he requested.

EXPLORE FURTHER

How do I register a domain name?

Assume you are planning to start a new business when you graduate. You know you will need to have a website but are not sure how to go about getting a domain name for your organization.

1. Find out how to check for an available domain name and how to register the name.

2. With millions of websites already in existence, the name you want to use may already be taken. Find out what alternatives you have if the domain name you want is already in use.

3. Create a document that summarizes in your own words what you have learned about domain names in Steps 1 and 2. At the end of the document include the URLs of the articles you used.

4. Save the document as **C2-Web-DomainNames-Your Name**.

5. Submit the document to your instructor in the manner she or he has requested.

Searching the Web

A **search engine** is a company that searches web pages and indexes the pages by **keywords** or by subject. When you type a search phrase at a search engine website, the results list that displays contains links to the web pages that have been associated with the keywords you used in your search phrase. To generate indexes, search engines use programs called **spiders** or **crawlers** that read web pages and other information to generate index entries. Generally, website owners submit their website information to search engines to make sure they are included in search results.

Some search engines display a subject directory that provides links to categories of information such as *Music, News, Shopping,* or *Travel.* Clicking a category brings you to another page with subtopics for that category. In most cases, you can specify if you want search results to come from the entire Web or from indexes associated with images, maps, news, shopping, or videos. Table 2.3 contains a list of five popular search engines; however, be aware that many other search engines exist.

Did You Know?

Some browsers contain an Instant Search text box usually located to the right of the Address bar. Type a search phrase in this box to search using a default search engine. If you prefer to use a different search engine, customize the browser options.

Did You Know?

According to Hitwise (a company that measures Internet traffic) Google (65%) and Bing (28%) were the two leading search engines used in June 2012. More than 50 percent of searches in the same period used only one or two words in the search phrase.

Table 2.3	Popular Search Engines
Search Engine	**URL**
Google	google.com
Bing	bing.com
Yahoo!	yahoo.com
Ask	ask.com
Dogpile	dogpile.com

You will get different results from various search engines. Figure 2.13 displays the search results from the same search phrase *xeriscape gardening* entered at two search engines, Yahoo! and Ask. Differences in results can occur for a variety of reasons. For example, spider and index program parameters differ by search engine, some search engines locate and index new or updated pages at different speeds or times, and page relevance to the search phrase may be ranked differently.

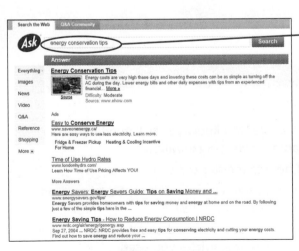

The same search phrase returns different search results at two search engines. Search engine spider and index programs vary.

Figure 2.13 Search engines provide different results for the same search phrase for many reasons, including the way in which spiders and indexers find and rank pages and keywords.

Fine-Tuning a Search

Regardless of the search engine you like to use, knowing how to fine-tune a search request will make your searching quicker and easier. With practice, you will develop a search technique that works best for you. Following are some guidelines for searching:

- A search phrase in quotations returns pages where the keywords are in the same sequence; otherwise, the search results may have the keywords in any order. For example, "endangered animals" returns pages with the word *endangered* immediately followed by the word *animals*.
- Type a minus symbol in front of a keyword to *exclude* the keyword from the search results; for example, "endangered animals" –tiger returns pages about endangered animals other than tigers.
- Rather than searching the entire Web, consider using a search engine's category such as News, Images, Videos, or Blogs to restrict the search results to a specific type of page or object (Figure 2.14).
- Check out a search engine's advanced search tools to further refine your search terms, domain, or region (Figure 2.14).
- Most search engines allow you to restrict searches to a specific time frame; for example, in Google's search tools you can filter results by *Past hour, Past 24 hours, Past week, Past month, Past year*, or *Custom date range* (Figure 2.14).
- Look for Help at the search engine's website to learn more about how the search engine indexes pages and the recommendations for searching at its site.

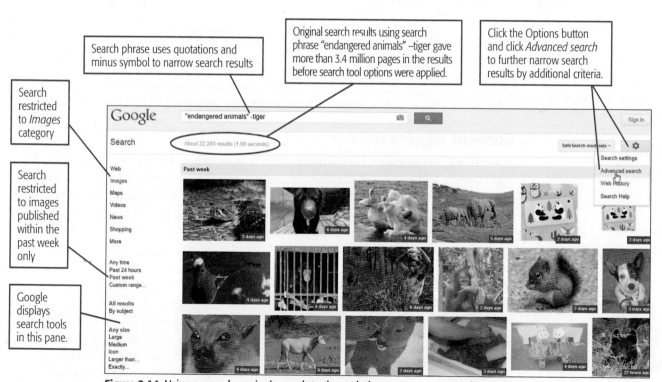

Figure 2.14 Using a search engine's search tools can help you narrow a search.

Some search engines are **metasearch search engines** that send your search phrase to other search engines and then compile the results in one list. Using a metasearch search engine allows you to type your search phrase once and access results from a wider group of search engines. Dogpile is an example of a metasearch search engine that provides search results in one place from Google, Bing, and Yahoo! among others.

Some metasearch search engines specialize in one type of search service such as KAYAK (kayak.com), which specializes in searching travel websites to provide you with a comparison of flights, hotels, and car rentals in one place (Figure 2.15).

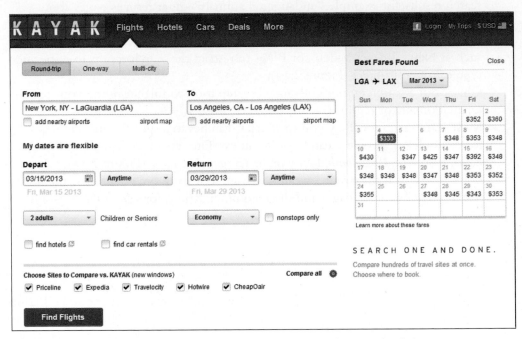

Figure 2.15 KAYAK, a metasearch search engine, specializes in searching travel websites.

Content Aggregators

A **content aggregator** is an organization that searches the Web for new content, and collects and organizes the content in one place. Some content aggregators send updates automatically to subscribers. Subscribers receive the updates, sometimes referred to as *feeds*, based on selections made for the type of information in which the subscriber is interested. For example, you can elect to receive new items related to news or music. Some content aggregators provide this service for free while others charge a fee to send out updates to subscribers. The advantage to subscribers is that the content aggregator does the work of searching the Web and organizing related information.

Really Simple Syndication (RSS) is a specification used by content aggregators to distribute updates to subscribers. Updates are read using an RSS reader (program used to read RSS feeds) on your PC or mobile device. Another reader by Google called Google Reader can be used to subscribe to updates at websites, which are viewed by signing in with your Gmail account at reader.google.com.

Click the RSS or Google Reader icon at websites to subscribe to update feeds.

Popurls.com is a content aggregator that lists on one page all of the latest headlines from the most popular sites on the Internet (Figure 2.16). Another aggregator, Techmeme (Techmeme.com), tracks changes to technology news and presents a summary each day.

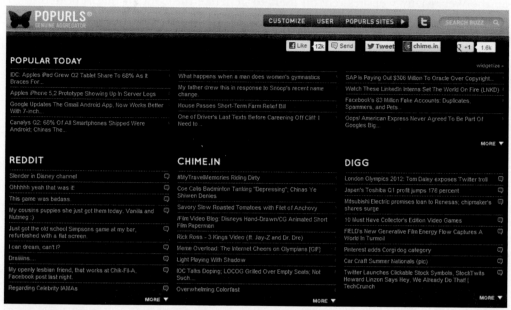

Figure 2.16 POPURLS is a content aggregator that lists all of the latest changes at popular websites.

EXPLORE FURTHER

Try out your search skills

Assume you need to find information on cybersquatting with respect to the concern that cybersquatting will increase in the future when ICANN releases new gTLDs. You need to find out what cybersquatting means and why it may become a greater concern. Only pages published within the past 12 months are desired.

1. Conduct a search using your favorite search engine using only a search phrase. What search phrase did you use and how many pages were in the search results list?

2. Next, explore the search engine's tools for conducting advanced searches and narrow your search results as specified above. How did you refine your search and how many pages were in the revised search results list?

3. Read one or two articles about the topic.

4. Create a presentation that summarizes in your own words a definition of cybersquatting and a few points about why cybersquatting is expected to rise with the release of new gTLDs. Include a slide for each of Step 1 and Step 2's answers. End your presentation with the URLs of the article(s) you read.

5. Save the presentation as **C2-Web-CybersquattingSearch-Your Name**.

6. Submit the presentation to your instructor in the manner she or he has requested.

TOPIC 2.6

Evaluating Web Content

Increasingly, the Web is becoming the only resource people turn to when looking for information, news, shopping, connecting with others, and sharing media. Anyone with an Internet connection and space allocated on a web server can publish a page on the Web. Many websites rely on users to generate the content that is posted. With thousands of new websites coming online every year, how can you be sure the information that is presented at a site is true, accurate, and timely?

Start at the Web Address

Look at the domain name in the web address. Is it an organization you recognize and trust? For example, an article published at nytimes.com would be associated with a highly recognizable media organization, The New York Times. A web address that ends with .gov, .org, or .edu would indicate the source is a government department or agency, a nonprofit organization, or an educational institution—all trusted sources.

Look at domain names for publishers of content in the print-based world with which you are familiar. For example, if you are familiar with *Psychology Today* magazine, then you will be comfortable reading content at psychologytoday.com (Figure 2.17).

Check the domain name in the web address for a recognizable name that you trust.

Figure 2.17 Begin evaluating web content by looking in the web address for a domain name that is an organization you recognize and trust.

If you do not recognize the domain name in the web address, consider doing a search for the domain name owner and searching the owner's name to find out whether the organization is reputable.

Look for an Author and the Author's Affiliation

Check for an author's name at the page. Is the author affiliated with the organization in the web address? Is the author an expert as evidenced by credentials after his or her name or evidenced in the introduction or other biographical information?

If no author name is found, try to determine if the information is credible by other means. For example, check for a link that describes the organization presenting the content. Most websites have an About Us or a Contact Us link (Figure 2.18). Check these sources to determine if a bias might exist for the information you are reading.

Figure 2.18 Check for an author's name on a web page; if the author has credentials or other biographical information, that helps you evaluate the validity of the content.

Check the Publication Date

In most cases you want to find the most recent information about a topic. Look for the date of publication on the page (Figure 2.19). Use the search engine's advanced search tool to filter your search results by a recent time frame and see if the page remains in the list. Sometimes, the original publication date may be older but a notation may appear (usually near the top or bottom of the page) that provides a date the content was updated. Finally, a clue to the date of publication may appear in the linked web address. For example, a linked page may have an address similar to: http://www.companyname.com/archives/2013/March/pagename.html.

If no date can be found, consider whether the content seems dated. For example, look for something in the article that may give a clue to the time frame it was published such as a reference to an event. When in doubt, corroborate the content by finding another source that is published with a recent date.

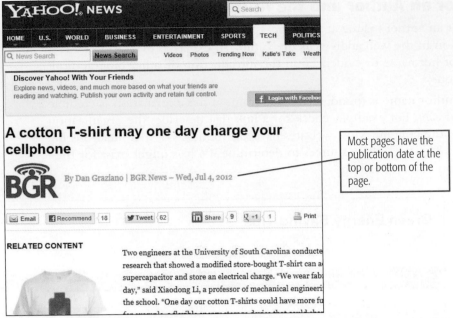

Figure 2.19 Always look for a publication date to evaluate if the content is current.

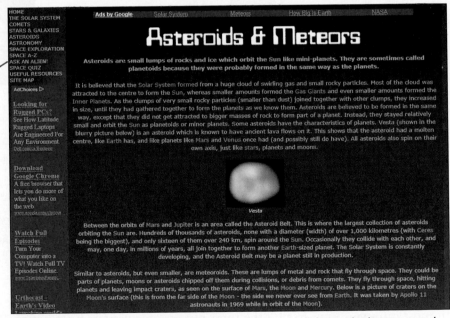

Figure 2.20 A page's design including layout, organization, and choice of colors can reveal whether the page has been published by a professional organization.

Purpose and Design of the Site

Finally, consider the purpose and design of the page you are reading. Is the organization that has published the page a company in the business of marketing a product or service? If yes, a bias may be present toward convincing you to buy the product or service.

A web page's design, spelling, and grammar will also indicate the page's credibility. A professionally designed, well written page will invite trust. The page shown in Figure 2.20 may indeed be presenting accurate information on asteroids and meteors; however, the page design uses layout, colors, and organization not used by professionals, and links such as *ASK AN ALIEN!* are cause for further inspection.

A poorly designed web page that is lacking a recognizable domain name, an author's name, and a recent publication date indicates a page that you need to be careful with. The information may indeed be accurate and credible, but you should do some additional checking to be sure.

 Blog Topic

Is Wikipedia a valid source of information for a research paper?

Wikis are websites where the page content is created by the user community. Generally, anyone can add content, and additions or changes that are wrong may be visible for a while before errors are caught. The openness of wikis has led some in the academic world to discredit sources such as Wikipedia (the most popular encyclopedia with content developed by volunteers). What do you think?

1. Go to wikipedia.org and read the information on the *About Wikipedia* page.

2. Create and post a blog entry with your opinion on whether Wikipedia content is an acceptable source for a research paper and state your rationale.

3. Read at least two of your classmates' blogs and post one comment to each.

4. Submit your blog URL and the URLs of your classmates' blogs for which you provided a comment.

EXPLORE FURTHER

Evaluate information on geocaching in your area

Geocaching is an outdoor activity where participants use a GPS or other mobile device to locate a container that has been hidden by other participants. The container usually contains a logbook and may also have a prize of small value. When a participant finds the geocache, he or she updates the logbook and trades or leaves the prize for the next person.

1. Find information on geocaching in your area. Pick a web page and evaluate the web page. Is it accurate? Is the page from a credible source? Is the information current?

2. Create a document with a screen capture of the web page and below the screen capture list the elements that you used to evaluate the web page in Step 1. Provide the URL at the bottom of the document. *Hint: One way to make a screen capture of a web page is to display the desired web page, press the Print Screen key on your keyboard, and then use the Paste button in Word to paste the image into a document.*

3. Save the document as **C2-Web-PageEvaluation-Your Name**.

4. Submit the document to your instructor in the manner she or he has requested.

Popular Web Plug-ins and Players for Multimedia Content

TOPIC 2.7

Most web pages have some multimedia content such as images, animations, audio, and video. This type of rich content enhances the experience. In order for some multimedia content to work, a **plug-in** (also referred to as an **add-on**) or **player** may need to be installed. Plug-ins, add-ons, or players all refer to the same type of program—a software program that allows the browser to display enhanced content that it cannot display on its own.

Some plug-ins and players are included in the browser or with your operating system (Windows Media Player); however, you may display a web page with a message similar to the one shown in Figure 2.21 indicating that you need to install a plug-in or player to view the content. When you encounter a message like this, a link will be provided to the source program, which you can download for free. Click or tap the link and follow the instructions to download and install the software (Figure 2.22).

Popular plug-ins and players used on the Web are listed in Table 2.4.

Table 2.4	Common Plug-ins and Players You May Be Prompted to Download and Install	
Plug-in or Player Name	**Description**	**URL**
Adobe Reader	Used to view PDF documents. PDF documents are popular for exchanging richly formatted documents on the Web. PDFs are formatted as they would look when printed without requiring the source program in which the document was created to view or print.	adobe.com
Adobe Flash Player	Used often for animations on web pages with high-quality graphics, sound, and interactivity. Many browsers include the Flash Player since it is a popular plug-in; however, some such as Firefox will require you to download and install the application.	adobe.com
Shockwave Player	Used for Web content that includes interactive games, high-quality video or audio	adobe.com
Java	Java is a programming language used on some web pages to add interactivity to applications run from web pages or play online games.	java.com
Microsoft Silverlight	Plug-in from Microsoft used for interactive applications and high-quality video or audio	microsoft.com
Real Player	Used to play video and music files such as MP3 files	real.com
QuickTime	QuickTime is from Apple and built into Mac computers and mobile devices. PCs will also need QuickTime if the web page has video or animation provided in the QuickTime format.	apple.com

Depending on the plug-in or player you have had to install, the content may become visible immediately, or you may need to close and reopen the browser and then return to the web page you were trying to view.

A link will be provided to the plug-in or player that is needed. Click the link to download and install the latest version from the software program's website. In this case clicking the link connects you to adobe.com.

Figure 2.21 A message such as this one will appear if you display a web page that requires a plug-in or player that is not installed.

Watch for messages that will add extra software or toolbars to your browser that you may not want. If necessary, deselect these options and then click the Download button.

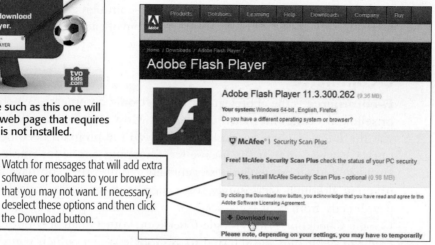

Figure 2.22 Install a plug-in or player by following the steps provided at the software program's website.

Plug-in and Player Updates

From time to time you will be prompted to install an update to a plug-in or player. Generally, when these messages occur, you should install the updates so that web pages work as expected.

Be Alert for Fake Plug-Ins and Players!

Some viruses appear on web pages as spoofs of popular plug-ins and players. These viruses look like the real player but clues will exist that they are not real. Look for typos in the name of the player (missing spaces between words) or linked web page. If in doubt, go directly to the source URL provided in Table 2.4 to download a plug-in or player.

EXPLORE   FURTHER

Add-on toolbars for your browser

Some programs, such as many antivirus applications, install add-on toolbars to your browser automatically. As shown in Figure 2.22, you may inadvertently install an add-on when you download a plug-in or player. Some browsers refer to add-ons as *extensions*.

1. Using your favorite browser, find out how to enable and disable add-ons/extensions.
2. Create a handout specifying the browser and version that provides step-by-step instructions for the reader on how to turn on or turn off additional toolbars in the browser.
3. Save the document as **C2-Web-AddOnToolbars-Your Name**.
4. Submit the document to your instructor in the manner she or he has requested.

E-Commerce, Messaging, and Internet Telephone and Conferencing Options

The Internet is not used just for connecting with others at social media websites or looking up information you need for work, school, or your personal life. Many people turn to the Internet for shopping (e-commerce), communicating using messaging services such as electronic mail (email), and for telephone calls or conferencing services.

E-Commerce

E-commerce is the abbreviation for electronic commerce, which involves buying or selling over the Internet (Figure 2.23). Most software is now purchased directly via the Internet where the link to download the program becomes available once you have paid for the license fee. Shopping online for music, videos, books, clothing, and other merchandise generally requires that you have a credit card for payment although, increasingly, some merchants are making available the ability to pay directly from your bank account or use a third-party payment service such as Google Checkout. With Google Checkout, your Gmail account can be linked to a credit or debit card and referred to as Google Wallet, which you can use to pay for purchases at websites. E-commerce on mobile devices is a fast-growing market as consumers love to shop for favorite apps or music to use on a smartphone or tablet. Table 2.5 describes three categories of e-commerce.

Table 2.5	Types of E-Commerce Transactions
E-Commerce Activity	**Description**
Business-to-consumer (B2C)	This is a familiar category of e-commerce if you have ever bought music, software, or other merchandise on the Web. A business such as Amazon sets up a website that is available to any consumer for purchasing merchandise or services. Businesses that sell online to consumers are often referred to as **e-tailers** (abbreviation for electronic retailers). Figure 2.23 illustrates the typical steps in a B2C transaction.
Business-to-business (B2B)	In this category, a business sells directly to other businesses using the Web. In some cases, B2B transactions occur at websites used by consumers. For example, if you are on a website where ads are shown and you click the ad, a payment is charged to the business that posted the ad. B2B ads at websites allow the website owner to provide the website free of charge to consumers.
Consumer-to-consumer (C2C)	C2C activity occurs at websites such as Craigslist or eBay where transactions occur directly between two consumers. C2C websites generally also involve B2C or B2B transactions since the website owner that provides the service charges fees to advertisers and/or sellers to post ads.

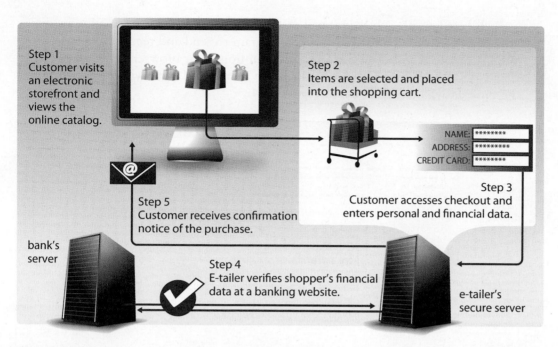

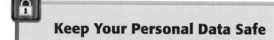

Figure 2.23 Steps in the online shopping process for B2C transactions

Keep Your Personal Data Safe

When paying online make sure you are using a secure website before entering personal data such as your credit card number. The Web address should start with https, and some browsers show an icon of a closed lock indicating your personal data is safe. You will learn about secure websites in Chapter 7.

Email

Electronic mail **(email)** is the sending and receiving of digital messages using the Internet, sometimes with documents or photos attached. Businesses were using the Internet for email long before consumers embraced the service when PCs became mainstream in the 80s and 90s. In today's workplaces, email is the standard communication medium and often is preferred over voice conversation since email provides a written record of what has been agreed upon.

When you sign up for an account with an ISP, one or more email accounts are included with your Internet service. An **email address** is used to connect to your email account at the ISP server and is generated in the format *username@mailserver. com* or *username@mailserver.net*. Your ISP will provide the means for you to create your own user name to include before the @ symbol. The text after the @ symbol is the ISP's server name. Once your email account is created you can use a program called an **email client** such as Microsoft's Outlook or Apple's Mail to send and receive messages.

Did You Know?

In 1971 the first message was sent across a network with the @ symbol used to separate the user name from the computer name.

Web-based email such as Hotmail or Gmail are popular among email users since you do not need a separate email client program to send and receive messages. When you use Hotmail or Gmail, you sign in from your browser to access email. Once logged in, all messages are created, sent, stored, and otherwise managed from the browser window as shown in Figure 2.24.

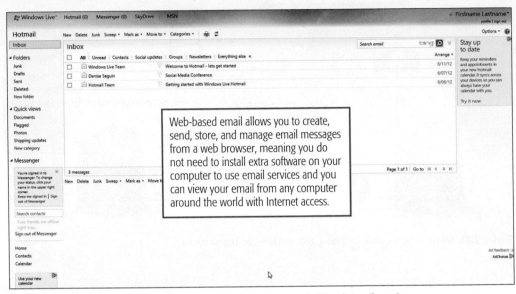

Web-based email allows you to create, send, store, and manage email messages from a web browser, meaning you do not need to install extra software on your computer to use email services and you can view your email from any computer around the world with Internet access.

Figure 2.24 Windows Live Hotmail is a popular choice for a web-based email service.

Text and Instant Messaging Messaging between mobile devices is often preferred over email since the messages can be sent more quickly without the need to go to a special email program. **Text messages** are short text exchanges, referred to as **texting**, that you send to another mobile device using a service called **Short Message Service (SMS)**. Some mobile devices provide the ability to use **instant messaging** (exchanging text messages in real time) between other users of similar devices. Examples of instant messaging services on mobile devices are BlackBerry's BBM and Apple's iMessage.

Internet Voice and Conferencing Services

The ability to call someone using the Internet and engage in a voice conversation is called **Voice over Internet Protocol (VoIP)**. Skype is a popular service for making free calls over the Internet and includes the ability to make video calls using web cameras to allow each party to see one another while chatting. Software and hardware on your PC or mobile device convert your voice and/or picture into digital signals that travel the Internet.

Skype is a popular choice for people who want to make video calls using the Internet.

Text or instant messaging from a mobile device is a popular method of communicating with others.

Web Conferencing **Web conferencing** is a program that allows a group of individuals to connect online to engage in a meeting. Web conferencing software similar to that shown in Figure 2.25 allows each participant to talk and share ideas and information using presentations or online whiteboards. A person's desktop can be shared so that others participating in the meeting can watch a demonstration. Online meetings allow businesses to save the cost of expensive travel to bring together a group of people.

Other services use the Internet such as newsgroups, chat rooms, and remote access support providers. New applications for the Internet that will make creative use of text, video, and audio are sure to be invented!

Web conferencing programs provide the ability to talk and share documents or presentations with a group of individuals. Tools are included to annotate and mark up the online whiteboard during the conference.

Participants can pose and answer questions with the group in this window.

Figure 2.25 Web conferencing software allows a group of individuals to connect and collaborate using the Internet.

EXPLORE   FURTHER

Netiquette Guidelines

With so much communication taking place over the Internet, rules for acceptable social interactions have been developed called **netiquette**, which is short for *Internet etiquette*. Without the visual cues that are present in face-to-face communication, messages can often be misunderstood. What are some common netiquette guidelines?

1. Research netiquette and pick what you think are the five most important rules.
2. Create a presentation with one rule per slide and provide an example of appropriate and inappropriate netiquette to demonstrate the rule. Include a slide at the end with the URLs of the sites from which you obtained your rules.
3. Save the presentation as **C2-Web-Netiquette-Your Name**.
4. Submit the presentation to your instructor in the manner she or he has requested.

Concepts Review

Topic	Key Concepts	Key Terms
Networks, the Internet, and the World Wide Web	Networks link computers together to share resources. The Internet is the physical structure that represents a global network linking other networks from around the world. Connection to the Internet is provided by ISPs for a fee. Web pages circulated on the Internet make up the World Wide Web. Web pages stored on web servers are viewed using a web browser. Websites are a collection of related web pages. Web 2.0 refers to a second generation of two-way communication using web pages. Web 3.0 is expected to incorporate automated agents that will adapt and learn the type of content you want to see on the Web.	Network Internet (Net) Internet Service Provider (ISP) Web page World Wide Web (Web or WWW) Web browser Website Web server Web 2.0 Web 3.0 Semantic Web
Connecting to the Internet	Computers sold today come equipped with a network interface card and/or a wireless interface card to facilitate connection to the Internet. ISPs provide the equipment and servers to connect to the Internet backbone. Fees for Internet access vary and are based on connection speed. High-speed Internet access is referred to as broadband. Internet access is measured in megabits per second (Mbps). Cable Internet access requires a cable modem that connects a coaxial cable from the cable company's network to your computer. A Digital Subscriber Line is provided by a telephone company, which supplies a DSL modem that uses twisted-pair cable to connect into the telephone jack and into your computer. Fiber-optic service requires that the ISP run a fiber-optic cable to your home, where a piece of equipment converts optical signals to electrical signals. Satellite Internet access is usually found in rural areas and requires the installation of a satellite dish and satellite modem. Fixed wireless Internet access requires you to install an antenna outside your home, and a wireless modem sends/receives radio signals. A Wi-Fi network uses wireless access points and is a popular choice for public spaces and homes. Mobile broadband sticks are portable modems that connect to the Internet via a cellular network. Smartphones and tablets connect using a third-generation (3G) or fourth-generation (4G) network.	Network interface card (NIC) Ethernet port Wireless interface card Bluetooth Broadband Megabits per second (Mbps) Cable Internet access Digital Subscriber Line (DSL) Fiber-to-the-Premises (FTTP) Fiber-to-the-Home (FTTH) Fiber-Optic Service (FiOS) Satellite Internet access Fixed wireless Internet access Wi-Fi Hotspot Mobile broadband sticks 3G 4G LTE network Dial-up

continued....

	A 4G LTE network is the fastest network for mobile devices. Where broadband is not available or is too expensive, you can connect to the Internet using a dial-up modem that uses your telephone line.	
Popular Web Browsers	Web pages are viewed using web browser software that interprets the code the page is stored in as text and multimedia content. HTML is a markup language used in many web pages that describes page content using tags. Internet Explorer is the browser included with Microsoft Windows. Chrome, provided free by Google, runs on Windows-compatible PCs and is becoming popular due to its fast page loading and ability to search in the Address bar. Firefox is a free browser for PCs, Macs, or Linux computers available from the Mozilla Foundation. Apple's Safari is used on Mac and Apple mobile devices such as iPads and iPhones. Mobile web browsers are designed to quickly display web pages optimized for much smaller screens.	HTML Internet Explorer (IE) Chrome Firefox Safari Mobile web browsers
Understanding Internet and Web Addresses and Navigating Web Pages	Every computing device connected to the Internet is assigned an IP address. ICANN is a nonprofit organization in charge of keeping track of IP addresses around the world. An IP address with four groups of numbers from 0 to 255 separated by periods is known as IPv4. IPv6 was developed because the number of unique IPv4 addresses was running out. A web address, also called a URL, is a text-based address used to navigate to a website. A DNS server holds the directory that associates an Internet address with a web address. The http in a URL refers to the Hypertext Transfer Protocol used for displaying pages. A domain name is the text-based name for an organization within the URL. The three- or four-character extension in a domain name is called the top-level domain and identifies the type of organization. Generic top-level domains are being expanded by ICANN. Two-character extensions in a domain name are country codes. The first page you see when you visit a web page is called the home page. Web pages contain hyperlinks that take you to a related web page when clicked or tapped.	Internet Protocol (IP) address ICANN (Internet Corporation for Assigned Names and Numbers) Web address Uniform Resource Locator (URL) Domain Name System (DNS) server Domain name Top-level domain (TLD) Generic top-level domain (gTLD) ccTLDs Home page Hyperlinks Links

continued....

Topic	Key Concepts	Key Terms
Searching the Web	Search engines read web pages and create indexes using keywords associated with the page. Spiders and crawlers are programs used by search engines to find and index web pages. Some search engines provide categories of topics and subtopics that you can use to narrow your search. You will get different results from different search engines using the same search phrase because spider and index programs vary, pages may be updated at different times, and rankings may differ. A metasearch search engine compiles results from other search engines in one place. Typing a quotation or minus symbol in the search phrase helps to narrow the results list. Use a search engine's advanced tools to fine-tune a search.	Search engine Keywords Spiders Crawlers Metasearch search engine Content aggregator Really Simple Syndication (RSS)
Evaluating Web Content	Domain names in the web address can provide clues to a web page's authenticity. Check a web page for an author's name and author's affiliation; if no name is present, try reading the About us or Contact links. Look for dates to make sure the information you are reading is the most recent; if no date exists look for clues in the content or web address. Evaluate the purpose of a website to help decide if a bias may exist in the information presented. A poorly designed website with errors in spelling and grammar should have its content corroborated by another source.	
Popular Web Plug-ins and Players for Multimedia Content	Plug-ins, players, and add-ons are all software programs needed by a browser to display multimedia content. Adobe Reader is a program used to view PDF documents. Adobe Flash Player and Shockwave Player are programs used to view animations with high-quality graphics, sound, and interactivity. Java is a programming language used to add interactivity to games and web page applications. Silverlight is a plug-in from Microsoft for interactivity applications and high-quality audio or video. Real Player is used for music files such as MP3s. QuickTime from Apple is used for videos or animations. Once installed, plug-ins and players will periodically require updating.	Plug-in Add-on Player
E-Commerce, Messaging, and Internet Telephone and Web Conferencing Options	E-commerce involves transactions online between businesses and consumers, businesses and other businesses, and consumers and other consumers. Shopping online generally requires a credit card or account with a third party payment service such as Google Checkout.	E-commerce E-tailers Email

continued....

E-Commerce, Messaging, and Internet Telephone and Web Conferencing Options	E-tailer is a term that refers to a business with an electronic storefront. Email is the sending and receiving of messages that can have attachments such as documents and photos. An email address connects you to your ISP's mail server to send and receive messages. An email client is a program used to compose and manage email messages. Texting involves sending short messages to a mobile device. Instant messaging allows you to send/receive text messages in real time. VoIP is a technology that allows you to make telephone calls over the Internet. Web conferencing software allows a group of individuals to collaborate online.	Email address Email client Text messages Texting Short Message Service (SMS) Instant messaging Voice over Internet Protocol (VoIP) Web conferencing Netiquette

Multiple Choice

1. The collection of networks that provides the pathway for data to travel is the _____.
   a. Web
   b. Internet
   c. Internet4
   d. Superhighway

2. This refers to the global collection of web pages circulated on the internet.
   a. Internet
   b. Superhighway
   c. World Wide Web
   d. Web server

3. High-speed Internet access is referred to by this term.
   a. Broadband
   b. Megabits per second (Mbps)
   c. Superhighway
   d. Baseband

4. Which of the following connections is *not* high speed?
   a. Cable
   b. DSL
   c. FTTP
   d. Dial-up

5. This is the web browser included with Microsoft Windows.
   a. Internet Explorer
   b. Chrome
   c. Safari
   d. Firefox

6. This browser allows you to type search phrases directly in the Address bar.
   a. Chrome
   b. Internet Explorer
   c. Firefox
   d. Safari

7. This is the nonprofit organization that keeps track of Internet addresses for the world.
   a. IPv6
   b. IPv4
   c. ICANN
   d. IPANN

8. A Web address is called a(n) _____.
   a. IP address
   b. URL
   c. DNS
   d. Hyperlink

9. A search engine uses this type of program to search the Web for keywords to index.
   a. Hyperlinks
   b. HTTP
   c. Metaindex
   d. Spider

10. A search engine that compiles results from other search engines is called a _____ search engine.
    a. category
    b. hypertext
    c. metasearch
    d. cybersearch

11. Which of the following is *not* a strategy to help you evaluate a web page's credibility?
    a. Look at the domain name for an organization you recognize.
    b. Check for an author's name and affiliation.
    c. Evaluate the page design.
    d. Look for the same page at a different search engine.

12. If a publication date is not on the web page, a clue may appear in this linked address.
    a. IP address
    b. Web address
    c. Mailing address for the organization
    d. DNS

13. This player allows you to read PDF documents.
    a. Adobe Reader
    b. Adobe Flash Player
    c. Shockwave Player
    d. Real Player

14. This player is a programming language used on web pages.
    a. QuickTime
    b. Real Player
    c. Silverlight
    d. Java

15. E-tailers are primarily involved in this category of e-commerce.
    a. B2C
    b. B2B
    c. B2W
    d. C2C

16. This type of software allows a group of individuals to collaborate online in a meeting.
    a. VoIP
    b. Email
    c. Instant messaging
    d. Web conferencing

Crossword Puzzle

ACROSS

3 emcp.com
7 First page that displays
9 A collection of related web pages
11 Company that sells Internet access
12 Program used to view web pages
13 Search engines index pages by these
14 Web address TLD indicating a trusted source
15 May indicate a page's credibility

DOWN

1 Player from Apple
2 Your Name@mailserver.com
4 Free browser from Google
5 Free browser from Mozilla
6 Company that finds and indexes web pages
8 Plug-in from Microsoft
9 Wireless network that uses access points and radio signals
10 Buying and selling on the Internet

Matching

Match the term with the statement or definition.

_____	1. Web 2.0	a.	Included with many browsers
_____	2. Wireless interface card	b.	eBay
_____	3. Mobile web browsers	c.	Indicates keyword to be excluded
_____	4. IPv6	d.	Optimized for smaller screens
_____	5. Minus symbol	e.	Evaluate web page's currency
_____	6. Publication date	f.	Equipment in mobile device
_____	7. Adobe Flash Player	g.	Second generation web pages
_____	8. C2C	h.	System of Internet addresses

Project 1 Broadband Options and Questions for ISPs

Individual, Pairs, or Team

Deliverable: Presentation

The manager at the local senior community center where you volunteer has asked you to prepare a presentation for the seniors that compares the various high-speed Internet connection options in your area. The manager wants you to include questions that seniors should ask an ISP before signing a contract for Internet access.

1. Research the available broadband connection options in your area.
2. Prepare a list of questions someone should ask an ISP before signing a contract. Consider services, speed, support, and cost questions.
3. Create a presentation that could be shown to seniors with the information from Steps 1 and 2.
4. Save the presentation as **C2-Project1-InternetConnections-Your Name**.
5. Submit the presentation to your instructor in the manner she or he has requested.

Project 2 Which Browser Is the Favorite?

Pairs or Team

Deliverable: Table or Chart

Conduct an informal survey of at least 20 friends, relatives, neighbors, or students in another class asking them which browser they use on the Web.

1. Compile your results and create a table or chart in a word processor, spreadsheet, or presentation program to show the results.
2. Save the table or chart as **C2-Project2-BrowserChart-Your Name**.
3. Submit the table or chart to your instructor in the manner she or he has requested.

Project 3 Google versus Bing

Individual or Pairs

Deliverable: Document or Presentation

Google and Bing are the two leading search engines used on the Web. Pick a topic you are interested in and perform searches for your topic using both search engines. Make sure to use each search engine's advanced tools to narrow the search results. When finished, compare and contrast the experience you had with each search engine. What did you like or dislike about each set of advanced search tools? Which search engine do you think gave the best results?

1. Create a document or presentation that summarizes your search experience at Google and Bing. Include

descriptions or examples of the advanced search tools you used and how the results improved. Provide answers to the above questions.

2. Save the document or presentation as **C2-Project3-GooglevsBing-Your Name**.
3. Submit the document or presentation to your instructor in the manner she or he has requested.

Project 4 Evaluating the Credibility of Content on a Web Page

Pairs or Team
Deliverable: Document or Presentation

Within your pair or team pick a topic of interest and search the Web for pages related to the topic you chose. Find a web page that you believe is missing key information that would help evaluate the page's credibility. For example, find a page missing an author or a publication date, a page published by an unknown organization, or a page with poor design or poorly written content.

1. Create a document or presentation that includes a hyperlink to the web page. Include a brief description of the page and the reasons why you believe the page's credibility needs to be verified.
2. Save the document as **C2-Project4-TeamPageEvaluation-Your Name**.
3. Submit the document to your instructor in the manner she or he has requested.

Project 5 Comparing C2C Options

Pairs or Team
Deliverable: Presentation

A neighbor wants your help selling her Xbox games online. She has never sold anything using the Web before and is not sure if she should use an auction, a classified ad, or an online marketplace. Learn about the differences between an auction site such as eBay, a classified ad site such as Craigslist, and an online marketplace such as Amazon Marketplace. Compare an ad for an Xbox game at each venue and the cash the neighbor may realize from a similar sale.

1. Create a presentation with a brief summary of how each type of C2C site operates. What are the advantages and disadvantages of each site? Which venue do you think would provide the best return for your neighbor?
2. Save the presentation as **C2-Project5-C2COptions-Your Name**.
3. Submit the presentation to your instructor in the manner she or he has requested.

Project 6 Greener Computing

Individual, Pairs, or Team
Deliverable: Blog Entry

You have just purchased a new 4G smartphone and are not sure what to do with your older 3G smartphone that you no longer want. Research ways in which you can recycle or reuse the 3G smartphone in your area.

1. Write and post a blog entry that describes what you learned and which method you would probably use if you had an older smartphone to discard and give your reasons.
2. Submit your blog URL to your instructor in the manner she or he has requested.

Optional

Read the blog entry for this project of at least two other classmates and post a comment to each. Submit the URLs of your classmates' blogs with Step 2.

Project 7 Online Meeting or Face-to-Face Meeting— Which Is Better?

Individual, Pairs, or Team
Deliverable: Blog Entry

The ability to collaborate using web conferencing software means a group of individuals could meet virtually any time, anywhere. The technology could even be used when a group is housed within the same building but prefers the online collaborative environment. When, if ever, is a face-to-face meeting more desirable than a web conference? Could web conferencing be used for all types of meetings? If necessary, consult a parent or relative, or interview someone with work experience that involves meetings.

1. Write and post a blog entry that describes your opinions about the above questions.
2. Submit your blog URL to your instructor in the manner she or he has requested.

Optional

Read the blog entry for this project of at least two other classmates and post a comment to each. Submit the URLs of your classmates' blogs with Step 2.

Project 8 Ethics Discussion—Posting Negative Reviews

Team
Deliverable: Document, Blog Entry, or Presentation

You overheard one of your colleagues at work while she was talking on the telephone to a friend telling the friend she has posted negative reviews about one of your company's products at various websites. She said she was doing it to get even with her manager for treating her poorly. What should you do?

1. Within your team discuss how you should handle this situation. Should you ignore the situation since the conversation did not directly involve you? Should you confront the person? Should you tell her manager? Is there any other option you should consider?
2. Prepare a summary of your team's discussion in a document, blog entry, or presentation.
3. Save the document or presentation as **C2-Project8-EthicsDiscussion-Your Name**.
4. Submit the document, presentation, or blog entry to your instructor in the manner she or he has requested.

Chapter 3

Computer Hardware

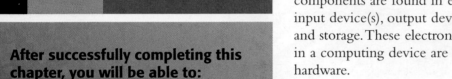

After successfully completing this chapter, you will be able to:

- Recognize and explain the purpose of the major components in a system unit

- List and recognize various types of input devices

- List and recognize various types of output devices

- Identify network adapters for connectivity purposes

- Understand how data is represented on a computer

- State various options for storage and storage capacities

As you learned in Chapter 1, computers come in all shapes and sizes. Whether you are working with a desktop, laptop, netbook, ultrabook, tablet, or other mobile device, certain components are found in each one. All computers have a CPU, input device(s), output device(s), memory, connectivity adapters, and storage. These electronic and physical components found in a computing device are collectively known as the computer's hardware.

Some hardware is visible to you such as the screen, keyboard, and mouse, while other hardware is housed inside the system such as the CPU, memory, network adapter, and some storage. Hardware used for input, output, connectivity, or storage that you plug in or connect to your computer wirelessly such as a USB storage medium or printer is called a **peripheral** device.

If you have looked at ads for computers you know that a basic understanding of the terminology and hardware components is helpful to making a purchase decision. In Chapter 1 you were introduced to many of the hardware components found in a PC. In Chapter 2 you learned about hardware such as cable modems and DSL modems that provide connectivity to the Internet. In this chapter you will explore what's inside the system unit, input and output devices, network adapters, digital data representation, and storage options in more detail. Appendix A contains tips for buying a computer or mobile device.

TOPIC 3.1

The System Unit

As stated in Chapter 1, the system unit is the horizontal or vertical (tower) case in which the computer's microprocessor, memory, and storage are located. In a mobile device such as a laptop, tablet, or smartphone, these components are inside the unit below the integrated keyboard and/or screen. In an all-in-one system, these components are mounted in the same case in which the monitor is housed. Regardless of the configuration, the main components in the system unit are the power supply with cooling fan, motherboard, ports for plugging in peripherals, and storage devices. In this topic you will learn about the power supply, motherboard components, and ports. In a later topic you will learn about storage.

Figure 3.1 shows the inside view of a notebook's system unit.

DVD drive

Hard drive

Motherboard

Cooling fan

Heat sink

Ports for plugging in peripherals

Figure 3.1 Inside view of a notebook

Power Supply

All computers need power to operate. In a tower or desktop the power supply is positioned at the back of the unit where you plug in the power cord. A notebook or tablet is powered by a charged battery or the power adapter when the power adapter is plugged into a power outlet. A cooling fan is located near a power supply to draw heat away from the CPU and prevent the CPU from overheating. A heat sink is also installed near a CPU to draw heat away from the processor.

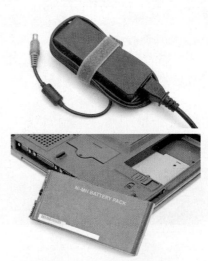

Notebooks are powered by a charged battery or by using a power adapter plugged into a wall unit.

Motherboard

The main circuit board in the computer is called the **motherboard**. All of the other devices plug directly into or communicate wirelessly with the motherboard. Figure 3.2 shows a typical motherboard you might find inside a PC.

Figure 3.2 The motherboard is the hub that connects all of the devices together and is designed to support a certain type of CPU.

The motherboard includes the CPU, memory, expansion slots, and circuitry attached to ports that are used to plug in external devices. Many computers integrate video and sound electronics into the motherboard's main circuit board while other computers may include these components as **expansion cards** that plug into an expansion slot on the motherboard. Expansion slots are used to plug in additional circuit boards to your computer to either add or improve functionality. Another common use of an expansion card in a tower unit is to provide a network adapter into which a cable, called an Ethernet cable, is plugged for connectivity to a network. Notebook computers also have built-in card readers that allow you to insert a memory card from a digital camera or plug in a card used for wireless networking.

Data travels between the components on the motherboard to the CPU and memory over wires called **data buses**. Think of a data bus as a highway upon which data is routed. The size and speed of a data bus affects performance since a data bus that can carry more data to the CPU and memory at a faster rate of speed performs better. Similarly, traveling by car on a four-lane highway at a high speed means you arrive at a destination faster than if you traveled on a two-lane highway at a slower speed.

CPU As you learned in Chapter 1, the CPU performs the processing cycle and is often referred to as the "brain" of the computer. Today's computers can do **parallel processing**, which involves having multiple microprocessor chips (more than one CPU chip on the motherboard), or a multi-core processor (one CPU chip separated into independent processor cores). Parallel processing provides the ability to execute multiple instructions at the same time. Most notebooks today are configured with a two- or four-core microprocessor. Parallel processing has vastly improved system performance when software has been written to take advantage of its capabilities.

Apple's A6 ARM CPU at the time of writing is expected to be the processor in iPhone5 and/or the next iPad. ARM processors use less energy, making them a popular choice for mobile devices such as iPhones and iPads.

A CPU goes through an **instruction cycle** that involves the CPU retrieving, decoding, executing, and storing an instruction. The speed at which a CPU operates is measured in the number of instruction cycles the CPU can process per second, referred to as **clock speed**. Clock speed is typically measured in **gigahertz (GHz)**, which is 1 billion cycles per second. A CPU in most notebooks and tablets sold today run at speeds between 1 and 2.5 GHz.

In Chapter 1 you were introduced to cache memory, which is memory either built into the CPU or stored next to the CPU on a separate chip on the motherboard that is used for storing frequently used instructions and data. Cache memory stored closest to the CPU is called **Level 1 (L1) cache**. L1 cache is memory built on the CPU chip and operates the fastest of all memory. Secondary cache memory either stored on the CPU chip or built on the motherboard is called **Level 2 (L2) cache**. L2 cache feeds the L1 cache. A third level of cache memory, called **Level 3 (L3) cache**, is usually built on the motherboard and feeds the L2 cache. The amount of L1, L2, and L3 cache affect performance since the CPU accesses cache memory faster than other memory.

Memory On the motherboard are two types of memory: **read-only memory (ROM)** and random access memory (RAM). ROM is used for storing instructions that the computer uses that do not change. For example, the programming code with the instructions used when starting a computer is often stored on a ROM chip, which is called the ROM BIOS, where **BIOS** stands for **Basic Input Output System**.

Recall from Chapter 1 that RAM is temporary memory where data and instructions are stored while processing and is erased when power is turned off. RAM is configured in modules that plug into slots on the motherboard (see Figure 3.2). Since all of the software and the data you are creating or editing while working on the computer must reside in RAM to access the CPU, the size and type of RAM in a computer affects its performance.

Today's desktop and notebook computers often have DDR3 SDRAM, which is the fastest RAM available at the time of writing; however, expect DDR4 RAM to crop up soon. DDR stands for Double Data Rate and refers to the ability to transfer data twice as often with 3 representing third generation DDR, which is twice as fast as DDR2. SDRAM means Synchronous Dynamic Random Access Memory and refers to a type of RAM that operates at higher clock speeds than older RAM technologies.

A memory module used in a notebook includes DDR3 SDRAM chips on a smaller circuit board than one used in a desktop.

Installing additional RAM into an empty module slot can improve a computer's performance, extending the life of an older system.

Motherboards also house other components such as drive controllers and interfaces used to connect a system's hard drive and DVD drive to the motherboard via cables.

Did You Know?

USB 3.0 (known as SuperSpeed USB) can operate approximately 10 times faster than a USB 2.0 device.

Ports

Ports are the connectors located at the back of a desktop PC or at the sides, back, and sometimes the front of a notebook or other mobile device. Ports are used to plug in external devices. The most common type of port is the **universal serial bus (USB) port**, which is used to connect an external device such as a keyboard, mouse, printer, smartphone, or external storage media to name a few.

Most computers today provide several USB ports to accommodate multiple USB devices being used simultaneously. A USB hub can be used to increase the number of USB ports if your computer does not provide enough to meet your needs.

A typical notebook also includes ports for plugging in an external monitor, connecting to a network using an Ethernet cable, connecting a telephone line for accessing a dialup network, an HDMI port for connecting to a high-definition TV, and a high-speed FireWire port to connect a digital camcorder or other device (Figure 3.3). Ports will also be found along the side or front of a notebook or other mobile device to plug in headphones, external speakers, or a microphone.

Plug in a USB hub to add more USB devices if you do not have enough USB ports.

Power adapter

USB ports

Video port

Network port

Dial-up modem port

HDMI port

FireWire port

Figure 3.3 Ports at the sides, back, and sometimes front of a notebook are used to plug in external devices.

In desktop PCs, the ports are often color coded to make it easy for someone to plug in a device with a similar end to the correct port. For example, on older desktop PCs the keyboard and mouse connectors are colored purple for the keyboard and green for the mouse so that the devices are not mixed up.

EXPLORE   FURTHER

What is a Thunderbolt port?

Apple's MacBook and iMac feature a new high-speed port named Thunderbolt. What is a Thunderbolt port? How fast does it operate? What kinds of Thunderbolt devices are available? Are there Thunderbolt devices available for a PC?

1. Go to apple.com/thunderbolt and read the information about Thunderbolt presented by Apple.

2. Next, find out if Thunderbolt is available for Windows-compatible computers and if so, for what kinds of devices.

3. Create a document that provides answers in your own words to the above questions. Include the URL of the article(s) you read about Thunderbolt devices for PCs.

4. Save the document as **C3-Hardware-Thunderbolt-Your Name**.

5. Submit the document to your instructor in the manner she or he has requested.

TOPIC 3.2

Input Devices

As stated in Chapter 1, any device used to enter raw data or communicate instructions to the computer is an input device. Several input devices exist with the most common being a keyboard and mouse. Other devices used for input are also described in this topic.

Keyboards and Mice

While wired keyboards and mice were the standard for traditional desktop PCs, today's computer users prefer to be untethered from their computer. A wireless **keyboard** and/or mouse can be used with any computer device. Wireless keyboards and mice use batteries as a source of power. A wireless receiver is plugged into a computer's USB port and connects with the wireless keyboard and mouse. Electronic signals from the keyboard are interpreted by the keyboard's device controller and sent to the computer's operating system via the wireless receiver, which in turn sends the keystrokes to the active running program for display on the screen.

Wireless keyboards and mice are popular for traditional PCs and as peripherals for mobile devices.

In addition to the alphabetic and numeric keys on a keyboard, special purpose keys such as Esc, Insert, Delete, function keys labeled F1 through F12, the Start key on a Windows-compatible computer, and the command key on an Apple computer allow commands to be sent to a program. Directional movement keys such as the up, down, left, and right arrow keys, and the Home, End, Page Up, and Page Down keys provide the ability to move around a screen. Finally, keys labeled Ctrl, Alt, and Shift allow you to use a combination of one or more of these keys with letters, numbers, and function keys to send instructions to the active program.

Notebooks include a built-in keyboard while some tablets and smartphones may or may not have integrated keyboards that are built in or slide out. Some tablets include a keyboard that you can use by plugging the tablet into a dock port on the keyboard. Finally, some tablets and smartphones with touch-enabled screens display a keyboard onscreen that you use by tapping the onscreen keys with your fingers or a stylus.

Today's tablets and smartphones offer onscreen keyboards, which you tap using your fingers or a stylus (digital pen).

A **mouse** is a device used to point, select, and manipulate objects on the screen. The mouse works by detecting the motion of the mouse in relation to the surface beneath it as you move the mouse. Most mice in use today track the movement using light technology, while older mice used a trackball to sense movement. As you move the mouse, the pointer on the screen moves in the same direction. Buttons on the mouse provide the ability to send a command when the pointer is resting on the target that you wish to manipulate. A wheel on the mouse facilitates scrolling.

On notebooks, a **touchpad** is located below the keyboard. This rectangular surface with buttons is used in place of a mouse to move the pointer on the screen and manipulate objects. The touchpad senses finger movement and taps similarly to a mouse. Depending on the touchpad device, multi-finger gestures and pinch and zoom movements can be used to scroll and zoom the display. Some notebooks and smartphones include a track pointer, which senses finger pressure for moving the pointer.

Touch-Enabled Devices

Many of today's mobile devices such as tablets, smartphones, and some portable media players include **touch-enabled displays**, also called **touchscreens**, for accepting input. A touch-enabled device has a layer of capacitive material below a protective screen. When you touch the screen with your finger or with a digital pen called a **stylus**, an electrical signal is sensed by the capacitive layer, which sends data about the location you touched and any gesture you used to the computer's touch processor and software that interpret the touch gesture.

On a notebook, a touchpad is used to move the pointer on the screen using finger movements, while taps and buttons allow you to manipulate objects.

Self-serve kiosks such as an airline check-in station or an ATM use touchscreens in combination with other input devices such as keypads, buttons, and magnetic strip readers to accept input.

Many mobile devices and self-serve kiosks are touch-enabled or can be operated with a stylus.

Scanners and Readers

A **scanner** is a device that uses optical technology to analyze text and/or images and convert them into data that can be used by a computer. Scanners can be a separate input device such as a flatbed scanner (a scanner that sits on a desk) or a handheld scanner. Many printers and photocopiers used today are multi-purpose devices that also incorporate scanners.

Bar code readers optically scan barcodes to identify products in warehouses or at checkout counters. Even smartphones include the ability to scan **QR (Quick Response) codes**, a type of barcode that looks like a matrix of black square dots. The smartphone reads the QR code that usually directs the device to display a website. **Magnetic strip readers** can read data from the magnetic strip on the backs of cards such as debit cards, credit cards, or cards used to open doors or parking gates. **Biometric scanners** are used to identify people by individual human characteristics such as a fingerprint, iris, or voice pattern. Finally, **Radio Frequency Identification (RFID) readers** scan an embedded RFID tag to identify an object. RFID readers and tags use tiny chips with antennas that are

Check This Out

www.rfidjournal.com
Go here to read the latest news on RFID technology innovation in various industries.

readable when the reader and tag are within range of each other. Typically, RFID technology is used to read tags up to 300 feet away.

Many different types of scanners and readers are used to generate input from documents, images, barcodes, biometrics, or wireless tags.

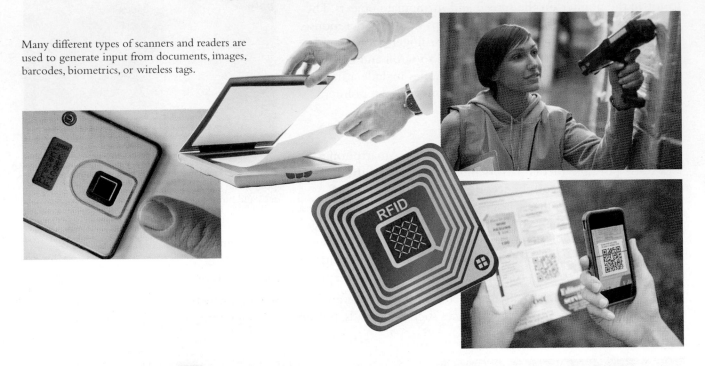

Keep Your Eyes on Your Cards

Protect cards with a magnetic strip that store personal data. These cards are targets for criminals who use skimmers to read the data. If you hand over a debit or credit card to a store clerk when making a purchase make sure you keep the card in your line of sight at all times.

Digital Cameras, Digital Camcorders, and Webcams

Digital cameras, camcorders, and webcams are used to convert images and live video into a digital format.

Digital cameras capture still images, while digital video cameras called **camcorders** capture live video and audio. Many of these devices are multi-purpose, meaning some digital cameras could be used to capture short live video segments and some camcorders double as digital cameras.

A **webcam** is a video camera built into a video display screen (mounted at the top center of the screen's edge), or plugged in as a peripheral and used to provide images to the computer during live web conferencing or chatting using a program such as Skype.

Smartphones and tablets have digital camera capabilities that allow you to snap pictures and record video and send them via messaging applications directly from the device.

Microphones and Voice Recognition

A **microphone** can be used in conjunction with software to create a digital audio file from voice input or other sounds captured by the device. You may also use a microphone to chat with someone online. Some games played online or with game systems accept voice commands. **Voice recognition technology** (also called **speech recognition technology**) is used to recognize voice commands as input for hands-free operation at work, with your car's navigation and communications system, or with your mobile device. Apple's Siri on the iPhone 4 uses voice recognition to send messages, schedule meetings, or make a call. A program such as Dragon NaturallySpeaking converts input you speak into your microphone into text and commands in documents or messaging applications.

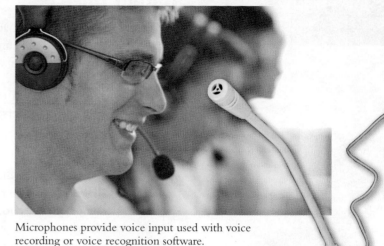

Microphones provide voice input used with voice recording or voice recognition software.

Microphones are built into notebooks and mobile devices. An external microphone or a headset with a microphone attached can also be plugged in as a peripheral.

Entertainment Controllers

Gaming systems accept input using a variety of methods such as wired or wireless game controllers, joysticks, and motion sensors. Some games have controllers such as guitars, other musical instruments, or a tennis racket. Some exercise games use pressure sensitive mats or boards.

Other devices such as keypads and magnetic ink character recognition systems are used in specialized applications to provide input. Futuristic input devices such as wearable keyboards and holographic inputs are already being developed and tested. Imagine in the future wearing your keyboard on your sleeve or entering data using a hologram!

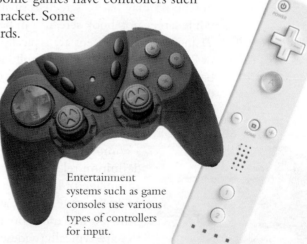

Entertainment systems such as game consoles use various types of controllers for input.

EXPLORE FURTHER

Virtual Reality Devices

Virtual reality devices are used with games and in commercial applications to train workers, such as simulating flights for pilots. Devices are worn on the body as headsets or as data gloves that detect input.

1. Research a virtual reality device for a game or training purpose.
2. Create a brief presentation that describes in your own words what you learned about the virtual reality device. Include a slide with a picture of the virtual reality device that you researched. Include the URL(s) of the sites from which you obtained information.
3. Save the presentation as **C3-Hardware-VirtualReality-Your Name**.
4. Submit the presentation to your instructor in the manner she or he has requested.

TOPIC 3.3

Output Devices

In Chapter 1 you learned that devices used to view the information processed and organized by the computer are output devices. The most commonly used output device is a monitor or other type of screen or display in a mobile device. Computer output can also be connected to high-definition televisions, projectors, or interactive whiteboards. Other types of output devices explored in this topic include speakers, headsets, printers, and copiers.

Video Displays

Video displays are electronic devices that present information from a computer visually. Desktop PCs connect a device called a **monitor** to the computer's video port. Notebooks and other mobile devices have a built-in video display screen. Other electronic devices with built-in display screens include eReaders and portable media players.

Video displays come in many different sizes, where the size is the diagonal length of the viewing area. For a mobile device, the size of the video display is constrained by the size of the notebook, tablet, or smartphone. Smaller notebooks may have a screen as small as 11 inches, while larger notebook screens can be as large as 21 inches. Tablet screens are typically in the range of 7 to 11 inches, while a smartphone screen can be as small as a few inches with newer phones breaking in near 5 inches.

Notebooks are often connected to external video displays such as a computer monitor or a high-definition television screen to take advantage of larger viewing areas or to use two screens at the same time. Newer monitors for a desktop PC are typically widescreen **Liquid Crystal Displays (LCD)**, which is a flat-panel technology in various sizes upward from 20 inches. LCDs are popular because they do not experience flicker or glare. Older PCs may have rectangular-shaped LCD screens from 14 to 17 inches.

The size of display screens varies by device with some smartphones as small as a few inches, and notebooks with display screens that could rival a desktop monitor.

Other flat-panel display screens are **Light-Emitting Diode (LED)** displays and **plasma** displays. These types of flat panel technology are more expensive and often used for televisions. Each has its advantages, with LED screens consuming less energy and plasma providing truer color representation.

A newer technology known as **Organic Light-Emitting Diode (OLED)** may eventually replace LCD display screens in mobile devices because this technology does not require backlighting like LCDs do, making them far more energy efficient for any device that runs off battery power.

Connecting two display screens to a PC or notebook is becoming more common as well as watching movies or images from a computer on a high-definition television.

Video Display Resolution A video display's **resolution** setting will affect the quality of output viewed on the display screen. Resolution refers to the number of picture elements, called **pixels**, that make up the image shown on the display screen. A pixel is square with red, green, and blue color values (called RGB) that represent each color needed to form the image. A resolution setting is expressed as the number of horizontal pixels by the number of vertical pixels. For example, a typical 20-inch widescreen monitor would have a resolution of 1600 x 900 pixels. The more pixels used to render the output, the sharper the image as shown in Figure 3.4. Also, at higher resolutions more content can be displayed on the screen than at lower resolutions. While displays typically default to recommended settings, the resolution can be changed using the operating system software to a higher or lower resolution.

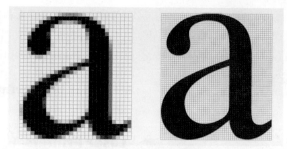

Figure 3.4 A character displayed at a low resolution using fewer pixels to form the character appears fuzzy (left) compared to the same character at a higher resolution using more pixels (right).

Video Display Projectors and Interactive Whiteboards

A **video display projector (VDP)** is used when a computer's output needs to be projected on a large screen when making presentations to groups. VDPs are often ceiling mounted in classrooms and boardrooms, while portable projectors are available for other venues. A PC or notebook connects to the projector via a video output cable.

An **interactive whiteboard** displays the computer's output on a large whiteboard. Special pens are used to annotate on the whiteboard while the image is displayed, making it easier for a presenter to make notes or draw attention to objects on the display. In these instances, the whiteboard is acting as both an output and an input device since the annotations can be saved with the images as electronic files that can be viewed at a later time. Interactive whiteboards also include tools that allow touch gestures for interaction with the computer while the display is being viewed.

A computer's image can be directed to display on a video display projector or an interactive whiteboard when making presentations to groups.

Speakers and Headphones

Audio output from the computer such as music, voice, or sound effects is heard through the computer's internal speakers, external speakers, or headphones. PC monitors generally include built-in speakers. Notebooks and other mobile devices have speakers integrated into the device. Plug the headphones or earbuds into the audio port of a computer or mobile device to redirect the audio output to your headset when others are around you. High-quality headphones reduce background noise to improve the audio experience. Headsets are headphones that include a microphone.

Often when playing games, watching movies, or playing music on a computing device, higher-quality external speakers are used to achieve home theater quality sound. External speakers can be wired or wireless.

A **Bluetooth headset** can be paired with a smartphone to enable the user to hear a conversation when making and receiving voice calls.

External speakers, earbud headphones, and a Bluetooth headset are common ways to hear audio output from a computing device.

Printers and Copiers

Video displays provide output that is temporary. When the computer is turned off, the output disappears. Often, a printed copy of a document or an image is desired. Printed copies of computer output are called **hard copy**. Hard copy can be generated by a laser printer, inkjet printer, photo printer, thermal printer, plotter, or digital photocopier.

A laser printer is a popular choice for high volume output.

Laser Printers **Laser printers** are a popular choice for producing hard copy in offices and homes. A laser beam electrostatically charges a drum with the text and images sent for printing. A dry powder called toner sticks to the drum and is transferred to the paper as the paper passes through the printer. Paper feels warm when it comes out of a laser printer since heat is applied to the page to permanently adhere the toner to the paper. Although expensive, color laser printers are starting to increase in popularity.

Inkjet Printers The most common type of printer found in a home is an **inkjet printer**. These printers form text and images on the page by spraying drops of ink from one or more ink cartridges that move back and forth across the page. Inkjet printers allow home users to print in color relatively inexpensively.

Inkjet printers spray drops of ink on the page to form text and images.

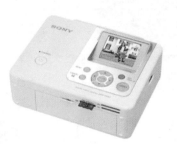

Photo printers print directly from your camera or your camera's memory card.

Photo Printers A **photo printer** generally connects directly to a digital camera to print high-quality photos on photo paper usually using inkjet technology. Professional photo-printing service companies use higher-end photo printers that produce a high-quality image on specially treated paper for prints that last longer than those produced by inkjet printers.

Thermal Printers Most receipts you receive from retail stores or services are printed on **thermal printers**. These printers produce output by heating coated paper as the paper passes over the print head. These printers produce receipts quickly; however, the image fades away over time.

Thermal printers are used to print receipts and barcode labels.

Plotters are used to print blueprints or other large technical drawings.

Plotters Blueprints and technical drawings are often produced on **plotters**. A plotter moves one or more pens across the surface of the paper to produce the drawing. Plotters are slow as the movement of the pen or pens across the page takes a longer time.

Digital Copiers A **digital copier** in an office can now double as both a traditional paper photocopier and, by being connected to a network, can also accept output from computers for printing. Often these copiers are used to share color printing capabilities in a workplace.

Digital copiers in modern offices are connected to a network to print computer output.

All-in-One Printers Many laser and inkjet printer models are multipurpose, meaning that in addition to printing, the device can be used for scanning, photocopying, and sending/receiving faxes. Having a multipurpose printer saves desktop space, cuts down on multiple supply costs, and means you only have to learn to operate one device. The downside is that you cannot do multiple functions at the same time. For example, you cannot copy a document while another one is printing.

Other special-purpose printers are also used such as label printers and portable printers for carrying out specific tasks. In addition, other output devices are available such as a document camera that displays an image from hard copy on a video display. Some virtual reality devices provide output, and 3-D technology for displaying and printing output is being further developed.

Many printers have multifunction capability for printing, copying, scanning, and faxing.

 Blog Topic

Are you 3-D-ready?

3-D technology is available for display and printing purposes but is not yet commonplace. As the technology improves and newer devices develop that become less expensive, 3-D is sure to find its way into our homes and offices. Do you already own 3-D glasses and a 3-D monitor? Will you embrace 3-D in your computer world?

1. Research the current offerings for either 3-D displays or 3-D printing technology.

2. Write and post a blog entry that briefly describes what you learned about 3-D displays or 3-D printers. Provide your opinion on whether you are ready to embrace 3-D technology and give your reasons.

3. Read at least two of your classmates' blogs and post one comment to each.

4. Submit your blog URL and the URLs of your classmates' blogs for which you provided a comment to your instructor in the manner she or he has requested.

EXPLORE FURTHER

What is a video card and do I need one?

A computer uses a **video card** to process the data needed to display text and images on your monitor, projector, or television. These cards are also referred to as graphics accelerators. Most computers integrate the video circuitry directly on the motherboard. What are the advantages and disadvantages of this? Do you need to add a video expansion card to a computer? Why or why not?

1. Research video cards to find out the answers to the above questions. Also find out what GPU means and how the amount of memory on video cards affects graphics performance.

2. Create a document that summarizes in your own words what you learned about video cards. Include the URLs of the websites you used for information.

3. Save the document as **C3-Hardware-VideoCards-Your Name**.

4. Submit the document to your instructor in the manner she or he has requested.

TOPIC 3.4

Network Adapters

Recall from Chapter 1 that the term *communications device* refers to any component or device used to facilitate the transmission of data. In Chapter 2, the various types of Internet connection options were explored, and you learned about hardware used for accessing the Internet such as cable modems, DSL modems, mobile broadband sticks, and so on. A communications device can be thought of as both an input and an output device since the device receives (input) and sends (output) data to/from the computing device and other computers via a network. In this topic you will examine further the hardware provided in a notebook, tablet, or mobile device that enables connectivity to a network.

Network Adapters

Any device used to connect a computer to a network is called a **network adapter** (also called a **network card**). The network adapter is the interface between your computer and the other networking equipment such as the modem or router that provides the pathway for data to travel to/from the network. All networking equipment communicates with each other using a set of standards called **protocols**. Protocols can be thought of as a set of rules that define how data is exchanged between two devices. A network adapter has to use the same protocols as the modem or router with which the adapter is trying to communicate for each device to "understand" the other. This usually becomes a factor when an older wireless network adapter does not work with a newer router that uses a faster data transfer protocol. In that case, a newer adapter that supports the faster protocol can be purchased.

Network Adapters for Wired Connectivity

A network adapter for a wired connection is called an Ethernet port (sometimes referred to as an RJ45 port). One end of a network cable is plugged into the network port on the computer or mobile device and the other end into a modem or router to provide the communications channel as shown in Figure 3.5.

Ethernet refers to the type of cable used to connect two devices and the data transfer speed that the media can support. Typical ads for a computer will state Ethernet 10/100 or 10/100/1000. The numbers after Ethernet refer to the data transfer speed the adapter can support with 10 indicating 10 Mbps, 100 indicating 100 Mbps, and 1000 indicating 1,000 Mbps (or 1 Gbps, called Gigabit Ethernet).

> With a wired network adapter, plug one end of a network cable into the network port of a computer and the other end into a modem or router to provide the communications pathway.

Figure 3.5 With a wired network adapter, a network cable connects two devices in a network.

Network Adapters for Wireless Connectivity

Wireless connectivity is preferred by people who do not want their movements constrained by the length of a physical cable. At home, at work, or when you are on the go, a wireless network allows you the freedom to move around. Today's computers come equipped with a wireless interface card that is integrated into the system unit as either Wi-Fi or Bluetooth.

Check This Out

www.wirelessindustrynews.org
Go here to find articles on recent news in the wireless industry.

Use Wireless Wisely

Wi-Fi hotspots in public areas are not secure networks. Never enter personal data at a website, in a text, or in an email message sent from a public location. Do not perform any financial transactions in a public Wi-Fi network. At home, make sure your wireless network's identification name is not obvious to your household and is secured with a strong password.

A USB wireless adapter or a wireless ExpressCard are often used to provide wireless connectivity or upgrade an existing Wi-Fi adapter.

Wi-Fi Adapters A **Wi-Fi adapter** communicates with a wireless access point or wireless router using radio frequencies to transfer data. Wi-Fi is often referred to as the **802.11 protocol**, which is the name of the standard developed to facilitate wireless communication among several hardware providers. As the protocol was improved to transmit data at faster rates, version letters were added to the 802.11 standards. At the time of writing, the latest Wi-Fi standard is 802.11n. A computer ad may state that the integrated Wi-Fi adapter is 802.11 a/b/g/n, which means the adapter can communicate with older Wi-Fi networks as well as the newer wireless networks.

If the integrated wireless adapter does not support a newer wireless network, or you have a desktop PC that does not have a wireless interface, you can purchase an **external wireless adapter**. External wireless adapters have built-in radio transmitters and receivers to allow you to connect to a wireless modem or wireless router. The most common type of external wireless adapter is a **USB wireless adapter**, also referred to as a **USB dongle** or USB mobile broadband stick. A **wireless ExpressCard** adapter plugs into a narrow slot on a notebook or other mobile device.

Connecting with Bluetooth Bluetooth is a communications technology for short range distances. With Bluetooth, one device is paired to another Bluetooth-enabled device that is usually within a 30-foot range. When the adapter is activated and another Bluetooth device is turned on, the adapter detects the wireless signal and the two devices are paired, meaning they can exchange data. Bluetooth is a popular way of connecting a smartphone to a communications system inside a car; however, the technology is also used to provide network access on other mobile devices such as a notebook or tablet. Newer notebooks and mobile devices include an integrated Bluetooth adapter, but you can purchase a USB Bluetooth adapter if needed.

Did You Know ?

The name Bluetooth came from 10th Century King Harold Bluetooth who was instrumental in uniting warring countries in Europe. Bluetooth seemed an appropriate name as hardware competitors had to collaborate to make devices that work with each other.

A USB Bluetooth adapter can be used to provide connectivity with another Bluetooth device.

EXPLORE **FURTHER**

Which network adapters do you have?

Do you know the type of network adapters installed on the computer you are using at home?

1. Find out the network adapters installed on the computer or tablet you use. If you do not own a computer or tablet, use a computer at your school or public library. On a Windows-compatible computer use Device Manager in the Control panel and expand the list of network adapters. On a Mac, open the System Profiler. ***Note: Some schools and public libraries prevent users from viewing a computer's devices. If necessary, look up ads for a newer notebook or tablet and identify the network adapters supplied with the computer.***

2. Create a document with a list of the network adapters installed on the computer. If you have purchased an external adapter, include a description of the external adapter you use.

3. Save the document as **C3-Hardware-MyNetworkAdapters-Your Name**.

4. Submit the document to your instructor in the manner she or he has requested.

Digital Data

When you type a document on a computing device, you see the characters as you type them displayed on the video display screen. However, the digital data temporarily stored in RAM, processed by the CPU, and eventually saved to permanent storage when you save the document is stored using the **binary system**. In the binary system, only two possible values exist—0 and 1. Every document you save, picture on your camera, or message you send is really a series of 0s and 1s according to the computer. Understanding the way digital data is represented is helpful to put context to the speed of an Internet connection and the capacity of storage devices and memory.

Binary's Bits and Bytes

The smallest unit for digital data in the binary system is called a **bit**. Bit is derived from *bi*nary digi*t*. A bit is either 0 or 1. By itself, a single bit of 0 or 1 is not meaningful because only two possibilities exist. However, by adding additional bits to form a group, more possibilities to represent data are available because different combinations of 0s and 1s can be created to represent something. By grouping 8 bits together, 256 possibilities for combinations of 0s and 1s are created. This provides enough combinations to represent each letter of the alphabet in both upper and lower case, each number, and symbols such as $, ?, and !. Each group of eight bits is called a **byte** and represents one character. When you type the letter A on the keyboard and see A appear on the screen, one byte of RAM memory is being used to store the letter. Table 3.1 illustrates the binary equivalents for the two forms of the letter A, the number 4, and the $ symbol.

Table 3.1	Binary Equivalents for Letter a, Number 4, and Dollar Symbol
You type . . .	**Computer stores in RAM . . .**
a (lower case)	01100001
A (upper case)	01000001
4	01100100
$	00100100

Did You Know ?

A coding system called Unicode based on binary was developed to accommodate every letter in every language. More than 100,000 characters are represented in Unicode, with some requiring two 16-bit groups to represent a character! Unicode is the standard for programming characters in browsers and operating systems.

An average speed of 20 Mbps means 2.5 million characters per second are being transmitted!

Measuring Internet Speed and Data Caps

Bits are used to measure speed for transmitting data on the Internet. Recall in Chapter 2 when discussing broadband, average speeds were measured in mega*bits* per second (Mbps). One megabit was defined as 1 million bits. If it takes eight bits to represent one character, then one megabit transfers 125,000 characters. If your cable modem performs at an average speed of 20 Mbps, that means your cable modem is transmitting 2,500,000 characters per second.

Some ISPs put a limit on your monthly data transfer capacity. These limits are called data caps and are expressed in gigabytes. For example, a data cap of 100 GB means the ISP is limiting data transfer to 100 gigabytes in the billing period. Gigabytes are described in the next section.

Measuring File Size and Storage Capacity

A document such as an essay that you create in a program like Word is simply a collection of characters (bytes). When saved, the collection of bytes that comprise the document is called a **file**. The unique name that you assign to the document when you save it is called a **file name**, which allows you to identify one file from another on your storage medium. A file could potentially hold several thousand characters. Similarly, memory such as RAM and a permanent storage medium such as a hard disk drive can store several thousands of characters.

Prefixes added to the word byte describe progressively larger storage capacities. For example, adding *kilo* in front of byte creates the word **kilobyte**. One kilobyte, abbreviated as KB, is 1,024 bytes, but people use the approximated value of 1,000 characters when calculating storage capacity. The next prefix is *mega*, creating the term **megabyte**. One megabyte is approximately 1,000,000 bytes. Table 3.2 summarizes storage units including **gigabyte** and **terabyte** with their corresponding capacities for the types of storage mediums you would encounter at home or at work.

Storage capacities for USB flash drives such as this one are measured in megabytes or gigabytes.

Table 3.2	Storage Units and Capacities in Bytes		
Storage Unit	**Abbreviation**	**Popular Reference**	**Approximate capacity in bytes**
Kilobyte	KB	K	1,000 (one thousand)
Megabyte	MB	meg	1,000,000 (one million)
Gigabyte	GB	gig	1,000,000,000 (one billion)
Terabyte	TB	TByte	1,000,000,000,000 (one trillion)

Adding Context with Storage Capacity

Understanding that a megabyte is approximately 1 million characters is more helpful to you if you can put this value into some meaningful context. According to ehow.com, one megabyte equals approximately 500 typed pages of text with no images. However, most documents created today have some images or other graphics added to the text to make the documents more appealing to read. The picture shown of Balancing Rock uses 1.29 megabytes of storage space. One picture needs more space than 500 typed pages of text!

Many people like to download and store music and videos. It is not uncommon for one mp3 song to use more than 8 megabytes of storage and a movie file to require more than 4 gigabytes. If you like to use your computer to store pictures, music, and movies you will need a storage medium with a large capacity.

This picture of Balancing Rock in Nova Scotia, Canada, uses 1.29 MB of storage space.

Did You Know

According to informationweek.com, storage used to house the data of top corporations requires many petabytes. One petabyte is approximately 1,000 terabytes!

EXPLORE FURTHER

Compressing Digital Photos

Picture files are large because of the number of bytes needed to digitize an image. Digital image sizes are measured in pixels. For example, a typical photo taken with a digital camera may be in the range of 3000 x 2000 pixels. Such a photo would be 6 million pixels, where each pixel needs to be represented by its RGB color values. RGB color information uses 24 bits for each pixel (or 3 bytes). Therefore, the file size is 18 million bytes or 18 MB (6 million pixels times 3 bytes per pixel). However, if you were to look at the file size of the picture on your digital camera's memory card, the file size would be much lower than 18 MB. This occurs because of the image file format's compression scheme.

1. Find out about the JPEG (pronounced *jay-peg*) file format used to store pictures for most digital cameras and for displaying pictures on websites. How does JPEG compression reduce file size? What is the sacrifice made to achieve the smaller file size? What are some other file formats used for digital images?

2. Create a document that describes in your own words what you learned about JPEG image files. Include the URLs for the articles you read.

3. Save the document as **C3-Hardware-JPEG-Your Name**.

4. Submit the document to your instructor in the manner she or he has requested.

TOPIC 3.6

Storage Options

Saving a document, spreadsheet, or presentation makes a permanent copy of the work in a file that is available after power to the computer is turned off. When saving, you identify the **storage device** upon which the file should be saved. A storage device is a piece of hardware with the means to write new data to and read existing data from storage media. Storage devices are often referred to as **drives**. Each drive is identified by a unique letter and label on a Windows-compatible computer (Figure 3.6). On a Mac computer, each storage device is assigned a name, such as Macintosh HD for a hard disk drive.

Several storage options for saving a permanent copy of a file are available, such as internal and external hard disk drives, solid-state drives, network storage, USB flash memory, optical discs, flash memory cards, and cloud storage. In this topic you will learn about each of these storage options.

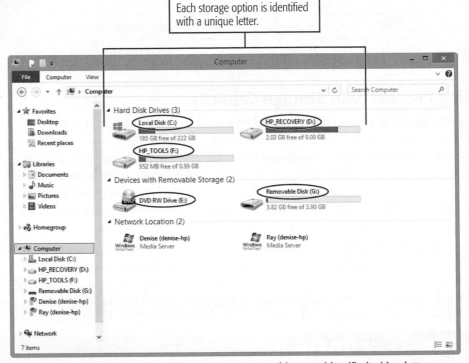

Each storage option is identified with a unique letter.

Figure 3.6 In a Windows-compatible computer, storage drives are identified with a letter.

Did You Know?

Notice the first drive letter used is C. Early PCs did not have hard disk drives and operated with one or two floppy disks (soft plastic disks that you inserted into a drive slot) that were assigned the letters A and B. When floppy disks became obsolete, A and B were not reused.

Hard Disk Drives

Inside the system unit of a PC is an internal **hard disk**, also called **hard drive** and **hard disk drive (HDD)**. The internal HDD is usually the largest storage device on a standalone PC and is assigned drive letter C on Windows-compatible computers. This is the storage medium upon which the operating system and application software programs are stored as well as data files. Hard disks are round pieces of metal called platters stacked inside a sealed unit with a magnetic coating on their surface. The disks spin and a read/write head moves across the surface of the disk magnetizing the data to the surface.

Internal hard disk with top cover plate removed to show platters and read/write head; a read/write head for each surface moves over the disks together as the platters spin.

An external hard disk drive is a storage device that you attach to the computer as a peripheral using a USB or FireWire port. External HDDs are a popular option for extending the storage capacity of a PC and/or for backing up documents, photos, videos, music, and other files.

Storage capacities for hard disk drives vary but are typically in the range of several hundred gigabytes with some newer computers having HDDs in the range of one to three terabytes.

External HDDs are often used to back up an entire computer.

Solid State Drives

A newer type of hard disk drive technology called **solid-state drive (SSD)** is increasingly being used in portable computers. SSDs use **flash memory**. Flash memory is chip-based technology where data is stored electronically on a chip instead of magnetically like a traditional HDD. With chip-based flash memory no mechanical parts are required inside the drive, making the device more durable. SSDs also weigh less than traditional HDDs, they make no noise when operating, and require less power. These qualities make SSDs popular for mobile devices. Internal and external SDDs are available in similar storage capacities as traditional HDDs.

Solid-state drives are popular in Ultrabooks because they weigh less and use less power than traditional HDDs.

Network Storage

In some workplaces, data is often required to be stored on a network drive for security and cost reasons. Network drives are hard disk drives installed in a network server and made available to users who have been granted access to the server's storage with their user name and password. A network drive will often have a letter assigned that is higher in the alphabet such as drive R or drive S. Networked storage is automatically backed up daily at the server. Centralized network storage is also considered more secure than leaving data on individual HDDs scattered about a workplace.

USB Flash Drives

A **USB flash drive** is a portable storage device that contains flash memory inside the case. USB as a storage option is popular because the drive is easy to use, small enough to carry easily, and inexpensive. The drive is powered through the USB port of the computer. When you plug in a USB flash drive, a drive letter is assigned to the device that is usually E, F, G, or another higher letter depending on the number of USB ports and other devices.

USB flash drives are made in all kinds of shapes, sizes, and colors. Some are disguised inside toys or cartoon characters. Storage capacities are available to meet several needs including 8 GB, 16 GB, 32 GB, 64 GB, and 128 GB. USB flash drives are called by many other names such as thumb drive, memory stick, jump drive, key drive, and pen drive.

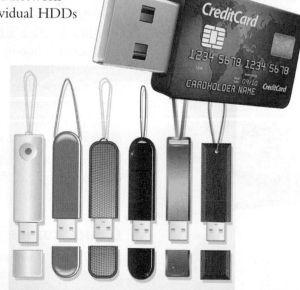

USB flash drives come in all shapes, sizes, colors, and capacities.

With Blu-ray's higher storage capacity and better quality video and audio, Blu-ray media are fast replacing DVDs.

Optical Discs

An **optical disc** is a CD, DVD, or Blu-ray disc. Note that the spelling of this storage media is *disc* (not *disk*). An optical drive is internally mounted inside the system unit, though external drives are also available for plugging into a USB or FireWire port. Most PCs include an optical drive except netbooks and many ultrabooks. Optical drives are usually identified with the letter E or F, although this could vary depending on the number of other installed devices. A laser beam is used to read and write data on optical discs. Recording to an optical disc is referred to as *burning a disc.*

Optical discs are sometimes used to back up important data or for making copies of music, pictures, or movies since the removable media can be used in other devices and players and is relatively inexpensive. Optical disc types and storage capacities are listed in Table 3.3.

Table 3.3	Recordable Optical Discs and Storage Capacities	
Type of Optical Disc	**Media Options**	**Storage Capacity**
Compact Disc (CD)	CD-R (write once) CD-RW (rewritable up to 1000 times)	700 MB
Digital Versatile Disc/Digital Video Disc (DVD)	DVD +R or –R (write once) DVD +RW or –RW (rewriteable up to 1000 times)	4.7 GB for single-layer 8.5 GB for dual-layer
Blu-ray disc (BD)	BD –R (write once) BD –RE (erase and re-record multiple times)	25 GB for single-layer 50 GB for double-layer

Flash memory cards are used for storage in digital cameras, smartphones, and other portable devices.

Flash Memory Cards

The most common type of storage for a digital camera, smartphone, or other portable device is a **flash memory card**. A flash memory card is a small card that contains one or more flash memory chips (similar to SSDs and USB flash drives). Flash memory cards come in a variety of formats such as Secure Digital (SD), CompactFlash (CF) and proprietary formats made by Sony and Olympus for their digital cameras. Capacities for flash memory cards can range from 1 GB to more than 60 GB. The type of flash memory card you would buy for a device is dependent on the formats the device can read.

Some computers and notebooks have a card reader built in for easy transfer of files stored on a flash memory card's portable device (such as a digital camera) and the PC. Some USB hubs also contain readers.

Cloud Storage

Recall from Chapter 1 that cloud computing involves accessing software and storage services from the Internet. Some cloud computing providers allow you access to free storage with subscription plans available for those with higher capacity level needs. For example, at both Google Drive and Microsoft's SkyDrive you can store files for free up to a specified capacity limit (5 GB at Google and 7 GB at Microsoft at the time of writing). The main advantage with storing your documents using a cloud provider is the ability to access the files using a web browser from any location at which you have an Internet connection. You can also sync documents between multiple devices and easily share files with others. Transferring files via an Internet connection is fast and easy and you no longer need to buy, organize, and store media such as USB flash drives, CDs, DVDs, or BDs. Popular cloud storage providers besides Google and Microsoft are Dropbox and Box.net.

Storage capacities continue to grow to meet demands by consumers and businesses to store increasing amounts of data. The typical storage capacities mentioned here are likely soon to be replaced by higher capacity drives or media.

Storing files using a cloud storage provider is one way to access documents from multiple devices and easily share pictures or other files.

Career Connection

Computer Technician

If you like hardware and are a good communicator you may want to consider a career in computer hardware repair. Computer technicians troubleshoot and repair PCs and mobile devices. To succeed as a computer systems technician you need to like working with customers as well as hardware. CompTIA's A+ certification validates entry-level knowledge and skills for computer support. Consider also enrolling in a program at a community college in PC/Desktop Support or PC Support Technician.

EXPLORE   FURTHER

Comparing Cloud Storage Providers

Using a cloud storage provider to keep a copy of important documents or other media files such as pictures, music, and videos has many advantages, but which provider offers the best deal?

1. Research at least five cloud storage providers besides Google and Microsoft. Find out how much, if any, free storage space is offered and the costs to purchase additional storage. Also learn the limit imposed on the file size that can be transferred to their servers.

2. Create a presentation with one slide per provider. Describe the features, benefits, costs, and file size limit for each provider. Include the URL at the provider's website where you found the information described. Conclude the presentation with a slide that states your recommendation for a cloud storage provider and give your reasons.

3. Save the presentation as **C3-Hardware-CloudStorage-Your Name**.

4. Submit the presentation to your instructor in the manner she or he has requested.

Concepts Review

Topic	Key Concepts	Key Terms
The System Unit	A peripheral device is hardware used for input, output, connectivity, or storage. The power supply is where you plug in the power cord. A cooling fan near the CPU prevents the CPU from overheating. A motherboard is the main circuit board into which all other devices connect. Expansion cards are plugged into expansion slots on the motherboard to provide or improve functionality. Data travels between components on the motherboard and the CPU via data buses. Parallel processing means the CPU can execute multiple instructions simultaneously. The instruction cycle is the process the CPU goes through to retrieve, decode, execute, and store an instruction. Clock speed refers to the speed at which the CPU operates and is measured in gigahertz. L1, L2, and L3 cache affect system performance since the CPU accesses cache memory faster than RAM. Read-only memory stores instructions that do not change, such as the BIOS instructions used to start up a computer. RAM is configured in modules that plug into the motherboard. The size and type of RAM affects system performance. External devices plug into a port attached to the motherboard. USB ports are the most common type of port.	Peripheral device Motherboard Expansion cards Data buses Parallel processing Instruction cycle Clock speed Gigahertz (GHz) Level 1 (L1) cache Level 2 (L2) cache Level 3 (L3) cache Read-only memory (ROM) BIOS (Basic Input Output System) Ports Universal Serial Bus (USB) port
Input Devices	Wireless keyboards and mice communicate with a wireless receiver plugged into a USB port. Special purpose keys on the keyboard are used to send commands to the computer. Some tablets and smartphones display an onscreen keyboard. A mouse detects movement using light technology and moves the pointer in the same direction you move the mouse. Buttons and a scroll wheel on a mouse are used to manipulate objects or send commands. On notebooks, a touchpad or track pointer senses finger movement and taps or finger pressure in place of a mouse. A touch-enabled device accepts input from finger gestures or a stylus (digital pen). A scanner uses optical technology to convert text and images into data. Other readers used for input are bar code, QR code, magnetic strip, and RFID readers, and biometric scanners. Digital cameras, camcorders, and webcams are input devices used to provide pictures or live video to the computer. Microphones combined with voice recognition technology are used to create data from audio sources. Various game controllers provide a means to input commands to entertainment systems.	Keyboard Mouse Touchpad Touch-enabled displays Touchscreens Stylus Scanner Bar code readers QR (Quick Response) codes Magnetic strip readers Biometric scanners Radio Frequency Identification (RFID) readers Camcorders Webcam Microphone Voice recognition technology Speech recognition technology

continued....

Output Devices	Video display screens connect to a video port on a PC or are integrated into a notebook or mobile device.	Video displays
	Newer monitors for PCs are widescreen LCD displays.	Monitor
	LED and plasma displays are often used for televisions.	Liquid Crystal Displays (LCD)
	OLED displays do not require backlighting and are expected to eventually replace LCD screens in mobile devices.	Light-Emitting Diode (LED)
		Plasma
	Resolution is the measurement of horizontal and vertical pixels used to render an image on a video display.	Organic Light-Emitting Diode (OLED)
	Video display projectors and interactive whiteboards are used to display computer output on large screens.	Resolution
		Pixels
	Audio output is heard from speakers, headphones, or headsets.	Video display projector (VDP)
	A Bluetooth headset is used with a smartphone to hear a conversation when making a voice call.	Interactive whiteboard
		Bluetooth headset
	Printed copy of computer output is called hard copy.	Hard copy
	A laser printer uses a laser beam to charge a drum to which toner is applied and then heated as the paper passes through the printer.	Laser printer
		Inkjet printer
	Inkjet printers form text and images by spraying drops of ink from ink cartridges onto a page.	Photo printer
		Thermal printer
	Photo printers are used to print high-quality pictures from digital cameras.	Plotter
	Thermal printers heat coated paper and are often used to print receipts at retail stores.	Digital copier
		Video card
	Blueprints and technical drawings are printed on plotters that move a pen across the page.	
	Digital copiers connected to a network can be used to print output.	
	Multipurpose printers include printing, scanning, copying, and faxing capabilities in one device.	
	A video card processes the data needed to display text and images on your screen.	
Network Adapters	A network adapter is any device used to connect to a network.	Network adapter
	The network adapter is the interface between a computer and a modem or router that allows data to be exchanged.	Network card
		Protocols
	Data is exchanged in a network using a system of rules called protocols.	Wi-Fi adapter
		802.11 protocol
	A network connection for a wired connection is called an Ethernet port.	External wireless adapter
	Ethernet refers to the physical cable used for the connection.	USB wireless adapter
	Wi-Fi adapters are used to communicate with a wireless network.	USB dongle
		Wireless ExpressCard
	The 802.11 protocol is the name of the standard used for wireless communications in Wi-Fi networks.	
	A USB wireless adapter or a wireless ExpressCard are external wireless adapters used to connect to a wireless network.	
	A Bluetooth adapter is used to provide connectivity to other Bluetooth-enabled devices.	

continued....

Topic	Key Concepts	Key Terms
Digital Data	Computers understand the binary system, which uses only 0s and 1s. The smallest unit in the binary system is a bit, which can have one of two values: either 0 or 1. A group of 8 bits equals a byte and represents one character, number, or symbol. Internet speed is measured in megabits per second, which is 1 million bits transferred per second. Files are permanent copies of documents, photos, or videos assigned a file name and measured in bytes. A kilobyte is approximately 1,000 bytes. A megabyte is approximately 1 million bytes. A gigabyte is approximately 1 billion bytes. A terabyte is approximately 1 trillion bytes. One megabyte can store approximately 500 pages of text. Images, music, and videos require many megabytes of storage space.	Binary system Bit Byte File File name Kilobyte Megabyte Gigabyte Terabyte
Storage Options	A storage device provides the means to read data from and write data to a permanent storage medium. Storage devices are referred to as drives. An internal hard disk drive is usually the largest storage device on a standalone PC. Traditional hard disk drives are magnetic storage mediums. External hard disk drives can be connected via a USB or FireWire port. Solid-state drives use chip-based flash memory to store data, are more durable, and use less power than HDDs. Some workplaces require data to be stored on network servers. USB flash drives are portable, easy to use, and come in all shapes, sizes, and storage capacities. CDs, DVDs, and Blu-ray discs use optical technology to read and write data to recordable discs. Flash memory cards are used in portable devices such as digital cameras. Some computers have a card reader built in for easy transfer of data from portable flash memory cards. Cloud storage providers allow you to store and share files that are accessible from any device with an Internet connection. Some cloud providers allow you access to free storage space, with higher capacities available for a subscription fee.	Storage device Drives Hard disk Hard drive Hard disk drive (HDD) Solid-state drive (SSD) Flash memory USB flash drive Optical disc Flash memory card

Multiple Choice

1. Which of the following is *not* found inside a system unit?
   a. Motherboard
   b. Power supply
   c. RAM
   d. USB flash drive

2. Additional circuit boards that add functionality are plugged into the motherboard in these slots.
   a. Data bus
   b. Expansion
   c. Parallel processing
   d. BIOS

3. A notebook computer senses finger movement from this device and moves the pointer.
   a. Touchpad
   b. Special purpose keys
   c. Biometric scanner
   d. Stylus

4. A smartphone can scan this type of matrix of black dots that usually directs the computer to display a website.
   a. UPC code
   b. QR code
   c. Magnetic strip
   d. RFID tag

5. This newer technology is expected to eventually replace screens in portable devices because it does not require backlighting.
   a. LED
   b. Plasma
   c. OLED
   d. LCD

6. This term refers to the measurement of horizontal and vertical pixels used to make up an image on a video display screen.
   a. Plasma
   b. Bytes
   c. Pixelation
   d. Resolution

7. A wired network adapter is referred to as this type of port.
   a. USB
   b. Wi-Fi
   c. ExpressCard
   d. Ethernet

8. A wireless USB adapter is sometimes referred to by this term.
   a. USB dongle
   b. USB pendrive
   c. USB memory stick
   d. USB flash drive

9. This is the term used to refer to data represented as a series of 0s and 1s.
   a. Microprocessing
   b. Binary system
   c. Character recognition
   d. Random access memory

10. Internet speed is measured in this type of unit.
    a. Bytes per second
    b. Megabits per second
    c. Terabytes per second
    d. Kilobytes per second

11. An internal hard disk drive is usually referred to by this drive letter in a standalone PC.
    a. A
    b. B
    c. C
    d. G

12. Solid-state drives use this type of technology.
    a. Flash memory
    b. Laser memory
    c. Optical memory
    d. Magnetic memory

Crossword Puzzle

ACROSS

2 Term for network connectivity device
10 External wireless adapter
11 Prints on coated paper
12 A group of 8 bits

DOWN

1 Workplace storage requirement
3 Power cord plug
4 Reads embedded tags with antennas
5 Digital pen
6 Approximately 1,000 characters
7 Optical disc replacing DVDs
8 Measures clock speed
9 Typical monitor for PC

Matching

Match the term with the statement or definition.

_____ 1. Wi-Fi standard
_____ 2. Networked photocopier
_____ 3. Fingerprint reader
_____ 4. SkyDrive
_____ 5. Two CPU chips
_____ 6. Charged drum
_____ 7. Digital pen
_____ 8. Main circuit board

a. Parallel processing
b. Motherboard
c. Stylus
d. Biometric scanner
e. Laser printer
f. Digital copier
g. 802.11
h. Cloud Storage

Project 1 My Computer's Hardware

Individual
Deliverable: Document

Find out the specifications for all of the hardware and peripherals on the computer or mobile device that you use for school or personal use. Organize the information into the following categories: CPU, RAM, Input Devices, Output Devices, Ports, and Storage Options. If you do not own a computer, use one in a computer lab at school or in a public library. List all of the devices and any information you can learn about each device's capacity or speed. *Hint: In a Windows-compatible computer you can find storage options by opening a Computer window, and other hardware by exploring the System category in the Control Panel. In a Mac computer, open System Preferences.* If necessary, find a computer ad for a new notebook computer and use the ad to complete this project.

1. Create a document in a table format that describes all of the hardware you were able to identify in your computing device. Include as many specifications as possible such as CPU clock speed, amount of RAM, and so on.
2. Save the document as **C3-Project1-MyComputerSpecs-Your Name**.
3. Submit the document to your instructor in the manner she or he has requested.

Project 2 Adaptive/Assistive Technologies

Pairs or Team
Deliverable: Presentation

Adaptive technologies are also referred to by the term assistive technologies and refer to devices used by persons with disabilities to interact with a computer or mobile device. For example, technology exists to read text from a screen to an individual who is visually impaired. Choose the category of adaptive input devices or adaptive output devices and research a minimum of two technologies that are available to assist individuals with disabilities.

1. Create a presentation that describes the technologies you researched. Include the URLs of the websites from which you obtained information.
2. Save the presentation as **C3-Project2-AdaptiveTechnology-Your Name**.
3. Submit the presentation to your instructor in the manner she or he has requested.

Project 3 Laser or InkJet?

Individual or Pairs
Deliverable: Comparison Table in a Document or Presentation

You have been asked by the office manager at a small travel agency to research the costs of a laser printer versus an inkjet printer. The office manager is planning to replace all of the printers in the office and your analysis will help her decide the type of printer to buy.

1. Choose a manufacturer of printers such as HP, Canon, Epson, or another supplier and pick one laser printer and one inkjet printer from the company's website to compare for this project. Compare the features of each printer and the specifications for print speed. Compare the current cost to buy the printer as well as the cost of replacement toner and ink cartridges. Based on what you have researched, choose the laser or the inkjet printer as your recommendation.
2. Create a comparison table in a document or presentation with a summary of your work including your recommendation along with your reasons. Include the URLs of the websites you used for this project.
3. Save the document or presentation as **C3-Project3-LaserOrInkJet-Your Name**.
4. Submit the document or presentation to your instructor in the manner she or he has requested.

Project 4 Connecting Your Notebook to HDTV

Individual or Pairs
Deliverable: Instructional Handout

Your family just purchased a new high-definition television. You decide you want to watch movies from your notebook on the television video display, but you do not know how to connect the notebook to the television. Your notebook has an HDMI port and you have bought an HDMI cable. Now all you need to do is figure out how to connect the two devices.

1. Go to YouTube, and find and watch at least two videos that demonstrate how to connect a laptop computer to a high-definition television using HDMI.
2. Create a step-by-step instructional document for your family so that each person will be able to connect the notebook to the HDTV without difficulty. Make sure the instructions are written in your own words in clear language. Include graphics to illustrate your instructions to ensure the steps could be followed by anyone in your family.
3. Save the document as **C3-Project4-NotebookToTV-Your Name**.
4. Submit the document to your instructor in the manner she or he has requested.

Project 5 Upgrading Laptop RAM

Individual or Pairs
Deliverable: Presentation

Assume that a friend has asked for your help to upgrade RAM in her laptop. She has an IBM ThinkPad T60 laptop with 1 GB of RAM. She wants to add another 2 GB to improve the computer's performance. She has asked you to help her determine what type of RAM to buy and how to install the new RAM module.

1. Research RAM upgrades for an IBM ThinkPad T60. Find a website that advertises the RAM upgrade module and the current price.
2. Go to YouTube, and find and watch at least two videos that demonstrate how to replace the RAM module in an IBM ThinkPad.
3. Create a presentation with one slide that describes the type of RAM module, price, and company website URL for the RAM module you found. On the next slide, link to the YouTube video you thought best showed the process for upgrading the RAM module.
4. Save the presentation as **C3-Project5-RAMUpgrade-Your Name**.
5. Submit the presentation to your instructor in the manner she or he has requested.

Project 6 Storage Options

Team
Deliverable: Document, Blog Entry, or Presentation

Your team has been asked by a local accountant to educate him on storage options for his accounting firm. The accountant runs a small office with three staff members who currently save all clients' accounting work on individual internal hard drives. The accountant would like to move to a centralized storage system so that each person has access to all client files in case someone is absent. The accountant has heard of cloud storage and network storage and would like to know more about these options. Since the accountant stores the personal financial data of his clients, security and backup of data is a main concern for him.

1. Within your team discuss cloud storage and network storage options for the accountant. What are the advantages and disadvantages of each type of storage? Which option would best meet the security and backup needs or do both options adequately meet those needs? Which option might be more cost-effective? What would be the team's recommendation to the accountant? If necessary, conduct research to answer the questions posed.

2. Prepare a summary of your team's discussion in a document, blog entry, or presentation.
3. Save the document or presentation as **C3-Project6-Storage-Your Name**.
4. Submit the document, presentation, or blog entry to your instructor in the manner she or he has requested.

Project 7 Greener Computing

Individual, Pairs, or Team
Deliverable: Blog Entry

You are ready to purchase a new notebook computer and want to buy one that will have a minimal impact on the environment. A friend has told you about epeat.net, a rating system/registry for green electronics. Go to epeat.net and learn about the criteria by which products are rated for the EPEAT registry. Next, click the link to Search the Registry and choose the option to search by Manufacturer/Country (the list defaults to the United States). Click the number in the Notebooks column next to a manufacturer's name you recognize. Then, click the link to a product that has been evaluated with a Gold rating. Read the information on the next screen about the product and its individual scores by criteria.

1. Write and post a blog entry that describes what you learned about EPEAT. Would you use this registry to help you choose a new notebook? Why or why not? Were you surprised by any of the individual scores on the product you reviewed? Why or why not? (For example, a product can receive a Gold rating but score 0 on an individual criterion such as materials selection.)
2. Submit your blog URL to your instructor in the manner she or he has requested.

Optional

Read the blog entry for this project of at least two other classmates and post a comment to each. Submit the URLs of your classmates' blogs with Step 2.

Project 8 Ethics Discussion on Using Color Copier for Personal Use

Team
Deliverable: Document, Blog Entry, or Presentation

A coworker's daughter is getting married and you learned recently that your coworker used the company's high-quality color digital copier to print 200 wedding invitations.

1. Within your team discuss the ethics involved in using the company's high-quality color digital copier for personal use. Is it acceptable or not? If she only printed one copy, would that be acceptable? What should you do? Should you confront her and demand she reimburse the company for the cost of the paper and color toner? Should you tell her manager? Would any of your answers change if you knew you were going to be invited to the wedding?
2. Prepare a summary of your team's discussion in a document, blog entry, or presentation.
3. Save the document or presentation as **C3-Project8-PersonalUsePrinting-Your Name**.
4. Submit the document, presentation, or blog entry to your instructor in the manner she or he has requested.

Chapter 4

The Operating System and Utility Programs

After successfully completing this chapter, you will be able to:

- Identify system software and describe the role an operating system fulfills in computer operations

- List and describe the major functions of operating system software

- Identify the operating systems in use for personal computers and mobile devices

- Explain the purpose of an embedded operating system and a cloud operating system

- Describe and explain common utility programs used to maintain a computer

- Use troubleshooting tools found in the operating system to solve computer problems

A computing device needs software installed on it for the device to work. Software is the term that describes the set of programs that contains instructions that tell the computer what to do and how to perform each task. **System software** includes the operating system that is designed to work with the hardware that is present as well as a set of utility programs that are used to maintain the computer and its devices. The **operating system (OS)** program provides the user interface that allows you to work with the computer, manages all of the hardware resources, and provides the platform for managing files and application programs (the programs you use to perform tasks). It is the most important software on your computer because without an operating system, the hardware and other software programs you want to use would not work.

For example, most people go to their computing device because they have a specific task they want to do. Assume you want to log in to Facebook to check for updates on your friends. To do this, you start your computer and connect to the Facebook website. The computer first has to start the operating system before you see the interface that allows you to launch the Internet browser program such as Internet Explorer. Without the operating system, the interface would not appear and the browser would not be able to connect to the Internet to load the Facebook page. In this chapter, you will learn the various operating systems available for computers, the typical tasks that operating systems perform, and how to use a few utility programs to maintain and troubleshoot your computer.

Introduction to the Operating System (OS) and the OS Functions

TOPIC 4.1

The operating system manages all of the activities within the computer. The OS routes data between the hardware resources and the application programs as shown in Figure 4.1. The OS also starts the user interface and properly shuts down the hardware. Files that are stored on devices are managed by the OS, and while you are working the OS controls the flow of data between memory and the CPU. If you plug a new device into the computer, the OS looks for and installs the software that allows the device to work. Consider the OS as the conductor of a symphony; each instrument (hardware component and application program) needs the conductor (the OS) to direct when and how to "play" its individual piece so that the song plays correctly.

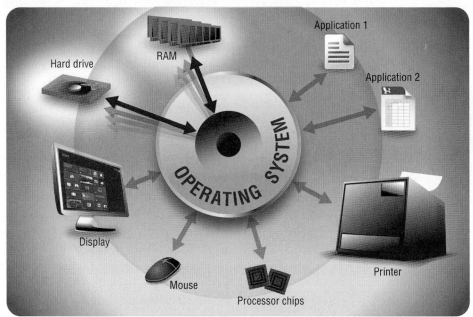

Figure 4.1 The operating system controls the flow of data and manages programs and memory.

Starting a Computer

Starting a computer is called **booting**. If you are turning on a computer that has been shut off, you are doing a **cold boot**. If you are restarting a computer without turning off the power, you are doing a **warm boot**. The instructions for booting are stored on the BIOS chip that resides on the motherboard. These instructions load the OS's **kernel** (the core of the OS that manages memory, devices, and programs and assigns resources) into RAM where it remains until you power off. Other parts of the OS are copied into RAM only when needed.

As the computer is booting, a series of messages may appear on the screen depending on the OS you are using. When the boot process is completed, the screen will display the user interface or the login screen. For example, on a computer running the Windows OS, the user interface is the Start Screen shown in Figure 4.2 (Windows 8.1) or the Desktop (Windows 7 and earlier).

Shutting Down a Computer If you decide to turn off the power to your computer, you should always perform a proper shut down command so that programs and files are properly closed. Depending on the OS, you can choose to *Shut Down*,

Figure 4.2 The Windows 8.1 Start Screen shown after booting and logging in to the system

which means you want to power off the computer, or invoke a power-saving mode such as *Sleep* where open documents and programs are saved but unnecessary functions and devices are turned off.

Functions of the Operating System

Although different operating systems are available for computers, most OS's perform similar functions. Most of these functions are performed automatically in the background, often without the user's awareness.

Providing a User Interface The **user interface (UI)** is the means with which you interact with the computer. For example, in Windows 8.1 with a touch-enabled computer, you tap a tile to launch an app; on a computer that is not touch-enabled, you click the tile to launch the app. In Windows 7 or earlier, you click or double-click an icon on the desktop or use the Start menu system to start an application. Most OS's provide the user with a **graphical user interface** (**GUI**, pronounced *gooey*) that presents visual images such as tiles, icons, or buttons that you tap or click to tell the OS what you want to do.

Sometimes a **command-line interface** similar to the one shown in Figure 4.3 is used to interact with an OS, where you type commands on the keyboard at a prompt to tell the OS what to do. Network specialists will sometimes use a command-line interface to configure or troubleshoot a network device.

Figure 4.3 A command-line interface requires that you type commands from the keyboard at a prompt such as C:\Users\Firstname> shown at the bottom of the window.

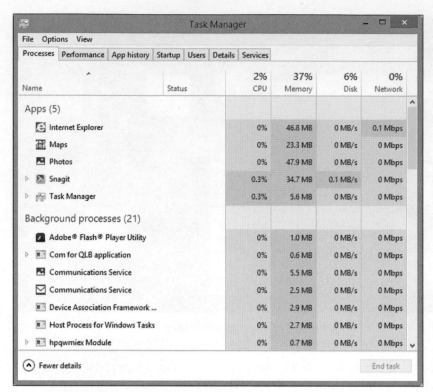

Figure 4.4 The Windows 8.1 Task Manager shows the many tasks the OS has to manage while you are working.

Managing Application Programs and Memory, and Coordinating the Flow of Data The OS manages the installed application programs and provides you with the ability to run a program, install a new program, and uninstall a program no longer desired. When working at a computer, many people will have more than one program running at the same time. The OS manages the computer's resources (Figure 4.4), allocating data and software to/from the CPU and memory as needed, and determines the order in which tasks are performed. The OS manages the flow of data between the CPU, cache memory, RAM, and the input and output devices. If you exceed the capacity of RAM, the OS uses space on the hard disk to store overflow data. The hard disk space allocated to store RAM contents is called **virtual memory**.

Figure 4.5 When new hardware has been plugged in and a device driver has been installed, the OS displays a message indicating the device is ready for use.

Configuring Hardware and Peripheral Devices The OS configures all devices that are installed or connected to the computer. Small programs called **drivers** contain the instructions the OS uses to communicate and route data to/from the device. When the computer is booted, the OS loads each device driver. If you plug in a new device after the computer is started, the OS searches the device for the driver, loads it automatically, and displays a message when the device is ready to use (Figure 4.5). This is called **Plug and Play**. If a device driver is not found, the OS will prompt you to install the driver from another source.

Providing a File System The OS keeps track of the files stored on a computer's storage devices and provides tools with which you can find and then manage those files by moving, copying, deleting, or renaming. In addition, utility programs to search, back up, restore, clean up, and defragment storage devices are also included in the OS package. Figure 4.6 shows the Windows 8.1 ribbon in a Pictures window with buttons shown to perform file management tasks.

Software Updates and Security Software often needs to be updated as program fixes, security enhancements, and new or modified device drivers become available. By default, the OS is generally set up to download updates automatically, as shown in Figure 4.7, free of charge to registered users who have activated the software.

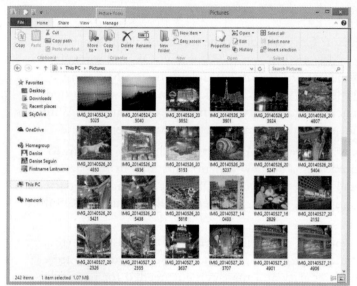

Figure 4.6 The Windows 8.1 Pictures Window shows the ribbon's Home tab buttons used to manage files and folders.

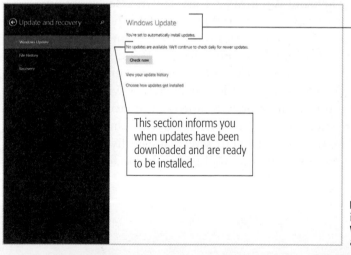

By default, Windows is set to automatically download and install updates.

This section informs you when updates have been downloaded and are ready to be installed.

Figure 4.7 Windows Update window in Windows 8.1 with the message that Windows Update is currently set to automatically install new updates

EXPLORE FURTHER

Look up the steps in the boot process

1. Using your favorite search engine, look up an article on the Web that explains the steps involved in the boot process when you turn on a computer.

2. Draw a flow chart or create a table that lists each step and explains what occurs in your own words.

3. Save the document as **C4-OS-BootProcess-Your Name** and submit it to your instructor in the manner she or he has requested.

TOPIC 4.2

Check This Out

www.windows.microsoft.com/ en-us/windows/history

Go here to read the history of Windows developments from 1975 to today.

Did You Know?

Microsoft will stop providing support to Windows XP in 2014. Home and business users are advised to upgrade to Windows 7 or Windows 8 beforehand to avoid problems that occur when updates are no longer provided.

Popular Operating Systems for Computing Systems

When you purchase a new computing device, an operating system is preinstalled so that the device will work when you turn it on. The OS that is preinstalled may depend on the hardware since some hardware is designed specifically for a particular OS. This is known as a **computing platform**, which refers to the combination of hardware architecture and software design that allows applications to run. For example, buying an iMac computer means you will have the Mac OS installed since Apple computers are not designed to run Windows software. Four operating systems that you may encounter in your work or personal life are Windows, Mac OS, Unix, and Linux.

Windows

Windows, created by Microsoft Corporation, is the most popular OS because a wide variety of hardware is designed to run the Windows OS, and software applications designed for Windows are plentiful. Windows has evolved from Windows 1.0, released in 1985, to Windows 8.1, released in 2013 with an update in April of 2014. You will encounter a variety of Windows OS's since the Windows brand is so prevalent and not everyone upgrades to the most current release.

Windows is updated every few years as Microsoft develops new versions to keep up with hardware innovations, adds new functionality and/or redesigns existing functions, and overall strives to make the OS faster and more user-friendly. Generally, a new release is assigned a version number to differentiate the OS from earlier editions.

Each Windows version generally comes in a variety of editions for various home and business environments. In addition, Windows Server editions are available to provide advanced security and management needed for networks.

Windows 7, released in 2009, and Windows 8.1 are shown side-by-side in Figure 4.8. You can see the vast difference in the user interface between these two releases. While prior updates to Windows typically involved a fairly fast learning curve for users, Windows 8.1 is definitely a game changer. Windows 8.1 is focused on touch-enabled mobile devices, meaning the OS runs faster and integrates more easily with other apps and devices. The cloud is a major factor with Windows 8.1 since the OS is designed to store your favorite online services accounts (such as Facebook) so that when you sign in to a Windows 8.1 device, these services are automatically connected. The tiles on your Start screen stream live updates so you instantly know when someone posts on your wall in Facebook, for example.

Figure 4.8 Windows 7 Desktop (left) and Windows 8 Start Screen (right)

Mac OS

The **Mac OS** is a proprietary OS created by Apple, Inc. with the first release in 1984 for Apple's Macintosh computer. The first Macintosh computer used a GUI interface and became the basis for the design of other GUI OS's down the road.

The Mac OS X family is the most recent OS, with the Mavericks version released in October 2013 shown in Figure 4.9. Apple uses a unique naming convention for Mac OS X with a version sporting an animal's name such as Leopard (2007), Snow Leopard (2009), and Mountain Lion (2012), or a popular place such as Mavericks (2013, or Yosemite (2014). Like Microsoft, Apple releases new versions to update functionality, responsiveness, and efficiencies to strive for faster, more user-friendly experiences. Server versions of Mac OS X are also available.

Historically, Macs were less prone to viruses since hackers went after Windows software because of its prevalence in the marketplace; however, with the rise in Mac sales in the past few years, virus attacks are now hitting the Mac world.

Mac computers have always been popular with graphic artists and those working in multimedia environments since the hardware is designed with high-end graphics processing capability. Consumer demand for Apple's products has resulted in an increased Mac brand presence in the marketplace.

Figure 4.9 Mac OS X Mountain Lion, released in July 2012

UNIX

UNIX is an operating system that has been around since the late 1960s and is designed for servers. Originally designed to be multi-user and multitasking, the OS is often used for web servers because of the OS's robust ability to support many users. UNIX is available in several versions and is able to run on a variety of devices, including hardware built for Windows and Macs. In fact, Apple's Mac OS is based on the UNIX OS. Although UNIX is a highly stable OS, the cost and higher level of skill required to install and maintain a UNIX computer make it less prevalent for typical computer users.

UNIX was designed as a server operating system.

Linux

Linux was created by Linus Torvalds in 1991 and is based on UNIX. Linux can be used as a standalone OS or as a server OS. What makes Linux preferable to some users is that the OS is an **open source program**, meaning that the source code is available to the public and can be freely modified or customized. Linux, like UNIX, can run on a variety of devices and is available as a free download on the Web as well as by purchase from Linux vendors. Linux, because of its open source design, is available in many distributions (versions) such as Red Hat and Ubuntu. Figure 4.10 illustrates PCLinuxOS. You can order some computers with Linux preinstalled upon request.

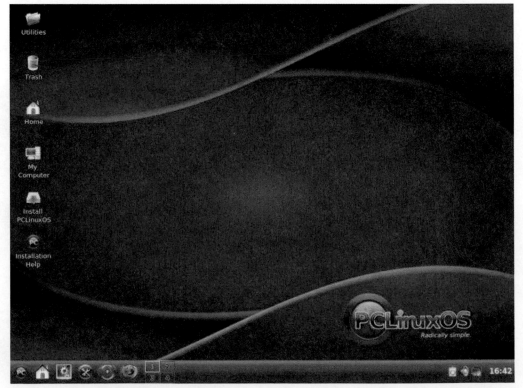

Figure 4.10 PCLinuxOS, one of the many distributions available for this open source operating system

The open source software movement is increasing in large part due to the lower costs associated with using free software. Linux can be found in use at companies such as IBM and HP, and a popular mobile OS is based on Linux.

Check This Out

www.webopedia.com/ TERM/N/network_ operating_system_NOS.html

Go here to read a definition of a network operating system (NOS).

Blog Topic

To upgrade or not to upgrade—which side are you on?

When a newer version of an operating system is released, some people jump on the bandwagon and immediately upgrade, relishing the opportunity to be on the leading edge and experience what's new. Others prefer to wait a while and stick with the tried and true, assuming that it is more prudent to wait for the manufacturer to work out all of the bugs.

1. Assuming that cost is not a factor in the decision to upgrade, write and post a blog entry that supports immediately upgrading or taking the wait-and-see approach. Give your reasons for your position.

2. Read at least two of your classmate's blogs and post a comment to each.

3. Submit your blog URL and the URLs of the two classmates' blogs for which you provided a comment to your instructor in the manner she or he has requested.

EXPLORE FURTHER

Conduct a survey and look up statistics on OS usage

1. Survey a minimum of 10 friends, family, or classmates outside your class to find out which OS they use on their primary computing device.

2. Next, using your favorite search engine, look up current statistics on OS market share on the Web.

3. Create two charts in a new document or presentation that show the compiled results of your personal survey and the results you found on the Web.

4. Add a short paragraph that describes the comparisons you found. Include the URL of the site you used for your web research.

5. Save the document or presentation as **C4-OS-OSStats-Your Name** and submit it to your instructor in the manner she or he has requested.

Popular Operating Systems for Mobile Devices

A variety of mobile devices such as smartphones and tablets use a **mobile operating system**, an operating system designed specifically for a mobile device. The OS is stored on a ROM chip. These operating systems are designed to manage hardware and applications with less memory than a personal computer operating system yet run fast and efficiently. The mobile OS often manages input from a touchscreen and/or voice command and routes data to/from wireless connections including web browsing. Mobile devices also generally include cameras that can be used for video calling or taking pictures. Mobile OS's manage small application programs, called **apps**, with support for multitasking contacts, messages, calendars, music, video, social media updates, and numerous other mobile tools. Several hardware manufacturers produce mobile devices, and some have developed their own operating systems for use on their hardware. The most common mobile operating systems include Android, iOS, BlackBerry OS, and Windows Phone.

The mobile market changes rapidly as wireless technologies and software develop to take full advantage of faster speeds and capabilities. Competition in the industry is fierce and companies that lag in new development quickly run into trouble. For example, Symbian, a mobile operating system once used on most Nokia phones that was popular in Europe, has seen significant decline after Nokia announced a new partnership with Windows Phone. Consider also the struggle by Research in Motion's BlackBerry to remain viable. RIM's predicament is largely attributed to a failure to keep up with touch-enabled multimedia, web browsing, and apps consumers love on Apple and Android phones.

Secure Your Mobile Device!

Imagine your lost smartphone or tablet resulting in someone posting embarrassing updates or photos on your Facebook account! Secure your device by locking it in case it falls into the wrong hands. Some devices provide for a touch or swipe motion to unlock; others require a typed password.

Android is the operating system of choice for mobile devices.

Android

Android is the mobile operating system of choice for many smartphones and tablets. The OS is based on Linux, making it an open source OS. In 2007 Android was released by the **Open Handset Alliance**, which is a consortium of several mobile technology companies of which Google is a member. The goal of the alliance is to develop open standards for mobile devices. Android is now maintained and developed by the **Android Open Source Project (AOSP)**, which is led by Google.

Android currently enjoys the highest market share for mobile devices, and Google Play, the website where you download apps for Android devices, lists more than 450,000 apps.

iOS

Apple developed **iOS** as the mobile operating system for its iPhone, iPod Touch, and iPad. The OS is based on the Mac OS X operating system and is a proprietary OS. Users can only download apps for their Apple devices from the App store in iTunes. Development of new apps for Apple devices is tightly controlled by Apple, meaning that that new apps are generally virus-free, stable, and reliable. The Apple website indicates that more than 500,000 apps and games are available in iTunes for Apple devices.

Apple's iPad 3

BlackBerry OS

Research in Motion (RIM) developed the BlackBerry and the **BlackBerry OS**, which is the operating system designed for BlackBerry devices. Although known for its superior messaging security and its popular BlackBerry Messenger (BBM) tool, this smartphone has been experiencing a market decline. BlackBerry OS, like iOS, is proprietary. Apps available at BlackBerry's App World number more than 70,000.

Windows Phone

Windows Phone is the mobile operating system developed by Microsoft that replaced its earlier OS, Windows Mobile, which was used on Windows smartphones. Windows Phone introduced the tile interface, which is the basis for Windows 8.1 for standalone computers in which live tiles stream updates to the user's mail, calendar, and web apps.

BlackBerry was popular with businesses because of its superior security and popular BBM messenger tool; however, recently it has experienced declining sales.

Windows Phone uses a live tile interface.

EXPLORE FURTHER

Which smartphone would you choose?

1. Assume you have just won a contest where the prize is to buy any smartphone you want with a fully paid talk, text, and data plan for one year that more than meets your needs. Visit your preferred smartphone provider store or use the Internet to conduct your survey of smartphone providers.

2. Once you have made your selection, create a new document that explains your smartphone choice, the features of the smartphone, and your rationale. Include in your rationale the mobile OS that resides on the smartphone and whether the mobile OS had any influence on your choice.

3. At the end of the document, include the URL(s) of any websites you used and/or the name and location of the store you visited.

4. Save the document as **C4-OS-Smartphone-Your Name** and submit it to your instructor in the manner she or he has requested.

TOPIC 4.4

Embedded Operating Systems and Cloud Operating Systems

Computing consoles such as automated tellers, GPS navigation systems, smart appliances, video game controllers, medical equipment devices, point-of-sale cash registers, digital cameras, and a multitude of other consumer and commercial electronics need a specialized operating system designed for the device's limited use. In these computing devices, an **embedded operating system** is installed. Embedded operating systems are smaller and interact with fewer resources to perform specific tasks fast and reliably.

Windows Embedded

Windows Embedded is a family of operating systems based on the familiar Windows operating system designed for use in a variety of devices. For example, Windows Embedded, Windows Embedded POSReady, and Windows Embedded Compact are all variations recommended by Microsoft for an ATM, a kiosk, or a digital picture frame.

Embedded Linux

Embedded Linux applications can be found running smart appliances, in-flight entertainment systems, personal navigation systems, and a variety of other consumer and commercial electronics. Similar to the standalone Linux operating system, embedded Linux is available in many different distributions since it is an open source program.

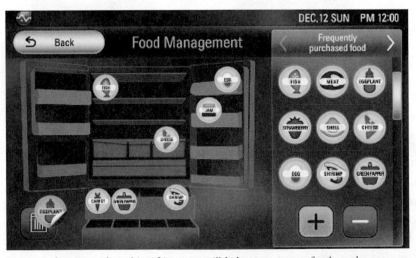

Smart appliances, such as this refrigerator, will help you manage food purchases.

ATMs are just one of many electronic devices that require an embedded operating system.

In-flight entertainment systems are popular with travelers.

Android is the operating system used on some netbooks.

Android

Android, an operating system based on Linux, is a popular choice for electronic devices beyond smartphones such as tablets, set-top boxes, and netbooks. Recently, Google announced its Android@Home project with the goal of controlling household objects such as your dishwasher, lighting, heating, and air conditioning systems using an Android device.

Cloud Operating Systems

Some companies, such as Google, are developing operating systems that operate like a virtual desktop. The interface may look and feel like a traditional desktop, but your settings, documents, pictures, contacts, and other files are stored in the cloud. This means you can access the objects from any device anywhere you have an Internet connection. These **web-based operating systems** are not true operating systems like Windows since you still need a standalone operating system on the computer you are using to access the web browser. However, the appeal of these systems is that extra software for applications does not have to be installed, and the ability to synchronize documents among multiple devices seamlessly is worthwhile as more people use multiple computers.

Cloud operating systems are like a virtual desktop with all settings, applications, and documents stored on cloud servers.

Protect Your Documents in the Cloud

Storing all your files in the cloud is not without risk of hackers or other unwanted intrusions into your personal data. Make sure the service provider encrypts data and choose a password that is difficult to hack. See Chapter 7 for information on encryption and creating strong passwords.

Figure 4.11 After logging in with your Apple ID, the iCloud website connects you to Mail, Contacts, Calendar, Find My iPhone, and Documents from any other Apple device or PC.

iCloud Apple's **iCloud** is built into every new iOS device. Once set up, the iCloud provides access to your email, contacts, calendar, documents, and more as shown in Figure 4.11. You can work on documents in the cloud and have access to them on any device—including a Windows-based PC. If you download an app on one device, you have access to it on your other devices too. Apple includes 5 GB of free storage when you sign up for iCloud.

Chrome OS Google's **Chrome OS** is a Linux-based operating system available on specific hardware called Chromebooks. Chromebooks boasts fast startup with built-in virus protection, automatic updates that promise not to slow down your device over time, and cloud-based applications such as Google Docs, Gmail, Google Drive, and Cloud Print. You also have the ability to sync your favorite websites, documents, and settings with other devices that use the Chrome browser.

Google is constantly updating Chrome OS as it receives feedback from users and reviewers. Figure 4.12 shows the desktop available in version 19 for an operating system that was first released in 2009!

Did You Know

Chrome OS led to the establishment of the Chromium projects with the goal to develop a fast, simple, and secure open-source OS for people who spend most of their time on the Web.

Check This Out

www.jolicloud.com/jolios
Go here to learn about Joli OS, a free cloud-based operating system.

Figure 4.12 A desktop image from version 19 of Google's Chrome OS

Career Connection

Careers in the Cloud

Cloud computing is a growing trend and businesses that use and supply cloud services are looking for IT professionals with the right cloud technology skill sets. These skills include knowledge of networks, security, data migration, and web programming languages. The Global Science and Technology Forum has created three certifications to demonstrate mastery of cloud computing and its applications: Certified Cloud Computing Associate (CCCA), Certified Cloud Computing Specialist (CCCS), and Certified Cloud Computing Professional (CCCP).

 Blog Topic

Is there a future for cloud-based operating systems?

Within a team discuss the following question: *Will cloud-based operating systems eventually take over from traditional computing environments where all of the software and files are stored on a local hard drive?* Consider the advantages and disadvantages of using a system where all settings and files are stored in the cloud. What, if any, barriers will prevent these working environments from becoming commonplace?

1. Write and post a blog entry for your team with a summary of your team's position.

2. Read at least two of your classmates' team blogs and post one comment from your team to each.

3. Submit your team's blog URL and the URLs of the two classmates' team blogs for which you provided a comment to your instructor in the manner she or he has requested.

EXPLORE **FURTHER**

Favorite Electronic Devices

1. Ask at least 10 family or friends to name their favorite electronic device other than a smartphone or tablet. Examples can include mp3 player, GPS, gaming system, digital camera, and so on.

2. Compare the results of your informal survey with a classmate's results and discuss the following questions: Which devices seem to be the most popular? Were there devices that were unique in each list? Was there a response that surprised you?

3. Create a document that summarizes the two survey results and the discussion.

4. Save the document as **C4-OS-FavoriteDevices-Your Name** and submit it to your instructor in the manner she or he has requested.

Utilities in Your OS Package for Maintaining System Performance

TOPIC 4.5

Just as a car needs regular tune-ups to keep the vehicle running smoothly and efficiently, so do computers. Files on the computer should be regularly maintained to remove unwanted files, and regular backups should be done to prevent loss of data. Most operating systems provide a utility that allows you to schedule regular maintenance. File maintenance utilities often include a file manager, a utility to clean up unwanted files, a disk defragmenter, and a backup and restore program.

Utilities that protect your computer from malware such as viruses and spyware are discussed in Chapter 7, *Computer Security and Privacy*.

File Manager

In Windows 7 you open **Windows Explorer** (Figure 4.13), and in Windows 8.1 open **File Explorer** (Figure 4.13) to perform file management tasks such as moving, copying, deleting, and renaming files. You can also set up your filing system by creating a new **folder**, which is a placeholder name for where you want to store related files. A folder on a computer is similar to a paper file folder you would use in an office for paper documents you want to keep together.

In Mac OS X, use the Finder utility to perform file management routines.

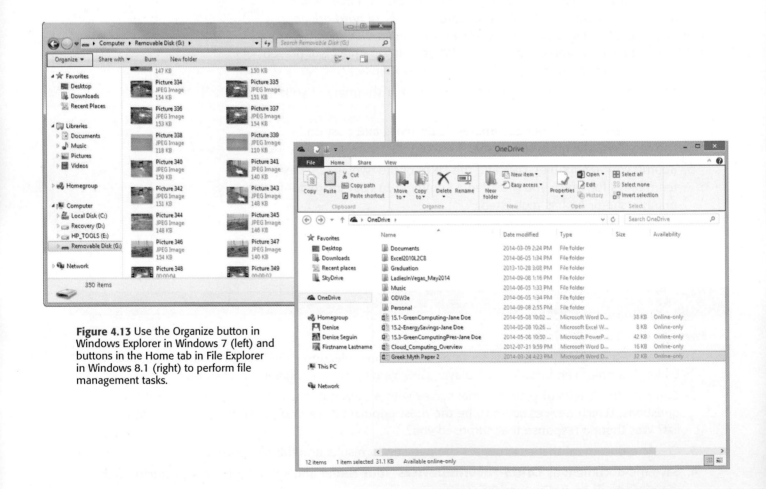

Figure 4.13 Use the Organize button in Windows Explorer in Windows 7 (left) and buttons in the Home tab in File Explorer in Windows 8.1 (right) to perform file management tasks.

Disk Cleanup

The Windows **Disk Cleanup** utility (Figure 4.14) allows you to scan a particular storage device or drive to select various types of files to be deleted. Files the utility will flag for deletion include temporary Internet files, temporary application files, downloaded files, files moved to the Recycle Bin, and offline web pages.

In Mac OS X, use the Repair Disk utility to clean up unwanted files.

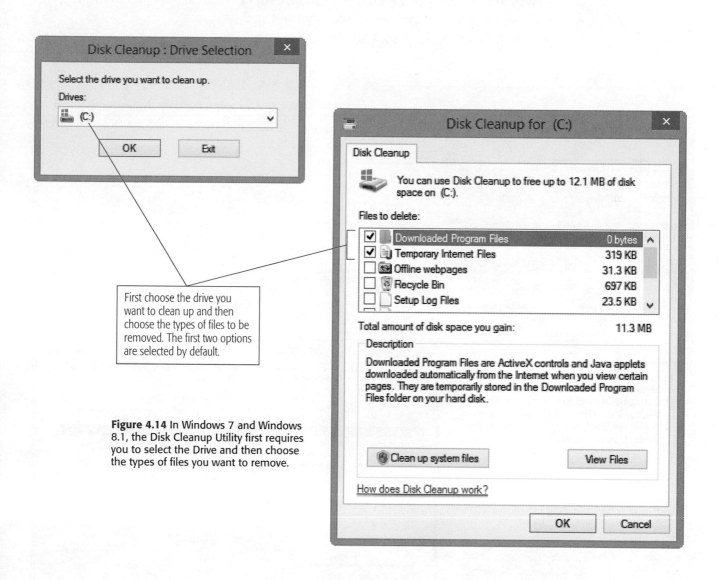

First choose the drive you want to clean up and then choose the types of files to be removed. The first two options are selected by default.

Figure 4.14 In Windows 7 and Windows 8.1, the Disk Cleanup Utility first requires you to select the Drive and then choose the types of files you want to remove.

Disk Defragmenter

As time passes, a disk can become fragmented as a result of files being moved or deleted. Files are stored on a disk in groups called clusters, and several clusters are sometimes needed to store one document. Sometimes, the clusters needed for a document are not stored adjacent to each other. This is called a **fragmentation**. When you reopen a document that has been fragmented, the OS has to gather back together all of the fragmented clusters and arrange them in the correct order. As more fragmentation occurs, disk efficiency decreases. A **disk defragmenter** rearranges the fragmented files back together to improve file retrieval speed and efficiency. Figure 4.15 shows the Windows 7 Disk Defragmenter window and the Windows 8.1 **Optimize Drives** window, both of which are opened from the System and Security section of the Control Panel.

In Mac OS X, use Disk Utility to defragment a disk.

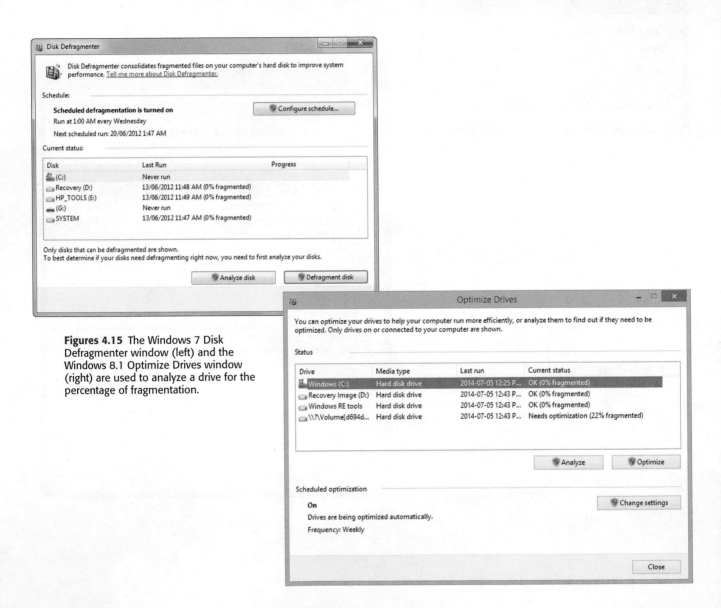

Figures 4.15 The Windows 7 Disk Defragmenter window (left) and the Windows 8.1 Optimize Drives window (right) are used to analyze a drive for the percentage of fragmentation.

Back Up and Restore

Regular backing up of important files is something all computer users should do to prevent loss of data from disk corruption, accidental deletion, or other damage that prevents the files from being usable. A **backup utility** is a program that allows you to back up selected files or an entire disk to a removable storage medium. To begin a backup, in the System and Security section of the Control Panel open **Windows Backup** (in Windows 7) or **File History** (in Windows 8) as shown in Figure 4.16.

Files backed up using a backup utility are not stored in a readable format since the files are compressed to save space. Open the operating system **restore utility** if you need to copy files from a backup back to a disk drive in their original state.

In Mac OS X, use Time Machine to back up and restore files.

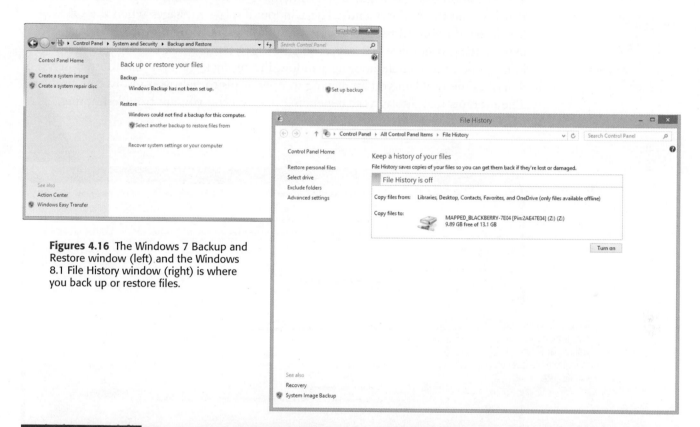

Figures 4.16 The Windows 7 Backup and Restore window (left) and the Windows 8.1 File History window (right) is where you back up or restore files.

EXPLORE FURTHER

Develop a Computer Maintenance Checklist

1. In this topic you have seen a sampling of a few common utility programs provided with the operating system that are used to perform computer maintenance. A comprehensive computer maintenance plan includes other tasks such as wiping clean the screen and other peripherals. Search the Web for articles on computer maintenance to learn about other tasks recommended by computer experts.

2. Individually or in pairs, develop a computer maintenance checklist that you could use at home or at work to maintain your computer. Consider grouping tasks by frequency such as Daily, Weekly, Monthly, and Yearly.

3. Create the checklist in a document or in a spreadsheet. Set the checklist up to be easy to follow and user-friendly such as by providing check boxes you can check off when the task is completed.

4. Save the document as **C4-OS-MaintenanceChecklist-Your Name** and submit it to your instructor in the manner she or he has requested.

Using Operating System Tools to Troubleshoot Computer Problems

TOPIC 4.6

In a perfect world the printer would always print, the connection to the Internet would always work, and your computer would always operate at blazing fast speed! Causes of computer problems can be complex and not easily resolved; however, knowing how to use a few of the tools provided in the operating system package can help you fix the problem and get back to work.

Windows Action Center

The **Action Center** (available in Windows 7 and Windows 8.1) shown in Figure 4.17 is a good place to begin when something is not working. Open the Control Panel to find the Action Center. The window displays messages when the OS has detected potential issues that need your attention. If the problem you are experiencing is not listed in one of the messages, tap or click the Troubleshooting link to open the Troubleshooting window. Tap or click the link that most closely describes the problem you are having to open tools to help you resolve the problem. The prompts that display vary depending on the issue you are troubleshooting.

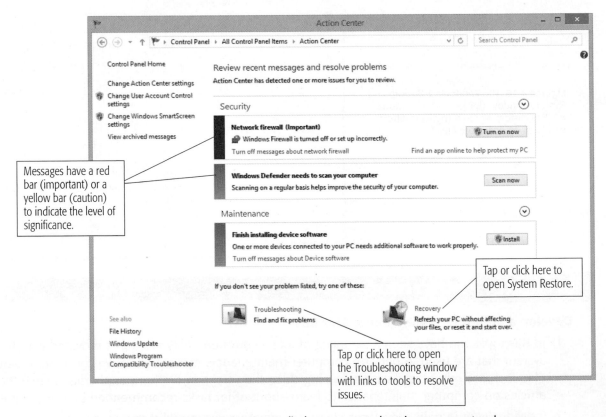

Figure 4.17 The Windows Action Center displays messages about issues encountered on your computer and provides buttons and links to tools that can be used to resolve the issues.

System Restore

Sometimes a problem will occur after you have installed something new like a device driver, a new application, or have run updates that inadvertently caused a problem with something else. Or you may have accidentally deleted or overwritten a system file that has rendered a program or device unusable. In these cases, **System Restore** is a way for you to turn back the clock to when the computer was functioning normally. System Restore will undo a recent change while leaving all documents intact. You will find System Restore in Windows 7 and Windows 8.1 in the Action Center. Tap or click the Recovery link located at the bottom right of the window. The System Restore window in Windows 7 and Windows 8.1 is the same in both versions (Figure 4.18). You select an event from a list of changes that have been made to your system (Figure 4.19 shows Windows 7 restore points) and then follow the prompts that appear.

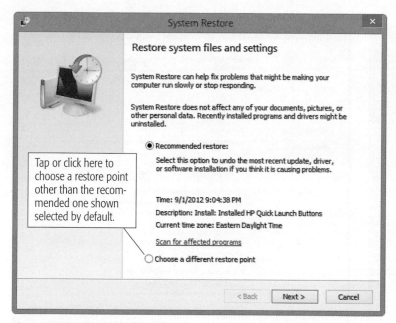

Figures 4.18 Windows 8.1 System Restore window used to undo changes made to your computer

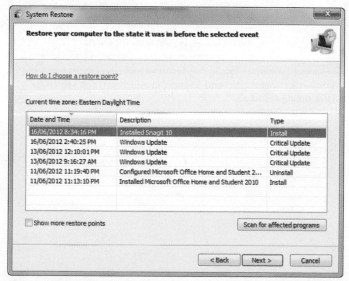

Figure 4.19 In both Windows 7 (shown) and Windows 8.1 System Restore, you can select the restore point from the event list and then click Next to begin the undo process.

Help and Support

Operating systems offer extensive help and support that you can search to find answers to most questions and issues. In Windows 8.1, you can access **Help and Support** by tapping or clicking the Search charm and typing *Help* in the Search text box. In Windows 7, click the Start button and then click Help and Support at the Start menu. In the Help and Support window, type a short phrase to describe the issue in the *Search* text box and then press Enter or tap or click the Search button. Navigate through Help information by tapping or clicking the links that appear in the Search results list. Figure 4.20 shows a list of help topics associated with a search in Help using the phrase *fix sound* in the Windows 7 and Windows 8.1 Help and Support windows.

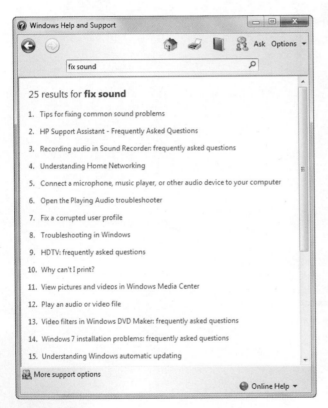

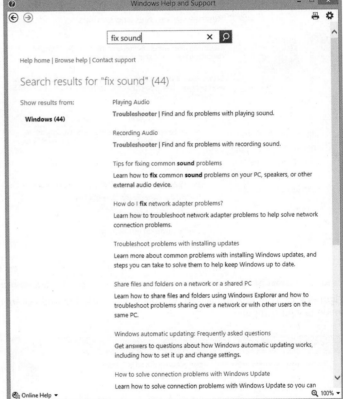

Did You Know?

Mac Help and support.apple.com contain extensive resources to assist Mac users with resolving computer issues.

Figures 4.20 Windows 7 (left) and Windows 8.1 (right) Help and Support in which you can search for solutions to a computer issue in extensive online resources

Career Connection

Careers in Technical Support

Computer technicians and help desk technical support specialists that can solve computer problems are always in demand. In the Top IT Skills in Demand for 2012 Computerworld survey, IT executives reported that mobile devices have added complexity to this in-demand role. Certifications to demonstrate your ability to work well in this field include CompTia's A+ certification geared toward workers in desktop support, and Microsoft's MCTS (Microsoft Certified Technology Specialist), which validates your skills in troubleshooting Microsoft technology. Go to microsoft.com/learning to learn more about Microsoft certifications.

Blog Topic

How I Fixed My Computer

Almost everyone has had to troubleshoot a computer issue at some point. Think about the last time you had a problem with your computer and how you resolved the problem. If you do not have an experience that you can recall, ask a family member or friend to describe his or her experience to you.

1. Write and post a blog entry that relates the issue and the resolution. Include tips or techniques learned from the experience to prevent the problem from reoccurring.

2. Read at least two of your classmates' blogs and post one comment to each.

3. Submit your blog URL and the URLs of the two classmates' blogs for which you provided a comment to your instructor in the manner she or he has requested.

EXPLORE   FURTHER

Common Computer Problems

1. Look up articles on the Web that describe five common computer problems and how to fix them.

2. Create a presentation with one issue per slide and include the recommendations for how to fix the problem.

3. Add a slide to the end of the presentation that includes the URL(s) of any websites that you used.

4. Save the presentation as **C4-OS-ComputerProblems-Your Name** and submit it to your instructor in the manner she or he has requested.

Concepts Review

Topic	Key Concepts	Key Terms
Introduction to the Operating System (OS) and the OS Functions	The OS provides the user interface. The OS coordinates the data and activities between hardware resources and application programs. Starting a computer is called booting. The Shut Down command turns off the power to a computer, properly closing all files and programs. The user interface is what you use to interact with the computer. The OS manages all of the application programs and memory, and coordinates the flow of data. The OS configures hardware. The OS keeps track of files. Automatic updates ensure the OS has all program fixes, security enhancements, and new or modified drivers.	System software Operating system (OS) Booting Cold boot Warm boot Kernel User interface (UI) Graphical user interface (GUI) Command-line interface Virtual memory Drivers Plug and Play
Popular Operating Systems for Computing Systems	A computing platform is a combination of hardware architecture and software design. Windows is the most popular OS since a wide variety of hardware is designed to run Windows OS and Windows applications. Windows 8.1 is focused on touch-enabled mobile devices with a redesigned Start screen that contains live tiles and automatically connects to online accounts. Mac OS is the proprietary OS used for Apple computers such as the iMac and MacBooks. UNIX was developed in the 1960s for servers and is a popular choice for web servers. Linux was created in 1991 and is an open source program that can run on a variety of devices. Several versions of Linux are available because it is able to be freely modified and distributed.	Computing platform Windows Mac OS UNIX Linux Open source program
Popular Operating Systems for Mobile Devices	Mobile operating systems are designed specifically to handle smaller hardware and apps with less memory. Most mobile OS's include support for cameras, touch screen and/or voice commands, and video calling. Android is the mobile OS of choice for many smartphones and tablets. The Android Open Source Project is now tasked with maintaining and developing Android. iOS is the proprietary mobile OS developed by Apple for the iPhone, iPod Touch, and iPad. Research in Motion developed the proprietary BlackBerry OS to support its family of BlackBerry devices. Windows Phone is the mobile OS developed by Microsoft for Windows smartphones.	Mobile operating system Apps Android Open Handset Alliance Android Open Source Project (AOSP) iOS BlackBerry OS Windows Phone

continued....

Embedded Operating Systems and Cloud Operating Systems	Consumer and commercial electronic devices need a specialized OS designed for their limited use. Windows Embedded is a family of embedded OS's used on a variety of devices. Embedded Linux is similar to standalone Linux. Android is used for electronic devices beyond smartphones and tablets. Cloud OS's operate like a virtual desktop, providing access to files and apps anywhere you have Internet access. iCloud is built into every iOS device and syncs documents in the cloud to all devices, including PCs. Chrome OS is available on Chromebooks and supports Google's cloud-based apps.	Embedded operating system Windows Embedded Embedded Linux Web-based operating system iCloud Chrome OS
Utilities in Your OS Package for Maintaining System Performance	File Managers such as Windows Explorer in Windows 7 and File Explorer in Windows 8.1 provide file-maintenance tools. Disk Cleanup is a utility used to remove unwanted files. Disk Defragmenter is a utility used to increase disk speed and efficiency by rearranging files. Backup and Restore are utilities used to back up files and restore backed up files to their original state.	Windows Explorer File Explorer Folder Disk Cleanup Fragmentation Disk Defragmenter Optimize Drives Backup utility Windows Backup File History Restore Utility
Using Operating System Tools to Troubleshoot Computer Problems	The Action Center in Windows is used to view messages about issues and access tools to resolve problems. System Restore will undo a recent change leaving all documents intact. Windows Help and Support can be used to find answers to problems occurring on your computer.	Action Center System Restore Help and Support

Multiple Choice

1. Which of the following is *not* a function of the operating system?
   a. Provides a user interface
   b. Booting
   c. Configures hardware devices
   d. Manages memory

2. This term describes the process of automatically installing a device driver when new hardware is plugged into the computer.
   a. Soft boot
   b. Virtual memory
   c. Driver
   d. Plug and Play

3. Which of the following is *not* one of the popular operating systems for standalone computers?
   a. iOS
   b. Windows
   c. UNIX
   d. Linux

4. Linux is based on which other operating system?
   a. Windows
   b. Mac OS X
   c. UNIX
   d. Chrome OS

5. This mobile operating system currently enjoys the highest market share.
   a. iOS
   b. BlackBerry OS
   c. Windows Phone
   d. Android

6. This mobile operating system displays a live tile interface.
   a. Android
   b. Windows Phone
   c. BlackBerry OS
   d. iOS

7. This term describes an operating system designed for a device that performs a specific task such as an ATM or a GPS.
   a. Open source operating system
   b. Embedded operating system
   c. Cloud operating system
   d. Standalone operating system

8. This term describes an operating system that operates like a virtual desktop where you access all files and applications using a web browser.
   a. Server operating system
   b. Embedded operating system
   c. Standalone operating system
   d. Cloud operating system

9. This utility program is used to remove unwanted files from your computer.
   a. Windows Explorer
   b. Disk Defragmenter
   c. Optimize Drives
   d. Disk Cleanup

10. This utility program is used to increase disk efficiency by rearranging files that have been split up.
    a. Optimize Drives
    b. Disk Defragmenter
    c. Disk Cleanup
    d. Windows Explorer

11. Open this window to view messages that describe issues the OS has detected.
    a. Help and Support
    b. Action Center
    c. System Restore
    d. Windows Explorer

12. You can undo a recent change made to your computer, such as installing a new driver, by opening this window.
    a. Disk Cleanup
    b. Windows Explorer
    c. Help and Support
    d. System Restore

Crossword Puzzle

ACROSS

1 Cloud OS developed by Google
4 Term that describes a file broken up into nonadjacent clusters
5 RAM contents stored on the hard disk
8 Apple's OS for the iMac and MacBooks
9 Mobile OS for the iPhone
11 Interface where you type instructions at a prompt
12 Microsoft's family of OS's for consumer electronics

DOWN

2 Includes OS and utility programs
3 Small program used to configure hardware
6 BlackBerry manufacturer
7 Starting a computer
10 OS developed in the 1960s

Matching

Match the term with the statement or definition.

_____ 1. Kernel
_____ 2. Open source program
_____ 3. Open Handset Alliance
_____ 4. iCloud
_____ 5. Restore
_____ 6. Control Panel

a. Built into every new iOS device
b. Utility to copy files back to their original state
c. Window to open to find the Action Center utility
d. Source code that can be modified by anyone
e. Core of the OS loaded into RAM
f. Released Android in 2007

Project 1 Training for the Windows GUI

Individual, Pairs, or Team
Deliverable: Presentation

You work in the IT department of a local travel agency. The owner of the agency has asked you to prepare a training presentation for new employees who need to learn how to use the Windows interface. Specifically, consider that the new employees have never before used Windows software and need to know the basics of how to run application programs, open and close windows, switch between open programs, and properly shut down the computer system.

1. Create a presentation that could be used as a self-guided training program on how to use Windows 7 or Windows 8.1 to perform the basic tasks described. Include an introductory slide that explains the purpose of the Windows software. Be creative in your approach and make sure the information is presented in such a way that someone reading the slides could learn the material on his or her own.
2. Save the presentation as **C4-Project1-WindowsGUI-Your Name**.
3. Submit the presentation to your instructor in the manner she or he has requested.

Project 2 Comparison of Features in Mobile Operating Systems

Pairs or Team
Deliverable: Table in Word Processor or Spreadsheet

The business manager of a new documentary film-making company has asked your group to assist him with research for new mobile device purchasing decisions by developing a comparison of features available by mobile operating systems. He has asked your group to develop a table that compares the popular mobile operating systems by four criteria: Ease of Use, App Availability, Connectivity Options such as tethering and WiFi hotspots, and Security.

1. Create a table in a word processor or spreadsheet that shows a comparison of at least three popular mobile operating systems by the four criteria. Use the Web to research current features and standards for the mobile OSs you want to compare and to look up the definition of features you may not understand such as tethering and WiFi hotspots. Make sure the table is easy to read and understand and provides complete information for a comparison. Below the table, include the URLs of the main websites from which you obtained your information.
2. Save the document or spreadsheet as **C4-Project2-MobileOSComparison-Your Name**.
3. Submit the document or spreadsheet to your instructor in the manner she or he has requested.

Project 3 Utility Programs to Speed Up Computer Performance

Individual, Pairs, or Team
Deliverable: Document

You volunteer at a local senior citizen community center. Many of the seniors you meet ask you why their computer's performance declines over time and how they can improve the computer's speed. You explain that most computers slow down because of virus or spyware infections, too many programs included in the startup process, undersized RAM, and the hard disk running out of space and/or becoming fragmented. The manager of the community center has asked you to create a document that can be used by the seniors to help them tune up their computers.

1. Research utilities within the operating system package with which you are familiar that do the following: scan for viruses and spyware, remove unused programs from the computer, and increase disk space and efficiency. (Assume that the amount of RAM cannot be upgraded for most seniors so you decide to leave out this option for improving speed.)
2. Create a document that specifies the operating system and explains the utilities you researched and how to use each program. Make sure the document is presented in a style that can be easily read and understood by seniors.

3. Save the document as **C4-Project3-PerformanceUtilities-Your Name**.
4. Submit the document or spreadsheet to your instructor in the manner she or he has requested.

Project 4 Help! My Computer Will Not Start

Individual or Pairs

Deliverable: Flowchart, Table, or Decision Tree in a Document or Presentation

The manager at the IT call center where you work has asked you to prepare a flowchart or decision tree to be used for training new help desk employees on how to question callers to help resolve why their computer is not booting up properly.

1. Research on the Web possible problems with computers that will not boot properly.
2. Develop a progressive list of questions that a person could ask someone on the telephone to help guide him or her to the root of the startup problem. Begin with simple questions that gradually progress to more complex questions. Assume the caller begins with the statement, "*My computer turns on but the screen remains blank.*"
3. Create a document or presentation with a flowchart, table, or decision tree with the questions in the order the help desk specialist should ask callers.
4. Save the document or presentation as **C4-Project4-TroubleshootBoot-Your Name**.
5. Submit the document or presentation to your instructor in the manner she or he has requested.

Project 5 Virtualizing Your Desktop for Students

Pairs or Teams

Deliverable: Presentation including a Video

Your group wants to switch to a cloud operating system as a way to save money on upgrading your PC or Mac. Before you dispense with your comfortable standalone operating system, you decide it would be prudent to learn more about these systems.

1. Research on the Web free cloud operating systems. Choose three services and explore them further to learn as much as you can about how they work.
2. At YouTube, search and watch videos that describe and show the three cloud operating systems functioning on a computer.
3. Within your team, discuss the cloud operating system that you think best meets your needs as a student.
4. Create a presentation that includes a slide describing each cloud operating system, one slide with your team's recommendation and rationale for the recommendation, one slide with the link to the YouTube video that best showcases your team's choice, and one slide with the URLs of the websites you used for this project.
5. Save the presentation as **C4-Project5-CloudOSServices-Your Name**.
6. Submit the presentation to your instructor in the manner she or he has requested.

Project 6 Greener Computing

Individual

Deliverable: Blog Entry

All operating systems provide tools to manage power on your computing device. Changing power options, sleep settings, and adjusting your screen settings can help with conserving energy use. Adjusting power options on your notebook or tablet will help prolong the life of the battery.

1. Learn more about the power options in the operating system on your desktop, notebook, or tablet.
2. Read at least two articles on the Web that recommend the best power settings for your computer.
3. Write and post a blog entry with a summary of what you learned and what you will set your power options to for your computer.
4. Submit your blog URL to your instructor in the manner she or he has requested.

Optional
Read the blog entry for this project of at least two other classmates and post a comment to each. Submit the URLs of your classmates' blogs with Step 4.

Project 7 Ethics Discussion on Copying OS

Team
Deliverable: Document, Blog Entry, or Presentation

At a party recently you overheard your neighbor bragging to someone that she had upgraded her computer to Windows 8.1 by using her company's site license product key and Windows 8.1 DVD to install the software on her notebook. She stated that since she often worked at home on her personal time she felt there was nothing wrong with using her company's software and license. She admitted that her work from home involved using documents and spreadsheets that worked fine under Windows 7; however, she wanted the new Windows 8.1 interface.

1. Within your team discuss the ethics involved in the neighbor's behavior. If the company's site license covers enough installations, is the neighbor justified in installing the software on her personal device? If yes, what should the neighbor do at her workplace to make sure she is acting ethically? If no and if this practice is commonplace, does that make it OK? Would any of your answers change if the neighbor was copying the word processing and spreadsheet applications and not the OS?
2. Prepare a summary of your team's discussion in a document, blog entry, or presentation.
3. Save the document or presentation as **C4-Project7-CopyOSEthics-Your Name**.
4. Submit the document, presentation, or blog entry to your instructor in the manner she or he has requested.

Project 8 Ethics Discussion on Upgrade Resisters

Team
Deliverable: Document, Blog Entry, or Presentation

At your workplace, company training is currently being conducted for all employees on Windows 8.1. Some employees are resistant to change as they are comfortable with Windows 7 and do not want to upgrade since the new interface is quite different. These resisters are constantly complaining during the training sessions and always finding fault with the trainer's presentations. The mood in the training room is deteriorating. You and a few other colleagues have heard that these employees are telling their managers that the trainer is not competent and that the upgrade to Windows 8.1 should be delayed as they are not ready for the conversion.

1. Within your team discuss the ethics involved in the resisters' behavior. What should you and your colleagues do? Would it be wise to tell management of their tactics, or should you try to win them over to Windows 8.1 without turning them in? Would your strategy be different if you work closely with the resisters or if they were in another department? If you decide to win them over, how will you accomplish this if they are so resistant to changing their methods? What role should the trainer be playing in this scenario?
2. Prepare a summary of your team's discussion in a document, blog entry, or presentation.
3. Save the document or presentation as **C4-Project8-Win8ResistorsEthics-Your Name**.
4. Submit the document, presentation, or blog entry to your instructor in the manner she or he has requested.

Chapter 5

Application Software

After successfully completing this chapter, you will be able to:

- Identify productivity application programs used in workplaces

- Distinguish various multimedia applications

- List and explain types of applications used by individuals

- Recognize web-based and open source applications

- Explain how to acquire, install, uninstall, and upgrade software programs

- Describe a mobile application and provide examples of mobile apps

Whether you turn on a computing device for work, for school, for personal tasks, or for entertainment, it is **application software** that you are using. Application software, also called **apps**, are programs used by individuals to carry out tasks or otherwise get things done. For example, if you need to update your budget, you might open a financial program. If you have a photograph with red eye, you might open a graphics editing application to edit the picture. An application exists for just about any purpose. Software is what makes our computers useful to us since it is the programs that provide us with the ability to create, write, calculate, draw, edit, manipulate, and otherwise work with text, graphics, audio, and video.

In Chapter 4 you learned about system software and the role of the operating system to route and manage data between the hardware and the other programs that are running. Once a computer is started and the OS is loaded, you are ready to start the application in which you want to work. In this chapter you will learn about software applications commonly used in the workplace and by individuals. You will also learn how to manage the software on your computing device and survey mobile apps for a smartphone or tablet.

TOPIC 5.1

Productivity Applications for the Workplace

Software for the workplace generally includes word processing (working with text), spreadsheets (calculating and managing numbers), presentations (slide shows), and database management (keeping track of data). This group of software programs is referred to as **productivity software** because it is used in the workplace to efficiently perform a wide variety of business-related tasks.

A group of productivity software applications will typically be bundled together in what is called a **software suite** or **productivity suite**. For example, the Microsoft Office Suite includes Microsoft Word for word processing, Microsoft Excel for spreadsheets, Microsoft PowerPoint for presentations, and Microsoft Access for database management. Microsoft's suite is available in several different configurations (called editions) to provide bundles of programs needed in different office environments. Apple computer users have a software suite called iWork that runs on Apple computers.

Regardless of the suite you use, features available for each type of productivity application are generally the same. In this topic, you will learn the basic features and uses for four commonly used productivity applications.

Word Processing

A **word processing application** is software used to create documents containing mostly text, although images are also included to add visual appeal and promote understanding of content. Figure 5.1 presents a cottage rental agreement document in Microsoft Word. Apple's word processor is called Pages. With a word processing program, individuals create a variety of documents such as essays, reports, letters, memos, contracts, brochures, catalogs, menus, newsletters, mailings, labels, articles, blogs, and journals. Features of word processing programs generally include:

- text formatting options to change the typestyle, color, size, and style of text called fonts and font attributes
- bold, underline, italic, and other text effects such as shadow and strikethrough
- spelling and grammar checking as well as synonyms from a thesaurus
- paragraph alignment options, spacing, tabs, indents, borders, and shading
- page numbering, margins, columns, and page breaks for formatting pages
- bulleted or numbered lists, tables, images, charts, and other graphics

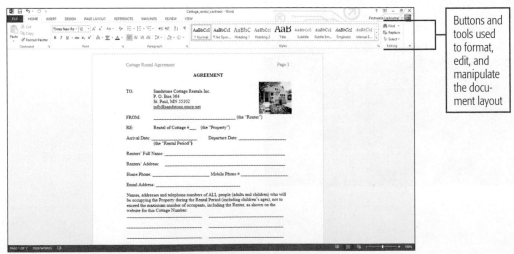

Buttons and tools used to format, edit, and manipulate the document layout

Figure 5.1 A word processor is used to create any kind of document that is mostly text such as this cottage rental agreement created in Microsoft Word.

- footnotes, endnotes, captions, and citations
- pre-formatted templates for cover pages, reports, letters, and other documents
- standard documents and labels for a mailing
- collaboration tools such as track changes, comments, share, and compare

Spreadsheet Programs

A software program in which you work primarily with numbers that you organize, calculate, and chart is called a **spreadsheet application**. Data is entered in a worksheet, which is a grid of columns and rows. Each intersection of a column and row is a placeholder for data called a cell and is addressed by the column letter and row number. For example, A1 is the cell for the intersection of column A and row number 1. You perform calculations on values stored in cells that can be simple mathematical operations or complex formula statements for advanced data analysis. Spreadsheets automatically recalculate whenever you change a number. People like to perform "what-if" analysis with spreadsheets, which involves changing a value or formula to see what will happen to another value. For example, you could increase your salary to see how much more money you will have after paying expenses. Spreadsheet programs also have charting capabilities so you can graph the values in a pie or column chart. Figure 5.2 illustrates a worksheet in Microsoft Excel. Apple's spreadsheet program is called Numbers.

Spreadsheets are used for any work that primarily tracks numbers such as budgets, revenue, expenses, asset tracking, inventory control, production control, gradebooks, research data, payroll, billing, costing, estimating, attendance recording, and scheduling. Features of spreadsheet programs generally include:

- pre-programmed functions for advanced formulas such as those used in statistics, finance, math, date, and logic analysis
- formatting options for text and numbers to change typestyle, color, size, alignment, and numeric options
- sorting and filtering options to organize large blocks of data
- various chart styles and options to graph data
- multiple worksheets for grouping, consolidating, and managing data
- shapes and other graphics to enhance a worksheet's appearance
- page layout and format options for printing large worksheets

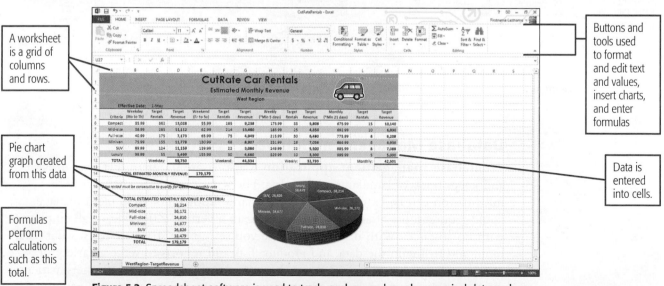

A worksheet is a grid of columns and rows.

Pie chart graph created from this data

Formulas perform calculations such as this total.

Buttons and tools used to format and edit text and values, insert charts, and enter formulas

Data is entered into cells.

Figure 5.2 Spreadsheet software is used to track, analyze, and graph numerical data such as this car rental pricing worksheet shown in Microsoft Excel.

- tools to perform what-if analysis
- collaboration tools such as track changes, comments, and share

Presentation Software

Slides for an electronic slide show that may be projected on a screen during an oral presentation or on a video display at a self-running kiosk are created in a **presentation application** like Microsoft's PowerPoint or Apple's Keynote. Presentation software helps you organize, describe, and explain key points, facts, figures, messages, or ideas. Slides can have images, audio, and video as well as text to provide a dynamic presentation experience. Figure 5.3 shows a group of slides in a presentation created with Microsoft PowerPoint. Features of spreadsheet programs generally include:

- several slide layouts for arrangement of titles and content
- predesigned presentation designs and themes for backgrounds, colors, fonts, and effects
- formatting options to change typestyle, color, size, and alignment of content
- pictures, clipart, photos, shapes, charts, tables, and other graphics
- sound and video media options
- slide transition and animation schemes to enhance presentations
- options for customizing presentation slide shows
- collaboration tools such as track changes, comments, and share

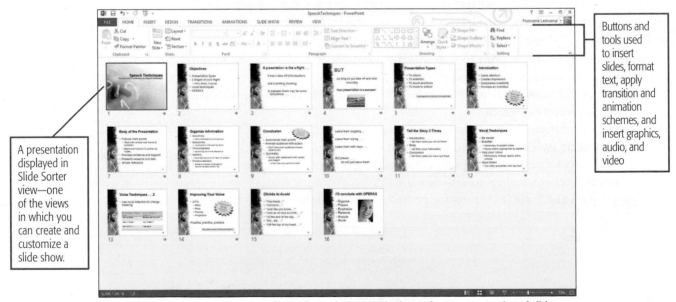

A presentation displayed in Slide Sorter view—one of the views in which you can create and customize a slide show.

Buttons and tools used to insert slides, format text, apply transition and animation schemes, and insert graphics, audio, and video

Figure 5.3 Presentation software such as Microsoft PowerPoint is used to create a series of slides that are presented in a slide show.

Database Management Software

A **database management application** is a software program that organizes and keeps track of large amounts of data. The data is stored in such a way that information can be extracted in useful lists and reports. For example, a manager could request a list of all customers residing in a certain ZIP code, or all employees with no absences. With database software you set up the structure for storing data, input and maintain the data, and produce lists and reports to serve a variety of purposes. Businesses use databases to keep track of data such as customers, patients, clients, vendors, employees, products, inventory, assets, contacts, claims, equipment, and service records. Any data that needs to be organized and stored can be set up in a database. Figure 5.4 illustrates a database created in Microsoft Access to keep track of computer service work orders. Features of database applications generally include:

- tables for designing the structure of data in columns (called fields) and rows (called records)
- forms for entering and maintaining data in a user-friendly interface
- queries for extracting and displaying data by criteria
- reports for printing or displaying data with rich text formatting options
- the ability to join related tables for queries and reports that extract data from multiple objects

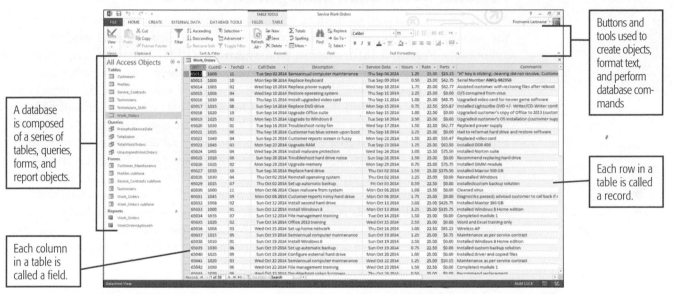

A database is composed of a series of tables, queries, forms, and report objects.

Each column in a table is called a field.

Buttons and tools used to create objects, format text, and perform database commands

Each row in a table is called a record.

Figure 5.4 Database management software helps a business track and organize data such as this computer service database shown in Microsoft Access.

Microsoft also publishes a version of Office designed for Mac computers. Alternatives to Microsoft Office and Apple iWork include OpenOffice, a free productivity suite made available by the open source community, and web-based productivity software offered by cloud providers such as Google and Zoho. These applications are introduced in a later topic.

EXPLORE FURTHER

Corel WordPerfect Office versus Microsoft Office

Corel is a software company that publishes the WordPerfect Office Productivity suite. How does WordPerfect Office compare to Microsoft's suite?

1. Research the features in the most recent professional editions of the Office suite offered by Corel and Microsoft. Find out what applications are included and the price for each suite.
2. Create a table in a document or spreadsheet that compares the features of the two productivity suites and the price for each. Below the table indicate which suite you think offers the better deal and give your reasons.
3. Save the document or spreadsheet as **C5-Apps-CorelvsOffice-Your Name**.
4. Submit the document or spreadsheet to your instructor in the manner she or he has requested.

TOPIC 5.2

Other Workplace-Oriented Productivity Applications

Businesses need applications beyond the basic word processing, spreadsheet, presentation, and database management programs. Software applications to manage communications, calendars, contacts, financial information, projects, and documents are also used. In some industries, specialized software is designed to complete tasks unique to the industry, and large companies use enterprise-wide software programs to manage large-scale operations. In this topic, you will be introduced to a sampling of other types of applications found in a workplace.

Personal Information Management Software

Managing one's messages, schedule, contacts, and tasks can be onerous with the volume of emails, appointments, contacts, and to-do lists a typical worker encounters. **Personal information management (PIM) software** helps you organize this type of information. Reminders and flags help you remember and follow up on important emails, appointments, events, or tasks. Figure 5.5 displays the Calendar in Microsoft Outlook. Microsoft Outlook is part of the Microsoft Office suite. Outlook can be used by individuals at home to manage personal information or, when Outlook is used in a workplace, an Exchange server allows you to send and track meeting requests and tasks to other employees. Lotus Notes by IBM is another PIM application. Apple devices include iCal, Contacts, and Mail programs. PIM apps are also included on smartphones. Syncing of calendars, contacts, and emails on multiple devices is important so that you have access to the latest information wherever you may be. Some PIMs also provide the ability to share your calendar or contact information with other people outside your workplace.

Buttons and tools used to create, navigate, arrange, and manage Outlook items

The day's appointments are displayed with the outstanding tasks shown below the schedule.

Navigate to e-mails, calendar, contacts, or tasks with these buttons.

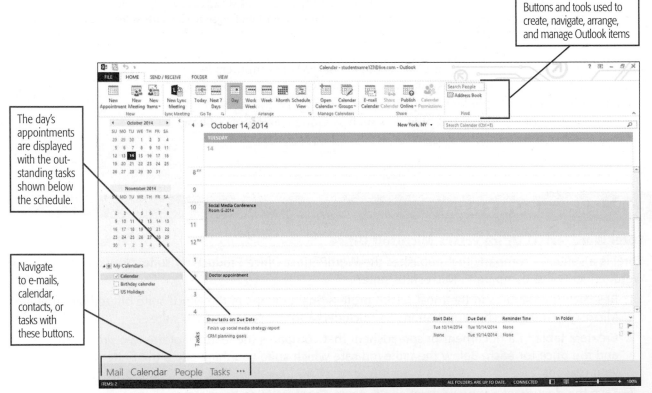

Figure 5.5 Microsoft Outlook is an application in which you can manage messages, schedules, contacts, and tasks. Here, the Calendar is displayed in Day view with tasks displayed below the day's appointments.

Accounting Software

All businesses need an **accounting software application** to record and report financial information related to assets, liabilities, equity, revenue, and expenses. These programs provide the basis for financial reporting and tax calculations. Accounting software is generally organized by accounting activity such as invoicing, purchasing, inventory, payroll, banking, paying bills, receiving payments, and processing memos. Accounting programs also support costing and estimating features for customer and vendor-related functions. Several accounting software programs are designed for small, medium, and large businesses. Figure 5.6 shows the home screen for QuickBooks, an accounting program used by many small businesses.

In QuickBooks use the menu system, buttons on the toolbar, or icons to open forms in which you enter financial transactions or display reports.

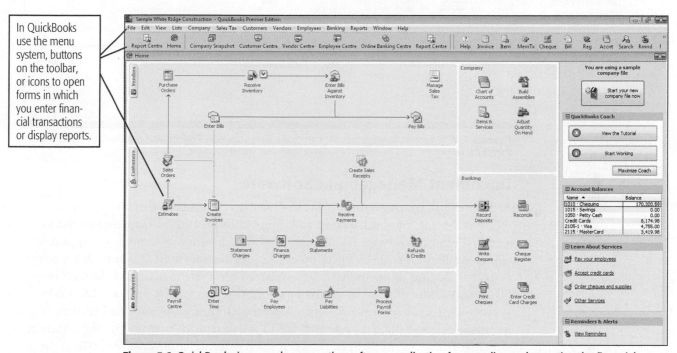

Figure 5.6 QuickBooks is a popular accounting software application for recording and reporting the financial activities for a business.

Project Management Software

Large projects that need several resources and are to be completed on a schedule and within a budget are often managed using **project management software**. Project management software such as Microsoft Project shown in Figure 5.7 allows you to enter all of the tasks needed to get a project done, establish time frames, assign resources, and allocate budget money to each task. Once the project is created, the program develops a project schedule and shows you interdependencies between tasks. A typical way to display a schedule is in a Gantt chart, which plots tasks in time lines as shown in Figure 5.7. Maintaining the data also allows you to view the impact on the schedule or budget if changes are made to tasks, resources, or time lines. Several project management software programs are available including the popular web-based application called Basecamp.

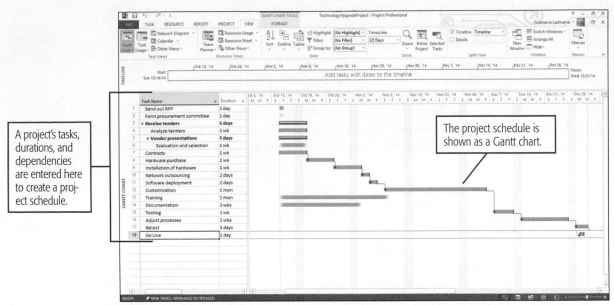

A project's tasks, durations, and dependencies are entered here to create a project schedule.

The project schedule is shown as a Gantt chart.

Figure 5.7 With project management software, such as Microsoft Project, you can manage a project's schedule, resources, and budget to finish on time and within budget.

Document Management Software

A **document management system (DMS)** is a program that manages the creation, storage, retrieval, history, and eventual disposal of information stored in a central repository. Paper documents are scanned, coded or tagged, and stored electronically in the DMS. DMS programs provide advanced search tools for retrieval as well as sharing of documents. A document's life cycle is managed through the DMS, and all documents are stored in a common file format such as PDF. DMS systems use secure servers and controlled access to ensure privacy and security. Some industries, such as the legal industry, use DMS systems to manage the thousands of documents that are exchanged between lawyers in litigation cases. A DMS is the cornerstone of a paperless office. The DMS called Dokmee is shown in Figure 5.8.

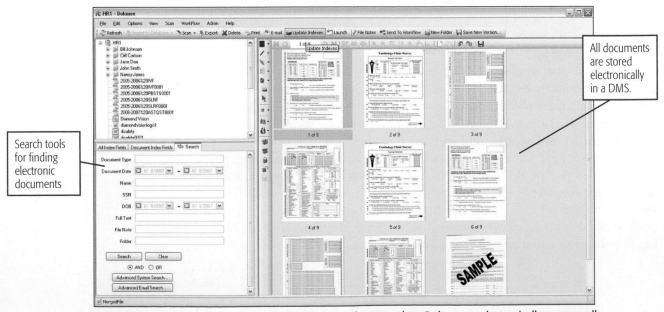

Search tools for finding electronic documents

All documents are stored electronically in a DMS.

Figure 5.8 Companies use Document Management Software such as Dokmee to electronically manage all documents, including paper documents that are scanned, coded, and stored on central servers.

Other Specialized Software

Industries such as automotive, construction, manufacturing, and engineering firms use industry-specific software such as computer-aided design (CAD) or computer-aided manufacturing (CAM) programs to create complex designs and drawings. Medical establishments use medical software programs to track patient records, billings, and insurance claims. Hotels and travel agencies use programs to manage bookings, guests, and resources. These are just a few examples of industry-specific software applications.

Large companies, referred to as enterprises, have higher-level needs to manage the multitude of activities and processes involved in transactions with customers, vendors, inventories, and human resources. These companies often use a category of software called **enterprise resource planning (ERP)**, which is a software solution designed for large-scale organizations. Companies such as SAP and Oracle provide ERP software for these environments, which often involve extensive customization, training, and support.

Career Connection

Project Management Skills in Demand for All Sectors

Any organization that launches a large project involving many resources and multiple teams needs to have a skilled project manager to keep the project on time and on budget. According to WANTED Analytics (a company that provides business intelligence for talent supply and demand), in May 2012 there were more than 235,000 online job listings that included a need for project management skills. The Project Management Professional (PMP) certification is recognized by industry as providing evidence of one's competency to lead large project teams. Consider investigating what it takes to be a project manager if you like to be well-organized, lead groups of diverse teams, and have excellent communication skills.

EXPLORE   FURTHER

Which industry-specific software will you use?

Chances are industry-specific software is used in your field of study. For example, contractors use materials and labor estimating software, restaurants use meal service software, and airlines use reservation systems. What industry-specific software will you be required to use in your future career?

1. Research industry-specific software applications used in your field of study. If possible, interview someone who works in your field and ask him or her to describe specialized software used in the workplace.
2. Create a document that describes the software applications used in your field and how they are used to track, manage, and report information.
3. Save the document as **C5-Apps-IndustrySpecificSoftware-Your Name**.
4. Submit the document to your instructor in the manner she or he has requested.

TOPIC 5.3

Applications for Working with Graphics, Multimedia, and the Web

Software programs for creating, editing, and manipulating drawings, photos, clip art, and scanned images are called **graphics software**. **Desktop publishing software** is an application that incorporates text, graphics, and the use of colors for creating high-quality documents for marketing, communication, or other commercial purposes. **Multimedia software** includes programs that use text and images with video, audio, and animations to create engaging and interactive applications that market products or services, educate, or entertain users. **Web authoring software** is a program designed to create content to be provided over the Internet.

In this topic you will be introduced to applications used by businesses and individuals to work with graphics, audio, video, animations, and for creating web pages.

Graphics Software

Graphic artists, illustrators, photographers, and other professionals use specialized software to create and edit images. Painting and drawing programs provide tools for artists to draw pictures, shapes, and other images to which they can add special effects. Adobe Illustrator is an example of a graphics program used to create, edit, and manipulate illustrations.

Photo editing software is used by photographers and others to edit pictures and add special effects and text to pictures taken with a digital camera. Adobe Photoshop is a popular choice for editing photos by professionals and individuals. Tools are available in Photoshop to crop out unwanted portions of a picture, remove red eye, retouch areas, correct color brightness and contrast, add text, add special effects, and even add in a person or object copied from another photo. Figure 5.9 shows an artistic filter effect applied to a photo using Adobe Photoshop.

Figure 5.9 An artistic filter effect called Poster Edges is applied to a picture in Adobe Photoshop.

Desktop Publishing Software

Although word processing software provides tools to arrange text and graphics in a document, these programs do not let you precisely position objects and control text flow around objects. For professional publications, desktop publishing (DTP) software is used for producing a print-based document such as a corporate newsletter, annual report, price list, restaurant menu, catalog, brochure, or book. Programs such as Adobe's InDesign or Microsoft's Publisher are popular choices for advanced page layout. DTP programs use rulers, grids, and guides as well as other tools and features that allow DTP professionals to precisely place text and graphics on a page. In addition, the software provides more control over spacing between and around objects and text, and a wider range of fonts, sizes, and colors for text formatting. Figure 5.10 illustrates a newsletter in Adobe's InDesign application.

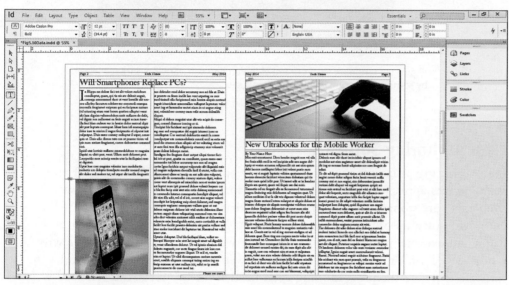

Figure 5.10 Adobe's InDesign application is used by desktop publishers to do page layout for professional publications such as this technical newsletter.

Multimedia Software

For content delivered via the Web or distributed on CD, DVD, or Blu-ray discs, multimedia programs are used by professionals to create animations, add audio and video, and author multimedia applications. **Animation software** is used to create images or objects that have movement or otherwise interact with users. Adobe's Flash application is often used to create interactive applications delivered over the Web. In Flash, the designer works with a time line and a stage in which text, graphics, and other objects are placed in the sequence for which the movement or interaction is to occur.

Video editing software such as Apple's Final Cut Pro (Figure 5.11) or Adobe's Premiere Elements provides tools to create videos referred to as clips. Video shot with a camcorder can be manipulated by cutting, adding, or moving scenes, creating split screens, or adding music, audio effects, or text for titles or credits. Some audio editing capability generally is also included as well as the capability to organize content on DVD and Blu-ray discs. For example, video editing programs also create the menus and burn the content to a DVD or Blu-ray disc. **Audio recording and editing software** such as free, open source Audacity or Adobe's Audition include tools for recording and editing music, sound clips, and podcasts (audio clips posted on the Web).

Other multimedia applications capture screen images and computer activity for creating training segments and demonstrations.

Figure 5.11 Apple's Final Cut Pro video editing software is a package used by some professional multimedia producers.

Web Authoring Software

Web authoring programs such as Adobe's Dreamweaver and Microsoft's Expression Web are two applications used to create and maintain today's interactive websites. Web pages are stored in programming code that is interpreted by browsers. Web authoring software provides tools for individuals to create and manage all of the pages and external resources for a website by working in either Design view or Code view. Non-programmers can create a web page in Design view and let the software generate the programming code needed for browsers. Experienced web developers can choose to work in Code view and often switch between views as pages are fine-tuned. Figure 5.12 is a web page with a reservation form with Design view and Code view shown side by side in Adobe Dreamweaver.

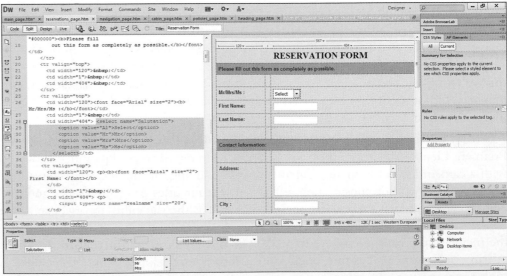

Figure 5.12 A reservation form for a website created in Adobe's Dreamweaver software is shown with Design view and Code view displayed.

Multimedia for the Non-Professional

A variety of graphics and multimedia programs are available to meet the needs of both professional and non-professional users. The Adobe and Apple programs showcased in this topic are more expensive software programs geared toward professionals or hobby enthusiasts. Less expensive or free programs are used by non-professionals or individuals who want to work with multimedia at home. For example, Windows Live Essentials is a free suite offered to Windows users that includes a program to work with video (Windows Live Movie Maker) and photos (Windows Live Photo Gallery). The Windows OS also includes programs for drawing (Windows Paint) and recording sound (Windows Sound Recorder). In Figure 5.13, a photograph's color is shown being adjusted using Windows Live Photo Gallery. Apple devices are packaged with the iLife suite that includes iPhoto, iMovie, and GarageBand for working with photos, video, and audio.

Check This Out

www.windows.microsoft. com/en-US/windows-live/ essentials-home

Go here to download Windows Live Essentials for free.

Figure 5.13 A photo's color is adjusted using Windows Live Photo Gallery, part of the free Windows Live Essentials suite from Microsoft.

EXPLORE FURTHER

Are you a skilled photo editor?

Web-based photo editing software programs allow you to edit photos without downloading and installing software on your computer. Tools may vary between services, but each offers a basic set of tools that do an adequate job for non-professionals.

1. Do a search for free online image editing programs and choose one with which to experiment for this activity.

2. Take a picture with a digital camera of something related to your field of study. For example, take a picture of a park if you are going to be a landscape designer or a house if you are going to work in construction. Upload the photo to the image editing website and experiment with the software's editing tools to edit the image. For example, crop out a part of the picture, change the color, retouch the photo, add shapes, special effects, text, and so on.

3. Save the revised image as **C5-Apps-EditedPhoto-Your Name**.

4. Submit the original photo and the edited photo to your instructor in the manner she or he has requested.

TOPIC 5.4

Software Applications for Personal Use

Software programs for personal use include a wide range of applications that cover every hobby, interest, and need. For example, you can install software to help you manage personal notes, ideas, and thoughts at work, at school, or at home, manage your personal finances, prepare tax returns, play games, design a garden, and create a genealogy map. Programs help you organize recipes and plan trips as well as educate and provide reference information. In this topic you will survey a variety of applications for personal use.

Note-Taking Software

While in meetings, classes, or at home you often need a place to record notes, thoughts, or ideas. **Note-taking software** such as Microsoft's OneNote (Figure 5.14) is used to store, organize, search, and share notes of any type. Notes can be entered by clicking anywhere on the screen and typing or writing by hand using a stylus. Documents, audio, video, images, emails, appointments, contacts, and web links can be attached to a note to collect everything related to a topic in one place. You can organize notes into notebooks and tabs and use search and share tools.

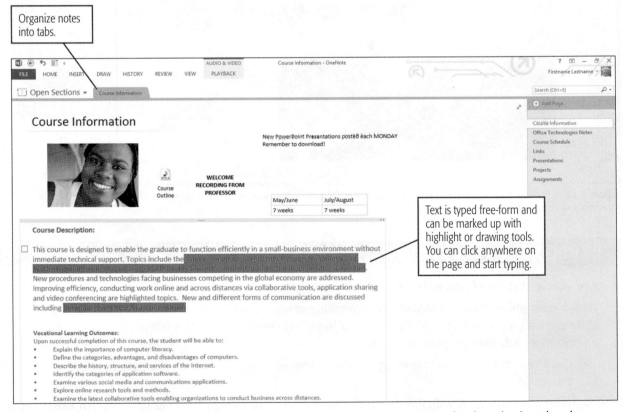

Figure 5.14 Microsoft's OneNote application is a useful tool to organize notes on any topic related to school, work, or home.

Software to Manage Personal Finances and Taxes

Keeping track of a checking or savings account and personal investments is accomplished with **personal finance software**. Most personal finance software programs allow you to download activity from your banking account directly into the personal finance program. You can balance your checking account, analyze home expenses, and track investments. Quicken is a popular program used for managing finances.

Tax preparation software guides you through the completion of the complex forms required to file your income taxes with the government. These programs generally estimate your tax bill using an interview-style series of questions and input boxes. Programs generally alert you to missing information and/or deductions that can help minimize taxes. Tax forms can be printed or, with some programs, filed with the government electronically.

Personal finance and tax preparation software help you manage your money.

Legal Software

Legal software such as Quicken's WillMaker, MyAttorney, or Family Lawyer help you prepare legal documents such as wills, contracts, leases, loan agreements, and living trusts. Standard contracts and other legal documents are provided that you customize for your purposes through a series of questions, forms, or dialog boxes that prompt you for input.

Legal software programs help individuals create legal documents such as this contract.

Hobby Software

Software applications for creating a family tree; scrapbooking; planning trips; managing recipes and meal planning; designing homes, decks, and gardens; and creating and printing custom greeting cards are just a few **hobby software applications** you can use to pursue your favorite leisure activities.

Entertainment and Games

Entertainment software includes programs for playing interactive games and videos. Some games are designed to be played individually while others involve subscribing to online services where you can join hundreds of thousands of other game enthusiasts and play against others online. For example, with more than 10 million subscribers, World of Warcraft (WoW) is a highly successful online multiplayer role-playing game.

Software is available to help individuals with just about any hobby imaginable.

Angry Birds is an example of entertainment software that is available in multiple versions.

Games are often available in multiple versions such as an edition for a PC, a version that can be played online through a browser, or as a smaller app for downloading to a smartphone. Angry Birds is one example of a game that is available in all of these flavors.

Education and Reference

Educational software designed for children and adults to learn about subjects such as math, spelling, grammar, geography, and history are available as interactive references or games. You can also find software to help you learn a foreign language and teach you how to type. **Reference software** programs use multimedia tools to provide rich content information in encyclopedias, dictionaries, translation guides, atlases, and other reference resources.

If you have an interest or a hobby that has not been mentioned here, chances are that a software program has been created that is related to your area of interest. Use the Web to search for an application if you have not already found one.

Education and reference software use multimedia to help with understanding complex information.

Be Cautious with Free Software!

The lure of free software can be enticing. Be cautious with offers found on the Internet for free software of any type but especially those that offer to manage personal finances for free. Read the details including the fine print before downloading or submitting your email address or any other personal information to obtain free software. Often these programs are used to collect personal information for resale or they may contain malicious code such as viruses.

Blog Topic

What is your favorite game?

Do you play Facebook games? If yes, which game is your favorite? Do you play other games online? If yes, which game do you find most challenging? Most relaxing? How much time per week do you spend playing games?

1. Write and post a blog entry with your answers to the above questions. If you do not play computer games, ask someone you know who does to describe a favorite game for you.

2. Read at least two of your classmates' blog entries and post one comment to each.

3. Submit your blog URL and the URLs of the two classmates' blogs to your instructor in the manner she or he has requested.

EXPLORE FURTHER

Survey note-taking software

The ability to organize, store, sort, and search notes electronically can save you time finding information. Is there a free note-taking software application that you might like to use?

1. Search for free note-taking software reviews and read at least two articles.

2. Decide on one program that you think would work best for you as a note-taking application. Consider the program's features and ease of use while considering your preference.

3. Create a document that describes the note-taking application you selected and give your reasons. Include the URLs of the articles you read for this topic.

4. Save the document as **C5-Apps-NoteTakingSoftware-Your Name**.

5. Submit the document to your instructor in the manner she or he has requested.

TOPIC 5.5

Cloud and Open Source Applications

In Chapter 1 you were introduced to Cloud Computing and the SaaS delivery model for software applications. Recall that SaaS stands for software-as-a-service and means that the software you are using is not installed on your computing device. SaaS applications are hosted by a third party and made available to you from a web browser. Open source programs are often provided for free, meaning that one can download and install the software on a computer without paying a license fee. In this topic you will survey three web-based and three open source software alternatives for productivity applications.

Web-Based Productivity Applications

The main advantage to using web-based applications is that you have access to the software application and your documents from any location at which you have an Internet connection. Table 5.1 provides a summary of three popular web-based productivity application alternatives. If you decide to use a cloud application, consider spending time working with a few different suites until you find the one with the features and interface that works best for you. In Figure 5.15 the same text is shown in the word processing application from each of the three providers summarized in Table 5.1.

Table 5.1	Summary of Three Popular Web-Based Productivity Applications		
Criterion	**Google Drive**	**Office Online**	**Zoho**
Free storage offered at time of writing	15 GB	15 GB	5 GB
Applications	Documents Spreadsheets Presentations Drawings	Word Excel PowerPoint OneNote	Calendar Notebook Planner Sheet (Spreadsheet) Show (Presentation) Writer (Word Processor) Plus several apps for collaboration and business processes
URL and sign-in for applications	google.com Sign in with your Gmail account, then click Documents.	onedrive.live.com Sign in with your Windows Live ID, then click Create to choose Word, Excel, PowerPoint, or OneNote.	zoho.com Sign in with your Zoho account, then click the Application you want to work in (you may need to scroll down the page to see the list of applications).

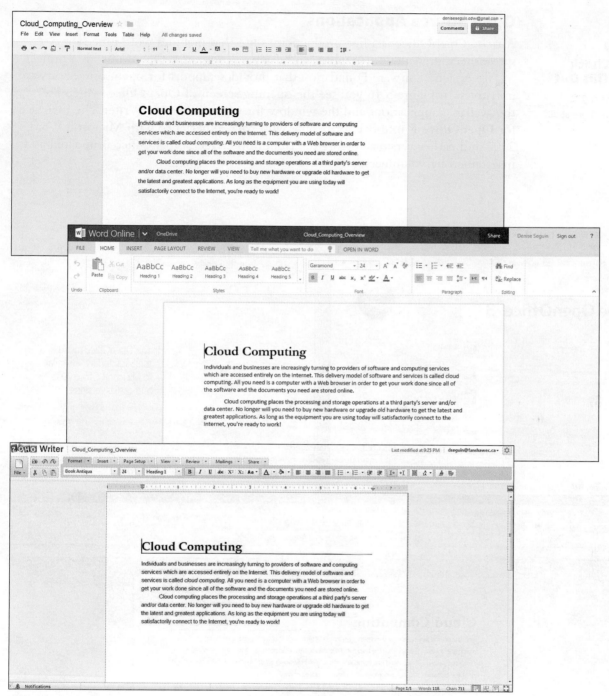

Figure 5.15 Each web-based application is slightly different as shown here with the same text formatted in Google's (top), Microsoft's (middle), and Zoho's (bottom) cloud word processor.

www.openoffice.org

Go here to learn more about OpenOffice.

Open Source Applications

Apache OpenOffice is a free productivity suite that includes word processor, spreadsheet, presentation, graphics, and database programs. OpenOffice is a project of The Apache Software Foundation that provides support for open source software initiatives. In Figure 5.16 you see the opening screen of OpenOffice, which lists the available applications and the window for OpenOffice.org Writer. The interface for OpenOffice is intuitive for people who have experience with Microsoft Word 2003 and earlier versions (before the ribbon interface). OpenOffice is updated and maintained by volunteers.

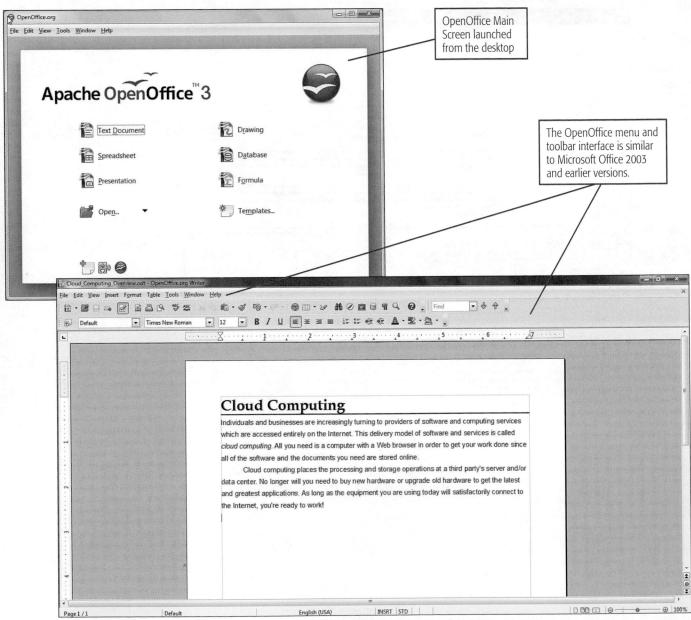

Figure 5.16 OpenOffice is a free open-source productivity suite that is updated and maintained by volunteers.

OpenOffice has been modified and packaged under the name Lotus Symphony offered by IBM at ibm.com/software/lotus/symphony. Lotus Symphony includes documents, presentations, and spreadsheets in a free download.

Another free open-source productivity suite is LibreOffice. LibreOffice runs on Windows, Macintosh, and Linux computers and includes the applications Writer, Calc, Impress, Draw, and Base. LibreOffice is a project of The Document Foundation.

Several other web-based and open source applications are available. Consider searching for a free cloud or open source application the next time you need to acquire new software for your computing device.

Check This Out

www.libreoffice.org

Go here to learn more about LibreOffice.

EXPLORE FURTHER

Discover Zoho

Zoho is a popular web-based applications provider with several programs beyond the standard word processor, spreadsheet, and presentation software. Try out Zoho and compare it to what you are using now for productivity applications. *Note: **If you are already a Zoho user, complete this activity using another web-based productivity application.***

1. Go to zoho.com, sign up, and activate a free account.

2. Once signed In, launch one of the productivity applications that you want to use for your comparison. Experiment with the program to see how it works and the features that are available. For example, enter some sample text and try formatting options and spell check features.

3. Create a document that compares your Zoho experience with the equivalent productivity application that you normally use. Consider doing the comparison in a table or chart to compare each program that you tested feature by feature.

4. Save the document or spreadsheet as **C5-Apps-ZohoComparison-Your Name**.

5. Submit the document or spreadsheet to your instructor in the manner she or he has requested.

Acquiring, Installing, Uninstalling, and Upgrading Software

TOPIC 5.6

Software applications can be acquired in various ways such as purchasing an application from a retailer either in the store or online, buying directly from the publisher, or buying from software download websites such as Tucows where people look for software that is low cost or free (Figure 5.17). Software is a licensed product, meaning that when you install software you have paid for the right to use the product while ownership remains with the publisher that created the software. In this topic you will learn the various models for distributing software and the general steps that you take to install, uninstall, or upgrade an application.

Figure 5.17 Tucows downloads has been a popular site for finding low-cost and free software since 1994.

Software Distribution Models

Traditional software suites like Microsoft Office or Adobe Creative Suite can be purchased as **packaged software** at a retailer's store or from several e-commerce websites. You can also buy the software online directly from the company that published it. Pricing for software suites can vary, so it is wise to check out a few options before making a purchase.

Other ways to acquire software include the following:

- **Shareware** software is available to download for a free trial period. Once the trial period expires, you need to pay a fee to the software publisher to unlock the application. Other forms of shareware continue to work beyond the trial period but generally have features made inaccessible until the fee payment is made.
- **Freeware** software can be downloaded and installed at no cost and without restrictions. An example of a popular freeware program is Apple's iTunes.
- Open source software is generally available for free and downloaded from a website.
- **Subscription software** is purchased from cloud computing providers who generally charge a monthly fee per user for access to the provider's software and storage services. Fees vary based on the number of users and the amount of storage space required.

Did You Know?

You should check the system requirements before paying for packaged software to make sure the software will work with your PC's hardware and with your OS. Software packages that have been opened are generally not returnable.

Installing Software

When you buy packaged software at a retail store, you receive a DVD inside the package. Insert the DVD into the appropriate drive on your computing device and the software will automatically begin the installation process. Follow the prompts that appear to complete the installation routine.

If you have downloaded software from a website, you generally have two methods for installing the software:

■ You can opt to run the installation program directly from the website. After clicking the download link, you'll be presented with the option to Run or Save the installation file. Click Run to run the program directly from the source website and then follow the prompts that appear. In the Windows OS you will be prompted with a security warning message and will have to allow the installation to proceed.

Packaged software purchased at a retailer generally includes a DVD that you use to install the software.

■ Alternatively, you may opt to save the downloaded file to your hard drive and run the installation later. After clicking the download link, select the option to Save or to Save As and navigate to the drive and folder in which to store the file. When the download is complete, open the window that you use to view files and display the location where you saved the downloaded file name. Double-click the file name to start the installation routine (Figure 5.18). Follow the prompts that appear. In the Windows OS you need to

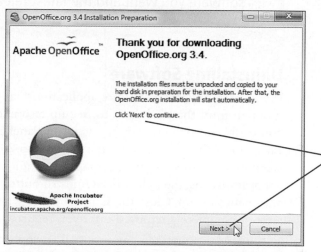

Software installers generally provide a series of prompts in dialog boxes to guide you through the installation process.

Figure 5.18 Installing software you have downloaded generally involves proceeding through an installer wizard that prompts you along the way.

click the option to allow the installation to proceed at the security warning message. Generally, you choose this method if you want to make sure you have the software program's installation file saved in case you need to reinstall it again at a later date.

Software License Agreements When you install software you are required to accept a license agreement (unless the software product is open source) similar to the one shown in Figure 5.19. License agreements, called **Software License Agreements (SLAs)** or **End User License Agreements (EULAs)**, vary by software publisher. Although the terms and conditions are generally long and filled with legal terminology, you

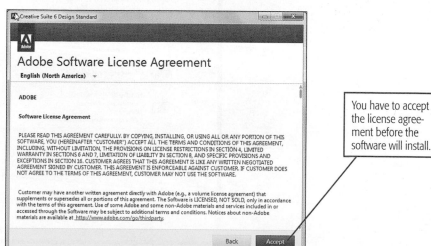

You have to accept the license agreement before the software will install.

Figure 5.19 Proprietary software such as Adobe requires that you accept a license agreement for the software installation to proceed.

should read the agreement and not just blindly click I accept/I agree to move on. The SLA or EULA specifies the number of computers upon which you can legally install the software. For example, some publishers will allow installation on up to three computers while others may restrict you to one.

Download Beware!

Exercise caution at software review websites that provide links to download free software. Many of these sites have ads that look deceptively similar to the actual download link you are supposed to click. Clicking the ad by mistake means you often end up with other software on your PC that you do not want and that is difficult to remove completely. To be safe, download a program from the actual company's website to make sure you are getting only the software you want and the latest release.

Uninstalling Software

If you have installed a software application that you no longer use, uninstall the program from the hard drive to free up resources. To do this on a Windows-compatible computer, open the Control Panel and click the link to Uninstall a Program in the Programs category (Figure 5.20). At the Programs and Features window, click to select the program you want to remove in the list of software applications and then click the Uninstall button. An uninstall routine will automatically run. Close the Control Panel when finished. In some cases, programs are not completely removed until you restart your computer.

On a Mac computer, you uninstall an application by finding the application icon (in the Finder window) and dragging the icon to the Trash. The icon is a shortcut to the program's installation bundle, which includes all related program files. To remove a program's shortcut icon from the dock, simply drag the icon off the dock.

Click here to open a window with a list of installed software to uninstall a program.

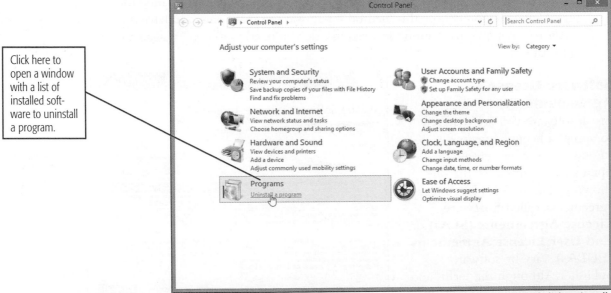

Figure 5.20 Open the Control Panel on a Windows-compatible computer and click Uninstall a program to open the Programs and Features window and remove software you no longer want.

Upgrading Software

Upgrading software simply means installing a newer version of a program you are already licensed to use (not to be confused with updating, which simply installs fixes or patches to the existing version). Usually, when you install an upgrade, the older version is replaced; however, in some applications, you can opt to keep the older version and the newer version on the same computer. Some software applications prompt you when an upgrade is available, and clicking the prompt will take you to the website where you can download the newer version (Figure 5.21). Some upgrades are free, while others require payment for the upgrade at a price lower than the original purchase. Registering software when you buy it is a good idea so that you are notified of upgrades and qualify for reduced pricing.

⚠ A new version of AnyDVD is available! ✕
Your current Version: 7.0.4.0
New version available for download: 7.0.6.0

Click here to visit the SlySoft download page!

Figure 5.21 Software usually installs with a setting that checks automatically for newer versions and prompts you to download the upgrade when it becomes available.

Blog Topic

Why pay for software?

As you have learned in this chapter, there are several alternatives to paying for a software license for a traditional packaged suite like Microsoft Office. Despite these free alternatives, software suites like Microsoft Office have loyal supporters that consistently buy upgrades. Why do you think people pay for software? What benefits do paying customers receive that users of freeware do not?

1. Write and post a blog entry with your thoughts on why people prefer to pay for software like Microsoft Office instead of using OpenOffice or free web-based applications.

2. Read at least two of your classmates' blog entries and post one comment to each.

3. Submit your blog URL and the URLs of the two classmates' blogs to your instructor in the manner she or he has requested.

EXPLORE FURTHER

EULAs for Retail Editions of MS Office and Apple Software

Do you know the usage rights in the Microsoft Office retail edition EULA? For example, if you purchased the Home and Student edition of Microsoft Office, can you legally install the software on more than one computer? Does Apple's SLA have the same terms and conditions as Microsoft?

1. On your home computer in the Help screen of Microsoft Word or at microsoft.com, find and read the software license terms section titled *Installation and Use Rights*. Next, find the application software license agreement for Pages at apple.com. Read the section titled *Permitted License Uses and Restrictions*.

2. Compare and contrast the two license agreements. Are they the same or do they specify different terms? How do the two license agreements vary for the specified sections?

3. Create a document with a brief summary in your own words of the specified sections and your answers to the above questions.

4. Save the document as **C5-Apps-MSandAppleEULAs-Your Name**.

5. Submit the document to your instructor in the manner she or he has requested.

TOPIC 5.7

Mobile Apps

Mobile devices such as smartphones require a different edition of software that is designed specifically for mobile use. These programs are **mobile applications**, or more generally referred to as *apps*. Apps are designed to work on smaller screens and accept touch input from finger gestures. Functionality for on-screen keyboards, handwriting recognition, and speech recognition capabilities are also part of app design. Other important features include compatibility and synchronization with PC software and sharing information from the smartphone with other programs and users.

Apps by the thousands are available for Android, Apple, BlackBerry, and Windows devices for just about any type of task you can imagine. For example, built-in or downloadable apps are available for mail, scheduling, contacts, maps, GPS, weather, news, travel, games, mobile banking, calculators, currency conversion, messaging, and connecting with social media such as Facebook and Twitter. These are just a few of the categories of apps you will find at the Android, Apple, BlackBerry, and Windows Phone stores (Figure 5.22). In this topic you will survey a sampling of built-in and productivity apps for mobile devices.

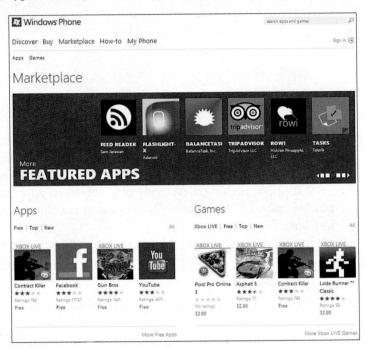

Figure 5.22 Apps for smartphones are downloaded from app stores such as Windows Phone Marketplace shown here. New apps are added frequently, with many offered for free or at a low cost.

Built-in Apps

Apple, Android, BlackBerry, and Windows smartphones and tablets come equipped with several built-in apps such as the ones shown on the iPhone 4 in Figure 5.23. Typically, personal information management apps for keeping track of appointments, contacts, to-do lists, reminders, and notes are standard as well as apps for mail, messaging, maps, music, and games.

Figure 5.23 Smartphones and tablets come equipped with several built-in apps such as the ones shown here that are included with Apple's iPhone4.

Mobile Productivity Apps

Microsoft Office Mobile has Word, Excel, PowerPoint, and OneNote editions designed for a smartphone. You can review, edit, and sync documents to and from email, SkyDrive, Sharepoint, or other web-based services. Apple's iWork for iOS is the mobile edition of Pages, Keynote, and Numbers. Zoho provides mobile editions of Mail, Calendar, Creator, Writer, Sheet, and Show at m.zoho.com. Google Mobile is a suite of productivity apps for Android devices. Figure 5.24 shows the app screen for Excel Mobile and Zoho Mobile Writer.

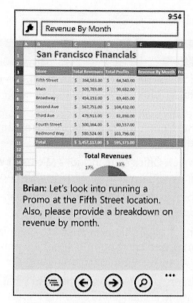

Figure 5.24 Microsoft Excel Mobile (left) and Zoho Writer Mobile (right) allow you to view, edit, and create spreadsheets and documents on your smartphone.

Blog Topic

My Favorite App

What is your favorite smartphone or tablet app? Why? How often do you use the app in a typical day?

1. Write and post a blog entry that describes your favorite app, why it is your favorite, and how often you use it in a typical day.

2. Read at least two of your classmates' blog entries and post one comment to each.

3. Submit your blog URL and the URLs of the two classmates' blogs to your instructor in the manner she or he has requested.

Did You Know?

Quickoffice, a mobile productivity suite with Quickword, Quicksheet, and Quickpoint apps that are compatible with Google Docs and Microsoft Office, was acquired by Google in June 2012. Watch for changes to Quickoffice that involve rebranding within Google Apps.

EXPLORE FURTHER

Popular Apps for Android, Apple, BlackBerry, or Windows Devices

With thousands of apps available for mobile devices, finding the most useful apps for one's smartphone or tablet might not be an easy task.

1. Find and read at least two articles that rate the top five apps for an Android, Apple, BlackBerry, or Windows mobile device.

2. Create a presentation that describes the five apps (one app per slide) you found most interesting. Include a sixth slide with the URLs of the articles you used.

3. Save the presentation as **C5-Apps-Top5Mobile-Your Name**.

4. Submit the presentation to your instructor in the manner she or he has requested.

Concepts Review

Topic	Key Concepts	Key Terms
Productivity Applications for the Workplace	Application software, or apps, are programs used by individuals to carry out tasks or otherwise get things done.	Application software
	A productivity suite generally includes a word processor, spreadsheet program, presentations program, and database management program.	Apps
	The Microsoft Office suite includes Microsoft Word, Microsoft Excel, Microsoft PowerPoint, and Microsoft Access.	Productivity software
	A word processing program is used to create, edit, and format documents that are mostly text.	Software suite
	Spreadsheet applications are used to organize, calculate, edit, format, and chart numbers that are entered in cells within a worksheet grid of columns and rows.	Productivity suite
	Spreadsheets are often used to perform what-if analysis where a value is changed to view the impact on other values.	Word processing application
	Presentation software is used to create slides for an electronic slide show that communicate key points, facts, figures, messages, or other ideas.	Spreadsheet application
	Large amounts of data are organized, stored, and maintained in software called database management applications.	Presentation application
	In database software you set up the structure to store data, input data, maintain data, and produce lists and reports for various purposes.	Database management application
	Microsoft publishes a productivity suite used on Apple computers.	
Other Workplace-Oriented Productivity Applications	Personal information management (PIM) software is used to organize emails, appointments, contacts, and to-do lists.	Personal information management (PIM) software
	Accounting software applications are used to record and report the financial activities of a business related to assets, liabilities, equity, revenue, and expenses.	Accounting software application
	A business will use project management software to create and maintain a project schedule and budget.	Project management software
	Document management software is used for managing the storage, retrieval, history, and eventual disposal of documents stored in a central repository.	Document management system (DMS)
	Industry-specific software applications are programs used to perform tasks unique to a specific business environment.	Enterprise resource planning (ERP)
	Enterprise resource planning (ERP) software is designed to support large-scale operations with higher level needs.	

continued....

| Applications for Working with Graphics, Multimedia, and the Web | Painting and drawing software provides tools for artists to create, edit, and apply special effects to pictures, shapes, or other images.

Photo editing software is used to edit pictures and add special effects and text.

Desktop publishing (DTP) software provides tools to place text and graphics on a page with more control over spacing and a wider range of fonts, sizes, and colors for professional publications.

Animation software applications allow a multimedia professional to create images with movement or otherwise interact with users.

Video editing software is used to manipulate video recorded with a camcorder and add music, audio effects, and text to create videos called clips.

Recording and editing music clips, sound clips, or podcasts is done using audio recording and editing software.

Websites and web pages are created and maintained using web authoring programs.

Non-programmers can create a web page in web authoring software without having to know the programming code used by browsers.

Low-cost or free multimedia programs are available for non-professionals to work with graphics, pictures, video, and sound. | Graphics software
Desktop publishing software
Multimedia software
Web authoring software
Photo editing software
Animation software
Video editing software
Audio recording and editing software |
| Software Applications for Personal Use | Note-taking software provides a way to store, organize into notebooks and tabs, search, and share notes of any type.

Personal finance software allows you to balance your bank accounts and manage personal investments.

Prepare and file your tax returns using tax preparation software.

Legal documents such as wills and contracts can be prepared using legal software, which contains forms for completing legal documents.

Hobby software applications are available to help you with just about any type of leisure activity such as scrapbooking, meal planning, or genealogy.

Programs for playing games and videos are referred to as entertainment software.

Learning about subjects such as math and geography is made easier using educational software programs that use multimedia to incorporate interactivity and games.

Reference software programs use multimedia tools to provide rich content in encyclopedias, translation guides, and other references. | Note-taking software
Personal finance software
Tax preparation software
Legal software
Hobby software applications
Entertainment software
Educational software
Reference software |

continued....

Topic	Key Concepts	Key Terms
Cloud and Open Source Applications	The main advantage to using web-based applications is that you have access to the software and your documents from any location with an Internet connection. Google Drive, Office Online, and Zoho are all cloud providers that offer free storage space and a suite of productivity applications for free. Apache OpenOffice is a free, open source productivity suite updated and maintained by volunteers. IBM's Lotus Symphony is a free suite with word processing, spreadsheets, and presentations based upon the OpenOffice package. LibreOffice, a project of The Document Foundation, includes Writer, Calc, Impress, Draw, and Base.	
Acquiring, Installing, Uninstalling, and Upgrading Software	Software is a licensed product, meaning that you pay for the right to use the software but you do not own the program code. Packaged software can be purchased in a retail store, at e-commerce websites, or directly from the software publisher. Shareware is downloadable software for which you pay a small fee if you decide to keep the program after a trial period. Freeware is software provided for your use without restrictions such as Apple's iTunes program. Subscription-based software is generally purchased from cloud computing providers, and there is a monthly charge per user. Packaged software contains a DVD inside the package with which you install the software application. Download and install software directly from a website by running the install program at the source website, or by saving the install program on your hard disk drive and then installing it at a later time. To install all software programs except open source applications, you are required to accept a Software License Agreement (SLA) or End User License Agreement (EULA). The EULA will specify the number of computers upon which you can legally install the software program. Remove software from the computer when you are no longer using it to free up computer resources. In a Windows-compatible computer, open the Control Panel to uninstall a software program. On a Mac computer, drag the program's icon and dock shortcut to the trash. Installing a newer version of a software program is called upgrading; upgrades are available free or at a price lower than purchasing the software new.	Packaged software Shareware Freeware Subscription software Software License Agreement (SLA) End User License Agreement (EULA)

continued....

Mobile Apps	Mobile applications specifically designed for use on a mobile device such as a smartphone are designed to work on smaller screens. They accept input from touch, handwriting, and voice, and include compatibility with PC software.	Mobile applications
	All smartphones and tablets come equipped with several built-in apps that typically include PIM, communication, music, and game apps.	
	Microsoft Office Mobile, iWork for the iOS, Zoho, and Google Mobile all have separate mobile apps for smartphones.	

Multiple Choice

1. Which of the following applications is *not* generally included in a productivity suite?
   a. Word processor
   b. Tax preparation
   c. Database management program
   d. Spreadsheet

2. This software application included with a productivity suite is used for organizing, storing, and maintaining large amounts of data.
   a. Presentation
   b. Word processor
   c. Personal information management
   d. Database management

3. A business will use this type of application to keep a project on time and on budget.
   a. Project management
   b. ERP
   c. Accounting software
   d. Industry-specific software

4. Outlook is an example of this type of application.
   a. Personal finance
   b. Personal information management
   c. Spreadsheet
   d. Database management

5. This type of software is used to create images with movement.
   a. Web authoring applications
   b. Desktop publishing applications
   c. Animation software applications
   d. Video editing software applications

6. Adobe Dreamweaver is an application used for this type of work.
   a. Web authoring
   b. Graphics editing
   c. Desktop publishing
   d. Audio recording and editing

7. This is the note-taking software application published by Microsoft.
   a. OneNote
   b. LibreOffice
   c. OpenNote
   d. OfficeNote

8. This type of software is used to manage personal investments.
   a. Reference software
   b. Tax preparation software
   c. Legal software
   d. Personal finance

9. Which of the following is *not* a cloud-based productivity suite?
   a. Zoho
   b. Office Online
   c. OpenOffice
   d. Google Drive

10. IBM's Lotus Symphony productivity suite is based on this open source application.
    a. OpenOffice
    b. OpenSuite
    c. LibreSuite
    d. Quickoffice

11. This type of software is made available for a trial period after which a license fee is paid to unlock the software.
    a. Shareware
    b. Freeware
    c. Subscription software
    d. Packaged software

12. Open this window on a Windows-compatible computer to remove a software application that you no longer use.
    a. Documents window
    b. Computer window
    c. Windows Explorer
    d. Control Panel

13. This is the name of the mobile application of Microsoft Office.
   a. Microsoft Office Mobile
   b. Microsoft Quickoffice
   c. Microsoft GoOffice
   d. Microsoft SmartOffice

14. Typically, a smartphone is preinstalled with built-in apps for everything except which type of software?
   a. Personal information management
   b. Communications
   c. Games
   d. Hobby apps

Crossword Puzzle

ACROSS
2 Cloud productivity suite
7 Category of software for wills or contracts
9 Created with Microsoft PowerPoint
11 Means mobile application
12 Software with no license restrictions

DOWN
1 Record and report financial activities in this type of application
3 Open source productivity suite
4 Photo editing program from Adobe
5 License agreement
6 Software with initial trial period
8 Used to do advanced page layout
10 Software used to manage large-scale operations

Matching

Match the term with the statement or definition.

_____ 1. Productivity suite
_____ 2. Subscription-based software
_____ 3. ERP
_____ 4. Multimedia
_____ 5. LibreOffice
_____ 6. Mobile apps
_____ 7. Document management software
_____ 8. Reference software

a. Manage large-scale operations
b. Designed for smaller screens
c. Open source software suite
d. Manage central document repository
e. Multimedia-enriched encyclopedia
f. Cloud computing
g. Microsoft Office
h. Text, graphics, video, and audio

Project 1 Learning Microsoft Office

Individual or Pairs
Deliverable: Document or Presentation

You have a friend who has asked for your help with learning how to use Microsoft Office. You want to provide her with a description of online learning tools available from Microsoft to help her learn how to use features in the software suite.

1. Go to www.office.microsoft.com and click the Support link. At the Support page, click a Training link to browse tutorials by application. Choose a tutorial that interests you and complete the course. Next, find and watch an Office video demo.
2. Create a document or presentation that describes each learning tool and provides an overview of how to access the resource. Include the features you liked the most about each resource as well as any weaknesses you noticed so that your friend can make an informed choice about which resource to use on her own. Be creative with the document or presentation to make the guide clear, interesting, and easy to follow. Include links to the tutorial and video that you watched.
3. Save the document or presentation as **C5-Project1-MSOfficeTraining-Your Name**.
4. Submit the document or presentation to your instructor in the manner she or he has requested.

Project 2 Managing Events Using Web-Based Software

Individual, Pairs, or Team
Deliverable: Document or Presentation

A charity at which you volunteer is planning a free seminar to promote awareness of the services that the charity provides to the general public. The seminar will be offered for free but you are requesting that people register in advance so that proper facilities are booked to accommodate everyone planning to attend. You will be assisting with the organization of the seminar and want to find an online event management software application that will help you manage online marketing, registrations, communications, and reports on participants.

1. Search for a free web-based event management application. Choose two programs to review, visit the websites and learn about the features and usability of each program.
2. Create a document or presentation that describes each program you reviewed, links to the source applications, and concludes with your recommendation and rationale for the application the charity should use to manage its seminar.
3. Save the document or presentation as **C5-Project2-EventManagement-Your Name**.
4. Submit the document or presentation to your instructor in the manner she or he has requested.

Project 3 Word Processor or Desktop Publisher?

Individual or Pairs
Deliverable: Document or Presentation

Word processing software includes many features that allow the formatting of text and placement of graphics to create documents such as newsletters, brochures, price lists, or catalogs. What distinguishes a word processing application from a desktop publishing application? Does a business need both programs? Assuming you are the creator of a monthly newsletter for a charity for which you volunteer, which program would you use to produce the newsletter each month? Why?

1. Search for information on the differences between desktop publishing and word processing software applications to find answers to the above questions.
2. Create a brief document or presentation that informs the reader as to the differences between the two types of software applications, states the application you would use for your monthly newsletter, and includes your rationale. Provide the URLs used for your research.
3. Save the document or presentation as **C5-Project3-WPvsDTP-Your Name**.
4. Submit the document or presentation to your instructor in the manner she or he has requested.

Project 4 Home or Hobby Software

Individual

Deliverable: Document, Presentation, or Blog Entry

You want to find software to help you with your personal finances, home, or hobby activities such as gardening, cooking, crafts, travel planning, genealogy, or other hobby.

1. Search for a personal, home, or hobby software application that is of interest to you that was not described in this textbook. Learn about the software application's system requirements, features, and cost. Find and read at least two reviews or articles about the application.
2. Create a document, presentation, or blog entry that provides a summary of what you learned at Step 1. Include a link to the page at the software company's website that features the product and the URLs of the reviews or articles you read.
3. Save the document or presentation as **C5-Project4-PersonalSoftware-Your Name**.
4. Submit the document, presentation, or blog URL to your instructor in the manner she or he has requested.

Project 5 Using Cloud Collaboration Tools to Evaluate Shareware Usefulness

Pairs or Team

Deliverable: Collaborative Presentation Using Cloud Software

Shareware has been a popular alternative to packaged software for many individuals and businesses that want to try out a software application before paying for a license. What are the advantages and disadvantages of shareware?

1. Each person will find and read at least two articles on the advantages and disadvantages of shareware.
2. Using a web-based presentation application such as Google Presentations, PowerPoint Online, or Zoho's Show, one person in the pair or team will create the initial presentation that describes advantages and disadvantages of shareware. Save the presentation as **C5-Apps-Project5-Shareware-Your Name**.
3. The creator of the presentation will share the file with his or her partner or team members.
4. The partner, or each of the other team members, will modify the presentation to add additional advantages, disadvantages, or other information about shareware that is considered important to know. If no new advantages and disadvantages can be added, the individual will add information to the existing points already contributed or format the presentation to include graphics and other effects to make the presentation engaging and interesting to view.
5. Include a slide at the end of the presentation that has a table with each team member's name and the links to at least two articles he or she used for their contributions.
6. Share the final copy of the presentation by emailing a link to your instructor or by submitting the presentation in some other manner that she or he has requested.

Project 6 Podcast or Video Commercial for Mobile App

Individual, Pairs, or Team

Deliverable: Podcast or Video

Research free tools for creating and editing podcasts and videos to help you complete this project. Consider your favorite mobile app that could be used in a commercial by your smartphone manufacturer.

1. Write a storyboard for a one-minute commercial that promotes your favorite mobile app. Save the storyboard document as **C5-Apps-Project6-MobileAppStoryboard-Your Name**.
2. Use the storyboard to produce a one-minute podcast or video.

3. Upload the podcast to a free podcast-hosting website such as podbean.com or upload your video to YouTube.

4. Submit your storyboard document and the podcast or video link to your instructor in the manner she or he has requested.

Project 7 Greener Computing

Individual, Pairs, or Team
Deliverable: Presentation or Blog Entry

Assume you work in Marketing for a software company that publishes hobby software application packages that are sold primarily through electronics retail stores such as Best Buy. As a green computing initiative, you want to discontinue the packaged software model to stop the oversized box and plastic packaging and DVDs that are discarded in landfills. To do this, you have to convince management to move to a download-only software distribution model. Consider key points that support your initiative and also any barriers that may prevent management from approving the plan.

1. Create a presentation or write and post a blog entry that convinces management to approve the new software distribution model.

2. Save the presentation as **C5-Apps-Project7-GreenComputingSoftware-Your Name**.

3. Submit the presentation or your blog URL to your instructor in the manner she or he has requested.

Optional

Read the blog entry for this project of at least two other classmates and post a comment to each. Submit the URLs of your classmates' blogs with Step 2.

Project 8 Ethics Discussion on Downloading TV Shows and Movies

Team
Deliverable: Document, Blog Entry, or Presentation

A friend of yours regularly uses a bit torrent client program (a file sharing tool used to download large files on the Internet) to download television show episodes and movies. She has a large collection of her favorite television shows and movies stored on her PC. She has a copy of the most recent season of a television show you want to watch. Is it OK for you to copy her files to watch the season? Why or why not? Should you try to convince your friend to stop downloading television shows and movies? What are the ethics involved in bit torrent search engine and indexing websites that enable the sharing of copyrighted content? How should these companies ensure that individuals are not using their website to infringe on copyrighted content?

1. Within your team discuss the ethics involved in bit torrent file sharing of movies and television shows with respect to the above questions. If necessary, search for information on bit torrents and copyright infringement.

2. Prepare a summary of your team's discussion in a document, blog entry, or presentation.

3. Save the document or presentation as **C5-Project8-BitTorrentDiscussion-Your Name**.

4. Submit the document, presentation, or blog entry to your instructor in the manner she or he has requested.

Chapter 6

Using Social Media to Connect and Communicate

In Chapter 2 you learned that Web 2.0 refers to second-generation websites that provide for two-way communication, where individuals interact with organizations and with each other by sharing ideas, feedback, content, and multimedia. A large component of Web 2.0 involves social networking sites such as Facebook and Twitter that are used daily by millions of people of all ages all over the world. Businesses and other organizations also use social media technologies to connect with existing and potential customers or clients. Media sharing, blogs, and wikis are other components of Web 2.0 that focus on user-generated content.

In this chapter you will learn about social networking, social bookmarking, media sharing, blogging, and wikis. You will also be introduced to ways in which various organizations have incorporated social media technologies into their business strategies.

NOTE: The nature of social media websites is that they constantly evolve in response to innovation or new trends. The screens shown and instructions provided in this chapter are subject to change. Often, updates or changes to software mean that changes occur to the layout, design, or procedures. If necessary, use the Help function at a website if the screens shown or steps provided are no longer applicable.

After successfully completing this chapter, you will be able to:

- List and describe popular social networking websites
- Explain how social bookmarking is used to track and share information
- List popular websites used for sharing music, videos, and photos
- Identify websites for blogging and know how to create a blog and blog post
- Describe how wikis generate content from users and list popular wiki websites
- Provide examples of social media strategies used by businesses

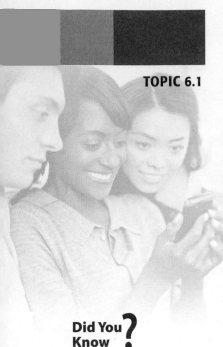

Social Networking

Social media is a term used to describe any online tool in which users generate content and interact with others. A website that provides tools for people to connect with groups of people and interact is called a **social networking website**. Generally, social networking sites provide a means to build a list of friends with whom you share information and publish a profile that contains information about you. In this topic you will be introduced to three social networking sites: Facebook and Google+ to connect with friends and family, and LinkedIn to connect with business contacts.

Facebook

Facebook is one of the most popular social networking sites used by people who want to connect with friends and family. A new user starts by creating an account, setting up his or her profile with personal information, and adding friends to his or her Friends list. To add friends, you search by the person's name and look at his or her profile page. If the person is someone you want to add to your Friends list, click the Add Friend button. A friend request is sent to the individual to accept or ignore. Once accepted as a friend, you and the other person can see each other's Facebook activity.

Facebook logo

People post updates in Facebook about what they're doing and share interesting links, photos, videos, music, games, news items, quotes, or just about anything else that appears to be of interest. People comment on a person's wall (their Facebook page) or a photo and generally post messages back and forth to each other. You can chat with friends who are online or use Facebook's Message tool to send private messages.

Users can create or join Facebook groups to gather with people that share a similar interest or goal. Businesses and other organizations create Facebook pages to share information and interact with customers, clients, or other interested visitors. For example, in Figure 6.1 the Facebook page for the U.S. Department of Education is shown.

Did You Know?

Facebook reported 955 million monthly active users at the end of June 2012—that's more than three times the population of the United States in the same year!

Figure 6.1 Education news is shared and discussed in comments with the general public on the Facebook page for the U.S. Department of Education.

Google+

In 2011, Google launched a social networking site called
Google+. Sign in at Google+ with your Gmail account or create
a new account. Edit your profile and then start adding people to
your circles.

Google+ logo

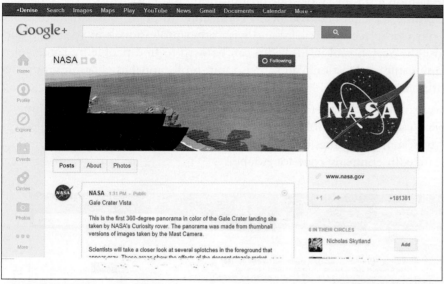

Figure 6.2 NASA's Google+ page is shown with a photo taken by the Curiosity rover on Mars
and a post describing the photo.

Circles In Google+, people or websites that you connect with are organized into
categories called circles. The default circles are Family, Friends, Acquaintances, and
Following. You can create your own new circles to group people with a similar
interest. When you add someone you want to connect with in Google+, you are
prompted to select the circle in which the individual should be associated. By
maintaining your social network in separate circles you can share activity with
only the people for whom the content is of interest. For example, you can post
information about a family reunion and share it only with your Family circle. This is
unlike Facebook, where a message you post is seen by everyone in your Friends list.

Add websites with which you want to keep up to date to your Following circle.
For example, adding a news website will ensure current news articles are added to
your Home page. Type a note, upload a photo or video, or enter a link at the *Share
what's new* box at the top of your page and then choose how to share the activity
by adding names, the names of circles, or email addresses. With Google+, you can
also use the Chat feature to talk with others online or use the Hangout feature to
conduct video chats.

As with Facebook, businesses and other organizations have created pages in Google+
to interact with interested users. Figure 6.2 shows the page for NASA in Google+.

LinkedIn

LinkedIn is the most visited business-related social networking site. It is a professional network where you connect with your business contacts. Creating an account with LinkedIn allows you to create a professional profile with your current and past employment positions, education credentials, and links to websites (such as your current company's website). Your profile can be expanded to represent in resume-like fashion a summary of your qualifications and prior work experiences. Once your profile is established, you begin connecting through LinkedIn with people in your workplace contacts list and with other professionals in your field and related fields. The Search tool in LinkedIn can be used to find people by name, job title, company name, or location. You can also join professional association groups to keep up with news in your field.

An Answers tool lets you post any type of question to the LinkedIn community so that experts can respond. A Jobs board shows current job listings and includes a search tool to search job listings by job title, keywords, or company name. Figure 6.3 shows the LinkedIn company page for Adobe.

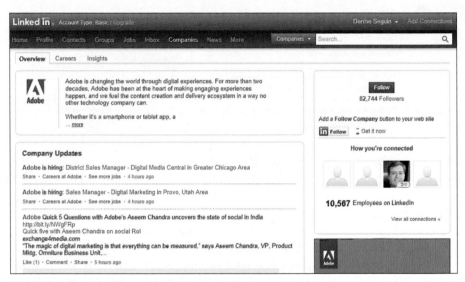

Figure 6.3 The LinkedIn page for Adobe provides a company overview, current job openings, and links to news, blogs, and articles related to Adobe products.

Mobile Apps for Social Networking

All of the popular social networking websites have free mobile apps that you download to your smartphone so that you can post messages, upload photos, or otherwise stay connected from your mobile device.

In this topic you have been introduced to three social networking websites. Table 6.1 lists three additional social networking websites that are also popular.

Social networking apps are free for your mobile device.

Table 6.1	Popular Social Networks
Social Network	**URL**
Bebo	bebo.com
Biznik	biznik.com
Facebook	facebook.com
Google+	plus.google.com
LinkedIn	linkedin.com
Tumblr	tumblr.com

Know Your Privacy Settings!

Make sure you check the privacy settings at the social networks that you use when you set up your account. You may be sharing more personal information than you intended. Ask your friends not to tag your name in photos they post if you don't want friends of friends to see what you've been up to.

EXPLORE **FURTHER**

Favorite Social Networking Websites

1. Conduct a survey with at least 10 relatives, friends, neighbors, or classmates to find out the social networking websites used by each individual and each person's estimate of the amount of time spent per week on social networking.

2. Compile the survey results in a table or chart in a document, spreadsheet, or presentation.

3. Save the document, spreadsheet, or presentation as **C6-SocialMedia-SocialNetworks-Your Name**.

4. Submit the document, spreadsheet, or presentation to your instructor in the manner she or he has requested.

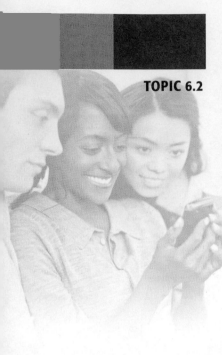

TOPIC 6.2

Social Bookmarking

A category of social networking that provides tools with which you can organize, store, and share content with others is known as **social bookmarking**. You have probably saved a link that you visit frequently to Favorites within your browser. These links are stored in folders on your local hard drive. Social bookmarking is similar to your Favorites list except that the links are called **bookmarks** and are saved in your social network so that you have access to them from anywhere and can share the links with others. At social bookmarking sites, you can search bookmarks that others have created.

Bookmarks are created by **tagging** a website. A **tag** is a keyword that you assign to the content to describe or categorize the photo, article, or item from a web page. The tags help users at the social bookmarking site find content. For example, if you find a recipe for Greek Soulvaki that you want to share you would tag the recipe at the source website with keywords such as *recipe, greek soulvaki, greek, entrée*.

Social bookmarking site icons called **bookmarklets** allow you to bookmark the page instantly by clicking the icon. The icons are copied from the social bookmarking website to your Favorites or Bookmarks toolbar in the browser. Some web pages include the more popular icons near the top of their pages. The icons have programming code attached that captures the site's references for bookmarking. In this topic, you will explore three social bookmarking sites: Pinterest, StumbleUpon, and Delicious.

Pinterest

According to Pinterest.com, **Pinterest** is a virtual pinboard. People pin pictures of things they have seen on the Internet that they like and want to share using the Pin It button. Pinterest users add the Pin It button (bookmarklet) to their browser's Favorites or Bookmarks toolbar. Click the Pin It button at a website with an image you like, select the image to pin, choose the board to pin the image to, and then type a description to pin a picture to your board. You can also upload your own pictures to share on a board.

Pinterest logo

A board is a name you assign to a collection of related pictures. For example, you can create a board for technology and collect pictures of cool gadgets. You can browse and follow boards created by other Pinterest users to get ideas for yourself. If you like something you find on someone else's board, you can repin the item to your own. Figure 6.4 displays a Pinterest board with bookmarked items.

Pin It bookmarklet added to Favorites bar in IE9

Click Add to create a new board, or to pin items by typing a URL or uploading from your PC or mobile device.

Figure 6.4 Pinterest is a visual social bookmarking site where users pin pictures to boards that link to items of interest.

StumbleUpon

By joining **StumbleUpon** you can browse recommended web pages and save the pages you like to your profile. When you join StumbleUpon, you choose categories for topics about which you want to see related content. Once your interests are established, navigate through various web pages StumbleUpon finds for you by clicking the Stumble! button in the black StumbleBar at the top of the screen (Figure 6.5). Use the like and dislike buttons on the StumbleBar as you view pages so that StumbleUpon can tailor the recommendations to your preferences. You can share a page you find with others and follow someone else if you like the same web pages as another StumbleUpon user (called a Stumbler). View web pages you have liked in the past using the History link in the left pane of your profile page.

StumbleUpon logo

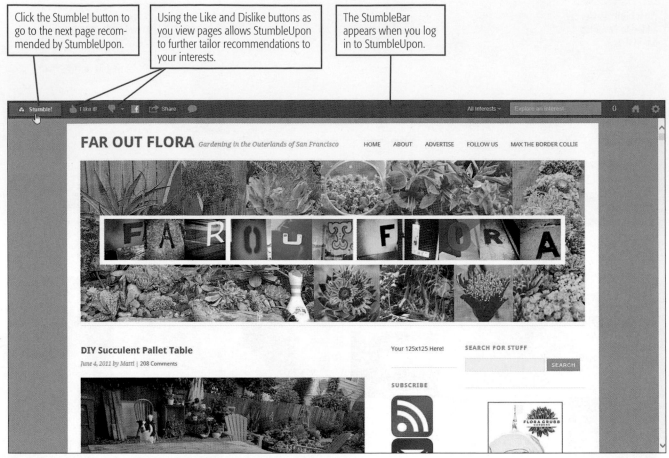

Click the Stumble! button to go to the next page recommended by StumbleUpon.

Using the Like and Dislike buttons as you view pages allows StumbleUpon to further tailor recommendations to your interests.

The StumbleBar appears when you log in to StumbleUpon.

Figure 6.5 StumbleUpon shows recommended web pages for you based on your likes and dislikes.

Delicious

Create an account at **Delicious** to save and share links to pages on the Web that have articles, pictures, videos, blogs, or some other content that you want to bookmark. Use the Delicious bookmarklet to save links to pages in your Delicious account. You will have to add the Delicious bookmarklet to your browser's Favorites or Bookmarks bar. Use the Add Link button on the Delicious toolbar to type a link directly that you want to save in Delicious. Delicious also has an import utility that will import bookmarks you have saved in your browser.

Delicious bookmarklet

When viewing a page on the Web that you want to save, click the Delicious bookmarklet, sign in to your account if you are not already logged in, enter tags or accept the default tags, type a description if desired, and click the Save button. You can mark links as private or public and follow other Delicious users.

Once you have a collection of links, you can sort and search through your personal collection or the collections of people you are following (use the Feed page). The Inbox contains private messages with links sent directly to you by other Delicious users. Figure 6.6 displays a Delicious page with saved bookmarks.

Some social bookmarking websites have connectors to Facebook and Twitter so that you can register using your existing Facebook or Twitter account instead of an email address.

Other popular social bookmarking sites are listed in Table 6.2.

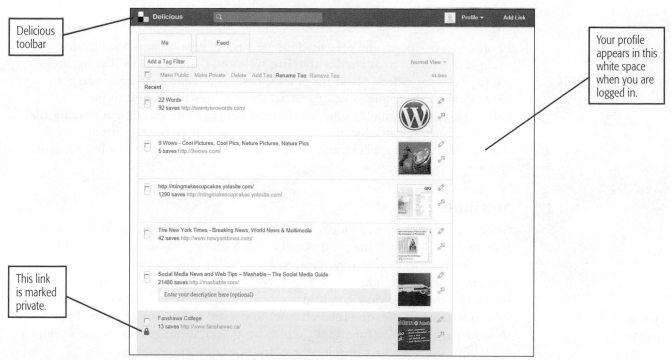

Figure 6.6 Use Delicious to collect pictures, videos, blog entries, articles, or anything else you have found that you want to save and/or share.

Table 6.2	Social Bookmarking Websites
Social Bookmark	**URL**
Clipboard	clipboard.com
Digg	digg.com
Delicious	delicious.com
Pinterest	pinterest.com
Reddit	reddit.com
StumbleUpon	stumbleupon.com

EXPLORE FURTHER

Start social bookmarking

As mentioned in the introduction to this topic, social bookmarks are available to you from any device, are searchable, and can be easily shared. If you have not yet experimented with social bookmarking, complete this activity to learn more about these websites.

1. Choose one of the social bookmarking websites listed in Table 6.2 and create an account at the website.

2. Experiment with the tools available at the site by adding at least 10 bookmarks to content that you like on the Web. Bookmark different types of content such as a blog, news article, picture, and video (unless you chose Pinterest, which bookmarks images only). Consider also customizing your profile and sharing some links with others.

3. Capture an image of your page at the social bookmarking website showing your saved links using a screen capture program such as Windows Snipping Tool or PrintScreen. Depending on the method used, save the image as a jpg file or paste the image into a document. Save the image or document as **C6-SocialMedia-Bookmarks-Your Name**.

4. Submit the image or document to your instructor in the manner she or he has requested.

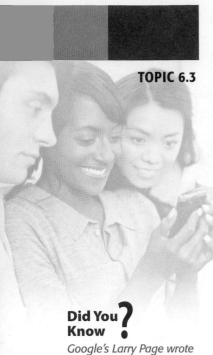

Sharing Media

Photos, videos, music, and presentations are shared, viewed, and downloaded using sites referred to as **media sharing** websites. Popular media sharing sites are YouTube for videos, Flickr for photos, Last.fm for music, and Slideshare for presentations. Sharing media using social sharing sites allows you to publish, collaborate, and distribute content to several people more easily than sending files or links as message attachments. In this topic you will survey the popular media sharing sites YouTube, Flickr, and Last.fm. In addition, Instagram, a photo sharing app for mobile devices, is introduced.

YouTube

Most people have viewed videos on **YouTube** (youtube.com). YouTube, which is owned by Google, is the most popular video sharing website in the world. Some YouTube videos become **viral videos** (video clips that spread quickly via forwarded or shared links or word-of-mouth). With a YouTube account you can search or browse for videos, upload a video you have created, rent full-length films, subscribe to someone's YouTube channel, and share videos with friends. Figure 6.7 shows a page from YouTube EDU, which hosts educational videos, some of which are lessons from teachers or full courses from leading universities.

Did You Know?

Google's Larry Page wrote in April 2012 that YouTube had 800 million-plus monthly users uploading more than an hour of video per second!

Choose Primary & Secondary Education, University, or Lifelong Learning here and then pick a subcategory to browse or search educational videos by topic.

Click Browse, and then click Education or type *youtube.com/education* to find the education channel.

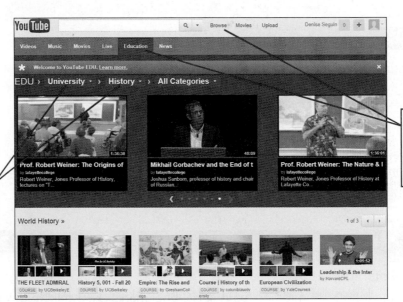

Figure 6.7 Go to YouTube EDU (youtube.com/education) to watch lectures, courses, or other educational videos.

Flickr

Sharing photos is one of the more popular media sharing activities on the Web since most people have digital photos they want to share with family and friends. Uploading photos to a sharing site lets you easily send a link to share your photo album with other people. Although social networking sites such as Facebook and Twitter let you upload and share photos, these sites generally have lower photo storage limits than dedicated photo sharing websites.

Many dedicated photo sharing websites are available, with **Flickr** being one of the popular choices. See Table 6.3 to review other photo sharing websites. Generally, photo sharing websites let you upload pictures organized into albums, sets, or folders; tag and comment on pictures; and share the photos with others. Sharing can be with other users of the site, or you can connect the photos to Facebook, Twitter, email, blogs, or other messaging tool. You can search for pictures uploaded by others, and sites such as Flickr include The Commons, which lets you search public photography archives. Figure 6.8 shows search results for *butterflies* in The Commons gallery in Flickr.

Some photo sharing websites such as Picasa include tools for editing photos.

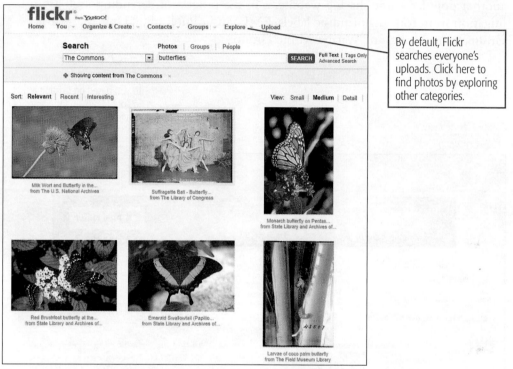

Figure 6.8 Some of the search results for *butterflies* in The Commons public photography archive in Flickr

Table 6.3	Sampling of Photo Sharing Websites	
Photo Sharing Website	**Restrictions for Free Accounts**	**URL**
Flickr	300 MB of photos and 2 videos *per month*	flickr.com
Photobucket	Unlimited photos and 500 videos for non-commercial users	photobucket.com
Picasa	1 GB of free storage space for photos and videos	picasa.google.com
Shutterfly	Unlimited photos	shutterfly.com
Snapfish	Unlimited photos	snapfish.com

Last.fm

Music fans who want to share their music discoveries or search for new music artists use one of many music sharing websites such as **Last.fm** (www.last.fm). Last.fm is a popular music streaming service. Using the site's software app called the Scrobbler, recommendations for new music are presented to you based on the types of songs you currently play (Figure 6.9). You can search for an artist or song, add a track to your library, and share it with another Last.fm user via Facebook, Twitter, Google+, or email.

Music sharing sites are often the target of litigation by major music recording labels for copyright violations. For example, at the time of writing, Grooveshark, another popular music sharing website, is in the process of defending itself against litigation from four major music labels: EMI Music Publishing, Universal Music Group, Sony Music, and Warner Music Group.

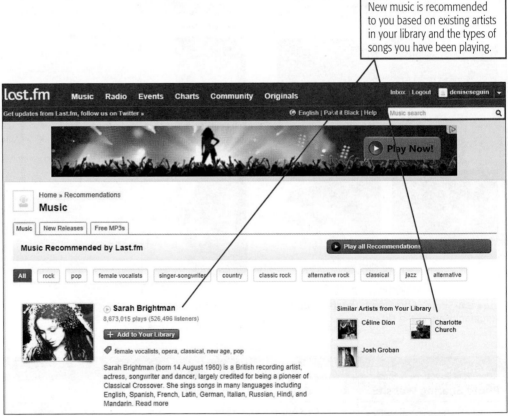

New music is recommended to you based on existing artists in your library and the types of songs you have been playing.

Figure 6.9 Last.fm is a popular music streaming and recommendation service based in the United Kingdom.

Sharing Photos from Mobile Devices

Instagram is a popular free app for sharing photos from your iPhone, iPad, iPod Touch, or Android phone. After taking a photo with your mobile device, you can use Instagram to add a special effect filter to the picture and then share the photo using your favorite social networking site. You can download the Instagram app from the iTune App store or Google Play. Instagram was purchased by Facebook in April 2012.

Instagram is a popular photo sharing app for mobile devices.

Check This Out

www.mashable.com

Go here for up-to-date news on digital culture, social media, and technology.

EXPLORE FURTHER

Sharing Presentations

Slideshare is a website at which you can upload and share presentations created in PowerPoint, PDF, Keynote, or OpenOffice. The slide hosting website also allows you to upload and share documents and videos. In 2012, Slideshare reported that 60 million people visited the site monthly.

1. Create a presentation with at least three slides that describes the methods or websites that you use to share media such as photos, videos, or music. If you do not share media, create one slide for each of the websites mentioned in this topic that summarizes what you learned.

2. Save the presentation as **C6-SocialMedia-MediaSharing-Your Name**.

3. Go to www.slideshare.net and sign up for a new account or log in if you already have an account.

4. Upload the C6-SocialMedia-MediaSharing-Your Name presentation. Add appropriate tags and a description and select the Education category.

5. Email the presentation to your instructor from slideshare.net or, alternatively, submit the presentation and a screen capture of your presentation uploaded in slideshare.net to your instructor in the manner she or he has requested.

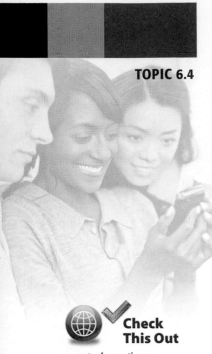

TOPIC 6.4

Blogging

Blogs are basically journals posted on a website with the most recent entry at the top of the page. Older blog entries are usually archived by month and can be displayed by clicking the month to expand the blog entry list. The word blog is derived from *web log*. The collection of all of the blogs on the Web is referred to as the **blogosphere**. Writing and maintaining a blog is called **blogging**. Entries in a blog are called **blog posts**, posts, or entries. The individual who writes the blog content is referred to as a **blogger**. Blogs exist on just about any topic one can think of and are mostly text and pictures; however, posts also contain links to other web pages and sometimes video and/or audio. Blog websites include tools that allow individuals to create, update, and maintain blogs without a programming background. Blogs are interactive, meaning that people can post comments below a blog post, and the author and his or her audience can have a conversation about the post.

Several popular blogs are viewed by millions of people every day. In this topic you will learn about two popular blog hosting websites: WordPress and Blogger. Twitter, a microblogging website, is also introduced.

WordPress

WordPress (wordpress.com) is a blog hosting website that uses the WordPress open source blogging software. Sign up for a free blog by providing a blog address, user name, password, and email address. A blog address begins with the domain you want to name your blog and ends with .wordpress.com. For example, if you type your name as the blog address, the URL you would give to people to find your blog would be *yourname.wordpress.com*. Once you activate the blog from the confirmation email message, choose a theme and start writing a post. A default post is created for you that you edit as your initial *About* entry, which generally describes you and the purpose of your blog. Click New Post to create a new blog post by typing a title and the body of the blog entry in a word processor–style window (Figure 6.10). Buttons are available to add a photo, video, quote, or link. Click the Publish Post button to add the entry to your blog.

Check This Out

www.technorati.com

Go here to find a blog. Technorati is a search engine that indexes more than a million blogs.

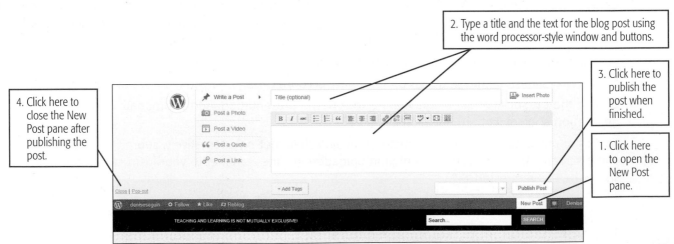

2. Type a title and the text for the blog post using the word processor-style window and buttons.

3. Click here to publish the post when finished.

1. Click here to open the New Post pane.

4. Click here to close the New Post pane after publishing the post.

Figure 6.10 New blog posts are created at Wordpress by typing inside a window similar to a word processor.

Blogger

Google's Blogger (blogger.com) is another popular choice for creating a blog. Sign up for the blog using your Gmail account. At the first screen, you can customize your profile or click the button to continue directly to Blogger. At the Blogger window, click the New Blog button to create a new blog. At the next screen, type a title for your blog, enter a blog address, choose the template with the colors and style you want to use, and then click Create blog! Blog addresses in Blogger end with .blogspot.com so the URL for your blog would be *yourblogaddress.blogspot.com* or *yourblogaddress.blogspot.ca* if you reside in Canada. Once the blog is created you can start publishing blog posts. Click the orange button with the icon of a pencil (Create a new post button) next to your blog title to create a new blog post. At the screen shown in Figure 6.11, type the post title and text in the word processor-style window. Add links, pictures, video, or quotes as needed and click Publish when finished.

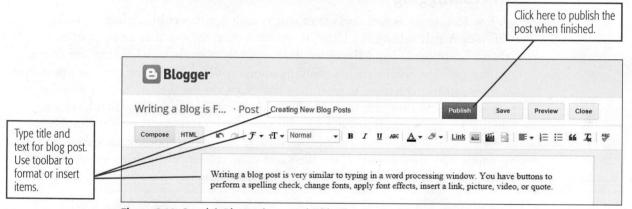

Click here to publish the post when finished.

Type title and text for blog post. Use toolbar to format or insert items.

Figure 6.11 Google's Blogger is a popular blog hosting service because the tools are easy to use and navigate for beginner bloggers.

Blogger is integrated with Google's other services and you may be prompted to share the blog on Google+ when you create it. Blogger uses a template design for blogs with a variety of colors for each template. You can change the template at any time in the Design window and see how the template will appear in both a PC and a mobile environment (Figure 6.12). Many other blog hosting websites are available such as those shown in Table 6.4.

Preview how your template design will look in both a PC and mobile environment.

Manage and customize your blogs in the Design window. Click Design while viewing the blog to see this window.

Figure 6.12 The template design can be changed at any time and you can preview how the blog will look on both a PC and a mobile device.

Table 6.4	Blog Hosting Services
Blog Hosting Service	**URL**
Blog.com	blog.com
Blogger	blogger.com
LiveJournal	livejournal.com
Squarespace	squarespace.com
Tumblr	tumblr.com
Twitter	twitter.com
Wordpress	wordpress.com
Xanga	xanga.com

Microblogging

A few blog services such as Twitter and Tumblr are **microblogging** hosting services. A **microblog** is a blog that restricts posts to a smaller amount of text than a traditional blog. **Microbloggers** typically post about what they are doing, where they are, what they are thinking about at the moment, or links to interesting content (stories, pictures, videos) they have seen on the Web. The most popular microblog is Twitter, although Tumblr is another highly popular microblog that includes social networking and social bookmarking features. A post in Tumblr is called a tumblelog. Many Tumblr users use their blogs to bookmark videos or pictures they have found on the Web and share them with their followers. Tumblr users also frequently reblog items seen on someone else's page at their own pages.

Twitter

By far, **Twitter** is the most popular microblog with posts limited to 140 characters or less. A post in Twitter is called a **tweet** and contains a short update on a breaking news story, opinion, a status update, or other topic the author finds interesting. Because of the short nature of a tweet, many users post to Twitter from their mobile devices. Clicking Compose New Tweet opens a small window in which you type your post. Twitter users type the **hashtag symbol (#)** preceding a keyword or topic (with no space) in a tweet to categorize messages. Clicking a hashtagged word in any post will show you all of the other tweets categorized with the same keyword.

Twitter logo

Many people like to follow other Twitter users to see their daily tweets, including popular businesses to find out about deals or specials (Figure 6.13). Twitter followers for some people reach millions. According to Twitter, at the 2012 Olympics in London, Usain Bolt set a new conversation milestone with 80,000 tweets per minute during his 200-meter run!

Figure 6.13 Businesses are using Twitter to post tweets with daily deals or news about products.

Be Careful What You Post Online

What you write in a blog or in comments at social media websites reflects on your ethics and your personality. Poor spelling and grammar portray sloppiness. Be mindful of your digital persona at all times. Do not engage in conversations or blogs that potential employers might read and use to decide that you are not a good fit for their organizations.

EXPLORE **FURTHER**

Tweet a social media fact

You may have been using blogs throughout this textbook but do you tweet? Complete this activity to post a tweet with an interesting fact about social media.

1. Search the Web for a fact about how Twitter has been used for social good.

2. Go to twitter.com and sign in or sign up for a new account if you do not already have one.

3. Compose a tweet to share the Twitter fact you found at Step 1. Precede your tweet with #courseidentifier so that your instructor can locate your tweet. Your instructor will provide you with the hashtag keyword to use for *courseidentifier*. For example, the hashtag keyword might be #comp100f2013.

4. In addition, or as an alternative, your instructor may request that you make a screen capture of your tweet and submit the screen capture as a jpg file or pasted in a document saved as **C6-SocialMedia-Tweet-Your Name**. In that case, submit the tweet in the manner she or he has requested.

TOPIC 6.5

Wikis for User-Generated Content

A **wiki** is a website with **wiki software** that allows anyone to create and edit content at the website. Clicking the edit tab, edit button, or edit link in a wiki opens the text in a word processor-style window where you can add, delete, or edit content. This type of open content is used for collaboration and knowledge sharing. Wikis that provide encyclopedic or other reference content have people that monitor postings to make sure entries are well written and accurate. In this topic you will explore two well-known wiki websites: Wikipedia and wikiHow.

Wikipedia

The most used online encyclopedia is **Wikipedia**, owned by the not-for-profit Wikimedia Foundation. Individuals looking for new information about a subject often start at Wikipedia. Content at Wikipedia can be created by anyone; however, thousands of editors regularly edit pages.

People who want to edit at Wikipedia are encouraged to create an account so that postings are identified with the individual either by name or alias. If you edit a page without being logged in to an account, the IP address for your PC is attributed to your content in the page history. New contributors to Wikipedia are encouraged to first post in the **Wikipedia Sandbox** (Figure 6.14).

Did You Know?

At the time of writing, 4,027,065 articles were available on Wikipedia.

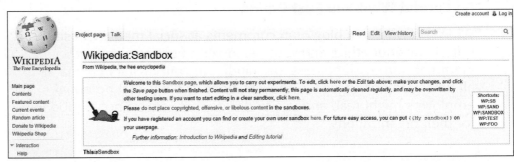

Figure 6.14 The Wikipedia Sandbox contains instructions on how to edit content and is where new contributors are encouraged to post a test edit before modifying a real article.

wikiHow

When a how-to instruction manual is needed, **wikiHow** is often where people look. The website contains more than 140,000 how-to articles. According to wikiHow, the mission of the website is to "build the world's largest, highest quality, how-to manual." You can search for the instructions you need using keywords or browse articles by category at the Home page. Figure 6.15 shows the beginnings of the how-to article titled "How to Change a Tire." wikiHow is a for-profit wiki that shows ads to users who are not registered to finance the operation of the website.

Other wikis that you might want to investigate are listed in Table 6.5.

Figure 6.15 wikiHow's user-generated articles are how-to instructions such as this article that describes the steps for changing a tire.

Table 6.5	Popular Wiki Websites	
Wiki	**URL**	**Purpose**
Wikibooks	wikibooks.org	Free textbooks and manuals
Wikimedia Commons	commons.wikimedia.org	Freely usable images, photographs, or videos
wikiHow	wikihow.com	How-to instructions
Wikipedia	wikipedia.org	Encyclopedia
Wikiquote	wikiquote.org	Collection of quotations from notable people
Wiktionary	wiktionary.org	Dictionary for words in all languages
WikiTravel	wikitravel.org	Worldwide travel guide

EXPLORE FURTHER

Explore a new wiki

Most people have experience looking up information at Wikipedia. In this activity you will explore another wiki of your choice.

1. Choose a wiki website from Table 6.5 other than Wikipedia that you have not used before and look up information on a topic or subject of interest to you. For example, you may want to use WikiTravel to find an article on a destination that you want to visit.

2. Read the article at the wiki website.

3. Create a document that provides a brief summary of the wiki you used, the information you researched, and your perception of the content's usefulness to you. Include the URL of the article at the end of the document.

4. Save the document as **C6-SocialMedia-WikiArticle-Your Name**.

5. Submit the document to your instructor in the manner she or he has requested.

TOPIC 6.6

Social Media Strategies in Business

Business strategies for using social media incorporate a wide variety of techniques such as using Facebook pages to provide customer support, invite feedback from customers, offer opportunities for new ideas, allow customers to share tips, or promote products. Businesses also offer coupons or information on specials using social media. In this topic, a sampling of selected companies' social media strategies is shown.

Amazon.com

Amazon's Facebook page provides a space for customers to post comments about interesting topics, showcase photos posted from customers, run contests, and provide customer service. In Figure 6.16, Amazon.com's Customer Service Support page is illustrated.

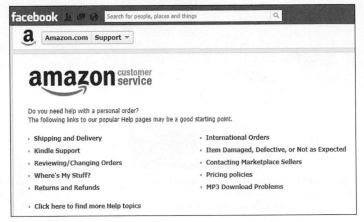

Figure 6.16 Amazon.com's Facebook page includes links to customer service Help pages.

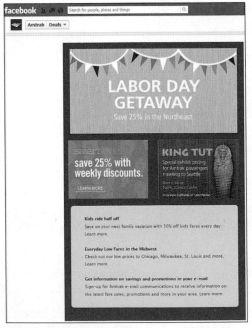

Figure 6.17 Amtrak's Deals are advertised on its Facebook page.

Amtrak

Amtrak's Facebook page engages customers in a variety of ways, including providing a place to leave comments; post photos, videos, and questions; learn about deals (Figure 6.17) and rewards; and book trips.

Coffee Groundz

A coffee shop in Houston called Coffee Groundz uses Twitter to tweet specials and promotions (Figure 6.18) and also was one of the first businesses to accept takeout orders from its customers in tweets.

Figure 6.18 Coffee Groundz in Houston tweets promotions and lets customers tweet their takeout orders.

Southwest Airlines

Southwest Airlines publishes a blog titled *Nuts About Southwest* (blogsouthwest.com), which uses a variety of multimedia (videos and podcasts) to engage readers who visit with information designed to build brand loyalty (Figure 6.19). Readers can create an account at the blog and exchange travel experiences with each other. At the Downloads page, people can download wallpapers and screen savers for their computing devices and install an app that notifies the user when new airfare deals are posted.

Figure 6.19 Southwest Airlines uses a blog to publish articles about the airline designed to build brand loyalty and provide a place for customers to exchange travel experience stories.

Career Connection

Social Media Managers

Businesses are increasingly aware of the need for a person to manage all of the social media feeds that can have a huge effect on their business strategies. A social media manager coordinates all of the social media networking and marketing for an organization. Typically, the social media manager is someone who enjoys spending a lot of time online, has excellent writing skills, and enjoys communicating and connecting with all types of people. Jobs in social media management or strategy typically ask for individuals with degrees or diplomas in communications, public relations, or marketing.

EXPLORE FURTHER

Find a business in social media

As you have seen in this topic, businesses use social media in a variety of ways. In this activity you will look for a business that you are familiar with on social media websites to find out how they are using the medium to promote products or services or build loyalty.

1. Choose a business that you are familiar with not profiled in this topic and find its presence in a social media venue such as Facebook, Twitter, LinkedIn, or some other network.

2. Examine the way in which the business is using social media to promote or otherwise engage its customers or find new customers. Do you think the strategy is successful? Would you engage with the business on its social media site? Why or why not?

3. Create a document or presentation that describes the results of your research in this activity and answers the questions posed in Step 2. Include a screen capture or URL of the page you reviewed.

4. Save the document or presentation as **C6-SocialMedia-BusinessStrategy-Your Name**.

5. Submit the document or presentation to your instructor in the manner she or he has requested.

Concepts Review

Topic	Key Concepts	Key Terms
Social Networking	A social networking website provides tools for people to connect and interact with one another. A social network provides a means to publish a personal profile and establish a list of people with whom you want to share activities and exchange updates. Facebook is the most popular social networking site used by people who want to connect with friends and family. Google+ uses circles to group people you want to connect with by categories such as Family, Friends, Acquaintances, and Following. LinkedIn is a social network used to connect with business contacts. Popular social networking websites provide free apps for downloading to a smartphone so that people can stay connected from their mobile devices.	Social media Social networking website Facebook Google+ LinkedIn
Social Bookmarking	Social bookmarking websites let you save and share links to content on the Web such as articles, pictures, videos, blogs, music, or other web pages. A saved link is called a bookmark. Bookmarks are created by tagging a website with one or more keywords called tags. Bookmarklets are icons installed on your Favorites or Bookmarks bar that are used to link a page to a social bookmarking website. Pinterest is used to pin images that you want to save and share to a board at your Pinterest account. StumbleUpon is a social bookmarking website that shows you pages that might be of interest to you based on categories that you like. Delicious is a social bookmarking site for saving and sharing links and one that can import links you have saved to Favorites in your browser. Social bookmarking websites have connectors to Facebook and Twitter.	Social bookmarking Bookmarks Tagging Tag Bookmarklets Pinterest StumbleUpon Delicious
Sharing Media	Media sharing websites let registered users upload photos, videos, music, or presentations and share the content with others. YouTube is owned by Google and is the most popular video sharing website in the world. Viral videos are videos that spread quickly via forwarded links, shared links, or word-of-mouth. Flickr is a popular photo sharing website that provides tools for users to upload, organize, and share photos. Last.fm is a music streaming and recommendation service based in the United Kingdom. Last.fm uses a software app called Scrobbler that tracks the music you play so that recommendations can be tailored to your interests. Instagram is a popular photo sharing app for use with a smartphone.	Media sharing YouTube Viral videos Flickr Last.fm Instagram

continued....

Blogging	Blogs are online journals created at blog hosting websites, with the most recent post at the top of the page.	Blogs
		Blogosphere
	Bloggers create blog posts that are composed of text, photos, videos, or links.	Blogging
		Blog posts
	Wordpress is a blog website that uses the open source WordPress blogging software.	Blogger
		WordPress
	A blog is generally typed inside a word processor-style window.	Google's Blogger
		Microblogging
	Blogger, owned by Google, is a popular blogging tool that uses templates and a user-friendly interface.	Microblog
		Microbloggers
	Microblogging websites such as Twitter and Tumblr are used to create short posts or share links or photos.	Twitter
		Tweet
	Twitter is the most popular microblog with posts limited to 140 characters or less.	Hashtag symbol (#)
	The hashtag symbol (#) in a tweet precedes a keyword that the author wants to use to categorize the tweet.	
Wikis for User-Generated Content	A wiki website uses wiki software that allows users to add or edit content.	Wiki
		Wiki software
	Wikis that provide encyclopedic information have thousands of editors that edit content to ensure postings are well written and accurate.	Wikipedia
		Wikipedia Sandbox
	Wikipedia is the most used online encyclopedia.	wikiHow
	New contributors are encouraged to do a test edit in the Wikipedia Sandbox before editing a real article.	
	wikiHow is a wiki website with thousands of how-to instruction articles on a wide range of topics.	
Social Media Strategies for Business	Businesses use social media networks in a variety of ways to engage customers or find new customers.	
	Amazon.com's Facebook page includes space for customers to interact with the company and find customer service support.	
	Amtrak uses its Facebook page to publish deals and allow customers to upload photos and videos or post questions.	
	A coffee shop in Houston uses Twitter to tweet promotions and allows customers to send their takeout orders by tweets.	
	Southwest Airlines publishes a blog that uses a variety of multimedia in articles that promote brand loyalty and allows customers to share travel experiences.	
	Southwest Airlines also provides downloads at its blog for wallpaper, screen savers, and an app that alerts the customer when airfare specials are published.	

Multiple Choice

1. Google+ organizes your contacts into categories referred to as _____.
   a. Social groups
   b. Circles
   c. Friend shares
   d. Address books

2. This website is the most visited business-related social network.
   a. Facebook
   b. Google+
   c. My Space
   d. LinkedIn

3. This is the term that refers to a social network used to save and share links.
   a. Social bookmarking
   b. Social tagging
   c. Social sharing
   d. Social wikis

4. Pinterest is this type of social networking website.
   a. Social Bookmarking
   b. Social Pin Sharing
   c. Blogging
   d. Social Pinning

5. YouTube is referred to as this type of website.
   a. Social networking
   b. Social bookmarking
   c. Media sharing
   d. Blogging

6. This is the name of a popular app for smartphones that you use to share photos.
   a. Flickr
   b. Instagram
   c. Picasa
   d. Shutterfly

7. Which of the following is *not* a blog hosting website?
   a. Xanga
   b. Blog.com
   c. Blogger
   d. StumbleUpon

8. This blog hosting website is owned by Google.
   a. WordPress
   b. Blogger
   c. Twitter
   d. Tumblr

9. This is the software used at websites where the content is generated by users.
   a. Media sharing
   b. Social sharing
   c. Wiki software
   d. Bookmarking

10. This website posts articles with how-to instructions that are created by users.
   a. Wikipedia
   b. wikiHow
   c. Wikimedia Commons
   d. WikiDo

11. Coffee Groundz was profiled in this chapter as a business that uses this social network to accept takeout orders.
   a. Facebook
   b. LinkedIn
   c. Delicious
   d. Twitter

12. Southwest Airlines was profiled in this chapter for its use of this type of social media to promote brand loyalty.
   a. Social bookmarking
   b. Blogging
   c. Tweeting
   d. Wikis

Crossword Puzzle

ACROSS

4 Social networking websites
6 Website that recommends pages
7 Most popular microblogging site
10 Open source blogging software
11 Most popular social network

DOWN

1 Button added to Favorites or Bookmarks bar
2 New contributors practice area in Wikipedia
3 Keywords used to create bookmarks
5 Type of media found at Last.fm
8 Precedes keywords in tweets
9 Popular photo sharing website
10 Website with user-generated content

Matching

Match the term with the statement or definition.

_____ 1. Social Networking	a. Social bookmarking
_____ 2. Google+	b. Targets for copyright litigation
_____ 3. Delicious	c. Photo sharing
_____ 4. Posts	d. Microblog
_____ 5. Twitter	e. Connecting with friends
_____ 6. Pinterest	f. Blog entries
_____ 7. Flickr	g. Virtual boards with pictures
_____ 8. Music sharing sites	h. Family, Friends, Acquaintances, Following

Project 1 Social Media at School, Work, or Volunteer Community

Individual
Deliverable: Presentation

How is social media used at your school, workplace, or volunteer organization? Does the school, business, or organization use Facebook, Twitter, LinkedIn, or blogs? If yes, how are these networks used to engage students, employees, customers, or other clients? Have you engaged with the school, workplace, or charity at these websites, and if so, how?

1. Create a presentation with your answers to the above questions summarizing your school, workplace, or volunteer social media activity only.
2. Save the presentation as **C6–Project1–SocialMedia–Your Name**.
3. Submit the presentation to your instructor in the manner she or he has requested.

Project 2 Establishing a Complete Profile at LinkedIn

Individual
Deliverable: Profile in PDF format

Having a complete profile on LinkedIn is a good idea since many businesses now use LinkedIn to look up prospective candidates. Starting now to build your professional presence before you graduate will give you a head start for your future job search.

1. Create a basic free account at LinkedIn if you do not already have one. If you already have a LinkedIn account, log in and go to your profile.
2. Edit your profile to enter a complete summary of your work experience and education by adding content similar to the information in your current resume. Make sure you have entered text for each of the LinkedIn headings *Summary*, *Experience*, *Education*, *Personal Information*, and *Skills & Expertise*. Be mindful of spelling, grammar, and writing style as this is your online resume.
3. Add a photo to your profile only if you have one that is of professional business quality. Consider asking a classmate to take a photo of you at school if you do not have a good quality picture suitable for a professional profile.
4. When you are finished polishing your profile, use the PDF button on the Profile page (located just above the Summary section) to export a copy of your profile in PDF format.
5. Choose the Save As option and name the PDF document **C6–Project2–MyLinkedInProfile–Your Name**.
6. Submit the PDF document to your instructor in the manner she or he has requested.

Project 3 Finding a Professional Blogger in Your Field of Study

Individual or Pairs
Deliverable: Document, Presentation, or Blog Entry

Blogging is an excellent forum for learning about new trends or issues in a field. Professional bloggers in many industries write regular posts about their fields. Specialized search engines that index blogs such as technorati.com can help you find a blog that is of interest to you.

1. Find a blog where the blogger writes about interesting topics or trends related to your field of study. Consider using technorati.com to locate a blog.
2. Read two to four blog posts and also read the comments posted as feedback.
3. Create a document, presentation, or blog entry with information about the blogger, the title of his or her blog, the two posts you read, the type of comments that were recorded, and your opinion on whether the blog is one that you will follow in the future. Provide the rationale for your decision to subscribe or not to subscribe to the blog. Include the URLs of the blog posts you read.

4. Save the document or presentation as **C6-Project3-ProfessionalBlogger-Your Name**.
5. Submit the document, presentation, or blog URL to your instructor in the manner she or he has requested.

Project 4 Social Media Policy for the Workplace

Pairs or Team
Deliverable: Document or Presentation

The popularity of social networking and blogging is blurring the lines between one's workplace and personal life. Organizations want to ensure that employees use web forums such as social networks and blogs to represent the organization in the best possible light and protect information that is considered confidential or intellectual property. How does a social media policy ensure employees do not post negative comments or photos, or misrepresent fellow colleagues or the organization in any way in social networks and blogs? How does the organization protect its intellectual property or confidential information from being disclosed by employees in blogs or on social networks?

1. Search the Web for examples of social media policies. Find and read at least two social media policy examples.
2. Within your team discuss each policy from both the employer's and the employee's point of view. What do you like and dislike about the policy for each side? Are there any parts of the policy you would rewrite? If yes, how would you rewrite the policy?
3. Create a document or presentation that links to the policies you reviewed and includes your assessment of the questions posed in Step 2.
4. Save the document or presentation as **C6-Project4-SocialMediaPolicies-Your Name**.
5. Submit the document or presentation to your instructor in the manner she or he has requested.

Project 5 Establishing a New Wiki on Green Computing

Pairs or Team
Deliverable: Document or Presentation

Assume that you want to establish a new wiki website with user-generated information about green computing. Are there existing wikis on green computing? If yes, how will you differentiate your wiki? What free wiki hosting sites are available that you can use to start a new wiki?

1. Search the Web for existing wikis on green computing and evaluate a wiki in terms of its organization and usefulness to someone interested in learning about green computing.
2. Plan the organization of pages at your wiki. Create a list of top-level headings or categories and subheadings that you might use for the structure of the new wiki.
3. Search the Web for free wiki hosting services. Choose one website and learn how to use the site to start a new wiki.
4. Create a document or presentation that summarizes your work in Steps 1 through 3. Include the URLs of all websites you used to help you complete this project.
5. Save the document or presentation as **C6-Project5-GreenComputingWiki-Your Name**.
6. Submit the presentation to your instructor in the manner she or he has requested.

Project 6 Greener Computing

Individual, Pairs, or Team
Deliverable: Blog Entry

Assume that you are an intern at a local business that sells pool care supplies. The company heavily promotes its pool maintenance products using print-based flyers with coupons that are distributed using direct mail campaigns. You want to convince the company to use social media tools to distribute coupon codes that people can use online or bring into the store instead of using the mass marketed print-based flyers.

1. Write and post a blog entry that will convince the management of the pool supplies store to consider using social networking tools to promote its products. Within your blog post include links to at least two companies that use social media for this purpose so that the manager can see a few models that support your suggestion.
2. Submit your blog URL to your instructor in the manner she or he has requested.

Optional

Read the blog entry for this project of at least two other classmates and post a comment to each. Submit the URLs of your classmates' blogs with Step 2.

Project 7 Ethics Discussion on Tagging Photos

Team
Deliverable: Document, Blog Entry, or Presentation

Assume that you and several workplace colleagues participated in a charity fundraiser that involved your team running a marathon. At the marathon event, a relative of one of your colleagues took several pictures of the team running at different points in the marathon. A few weeks later you found out that the relative uploaded the photos to his Facebook account and tagged your name in several pictures. You are upset because you never saw the photos, you were not in good running form near the end of the marathon, and you did not give your permission to have the pictures put on a social network where people you do not know will see them.

1. Within your team discuss the ethics involved in tagging someone in photos that are posted to a social network. Should you always get permission first before tagging someone in a photo? Is it OK to tag people in pictures they have not seen? Is it okay to tag people who are not in your network of friends or family? How should you share photos with your friends and family where someone else in the picture is a person they do not know? How should you handle this situation with your work colleague?
2. Prepare a summary of your team's discussion in a document, blog entry, or presentation.
3. Save the document or presentation as **C6-Project7-TagPhotoDiscussion-Your Name**.
4. Submit the document, presentation, or blog entry to your instructor in the manner she or he has requested.

Chapter 7

Computer Security and Privacy

After successfully completing this chapter, you will be able to:

- Explain various types of network risks that occur when computers are connected to a network or the Internet

- Describe techniques used to protect against network and Internet intrusions

- Distinguish various types of malware and methods to prevent malware

- Recognize privacy concerns when using the Internet and strategies for safeguarding personal information

- Identify mobile device security risks and techniques for minimizing risk

Chances are you spend most of your time online browsing the Web, social networking, messaging, shopping, or doing research. A network intrusion can occur any time you are online, leaving you vulnerable to security and privacy breaches. According to Interpol, **cybercrime** (illegal acts involving a computer) is one of the fastest-growing crime areas, with organized crime groups increasingly controlling these illegal activities. Given the prevalence of cybercrime and other malicious computer threats, every person needs to understand and protect his or her computing equipment, data, and personal information from theft or misuse.

Computer security, also known as information security, includes all activities related to protecting hardware, software, and data from loss due to unauthorized access or use, theft, natural disaster, and human error. In this chapter you will learn about the various security and privacy concerns associated with using a computer connected to a network or the Internet. You will also examine computer security issues related to mobile devices.

Unauthorized Access and Unauthorized Use of Computer Resources

TOPIC 7.1

Connecting to a network at home, at work, or at school has many advantages that include sharing access to the Internet and its resources, storage, and software. However, these advantages do not come without risk. Network attacks at business and government organizations occur often. In this topic you will learn about the types of risks associated with using a network, which include unauthorized access and unauthorized use, and ways in which a network can be protected from these threats.

No network is immune from the threat of intrusion by cybercriminals.

Unauthorized access is often the result of network intrusions from hackers.

War driving is when someone drives around a neighborhood looking for unsecured wireless networks.

Unauthorized Access

Using a computer, network, or other resource without permission is referred to as **unauthorized access**. Unauthorized access happens when someone using programming or other technical skills gains entry without permission into a computer or other resource through the network. The term **hacker** refers to an individual who accesses a network without permission, and **hacking** describes activities involved in gaining unauthorized entry into a network's resources. Some hackers have good intentions; they attempt to pinpoint weaknesses in network security and may even be hired by an organization to hack into the organization's network. These types of hackers are called **white hats**. Hackers who gain unauthorized access with malicious intent to steal data or for other personal gain are called **black hats**.

Wireless networks are used often in homes and workplaces. These networks become a target for hackers because wireless networks are easier to infiltrate. An individual with a portable computing device who drives around trying to connect to someone else's unsecured wireless network is **war driving**. Connecting to someone else's wireless network without the network owner's intent or consent to provide access is called **piggybacking** or Wi-Fi piggybacking. This often occurs when a neighbor is within range of another neighbor's or businesses' unsecured wireless network.

Unauthorized Use

Using a computer, network, or other resource for purposes other than the intended uses is referred to as **unauthorized use**. Unauthorized use can occur when an employee uses the employer's computer for activities such as personal emails, personal printing, or personal online shopping without the employer's permission. Another unauthorized use could occur when a student uses a computer on a school campus to send inappropriate messages or participate in other unacceptable conduct.

Strategies to Prevent Unauthorized Access

At home and in the workplace, unauthorized access is prevented by making sure that each person is assigned a unique user name and password. Family members and employees are advised to choose a password that is not easy to guess and never to reveal it to anyone else or write it down in a visible location. At some workplaces, passwords are required to be changed every month, and the reuse of a password may be prohibited. When a device is not in use, the screen should be locked so that the password is required to log back into the computer. Every computer user should choose a **strong password**, which is a password that is difficult to hack by humans or password detection software programs. A strong password meets the following criteria:

- is a minimum of eight characters
- uses a combination of uppercase letters, lowercase letters, numbers, and symbols
- does not contain any dictionary words or words spelled backward
- does not contain consecutive or repeated numbers or letters
- has no personal information such as a birthdate

In the workplace, entry to rooms with computing equipment is often secured with physical locks. Entry to these rooms may also require additional authentication before the door is unlocked. For example, the use of **biometric devices** is becoming more common. Biometric devices authenticate a person's identity using physical characteristics such as a fingerprint, iris scan, or voice recognition.

All networked computers should have user accounts with strong passwords to gain access.

All networked computers should also have a **firewall**, which is hardware, software, or a combination of hardware and software that blocks unwanted access to your network. Operating systems such as Windows install with the firewall feature turned on by default (Figure 7.1). Incoming and outgoing network traffic is

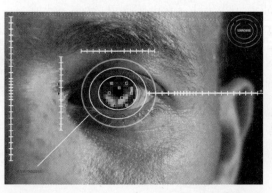

Access to computing equipment may also be controlled using biometric devices such as iris or hand scans.

routed through firewalls that examine each message and block any communication that does not meet the firewall's security criteria. Some routers that are used to share network or Internet access have a built-in firewall, which adds an extra layer of protection. Many organizations with large networks install a piece of networking equipment that is a dedicated firewall.

All networked computers should have a firewall that blocks outside access to your computer.

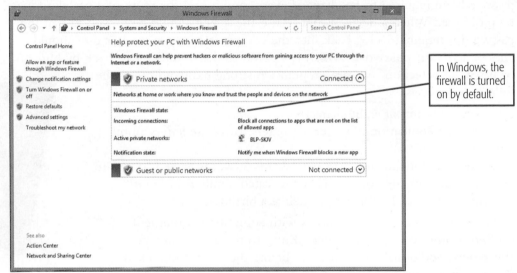

In Windows, the firewall is turned on by default.

Figure 7.1 In Windows, the firewall is turned on by default. You can view the status or change the firewall settings in the Control Panel.

Check This Out

www.onguardonline.gov/media/video-0009-wireless-security

Go here to watch a video on steps to take to protect a home wireless network.

Securing a Wireless Network

At home and at work, wireless routers and access points need to be secured from war drivers and piggybackers. The router or access point should require a security key to gain access. Some devices are sold with a preset password that should be changed to a strong password immediately upon installation. Wireless routers and access points should also be set to use the highest security and **encryption** standard available for the device. Encryption scrambles communications between devices so that the data is not readable. **Wi-Fi Protected Access (WPA)** and **WPA2** are the more recent security standards that authenticate users and employ sophisticated encryption techniques. Enable the WPA2 security standard if possible.

Organizations may also install **intrusion detection software** that analyzes network traffic for suspicious data and alerts network administrators to possible system threats.

A wireless access point should require a security key to connect and should use the highest level of security and encryption standard possible for the device.

Strategies to Prevent Unauthorized Use

An **acceptable use policy (AUP)** is a written policy that describes for employees, students, or other network users the permitted uses for computing equipment and networks. These policies will usually also spell out what is considered inappropriate use of the computers or networks. Some organizations allow employees to use a workplace computer for personal use while the employee is on breaks; however, other organizations prohibit personal use of any kind.

Some organizations use monitoring software that provides reports on activities at each computer. For example, some monitoring software will report on websites visited, web searches conducted, and may even record social networking activity. Email monitoring is also commonly practiced by employers.

Video surveillance, although usually part of a broader safety and security strategy, is another method that can be used by organizations to monitor authorized access and authorized use of computers and networks.

Acceptable use policies spell out authorized and unauthorized activities on a network.

 Blog Topic

Should employers monitor your smartphone?

Many employers provide mobile employees with company-paid smartphones for business use. Does the employer have the right to monitor your Internet and messaging use of the smartphone after business hours? Why or why not?

1. Write and post a blog entry that provides your response to the question.
2. Read at least two of your classmates' blogs and post one comment to each.
3. Submit your blog URL and the URLs of your classmates' blogs for which you provided a comment to your instructor in the manner she or he has requested.

EXPLORE FURTHER

How can I create a strong password that is easy to remember?

Passwords that are eight or more characters that meet all of the criteria mentioned in this topic can be difficult to remember. How can one create a strong password that is also easy to remember?

1. Search for and read a minimum of two articles that describe techniques for creating a strong password that you can remember.
2. Create a presentation that could be used as a self-guided tutorial for a new network user who needs to create a strong password. Include the URLs of the articles that you read.
3. Save the presentation as **C7-Security-StrongPasswords-Your Name**.
4. Submit the presentation to your instructor in the manner she or he has requested.

Botnets and Denial of Service Attacks

Two types of attacks on a computer network that cause disruption to network service are botnets and denial of service attacks. These malicious activities cause widespread network slowdowns and sometimes block authorized activity from taking place. In this topic you will learn how a botnet spreads and how to prevent your computer from becoming compromised. You will also learn how a denial of service attack disrupts a network.

Botnets

A computer that is connected to the Internet and is controlled by a hacker or other cybercriminal without the owner's knowledge is called a **zombie** computer. A collection of zombie computers that work together to conduct an attack on another network is a **botnet**. Botnets are used by hackers or cybercriminals to send spam emails, spread viruses, or steal personal data. In some cases, the botnet may be used to conduct a denial of service attack.

A computer becomes a zombie by becoming infected with software (usually a virus) that is hidden from the user and that is controlled remotely by the hacker or cybercriminal. Generally, the infection happens from one of the following events:

- The individual clicks a link in an email or opens an email attachment that contains the malicious program code, which is then installed on the computer.
- The individual downloads a video, image, or program from a website without realizing the file is a cover for the malicious program code; this method is often used at media sharing or peer-to-peer sharing websites.
- The individual simply visits a website without realizing that the malicious code is being downloaded in the background.

Figure 7.2 illustrates a botnet spreading malicious code to a target computer. Once the target computer is infected, it joins the botnet. Table 7.1 lists signs that may indicate your computer has become a zombie. Keep in mind that some of the symptoms listed in Table 7.1 could indicate other issues such as lack of memory. If necessary, have your PC checked by a professional to determine the cause of any symptoms.

Did You Know?

According to the Quarter 1 2012 McAfee Threats Report, between 4 and 5 million computers globally were infected by botnets, with Colombia, Japan, Poland, Spain, and the United States all seeing increases within the quarter.

To prevent your computer from becoming a zombie, make sure you have antivirus software automatically scheduled to scan and update, update the OS regularly, and have a firewall active at all times. If you think your computer is a zombie, immediately update your antivirus software and perform a full scan. In some cases, you may need to hire professional help to erase your hard disk drive and start from scratch by reinstalling legitimate programs and data.

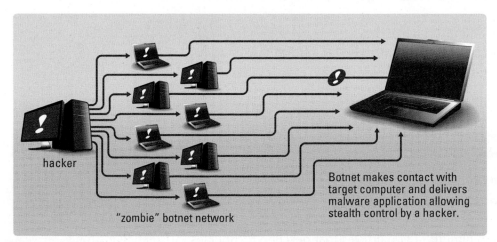

Figure 7.2 A zombie computer is a PC in which the owner is unaware that his or her computer is being used as part of a botnet to attack other computers.

Table 7.1	Signs That Your Computer May Be a Zombie
Your computer may be compromised if . . .	
Your Internet connectivity slows down consistently and dramatically	
Hard disk activity occurs when you are not running any programs (including automatic antivirus or software updates)	
Your computer or a device such as the keyboard or mouse becomes unresponsive	
Hard disk space is filling up unexpectedly	
A different default website appears when you open the browser window	
New desktop icons or toolbars appear that you did not install	
Undeliverable messages appear in your email inbox for people you did not email	

Denial of Service Attacks (DoS)

A **denial of service attack (DoS)** occurs when a network or web server is overwhelmed with network traffic in the form of a constant stream of bogus emails or other messages to the point that the server's response time becomes slow or shuts down completely. Legitimate users are denied access, usually receiving a message that the server is busy. Popular or well-known companies and government websites are often the target of DoS attacks conducted by botnets. Figure 7.3 displays how a DoS attack is orchestrated.

Hackers or other cybercriminals perform DoS attacks for a variety of reasons, some of which include to draw attention to a social or political cause, to embarrass a company or government, to gain notoriety, or to make demands on a company.

Organizations attempt to prevent DoS attacks by employing firewalls, intrusion detection software, and antivirus software tools.

Did You Know ?

In August 2012, WikiLeaks (a website that publishes whistleblower documents) was the victim of a DoS attack that disrupted service for more than a week. Its server was swamped with 10 Gbps of phony network traffic from thousands of Internet addresses.

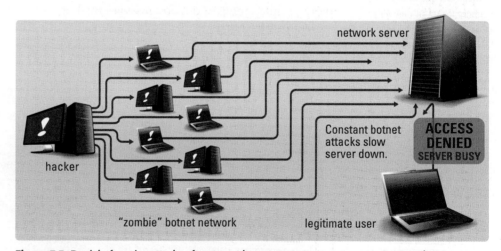

Figure 7.3 Denial of service attacks often target large corporate or government networks.

EXPLORE FURTHER

Best Practices for Preventing Botnets

In this topic you learned some strategies to avoid becoming a zombie computer that include regular updates to antivirus and OS software. Being diligent with email, downloading, sharing files, and web surfing will also help prevent botnets. What best practices should online users adopt?

1. Create a document or presentation with a list of Internet and Web use best practices that every computer user should adopt to help prevent the spread of botnets.
2. Save the document as **C7-Security-PreventBotnets-Your Name**.
3. Submit the document or presentation to your instructor in the manner she or he has requested.

Malware Infections

Any type of malicious software program that is designed to damage, disable, or steal data is called **malware**. Malware installs on your computer without your knowledge usually from email or online activities. Malware programs can delete files, damage files, steal personal data, track your activities, display pop-up windows or messages, or turn your computer into a zombie. In this topic you will learn about common malware that exists in the form of viruses, worms, Trojan horses, and rootkits as well as strategies to prevent malware from infecting your computer.

Viruses

A **virus** is a form of malware that, once installed on a host computer without the owner's knowledge, can replicate itself and spread to other media on the infected computer and to other computers on the network. A virus infects a computer through a variety of means, including:

- downloading and installing infected software
- opening an infected file attachment in an email message (Figure 7.4)
- visiting an infected website
- plugging in an infected USB or other peripheral device
- clicking links in messages (including instant messages) or at untrustworthy websites

A type of virus that is embedded in a document and infects the computer when the user opens the document and enables a macro is called a **macro virus**. Microsoft Office documents were once a favorite target for macro viruses because many people circulate documents via email attachments. Microsoft improved security in its Office programs so that macros are automatically disabled when a document is opened; however, one needs to be aware that enabling the macro may invoke the virus.

Check This Out

home.mcafee.com/virusinfo/

Go here for up-to-date virus information including recent threats, a virus threat meter, and a global virus map.

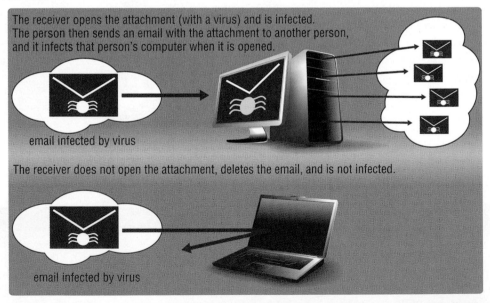

The receiver opens the attachment (with a virus) and is infected. The person then sends an email with the attachment to another person, and it infects that person's computer when it is opened.

email infected by virus

The receiver does not open the attachment, deletes the email, and is not infected.

email infected by virus

Figure 7.4 Opening an email attachment with a virus infects your computer and starts spreading the virus to others.

Worms

A self-replicating program that requires no action on the part of the user to copy itself to another computer on a network is called a **worm**. Your computer can become infected with a worm simply by being connected to an infected network (Figure 7.5). Worms typically exist to backlog network traffic or performance or may even shut down a network.

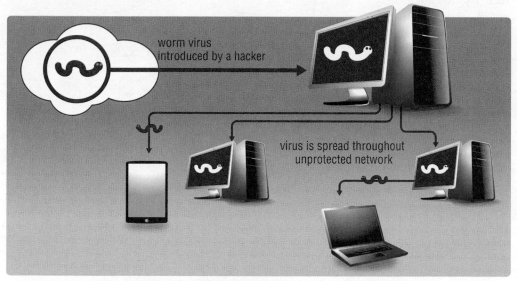

Figure 7.5 A worm automatically sends copies of itself to other computers on the network.

Trojan Horses

A program that disguises itself as a useful program but then infects your computer with malware when you run the application is called a **Trojan horse**. This type of malware is named after the legend in which Greeks concealed themselves inside a hollow wooden horse to invade the city of Troy. Residents of Troy thought the horse was a victory trophy and brought the horse inside the gates of the city, thereby allowing their city to be overtaken. Similarly, Trojan horse malware often appears as a useful program such as antivirus software or an OS update to entice you to run the application that installs the malware. Trojans do not replicate themselves, but nevertheless the damage done by a Trojan can be disastrous as some are designed to send personal information back to a cybercriminal.

A Trojan horse is disguised as a useful program, tricking you into running the program that installs the malware.

Did You Know?

Macs once considered safe from viruses have been the focus of new malware as hackers have turned their attention to popular Apple devices such as the iPad and iPhone.

Rootkits

A **rootkit** program hides on the infected computer and provides a **back door** (way to bypass computer security) for a hacker or other cybercriminal to remotely monitor or take over control of the PC. Using the remote access, the hacker or cybercriminal can run damaging programs or steal personal information. Unlike viruses and worms, the objective of a rootkit is not to spread to other computers but to control the target PC. Rootkits may end up on your computer by installing some other software in which the rootkit piggybacks or via a virus.

A hidden program called a rootkit can allow a hacker to monitor your activity or steal personal data.

Malware Protection

All computer users need to have an up-to-date **antivirus program** running on their computers at all times. Typically, these programs allow you to schedule automatic scans to run on a regular basis. Most programs are also set to scan all incoming emails automatically; however, you should check the settings in the program to ensure you have real-time protection turned on.

Most new computers are sold with an antivirus program already installed, and some OS's include malware protection. If you need an antivirus program or want to upgrade to a comprehensive suite of online threat protection, you can buy a program such as Norton 360 or McAfee All Access that includes protection for smartphones and tablets. You will also find antivirus software available free from companies such as Microsoft or AVG. Microsoft provides Windows Security Essentials free for computers using Windows 7 or earlier, and Windows Defender for computers using Windows 8. In Windows 8, Windows Defender (Figure 7.6) was enhanced to provide the same level of malware protection as Windows Security Essentials.

Norton 360 is a comprehensive package for protection from online threats including viruses, identity theft, and harmful websites.

Several other antivirus programs are available from reputable sources such as Sophos and Kaspersky; however, be wary of downloading free antivirus software from an ad or pop-up window that appears when you are on a website. Go directly to the website of a company that you know is trusted and download free software from there.

Regardless of the malware protection program you choose, make sure it is running automatically, scans regularly, and that a firewall is always active.

Check This Out

www.eset.com/us/online-scanner

Go here for a free on-demand scan of your computer that requires only your browser to work.

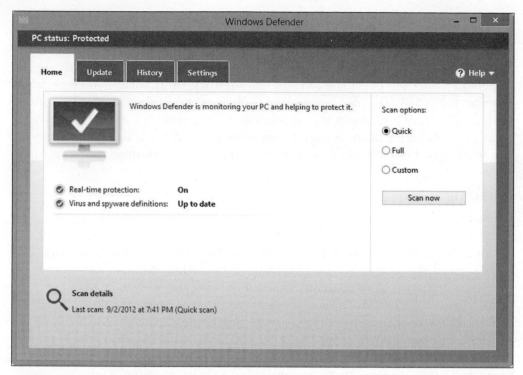

Figure 7.6 Windows Defender is included with Windows 8 and runs automatically to provide protection against malware and other unwanted software.

Do Regular Backups

Making regular backups of your data will provide the best protection of all. Create a routine to back up data regularly. Should malware strike your system, you will have another copy of important information safely stored somewhere else.

EXPLORE FURTHER

What is a logic bomb?

Another type of malware that can cause damage to your computer is a **logic bomb virus**. What are the characteristics of this type of malware? What is the most common type of activity that activates the virus? Are there uses for a logic bomb that are not malicious?

1. Search for information on logic bombs and read at least two articles to find answers to the above questions.

2. Create a document or presentation that summarizes in your own words what you learned about logic bombs. Include the URLs of the websites you used.

3. Save the document or presentation as **C7-Security-LogicBombs-Your Name**.

4. Submit the document or presentation to your instructor in the manner she or he has requested.

TOPIC 7.4

Phishing, Pharming, and Clickjacking Threats

A growing area of cybercrime involves online fraud or scams that are designed to trick unsuspecting users into revealing personal information so the criminal can steal money from the individual or engage in **identity theft**. Identity theft occurs when an individual's personal information is obtained by a criminal who then uses the information to buy products or services under the victim's name or otherwise pose as the victim for financial gain. In this topic you will learn about three scams that are designed to trick someone into revealing personal information.

Phishing

Phishing (pronounced *fishing*) is the term that describes activities that appear to be initiated by a legitimate organization (such as one's bank) in an attempt to obtain personal information that can be used in fraud, theft, or identity theft. A popular email phishing technique involves an individual receiving a message that appears to be from a bank or credit card company and directs him or her to click a link (Figure 7.7). The link goes to a bogus website that appears to be valid and may even include the real bank's logo and color scheme. At the phishing website, the user is prompted to enter his or her personal information such as a user name, password, bank account number, or credit card number. If the individual complies, he or she will have given critical personal information to a criminal who will use the information to transfer money from the individual's bank accounts or to charge purchases to a credit card.

Phishing is also growing on social networking sites such as Facebook and Twitter. With the high volume of activity at social networks, criminals are targeting these networks for new scams. One scam used a link to a video in a Facebook message that, when clicked, directed the person to a page that looked like the Facebook login page but was not genuine. Users typed in their email address and password thinking they were logging into Facebook but instead were providing the information to a cybercriminal.

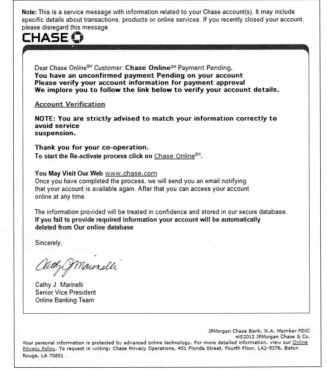

Figure 7.7 This message received by Chase customers was a phishing attempt to trick users into clicking the links and revealing account information.

Pharming

A **pharming** scam is similar to phishing except that the individual is tricked into typing in personal information at a phony website that appears to be the real website requested by the individual. For example, an individual enters a web address for his or her bank in the browser and is directed instead to a pharming website. The web page at the pharming website looks legitimate, so the individual proceeds to enter personal information.

Phishing and pharming scams employ **spoofing** techniques where a sender's email address is altered to a phony address that appears legitimate to the email recipient, or an IP address is altered to appear to be a trusted source.

Pharming scams redirect you to a phony website where you are prompted to enter personal information.

Clickjacking

Clickjacking occurs when a button, graphic, or link on a web page appears to be real but, when clicked, causes malicious software to run. The malicious software code is hidden on the web page so that an individual has no idea he or she is not clicking a real link. Clicking the bogus button, graphic, or link typically directs the person to another website where personal information is requested. Some clickjacks are used to download a virus onto a computer.

In January 2012, Facebook and the Washington State Office of the Attorney General filed a lawsuit against a company suspected of using clickjacking techniques. In one scheme, bogus Like buttons redirected users to advertising pages where the scammers received money for each wayward clicker.

Clickjacking scams use buttons, graphics, or links to redirect users from legitimate websites or run malicious software.

Phishing and clickjacking scams are often initiated in email. Delete messages you receive that ask you to click a link to update information. Never click links in unsolicited email messages. Before typing personal information, examine the URL and other text on the page. Phony websites usually have spelling or grammar errors, or the URL for a false website will have a slightly different domain name or character substitution in the name such as the number 1 instead of the letter i.

EXPLORE   **FURTHER**

What is social engineering?

Security experts know that the weakest link in computer security is humans. Unfortunately, cybercriminals also know this and employ **social engineering** tactics to gain unauthorized access to a network or trick individuals into revealing personal information. What is social engineering?

1. Search for articles on social engineering. Find and read at least two articles that describe social engineering tactics including tactics used at social networking websites.
2. Create a document or presentation that summarizes in your own words what you learned about social engineering. Include the URLs of the websites you used.
3. Save the document or presentation as **C7-Security-SocialEngineering-Your Name**.
4. Submit the document or presentation to your instructor in the manner she or he has requested.

TOPIC 7.5

Information Privacy

With so much information collected and stored online, individuals and companies are increasingly concerned with information privacy. **Information privacy** is the right of individuals or organizations to control the information that is collected about them. Consider all of the websites at which you have set up accounts and the personal information you provided at each site. Consider also that some websites track the pages you visit and store information about you. Software may be installed on your computer that is tracking everything you do. In this topic you will learn about privacy concerns related to online activities.

Cookies

A web server may send a small text file to be stored on your computer's hard disk that contains data about you such as your user name and the pages you visited. This text file is called a **cookie** and is used to identify you when you return to the website. In many cases, the use of cookies is welcomed to prefill a login or customize your viewing preferences at an e-commerce site. However, cookies might also be used for unwanted purposes such as tracking your activities or gathering information about you without your permission.

All Internet browsers provide the ability for you to control how cookies are handled. Figure 7.8 shows the Privacy tab where you can choose how to manage cookies in the Internet Options dialog box of Internet Explorer 10. The default setting is *Medium*, which blocks first- and third-party cookies that might be used to contact you without your consent or that have no compact privacy policy.

Dragging the slider up to the top changes the privacy setting to block all cookies and all the way down accepts all cookies. In between, options set the privacy setting to Low, Medium, Medium High, or High.

As you move the slider bar up or down, the description for each level of privacy displays here.

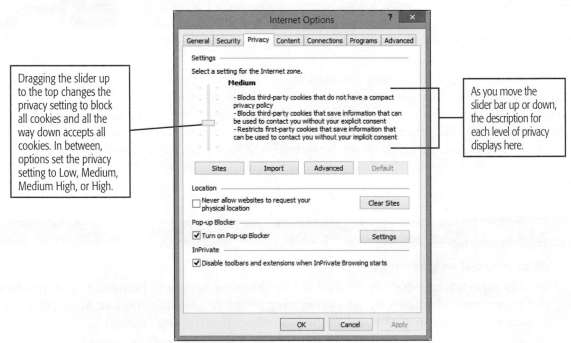

Figure 7.8 Internet browser software such as IE10 provides tools to help you manage cookies.

Spyware

Software programs that exist on your computer without your knowledge and track your activities are referred to as **spyware**. Some spyware may be on a workplace computer so that the employer can monitor your online activities. Other spyware may be used by websites to target ads to your preferences. Antivirus programs typically include spyware detection and removal.

Software programs responsible for pop-up ads that appear on your desktop or while viewing web pages are the result of software referred to as **adware**. These unwelcome ads often piggyback spyware onto your computer.

Spyware tracks your online activities.

Keystroke Loggers   A version of spyware called **keystroke logger**, or **keylogger**, may be activated as part of a rootkit or Trojan horse that records every keystroke you type and sends it back to a cybercriminal. Keystroke loggers may be used to obtain your bank account number and password or other personal information that leads to identity theft. Some keystroke logger software is promoted on the Internet to businesses as a computer security tool and to parents who want to monitor their children's online activity.

Spam

Spam is electronic junk mail—unsolicited emails sent to a large group of people at the same time. Spam messages entice readers to buy something or are phishing messages. Spam messaging has infiltrated social networks and text messages. According to Symantec, more than 60 percent of email is spam. **Twitter bots** are software programmed to follow people based on popular keywords. When a user clicks a link in the comment that appears as a response to a tweet, they receive spam or malware. Beware of followers with strange handles.

Obtaining a store loyalty card or registering for free accounts often requires you provide your email address. These databases of names and email addresses are sold for marketing purposes, which is how you end up with spam. Many people use a free web-based email account such as Windows Live Hotmail or Gmail for online activities only. This prevents spam from invading a regular email inbox. Sign up for a new account when spam at the free account becomes onerous.

Data Privacy in the Cloud

When storing pictures, documents, or other data at a cloud provider's website such as Flickr or Dropbox, find out the privacy and security policies that affect your data. Typically, you control the data privacy by restricting who can see a file. However, unanticipated issues could arise such as an employee of the cloud provider being able to view the contents of your files. To be safe, never post files at a cloud provider that contain sensitive information,

Did You Know ?

In October 2011, a keystroke logger virus was found in the U.S. military's network that recorded pilots' keystrokes as they flew drone missions over Afghanistan and other war zones.

Spyware called keystroke loggers record every keystroke you type.

Spam is estimated to account for more than 60 percent of all email traffic!

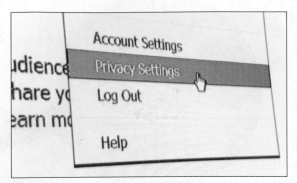

Change privacy settings at social networks such as Facebook and other cloud providers to control information about you that is available for anyone to view.

Check This Out

www.epic.org
Go here for up-to-date information on privacy issues.

such as your birthdate and social security number that could make you vulnerable to identity theft.

At social networks such as Facebook and Twitter, make sure you review and change privacy settings so that only the information you want public is viewable by anyone. When posting information at social networks, also consider that those friends who see the information could inadvertently share something personal about you with someone else. Cybercriminals are trolling social networks for personal data they can mine for financial gain.

Ways to Protect Personal Information

When shopping online or conducting other business that requires a financial transaction, make sure the URL at the website begins with *https* and that you see a small closed padlock next to the address bar or in the Status bar of the browser window. These signs indicate a secure website using a protocol that protects data sent to the site with **Transport Layer Security (TLS)**. TLS encrypts transmitted data so that the data is unreadable if intercepted.

Table 7.2 provides strategies you can use to protect personal information while pursuing online activities. Ultimately, the responsibility rests with you to keep sensitive information private and to be diligent at websites where you provide personal data. Check privacy policies and do not reveal information that you do not feel is necessary for the purpose of the visit.

Table 7.2   Strategies to Protect Personal Information
Ways to Minimize Tracking of Your Personal Information
Fill in only the fields marked with asterisks at websites that ask you for personal information when registering for an account; these are the minimum fields required to obtain an account.
Make sure the privacy setting for cookies in the browser you use is set to block cookies for sites that do not have a privacy policy or have not received your consent. You may want to consider blocking all cookies.
At websites that require a birthdate, such as Facebook, make sure you hide the date in your profile.
Have different user names and passwords for online shopping, social networks, and banking.
Do not allow apps or websites to tag your location. Geo-location apps on your smartphone sound cool, but consider that a third party could be tracking your every movement.
Use a free web-based email account for online shopping and social networks and keep your regular email address for other purposes.
If your ISP does not use a spam filter on your email account, find and install anti-spam software on your own.
Delete spam messages right away without opening them.
Unsubscribe to mailing lists that you think are selling your email address for marketing purposes.
Regularly clear the history in your browser.
Make sure the antivirus program you use includes anti-spyware and that the program is set to automatically update and scan your computer regularly.
Make sure a firewall is active at all times you are online.
Shred documents with personal information before discarding them.

Blog Topic

Should employers monitor employee activities?

Video cameras, email monitoring, website monitoring, and keystroke loggers are some of the ways in which employers can keep tabs on what their employees are up to at the workplace. Generally, employees should not have an expectation of privacy when using employer-owned computing equipment. Still, isn't all this monitoring of your activities an invasion of your privacy? What about using the employer's computer on your lunch hours and breaks? Shouldn't that be considered your personal time?

1. Write and post a blog entry that provides your opinion about the questions.

2. Read at least two of your classmates' blogs and post one comment to each.

3. Submit your blog URL and the URLs of your classmates' blogs for which you provided a comment to your instructor in the manner she or he has requested.

EXPLORE FURTHER

Learning about Privacy Notices

Websites that collect personal information also have a privacy notice that spells out how the organization will use the personal data you provide. Have you ever read a privacy notice? What should a typical privacy notice include?

1. Go to the website of an e-tailer that you have used in the past, and find and read the Privacy Policy or Privacy Notice link. If you have not made an online purchase, visit the website of a well-known e-tailer such as Amazon.

2. Create a document or presentation with a summary of how personal information will be used, stored, and safeguarded by the e-tailer. Include the URL to the policy you used.

3. Save the document or presentation as **C6-Security-PrivacyPolicy-Your Name**.

4. Submit the document or presentation to your instructor in the manner she or he has requested.

Mobile malware is on the rise! Make sure your smartphone or tablet has mobile security software to stop the spread of viruses and spyware.

Mobile Device Security

Portable devices such as notebooks, ultrabooks, tablets, and smartphones have unchained people from their homes and offices; however, the portable nature of these devices makes them vulnerable to security risks. In this topic, you will examine the various security risks for mobile workers and methods used to protect hardware and data.

Mobile Malware

According to McAfee Security, **mobile malware** (viruses designed for mobile devices) increased 1,200 percent in the first quarter of 2012. Some of the increase is attributed to improved detection methods; however, a massive increase in viruses for mobile devices is still evident. Additionally, McAfee reported finding the first Android Trojan horse virus in 2012. Most mobile malware targets Android devices because of the open source nature of the mobile OS; however, no mobile OS is without risk. Make sure all mobile devices, including tablets and smartphones, have mobile security software to prevent malware infections.

Lost or Stolen Mobile Devices

Securing a mobile device with locks, biometrics, or remote tools is a necessity to protect against the loss of a smartphone, tablet, or notebook computer due to theft or absentmindedness. Recent reports have shown an increase in the theft of mobile devices. While the hardware is easily replaced, the personal information and data stored on these devices is a major risk for individuals and employers. The following tools assist with securing mobile devices and data:

- Physical locks with cables that attach a notebook to a table or desk in a public place are a deterrent to thieves looking for an easy target.
- Many devices now come equipped with fingerprint readers that restrict access to the authenticated user only.
- Technology for remote wiping, locking, and tracking of a lost or stolen mobile device allows the owner to wipe the device clean of data and track the device's location.
- A strong password or passcode for access to the data should be enabled on all devices; should the device be stolen or lost, the password/passcode may provide enough time to employ remote wiping utilities.
- Regular backups of data stored on mobile devices should be mandatory.

Mobile devices can be secured with fingerprint readers, passcodes, and physical cable locks to restrict access.

Bluetooth Risks

Bluetooth technology, which wirelessly connects and exchanges data between two devices in close proximity, is subject to risk from intrusion from others within range. Bluetooth range is approximately 30 feet. When using Bluetooth in a public space with many people nearby, a risk exists that someone else can connect to your device and send you a virus or access personal data. Turn Bluetooth on only when needed and turn it off as soon as you are finished with it to prevent others from accessing your device. Consider installing a Bluetooth firewall app that will secure your device from unwanted intrusions.

Mobile devices carry risks unique to their portable nature. Employers may require employees with mobile devices to abide by a mobile computing policy that requires employees to take responsible measures to secure notebooks, tablets, or smartphones while away from the office, make frequent backups to a secure site, and password-protect all sensitive company documents stored on the device.

Turn off Bluetooth when using a mobile device in a crowded place.

Be Aware of Shoulder Surfers!

If you are viewing sensitive information on a mobile device, protect your screen from shoulder surfers. Privacy screens for notebooks, tablets, and smartphones prevent shoulder surfers from seeing personal or confidential information.

Career Connection

Computer Security Experts

Symantec CEO Enrique Salem told a New York Technology Summit group in June 2012 that the United States does not have enough security professionals. Computer security is a top priority for many organizations to combat the increase in network attacks and cybercrime. Security professionals are among the highest paid IT workers. A bachelor's degree in computer science or computer security is generally required for a computer security career. Certifications attract higher salaries with the Certified Information Security Manager (CISM) and Certified Information Systems Security Professional (CISSP) the most widely recognized security certifications.

EXPLORE FURTHER

Using Public Wi-Fi Wisely

Many public places now provide free access to Wi-Fi networks. These networks are unsecured to make them as convenient to use as possible. What precautions should you take when using a public Wi-Fi network to connect your notebook, tablet, or smartphone?

1. Search for articles on public Wi-Fi hotspot security. Find and read at least two articles with tips for using these networks safely. Choose five tips you think are the most important.

2. Create a presentation with one slide for each tip where you describe how to use public Wi-Fi safely and securely. Include a sixth slide with the URLs of the articles you used.

3. Save the presentation as **C7-Security-PublicWi-Fi-Your Name**.

4. Submit the presentation to your instructor in the manner she or he has requested.

Concepts Review

Topic	Key Concepts	Key Terms
Unauthorized Access and Unauthorized Use of Computer Resources	Unauthorized access occurs when someone, usually a hacker, gains entry without permission to a computer through a network (referred to as hacking).	Cybercrime
	White hats are hackers that gain entry into a network to pinpoint weaknesses in the network security.	Computer security
		Unauthorized access
	Black hats are hackers that gain entry into a network with malicious intent.	Hacker
		Hacking
	Wireless networks are often the target of war drivers or piggybackers because unsecured wireless networks are easy to infiltrate.	White hats
		Black hats
	Unauthorized use is performing activities on a computer other than the intended uses.	War driving
		Piggybacking
	A strong password is difficult to hack by humans or password detection software programs.	Unauthorized use
		Strong password
	Physical entry to rooms with computing equipment at workplaces is secured by locks and biometric devices.	Biometric devices
		Firewall
	A firewall is hardware, software, or a combination of hardware and software that blocks unauthorized access.	Wi-Fi Protected Access (WPA)
		WPA2
	Wireless routers and access points should be protected with security keys and the highest possible encryption standards.	Encryption
		Intrusion detection software
	Organizations may use intrusion detection software to thwart network attacks.	Acceptable use policy (AUP)
	An acceptable use policy spells out appropriate and inappropriate use of computing equipment in the workplace.	
Botnets and Denial of Service Attacks	A zombie is a computer controlled by someone else without the owner's knowledge.	Zombie
		Botnet
	A collection of zombie computers that attack a network is called a botnet.	Denial of service attack (DoS)
	A computer becomes a zombie by being infected with software that is hidden from the user and is controlled remotely by the hacker or cybercriminal.	
	To prevent a computer from becoming a zombie, scan regularly with up-to-date antivirus software, update the OS regularly, and make sure a firewall is always active.	
	A denial of service attack (DoS) occurs when a botnet attacks a network by sending a constant stream of messages that slow down or completely shut down a server.	
	Corporate and government networks are often the target for DoS attacks.	
	Organizations use firewalls, intrusion detection software, and antivirus tools to prevent DoS attacks.	

continued....

Malware Infections	Malware refers to any type of malicious software.	Malware
	A virus is a form of malware that replicates itself, spreading to other media on the infected computer and to other computers.	Virus
		Macro virus
	A macro virus is a virus that is embedded in a macro in a Microsoft Office document; when the user enables the macro, the virus infects the computer.	Worm
		Trojan horse
	A worm is a self-replicating program that infects other computers on a network without user action.	Rootkit
		Back door
	A Trojan horse is a program that appears to the user to be a useful program but which in fact is malware.	Antivirus program
		Logic bomb virus
	Rootkit programs are hidden from the owner and are used by a hacker or cybercriminal to control a computer remotely.	
	Antivirus programs detect and remove malware.	
Phishing, Pharming, and Clickjacking Threats	Identity theft occurs when personal information is obtained by a criminal who uses the information for financial gain.	Identity theft
		Phishing
	Phishing messages include links to websites that appear legitimate but are intended to steal personal information.	Pharming
		Spoofing
	Phishing is increasing on social networks.	Clickjacking
	Pharming is where a phony website appears after the user types a web address into the address bar of a browser.	Social engineering
	Spoofing techniques alter a sender's email or web address to appear legitimate.	
	Clickjacking occurs when a user clicks a phony button, image, or link and is redirected to another website or a virus downloads.	
	Phishing and clickjacking scams are often initiated in email messages.	
Information Privacy	Information privacy refers to the rights of individuals to control information that is collected about them.	Information privacy
		Cookie
	A cookie is a small text file placed on your hard drive by a web server with information about your user name and the pages you visited.	Spyware
		Adware
	Spyware tracks your activities without your knowledge.	Keystroke logger
	Adware displays pop-up ads on your desktop or at web pages.	Keylogger
	Adware will sometimes piggyback spyware onto your computer.	Spam
	Keystroke loggers, or keyloggers, record every keystroke you type and send the data to a cybercriminal.	Twitter bots
		Transport Layer Security (TLS)
	Spam is unsolicited email sent to large groups of people.	
	Find out the privacy and security policies in effect at cloud providing websites where you store pictures and documents.	
	Review and change privacy settings at social networks like Facebook and Twitter.	
	Make sure *https* is the beginning of an address at any website at which you enter personal information for a financial transaction and that a closed padlock icon displays.	
	Transport Layer Security (TLS) encrypts data transmitted to a secure website.	

continued....

Topic	Key Concepts	Key Terms
Mobile Device Security	Mobile malware are viruses designed for mobile devices.	Mobile malware
	All mobile devices including tablets and smartphones should have mobile security software installed.	
	Android devices are attacked more frequently due to their open source mobile operating system.	
	Mobile devices should be secured with locks, biometrics, or remote wiping and tracking tools in case of loss or theft.	
	Using Bluetooth in a public space leaves you vulnerable; someone else with a Bluetooth device can access your smartphone, tablet, or notebook and send you a virus or steal personal data.	
	Employers may require mobile workers to abide by a mobile computing policy that requires them to take responsible measures to secure their devices.	
	Regular backups of data on mobile devices may be required as part of a mobile computing policy.	

Multiple Choice

1. A type of hacker that breaks into a computer network to pinpoint network weaknesses is known as a _____.
   a. Piggybacker
   b. Black hat
   c. White hat
   d. War logger

2. Hardware or software that blocks unwanted access to a network is a(n) _____.
   a. War driver
   b. Firewall
   c. Encrypter
   d. White hat

3. This term refers to a computer that is controlled by a hacker without the owner's knowledge.
   a. Botnet
   b. DoS
   c. Bot
   d. Zombie

4. This type of attack overwhelms a network server with the intent of slowing or shutting down the server.
   a. Denial of service
   b. Bot attack
   c. Piggybacking
   d. War driving

5. This type of virus is often embedded in a Microsoft Office document.
   a. Rootkit virus
   b. Worm virus
   c. Trojan horse virus
   d. Macro virus

6. This type of virus is hidden from the owner and allows the computer to be controlled remotely.
   a. Rootkit virus
   b. Worm virus
   c. Macro virus
   d. Logic bomb virus

7. This term describes activities that appear to be from legitimate organizations but that have malicious intent.
   a. Rootkit virus
   b. Logic bomb virus
   c. Phishing
   d. War driving

8. A phony button, graphic, or link on a website is used for _____.
   a. Phishing
   b. Pharming
   c. Spoofing
   d. Clickjacking

9. This is a small text file placed on your hard drive after visiting a website.
   a. Spyware
   b. Cookie
   c. Adware
   d. Spam

10. This type of spyware records everything you type.
    a. Adware
    b. Spam
    c. Cookie
    d. Keylogger

11. Bluetooth range is approximately _____ feet.
    a. 10
    b. 20
    c. 30
    d. 40

12. Viruses designed for a notebook, tablet, or smartphone are referred to by this term.
    a. Mobile malware
    b. Mobile mania
    c. Mobile risk
    d. Mobile software

Crossword Puzzle

ACROSS

7 Program disguised as useful software
8 Desktop pop-up ad
9 Software that tracks your activities
11 Scrambles data to make it unreadable
12 Bogus buttons at websites

DOWN

1 Devices frequently targeted for mobile malware
2 Malicious software
3 Wireless technology for short ranges
4 Often used to conduct DoS attack
5 Device authenticates physical characteristic
6 Junk mail
10 Links to phony websites in emails

Matching

Match the term with the statement or definition.

_____ 1. Mobile malware
_____ 2. WPA2
_____ 3. Denial of service
_____ 4. Worm
_____ 5. Botnet
_____ 6. Pharming
_____ 7. War driving
_____ 8. Https

a. Collection of zombies
b. Self-replicating virus
c. Spoofing a web address
d. Android Trojan horse
e. Transport Layer Security (TLS)
f. Breaking into a wireless network
g. Server is busy messages
h. Wireless security standard

Project 1 Computer Security Risks for Small Businesses

Individual or Pairs
Deliverable: Presentation

Assume you are helping an aunt who is working on opening a new café in your area. The café will feature daily lunch specials in addition to dessert treats, cold drinks, and fair trade coffee beverages. Free Wi-Fi access will be available to customers in the café. At a secure website, customers will be able to order and pay for lunch as well as receive daily coupons and specials at a Facebook page. Your aunt is also considering using Twitter to promote daily specials. To properly plan for her computing needs, your aunt has asked for your help in assessing the computer security risks that she may encounter.

1. Create a presentation that will summarize all of the risks and strategies for mitigating risks that have been explored in this chapter. The information presented should be a summary only of high-level points for your aunt to consider as she plans her business needs.
2. Save the presentation as **C7-Project1-SummaryOfSecurityRisks-Your Name**.
3. Submit the presentation to your instructor in the manner she or he has requested.

Project 2 Acceptable Use and Computer Security Policies

Individual or Pairs
Deliverable: Document or Presentation

Assume the aunt you have been helping launch a new café is now ready to hire staff and wants to have a solid Acceptable Use Policy and Computer Security Policy in place before employee training begins. She has asked you to develop a list of points that should be included in the two policies that include appropriate and inappropriate use of computer and network resources and responsibilities related to ensuring that the computing resources are not compromised with malware.

1. Create a document or presentation that provides your aunt with a list of points that should be included in the Acceptable Use Policy and a second list of points that should be included in the Computer Security Policy. *Hint: Use your school's AUP as a guideline.*
2. Save the document or presentation as **C7-Project2-AUPandSecurityPolicy-Your Name**.
3. Submit the document or presentation to your instructor in the manner she or he has requested.

Project 3 How Does AntiVirus Software Detect and Remove Viruses?

Individual or Pairs
Deliverable: Document or Presentation

The importance of regularly updating antivirus programs has been stressed throughout this chapter. How do antivirus programs work to detect a new virus on your computer? Why is updating the software so important? When a virus is found, how does the software remove the virus from your computer?

1. Search for information on how antivirus programs work to find answers to the above questions.
2. Create a document or presentation with a summary in your own words that describes the detection and removal techniques used by antivirus programs. Include the URLs of the websites you used.
3. Save the document or presentation as **C7-Project3-AntiVirusPrograms-Your Name**.
4. Submit the document or presentation to your instructor in the manner she or he has requested.

Project 4 College Students the Target of Identity Thieves

Pairs or Team

Deliverable: Information Flyer for New Students

According to the U.S. Department of Justice, individuals 18 to 24 years old are more likely to experience identity theft than others. College-age students represent one-quarter of identity theft victims. Why are college students the frequent targets of identity thieves? What can a college student do to minimize his or her risk of identity theft?

1. Search for information related to identity theft aimed at college-age students to find answers to the above questions.
2. Create a flyer that your school could insert in a new student's orientation package that warns students of the risk of identity theft and provides information on how to prevent it.
3. Save the flyer as **C7-Project4-StudentIdentityTheft-Your Name**.
4. Submit the flyer and the URLs for the websites you used to your instructor in the manner she or he has requested.

Project 5 Public Key and Symmetric Key Encryption

Pairs or Team

Deliverable: Document or Presentation with Diagrams

Encryption, a part of cryptography, is a method used to protect data as it is transmitted across a network. Encrypted data is scrambled so that a hacker will not be able to read intercepted messages. In this chapter, encryption was recommended to secure data transmitted on a wireless network and when conducting online financial transactions. Computer encryption systems are generally based on public key or symmetric key categories. How do these two encryption models differ?

1. Search for information on public key and symmetric key encryption. Read at least two articles that describe each encryption model process.
2. Next, search for images that diagram public key and symmetric key encryption models. Choose a diagram for each model that you think best illustrates each encryption model.
3. Create a document or presentation that summarizes in your own words how each encryption model works and include the diagram that you selected to illustrate the process. Be sure to cite the diagram in your document or presentation and include the URLs of the websites that you used.
4. Save the document or presentation as **C7-Project5-Encryption-Your Name**.
5. Submit the document or presentation to your instructor in the manner she or he has requested.

Project 6 Greener Computing

Individual, Pairs, or Team

Deliverable: Blog Entry

Cloud computing has been advocated as a way to practice green computing. By using SaaS tools at a cloud provider, a business or individual has no need for high-end computing devices to act as servers or PCs. Lower-powered hardware is a viable option that reduces an individual's or company's carbon footprint. Another advantage is the benefit of online collaboration reducing the need for travel by team members. However, adopting SaaS does not come without security and privacy risks. What are the risks and how can risks be mitigated?

1. Search for information on cloud computing security and privacy risks and methods to minimize risk. Read at least two articles that provide information to answer the above question.

2. Write and post a blog entry that describes in your own words cloud computing security and privacy risks and strategies for minimizing the risks.

3. Submit your blog URL to your instructor in the manner she or he has requested.

Optional

Read the blog entry for this project of at least two other classmates and post a comment to each. Submit the URLs of your classmates' blogs with Step 3.

Project 7 Ethics Discussion on Revealing Company Secrets

Team
Deliverable: Document, Blog Entry, or Presentation

You work in a company that is developing web-based software that homeowners can use to remotely adjust heating, lighting, and security systems in their homes. The software program is easier to use than others on the market and will be priced competitively. You have recently learned that a member of the team has been talking about the new software with her friends on Facebook. Another person in the company who is on the colleague's friends list has told you that she is revealing information about the program features and pricing. You have mentioned to her that she should not be discussing the project on a social network. She replied that it's OK because it's only her friends that see the postings.

1. Within your team discuss the ethics involved in revealing company secrets on a social network. Is it okay to discuss a project since only people in a friends list see the postings? Why or why not? Are there security and privacy issues the colleague is not considering when she responded that it was OK? How should you handle this situation? Is there any action the individual who told you about the matter should have taken? How can a company prevent an individual from revealing company secrets on a social network?

2. Prepare a summary of your team's discussion in a document, blog entry, or presentation.

3. Save the document or presentation as **C7-Project7-CompanySecretsDiscussion-Your Name**.

4. Submit the document, presentation, or blog entry to your instructor in the manner she or he has requested.

Appendix A

Buying a New Computing Device

Buying a new notebook, tablet, or smartphone requires an understanding of some of the technical jargon that fills a computer ad. An experienced electronics sales associate will help you choose the right device; however, some people like to shop online or know in advance the features that are important to consider. In this appendix you will learn tips for shopping for a device that meets your needs in a step-by-step buying process model.

Buying a New PC, Tablet, or Smartphone

Are you in the market for a new computer or are you looking to add a second device to supplement a computer you already own? Many people own more than one computing device. Perhaps you have a desktop PC and want a notebook or tablet to use for school. You may have an older cell phone and want a newer smartphone that you can use to access the Internet or view documents while you're on the go. The following pages will guide you through a decision-making process that will help you make an informed purchase. Spending a little time planning your requirements will save time and money and help you avoid making an impulse purchase that you may regret.

A section with tips for making a smartphone purchase is included at the end of the appendix. The following steps are geared toward deciding how to buy a personal computer or tablet.

Step 1 Determine Your Maximum Budget

Before you start browsing computer ads, know how much money you can afford to spend. Computers are sold in a wide range of prices from a few hundred dollars to a few thousand dollars to suit a variety of budgets. Setting the maximum price will help narrow the search when you are ready to shop.

Start by setting the maximum budget.

Step 2 Decide on a Desktop, Notebook, Ultrabook, Netbook, or Tablet

Desktop PCs are declining in usage, but nevertheless, some people prefer the stationary system unit that sits on or under a desk with an attached monitor, keyboard, and mouse. If you normally work in one place and have the physical space to accommodate the larger PC, a desktop is a good value. The desktop PCs of today last longer than earlier desktops and are easier to upgrade than most mobile devices. All-in-one PCs pack all of the system unit components behind the monitor, which requires less desktop. Desktop PCs also generally include a large screen.

Decide between a desktop PC, notebook, Ultrabook, netbook, or tablet.

If you are looking for a portable computer for school or work, or one that you can move around your house, then a notebook, Ultrabook, or netbook is a good choice. Which option you choose will depend on how you plan to use it. A notebook computer provides everything that a traditional desktop PC provides in a portable case that you can carry around. An Ultrabook is lighter and slimmer than a notebook but sacrifices an optical drive to achieve the slim, lightweight design. Consider if you want to watch DVD or Blu-ray movies on your computer; if you do, you'll need a notebook. If your computing needs are primarily just surfing the Web and sending and receiving email, a netbook with its smaller screen size may be for you. A netbook will limit your choice of applications and does not include a DVD or Blu-ray drive, so if you have the money to afford a notebook, you may be better off with a more powerful unit.

Tablets are smaller and lighter than notebooks. If screen size is important to you, a notebook or Ultrabook will be your preference. Typically, people buy a tablet as a secondary device to a desktop or notebook PC. However, newer tablets, convertible tablet PCs (screens rotate 180 degrees to fold over a keyboard), and tablets that are supplied with a docking station that includes a full-size keyboard are available. If you want to use touch-enabled screens or a stylus to handwrite notes, a tablet is the way to go.

Step 3 Decide on the Software Applications and Operating System

Computers come with an operating system and some software applications preinstalled so you may be tempted to skip over this step. However, watch for systems that preinstall limited trial editions of software applications. These applications usually expire within a short time frame such as 90 days or at some point within the first year after purchase. Following expiration, you have to pay a software license fee to continue using the software. This will affect your budget, so you need to find out in advance if you will need to set aside money to pay for software applications separately.

Choosing the software applications you need will determine the hardware and operating systems requirements.

Check your school's computer store to see if you can buy software applications at academic pricing. Some academic licenses have to be purchased, through your school to qualify for student discounts; however, increasingly, retailers are able to offer the same pricing upon proof of student registration.

It pays to shop around for the best price on the software application you want to install. Some software publishers offer coupons for web-based purchases and some retailers can offer attractive pricing when you package the software with your hardware. Look for a software suite that will bundle together multiple applications in one product. These are always a better value than buying individual applications.

Deciding on the software applications you want to use will help you choose the appropriate hardware and OS. All software applications will specify the system requirements that are needed to run the software. You will notice that software companies will specify minimum and recommended system requirements. Go for the recommended requirements in a new purchase since the minimum requirements usually mean performance is slower than the recommended requirements. Pay particular attention to the specified operating system that is needed to run the application, the amount of RAM, the processor speed, and the disk storage used by the application(s).

Apple PCs and mobile devices are generally more expensive than Windows-compatible computers.

Mac versus PC Software applications are typically available in a Mac or a Windows-compatible PC edition. With the popularity of cloud-based software solutions, the computer platform is becoming less of an issue than it was for early computers. Deciding between Mac and PC is becoming more a personal choice and a budget issue. Apple PCs are more expensive than Windows-compatible PCs. Apple's iPad and iPhone are also more expensive than Windows-compatible or Android tablets and smartphones.

Apple fans are fiercely loyal to the brand and will argue that the extra money for Apple is well worth the investment. Ultimately, if you are not partial to either platform or OS family of products, you should try both environments at your school or at a store to determine if you become a Mac or a PC owner.

Step 4 Compare Hardware Components to Match Software Needs

Table A.1 provides an overview of specifications you should check in a typical ad for a Windows-compatible notebook computer. If necessary, review Chapter 3 for more information on any of the hardware components that are listed.

If you can afford to spend more, buy more than you need to meet the recommended requirements. This will ensure you have a computer that will meet your needs into the future. In a nutshell, go for the computer with the fastest processor, most RAM, and largest internal hard disk drive. These systems will typically be packaged with other components that will be adequate for an average computer user who needs a device to use Office applications and the Internet. If you cannot afford to spend more now, look for a computer ad that says the RAM is expandable. This will be a better choice than one that cannot be upgraded or that can have only a limited amount added later.

Look for the Energy Star logo or something in the ad that says the device is Energy Star qualified. This means the computer will use less energy than one that is not rated.

Examine the width, height, and weight specifications to get an idea of the physical characteristics. Pay particular attention to weight and screen size if you will be carrying the notebook around at school in a backpack.

Table A.1	Hardware Components Typically Advertised for a Notebook PC
Processor	Intel Core, Atom, AMD, or ARM processors are commonly found in notebooks and tablets. Notebooks and tablets are sold with multiple-core CPUs, usually dual- or quad-core at the time of writing. Look for the amount and type (L1, L2, or L3) of cache memory with the CPU and the highest processor speed (1.5 GHz and higher).
RAM	RAM works with the CPU to give you high-speed performance. The more RAM you have, the better your system will perform. Look for a minimum of 4 GB of RAM on a notebook and 1 to 2 GB on a tablet. Check if RAM is expandable in modules that can be added to the device at a later time. A system with a higher level of expandable RAM will last longer.
Screen	A desktop PC will have a larger screen than a notebook or tablet, typically 19 inches or higher. A notebook or Ultrabook will have a screen size in the range of 15 inches or higher. Netbook and tablet screens are the smallest in the range of 9 to 12 inches. Recall that screen size is measured diagonally from corner to corner.
Video Card	In most cases, the video card supplied with a notebook is adequate; however, if you are going to use your computer for gaming or high-end graphics design, pay attention to the graphics card, video memory, and the GPU. Look for higher specifications for these items to achieve faster graphics processing capabilities.
Hard Disk Space	The larger amount of hard disk storage space you can get the better; however, keep in mind that you can always buy external hard disk drives to store all of those digital photos, videos, and music files. Higher end notebooks at the time of writing are supplied with 1 TB HDDs, while lower end notebooks may only have 500 GB.
Optical Disc Drives	Notebooks include a DVD or Blu-ray Disc drive. If watching movies on your computer is important, remember that Ultrabooks and Netbooks do not have optical drives (although you can purchase one as a peripheral).
Digital Media Reader	Transferring data from a digital camera or smartphone is easier if the notebook has a digital media card reader. Most notebooks are equipped with a reader or include a slot for one.
Networking Capabilities	Notebooks and tablets are equipped with wireless networking capabilities. Some also come with Bluetooth-enabled connectivity. An Ethernet port will provide you with the added capability of plugging in to a wired network using a twisted-pair cable (sometimes called an RJ-45 connector). At school, some classrooms, lounges, or libraries may be equipped with network plug-ins that will give you faster Internet access than the wireless network.
Battery Life	Check the battery life to see how long the computer will operate before requiring power from an outlet. Battery life is important if you will be using the notebook away from power outlets for most of the day or evening.
Ports	Check the number and type of ports that are available on the notebook. The more USB ports the better, although you can buy an inexpensive USB hub if you need to expand the port availability. An HDMI port will allow you to plug in the notebook to a high-definition television screen for watching movies. A video port is also typically included to allow you to plug in an external monitor. Look for a FireWire port if you plan to transfer digital video from a peripheral device to the PC.
Integrated Web Cam	Most notebooks are equipped with a web cam. If you plan to do video calling, this feature will be important to you.

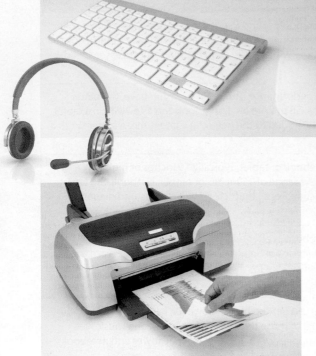

Choose the options you want to purchase in addition to the computer.

Step 5 Choose Options

If you will be using the notebook in place of a desktop PC, you may want to consider buying an external monitor, keyboard, and mouse. These peripherals will allow you to design an ergonomically correct workspace at home to avoid the repetitive strain and eye strain that occur from prolonged use of notebooks. Wireless keyboards and mice allow you to adjust your workspace to more comfortable positions. If you like listening to music or watching movies, you may want to invest in external speakers or high-quality, noise-canceling headphones. A headset with a microphone is desirable if you plan to use voice technology in many applications.

If you need to print at home, consider whether you want a laser or inkjet printer. Compare the cost of toner versus ink and the number of pages you can print before replacing supplies to help you decide on the type of printer. Some computers are bundled with a printer. Make sure the printer included in such a package is one that you want, and if it isn't, negotiate a discount on a better quality printer rather than accepting the packaged device. Consider an all-in-one printer that includes scanning and copying capabilities. All-in-one printers are a good value and will use less desk space than having multiple devices.

Think about how you will carry the device, and buy a well-padded case or backpack. Consider buying a case with wheels if you will be carrying the notebook along with your textbooks at school. For tablets, consider buying a sleeve or case that you can use to protect the screen's surface.

Many mobile devices are subject to theft or loss. Consider biometric options such as a fingerprint reader or tracking software and hardware that will allow you to remotely monitor or wipe the device should it be stolen or lost.

Step 6 Decide Whether to Buy an Extended Warranty

Computers come with a limited parts and labor warranty that is typically good for one year. Consider if you want to buy the extended warranty plans that are offered when you buy a new computer. These warranties are priced depending on the notebook's value, and some retailers' warranties will fix mishaps not covered by the manufacturer. Decide if you want to spend the money on these plans. Some people believe extended warranties are a waste of money, while others prefer the peace of mind knowing they are covered for anything that might happen.

If you have a credit card that includes a buyer protection plan, check the policy first to see if the credit card insurance will cover you for any accidental damage or loss. Sometimes these policies supply enough coverage that you do not need the extra protection from a retailer's extended warranty.

Most computer equipment carries a one-year parts and labor warranty.

Step 7 Shop Around, Ask About Service, and Check Reviews

Spend some time on the Web before deciding what to purchase by comparing two or three notebooks in the same price range that you can afford. Compare the pricing at in-store electronics retailers and online etailers. Be mindful of shipping costs that you may incur if you buy from a web-based store. Consider creating a spreadsheet to compare a few options side by side.

Make sure to visit your school's computer store. Schools often offer attractive deals from hardware manufacturers that have discounts negotiated for the large school audience. School staff will also be able to help you choose a computer for programs with specialized hardware or software requirements.

If you are comfortable negotiating at an electronics store, find a retailer that you may be able to convince to upgrade some options for you in a package price. For example, it won't hurt to ask the sales associate if he or she will throw in a wireless keyboard or mouse or a set of speakers with a new notebook PC.

Make sure to inquire about service options. If the computer you buy requires repairs, ask where the warranty work is performed. Some stores will do warranty repairs or out-of-warranty repairs onsite, while others have to ship the PC back to the manufacturer. If the retailer ships the computer elsewhere, ask how long a typical repair will take. In some cases, you could be without your PC for more than week if the store ships the repair offsite. Ask who pays for the shipping to and from the repair center. Finally, some stores do not offer any assistance with repairs—avoid these locations if you are not technically savvy or are adverse to risk.

Some people prefer to pay a little more for a computer that they can have serviced at the store of purchase in case of malfunction. You will have to decide how important the repair facility is to you before making a purchase. Be sure to ask all of these questions to help you make the choice with which you are most comfortable.

Search the Web for reviews of the product you are considering and the retailer from which you want to purchase it. While reviews are not always helpful (many are negative and the positive ones may not be authentic), they do provide insight into the questions you should ask and the issues for which you want to be on the alert.

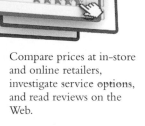

Compare prices at in-store and online retailers, investigate service options, and read reviews on the Web.

Considerations for Buying a Smartphone

Before choosing a smartphone, choose the provider with which you want to subscribe and the data plan that will meet your needs. Often, the wireless provider will provide a base model smartphone free of charge or upgraded models at a low price if you sign up for a specified contract period. If you are willing to commit to a long-term plan, you may be satisfied with the smartphone that comes free with the plan. Watch for limits, caps, and time-of-use charges that may apply. For example, a plan may advertise unlimited use, but the unlimited use may apply in certain hours only. Note that some tablets may also need a data plan from a wireless carrier.

Once you have chosen a data plan, compare the smartphones the carrier is offering. Visit a store where you can try out a few smartphone models in advance. You will want to note the screen size and the type of input. Some smartphones have smaller screens than others. You will want to try out messaging and browsing on different size screens to find the one with which you are comfortable. Input can be touch-based with an onscreen keyboard or a keyboard with trackpad input. Keyboards may slide out or be built in below the screen. Try a few tasks with a touch screen to make sure you are comfortable with touch input. Some people prefer keyboards over touch; however, touch-enabled screens are definitely the mode of input for future devices.

Compare the battery life of various smartphone models. Battery technology is improving and newer batteries last longer, but often battery life does not live up to the advertised specifications. Talk time is the standard by which to base comparisons. Look for reviews on the Web that have tested models and provide actual talk time statistics. You may want to inquire about purchasing a second battery if you will often be away from charging stations and think you will use the phone more robustly than the advertised specifications.

People often want to take pictures with their smartphones, use them to play music, and communicate using messaging applications. These apps need storage space on a memory card. Check the size of the memory card that comes with the smartphone and consider if you will need to buy a larger memory card. Check the compatibility of the memory card with your notebook or other computing devices so that you can easily exchange media files among them.

When acquiring a smartphone, start with a data plan and then try out various smartphones to choose the one that suits you. Consider the screen size, input method, battery life, and memory card options.

Ask if a car charger adapter comes with the smartphone or if you have to buy the car charger separately. This could be a negotiating item if you think you will use a car charger often.

Replacing an Older Device?

Try selling your older device using online classified ads or donate the equipment to a charity. If you cannot sell, give away, or trade in older electronics, remember to look into disposal options for e-waste that will properly recycle the device. Go to www.epa.gov/epawaste/conserve/materials/ecycling for more information on recycling electronics.

Appendix B

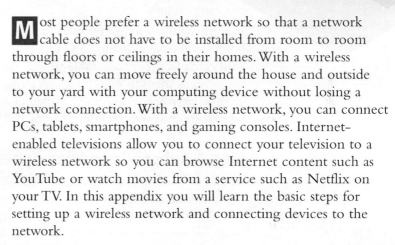

Wireless Networking

Most people prefer a wireless network so that a network cable does not have to be installed from room to room through floors or ceilings in their homes. With a wireless network, you can move freely around the house and outside to your yard with your computing device without losing a network connection. With a wireless network, you can connect PCs, tablets, smartphones, and gaming consoles. Internet-enabled televisions allow you to connect your television to a wireless network so you can browse Internet content such as YouTube or watch movies from a service such as Netflix on your TV. In this appendix you will learn the basic steps for setting up a wireless network and connecting devices to the network.

Setting Up a Wireless Network at Home

Most home networks are a Wi-Fi network. Wi-Fi uses a combination wireless router/wireless access point and radio signals to transmit data. Wi-Fi networks have a limited range and a connection speed that vary depending on the equipment. Most routers used today are referred to as Wireless N (802.11n) routers and have the ability to support speeds up to 300 Mbps. A new technology called Wireless AC (802.11ac) is coming into the marketplace at the time of writing. Expect to see this technology become popular as it is estimated that Wireless AC is capable of delivering speeds of more than 6.0 Gbps. While this speed sounds lightning fast, bear in mind that the equipment can only deliver the Internet speed for which you have subscribed (see Step 1). You also need to have devices that are compatible with the wireless router to take advantage of newer technology.

A modem provides Internet access. A wireless router allows you to share that access among multiple devices.

Even with a wireless network, some homes will have a desktop PC that is connected by a network cable to the wireless router. In the steps that follow, the process to set up a wireless network is described. Different routers provide slightly different software interfaces; however, the general steps will be the same.

Step 1 Subscribe to High-Speed Internet Service with an ISP

As you learned in Topic 2.2 in Chapter 2, to connect to the Internet you need an account with an Internet Service Provider (ISP). Contact your telephone or cable provider for high-speed Internet access. Each provider will offer different pricing levels for Internet access that vary according to the speed you want, with faster speeds costing more per month than slower speeds.

A telephone company will provide you with a DSL modem and a cable company will provide you with a cable modem. Newer modems provided by ISPs are a combination wireless router and modem in one piece of equipment called a *modem router*. Some installations may require two pieces of equipment: a DSL or cable modem plus an additional wireless router. To proceed to Step 2 you need the ISP service activated, as well as a DSL or cable modem router or modem plus wireless router. If necessary, you can buy a wireless router at an electronics store if your ISP does not provide one. Brand names for wireless routers that are popular are Linksys, D-Link, and Cisco.

Your ISP will also provide instruction documentation when you subscribe for service and may give you a USB or DVD that automates the setup process. If the documentation from your ISP contains instructions that vary from the steps below, complete the steps according to the ISP's instructions.

A modem router or cable modem provide high-speed Internet access.

Step 2 Connect the Networking Hardware Equipment

Connect one end of a coaxial cable (cable modem) or twisted-pair cable (DSL modem) to the modem and the other end to the cable or telephone line coming into your house. Plug the power adapter into the modem and into a power outlet. You should see lights illuminate on the front of the modem, indicating power and connectivity are live.

Next, connect the modem to the wireless router if you need a standalone router (your ISP did not provide you with a modem router device). To do this, plug one end of a network cable into the back of the modem and the other end into the back of the wireless router. Plug the power adapter into the wireless router and into a power outlet. You should also see lights illuminate on the front of the standalone router.

Connect a cable or DSL modem to a wireless router using a network cable.

If you have a desktop PC in the same room as your networking equipment, you can connect the PC to the integrated modem router or standalone router by plugging one end of a network cable into the PC's network port and the other end into the back of the modem router or standalone router. This allows the PC to use a wired connection to the router, while the remaining devices in your home will use a wireless connection.

Once the networking equipment is connected and has power, you can move on to Step 3, where you will configure the router.

Step 3 Configure the Wireless Router

Integrated modem routers or standalone routers all come with an installation CD, DVD, or USB flash drive that walks you through the steps to set up the router. One computer used to configure the wireless router will need to be plugged into the wireless router while you configure it. After this step, you can unplug the PC from the router and connect wirelessly afterward.

If you have a desktop PC already connected to the router, proceed to insert the installation medium into the desktop PC and begin the configuration process. If you do not have a PC connected to the router, attach a network cable from an open port on the back of the wireless router to the network port on your notebook, insert the installation medium, and begin the configuration process (Figure B.1).

To configure the wireless router, follow the instructions that appear in the setup program. The software interface is user-friendly and prompts assist you at each step. Generally, you need to do three tasks: assign the router a name (called the SSID) and security key, change the router's administrative password, and choose the security standard you want to use.

If you did not receive an installation medium with a preprogrammed setup process, look for instructions that came with the equipment that provide a URL or

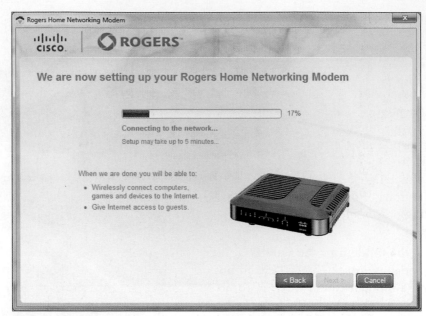

Figure B.1 Insert the CD, DVD, or USB flash drive into a PC to start the router's setup program.

IP address to configure the router. Open a browser window and type the URL or IP address to start the software interface.

Wireless routers come with a default user name and password that is usually *admin* (for both user name and password) or *admin* and *password*. Log on to the router device and proceed to change the settings as needed.

When giving the router a new name, try not to use obvious names that will identify you with the router. For example, do not use your name or your address. This way when someone is within range of your router, they will not associate the network name with you and try to break into your Internet access (such as a neighbor trying to piggyback your connection). A good idea is to prevent the router from broadcasting the router's SSID. Free public Wi-Fi networks such as those at airports, coffee shops, and libraries use a recognizable name because they provide unsecured network access to everyone who is within range. Also assign a security key that your neighbors or anyone who knows you would not be able to guess.

Wireless routers generally include a setup CD that automates the configuration process.

Change the default administrator password to a strong password known only to you. The administrative password will be needed if you ever want to change the router settings in the future. If necessary, write down the user name and password for administering the router and store it in a secure location.

Activate the router's security standard using Wi-Fi Protected Access WPA2 if possible. Some older devices may not support WPA2 and you may need to use WPA instead. Avoid using the less secure WEP standard. WPA2 secures your wireless network with encryption. People will not be able to connect to the wireless router unless they know the security key, and data transmitted across the wireless network will be encrypted.

When you have finished configuring the wireless router, unplug the notebook PC used to configure the wireless router and proceed to connect each wireless device to the router as per Step 4. You can leave a desktop PC plugged into the router if the desktop PC does not have a wireless network adapter or you do not want to use it wirelessly.

Step 4 Connect Individual Devices to the Wireless Router

Notebooks, tablets, and smartphones come equipped with a built-in wireless interface card, called a network adapter. Generally, the wireless network adapter turns on by default when the device is powered on. For smartphones and some tablets you may need to turn on Wi-Fi.

If a PC or other computing device does not have a built-in wireless interface card, you can purchase a network adapter for wireless networking. For a desktop PC, buy a USB wireless network adapter; for a notebook PC, buy a wireless network card adapter. A tip for ensuring a smooth setup process is to buy a wireless network adapter made by the same manufacturer as your wireless router.

Generally, the installation medium you used to set up your wireless router can be used in each other device that you want to connect to the network. If necessary, you can manually connect to the router by following the steps shown in Figure B.2 for Windows 7 and Figure B.3 for Windows 8.

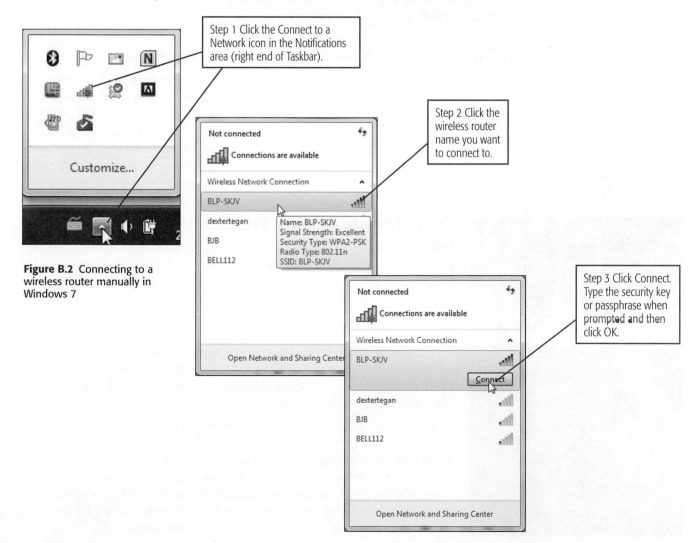

Figure B.2 Connecting to a wireless router manually in Windows 7

Step 1 Swipe in from the right edge of the Start screen or point at the top right or bottom right screen edge to display charms, tap or click the Settings charm, and then tap or click the Networks icon.

Step 2 Tap or click the wireless router name you want to connect to.

Step 3 Tap or click the Connect automatically check box and then tap or click Connect. Type the security key or passphrase when prompted and then tap or click OK.

Figure B.3 Connecting to a wireless router manually in Windows 8

Connect a computing device, television, or gaming console by following instructions provided by the device manufacturers. In most cases, you have options to use a push button on the router to automatically detect the wireless router or to manually connect by providing the device name and security key by using buttons on a remote control and on-screen menu.

Setting Up a Wireless Network on Apple Equipment

To set up a wireless network with Apple computers, you will need to purchase and configure a Wi-Fi base station (called Airport Express, Airport Extreme, or Time Capsule) that connects to your high-speed cable or DSL modem. Plug in the networking equipment by following steps similar to Step 2 above and then go to www.apple.com/findouthow/mac/#wirelesssetup to watch a video that shows you the steps to configure the wireless network on an Apple computer using the Airport Utility software.

Connecting to a Public Wireless Hotspot

Follow the steps to manually connect to a public wireless hotspot as shown in Figure B.2 for a Windows 7 device and Figure B.3 for a Windows 8 device. The network name should be obvious in the list of available networks; however, if necessary you can ask a store clerk, hotel clerk, or airport staff member for the network name and password. Exercise caution when using a public Wi-Fi hotspot, and do not transmit personal or confidential data as these networks are not secured with encryption and are at risk of interception by hackers. Never perform financial transactions or log on to websites where you need to provide your user name and password.

Wireless networking has unchained people from fixed locations and allowed for freedom of movement without losing Internet access. With more home devices becoming Internet-enabled, such as smart appliances and televisions, wireless networking is becoming even more advantageous. Setting up a wireless home network is relatively straightforward. Always implement wireless network security to ensure your personal data is not subjected to unwanted access.

Glossary

A

acceptable use policy (AUP) a written policy that spells out for employees, students, or other network users the permitted uses for computing equipment and networks.

accounting software application business software used to record and report financial information related to assets, liabilities, equity, revenue, and expenses.

adware software programs responsible for pop-up ads that appear on your desktop or while viewing web pages.

Android the mobile operating system for many smartphones and tablets.

Android Open Source Project (AOSP) a program operated by Google through which the Android is maintained and developed.

animation software programs used to create images or objects that have movement or otherwise interact with users.

antivirus program a program that detects and removes malware.

application software (apps) programs used by individuals to carry out tasks or otherwise get things done.

audio recording and editing software programs that include tools for recording and editing music, sound clips, and podcasts.

B

back door a way to bypass computer security.

backup utility a program that allows you to back up selected files or an entire disk to a removable storage medium.

bar code reader a device that optically scans bar codes to identify products in warehouses or at checkout counters.

binary system the location for the digital data temporarily stored in RAM, processed by the CPU, and eventually saved to permanent storage when you save the document. In the binary system, only two possible values exist—0 and 1.

biometric device a tool that authenticates a person's identity using physical characteristics such as a fingerprint, iris scan, or voice recognition.

biometric scanner a device used to identify people by individual human characteristics such as a fingerprint, iris, or voice pattern.

BIOS (Basic Input Output System) programming code stored on a ROM chip that includes instructions used when starting a computer.

bit the smallest unit for digital data in the binary system.

black hats hackers who gain unauthorized access with malicious intent to steal data or for other personal gain.

BlackBerry OS the operating system designed for BlackBerry devices.

BlackBerry thumb the pain that develops in BlackBerry users in the thumb or wrist from excessive texting.

blog a journal posted on a website.

blog posts entries on a blog.

blogger an individual who writes blog content.

blogging writing and maintaining a blog.

blogosphere the collection of all of the blogs on the Web.

Bluetooth a technology that offers the ability to connect to another Bluetooth-enabled device such as your smartphone.

Bluetooth headset a device that can be paired to a smartphone to hear a conversation when making and receiving voice calls.

bookmark a link on a social bookmarking site.

bookmarklet a social bookmarking site icon that allows you to bookmark the page instantly by clicking the icon.

booting starting a computer.

botnet a collection of zombie computers that work together to conduct an attack on another network.

broadband any always-on connection capable of carrying a large amount of data at a fast speed.

byte each group of eight bits that represents one character.

C

cable Internet access Internet access provided by the same cable company with which you subscribe for television service.

cache memory a system that stores frequently used data.

carpal tunnel syndrome (CTS) a common computer-related RSI injury that occurs when the nerve that connects the forearm to the palm of the hand becomes inflamed. It is caused by excessive typing, mouse scrolling, mouse clicking, and thumb typing/movements on mobile devices.

ccTLDs two-character TLDs that are country codes such as us and ca.

central processing unit (CPU) a computer chip that carries out the instructions given by the software to perform the processing cycle.

Chrome Google's free Web browser that runs on Windows-compatible PCs.

Chrome OS Google's Linux-based cloud operating system that is available on specific hardware called Chromebooks.

clickjacking when a button, graphic, or link on a web page appears to be real, but when clicked causes malicious software to run.

client a computer that connects to a server.

clock speed the number of instruction cycles the CPU can process per second, typically measured in gigahertz (GHz).

cloud computing software and computing services accessed entirely on the Internet.

cloud storage a storage option in which you log in to a website and copy documents, photos, or other information to a web service.

cold boot turning on a computer that has been shut off.

command-line interface a system used to interact with an OS in which you type commands on the keyboard at a prompt to tell the OS what to do.

communications device any component used to facilitate the transmission of data such as a cable modem, DSL modem, or router.

computer an electronic device that has been programmed to process, store, and output data that has been accepted as input. It needs hardware and software to work.

computer security all activities related to protecting hardware, software, and data from loss as a result of unauthorized access or use, theft, natural disaster, and human error. Also known as information security.

computer vision syndrome (CVS) a temporary condition caused by prolonged computer use that involves eye strain; weak, blurred, itchy, burning, or dry eyes; double vision; difficulty with focus; sensitivity to light; headaches; and neck pain.

computing platform the combination of hardware architecture and software design that allows applications to run.

content aggregator an organization that searches the Web for new content, and collects and organizes the content in one place.

cookie a small text file stored on your computer's hard disk that contains data about you such as your user name and the pages you visited.

cybercrime illegal acts involving a computer.

D

data buses wires that allow data to travel between the components on the motherboard to the CPU and memory.

database management application software that organizes and keeps track of large amounts of data.

Delicious a social bookmarking website that allows you to save and share links to pages on the Web that have articles, pictures, videos, blogs, or some other content that you want to bookmark.

desktop computer a PC that includes a system unit and a separate monitor, keyboard, and mouse.

desktop publishing software an application that incorporates text, graphics, and colors to create high-quality documents for marketing, communication, or other commercial purposes.

dial-up Internet access in which you connect your PC to your telephone system via a modem built into your PC.

digital copier an output device that can be used as a traditional paper photocopier and also accept output from computers for printing.

Digital Subscriber Line (DSL) Internet access provided by your telephone company that connects using telephone lines.

Disk Cleanup a Windows utility that allows you to scan a particular storage device or drive to select various types of files to be deleted.

disk defragmenter a utility that rearranges fragmented files back together to improve file retrieval speed and efficiency.

document management system (DMS) a program that manages the creation, storage, retrieval, history, and eventual disposal of information stored in a central repository.

Domain Name System (DNS) a server that holds the directory that associates an Internet address with a Web address.

drive a storage device that is identified by a unique letter and label or assigned a name.

drivers small programs that contain the instructions the OS uses to communicate and route data to/from the device.

E

e-commerce (electronic commerce) buying or selling over the Internet.

e-tailers (electronic retailers) businesses that sell online to consumers.

e-waste (electronic waste) discarded or unwanted electrical items. Also known as e-trash.

educational software programs designed for children and adults to learn about subjects such as math, spelling, grammar, geography, and history.

802.11 protocol the standard developed to facilitate wireless communication among several hardware providers.

email (electronic mail) the sending and receiving of digital messages, sometimes with documents or photos attached.

email address used to connect to your email account at the ISP server.

email client a program such as Microsoft's Outlook or Apple's Mail that sends and receives messages.

embedded computer a processor programmed to perform a particular task that is incorporated into a household appliance and consumer electronic.

Embedded Linux applications that run smart appliances, in-flight entertainment systems, personal navigation systems, and a variety of other consumer and commercial electronics.

embedded operating system a specialized operating system designed for the limited use of a specific device.

encryption the act of scrambling communications between devices so that the data is not readable.

enterprise resource planning (ERP) a software solution designed for large-scale organizations.

entertainment software programs for playing interactive games and videos.

ergonomics strategies involving the design of equipment and a person's work space to promote safe and comfortable operation.

Ethernet port a device that facilitates connection to the Internet. Also known as a network interface card (NIC).

expansion card a device that plugs into an expansion slot on the motherboard to provide or improve functionality.

external wireless adapter a device that has a built-in radio transmitter and receiver that allow you to connect to a wireless modem or wireless router.

F

Facebook one of the most popular social networking sites used by people who want to connect with friends and family.

Fiber-to-the-Premises (FTTP) Internet access that involves the ISP running a fiber-optic cable directly to your home or business. Also known as Fiber-to-the-Home (FTTH) or Fiber-Optic Service (FiOS).

file the collection of bytes that comprise the saved document.

File Explorer a file management system in Windows 8 in which you can move, copy, delete, and rename files.

File History the location where you back up or restore files.

file name the unique name assigned to a document when you save.

Firefox the Mozilla Foundation's free Web browser.

firewall hardware, software, or a combination of hardware and software that blocks unwanted access to your network.

fixed wireless Internet access Internet access that involves installing an antenna outside your home to send and receive radio signals.

flash memory chip-based technology where data is stored electronically on a chip instead of magnetically like a traditional HDD.

flash memory card a small card that contains one or more flash memory chips.

Flickr one of the most popular dedicated photo-sharing websites.

folder a placeholder name for where you want to store related files.

4G (fourth generation) a network for mobile devices that provides Internet access through cell towers. The average speed for 4G devices is often advertised as 10 times faster than 3G.

fragmentation occurs when file clusters needed for a document are not stored adjacent to each other.

Freeware software that can be downloaded and installed at no cost and without restrictions.

G

generic top-level domains (gTLDs) TLDs with three or more characters such as com, gov, and edu.

gigabyte approximately 1 billion bytes.

gigahertz (GHz) 1 billion instruction cycles per second.

Google's Blogger a popular choice for creating a blog.

Google+ a Google social networking site.

graphical user interface (GUI) a system that presents visual images such as tiles, icons, or buttons that you tap or click to tell the OS what you want to do.

graphics software programs for creating, editing, and manipulating drawings, pictures, photos, clip art, and scanned images.

green computing the use of computers and other electronic devices in an environmentally responsible manner.

H

hacker an individual who accesses a network without permission.

hacking activities involved in gaining unauthorized entry into a network's resources.

hard copy a printed copy of computer output.

hard disk the storage medium upon which the operating system and application software programs are stored as well as data files. Also known as a hard drive or hard disk drive (HDD).

hashtag symbol (#) precedes a keyword or topics in a tweet to categorize messages.

Help and Support a program that allows you to search for solutions to a computer issue in extensive online resources.

hobby software applications programs that support leisure activities such as creating a family tree, scrapbooking, planning trips, and creating custom greeting cards.

home page the first page of a website that displays when the Web address is requested.

hotspot an area where a Wi-Fi network is within range.

HTML (Hypertext Markup Language) markup language used to create web pages.

hyperlinks addresses that when clicked or tapped on a touchscreen take you to a related Web page.

I

ICANN (Internet Corporation for Assigned Names and Numbers) a nonprofit organization that keeps track of the Internet addresses and names all around the world.

iCloud Apple's cloud operating system that provides access to email, contacts, calendar, documents, and more.

identity theft when an individual's personal information is obtained by a criminal who then uses the information to buy products or services under the victim's name or otherwise pose as the victim for financial gain.

information the result of software programs providing instructions for a computer to process and organize the data into a meaningful and useful way.

information privacy the right of individuals or organizations to control the information that is collected about them.

Information Processing Cycle four operations—input, processing, output, and storage—involved in transforming data into information.

information technology (IT) the use of computers, software, networks, and other communication systems and processes to store, retrieve, send, process, and protect information.

inkjet printer an output device that forms text and images on the page by spraying drops of ink from one or more ink cartridges that move back and forth across the page.

input device any device used to enter raw data or communicate instructions to the computer.

Instagram a popular, free app for sharing photos from your iPhone, iPad, iPod Touch, or Android phone.

instant messaging exchanging text messages in real time.

instruction cycle an action in which the CPU retrieves, decodes, executes, and stores an instruction.

interactive whiteboard a device that displays the computer's output on a large whiteboard, on which special pens can be used to annotate and draw.

Internet (Net) a global network that links together other networks such as government departments, businesses, nonprofit organizations, educational and research institutions, and individuals.

Internet Explorer (IE) the web browser included with Microsoft Windows.

Internet Protocol (IP) address a unique address assigned to a computing device when it is connected to the Internet so that the device can communicate with other computers. An IP address is a series of four numbers from 0 to 255 separated by periods.

Internet Service Provider (ISP) a company that provides access to the Internet's infrastructure for a fee.

intrusion detection software programs that analyze network traffic for suspicious data and alert network administrators to possible system threats.

iOS Apple's mobile operating system used for its iPhone, iPod Touch, and iPad.

K

kernel the core of the OS that manages memory, devices, and programs, and assigns resources.

keyboard a device used to type and input data into a computer.

keystroke logger spyware that is activated as part of a rootkit or Trojan horse that records every keystroke you type and sends it back to a cybercriminal. Also known as a keylogger.

kilobyte (KB) approximately 1,000 bytes.

L

laptop computer a PC that has a monitor that when swiveled up reveals a keyboard with the remaining components housed below. Also known as a notebook.

laser printer an output device in which a laser beam electrostatically charges a drum with the text and images sent for printing. A dry powder called toner sticks to the drum and is transferred to the paper.

Last.fm an example of a music-sharing website.

legal software programs that help you prepare legal documents such as wills, contracts, leases, loan agreements, and living trusts.

Level 1 (L1) cache cache memory that is built on the CPU chip and operates the fastest of all memory.

Level 2 (L2) cache cache memory stored on the CPU chip or built on the motherboard that feeds the L1 cache.

Level 3 (L3) cache cache memory that is usually built on the motherboard and feeds the L2 cache.

Light-Emitting Diode (LED) a flat-panel technology that consumes less energy and costs more than LCD.

LinkedIn a professional network through which you connect with your business contacts.

Linux an operating system created by Linus Torvalds and based on UNIX; it can be used as a standalone OS or as a server OS.

Liquid Crystal Displays (LCD) flat-panel, widescreen technology widely used for new desktop PC monitors.

LTE network the fastest network for mobile devices.

M

Mac OS a proprietary operating system created by Apple.

magnetic strip reader a device that can read data from the magnetic strip on the backs of cards such as debit cards, credit cards, or cards used to open doors or parking gates.

mainframe a large, powerful, and expensive computer used by the government and large organizations such as banks, insurance companies, and other corporations to connect hundreds or thousands of users simultaneously.

malware any type of malicious software program that is designed to damage, disable, or steal data.

media sharing websites that allow you to share, view, and download photos, videos, music, and presentations.

megabits per second (Mbps) the speed for broadband connectivity in which data transfers at the rate of 1 million bits per second.

megabyte approximately 1 million bytes.

metasearch search engines search engines that send your search phrase to other search engines and then compile the results in one list.

microblog a blog that restricts posts to a smaller amount of text than a traditional blog.

microblogger individuals who create posts that are typically about what they are doing, where they are, what they are thinking about in the moment, or links to interesting content they have seen on the Web.

microphone a device used in conjunction with software to create a digital audio file from voice input or other sounds.

microprocessor a silicon chip. Also known as a central processing unit.

midrange server used in small and medium organizations that need to connect hundreds of client computers at the same time.

mobile applications a different edition of software that is designed specifically for mobile use.

mobile broadband sticks portable modems that plug into a USB port on your mobile device and connect via a cellular network.

mobile computer a PC that can be moved from place to place.

mobile device a handheld computing device smaller than a notebook.

mobile malware a virus designed for mobile devices.

mobile operating system an operating system designed specifically for a mobile device.

mobile web browser a browser designed to quickly display web pages optimized for the smaller screens on devices such as tablets and smartphones.

monitor an output device that houses the screen on a desktop PC.

motherboard the main circuit board in the computer.

mouse a device used to point, select, and manipulate objects on the screen.

multi-core processor independent units on the same chip that can process data simultaneously, which significantly increases speed and performance.

multimedia software programs that use text and images with video, audio, and animations to create engaging and interactive applications that market products or services, educate, or entertain users.

N

netbook a smaller version of a notebook designed for people who primarily need access only to web-based applications such as email and the Internet.

netiquette short for *Internet etiquette*; rules for acceptable social interactions over the Internet.

network two or more computers or other devices (such as a printer) that are linked together to share resources and communicate with each other.

network adapter any device used to connect a computer to a network. Also known as a network card.

network interface card (NIC) facilitates connection to the Internet. Also known as an Ethernet port.

note-taking software programs used to store, organize, search, and share notes.

O

Open Handset Alliance a consortium of several mobile technology companies of which Google is a member.

open source program a program in which the source code is available to the public and can be freely modified or customized.

open source software programs that generally are available for free and downloaded from a website.

operating system (OS) a system that provides the user interface that allows you to work with the computer, manages all of the hardware resources, and provides the platform for managing files and application programs.

optical disc a CD, DVD, or Blu-ray disc.

Optimize Drives a utility used to analyze a drive for the percentage of fragmentation.

Organic Light-Emitting Diode (OLED) a newer flat-panel technology that does not require backlighting like an LCD.

output device anything used to view the information processed and organized by the computer.

P

packaged software a bundle of traditional software suites.

parallel processing a procedure that involves having multiple microprocessor chips or a multi-core processor to execute multiple instructions simultaneously.

peripheral hardware used for input, output, connectivity, or storage that you plug in or connect to your computer wirelessly.

personal computer (PC) a computer in which the input, processing, storage, and output are self-contained.

personal finance software programs that allow you to download activity from your banking account directly into the software.

personal information management (PIM) software programs that help you organize messages, schedule, contacts, and tasks.

petaflop a measurement used in scientific calculations that represents a quadrillion floating point operations per second.

pharming a scam in which an individual is tricked into typing in personal information at a phony website that appears to be the real website requested by the individual.

phishing activities that appear to be initiated by a legitimate organization in an attempt to obtain personal information that can be used in fraud, theft, or identity theft.

photo editing software programs used to edit and add special effects and text to photos.

photo printer an output device that connects directly to a digital camera to print high-quality photos on photo paper using inkjet technology.

piggybacking connecting to someone else's wireless network without the network owner's consent.

Pinterest a virtual pinboard on which people pin pictures of things they have seen on the Internet that they like and want to share using the Pin It button.

pixels the picture elements that make up the image shown on the display screen. A pixel is square with red, green, and blue color values that represent each color needed to form the image.

plasma a flat-panel technology that provides truer color representation and costs more than an LCD.

plotter an output device that moves one or more pens across the surface of the paper to produce a drawing.

Plug and Play a platform in which the OS searches a newly plugged-in device for the driver, loads it automatically, and displays a message when the device is ready to use.

plug-in a software program that allows the browser to display enhanced content that it cannot display on its own. Also known as add-on or player.

port a connector located at the back of a desktop PC or at the sides, back, and sometimes the front of a notebook or other mobile device that is used to plug in external devices.

Portable Media Player a device on which to play music, watch videos, view photos, play games, and/or read electronic books.

presentation application software used to create slides for an electronic slideshow that may be projected on a screen.

processing a cycle carried out by the central processing unit.

productivity software a group of programs that includes word processing, spreadsheets, presentations, and database management.

project management software programs that allow you to enter all of the tasks needed to get a project done, establish time frames, assign resources, and allocate budget money to each task.

protocol a set of rules that defines how data is exchanged between two devices.

Q

QR (Quick Response) code a type of bar code that looks like a matrix of black square dots.

R

Radio Frequency Identification (RFID) reader a device that scans an embedded RFID tag to identify an object.

random access memory (RAM) temporary storage for instructions and data that is emptied when power to the computer is lost.

raw data characters that are typed or otherwise entered into a computer.

read-only memory (ROM) memory built on the motherboard that is used for storing computer instructions that do not change.

Really Simple Syndication (RSS) a specification used by content aggregators to distribute updates to subscribers.

reference software programs that use multimedia tools to provide rich content information in encyclopedias, dictionaries, translation guides, atlases, and other reference resources.

repetitive strain injury (RSI) an injury or disorder of the joints, nerves, muscles, ligaments, or tendons.

resolution the number of pixels that make up the image shown on the display screen, which affects the quality of output.

restore utility a program that allows you to copy files from a backup to a disk drive in their original state.

rootkit a program that hides on an infected computer and provides a back door for a hacker or other cybercriminal to remotely monitor or take control of the PC.

S

Safari Apple's browser for mobile devices.

satellite Internet access Internet access available to those who live in a rural area where cable or DSL is not available.

scanner a device that uses optical technology to analyze text and/or images and convert them into data that can be used by a computer.

search engine a company that searches Web pages and indexes the pages by keyword or subject.

server a computer with hardware and software that allows it to link together other computers to provide services and share resources.

server room a controlled room where high-performance computers are stacked in racks and stored to avoid heat, humidity and dust.

Shareware software that is available to download for a free trial period.

Short Message Service (SMS) a service that facilitates texting.

smartphone a cell phone with a built-in camera that offers apps, web browsing, and messaging capabilities.

social bookmarking a category of social networking that provides tools with which you can organize, store, and share content with others.

social media any online tool in which users generate content and interact with others.

social networking website a website that provides tools for people to connect and interact with groups of people.

Software License Agreement (SLA) a license agreement that you are required to accept when you install software. Also known as End User License Agreement (EULA).

software suite a bundled group of productivity software applications. Also known as productivity suite.

software-as-a-service (SaaS) the delivery of software applications using the Internet.

solid-state drive (SSD) a newer type of hard disk drive technology that uses flash memory.

spam electronic junk mail.

spiders programs that read Web pages and other information to generate index entries. Also known as crawlers.

spoofing techniques in which a sender's email address is altered to a phony address that appears legitimate to the email recipient, or an IP address is altered to appear to be a trusted source.

spreadsheet application software in which you work primarily with numbers that you organize, calculate, and chart.

spyware software programs that exist on your computer without your knowledge and track your activities.

storage device the piece of hardware with the means to write new data to and read existing data from storage media.

storage media any device where data and information are saved for later use.

strong password a password that is difficult to hack by humans or password detection software programs.

StumbleUpon a social bookmarking website on which you can browse recommended web pages and save the pages you like to your profile.

stylus a digital pen.

subscription software programs purchased from cloud computing providers who generally charge a monthly fee per user for access to the provider's software and storage services.

supercomputer the fastest, most expensive, most powerful computer, capable of performing trillions of calculations per second.

System Restore a program that will undo a recent change while leaving all documents intact.

system software programs, including the operating system, that are designed to work with the present hardware as well as a set of utility programs that are used to maintain the computer and its devices.

system unit a horizontal or vertical case in which the computer's processing, memory, and main storage device are housed.

T

tablet PC a lightweight notebook with a smaller screen that you interact with using a touch screen or stylus.

tag a keyword you assign to content to describe or categorize a photo, article, or item from a Web page.

tagging creating bookmarks on a website.

tax preparation software programs that guide you through the completion of the complex forms required to file your income taxes.

technological convergence the place where innovation merges several technologies into a single device.

tendonitis a common computer-related RSI injury that occurs when a tendon in the wrist becomes inflamed. It is caused by excessive typing, mouse scrolling, mouse clicking, and thumb typing/movements on mobile devices.

terabyte approximately 1 trillion bytes.

text messages short text exchanges using mobile devices.

texting sending text messages to another mobile device.

thermal printer an output device that heats coated paper as the paper passes over the print head; usually used for receipts.

thin client a computer connected to a network that does not store any data or software on the local PC.

3G (third generation) a network for mobile devices that provides Internet access through cell towers. Average speed for a 3G connection is around 1 Mbps.

top-level domain (TLD) the part of the domain name that identifies the type of organization associated with the domain name.

touch-enabled display a technology that accepts input from finger gestures and is found on many of today's mobile devices. Also known as touchscreens.

touchpad a rectangular surface with buttons, located below the keyboard on a notebook, that is used in place of a mouse to move the pointer on the screen and manipulate objects. The touchpad senses finger movement and taps similar to a mouse.

Transport Layer Security (TLS) a program that encrypts transmitted data so the data is unreadable if intercepted.

Trojan horse a program that disguises itself as a useful program that infects your computer with malware when you run the application.

tweet a post on Twitter.

Twitter the most popular microblog, with posts limited to 140 characters or less.

Twitter bots software programmed to follow people based on popular keywords.

U

ubiquitous computing an idea that computing technology is everywhere within our environment and used all of the time.

Ultra-Mobile PC (UMPC) a small handheld computer that supports touch or digital pen input, or includes a compact keyboard.

ultrabook a type of notebook that is thinner and lighter, but just as powerful as a traditional notebook.

unauthorized access using a computer, network, or other resource without permission.

unauthorized use using a computer, network, or other resource for purposes other than the intended use.

universal serial bus (USB) port the most common type of port that is used to connect an external device such as a keyboard, mouse, printer, smartphone, or external storage media to a computer.

UNIX an operating system designed for servers that originally was designed to be multi-user and multitasking.

USB flash drive a portable storage device that contains flash memory inside the case.

USB wireless adapter the most common type of external wireless adapter. Also known as a USB dongle.

user interface (UI) the means with which you interact with the computer.

V

video card a device used to process the data needed to display the text and images on your monitor, projector, or television.

video display an electronic device that visually presents information from a computer.

video display projector (VDP) a device used when a computer's output needs to be projected on a large screen.

video editing software programs that provide tools to create video clips.

viral videos video clips that spread quickly via forwarded or shared links or word-of-mouth.

virtual memory the hard disk space allocated to store RAM contents.

virus a form of malware that can replicate itself and spread to other media on the infected computer and to other computers on the network.

Voice over Internet Protocol (VoIP) the ability to call someone using the Internet and engage in a voice conversation.

voice recognition technology used to recognize voice commands as input for hands-free operation at work, with your car's navigation and communications system, or with your mobile device. Also known as speech recognition technology.

W

war driving the act of driving around trying to connect to someone else's unsecured wireless network.

warm boot restarting a computer without turning off the power.

wearable computer a computing device that can be worn on the body and functions while the individual is walking or otherwise moving around.

Web 2.0 websites that encourage and facilitate collaboration and sharing and allow users to add or edit content.

Web 3.0 the next generation of the Web that is under development in which meaningful connections between data and web pages will exist, allowing you to find more complex information more easily and more quickly. Also known as Semantic Web.

Web address a text-based address to navigate to a website. Also known as uniform resource locator (URL).

web authoring software a program designed to create content to be provided over the Internet.

web conferencing a program that allows a group of individuals to connect online to engage in a meeting.

web page a document that contains text and multimedia content such as images, video, sound, and animation.

web server a special server where all the web pages and resources that make a website work are stored.

web-based operating system an operating system that operates like a virtual desktop where settings, documents, pictures, contacts, and other files are stored in the cloud.

webcam a video camera built into a video display screen or plugged in as a peripheral and used to provide images to the computer.

website a collection of related web pages for one organization or individual.

white hats hackers who pinpoint weaknesses in network security and may even be hired by an organization to hack into the organization's network.

Wi-Fi a network in which wireless access points and radio signals are used to transmit data Wi-Fi adapter a device that communicates with a wireless access point or wireless router using radio frequencies to transfer data.

Wi-Fi Protected Access (WPA or WPA2) security standards that authenticate users and employ sophisticated encryption techniques.

wiki a website that allows anyone to create and edit content.

wiki software programs that allow anyone to create and edit content on the website.

wikiHow a website that contains more than 140,000 how-to instruction articles.

Wikipedia Sandbox a Wikipedia entry that contains instructions on how to edit content.

Wikipedia the most-used online encyclopedia on which content can be created by anyone.

Windows Action Center used to view messages about issues encountered on your computer and provides buttons and links to tools that can be used to resolve the issues.

Windows an operating system created by Microsoft Corporation that is the most popular OS because a wide variety of hardware is designed to run it.

Windows Backup where you back up or restore files.

Windows Embedded a family of operating systems based on the familiar Windows

Windows Explorer a file management system in Windows 7 in which you can move, copy, delete, and rename files.

Windows Phone Microsoft's mobile operating system used on Windows smartphones.

wireless ExpressCard an adapter that plugs into a narrow slot on a notebook or other mobile device.

wireless interface card allows you to connect to a network using wireless technology.

word processing application software used to create documents containing mostly text.

WordPress a blog-hosting website that uses the WordPress open source blogging software.

World Wide Web the global collection of electronic documents circulated on the Internet in the form of web pages. Also known as Web or WWW.

worm a self-replicating program that requires no user action to copy itself to another computer on a network.

Y

YouTube the most popular video sharing website; owned by Google.

Z

zombie a computer that is connected to the Internet and is controlled by a hacker or other cybercriminal without the owner's knowledge.

Index

PART II

Computer Applications with Microsoft Office 2013

Chapter 1

Using Windows 8.1 and Managing Files

After successfully completing this chapter, you will be able to:

- Navigate Windows 8.1 using touch, a mouse, or a keyboard
- Start Windows 8.1 and sign in
- Launch an app, switch between apps, and close apps
- Reveal the Charms bar and use the Search charm
- Lock the screen, sign out, and shut down Windows 8.1
- Customize the Start screen and Lock screen
- Launch and close Desktop apps
- Browse files with File Explorer
- Create new folders and copy, move, rename, and delete files and folders
- Eject a USB flash drive
- Use Windows Help

Windows 8.1 is the operating system (OS) software published by Microsoft Corporation. An OS provides the user interface that allows you to work with the computer or mobile device. The OS also manages all of the hardware resources, routes data between devices and applications, and provides the tools for managing files and application programs. Every computing device requires an OS; without one your computer would not function. Think of the OS as the data and device manager that ensures data flows to and from each device and application. When you touch the screen, click the mouse, or type words on a keyboard, the OS recognizes the input and sends the data to the application or device that needs it. If a piece of hardware is not working, the OS senses the problem and displays a message to you. For example, if a printer is not turned on, the OS communicates that the printer is offline. When you power on a computer or mobile device, the OS loads automatically into memory and displays the user interface when the computer is ready.

Computers and mobile devices have an OS preloaded and ready to use. Some tasks you perform require that you interact with the OS directly such as when you launch applications (called "*apps*" in Windows 8.1), switch windows, and manage your files and folders. In this chapter you will learn to navigate in Windows 8.1 and work with files.

Note: You will need a removable storage medium (USB flash drive) with enough space to copy the student data files for this textbook.

Windows 7 Users?

A version of Chapter 1 written for Windows 7 users is available. For instructors who ordered the supplement, this version of Chapter 1 is packaged with the textbook. Windows 7 users should read and complete the topics in the Windows 7 supplement rather than those in the textbook chapter.

TOPIC 1.1

SKILLS

Describe touch gestures for Windows 8.1

Describe basic mouse actions

List common keyboard commands for Windows 8.1

You can adjust settings for some touch actions in the Pen and Touch dialog box accessed from the Control Panel.

Using Touch, Mouse, and Keyboard Input to Navigate Windows 8.1

Windows 8.1, released in October 2013, is the latest edition of Microsoft's popular OS for PCs and mobile devices. The Windows 8 or 8.1 **user interface (UI)** has been redesigned with a new **Start screen**, which users of earlier Windows editions will notice first. The Start Screen contains **tiles** that are used to start **applications**, called **apps**. Some tiles display updates in real time so that you are immediately informed when a new message arrives, a news story is released, the weather updates, or a friend posts a new status in Facebook. Tiles let you see all of your programs in one place as opposed to using the Start button and navigating menus to find a program, as was the case in earlier Windows versions.

Windows 8.1 is designed to work with devices capable of touch screen input, mouse input, and keyboard input. Before starting Windows 8.1, becoming familiar with input actions using touch, the mouse, and the keyboard will assist with navigating the user interface.

Using Touch to Navigate Windows 8.1

On touch-enabled PCs or tablets you perform actions using **gestures**. A gesture is an action or motion you perform with your finger(s), thumb, stylus, or mouse. In some cases, users with a touch-enabled device will still use a mouse or keyboard for some purposes. Windows 8.1 accommodates all three input methods. Table 1.1 explains the touch gestures used to interact with the Windows 8.1 interface on a touch-enabled PC or mobile device.

In Windows 8.1, touch actions are called *gestures*.

You can perform the gestures with one or two fingers or by using a stylus. For tasks that require typed characters such as email addresses, message text, or web addresses, the **touch keyboard** shown in Figure 1.1 is used. Tapping in an area of the screen that requires typed input generally causes the touch keyboard to appear. The touch keyboard is also available in thumb keyboard mode (Figure 1.2) and in handwriting mode (Figure 1.3).

Performing tasks such as typing an essay for a school project, or doing precise graphics editing, may be easier with a full-size keyboard or mouse. Connect a USB or wireless mouse and/or keyboard for intensive work where touch input is not as productive.

Figure 1.1 The full touch keyboard in Windows 8.1 appears whenever typed characters are expected. You can also launch the touch keyboard from the Touch Keyboard icon in the Taskbar of the Desktop app.

Table 1.1	Windows 8.1 Touch Gestures		
Gesture	**Description and Mouse Equivalent**	**What It Does**	**What It Looks Like**
Tap or Double-tap	One finger touches the screen and immediately lifts off the screen once or twice in succession. **Mouse:** Click or double-click left mouse button.	Launches an app Follows a link Performs a command or selection from a button or icon	
Press and hold	One finger touches the screen and stays in place for a few seconds. **Mouse:** Point or right-click.	Shows a context menu Shows pop-up information or details	
Slide	Move one or two fingers in the same direction. **Mouse:** Drag (may need to drag or scroll using scroll bars).	Used to drag, pan, or scroll through lists or pages	
Swipe	Move one finger in from the left or right, up from the bottom, or down from the top a short distance. **Mouse:** Point to upper right corner or lower right corner to reveal Charms bar.	In from the right reveals the Charms bar with system commands	
	Mouse: Point at upper left corner and click.	In from the left switches between open apps	
	Mouse: Point at upper left corner and slide down along left edge to view list of open apps.	In and back out quickly from the left shows a list of open apps	
	Mouse: Right-click.	Up from the bottom or down from the top shows app commands	
Pinch	Two fingers touch the screen apart from each other and move closer together. **Mouse:** Ctrl + scroll mouse wheel toward you.	Shrinks the size of text, an item, or tiles on the screen	
Stretch	Two fingers touch the screen together and move farther apart. **Mouse:** Ctrl + mouse scroll wheel away from you.	Expands the size of text, an item, or tiles on the screen	

Figure 1.2 The Windows 8.1 touch keyboard in thumb mode with the keys split on either side of the screen for comfortable typing while using the device for text messaging or similar application.

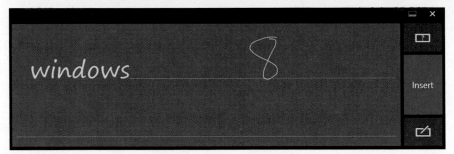

Figure 1.3 The Windows 8.1 touch keyboard in handwriting mode. Text can be inserted into an application by writing in the keyboard area using a stylus or your finger. When you stop writing, Windows converts the handwriting to text.

Using a Mouse to Navigate Windows 8.1

For traditional desktops, laptops, or notebook PCs, navigating the Windows 8.1 user interface requires the use of a **mouse**, **trackball**, **touchpad**, or other pointing device. These devices are used to move and manipulate a **pointer** (displayed as ⬚) on the screen; however, the white arrow pointer can change appearance depending on the action being performed.

To operate the mouse, move the device up, down, right, or left on the desk surface to move the pointer on the screen in the corresponding direction. A scroll wheel on the top of the mouse can be used to scroll up or down. Newer mice include the ability to push on the left or right side of the scroll wheel to scroll right or left. Left and right buttons on the top of the mouse are used to perform actions when the pointer is resting on an item. Table 1.2 provides a list and description of mouse actions.

To use a touchpad, move your finger across the surface of the touchpad in the direction required. Tap the touchpad or a button below the touchpad to perform an action.

A mouse, trackball, or touchpad can be used as a pointing device to navigate Windows 8.1.

App Tip

If you run out of desk surface, lift the mouse up off the desk, place it back down, and then continue moving in the same direction to extend the mouse movement further.

Using a Keyboard to Navigate Windows 8.1

Most actions in Windows 8.1 are easier to perform using touch gestures or a mouse; however, some **keyboard commands** are fast and easy to use. The Windows logo key is positioned at the bottom left of a keyboard between the Ctrl or Function key (labeled Fn) and the Alt key. Many keyboard shortcuts use the Windows logo key. For example, press the Windows logo key in any app to bring up the Start Screen. Pressing the Windows logo

Press the Windows logo key with a letter to perform an action.

key toggles between the Start Screen and the most recently opened app. The Menu button at the right side of the keyboard (between Alt and Ctrl) brings up context menus (similar to right-clicking with the mouse). Useful keyboard shortcuts are described in Table 1.3.

If you prefer using keyboard shortcuts, use the Help system (see Topic 1.11) to search for other keyboard navigational commands.

Note: Instructions in this textbook are written with touch gestures and mouse actions. If necessary, check with your instructor for the equivalent touchpad or other pointing device action.

Table 1.2	Mouse Movements and Actions
Term or Action	**Description**
Point	Move the mouse in the direction required to rest the white arrow pointer on a button, icon, option, tab, link, or other screen item.
Click	Quickly tap the left mouse button once while the pointer is resting on a button, icon, option, tab, link, or other screen item.
Double-click	Quickly tap the left mouse button twice. On the desktop, a program is launched by double-clicking the program's icon.
Right-click	Quickly tap the right mouse button. A right-click in Windows 8.1 or Windows 8.1 app reveals app controls or options. Within a software application such as Microsoft Word or Microsoft Excel, a right-click causes a shortcut menu to appear. Shortcut menus in software applications are context-sensitive, meaning that the menu that appears varies depending on the item the pointer is resting upon when the right-click occurs.
Drag	Hold down the left mouse button, move the mouse up, down, left, or right, and then release the mouse button. Dragging is an action often used to move or resize an object.
Scroll	Use the scroll wheel on the mouse to scroll in a window. If the pointing device you are using does not include a scroll wheel, click the scroll arrows on a horizontal or vertical scroll bar at the right or bottom of a window, or drag the scroll box in the middle of the scroll bar up, down, left, or right.

When navigating Windows 8.1 with a mouse, point to the corners of the screen (referred to as *hot corners*) to access Start and system commands and to switch apps.

Table 1.3	Keyboard Commands or Shortcuts
Keyboard Shortcut	**What It Does**
Windows logo key	Displays Start screen. Pressing the Windows logo key also toggles between the Start screen and the most recently used app.
Windows logo key + c	Reveals the Charms bar along the right side of the screen
Windows logo key + d	Goes to the desktop (similar window as the desktop in Windows 7 and earlier)
Windows logo key + e	Displays a This PC window on the desktop
Windows logo key + f	Searches the files on the PC or mobile device
Windows logo key + l	Locks the screen
Windows logo key + q	Searches everywhere including apps, settings, files, and the web
Alt + F4	Closes an app
Menu button	Reveals app controls and options (similar to a right-click)
Esc	Removes app controls, pane, or backs out of a menu or option
Up, Down, Left, or Right Arrow keys	Moves pointer to select a tile or charm; press the Enter key to launch the app or charm options.

To use a keyboard command, hold down the Windows logo key or Alt, press and release the letter or function key, and then release the Windows logo key or Alt.

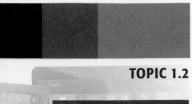

TOPIC 1.2

SKILLS

Start and sign in to
Windows 8.1

Launch an app

Switch apps

App Tip

Signing in with a Microsoft
account is considered
connecting to the cloud. Some
of your apps, games, music,
photos, files, and settings are
stored online and can be used
or viewed from any other
Windows 8.1 device.

Starting Windows 8.1 and Exploring Apps

Windows 8.1 starts up faster than earlier versions of Windows. If you are turning
on your PC from a no power state, the **Lock screen** shown in Figure 1.4 appears
in approximately 10 to 20 seconds. The Lock screen also appears if you resume
computer use after the system has gone into sleep mode. Depending on your PC
or mobile device, turning on or resuming system use from sleep mode involves
pressing the Power button or moving a mouse.

Each person who uses a PC or mobile device will have his or her own **user
account**. A user account includes a user name and a password. Windows stores
program and settings information for each user's account so that each person can
customize options without conflicting with the setttings for other people who use
the computer. In Windows 8.1, Microsoft provides for two types of user accounts at
sign-in: a Microsoft account or a local account.

Signing In with a Microsoft Account

A user account that has been set up as a **Microsoft account** means that you sign
in to Windows 8.1 using an email address from outlook.com, hotmail.com, or
live.com (referred to as a Windows Live ID). A Microsoft account means you can
download new apps from the Windows store, see live updates from messaging and
social media services in tiles, and sync some of your Windows and browser settings
online so that you see the same settings when you sign in on a different device.

Signing In with a Local Account

A user account that has been set up as a **local account** means that Windows and
browser settings on the PC or mobile device cannot be shared with other devices
and that automatic connections to messaging and social media services do not work.

*Note: The screens shown throughout this textbook show Windows 8.1 signed in with
a Microsoft account.*

1 Turn on the computer or mobile device, or resume system use from sleep mode.

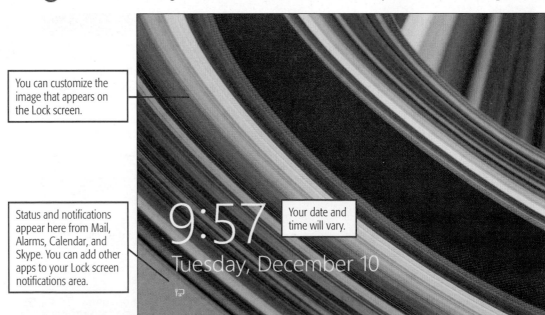

You can customize the
image that appears on
the Lock screen.

Status and notifications
appear here from Mail,
Alarms, Calendar, and
Skype. You can add other
apps to your Lock screen
notifications area.

Your date and
time will vary.

9:57
Tuesday, December 10

Figure 1.4 The Windows 8.1 lock screen appears after you start up the computer from
a no power state or when resuming use from sleep mode.

② At the Lock screen shown in Figure 1.4 on the previous page, swipe up from the bottom edge of the screen, click anywhere on the screen, or press any key on the keyboard to reveal the sign-in screen.

③ Depending on the system, the next step will vary. Complete the sign-in by following the steps in 3a, 3b, or 3c that match the configuration of your PC or mobile device:

a. Type your password in the *Password* text box below your Microsoft account name and email address and tap or press Enter, or tap or click the Submit button (displays as a right-pointing arrow).

Type your password and tap or press Enter, or tap or click the Submit button. The steps you complete to sign in may vary. If necessary, check with your instructor.

oops!

Your account is not shown on the sign-in screen? Tap or click Switch user (left-pointing arrow inside circle) next to the existing account name to see a list of accounts set up for the device. If necessary, check with your instructor for sign-in instructions.

b. Perform the touch gestures over your account's picture password.

c. If more than one user account is shown on the sign-in screen, tap or click the account picture or icon you want to use. Type your password in the *Password* text box and tap or press Enter, or tap or click the Submit button (displays as a right-pointing arrow).

The Start Screen

Once signed in, the Start screen, similar to the one shown in Figure 1.5, appears. The Start screen displays a series of tiles that are used to launch apps. A tile is a square or rectangle with an icon and name for an app.

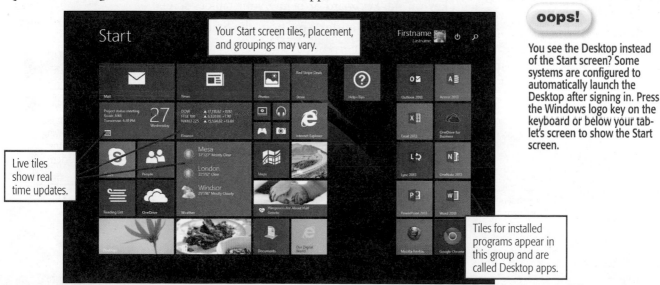

Live tiles show real time updates.

Tiles for installed programs appear in this group and are called Desktop apps.

oops!

You see the Desktop instead of the Start screen? Some systems are configured to automatically launch the Desktop after signing in. Press the Windows logo key on the keyboard or below your tablet's screen to show the Start screen.

Figure 1.5 The Windows 8.1 Start screen. Apps and programs are accessed from tiles, some of which display live updates.

Some tiles display status updates or notifications such as the number of new email messages, a weather update, a breaking news headline, or a status update from a Facebook friend. The Start screen and tiles are customizable. You will learn about customization in a later topic.

In the next steps, you will explore the Windows 8.1 environment by launching apps and switching between apps.

Launching an App

Built-in apps for Windows 8.1 include Mail, Calendar, Internet Explorer, Store, People, Photos, Maps, OneDrive, Desktop, Skype, Weather, News, Travel, Finance, Sports, Games, Camera, Music, Video, Food & Drink, Health & Fitness, Reading List, and Help + Tips. Apps automatically run in full-screen mode.

To launch an app, tap or click the app's tile from the Start screen. You can return to the Start screen using a touch gesture or mouse action, or by pressing the Windows logo key on the keyboard.

4 Tap or click the **Photos app** from the Start screen.

The Photos app shows thumbnails of the photos stored in the Pictures library on the PC or mobile device, or in the Pictures folder in OneDrive.

Step 4

Your Photos tile may vary, showing images if the tile is live.

Tap or click here to choose to display photos from OneDrive if you are signed in with a Microsoft account.

Your Photos app may show pictures in Details view instead of Thumbnails view shown here.

5 Swipe in from the right edge of the screen and tap Start, or press the Windows logo key on the keyboard or below your tablet's screen.

6 Tap or click the **Calendar app** from the Start screen.

The Calendar for the current day and the next day loads. Those connected to social networks such as Facebook see birthday reminders in their calendars.

Step 6

Your Calendar tile will vary, showing reminders from your connected services.

Your date and calendar entries will vary.

Your Calendar may appear in What's next view instead of Day view shown here.

7. Swipe in from the right edge of the screen and tap Start, or move the pointer to the lower left corner of the screen until the **Start button** appears (displays as the Windows icon) and then click the left mouse button.

Step 7

8. Tap or click the **Store app** from the Start screen.

In the Store you can search for and download new apps for your PC or mobile device.

9. Swipe in from the right edge of the screen and tap Start, or move the pointer to the top right or bottom right corner, slide the pointer down or up along the right edge when you see the five icons (called charms) appear in a column, and then click the Start charm (third from the top).

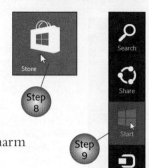

Step 8

Step 9

Switching between Apps

You can switch to an open app using touch gestures or mouse actions, or by clicking the program's button on the Taskbar. In the next steps you will switch between the Photos, Calendar, and Store apps.

10. Swipe in from the left edge of the screen a short distance and immediately swipe back to the left edge, or move the pointer to the top left corner of the screen until a thumbnail of the Store app appears and then move the pointer down along the left edge to see thumbnails of all open apps.

11. Tap or click the Photos app.

12. Move the mouse down towards the bottom of the screen until the Taskbar appears if the Taskbar is not currently visible, and then click the Calendar button on the Taskbar. Skip this step if you are using a tablet without an external mouse attached.

13. Press the Windows logo key on the keyboard or below your tablet's screen to return to the Start screen.

This pane is called the Switch list.

Step 11

Step 12

App Tip

With a touch-enabled device, you can switch between open apps by swiping in (also called thumbing in) from the left edge of the screen. As you swipe inward, the last open app comes into view and fills the screen as you continue moving your finger or thumb inward. Repeat the motion until you return to the desired app.

Beyond Basics   **Displaying Apps View**

Switch from the Start screen to Apps view to see a list of all apps on your PC or mobile device in a columnar arrangement by tapping or clicking the down-pointing arrow inside a circle near the bottom left of the Start screen. You can customize Windows to show Apps view instead of the Start screen after you sign in.

Slide up from the middle or move the mouse downward if this button is not visible.

Revealing the Charms Bar, Searching for an App, and Closing Apps

When you swipe in from the right edge of the screen or move the pointer to the top right corner or bottom right corner, the **Charms bar** shown in Figure 1.6 appears.

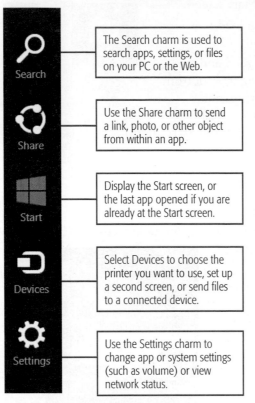

The Search charm is used to search apps, settings, or files on your PC or the Web.

Use the Share charm to send a link, photo, or other object from within an app.

Display the Start screen, or the last app opened if you are already at the Start screen.

Select Devices to choose the printer you want to use, set up a second screen, or send files to a connected device.

Use the Settings charm to change app or system settings (such as volume) or view network status.

Figure 1.6 The Charms bar displays when you swipe in from the right edge of the screen or point at the top right corner or bottom right corner.

Charms are used to access system resources and commands. As you saw in the previous topic, the Start charm is used to return to the Start screen. The Search charm is used to search for something in apps, settings, files, or the Web. You can use Search to find a program, a document or other type of file, a setting in an application or the control panel, or search for a word or phrase within an app. Search can be used to quickly find and launch a program rather than scrolling through the Start screen, or find a program that does not have a tile on the Start screen.

In Windows 8.1 you do not need to close apps. When you switch to another app, the app you switched from remains running in the background and will eventually close if not used. However, you can close an app if you are done with it by swiping from the top edge of the screen down to the bottom, or by revealing the Title bar by moving the mouse to the top of the screen and then clicking the Close button.

1. At the Start screen, display the Charms bar by swiping in from the right edge of the screen or by moving the pointer to the top right or bottom right corner and sliding down or up the edge of the screen.

2. Tap or click the Search charm.

App Tip

You can search from the Start screen without revealing the Charms bar by using the Search button at the top right of the screen next to your account name and picture, or by typing the first few characters of the app or file you are looking for at the Start screen to automatically open the Search pane.

Step 2

By default, Windows will search *Everywhere*, which means apps, programs, settings, files, and web searches display in the Search results list.

③ Type **map**. (If necessary, tap inside the text box to bring up the touch keyboard.)

As soon as you start typing, Windows returns a list of programs, files, settings, and web searches in the search results list within the Search pane. Each letter typed narrows the search results.

Your search results list may vary.

④ Tap or click *Maps* in the search results list to launch the Maps app. If prompted, tap or click Allow to use your location and turn on location services.

⑤ Swipe in from the right edge or point to the top right or bottom right corner and slide the mouse down or up to reveal the Charms bar, and tap or click the Search charm.

⑥ Type **weather** and tap or press Enter.

⑦ Swipe from the top edge of the screen all the way to the bottom, or move the mouse to the top edge of the screen until the Title bar appears and then click the Close button (red button with white ×) at the right end of the Title bar to close the Weather app.

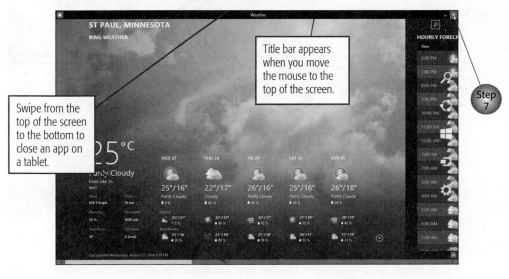

Swipe from the top of the screen to the bottom to close an app on a tablet.

Title bar appears when you move the mouse to the top of the screen.

⑧ Switch to the Calendar app and close the app by completing a step similar to Step 7.

⑨ Close the Photos app, the Store app, and the Maps app, and then display the Start screen if the desktop appears.

Quick STEPS

Reveal the Charms Bar
Swipe in from right edge of screen, or point at top right corner or bottom right corner and slide the mouse down or up along right edge.

Search for an App
1. Reveal Charms bar.
2. Tap or click Search charm.
3. Type name of app you want to find.

Close an App
Swipe from top edge of screen to bottom edge of screen, or move the mouse to the top of the screen until the Title bar appears and then click the Close button.

App Tip

You can also close an app by right-clicking the mouse over the app thumbnail in the Switch list and choosing *Close* at the shortcut menu.

App Tip

The keyboard command Alt + F4 closes an app.

Beyond Basics   Limiting the Search to One Category

You can limit a search to show results for only one category such as files or settings for your PC or mobile device. To do this, display the Search pane, tap or click the down-pointing arrow next to *Everywhere* above the search box, and then choose *Settings*, *Files*, *Web images*, or *Web videos* in the drop-down list.

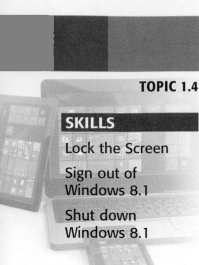

TOPIC 1.4

SKILLS

Lock the Screen

Sign out of
Windows 8.1

Shut down
Windows 8.1

Locking the Screen, Signing Out, and Shutting Down Windows 8.1

If you need to leave your PC or mobile device for a short period of time and do not want to close all of your apps and documents, you can lock the device. Locking the system causes the lock screen image to appear full screen so that someone else cannot see your work. All of your apps and documents are left open in the background so that you can resume work right away once you enter your account password.

1. At the Start screen, tap or click the Photos tile to launch the Photos app.

2. Press the Windows logo key on the keyboard or below your tablet's screen, or swipe in from the right and tap Start to return to the Start screen.

3. Tap or click your account name at the top right corner of the screen.

4. Tap or click *Lock* at the drop-down list.

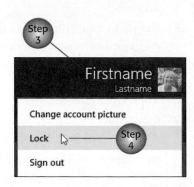

The Windows lock screen appears with the current date and time. Notifications appear below the date to show network connectivity status, power status, and updates from apps such as mail.

5. Swipe up, click anywhere on the lock screen, or press any key on the keyboard to display the sign-in screen.

6. Type your password in the *Password* text box and tap or press Enter, or tap or click the Submit button.

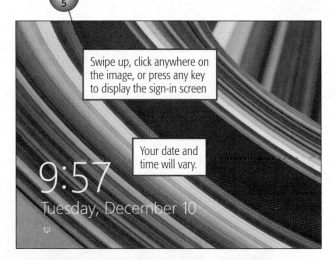

Swipe up, click anywhere on the image, or press any key to display the sign-in screen

Your date and time will vary.

9:57
Tuesday, December 10

7. Swipe in from the left edge or click at the top left corner of the screen when the Photos app thumbnail appears to return to the Photos app.

When you locked the screen, the Photos app stayed open in the background.

8. Display the Start screen.

Start

Signing Out of a Windows Session

When you are finished with a Windows session, you should **sign out** of the PC or mobile device. Signing out is also referred to as **logging off**. Signing out closes all apps and files. If a computer or mobile device is shared with other people, signing out is expected so that the next user can sign in to his or her account. Signing out and locking also provide security for your device because someone would need to know your password to access programs or files.

App Tip

If you have documents open, Windows prompts you to save changes before proceeding with the sign-out process.

⑨ At the Start screen, tap or click your account name and tap or click *Sign out* at the drop-down list.

The Windows lock screen appears; however, this time Windows closes the Photos app automatically.

⑩ Display the sign-in screen and sign back in to Windows. If your PC or mobile device goes to the desktop at sign in, display the Start screen.

⑪ Display the Switch list. Refer to Step 10 on page 11 if you need assistance displaying the Switch list. Notice that the Photos app thumbnail does not appear because it was closed when you signed out.

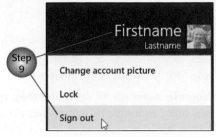

Lock PC or Mobile Device
1. Tap or click account name at top right corner of screen.
2. Tap or click *Lock*.

Sign Out of Windows
1. Tap or click account name at top right corner of screen.
2. Tap or click *Sign out*.

Shut Down PC or Mobile Device
1. Tap or click Power Options button.
2. Tap or click *Shut down*.

Shutting Down the PC or Mobile Device

If you want to turn off the power to your computer or mobile device, perform a **shut down**. Shutting down the system ensures that all Windows files are properly closed. The power will turn off automatically when shut down is complete.

⑫ Tap or click the Power Options button located next to your account name and picture at the top right of the screen.

Note: Check with your instructor before proceeding to Step 13 because some schools do not allow students to shut down computers. If necessary, tap or click in an unused area of the Start screen to remove the Power Options drop-down list and proceed to the next topic.

⑬ Tap or click *Shut down* at the drop-down list.

The system will perform the shut down operation, and in a few seconds the power will turn off. The Power Options drop-down list may indicate that the system will automatically perform updates as it is shut down or restarted.

⑭ Wait a moment or two and then press the Power button to turn the PC or mobile device back on.

⑮ When the lock screen appears, display the sign-in screen and sign back in to Windows. If your PC or mobile device goes to the desktop at sign in, display the Start screen.

In the *Balanced* power plan (the default power option), the system will automatically go into sleep mode after 15 minutes (battery power) or 30 minutes (plugged in).

 **Other Power Options**

Use the *Sleep* option from the Power Options drop-down list if you are leaving the computer for a while and want to leave all programs and documents open but use less power. Choose *Restart* to shut down Windows and immediately start it up again without turning off the power. A restart may be needed if the system is not performing correctly, hangs, or is otherwise not responding.

TOPIC 1.5

SKILLS

Pin/Unpin tiles to/from the Start screen

Move tiles

Resize tiles

Turn on and off live updates

Customizing the Start Screen

You can personalize the Start screen to suit your preferences by adding or removing tiles, rearranging tiles, resizing a tile larger or smaller, and by turning a live tile off to stop notifications and updates from appearing in the tile.

Note: In some school computer labs, the ability to change Windows settings is disabled. If necessary, complete this topic and the next topic on your PC or mobile device at home.

Selecting a Tile

Select a tile using a touch gesture by swiping up from the bottom of the screen, tapping the Customize button, and then tapping the tile(s) you want to customize. Right-click a tile to select the tile using a mouse. A selected tile displays a check mark in the upper right corner of the tile, and tile commands appear along the bottom of the screen on touch-enabled devices, or in a shortcut menu as shown in Figure 1.7.

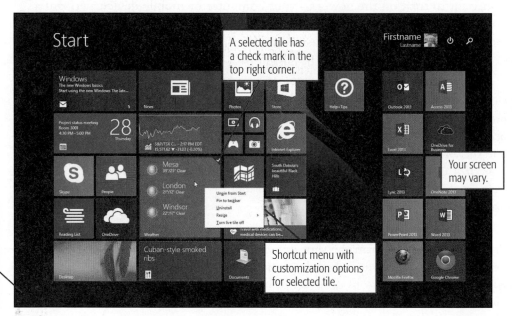

On touch-enabled devices, tile options appear along the bottom of the screen when a tile has been selected.

Figure 1.7 Selecting a tile on the Start screen displays tile options to unpin the tile from the Start screen, pin the app to the taskbar, uninstall the app, resize the tile, or turn on or off live updates.

Pinning and Unpinning Tiles to and from the Start Screen

Select a tile and choose **Unpin from Start** from the shortcut menu or from the Customize pane along the bottom of the screen to remove the tile from the Start screen. Add a tile to the Start screen by selecting the tile in Apps view and choosing **Pin to Start**.

oops!

No Weather tile on the Start screen? Select any other tile to remove. You will repin the tile to Start after you practice removing it.

App Tip

Pressing and holding a tile on a touch-enabled device automatically selects the tile and opens the Customize pane.

1. Select the Weather tile by swiping up from the bottom of the screen, tapping the Customize button located near the bottom right corner, and then tapping the tile; or, by right-clicking the Weather tile.

2. Tap Unpin from Start in the Customize pane, or click *Unpin from Start* at the shortcut menu.

③ Tap in an unused area of the Start screen to close the Customize pane if you are using touch gestures; otherwise, proceed to Step 4.

④ Slide right until you see the Apps button (down-pointing arrow inside circle) near the bottom left of the screen and then tap the button; or, move the mouse to the bottom of the screen and then click the Apps button when it appears.

⑤ In Apps view, select the Weather tile and then tap Pin to Start in the Customize pane, or click *Pin to Start* at the shortcut menu.

The Weather tile is added back to the Start screen placed at the right end of the tiles.

⑥ At the Start screen, slide or scroll right if necessary to see the Weather tile.

Rearranging Tiles

Tiles can be moved to a new location on the Start screen by swiping up, tapping the Customize button, selecting the tile, and then sliding the tile using touch, or by dragging the tile using the mouse to the desired location.

⑦ Swipe up, tap the Customize button, select the Weather tile, and then slide the tile down and across, or drag the tile with the mouse until the tile is back at its original location in the Start screen. Tap an unused area of the Start screen to close the Customize pane if you used a touch gesture for this step.

Resizing a Tile and Turning Off Live Updates

Tiles can be sized *Large*, *Wide*, *Medium*, or *Small* using the Resize option in the Customize pane or from the shortcut menu for a selected tile. Some tiles offer fewer size options.

Some tiles display live updates by default. For example, the Food & Drink tile shows a featured recipe. Other tiles show current news headlines or status updates. Live updates can be turned off or on as desired.

⑧ Select the Food & Drink tile, tap the Resize button in the Customize pane or point to *Resize* on the shortcut menu, and then tap or click *Medium*. (Choose another size if the tile is already Medium.)

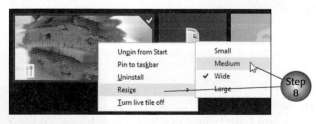

⑨ Select the Food & Drink tile and tap Turn live tile off in the Customize pane, or click *Turn live tile off* at the shortcut menu. Skip this step if live tile is already turned off.

⑩ Resize the Food & Drink tile back to *Wide* and *Turn live tile on* by completing steps similar to Step 8 and Step 9. If necessary, close the Customize pane.

SKILLS

Change the Lock
screen background
image

Add an app to
the Lock screen
notifications

Change the Start
screen design and
color scheme

Personalizing the Start and Lock Screens

Most people like to put a personal stamp on their PC or mobile device. In
Windows 8.1, you can personalize the Lock screen by changing the picture that
displays and the apps that provide notifications when the screen locks. The Start
screen can be personalized to a different color scheme and background design.

Display the Charms bar, tap or click the Settings charm, and tap or click **Change
PC settings** at the bottom right of the Settings pane to change the Lock screen
picture at the PC settings window, or tap or click *Personalize* near the top of the
Settings pane to change the Start screen design and color scheme.

1 At the Start screen, reveal the Charms bar
and tap or click the Settings charm.

2 Tap or click Change PC settings at the
bottom right of the Settings pane.

The current Lock screen image is shown
at the top of the Personalize pane in the PC
settings window as shown in Figure 1.8. You
can change the lock screen image to one of
five other images provided in Windows 8.1, or select a picture stored on your PC or
mobile device from the Browse button.

3 Tap or click PC and devices in the left pane of the PC settings window.

Categories for
system options
that can be
changed.

Figure 1.8 You can make changes to your system by choosing a category in the left pane of
the PC settings window and then changing options for the category in the right pane.

4 Tap or click any one
of the five background
thumbnails below the
current image shown
in the *Lock screen
preview* section of the
PC and devices
window.

By default, the Mail, Alarms, Calendar, and Skype apps provide quick status and notifications on the Lock screen.

5 Tap or click the first button with a plus symbol in the *Lock screen apps* section and tap or click *Weather* at the pop-up *Choose an app* list. (You may need to scroll up or down the list to find *Weather*.)

6 Display the Start screen, reveal the Charms bar, tap or click the Settings charm, and then tap or click *Personalize* near the top of the Settings pane.

7 Tap or click any one of the 20 tile designs in the Personalize pane.

8 Slide or drag the color slider below the *Background color* and *Accent color* palettes to change the color of the Start screen background and designs. You can also tap or click a color tile within the palette instead of using the slider.

9 Tap or click in an unused area of the Start screen to close the Personalize pane and view the new design and color scheme.

10 Tap or click your account name at the top right of the Start screen and tap or click *Lock* to view the new Lock screen image.

11 Sign back in with your password to unlock the system.

Note: Check with your instructor if you are completing this topic in a school computer lab to see if he or she wants you to restore the Lock and Start screen to the original settings by redoing Steps 1 through 9 and choosing the default Lock screen and Start screen options. Remove Weather from the lock screen notifications by tapping or clicking the Weather button in the **Lock** *screen apps section of the* **PC and devices** *window and tapping or clicking* **Don't show quick status here** *at the top of the Choose an app list.*

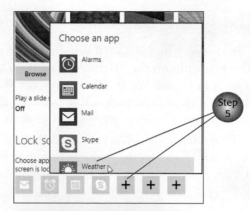

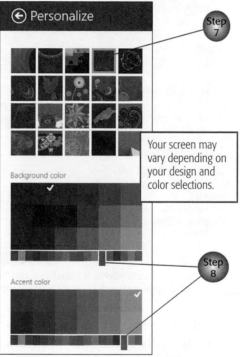

Your screen may vary depending on your design and color selections.

Adding a Picture for your Account

Tap or click *Accounts* in the left pane of the PC settings window to add a picture to your account name on the Start screen. Tap or click the Browse button below the Account picture box, tap or click the desired image in the Pictures window, and then tap or click the Choose Image button. You can also use the Camera button to take a new picture of yourself with your PC or mobile device camera.

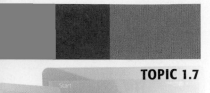

TOPIC 1.7

SKILLS

Display the desktop

Open and close desktop apps

View information in the Notifications area of the Taskbar

Using the Desktop

For people who have used Windows 7 or earlier, the desktop is a familiar place. The **Desktop** tile on the Start screen opens a window with the Windows 8.1 desktop, as shown in Figure 1.9. In many ways, the Windows 8.1 desktop functions the same as the desktop in Windows 7. You can even choose to show the desktop instead of the Start screen whenever you sign in to your PC or mobile device.

Programs such as Microsoft Word or Microsoft Excel are considered desktop apps, which means the desktop launches first, then Word or Excel. Even Windows 8.1 accessory programs such as Notepad or Paint open from the desktop.

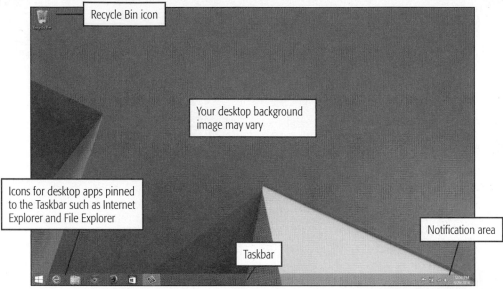

Recycle Bin icon

Your desktop background image may vary

Icons for desktop apps pinned to the Taskbar such as Internet Explorer and File Explorer

Notification area

Taskbar

Figure 1.9 The Windows 8.1 desktop with Taskbar and desktop icons is used for working in desktop apps such as File Explorer, in which you perform tasks such as copying or moving files.

App Tip

Some apps such as Internet Explorer offer both an app and a desktop version. Desktop apps offer the traditional user interface from Windows 7 and earlier and include more features.

1 Tap or click the Desktop tile from the Start screen.

The **Recycle Bin** icon is at the top left corner. Icons for other desktop programs that are installed on your computer may also appear on your desktop. The **Taskbar** along the bottom of the window contains an icon to launch Internet Explorer and **File Explorer**. Other program icons may also be pinned to the Taskbar. The **Notification area** at the right end of the Taskbar shows the current date and time, speaker icon, network status indicator, and Action Center flag. A power status indicator and other icons may also appear in your Notification area depending on the desktop programs installed on your PC or mobile device.

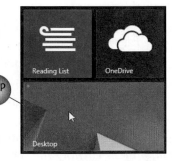
Step 1

2 Double-tap or double-click the Recycle Bin icon on the desktop.

Double-tapping or double-clicking launches programs from an icon on the desktop. Desktop apps window features are described in Figure 1.10 on the next page. You will learn more about desktop windows in the next topic.

Step 2

3 Tap or click the **Close button** (red button with white ×) at the top right corner of the Recycle Bin window.

Step 3

④ Tap or click the File Explorer icon on the Taskbar.

Programs with icons pinned to the Taskbar are opened with a single tap or click. You will learn more about File Explorer in the next three topics.

⑤ Tap or click the Close button at the top right corner of the This PC window.

⑥ Tap or click the current date and time at the right end of the Taskbar.

The current month's calendar appears above the date and time. You can change the date or time if necessary by tapping or clicking the <u>Change date and time settings</u> hyperlink to open a Date and Time dialog box.

⑦ Tap or click in an unused area of the desktop to remove the pop-up calendar.

⑧ Tap or click the Speakers icon at the right end of the Taskbar to open the Volume control slider.

You can slide or drag the slider up or down to raise or lower the volume.

⑨ Tap or click in an unused area of the desktop to remove the volume slider.

⑩ Reveal the Charms bar and tap or click the Start charm.

Quick STEPS

Show the Desktop
Tap or click Desktop tile.

Launch a Desktop App
Double-tap or double-click icon on desktop OR tap or click icon in Taskbar.

App Tip

The Settings charm on the desktop provides options to personalize the desktop window and access the Control Panel from which you can control more system features.

App Tip

The desktop is also opened automatically if you launch a desktop app from a Start screen tile or from the Search apps screen.

Title bar shows desktop app name. Slide or drag Title bar to move window to another location on the desktop.

Minimize button. Tap or click to reduce window to a button on the Taskbar.

Maximize button. Tap or click to have window fill entire desktop.

Close button. Tap or click to close the window.

Slide or drag the edge of any side or any corner to resize the window larger or smaller.

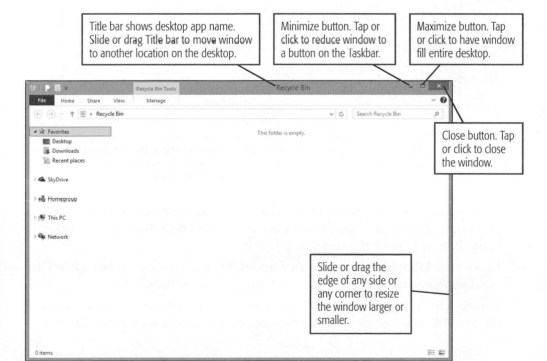

Figure 1.10 The Recycle Bin window. Desktop app windows contain standard features for moving, resizing, and closing windows.

SKILLS

Identify features in the File Explorer window

Browse content of devices using File Explorer

Browsing Files with File Explorer

As you work on a PC or mobile device you are creating and modifying files. A **file** is a document, spreadsheet, presentation, picture, or any other text and/or image that you have saved as digital data. Files are also videos and songs that you play on your PC or mobile device. Each file has a unique **file name**, which is a series of characters you assign to the file when you save it that allows you to identify and retrieve the file later. File Explorer is the utility used to browse the contents of various storage devices and perform file management routines.

Note: You will need the student CD that came with this textbook and a USB flash drive to complete the steps in this topic and the next two topics.

1. Tap or click the Desktop tile from the Start screen.

2. Tap or click the File Explorer icon on the Taskbar.

A This PC window opens. The features of the This PC window are identified in Figure 1.11. From a This PC window you can browse all of the files and folders stored on the hard drives, removable devices, and networked locations for which you have access.

In Windows 8.1, OneDrive was added to the Navigation pane to provide easy access to the files and folders you have stored in OneDrive provided you signed in with your Microsoft account.

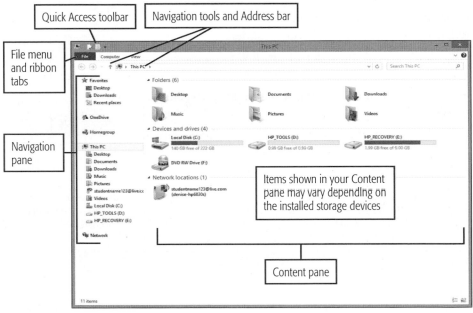

Each storage drive in the *Devices and drives section* of a This PC window is identified with an icon, a drive letter, the available storage capacity, and the total storage capacity.

Figure 1.11 A This PC window is divided into two panes. The Navigation pane at the left displays the list of places associated with your account. The right pane, called the Content pane, displays the folders, devices and drives, and network locations accessible to you with the PC or mobile device.

3. Insert the student resources CD that came with this textbook into the DVD or other optical drive. If a new window opens for the DVD drive, tap or click the Close button to close the window.

4. Insert your USB flash drive into an empty USB port. If a new Removable Disk window opens, tap or click the Close button to close the window.

5. Double-tap or double-click the DVD drive in the *Devices and drives* section in the This PC window to view the contents of the student resources CD.

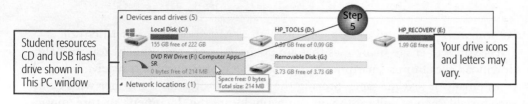

Student resources CD and USB flash drive shown in This PC window

Step 5

Your drive icons and letters may vary.

Browse Files in File Explorer
1. Display the desktop.
2. Tap or click File Explorer in the Taskbar.
3. If necessary, insert a removable storage medium such as a DVD or USB flash drive.
4. Tap or click desired location or device in Navigation pane OR double-tap or double-click a folder or device name in Content pane.

The Content pane shows the names of the files and folders on the student resources CD. A **folder** is a name assigned to a placeholder or container in which you store a group of related files. Think of a folder on the computer in the same way you consider a paper file folder in a desk drawer in your home. You might have one file folder for your household bills and another file folder for your school documents. Separating documents into different file folders makes storage and retrieval quicker and easier. Similarly, electronic files on a storage medium are organized into folders.

⑥ Double-tap or double-click the folder named *Student_Data_Files*.

A list of folders stored within the Student_Data_Files folder appears. A folder within another folder is sometimes referred to as a **subfolder**.

⑦ Double-tap or double-click the folder named *Ch1*.

A list of files stored in the Ch1 subfolder appears in the Content pane.

⑧ Tap or click *This PC* in the Navigation pane.

You can browse content by tapping or clicking names in the Navigation pane or by double-tapping or double-clicking names in the Content pane.

Step 6

Folders

Step 7

Name

▲ Files Currently on the Disc (15)

Ch1

Type: File folder
Date modified: 4/26/2013 8:31 AM
Size: 104 MB
Files: Apollo11_NYParade.jpg, ...

Ch7
Ch8
Ch9
Ch10
Ch11
Ch12
Ch13
Ch14
Ch15
Summary_Table_Student_Data_Files.docx

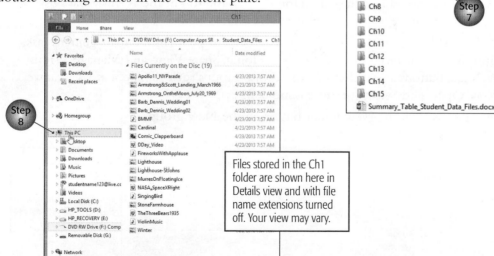

Step 8

Files stored in the Ch1 folder are shown here in Details view and with file name extensions turned off. Your view may vary.

⑨ Tap or click the Close button in the This PC window Title bar.

⑩ Display the Start screen.

Note: Leave the Student Resources CD and your USB flash drive in the PC or mobile device for the next topics.

oops!

Using a tablet or other device with no DVD drive? Check with your instructor for information on where you will look for the student data files. You may be directed to a website or network location. If necessary, practice the remaining steps using folder names on your local disk drive.

App Tip

Double-tapping or double-clicking a file name opens the program associated with the file and automatically opens/plays the document, image, video, or sound.

App Tip

Tap or click the View tab to change the way the Content pane displays the file list. You can choose to display the files with different sized icons as well as a Preview pane or Details pane.

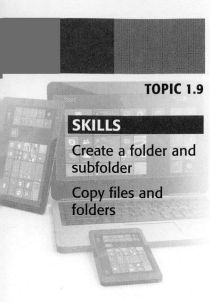

TOPIC 1.9

SKILLS

Create a folder and subfolder

Copy files and folders

Creating Folders and Copying Files and Folders

As you work with software applications such as Microsoft Word or Microsoft Excel you will create many files that are documents or spreadsheets. You may also download files from a smartphone, digital camera, or website and receive other files from emails or text messages. Storing the files in an organized manner with easily recognizable names will mean you can easily locate the document, picture, music, or other item later. Creating folders in advance of creating files will mean you have an organizational structure already in place. From time to time you also need to rename, copy, move, or delete files and folders to maintain a storage medium in good order.

Creating a Folder

Creating a folder on a computer is like placing a sticky label on the outside of an empty paper file folder and writing a title on it. The title provides a brief description of the type of documents stored inside the file folder. On the computer, in File Explorer, you tap or click a **New folder** button and then type a name for the folder to set up the electronic equivalent of a paper filing system.

1. Tap or click the Desktop tile from the Start screen and then tap or click the File Explorer icon in the Taskbar.

2. Double-tap or double-click the Removable Disk representing your USB flash drive in the *Devices and drives* section of the This PC window.

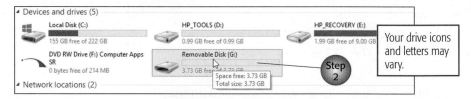

Tabs and/or buttons in the ribbon change and become available or unavailable depending on what is selected in the window.

3. If necessary, tap or click the Home tab at the top of the Removable Disk window to display the ribbon interface.

The **ribbon** provides the buttons you need to perform file management tasks. Buttons are organized into tabs such as Home, Share, View, and Manage. Within each tab, buttons are further organized into groups such as Clipboard, Organize, New, Open, and Select (on the Home tab).

4. Tap or click the New folder button in the New group.

In the folder structure you are creating, no spaces between words are used. Windows allows the use of spaces; however, common practice is to avoid spaces in folder names.

5. Type **ComputerCourse** and tap or press Enter.

(6) Tap or click the View tab and tap or click the List button in the Layout group.

List view displays names with small icons representing each file or folder and without details such as the date or time the file or folder was created or modified, the file type, and the file size. Each folder can have a different view.

(7) If necessary, tap or click the Home tab and tap or click the push pin icon at the right end of the ribbon below the Close button. This displays the ribbon permanently in the window.

(8) Double-tap or double-click the *ComputerCourse* folder name in the Content pane.

You have now opened the ComputerCourse folder. File management tasks performed next will occur inside this folder.

(9) With the Home tab active, tap or click the New folder button, type **ChapterTopicsWork**, and then tap or press Enter.

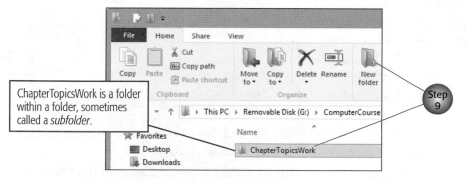

ChapterTopicsWork is a folder within a folder, sometimes called a *subfolder*.

(10) Tap or click the New folder button, type **ChapterProjectsWork**, and tap or press Enter.

You now have two subfolders within the ComputerCourse folder.

(11) Tap or click the Up arrow button at the left of the Address bar.

Notice you now see the ComputerCourse folder name only. The two folders created in Steps 9 and 10 are no longer visible because they are *inside* the ComputerCourse folder.

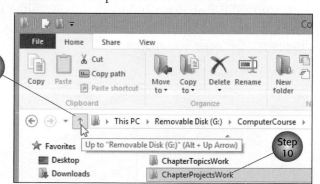

The Up arrow used in Step 11 moved the display up one level in the folder hierarchy as shown in the Address bar.

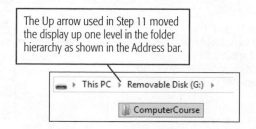

Copying Files and Folders

Copying a file or folder from one storage medium to another makes an exact copy of a document, spreadsheet, presentation, picture, video, music file, or other object. Copying is one way of making a backup copy of an important file on another storage medium. Windows provides multiple methods for copying files or folders.

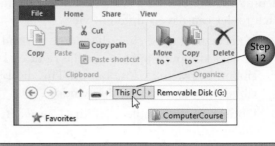

12 Tap or click *This PC* in the Address bar.

Tapping or clicking a name in the Address bar is another way to navigate to devices or folders.

13 Double-tap or double-click the DVD drive representing the student resources CD.

14 Tap once or single-click to select the folder named *Student_Data_Files*.

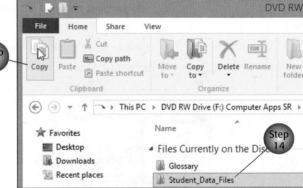

Before you can copy, you must first select a file or folder. A selected file or folder displays with a blue background in the Content pane.

Ctrl + C is the universal keyboard shortcut to Copy.

15 Tap or click the **Copy** button in the Clipboard group.

16 Tap or click This PC in the Address bar and then double-tap or double-click the Removable Disk representing your USB flash drive.

17 Double-tap or double-click the folder named *ComputerCourse* in the Content pane.

18 Tap or click the **Paste** button in the Clipboard group.

This step is copying all of the student data files you will need for your course onto your USB flash drive and placing them in the ComputerCourse folder. As the copying takes place, Windows displays a progress message. When the message disappears, the copy is complete.

Ctrl + V is the universal keyboard shortcut to Paste.

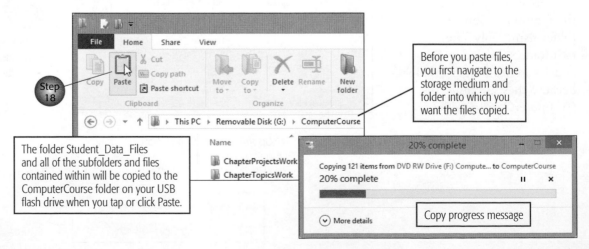

Before you paste files, you first navigate to the storage medium and folder into which you want the files copied.

The folder Student_Data_Files and all of the subfolders and files contained within will be copied to the ComputerCourse folder on your USB flash drive when you tap or click Paste.

Copy progress message

(19) Double-tap or double-click the *Student_Data_Files* folder name.

(20) Double-tap or double-click the *Ch1* folder name.

In the next steps you will copy individual files to a folder on the same storage medium.

(21) If necessary, tap or click the View tab and tap or click List in the Layout group to show only the file names in the Ch1 folder.

(22) Swipe your finger from the bottom of the list up over the file names starting at **Winter** and ending at **Lighthouse**; or single-click *Lighthouse*, hold down the Shift key, and single-click *Winter*.

This selects all of the files starting with **Lighthouse** and ending with **Winter**.

(23) If necessary, tap or click the Home tab.

(24) Tap or click the Copy button.

(25) Tap or click *ComputerCourse* in the Address bar and double-tap or double-click *ChapterTopicsWork* in the Content pane.

(26) Tap or click the Paste button.

The selected files are copied into the ChapterTopicsWork folder.

(27) Tap or click the Close button to close the ChapterTopicsWork window and return to the desktop.

(28) Display the Start screen.

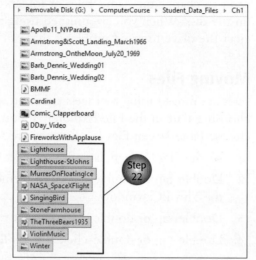

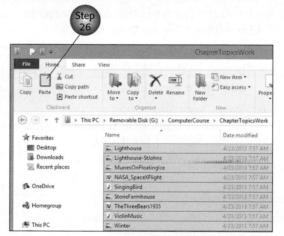

Quick STEPS

Copy Files or Folders

1. Display desktop.
2. Tap or click File Explorer.
3. Navigate to source data storage medium and/or folder.
4. Select files or folder to be copied.
5. If necessary, tap or click Home tab.
6. Tap or click Copy button.
7. Navigate to destination storage medium and/or folder.
8. Tap or click Paste button.

App Tip

Select multiple adjacent files using Shift + click. Use Ctrl + click to select multiple files that are not next to each other in the list.

App Tip

Touch-enabled devices display a check mark inside a check box next to each selected file.

ALTERNATIVE method

Windows provides multiple other methods for copying files:

■ Select files, choose the Copy to button in the Organize group, choose the destination folder;

■ Select files, display the shortcut menu, choose Copy, navigate to the destination folder, display the shortcut menu and choose Paste; or

■ Slide or drag and drop folders/files in the File Explorer window.

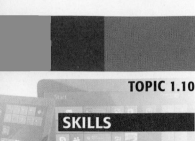

Moving, Renaming, and Deleting Files and Folders, and Ejecting a USB Flash Drive

File Explorer is also used to move, rename, and delete files and folders. Sometimes you will copy a file or save a file in a folder and later decide you want to move it elsewhere. You may also assign a file name to a file or folder and later decide you want to change the name. Files or folders no longer needed can be deleted to clean up the disk. When you are finished using a USB flash drive, you should properly eject the drive to avoid problems that can occur when files are not properly closed.

SKILLS

Move a file or folder

Rename a file or folder

Delete a file or folder

Empty the Recycle Bin

Eject a USB flash drive

Moving Files

Files are moved using a process similar to copying. Begin by selecting files and choosing **Cut** in the File Explorer ribbon. Navigate to the destination location and choose Paste. When files are cut they are removed from the source location.

1. At the Start Screen, launch the desktop and open File Explorer.

2. Double-tap or double-click the Removable Disk for your USB flash drive in the This PC window.

3. Double-tap or double-click *ComputerCourse* in the Content pane.

4. Double-tap or double-click *ChapterTopicsWork* in the Content pane.

Assume that you decide that the files copied from the Student_Data_Files Ch1 folder in the last topic should be stored inside a folder within ChapterTopicsWork.

5. Tap or click the New folder button in the ribbon, type **Ch1** and tap or press Enter.

6. Swipe your finger up over the file names starting at **Winter** and ending at **Lighthouse**; or single-click *Lighthouse*, hold down the Shift key, and single-click *Winter*.

App Tip

Ctrl + X is the universal keyboard shortcut to Cut.

7. Tap or click the Cut button in the Clipboard group.

8. Double-tap or double-click the *Ch1* folder.

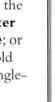
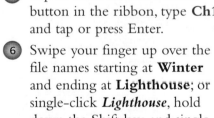
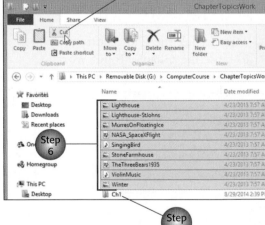

9. Tap or click the Paste button in the Clipboard group.

The files are removed from the ChapterTopicsWork folder and placed within the Ch1 folder.

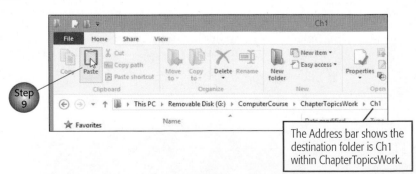

The Address bar shows the destination folder is Ch1 within ChapterTopicsWork.

10 Tap or click the Back
button to return to the
previous list.

Notice the files
are no longer in the
ChapterTopicsWork folder.

11 Tap or click the
Forward button (right-
pointing arrow next to
Back button) to return to
the Ch1 folder.

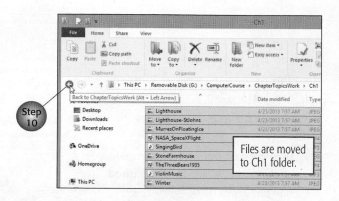

Files are moved
to Ch1 folder.

Step
10

Renaming Files and Folders

At times you will receive a file from someone else and decide you want to rename
the file to something more meaningful to you, or you may decide upon a new
name for a file or folder after the file or folder was created. A **Rename** button is in
the Organize group in the Home tab of the File Explorer ribbon.

12 Double-tap or double-click the file named *Winter* in the Content pane. The
photograph opens in the Photos app or in Windows Photo Viewer, depending
on the setup for the computer you are using.

Assume a friend sent you this picture of a weeping birch tree laden with snow in
a winter scene. You decide to rename the picture.

13 Close Windows Photo Viewer
or close the Photos app. If
necessary, switch back to
the desktop to return to
File Explorer.

14 If necessary, tap once or
single-click to select the
file named *Winter* in the
Content pane.

15 Tap or click the Rename
button in the Organize
group.

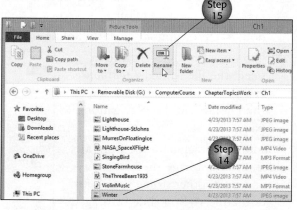

Step
15

Step
14

16 Type **TreeCoveredWithSnow** and tap or press
Enter.

17 Tap once or single-click to select the file named
ViolinMusic.

Assume this file is the song Donny Boy played on
a violin and recorded by you as you heard the song
at an outdoor event.

Step
16

⑱ Tap or click the Rename button, type **DonnyBoyViolinMusic**, and tap or press Enter.

⑲ Tap or click *ComputerCourse* in the Address bar.

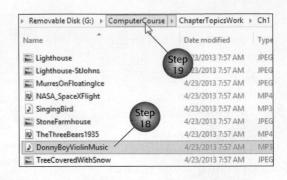

You can rename a folder as well as a file.

⑳ If necessary, tap once or single-click to select the folder named *ChapterTopicsWork*.

㉑ Tap or click the Rename button, type **CompletedTopicsByChapter**, and tap or press Enter.

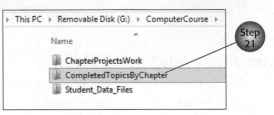

Deleting Files and Folders

Delete files or folders when you no longer need to keep them, or if you have copied files or folders to a removable storage medium for archive purposes and want to delete them from the local disk to free up space. Files and folders deleted from the local hard disk are moved to the Recycle Bin. While it is in the Recycle Bin, you can restore the file back to its original location if you deleted the file in error. Files deleted from a USB flash drive are not sent to the Recycle Bin; therefore, exercise caution when deleting a file from a USB flash drive.

㉒ Double-tap or double-click the folder named *CompletedTopicsByChapter*, and double-tap or double-click the folder named *Ch1*.

㉓ Tap once or single-click to select the file named **Lighthouse** and then slide or drag the file to the Desktop in the Navigation pane.

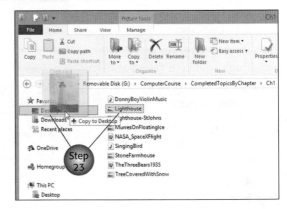

Sliding or dragging a file from a folder on one storage medium to a location on another storage medium copies the file. As you slide or drag, Windows shows a thumbnail of the picture.

㉔ Tap once or click Desktop in the Navigation pane.

㉕ Tap once or click **Lighthouse** to select the file and tap or click the **Delete** button in the Organize group (tap or click the top of the button—not the down-pointing arrow).

App Tip

The Recycle Bin is set to hold a maximum size of deleted files. Be aware that when the maximum is reached, some files will be permanently deleted to make room for new deleted files.

App Tip

Dragging a file or folder on the same storage medium moves the file. To be sure of the operation you want to perform, drag a file or folder to another location using the right-mouse button. When you release the mouse, a shortcut menu appears at which you can choose to Copy or Move.

26. Tap or click This PC in the Navigation pane and double-tap or double-click the Removable Disk for your USB flash drive.

27. Double-tap or double-click *ComputerCourse, CompletedTopicsByChapter*, and *Ch1*.

28. Tap once or single-click to select ***SingingBird*** and tap or click the Delete button.

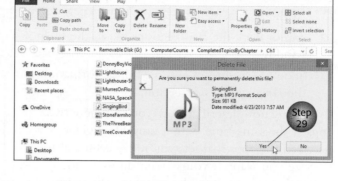

29. Tap or click Yes at the Delete File message box that appears.

The confirmation message appears when you delete a file from a USB device because the files are permanently deleted, not sent to the Recycle Bin from which they could be restored.

30. Close the Ch1 File Explorer window.

31. Double-tap or double-click the Recycle Bin icon on the desktop.

32. Tap or click the Empty Recycle Bin button in the ribbon.

File deleted at Step 25 was moved here.

33. Tap or click Yes to permanently delete the file at the Delete File message box.

34. Close the Recycle Bin window.

35. Tap or click the Show hidden icons button (up-pointing arrow) in the Notification area of the Taskbar and tap or click the **Safely Remove Hardware and Eject Media** icon.

36. Tap or click *Eject Mass Storage* at the pop-up menu. For some USB flash drives, the Eject message varies.

If multiple USBs are plugged in, tap or click the correct drive.

37. Remove your USB flash drive from the computer when the message appears that it is safe to do so.

38. Remove the student resources CD from the DVD drive and display the Start screen.

Message appears when USB can be safely removed.

Safe To Remove Hardware
The 'USB Mass Storage Device' device can now be safely removed from the computer.

Finding Help in Windows

Microsoft includes an extensive set of online resources to assist you as you learn Windows 8.1. You can access Help resources from the Help + Tips tile on the Start screen or by selecting Help in the Settings pane.

1. At the Start screen, tap or click the Help + Tips tile.

2. Tap or click the Basic actions tile in the Help + Tips window.

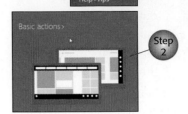

3. Slide or scroll right and read the information in the *Apps side by side* section.

This section describes how you can view two apps at the same time with a movable divider between the apps that lets you resize each app to the size you want. If your screen shows a video above this section, consider watching the video demonstration.

On touch-enabled devices, you can tap or click *Touch* or *Mouse* next to *Show content for* near the bottom left of the window to change the Help + Tips topic information to content optimized for the desired input method.

4. Use the Back button at the top left of the window to return to the Help + Tips window.

5. Tap or click another tile that interests you, scroll the help information and read a section and/or watch a video demonstration for a topic of your choice.

6. Close the Help + Tips app to display the desktop.

7. Reveal the Charms bar and tap or click Settings.

8. Tap or click *Help* in the top section of the Settings pane.

A Windows Help and Support window opens with three main gateways to help information: Get started, Internet & networking, and Security, privacy, & accounts.

9. At the Windows Help and Support window, tap or click Get started.

10. Tap or click Browse help near the top of the window.

11. Tap or click Performance and maintenance.

12. Tap or click the Back button twice.

13. Tap or click Touch: swipe, tap, and beyond.

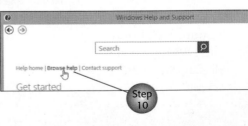

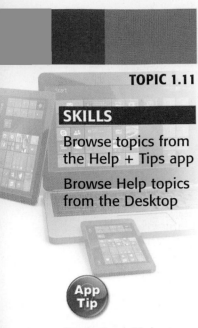

Quick
STEPS

Use Help from the Start Screen
1. Tap or click Help + Tips tile.
2. Tap or click desired category.
3. Read information, watch demos, follow links, OR use *Search* box to find other information at windows.com.

Use Help from the Desktop
1. Display desktop.
2. Reveal Charms bar.
3. Tap or click Settings charm.
4. Tap or click *Help*.
5. Tap or click link to help category, Browse help OR type search keyword or phrase in *Search* text box and tap or click Search button.

14 Slide or scroll down and view the information provided in the Help window.

15 Tap or click the Back button.

16 Tap or click in the Search text box, type **sound**, and tap or press Enter, or tap or click the Search button.

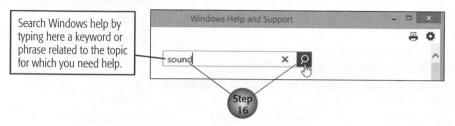

Search Windows help by typing here a keyword or phrase related to the topic for which you need help.

Step 16

17 Tap or click <u>Tips for fixing common sound problems</u>.

18 Tap or click <u>I can't hear any sound from my PC</u>.

19 Read the expanded information in the Help window.

As you have experienced in this topic, you can navigate Windows Help by following links to article titles or by searching by keyword or phrase.

20 Close the Windows Help and Support window.

21 Display the Start screen.

Figure 1.12 The How-to page at windows.com. The page is frequently updated and may not appear exactly as shown here.

Check This Out

youtube.com/windows
Go to the Windows YouTube channel to browse videos on Windows 8 and Windows 8.1. You can find how-to videos and tips videos. Use the *Search* box at the top of the Windows YouTube page to find a video on a topic that you need assistance with.

Beyond Basics

Windows Information on the Web

Go to <u>windows.com</u> and tap or click the <u>How-to</u> link near the top of the page to locate tutorials for Windows (see Figure 1.12). Use the links in the Navigation bar near the top of the page or use the *Search* box to find a tutorial. Windows is also on Facebook. Go to <u>facebook.com/windows</u> and explore the timeline for interesting ideas or links to resources Microsoft has put on its Facebook page. You can also follow Windows on Twitter at <u>twitter.com/windows</u>.

Concepts Review

Topic	Key Concepts	Key Terms
Using Touch, Mouse, and Keyboard Input to Navigate Windows 8.1	The Windows 8.1 user interface is a Start screen with tiles that are used to start apps.	Windows 8.1
	Some tiles display notifications or status updates in real time.	User interface (UI)
	A gesture is an action or motion you perform with your finger, stylus, or mouse on a touch-enabled device.	Start screen
	Touch gestures are tap, press and hold, slide or drag, swipe, pinch, and stretch.	Tiles
	The touch keyboard appears onscreen when typed characters are expected, such as in text messages.	Applications
	The touch keyboard is also available in thumb mode and handwriting mode.	Apps
	A mouse, trackball, touchpad, or other pointing device is used to navigate Windows 8.1 on traditional laptops, notebooks, or desktop PCs.	Gestures
	Mouse actions are point, click, double-click, right-click, drag, and scroll.	Touch keyboard
	Move the pointing device on a desk surface to move a white arrow pointer on the screen and use mouse buttons or scroll wheels to perform an action.	Mouse
	Pressing the Windows logo key brings up the Start screen.	Trackball
	Navigating Windows 8.1 with a keyboard command generally involves pressing the Windows logo key, Ctrl, Alt, or a function key with a letter.	Touchpad
		Pointer
		Keyboard commands
Starting Windows 8.1 and Exploring Apps	The Lock screen appears when you start Windows 8.1 or resume use from sleep mode.	Lock screen
	A user account is a user name and password used to sign in to Windows.	User account
	Signing in to Windows using an outlook.com, hotmail.com, or live.com email address is considered a Microsoft account and means that some settings are stored online.	Microsoft account
	Signing in with a local account means that some settings are not synced with other devices and you do not see live updates on some of the tiles in the Start screen.	Local account
	The Start screen appears once you have signed in to Windows.	Photos app
	Several built-in apps are included with Windows 8.1 and automatically run in full screen mode when launched.	Calendar app
	The Photos app shows pictures stored on the device and from OneDrive if you are signed in with a Microsoft account.	Start button
	The Calendar app is used to enter appointments or events and will show birthdays from Facebook if connected.	Store app
	Use the Store to search for and download new apps.	
	Return to the Start screen by tapping or clicking the Start button at the bottom left corner or the Start charm.	
	Switch between apps using touch gestures, the mouse, or by clicking the app's button on the taskbar.	

Topic	Key Concepts	Key Terms
Revealing Charms Bar, Searching for an App, and Closing Apps	Swipe from the right edge of the screen or point to the top right or bottom right corner to reveal the Charms bar.	Charms bar Charms
	Charms are used to access system resources or commands.	
	The Search charm is used to search for something in apps, programs, settings, files, or on the Web.	
	Inactive apps are eventually closed by Windows; however, you can close an app by swiping from the top of the screen down to the bottom, or by clicking the Close button in the Title bar that appears when you move the mouse to the top of the screen.	
Locking the Screen, Signing Out, and Shutting Down Windows 8.1	Lock the screen if you need to leave your PC or mobile device for a short period of time by tapping or clicking your account name and choosing Lock.	Sign out Logging off Shut down
	Locking leaves all documents and apps open but unavailable to anyone but yourself.	
	Tap or click your account name and choose Sign out to close all apps and documents (also referred to as logging off).	
	Perform a shut-down command if you want to turn off the power to the PC or mobile device.	
	Shut down is accessed from the Power Options button.	
Customizing the Start Screen	Customize the Start screen by adding or removing tiles, rearranging tiles, resizing a tile, and by turning off live updates.	Unpin from Start Pin to Start Turn live tile off
	Select a tile by swiping up from the bottom edge, tapping the Customize button, and then tapping a tile; or, by right-clicking the tile. A selected tile displays with a check mark.	
	Tile commands are revealed in the Customize pane when a tile is selected on touch-enabled devices, or in a shortcut menu for mouse users.	
	Unpin from Start removes the selected tile, and Pin to Start adds the selected tile to the Start screen.	
	Move a tile to a new location using touch by displaying the Customize pane and sliding the tile. Move a tile with a mouse by dragging the tile to a new location.	
	A selected tile can be resized Large, Wide, Medium, or Small.	
	Select a tile and choose the Turn live tile off command to stop a tile from displaying notifications or status updates.	
Personalizing the Start and Lock Screens	Tap or click Change PC settings from the Settings charm and then tap or click PC and devices to personalize the lock screen to one of five other pictures or browse to a picture on your PC or mobile device.	Change PC settings
	Tap or click the first plus symbol in the Lock screen apps section of the PC and devices window to add an app that will provide notifications to the Lock screen.	
	Choose from 20 different designs for the background of the Start screen and drag color sliders to change the color scheme used in Windows 8.1 in the Personalize pane accessed from the Settings charm.	

Topic	Key Concepts	Key Terms
Using the Desktop	The Desktop tile launches the Windows 8.1 desktop, which is similar to the Windows 7 desktop.	Desktop
	The desktop displays icons used to launch programs such as the Recycle Bin, Internet Explorer, or File Explorer, and displays a Taskbar along the bottom of the screen.	Recycle Bin
		Taskbar
	Desktop apps such as Microsoft Word or Microsoft Excel contain standard features for moving, resizing, and closing windows.	File Explorer
		Notification area
	The Close button displays at the top right corner of a desktop app window and is used to close the application.	Close button
	Some programs are pinned to the Taskbar. A notification area at the right end displays the current date and time along with icons to access volume control, network status, and the Action Center.	
Browsing Files with File Explorer	A file is any document, spreadsheet, picture, or other text or image saved as digital data.	File
	When you create a file, you assign a unique file name that allows you to identify and retrieve the file.	File name
		Folder
	File Explorer is the utility in Windows used to browse contents of storage devices and perform file management tasks.	Subfolder
	A This PC window opens when you launch File Explorer, which displays the Folders, Devices and drives, and Network locations accessible for your account on the PC or mobile device.	
	A folder is a name assigned to a placeholder or container that will store a group of related files.	
	A subfolder is a folder created inside another folder.	
	You browse content by tapping or clicking names in the Navigation pane or by double-tapping or double-clicking names in the Content pane of the This PC window.	
Creating Folders and Copying Files and Folders	Creating folders in advance of creating files sets up the organizational structure for later use.	New folder
	In File Explorer, a ribbon provides buttons organized into tabs and groups that are used to carry out file management tasks.	Ribbon
		Copy
	Tap or click the New folder button and type a folder name to create a new folder.	Paste
	Copying a file or folder makes an exact duplicate of a document, spreadsheet, presentation, picture, video, music file, or other object in another folder and/or storage medium.	
	Make copies of important files as backups.	
	Begin a copy task by first selecting the file or folder to be copied, then use the Copy and Paste commands.	

Topic	Key Concepts	Key Terms
Moving, Renaming, and Deleting Files and Folders, and Ejecting a USB Flash Drive	Files are moved by selecting the files or folders, choosing Cut, navigating to the new destination drive and/or folder, and choosing Paste. Use the Rename button to change the name of a file you have received from someone else, or that you have created and assigned a name that you later decide is not satisfactory. Select the file or folder to be renamed and tap or click the Rename button in the Organize group of the Home tab in File Explorer. Type a new name and press Enter. Files deleted from a hard disk drive are sent to the Recycle Bin and remain there until the Recycle Bin is emptied. Files deleted from a USB flash drive are not sent to the Recycle Bin. Select files or folders to be deleted and tap or click the Delete button in the Organize group of the Home tab. Open the Recycle Bin to view files deleted from the hard disk drive. Emptying the Recycle Bin permanently deletes the files or folders. Eject a USB flash drive using the Safely Remove Hardware and Eject Media icon in the Notification area of the Taskbar.	Cut Rename Delete Safely Remove Hardware and Eject Media
Finding Help in Windows	Help information is available from the Help + Tips tile, or by selecting Help from the Settings charm in the desktop. When Help is accessed from the desktop, a Windows Help and Support window opens in which you can browse help topics or search Help by typing a keyword or phrase in the Search text box. Help is also available at <u>windows.com</u>, on Facebook at <u>facebook.com/windows</u> and by following Windows on Twitter at <u>twitter.com/windows</u>.	Help

Multiple Choice

1. This term refers to an action or motion you perform with your finger or stylus on a touch-enabled device.
   a. Writing
   b. Gesture
   c. Navigate
   d. Interface

2. The white arrow on a Windows screen that appears when using a mouse is referred to as the _____.
   a. I-beam
   b. trackball
   c. scroller
   d. pointer

3. Signing in with this type of account means you can see live updates from social media services.
   a. Local
   b. Microsoft
   c. Facebook
   d. Twitter

4. Built-in apps for Windows 8.1 automatically run in this mode.
   a. Desktop
   b. Start screen
   c. Full screen
   d. Live

5. This bar displays along the right edge of the screen when you swipe in, or point to the top right or bottom right corner.
   a. Apps bar
   b. Charms bar
   c. Settings bar
   d. Switch list

6. This charm is used to find an app.
   a. Search charm
   b. Find charm
   c. Settings charm
   d. Share charm

7. If you are leaving your computer for a short period of time, you should do this so that someone else cannot see your work.
   a. Turn off the computer.
   b. Freeze the Start screen.
   c. Lock the screen.
   d. Hide your computer.

8. Do this action when you are finished with a Windows session for the day.
   a. Sign out.
   b. Lock the screen.
   c. Restart.
   d. Freeze the Start screen.

9. A selected tile displays with this symbol.
   a. ×
   b. ✓
   c. |
   d. #

10. Select this option to stop headlines from displaying on a selected Finance tile.
    a. Pin to Start
    b. Uninstall
    c. Turn live tile off
    d. Turn notifications off

11. Choose this option from the Settings charm to change the Lock screen picture.
    a. Change PC settings
    b. Personalize
    c. Lock screen
    d. Browse

12. The background of the Start screen can be customized with a different design and/or _____.
    a. pixel scheme
    b. tile scheme
    c. notification scheme
    d. color scheme

13. Launch this tile from the Start screen to find File Explorer.
    a. Computer
    b. Desktop
    c. Libraries
    d. Files

14. This is the name of the bar that displays along the bottom of the desktop.
    a. Taskbar
    b. Charms bar
    c. Notification bar
    d. System bar

15. A This PC window contains the Navigation pane and the _____ pane.
    a. Files
    b. Content
    c. Organize
    d. Tools

16. Tap or click this option in the Navigation pane to view all of the available storage options.
    a. Network
    b. Homegroup
    c. OneDrive
    d. This PC

17. This is the name for the area within the File Explorer window that organizes buttons into tabs and groups.
    a. Ribbon
    b. Organize
    c. Tools
    d. Menu

18. A folder created within another folder is sometimes referred to as a _____.
    a. folder path
    b. subfolder
    c. folder hierarchy
    d. structure

19. After choosing Copy and navigating to the destination folder, tap or click this button in the Clipboard group.
    a. Copy to
    b. Copy path
    c. Cut
    d. Paste

20. To move a file, use this button in the Clipboard group.
    a. Cut
    b. Move
    c. Delete
    d. Transfer

21. Use this button in File Explorer to change the name of a file or folder.
    a. New name
    b. Rename
    c. Change name
    d. Easy change

22. Deleted files from a hard disk drive are sent to this location.
    a. Taskbar
    b. Recycle Bin
    c. Trash
    d. USB flash drive

23. Use this charm to access Help from the desktop.
    a. Share
    b. Devices
    c. Settings
    d. Find

24. Help information is available by selecting this app from the Start screen.
    a. Reading List
    b. Help + Tips
    c. Windows
    d. Store

Crossword Puzzle

ACROSS

4 Name of Options button used to access Shut Down command

6 Name assigned for a place to store a group of related files

7 Used to access system resources and commands

8 Button used to move a file

9 Mouse button that selects a tile

10 Button that causes This PC window to open

DOWN

1 Option in Settings pane to change Start screen design or color

2 Area at right end of taskbar

3 Account in which settings cannot be shared with another device

5 Button to make selected tile size wide

Matching

Match the term with the statement or definition.

_____ 1. Start screen
_____ 2. Photos
_____ 3. Search charm
_____ 4. Sign out
_____ 5. Unpin
_____ 6. Change PC settings
_____ 7. Recycle Bin
_____ 8. File Explorer
_____ 9. Eject Mass Storage

a. Logging off
b. Personalize Lock screen
c. File management
d. Desktop app
e. Safely Remove Hardware
f. Find an app
g. User interface
h. Remove tile
i. Built-in app

Project 1 Exploring Windows 8.1 Apps

Individual

Deliverable: Screen capture of Start screen with Switch list

1. Start Windows 8.1 and sign in.
2. Find and launch the Travel app. Browse the list of featured destinations and tap or click a destination of your choice. Read the Overview, browse photos, panoramas, lists of attractions, and so on for the destination location.
3. Display the Start screen and launch the Food & Drink app. Slide or scroll right in the app and tap or click a recipe, tip & technique, food culture story, or chef biography that interests you.
4. Display the Start screen and launch the Store app. Slide or scroll to the Top free section and tap or click a tile to a free app that interests you.
5. Display the Start screen and reveal the Switch list in the left pane.
6. Press the Print Screen key on the keyboard to capture an image of your screen with the Switch list displayed. The key may be labeled Prt Sc, PrtScrn, or PrtSc and is generally located in the top row of keys at the right near the last function key. On some PCs or devices you may need to press Shift + Print Screen or a function key with Print Screen. If you are using a tablet without a keyboard or if the Switch list does not remain on screen when you press Print Screen, check with your instructor for instructions on how to submit projects with screen capture deliverables.
7. Use the Search charm to search for and launch the Paint app. Paint is a desktop app and will open in the Windows 8.1 desktop.
8. Tap or click the Paste button in the Home tab of the Paint ribbon.
9. Tap or click the Save button on the Quick Access toolbar. At the Save As dialog box, navigate to your USB flash drive, select the current file name in the *File name* text box, type **C1-Project1-AppsSwitchList-Your Name**, and tap or click the Save button. (You will move this file to another location in Project 4.)
10. Close the Paint window.
11. Switch to and close each of the three apps you launched in this project.
12. Submit the project to your instructor in the manner she or he has requested.

Project 2 Customizing the Start Screen

Individual

Deliverable: Screen capture with customized Start screen

Note: Skip steps in this project that ask you to customize a tile if the tile is already at the instructed setting.

1. At the Windows Start screen, select the Calendar tile and resize the tile to Medium.
2. Select the News tile, resize the tile to Large, and turn on live updates.
3. Select the Store tile and resize the tile to Wide.
4. Select the People tile and turn the live tile off.
5. Select the Photos tile and turn the live tile off.
6. Rearrange the tiles that you have customized in this project within the first group of tiles in a manner that suits you.
7. Capture an image of your customized Start screen and paste it into a new Paint document. See Project 1, Steps 6 to 8 if you need help.
8. Save the image in Paint on your USB flash drive as **C1-Project2-CustomizedStartScreen-Your Name**.
9. Close the Paint window and close the desktop app.
10. Submit the project to your instructor in the manner she or he has requested.
11. Restore the Calendar, News, Store, People, and Photos tiles to their original settings and rearrange the tiles back to their original locations.

Project 3 Browsing Files with File Explorer

Individual

Deliverable: Screen capture with File Explorer window

1. Start File Explorer.
2. Insert your USB flash drive into an empty USB port. If a new Removable Disk window opens, close the window.
3. At the This PC window, display in the Content pane the contents stored on your USB flash drive.
4. Navigate the following folders: ComputerCourse, CompletedTopicsByChapter, Ch1.
5. With the Ch1 files displayed in the Content pane, change the View to Large Icons.
6. Capture an image of the desktop with the File Explorer window open and paste it into a Paint document.
7. Save the image in Paint on your USB flash drive as **C1-Project3-FileExplorerWindow-Your Name**.
8. Close the Paint window, close the File Explorer window, and close the desktop app.
9. Submit the project to your instructor in the manner she or he has requested.

Project 4 Performing File Management Tasks

Individual

Deliverable: Screen capture with File Explorer window

1. Start File Explorer and display in the Content pane the ChapterProjectsWork folder on your USB flash drive.
2. Create a new folder named *Ch1*.
3. Navigate to the Student_Data_Files folder within the ComputerCourse folder and copy the Ch1 folder to the ComputerCourse folder.
4. Display in the Content pane the Ch1 folder within the ComputerCourse folder.
5. Select all files within the folder and move them to the Ch1 folder within the ChapterProjectsWork folder.
6. With the Content pane displaying the files in the Ch1 folder within ChapterProjectsWork, do the following:
   a. Delete the files named **FireworksWithApplause**, **Winter**, and **TheThreeBears1935**.
   b. Rename the file **MurresOnFloatingIce** to *BirdsOnIceFloe*.
   c. Rename the file **BMMF** to *DrumsSolo*.
   d. Create a new folder named *NASA*.
   e. Select and move the following files to the NASA folder: **Apollo11_NYParade**, **Armstrong&Scott_ Landing_March1966**, **Armstrong_OntheMoon_July20_1969**, **NASA_SpaceXFlight**.
   f. If necessary, change the View to List view.
7. Capture an image of the desktop with the File Explorer window showing the Content pane for the Ch1 folder within ChapterProjectsWork and paste it into a Paint document.
8. Save the image in Paint on your USB flash drive as **C1-Project4-Ch1FileExplorerWindow-Your Name**.
9. Close the Paint window.
10. Display in the Content pane the ComputerCourse folder and delete the folder named *Ch1*.
11. Create a new folder named *ScreenCaptures* within the Ch1 folder in ChapterProjectsWork and then move all of the Paint files created with screen captures to the new folder.
12. Close the File Explorer window.
13. Submit the project (from Step 8) to your instructor in the manner she or he has requested.
14. Eject the USB flash drive and close the desktop app.
15. Sign out of Windows.

Chapter 2

Navigating and Searching the Web

After succesfully completing this chapter, you will be able to:

- Describe the Internet, World Wide Web, web browser, web address, and hyperlink
- Navigate the Web using Internet Explorer
- View multiple websites within the same browser window
- Bookmark favorite websites
- Navigate the Web using Google Chrome
- Navigate the Web using Mozilla Firefox
- Use find and search tools to find information on the Web
- Print a web page
- Download content from web pages

For many people reading this textbook, the Internet is part of daily life, used to search for information, connect with friends and relatives, watch videos, listen to music, play games, or shop. Mobile devices such as tablets and smartphones allow people to browse the Web anywhere at any time. Being able to effectively navigate and search the Web is a requirement for all workers and consumers.

In this chapter you will learn definitions for Internet terminology and how to navigate the Web using the three most popular Web browsers. You will also learn to use search tools to find information quickly, print information from websites, view multiple websites in a browsing session, bookmark favorites, and copy information from websites to your local PC.

Notes: While the emphasis in this chapter is on using Internet Explorer 10, which is included with Windows 8, feel free to work through the topic activities and projects using Google Chrome or Firefox. In that case, be aware that for some topics, the steps provided may need to be altered to suit the Google Chrome or Firefox browser.

If you are using a computer with Windows 7 and an earlier version of Internet Explorer (such as version 9), the steps you complete and screens you see will vary from the ones shown in this chapter. If necessary, check with your instructor for alternate instructions.

No student data files are required to complete this chapter.

TOPIC 2.1

SKILLS

Define Internet

Define World Wide Web

Describe Web address

Introduction to the Internet and the World Wide Web

The **Internet (Net)** is a global network linking individuals, businesses, schools, governments, nonprofit organizations, research institutions, and others. The physical structure that connects thousands of other networks to make this worldwide network operational is known as the Internet. High speed communications and networking equipment is used on the Internet to transmit data from one computer to another. For example, a request sent from your computer to display a web page such as flight times from an airline's schedule would travel through several other networks such as telephone, cable, or satellite company networks to reach the airline's web server. This collection of networks that provides the pathway for data to travel is the Internet.

The World Wide Web

The collection of electronic documents circulated on the Internet in the form of **web pages** make up the **World Wide Web (Web** or **WWW)**. A web page is a document that contains text and multimedia content such as images, video, sound, and animation (Figure 2.1). Web pages also contain **hyperlinks** (referred to as **links**), which allow you to move from one page to another page. Web pages are stored in a format that is read and interpreted for display within a **web browser**, which is a software program used to view web pages. A website is a collection of related web pages for one organization or individual. For example, the collection of web pages linked to the main page for your school make up your school's website. All of the web pages and resources such as photos, videos, sounds, and animations that make the website work are stored on a computer called a web server. Web servers are connected to the Internet continuously.

You connect your PC or mobile device to the Internet by subscribing to Internet service through an **Internet Service Provider (ISP)**, a company that provides access to the Internet's infrastructure for a fee. The ISP will provide you with the equipment needed to connect to the ISP's network as well as instructions for installing and setting up the equipment to work with your computer or other mobile devices. Once your account and equipment are set up, you can start browsing the Web using a browser software program such as Internet Explorer, Google Chrome, or Firefox.

Many people connect wirelessly to the Internet from multiple mobile devices.

Web Addresses

Each web page has a unique text-based **web address** that allows you to navigate to the page. Web Addresses are also called **URLs (Uniform Resource Locators)**. One way to navigate the Web is to type a web address for an organization into the web browser's Address bar. For example, to view the main web page for the publisher of this textbook you would use the web address *http://www.emcp.com*. Since *http* and *www* are used in most web addresses, you can often navigate to a page by typing only the portion of the address after *www*. The parts of the web address (URL) http://www.nasa.gov/topics/universe/index.html shown in Figure 2.1 are explained in Table 2.1.

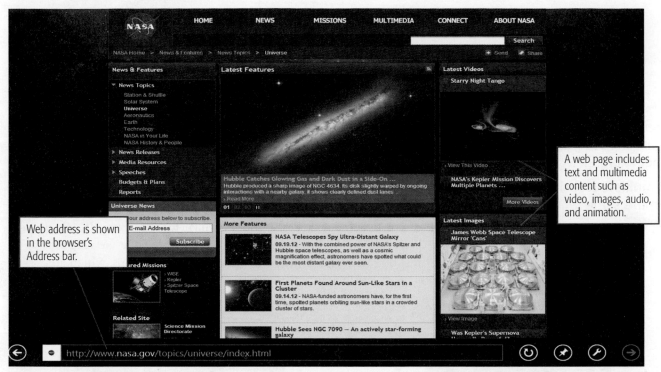

Figure 2.1 A web page such as this one from NASA includes text and multimedia content. Web pages are identified by a web address, which is typed into the browser's Address bar or shown in the Address bar when you navigate to the page from a search engine.

Table 2.1	The Parts of the Web Address (URL) **http://www.nasa.gov/topics/universe/index.html**	
Part of URL	**What It Means**	**Examples**
http://	Hypertext Transfer Protocol. A protocol is a set of rules that defines how data is sent over the Internet. Since http is used most of the time, you can omit this part of the web address. Other types of protocols are used to transfer files (ftp) or to send data securely (https).	http ftp https
www.nasa.gov	Domain name. A domain name is a text-based address that indicates the server on the Internet that stores the web page. The last three letters (gov) are called the extension and indicate the type of organization that owns the content. In the *Examples* column are popular extensions that you will recognize from your browsing experiences. Some domain names end with a two-character country code. For example: ebay.ca is the Canadian website for the popular online auction site ebay.	com (business) edu (education) gov (government) net (network providers) org (nonprofits)
/topics/universe/	Path to the web page. The forward slash (/) and text after the slash indicate the folder names on the web server in which the web page is stored. The number of folders and folder names indicate the organizational structure for the web pages that comprise a website.	path folder names will vary
index.html	Web page file name. The file name extension indicates the language used to create the web page. Html stands for *Hypertext Markup Language*, which uses tags to describe content and is widely used.	file names will vary

Many times when you open a web browser, you are looking for information and do not know the web addresses for the pages you want to view. In this case, you use search tools to find web pages that you want to view. You will learn to find web pages using search tools in Topic 2.5.

Navigating the Web Using Internet Explorer 10

Internet Explorer (IE) is the web browser included with Microsoft Windows. In Windows 8, IE version 10 is used. You can open Internet Explorer from a tile in the Start screen or from the Internet Explorer icon in the Windows 8 Desktop Taskbar.

The browser app that you launch from the Internet Explorer Start screen tile is slightly different than the browser you launch from the Desktop Taskbar, as shown in Figure 2.2. The Start screen app provides the most page viewing area because the Address bar is located at the bottom of the window and disappears as you scroll down a web page, meaning the web page will fill the entire window. Right-click the mouse or swipe from the bottom or top edge to reveal the Address bar and tabs for multiple page viewing in the window.

Using the Desktop IE window will feel more familiar for users with IE experience in Windows 7 or earlier. The Address bar and tabs for multiple page viewing are located at the top along with the Home, Favorites, and Tools buttons, which are located at the top right just below the Minimize, Maximize, and Close buttons.

SKILLS

Navigate the Web using Internet Explorer

View multiple websites within the same window

Add a page to Favorites

Start screen IE app has Navigation and Address bar at the bottom. This app provides the maximum page viewing area.

Navigation and Address bar are at the top with tabs for browsing multiple pages in the Desktop IE window.

Figure 2.2 The Internet Explorer app from the Windows 8 Start screen (left) varies from the IE window launched from the Desktop (right).

Starting Internet Explorer and Displaying a Web Page

1. Tap or click the Internet Explorer tile from the Start screen and review the layout and tools in the IE window, as shown in Figure 2.3 on the next page.

The IE window fills the screen with the default home page that is set for the browser.

oops!

Internet Explorer tile starts in Desktop version? This occurs when the default browser has been set to a browser other than IE. Change back to IE to complete this chapter by opening the Control Panel from the desktop, then choosing this sequence: Programs, Default Programs, Set your default programs, Internet Explorer (in Programs list), Set this program as default, OK.

Step 1

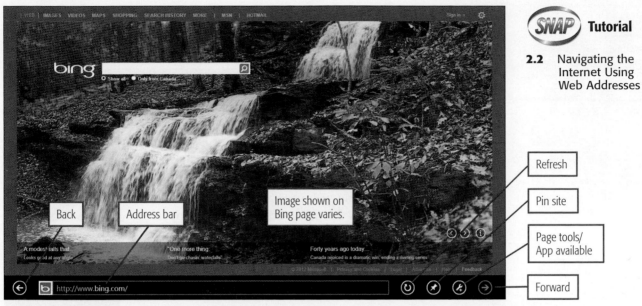

Refresh

Pin site

Page tools/
App available

Forward

Figure 2.3 Internet Explorer 10 app launched from Start screen. The default page that displays in your window may vary from the one shown.

(2) Drag to select the text in the **Address bar** or click to select the existing web address, type **www.loc.gov**, and then tap or press Enter (on the touch keyboard, the Enter key is labeled Go).

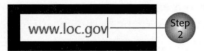

(3) Tap or click <u>Digital Preservation</u> in the *Resources & Programs* section at the right side of the Library of Congress page.

(4) Tap or click the **Back** control or slide right to return to the Library of Congress home page (move back one web page).

(5) Tap or click the **Forward** control or slide left to return to the Digital Preservation page (move forward one web page).

(6) Tap or click <u>View the tips</u> in the *Preserving Your Digital Memories* section.

The Personal Archiving page at the Library of Congress contains links to articles with useful information on how to preserve your personal memories. Consider further exploring the links at this web page if you have an interest in preserving personal information.

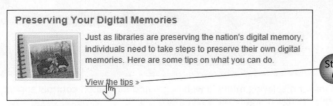

Preserving Your Digital Memories

Just as libraries are preserving the nation's digital memory, individuals need to take steps to preserve their own digital memories. Here are some tips on what you can do.

<u>View the tips »</u>

SNAP Tutorial

2.2 Navigating the Internet Using Web Addresses

oops!

Touch keyboard not active? You may need to tap inside the selected text to bring up the touch keyboard.

App Tip

As you begin typing a URL, IE displays matches above the Address bar that begin with similar text from the History list. Tap or click the page if it appears in the list.

App Tip

You may be prompted to turn on the Flip Ahead feature. Flip Ahead looks for the next page in a website, such as page 2 of an article, and lets you move to the next page without having to locate the next page hyperlink.

Resources & Programs

<u>American Folklife Center</u>
Preserving & presenting traditional culture

<u>Center for the Book</u>
Promoting books, reading & literacy

<u>Copyright Royalty Board</u>
Determining statutory royalty rates & distributing royalties

<u>Digital Preservation</u>
A national partnership to preserve new media

7 Drag to select the text in the Address bar or click to select the existing web address, type **www.nasa.gov/topics/universe/index.html**, and then tap or press Enter (Go on touch screen keyboard).

Step 7

8 If necessary, slide or scroll down to the *Latest Images* section at the right side of the page and tap or click the <u>View Archives</u> button link.

9 Slide or scroll down the web page and notice that the page fills the screen as the navigation controls disappear.

Step 8

Displaying Multiple Web Pages and Pinning a Site

Open multiple web pages within the same IE window by displaying each page in its own tab. Switch between web pages by displaying the tabs and clicking the tab control for the page you want to view. This is called **tabbed browsing**. Web pages you visit frequently can be pinned to the **Favorites** list or the Start screen.

10 Swipe up from the bottom edge of the screen or right-click to reveal the navigation controls and browser tabs, as shown in Figure 2.4.

11 Tap or click the **New Tab** control at the top right of the IE window that displays as a plus symbol inside a circle to open a new blank page.

Step 11

Browser tabs

New Tab

Tab tools

Images shown may vary.

Swiping up from the bottom edge or right-clicking reveals tab and app controls.

Figure 2.4 Browser tabs for displaying multiple web pages and navigation controls appear when you swipe up from the bottom edge or right-click a web page.

12 Type **www.flickr.com/commons** in the Address bar and then tap or press Enter.

The Commons at flickr contains collections of photos from the world's public photography archives. Images in the commons have no known copyright restrictions. The next time you need a picture or photo for a project, consider sourcing an image from this website.

13 Swipe up from the bottom edge of the screen or right-click to reveal the tabs and then click the tab with the title NASA - Archive to switch pages.

14 Reveal the tabs and tap or click the **Close Tab** control (displays with an × inside a circle) in the NASA - Archive tab.

15 Tap or click in an unused space on the page to hide the tab controls.

16 Swipe up from the bottom edge or right-click, tap or click the **Pin site** control (displays as a push pin inside a circle), and then tap or click *Add to favorites*.

17 Tap or click in the Address bar to display the *Frequent* and *Favorites* lists above the Address bar.

Slide or scroll if necessary to view all Frequent and Favorites tiles.

Your Frequent and Favorites tiles will vary.

18 Tap or click any tile in the *Frequent* section to display the web page.

19 Close the IE app.

TOPIC 2.3

Navigating the Web Using Google Chrome

Google Chrome is a free web browser for Windows-compatible PCs, Macs, or Linux PCs. The popularity of Google Chrome has been steadily increasing; the browser offers fast page loading and searching directly from the Address bar using Google. Complete the steps in this topic if you have the Google Chrome web browser installed on your device; otherwise, skip to the next topic.

SKILLS

Navigate the Web using Google Chrome

View multiple websites within the same window

Bookmark a page

Use the Find tool

Starting Google Chrome and Displaying a Web Page

1. Tap or click the Google Chrome tile from the Start screen and review the layout and tools in the Google Chrome window, as shown in Figure 2.5.

Step 1

The Google Chrome window is launched in the Desktop app. If Google Chrome is not currently set as the default browser, you may be prompted to set it as the default browser in a message bar below the omnibox. Do not set Google Chrome as the default browser until after you have completed all of the topics in this chapter.

2. If a message displays asking you to sign in to Google Chrome, tap or click <u>Skip for now</u>.

3. If necessary, tap or click in the **omnibox**, type **www.pinterest. com**, and then tap or press Enter.

Step 3

Pinterest is a social media website that is an online organizer for collecting your favorite pictures from the Web.

Check This Out

google.com/chrome

Go here to download and install Google Chrome on your PC or mobile device.

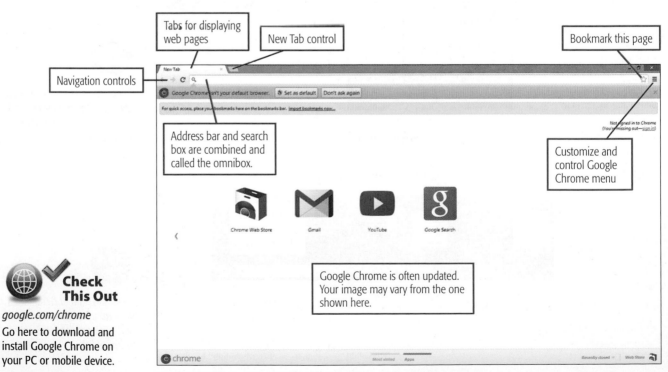

Figure 2.5 The Google Chrome window opens in the Desktop app.

4 Press and hold over <u>Categories</u> just below the Pinterest heading or point on <u>Categories</u> to see the drop-down list of headings by which images are grouped.

5 Tap or click a category heading that interests you. For example, tap or click the *Animals* category.

6 Slide or scroll down and view the pictures posted in the category you selected.

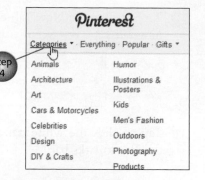

Displaying Multiple Web Pages and Bookmarking Pages

Similarly to IE, Google Chrome uses tabbed browsing to display more than one web page within the same browser window. Click a new tab and navigate to a web address to browse to a new site without closing the existing web page. Google Chrome displays a page name at the top of the tab along with a Close button. Web pages you visit frequently can be bookmarked by clicking the Bookmark this page icon (white star) at the right end of the omnibox.

7 Tap or click the **Bookmark this page** icon (white star) at the right end of the omnibox.

The white star changes to a gold star, and the Bookmark dialog box appears.

8 Tap or click Done to close the Bookmark dialog box.

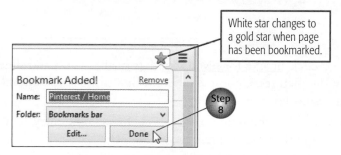

White star changes to a gold star when page has been bookmarked.

9 Tap or click the **Customize and control Google Chrome** button (displays with three short bars next to the star at the right end of the omnibox), tap or point to *Bookmarks* at the drop-down menu, and then tap or click *Show bookmarks bar*.

The **Bookmarks bar** appears below the omnibox.

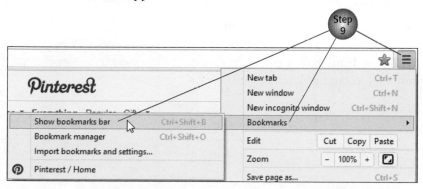

(10) Tap or click the New Tab control next to the Pinterest / Home tab to open a new tab, type **www.youtube.com**, and then tap or press Enter.

Step 10

(11) Tap or click the white star and then tap or click Done to add <u>youtube.com</u> to the Bookmarks bar.

Searching the Web from the Omnibox

Go to *Settings* from the Customize and control Google Chrome menu to change the default search engine.

Google Chrome allows you to type a search phrase directly in the omnibox, and search results from Google (or other default search engine) appear in the window.

(12) Tap or click the New Tab control next to the YouTube tab, type **seven wonders of the world**, and then tap or press Enter.

Notice that as you type, searches that match your entry appear in a drop-down list below the omnibox. If one of the searches is what you are looking for, tap or click the item.

Step 12

(13) Tap or click <u>Images for seven wonders of the world</u> and slide or scroll down to view the pictures. Choose a different link if the specified link is not shown in your results list.

(14) Tap or click in the omnibox to select the current entry, type **great wall of china**, and then tap or press Enter.

(15) Tap or click <u>Great Wall of China - Wikipedia, the free encyclopedia</u>.

Finding Text on a Page

Use the Find command to locate a specific word or phrase on a web page. The Find command is accessed from the Customize and control Google Chrome menu.

(16) Tap or click the Customize and control Google Chrome button and then tap or click *Find* at the drop-down menu.

This opens the **Find bar** at the right side of the window below the bookmarks bar.

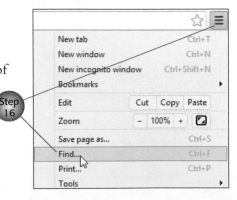

Step 16

(17) Type **ming dynasty** in the Find bar text box.

The currently selected match is shaded with an orange background, and the number of matches found on the web page displays in the Find bar next to the find text.

(18) Tap or click Next in the Find bar to scroll the page to the next occurrence of *ming dynasty*.

(19) Continue tapping or clicking Next until you have seen all occurrences.

(20) Tap or click the Close button at the top right of the Google Chrome window to close Google Chrome.

(21) Close the Desktop app.

ALTERNATIVE method   Use these shortcut keys to perform routine actions faster in Google Chrome:

Open a new tab	Ctrl + T
Show Bookmarks bar	Ctrl + Shift + B
Open Find bar	Ctrl + F

 **Google Chrome's Incognito Browsing**

Tap or click the Customize and control Google Chrome button and tap or click *New incognito window* to open a new tab for **private browsing**. Web pages you visit while incognito will not appear in the browser history or search history, and any cookies that are created are automatically deleted after all incognito windows are closed.

TOPIC 2.4

Navigating the Web Using Mozilla Firefox

Mozilla's Firefox is a free web browser that runs on Windows-compatible PCs, Macs, or Linux PCs. The software program is published by the nonprofit Mozilla Foundation. At the time of writing, Firefox was the third most popular web browser after IE and Google Chrome. Firefox fans use the browser for its speed in loading web pages. Complete the steps in this topic if you have the Firefox web browser installed on your device; otherwise, skip to the next topic.

Starting Firefox and Displaying a Web Page

SKILLS

Navigate the Web using Mozilla Firefox

View multiple websites within the same window

Bookmark a page

Use the Find tool

① Tap or click the Mozilla Firefox tile from the Start screen and review the layout and tools in the Firefox window, as shown in Figure 2.6. Tap or click No if prompted to set Firefox as the default browser.

The Firefox window is launched in the Desktop app.

② Tap or click in the **Location bar** that displays Go to a Website, type **commons.wikimedia.org**, and then tap or press Enter.

Wikimedia Commons is a media file repository maintained by volunteers. Go to this site to find images and sound and video clips that are free to use or copy by following the terms specified by the author, which often require only that you credit the source.

Check This Out

mozilla.org/firefox

Go here to download and install Mozilla's Firefox web browser on your PC or mobile device.

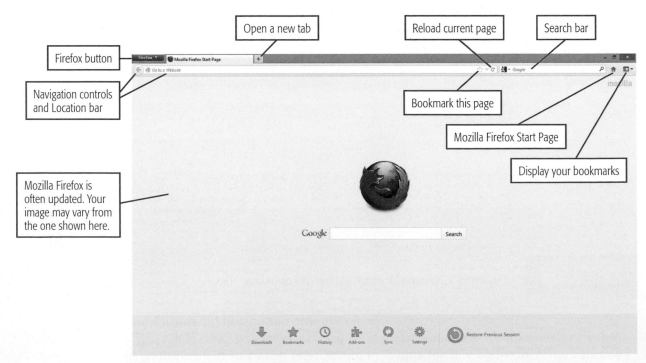

Figure 2.6 Mozilla Firefox is a free, open-source web browser that opens in the Desktop app.

3 Tap or click in the *Search Wikimedia Commons* text box near the top right of the Wikimedia Commons page that displays the word Search, type **clownfish**, and then tap or click the search icon (magnifying glass) or tap or press Enter.

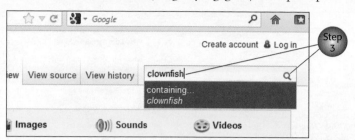

Did You Know ?

At the time of writing, more than 14 million free-use images, sound clips, and other media files were available at Wikimedia Commons.

4 Slide or scroll down and view the pictures of clownfish.

Displaying Multiple Web Pages and Bookmarking Pages

Similarly to IE and Google Chrome, Firefox provides for tabbed browsing. Tap or click the **Open a new tab** control (displays with a plus symbol) and type a web address in the Location bar. Firefox displays a title for a page in the tab along with a Close button. Web pages you visit frequently can be bookmarked by clicking the Bookmark this page icon (white star) at the right end of the Location bar.

5 Tap or click the Bookmark this page icon (white star) at the right end of the Location bar.

The white star changes to gold for bookmarked pages.

App Tip

Firefox includes a Bookmarks bar that displays below the Location bar. Turn on the Bookmarks bar from the Display your bookmarks menu. Add a web page to the Bookmarks bar by displaying the page and then dragging the page's icon from the Location bar onto the Bookmarks bar.

6 Tap or click the Open a new tab control (displays as a plus symbol) next to the Wikimedia tab.

7 Type **wikitravel.org** and then tap or press Enter.

Wikitravel is a worldwide travel guide written and updated by travelers.

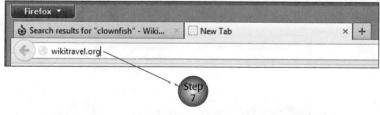

8 Tap or click the Bookmark this page icon (white star) to add the page to your bookmarks.

⑨ Tap or click the **Display your bookmarks** button at the right end of the Location bar (last button), tap or click *Recently Bookmarked*, and then tap or click *Search results for "clownfish" - Wikimedia Commons* at the side menu.

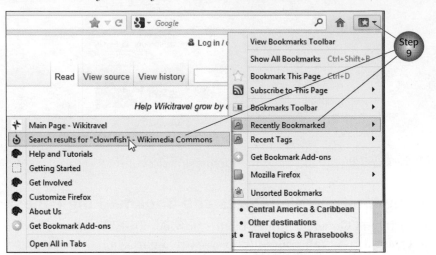

App Tip

To delete a bookmark, display the web page, tap or click the gold star in the Location bar, and tap or click Remove Bookmark in the Edit this Bookmark box.

⑩ Tap or click the Close Tab icon in the second tab titled Search results for "clownfish" - Wikimedia Commons to close the page.

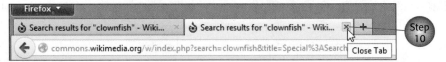

Finding Text on a Page

Open the Find bar in Firefox to search for all occurrences of a word or phrase on a web page. The Find bar is accessed from the Firefox button.

⑪ Tap or click the Firefox button at the top left of the window and then tap or click *Find* at the drop-down menu.

The Find bar opens at the bottom left of the Firefox window with an insertion point positioned in the Find text box. As you begin typing an entry in the text box, Firefox will immediately begin highlighting matches for the search text on the current web page. If no matches are found, Firefox sounds a chime and shades the Find box red.

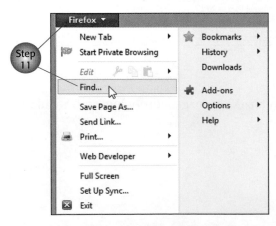

12 Type **ocellaris**.

The first matched occurrence of the search text is shaded green.

13 Tap or click Next to move to the next occurrence of *ocellaris* on the page.

14 Continue tapping or clicking Next until you return to the first occurrence near the top of the page.

15 Tap or click the Close Find bar button (displays with an ×) at the left end of the Find bar.

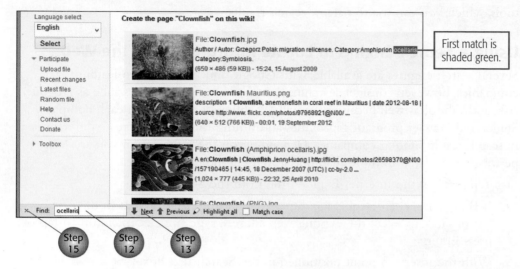

First match is shaded green.

Step 15   Step 12   Step 13

Start the Firefox App
Tap or click Mozilla Firefox tile from Start screen.

Display a Web Page
Tap or click in Location bar, type URL, and tap or press Enter.

Display Multiple Web Pages
1. Tap or click Open a new tab.
2. Type URL for new web page.
3. Tap or press Enter.

Bookmark a Web Page
1. Display desired web page.
2. Tap or click white star.

Display Bookmarks
1. Tap or click Display your bookmarks.
2. Tap or click *Recently Bookmarked*.
3. Tap or click desired book-mark.

Open the Find Bar
1. Tap or click Firefox button.
2. Tap or click *Find*.

Search Using the Search Bar
Type search phrase in Search bar and tap or press Enter.

Searching the Web Using the Search Bar

Search for information using a popular search engine such as Google or Bing by typing a search phrase in the **Search bar** near the top right of the Firefox window.

16 Tap or click in the Search bar near the top right of the window, type **tropical fish**, and then tap or press Enter, or tap or click the search button.

Choose a different search engine by tapping or clicking the search engine's icon in the Search bar and selecting a different search engine at the drop-down list.

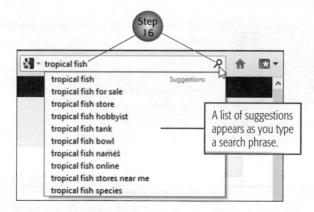

Step 16

A list of suggestions appears as you type a search phrase.

17 Tap or click a link to a web page that interests you from the search results list.

18 Tap or click the Close button at the top right of the Firefox window to close Firefox.

19 Close the Desktop app.

TOPIC 2.5

SKILLS

Use search tools to find information on the Web

Narrow search results by applying advanced search options

Print a web page, including selected pages only

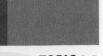 **Tutorials**

2.5.1 Finding Information Using Search Tools

2.5.2 Researching Information Using Advanced Search Tools

 **Check This Out**

dogpile.com
Go here to perform a search using a metasearch search engine. Metasearch search engines send your search phrase to other search engines and show you one list of search results from the wider group.

Searching for Information and Printing Web Pages

A **search engine** is a company that indexes web pages by keywords and provides a search tool with which you can search their indexes to find web pages. To create indexes, search engines use programs called **spiders** or **crawlers** that read web pages and other information supplied by the website owner.

Some search engines provide a list of topics or subjects by which you can navigate or search in addition to a search tool. Search engines also provide advanced tools, which you can use to narrow search results.

Using a Search Engine to Locate Information on the Web

Several search engines are available, with Google and Bing the two leading companies; however, consider searching using other search engines such as Dogpile, Ask, and Yahoo! as well because you will get different results from each company. Spider and crawler program capabilities and timing for indexing create differences in search results among companies. Depending on the information you are seeking, performing a search in more than one search engine is a good idea.

1. Tap or click the Internet Explorer tile from the Start screen.

2. If Bing is not the default page displayed, drag to select the text in the Address bar or click to select the existing web address, type **bing.com**, and then tap or press Enter.

3. With the insertion point positioned in the Search text box, type **cover letter examples** and then tap or press Enter (Enter key displays as *Search* on touch keyboard in Bing), or tap or click the Search button (magnifying glass).

Notice that Bing provides search suggestions that match the characters you type in a drop-down list below the Search text box as soon as you begin typing. Tap or click a search suggestion if you see a close match.

4. Slide or scroll down the search results page and tap or click a link to a page that interests you.

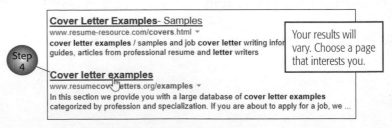

⑤ Read a few paragraphs about cover letters at the page you selected.

⑥ Tap or click the Back button or slide right to return to the search results list.

⑦ Select the text in the Address bar, type **yahoo.com**, and then tap or press Enter.

⑧ With the insertion point positioned in the Search text box, type **cover letter examples** and then tap or press Enter, or tap or click the Search button next to the text box.

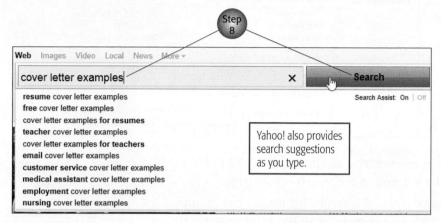

Yahoo! also provides search suggestions as you type.

⑨ Slide or scroll down the search results page. Notice that some links are to the same web pages that you saw in Bing's search results; however, the same page may be in a different order in the list or you may notice new links not shown by Bing.

Using Advanced Search Options

In both Bing and Yahoo!, the search results for the cover letter examples resulted in millions of links in the results page. Search engines provide tools to help you narrow the search results. Each search engine provides different tools. Explore the options at the search engine you prefer or look for a help link that provides information on how to use **advanced search tools**.

⑩ Slide or scroll to the top of the search results page and tap or click the Options link at the right of the Search button.

⑪ Tap or click Advanced Search at the drop-down list.

Your search results list will vary.

12. Tap or click the *Only .edu domains* option.
13. Tap or click the Yahoo! Search button at the top of the Advanced Web Search page.

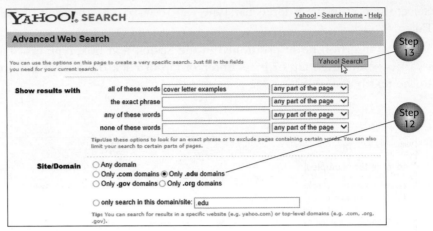

14. Tap or click *Past month* in the *FILTER BY TIME* section at the left side of the search results page.

   Notice the search results list is now significantly reduced from the millions in the prior results list.

15. Slide or scroll down the search results page and tap or click a link to a page that interests you.

Printing a Web Page

Printing a web page can sometimes be frustrating because web pages are designed for optimal screen viewing (not printing). Many times you may print a web page only to discard a second or third page that you did not need, or the content printed did not fit the width of the paper and the printout was unusable.

16. Select the text in the Address bar, type **studentaffairs.stanford.edu/cdc/resumes/cover-ltr-writing**, and then tap or press Enter.

   This page contains several tips for writing effective cover letters. Assume you decide to print the page for later use when you are looking for a job.

17. Reveal the charms and tap or click Devices. Skip to Step 23 if you are using Internet Explorer in the Desktop version.

   A list of installed printers appears in the Devices pane.

18. Tap or click the printer you want to use.

   The page displays in a Printer pane with a preview window that allows you to view how the page will print.

19 Slide left in the preview window or tap or click the Next Page arrow to view all of the pages that need to be printed.

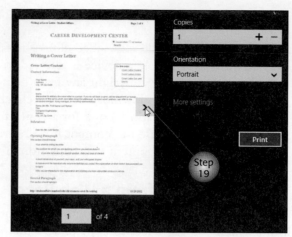

Step 19

The web page needs four pages to print, with the last page being unnecessary. The <u>More settings</u> link provides more print options; however, an option to control individual pages to print is not available. In the next steps, you will load the page in the Desktop IE app, which provides a Print dialog box.

20 Tap or click in an unused space on the web page to remove the Printer pane.

21 If necessary, swipe up from the bottom edge of the screen or right-click to display the navigation and app controls.

22 Tap or click the Page Tools control at the bottom right of the window (displays as a wrench) and then tap or click *View on the desktop*.

Step 22

23 Tap or click the Tools widget at the top right of the IE window (just below the Close button), tap or click *Print*, and then tap or click *Print* at the Print menu.

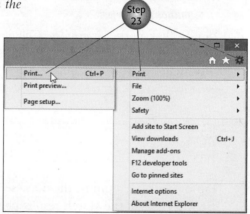

Step 23

24 Tap or click *Pages* in the *Page Range* section of the Print dialog box, type **1-3** in the *Pages* text box, and then tap or click the Print button.

Only pages 1, 2, and 3 of the web page print.

25 Close Internet Explorer.

26 Close the Desktop.

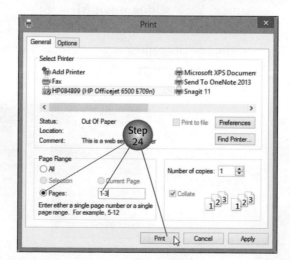

Step 24

App Tip

Use *Page setup* from the Print drop-down menu to change print options such as page orientation and margins.

Downloading Content from a Web Page

Copying an image, audio clip, video clip, or music file (such as MP3) from a web page to your PC or mobile device is referred to as **downloading** content. Most content is protected by copyright law from being used by someone else without permission. Before you download content, check the website for restrictions against copying information. Look for a contact link and request permission from the website owner to use the content if no restrictions are shown. Always cite the original source of any content you copy from a web page.

Saving a Picture from a Web Page

Saving content generally involves selecting an object and displaying a context menu from which you can select to copy or save the object.

① Tap or click the Internet Explorer tile from the Start screen.

  Assume you want to find an image of the Grand Canyon for a project. You decide to use the flickr Commons page to find a picture in the public domain that can be used without copyright restrictions.

② Select the text in the Address bar to reveal the Frequent and Favorites tiles.

③ Tap or click the Flickr: The Commons tile in the Favorites list (you added this tile to Favorites in Topic 2.2).

④ If necessary, slide or scroll down to the section titled *A Commons Sampler*.

⑤ Tap or click in the *Search The Commons* text box, type **grand canyon**, and then tap or press Enter, or tap or click the SEARCH button.

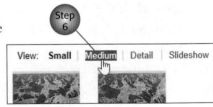
Step 3
Flickr: The Commons

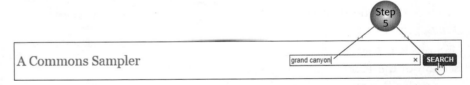
Step 5
A Commons Sampler   grand canyon   SEARCH

⑥ Tap or click <u>Medium</u> in the *View* section at the top right of the search results page if the current View setting is not Medium.

⑦ Slide or scroll down and view the images in the search results page.

⑧ Tap or click a picture that you like and want to save.

Step 6
View: **Small** | Medium | Detail | Slideshow

Step 8
Grand Canyon by The U.S. National Archives
Entering the Grand Canyon from The U.S. National Archives
Entering the Grand Canyon from The U.S. National Archives
Your list may vary. Choose any picture you want to save.

TOPIC 2.6

SKILLS

Download a picture from a web page

View the picture in the Pictures library

 **Tutorial**

2.6 Downloading Content from a Web Page

oops!

Don't have flickr The Commons in your Favorites list? If necessary, type *flickr.com/commons* in the Address bar and tap or press Enter.

9 At the next page, slide or scroll down if necessary and read the description below the photograph. Note the access and use restrictions, if any.

10 If necessary, slide or scroll back up the page and press and hold over the picture or right-click to reveal the context menu.

11 Tap or click <u>Medium 500</u> at the View menu that appears over the picture.

12 At the Photo / All sizes page, press and hold or right-click the picture to display the shortcut menu and then tap or click *Save to picture library*.

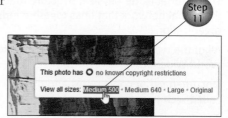

This photo has ○ no known copyright restrictions

View all sizes: Medium 500 · Medium 640 · Large · Original

Step 11

A Download link lets you choose to open the picture in a photo viewing application or save the file and specify the drive and/or folder location.

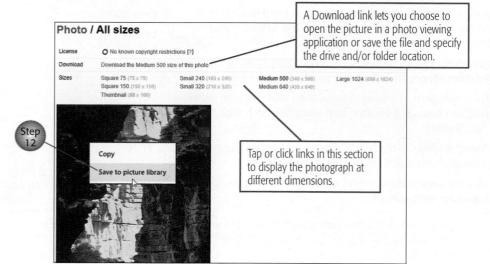

Photo / All sizes

| License | ○ No known copyright restrictions [?] |
| Download | Download the Medium 500 size of this photo |

Sizes
Square 75 (75 x 75)   Small 240 (163 x 240)   Medium 500 (340 x 500)   Large 1024 (698 x 1024)
Square 150 (150 x 150)   Small 320 (218 x 320)   Medium 640 (435 x 640)
Thumbnail (68 x 100)

Copy
Save to picture library

Step 12

Tap or click links in this section to display the photograph at different dimensions.

13 Close the IE app.

14 Tap or click the Photos app from the Start screen.

15 If necessary, tap or click the Pictures library in the Photos app window.

16 The Grand Canyon photo downloaded from the flickr Commons page is shown in the Pictures library. If necessary, slide or scroll right to view the picture.

17 Close the Photos app.

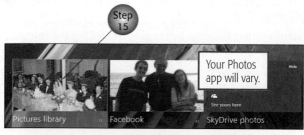

Step 15

Your Photos app will vary.

Hide

See yours here

Pictures library   Facebook   SkyDrive photos

← Pictures library 1 folder, 1 file

Your Pictures library will vary.

Step 16

Mom's Wedding Album

Concepts Review

Topic	Key Concepts	•	Key Terms
Introduction to the Internet and the World Wide Web	The Internet is the physical structure that represents the global network that links together individuals and organizations. All of the web pages circulated on the Internet form the World Wide Web. Documents that contain text and multimedia elements are called web pages. A web page also contains hyperlinks, which are used to move from one page to another. A web browser is a software program used to view web pages such as Internet Explorer, Google Chrome, and Mozilla Firefox. An Internet Service Provider is a company that provides Internet service to individuals and businesses for a fee. A web address is a unique text-based address, also called a Uniform Resource Locator, that identifies each web page on the Internet. A web address is made up of parts that define the protocol, domain, folder, and file name for the web page. You use search tools to find a web page when you do not know the web address.		Internet (Net) Web pages World Wide Web (Web or WWW) Hyperlinks Links Web browser Internet Service Provider (ISP) Web address Uniform Resource Locator (URL)
Navigating the Web Using Internet Explorer	Internet Explorer (IE) is the web browser included with Microsoft Windows. In Windows 8, Internet Explorer version 10 is included. The IE app launched from the Start screen varies from the IE app launched from the Desktop in the placement of the navigation tools and Address bar, as well as the page viewing area. Start Internet Explorer by tapping or clicking the Internet Explorer tile from the Start screen. Navigate to a web page by selecting the current text in the Address bar, typing the URL for the web page, and tapping or clicking Enter. Tap or click hyperlinks on web pages to navigate to the linked page. Tap or click the Back control or slide right to move back one page. Tap or click the Forward control or slide left to move forward one page. Tabbed browsing means you have multiple web pages open in an IE window, with each web page in a separate tab. Swipe up from the bottom or right-click to reveal controls and tap or click the New Tab control to open a new tab in which to display a web page. Close a web page by revealing the tab controls and tapping or clicking the Close Tab control for the page. Display a web page, reveal controls, tap or click the Pin site control, and tap or click Add to favorites to add a web page to the Favorites tiles.		Internet Explorer (IE) Address bar Back Forward Tabbed browsing Favorites New Tab Close Tab Pin site

Topic	Key Concepts	Key Terms
Navigating the Web Using Google Chrome	Google Chrome is a free web browser for Windows-compatible PCs, Linux PCs, or Macs.	Google Chrome
	Google Chrome is becoming more popular because of its loading speed for web pages and ability to search directly from the Address bar.	Omnibox
		Bookmark this page
	Start Google Chrome by tapping or clicking the Google Chrome tile from the Start screen. Google Chrome launches in the Desktop.	Customize and control Google Chrome
	In Google Chrome, the Address bar and Search box are combined and referred to as the omnibox.	Bookmarks bar
		Find bar
	Tap or click the Bookmark this page icon (white star) to add a web page to the Bookmarks bar.	Private browsing
	Use the Customize and control Google Chrome button to access the Bookmarks menu and turn on the display of the Bookmarks bar.	
	Tap or click the New Tab control to open a new tab in which to display another web page.	
	Open the Find bar from the Customize and control Google Chrome menu to locate all occurrences of a word or phrase in the current web page.	
	Private browsing with Google Chrome's incognito browsing feature lets you browse web pages without tracking history or saving cookies from the web pages visited.	
Navigating the Web Using Mozilla Firefox	Mozilla Firefox is a free web browser for Windows-compatible PCs, Linux PCs, or Macs.	Mozilla Firefox
	Start Mozilla Firefox by tapping or clicking the Mozilla Firefox tile from the Start screen. Mozilla Firefox launches in the Desktop.	Location bar
		Open a new tab
	Display a web page by typing the URL in the Location bar and tapping or pressing Enter.	Display your bookmarks
	Tap or click the Open a new tab control to display a web page in another tab.	Search bar
	Add a web page to the Bookmarks bar by tapping or clicking the Bookmark this page icon (white star).	
	Tap or click the Display your bookmarks button to show a bookmarked page from the Recently Bookmarked list.	
	Tap or click the Firefox button to open the Find bar to locate all occurrences of a word or phrase on the current web page.	
	Type a search word or phrase in the Search bar to search for information using the default search engine.	

continued....

Topic	Key Concepts	Key Terms
Searching for Information and Printing Web Pages	A company that indexes web pages by keywords using programs called spiders or crawlers and provides a search tool to find the pages is called a search engine.	Search engine Spiders Crawlers Advanced search tools
	Google and Bing are two leading search engines; however, several other companies provide search tools, such as Yahoo!, Ask, and Dogpile.	
	Use more than one search engine because you will get different results from each due to differences in spider and crawling programs and timing differentials.	
	To find information using a search engine, launch a web browser, type the URL for the desired search engine, type a search word or phrase in the search text box, and tap or press Enter.	
	Each search engine provides tools for advanced searching, which narrows the search results list. For example, at Yahoo!, the Advanced Web Search page provides options to include or exclude words in the search and restrict search results to types of domains, file formats, country, or language.	
	Print a web page by selecting a printer from the Devices list, which is accessed by revealing charms.	
	Printing selected pages from a web page requires that you display the page in the Desktop IE app and open the Print dialog box from the Tools widget.	
Downloading Content from a Web Page	Copying an image, audio clip, video clip, or music file from a web page to your PC or mobile device is called downloading.	Downloading
	Most content is protected by copyright law. Check a website for restrictions on copied content and request permission to use before downloading.	
	Saving content generally involves selecting an object and displaying a context menu at which you specify to copy to the clipboard or save the object as a file on your PC or mobile device.	
	Pictures downloaded from a web page are automatically saved to the Pictures library and can be viewed from the Photos app.	

Multiple Choice

1. Web pages are stored in a format that is read and interpreted for display by this type of software program.
   a. Hypertext
   b. Internet Reader Program
   c. Internet Service Provider
   d. Web browser

2. A web address is also referred to as a(n)
   _____.
   a. HTTP
   b. URL
   c. ISP
   d. WWW

3. Internet Explorer 10 can be launched from the Start screen or in this app.
   a. Desktop
   b. Photos
   c. People
   d. News

4. In Internet Explorer 10, use this control to display a second web page in the same window.
   a. New Tab
   b. Pin site
   c. Favorites
   d. Page tools

5. In Google Chrome you type the web address in this box.
   a. Find box
   b. Tab box
   c. Omnibox
   d. Bookmark box

6. Tap or click this icon in Google Chrome to add a web page to the bookmarks bar.
   a. Customize and control Google Chrome
   b. Refresh
   c. Start page
   d. White star

7. Firefox is published by this foundation.
   a. Wikimedia
   b. Open Source Alliance
   c. Mozilla
   d. Wikimedia Commons

8. Open the Find bar in Firefox by tapping or clicking this button.
   a. Search
   b. Firefox
   c. Bookmarks
   d. Reload

9. Search engines index web pages using this type of program.
   a. Spiders
   b. Browsers
   c. Trawlers
   d. Hypertext

10. Tap or click this charm in the IE app to select a printer to print a web page.
   a. Search
   b. Devices
   c. Printers
   d. Settings

11. Copying an image from a web page is referred to as _____.
   a. Uploading
   b. Freeloading
   c. Copyrighting
   d. Downloading

Crossword Puzzle

ACROSS
4 Address bar and search box combined in Google Chrome
7 Bookmark this page icon in Google Chrome
8 Company such as Google or Bing
10 Global network
11 Web address
12 Search text box in Firefox

DOWN
1 Library where downloaded pictures are saved
2 Add to favorites control in IE 10
3 Saving a picture from a web page
5 Type URL here in Firefox
6 Wrench control in IE 10
9 Plus symbol inside circle in IE 10

Matching

Match the term with the statement or definition.

_____ 1. Web address	a. Only edu domains
_____ 2. Internet Explorer 10 Start screen app	b. Used to print selected pages
_____ 3. Google's web browser	c. Bookmarks
_____ 4. Mozilla's web browser	d. URL
_____ 5. Saved links	e. Chrome
_____ 6. Advanced search options	f. Downloading
_____ 7. Tools widget in IE 10 Desktop app	g. Firefox
_____ 8. Save to picture library	h. Maximum page viewing

Project 1 Browsing Web Pages

Individual

Deliverable: Printed web pages, document with screen captures, or Microsoft XPS documents

1. Start Internet Explorer, Google Chrome, or Mozilla Firefox and navigate to **www.nga.gov**, which is the web page for the National Gallery of Art in Washington, D.C.
2. Navigate to the Exhibitions page and then tap or click the link to a current exhibition of your choosing.
3. Add the page to Favorites (IE) or bookmark the page (Google Chrome or Firefox).
4. Do ONE of the following tasks (check with your instructor for his or her preferred output method):
   a. Save a screen capture of the web page you visited in a file named **C2-Project1-WebBrowsing1-Your Name**.
   b. Select Microsoft XPS Document Writer from Devices and print the web page to an XPS document (.oxps). A file will be automatically saved in your Documents folder with a file name that is the title of the web page. Rename the file to **C2-Project1-WebBrowsing1-Your Name**. *This option is recommended if you are working on a tablet.*
5. Open a new tab and navigate to **www.navy.mil**, the web page for the U.S. Navy.
6. Add the page to Favorites (IE) or bookmark the page (Google Chrome or Firefox).
7. Navigate to one of the Navy News Service Top Stories.
8. Save a screen capture of the web page, or print the page to an XPS document. Use the same method you followed in Step 4 and name the new file **C2-Project1-WebBrowsing2-Your Name**.
9. Close the tab for the National Gallery of Art page.
10. Display the Favorites tiles (IE) or the bookmarks bar (Google Chrome or Firefox) and save a screen capture of the browser window in a file named **C2-Project1-WebFavorites-Your Name**.
11. Close Internet Explorer, Google Chrome, or Mozilla Firefox and any other apps you opened.
12. Submit the project to your instructor in the manner she or he has requested.

Project 2 Searching for Information on the Web

Individual

Deliverable: Document with search criteria and search results information

1. Start Internet Explorer, Google Chrome, or Mozilla Firefox.
2. Display the web page for your favorite search engine and search for information on resume writing tips.
3. Start a new WordPad (find using All Apps or Search charm) document and record the following information:
   a. The search engine you used and the search phrase you typed to find information.
   b. The number of pages returned in the search results list.

4. Next, return to the web browser and apply search options at the search engine website to help you narrow the search results. If necessary, use the Help feature for the search engine to learn how to specify advanced search options or use a different search engine that offers more options for narrowing a search.

5. Switch to the document window and type a description of the search options you applied and the number of pages returned in the new search results list.

6. Switch to the web browser, navigate to one of the links on the search results page, and read the information on resume writing tips. Select and copy the URL in the Address bar (IE), omnibox (Google Chrome), or Location bar (Firefox).

7. Switch to the document window, paste the URL of the page you visited below the search statistics, and add in your own words a brief summary of new information you learned by reading the web page.

8. Save the document as **C2–Project2–ResumeSearch–Your Name**.

9. Close the web browser and document apps.

10. Submit the project to your instructor in the manner she or he has requested.

Project 3 Downloading Content from a Web Page

Individual

Deliverable: Document with Downloaded Photograph of World War I Soldiers

1. Start Internet Explorer, Google Chrome, or Mozilla Firefox and navigate to The Commons page at flickr.

2. Search The Commons for pictures of soldiers from World War I.

3. Select and download a picture to the Pictures library.

4. Start a new WordPad document and paste the picture from the Pictures library into it. (Use the Picture button in the Home tab or the Insert tab, depending on the document app.)

5. Switch to the web browser, select and copy the URL for the photograph, and paste it below the picture in the document.

6. Save the document as **C2–Project3–WWIPicture–Your Name**.

7. Close the web browser and document apps.

8. Submit the document to your instructor in the manner she or he has requested.

Project 4 Exploring a New Search Engine

Individual or Pairs

Deliverable: Document with Comparison Information for two Search Engines

1. Start Internet Explorer, Google Chrome, or Mozilla Firefox, navigate to your favorite search engine web page, and search for information on job interview techniques.

2. Next, conduct a search using the phrase "top five popular search engines."

3. Read at least one article in the search results list. Choose a search engine from the article you read that you do not normally use. If you are doing this project in pairs, each person selects a different search engine.

4. Navigate to the web page for the new search engine that you selected and conduct a search on job interview techniques. Use the same search phrase at each search engine.

5. Compare the search results from each search engine. Was the number of pages in the search results close to the same number? On page one of search results at each search engine, how many web pages were repeated and how many web pages were different? Did one search engine seem to return more targeted results? Do you think you will use the new search engine in the future or will you revert back to the one you favored before?

6. Create a WordPad document with answers to the questions and, for the last question, provide your reasons. Include the two search engines and the search phrase you used to complete this project.

7. Save the document as **C2–Project4–SearchEngineComparison–Your Name**.

8. Close the web browser and document apps.

9. Submit the document to your instructor in the manner she or he has requested.

Chapter 3

Exploring Microsoft Office 2013 Essentials

After successfully completing this chapter, you will be able to:

- Identify various editions of Microsoft Office 2013 and the system requirements

- Start an Office program and identify common features

- Open, save, print, export, close, and start new documents in the Backstage view

- Customize the Quick Access toolbar (QAT)

- Perform commands using the ribbon, QAT, and Mini toolbar

- Select options in dialog boxes and task panes

- Copy text, an object, and formatting options using the Clipboard

- Use Microsoft Office Help

- Save and open files from OneDrive

- Set your display options to match the illustrations used in the textbook

Microsoft Office 2013 is a suite of software programs that includes applications such as Word, Excel, PowerPoint, Access, Outlook, and OneNote. The suite is available in various editions that package the programs in collections geared toward a home, business, or student customer using the programs under a traditional desktop installation or a subscription-based installation called Office 365. The Professional edition includes all of the programs included in this textbook.

Word is a program used to create, edit, and format text. Use Excel when your focus is to enter, calculate, format, and analyze numerical data. PowerPoint is an application used to create slides for an oral or kiosk-style presentation that includes text, images, sound, video, or other multimedia. Access is a database program in which you organize, store, and manage related data, such as information about customers or products. In addition to these four pillar applications, Outlook is included as a program to manage personal information such as mail, calendar, contacts, and tasks, and OneNote is included for storing and sharing information in notebooks.

One reason the Microsoft Office suite is so popular is because several features or elements are common to all of the programs. Once you learn your way around one of the applications in the suite, another application looks and operates similarly, making the learning process faster and easier.

In this chapter you will learn how to navigate the Microsoft Office 2013 interface and perform file-related tasks or routines common to all of the applications. You will customize the Quick Access toolbar and learn about choosing options using various methods. You will also learn how to save and open files to and from OneDrive as an alternative to using a USB flash drive.

TOPIC 3.1

SKILLS

Start an Office program

Switch between programs

Start a new presentation

Explore the ribbon interface

Starting and Switching Programs, Starting a New Presentation, and Exploring the Ribbon Interface

All of the programs in the Microsoft Office suite start the same way and share some common features and elements. Microsoft Office applications are desktop apps, meaning they are launched from the Windows 8.1 desktop.

Microsoft Office 2013 Editions

The Microsoft Office 2013 suite is packaged in various collections of programs, as shown in Table 3.1. The suite is also available through a subscription as Office 365. **Office 365** adds email, shared calendars, office web apps, instant messaging, and other web services to the standard productivity applications. An advantage to an Office 365 subscription is that these extras are accessible on more than one device with which you have Internet access, and updates to the suite are automatically pushed to the installed devices. For example, Office 365 Home Premium can be run on up to five devices with one subscription.

Table 3.1	Microsoft Office 2013 Editions
Edition	**What It Includes**
Office Home and Student 2013	Word, Excel, PowerPoint, and OneNote
Office Home and Business 2013	Word, Excel, PowerPoint, OneNote, and Outlook
Office Professional 2013	Word, Excel, PowerPoint, Access, Publisher, OneNote, and Outlook

The editions listed in Table 3.1 do not represent all of the available suites. For example, Microsoft also packages a suite called Microsoft Office University that is available only to verified students and faculty of postsecondary institutions, and an Office RT version for installation with Windows RT that is designed to conserve energy use on mobile devices.

Microsoft Office 2013 System Requirements

Table 3.2 on the next page provides the standard system requirements for installing Microsoft Office 2013. Generally, if the PC or mobile device is successfully running Windows 7 or Windows 8.1, then Office 2013 will also work on the same hardware provided there is enough free disk space for the program files. Note that Office 2013 cannot be installed on a computer running Windows XP or Windows Vista.

Starting a Program in the Microsoft Office 2013 Suite

To start any of the programs in the Microsoft Office 2013 suite, tap or click the program's tile on the Start screen. The Windows 8.1 desktop launches first, and the program opens within a window in the desktop.

You can also locate the program's tile in Apps view or tap or click the Search charm to locate the tile in the Apps list. Finally, type the first few characters of the program name at the Start screen to automatically start the Search feature at the Start screen. For example, typing *exc* at the Start screen or in the Search text box would show Excel 2013 in the results list.

oops!

Do you have Microsoft Office 2013 with **Windows 7**?

In Windows 7, you start at the desktop. To start an Office application:

1. Click the Start button.
2. Point to or click *All Programs*.
3. Click *Microsoft Office*.
4. Click the name of the desired program.

Table 3.2	Microsoft Office 2013 System Requirements
Hardware Component	**Requirement**
Processor	1 gigahertz (GHz) or faster processor
Memory	1 gigabyte (GB) of RAM for a 32-bit processor 2 gigabytes (GB) of RAM for a 64-bit processor
Disk space	3.0 gigabytes (GB) available free space
Operating system	Windows 7 or Windows 8.1
Internet browser	Internet Explorer (IE) version 8 or higher; Mozilla Firefox version 10 or higher; Google Chrome version 17 or higher; or Apple Safari version 5 or higher
Input devices	Touch-enabled input, mouse, or keyboard are all supported. Touch capability has been included in Office 2013 to work with touch gestures supported under Windows 8.1.

Quick **STEPS**
Launch an Office Application
Tap or click desired tile.
Switch between Applications
Tap button on Taskbar for desired application or, if multiple documents are open in application, point to button on Taskbar and tap or click thumbnail representing document.

1. At the Windows Start screen, tap or click the tile for **Word 2013**.

   You may need to slide or scroll the Start screen to find the tile. If necessary, swipe up or click the down-pointing arrow at the bottom of the screen to find the Word 2013 tile in the Apps list.

2. Notice that the Desktop launches first and then Microsoft Word opens inside a window within the desktop. If the Word screen does not fill the entire desktop above the Taskbar, tap or click the Maximize button 🗖 near the top right corner of the window (second button from right).

   Your window is already maximized if you see this button 🗗 near the top right corner of the window.

   Note: If asked to sign in, enter your Microsoft account email address and password.

3. Compare your screen with the **Word Start screen** shown in Figure 3.1.

4. Display the Start screen and tap or click the **Excel 2013** tile. If the Excel screen does not fill the desktop, tap or click the Maximize button.

5. Compare the Excel Start screen with the Word Start screen shown in Figure 3.1.

oops!

Windows 7 users at Steps 4, 6, and 8, start another program by clicking the Start button, pointing to or clicking *All Programs*, clicking *Microsoft Office*, and clicking the desired application.

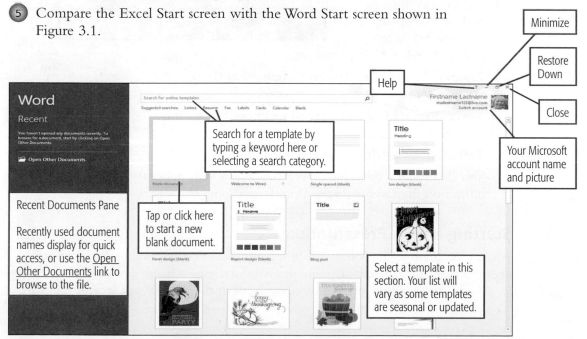

Figure 3.1 Word 2013 opens with the Word Start screen shown here. The Start screen for all Office apps shows the Recent list with the most recent documents opened next to the Templates gallery.

Each Office application opens in a Start screen. The left pane shows recent files opened and a link to open other files not shown in the recent documents list. Next to the recent files list, thumbnails for templates are shown with the first thumbnail used to start a new blank document, workbook, presentation, or database. At the top right of the Start screen are the Help, Minimize, Maximize, and Close buttons, with your Microsoft account name and picture below the buttons if you are signed in.

6 Display the Start screen and tap or click the **PowerPoint 2013** tile. If necessary, maximize the window.

7 Compare the PowerPoint Start screen window with the Word window shown in Figure 3.1 on the previous page.

8 Display the Start screen and tap or click the **Access 2013** tile. If necessary, maximize the new window and then compare the Access window with the Word window in Figure 3.1.

Switching between Office Programs

Because programs within the Microsoft suite open in the desktop, the Taskbar displays along the bottom of the screen with a button for each Office program. Switch to another open program by tapping or clicking the program's Taskbar button.

Point to a button on the Taskbar to see a thumbnail appear above the button with a preview of the open document. If more than one document is open, the button will appear cascaded as if multiple buttons are layered on top of each other. Point to the layered button to see a separate thumbnail for each open document.

9 Point to the Taskbar button representing Excel and tap or click the button to switch to the Excel window.

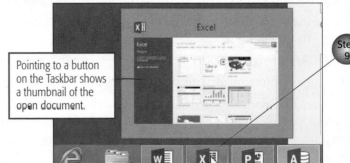

Pointing to a button on the Taskbar shows a thumbnail of the open document.

Step 9

10 Tap or click the Taskbar button representing Access to switch to the Access window.

11 Tap or click the Close button (× button) at the top right corner of the Access window.

Access closes and you are returned to Excel, which is the last program that you accessed.

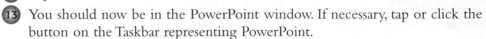

Step 11

Firstname Lastname
studentname123@live.com

Close

12 Tap or click the Close button to close Excel.

13 You should now be in the PowerPoint window. If necessary, tap or click the button on the Taskbar representing PowerPoint.

Starting a New Presentation

For any program in the Microsoft Office suite, start a new document, workbook, presentation, or database by tapping or clicking the new blank document, workbook, presentation, or database thumbnail in the *Templates* gallery of the Start screen.

(14) Tap or click *Blank Presentation* in the Templates and themes gallery of the PowerPoint window.

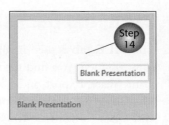

Start a new Office Document, Workbook, Presentation, or Database
Tap or click thumbnail for new blank document, blank workbook, blank presentation, or blank desktop database in Templates gallery.

Exploring the Ribbon Interface

The ribbon interface appears along the top of each Office application. Buttons within the ribbon are used to access commands and features within the program. The ribbon is split into individual tabs, with each tab divided into groups of related buttons, as shown in Figure 3.2. Word, Excel, PowerPoint, and Access all have the FILE and HOME tabs as the first two tabs in the ribbon. The FILE tab is used to perform document-level routines such as saving, printing, and exporting. This tab is explored in the next topic. The HOME tab always contains the most frequently used features in each application such as formatting and editing buttons.

Your background design may vary.

Ribbon Display Options

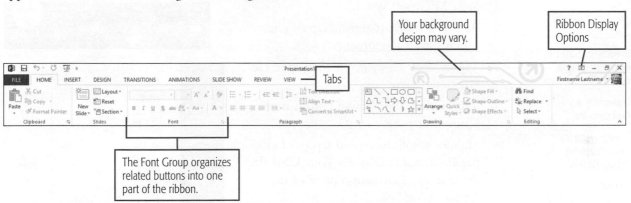

Tabs

The Font Group organizes related buttons into one part of the ribbon.

Figure 3.2 The ribbon in PowerPoint. The ribbon appears along the top of each Office application window and contains buttons to access features and commands.

The **Ribbon Display Options button** near the top right of the window is used to change the ribbon display from *Show Tabs and Commands* to *Show Tabs*, which hides the command buttons until you tap or click a tab, or *Auto-hide Ribbon*, which displays the ribbon only when you tap or click along the top of the window.

(15) Tap or click the INSERT tab to view the groups and buttons in PowerPoint's INSERT ribbon.

(16) Click the button on the Taskbar representing Word and tap or click Blank document to start a new Word document.

(17) Tap or click the INSERT tab to view the groups and buttons in Word's INSERT ribbon.

(18) Tap or click the DESIGN tab in Word and review the buttons in Word's DESIGN ribbon.

(19) Switch to PowerPoint and tap or click the DESIGN tab in PowerPoint.

(20) Spend a few moments exploring other tabs and then close PowerPoint.

(21) Spend a few moments exploring other tabs in Word and then close Word.

(22) Display the Start screen.

oops!

Ribbon is showing more or fewer buttons, or the buttons look different than shown here? The screen resolution for your PC or mobile device affects the ribbon display. In Topic 3.8 you will learn how to change the display. For now, the instructions will not ask you to tap or click anything you cannot see or identify by the button label or icon.

Using the Backstage View to Manage Documents

The **FILE tab** is used in all Office applications to open the **Backstage view**. Backstage view is where you find file management commands such as Open, Save, Save As, Print, Share, Export, and Close. If you have been working on a document within an application and want a blank document or template, you use the Backstage view to start a new document. You also use the Backstage view to display information about a document, protect the document, and manage document properties and versions.

Each application in the Microsoft Office suite provides options that you can personalize at the Backstage view through the Options dialog box. You also can manage your Microsoft account and/or connected services and change the background or theme for all of the Office applications in the Account tab of the Backstage view.

Note: Plug your USB flash drive into an empty USB port before starting this topic.

1. Start Microsoft Word.

2. At the Word Start screen, tap or click Open Other Documents.

3. Tap or click *Computer* in the Open tab Backstage view.

4. Tap or click the Browse button in the Computer pane.

5. Slide or scroll down and tap or click the Removable Disk for your USB flash drive in the Navigation pane of the Open dialog box.

6. Double-tap or double-click the *ComputerCourse* folder in the Content pane.

7. Double-tap or double-click the *Student_Data_Files* folder and then the *Ch3* folder.

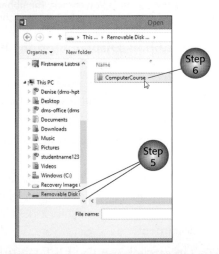

The Word document **Cottage_rental_listing** within the Ch3 subfolder is displayed in the Content pane. Within an Office application, the Open dialog box by default shows only files created in the active application.

8. Double-tap or double-click the Word document named **Cottage_rental_listing**.

In the next steps you will use the Save As command to save a copy of the document in another folder.

9. Tap or click the FILE tab to display the Backstage view.

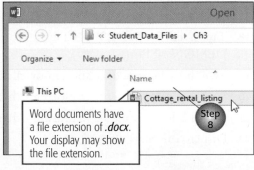

When a document is open, Backstage view displays the Info tab with document properties for the active file and buttons to protect, inspect, and manage versions of the document.

10 Tap or click Save As.

11 With *Computer* already selected in the Save As Backstage view, tap or click the *Ch3* folder in the *Current Folder* section or the Browse button in the Computer pane.

The Save As dialog box opens with the folder and drive selected from which the document was opened.

12 Tap or click the Up arrow button next to the Back and Forward buttons. Windows 7 users tap or click *Student_Data_Files* in the Address bar. (Windows 7 does not have an Up arrow button in the Open or Save As dialog boxes.)

The Up arrow button moves to the previous folder level.

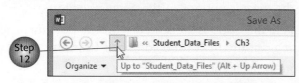

13 Tap or click the Up arrow button a second time. Windows 7 users tap or click *ComputerCourse* in the Address bar.

14 Double-tap or double-click the *CompletedTopicsByChapter* folder.

15 Tap or click the New folder button in the Command bar, type **Ch3**, and tap or press Enter.

16 Double-tap or double-click the *Ch3* folder.

17 Tap or click in the *File name* text box or select the current file name, type **3.2-CottageListing-Your Name**, and tap or press Enter, or tap or click the Save button.

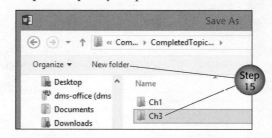

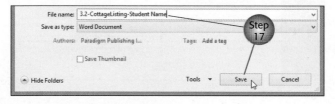

18 Tap or click in the document next to *List Date:* below the address *3587 Bluewater Road* (in the second column of the table) and type the current date.

19 Tap or click next to *Assigned Agent:* below the date (in the second column of the table) and type your name.

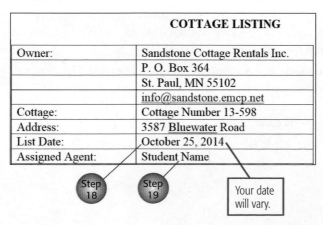

Printing a Document

Display the Print tab Backstage view when you want to preview and print a document. Before printing, review the document in the **Print Preview** pane of the Backstage view shown in Figure 3.3. The bottom of the Print Preview pane shows the number of pages needed to print the document, and navigation buttons are included to move to the next page and previous page in a multipage document.

Choose the printer on which to print the document in the *Printer* section and modify the print settings and page layout options in the *Settings* section. When you are ready to print, tap or click the Print button.

20 Tap or click the FILE tab to display the Backstage view and then tap or click Print.

21 Examine the document in the Print Preview pane, check the name of the default printer, and review the default options in the *Settings* section.

When print settings are changed, the options are stored with the document so you do not need to change them again the next time you want to print.

22 Tap or click the Print button to print the document.

The document is sent to the printer, and the Backstage view closes.

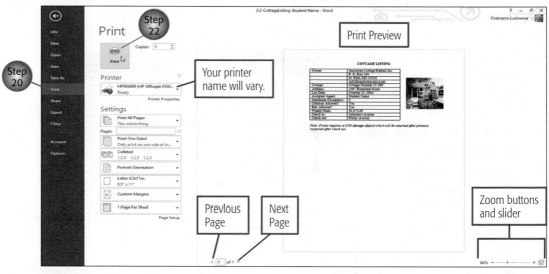

Figure 3.3 Print Tab Backstage View

Exporting a Document as a PDF File

Many people exchange documents in PDF format via email or websites. The advantage of a PDF file is that the document looks and prints as it would in the application in which it was created but without having to open or install the source program. A Word document can be sent to someone who does not have Word installed on his or her computer if the file is exported as a PDF.

A **PDF document** is a document saved in Portable Document Format, an open standard for exchanging electronic documents developed by Adobe systems. Anyone can view a PDF document with the free Adobe Reader application.

23 Tap or click the FILE tab and tap or click Export.

24 With *Create PDF/XPS Document* selected in the Export tab Backstage View, tap or click the Create PDF/XPS button.

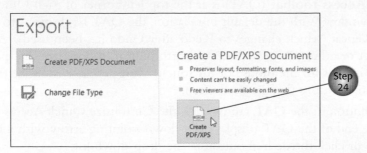

25 Tap or click the Publish button at the Publish as PDF or XPS dialog box.

By default, the PDF is created in the same drive and folder in which the Word document resides and with the same file name but with a file extension of *.pdf*. Because PDF files have a different file extension, the same name can be used for both the Word document and the PDF document.

26 By default, the published PDF document opens in the Windows Reader app (or Adobe Reader in Windows 7).

27 Close the Reader app and return to Microsoft Word.

28 Tap or click the FILE tab and then tap or click Close.

29 Tap or click the Save button when prompted at the message box asking if you want to save your changes. Leave Microsoft Word open for the next topic.

Close a document when you are finished editing, saving, printing, and publishing. A blank window displays when no documents are open.

 **Beyond Basics**   **Pinning Documents and Folders to Recent lists**

At the Open tab Backstage view, you can pin frequently used files to the *Recent Documents* list. Frequently used folders can be pinned to the Open or Save As tab Backstage views with *Computer* selected. Point to the file name or folder name and tap or click the push pin icon that displays at the right to pin the item to the list.

TOPIC 3.3

SKILLS

Add buttons to the Quick Access toolbar

Use buttons on the Quick Access toolbar to perform commands

 **Tutorial**

3.3 Customizing the Quick Access Toolbar

App Tip

Tapping or clicking a check-marked option removes the button from the QAT.

Customizing and Using the Quick Access Toolbar

The **Quick Access toolbar** (QAT) is at the top left corner of each Office application window. With the default installation, the QAT has buttons to Save, Undo, and Repeat (which changes to Redo after Undo has been used). A touch-enabled tablet or other device includes a fourth button to optimize the spacing between commands for the mouse or for touch. Most people customize the QAT by adding more buttons that are used often.

To add a button to the QAT, tap or click the Customize Quick Access Toolbar button at the end of the QAT (displays as a down-pointing arrow with a bar above) and then tap or click the desired button at the drop-down list.

Note: Skip this topic if the QAT on the computer you are using already displays the New, Open, Quick Print, and Print Preview and Print buttons in Word, PowerPoint, and Excel. Skip any steps in which a drop-down list option already displays with a check mark, which means the button is already added to the QAT.

1. At a blank Word screen, tap or click the Customize Quick Access Toolbar button at the end of the QAT.

2. Tap or click *New* at the drop-down list.

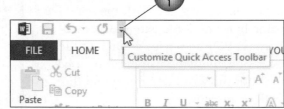

Options displayed with a check mark are already added to the QAT. Buttons added to the QAT are added at the end.

3. Tap or click the Customize Quick Access Toolbar button.

4. Tap or click *Open* at the drop-down list.

5. Tap or click the Customize Quick Access Toolbar button.

6. Tap or click *Quick Print* at the drop-down list.

7. Tap or click the Customize Quick Access Toolbar button.

8. Tap or click *Print Preview and Print* at the drop-down list.

Touch-enabled devices also show the Touch/Mouse Mode button.

QAT after buttons added in Steps 1–8

9. Tap or click the Open button on the QAT.

The Open tab Backstage view opens with the *Recent Documents* list. On a PC with Windows 7, the Open button on the QAT displays the Open dialog box.

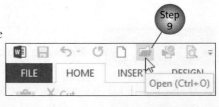

10. Tap or click the file named ***3.2-CottageListing-Student Name*** in the *Recent Documents* list, or double-tap or double-click the file in the Open dialog box for Windows 7 users.

11. Tap or click the Print Preview and Print button on the QAT.

    The Print tab Backstage view opens.

Step 11

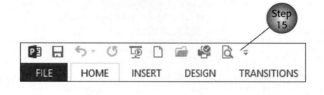

The Quick Print button added to the QAT automatically sends the current document to the printer using the active printer and print settings.

12. Tap or click the Back button (left-pointing arrow inside circle) to return to the document without printing.

Step 12

13. Display the Windows Start screen and start PowerPoint 2013.

14. Tap or click Blank Presentation at the PowerPoint Start screen.

    Notice the customized QAT does not carry over to other Microsoft applications.

 Print

Info

15. Customize the QAT in PowerPoint by adding the New, Open, Quick Print, and Print Preview and Print buttons.

Step 15

16. Close PowerPoint.

17. Display the Windows Start screen, start Excel 2013, and tap or click Blank Workbook at the Excel Start screen.

18. Customize the Excel QAT to add the New, Open, Quick Print, and Print Preview and Print buttons.

Step 18

19. Close Excel.

20. At the Word document, tap or click the FILE tab and then tap or click Close.

For Office applications, the keyboard command Ctrl + F4 closes the current document and Alt + F4 closes the program.

21. Tap or click the New button on the QAT.

    A new blank document window opens. Leave this document open for the next topic.

Step 21

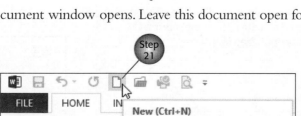

Selecting Text or Objects, Using the Ribbon and Mini Toolbar, and Selecting Options in Dialog Boxes

TOPIC 3.4

SKILLS

Select text and objects

Perform commands using the ribbon and Mini toolbar

Display a task pane and dialog box

Choose options in a dialog box

Creating a document, worksheet, presentation, or database involves working with the ribbon to select options or perform commands. Some options involve using a button, list box, or gallery, and some commands cause a task pane or dialog box to open in which you select options.

In many instances, before you choose an option from the ribbon, you first select text or an object as the target for the action. Select text by tapping or clicking within a word, paragraph, cell, or placeholder, or by dragging across the text you want to select. Select an object, such as a picture or other graphic, by tapping or clicking the object.

Selected objects display with a series of selection handles. A **selection handle** is a circle or square icon at the middle and/or corners of an object, or at the beginning and end of text on touch-enabled devices. Selection handles are used to manipulate the object or to define the selection area on touch-enabled devices. Table 3.3 provides instructions for selecting text using a mouse or touch and for selecting an object.

Table 3.3	Selecting Text and Objects Using the Mouse and Touch	
Selecting Text Using a Mouse	**Selecting Text Using Touch**	**Selecting Objects**
Point at the beginning of the text or cell to be selected. The pointer displays as I, called an I-beam in Word and PowerPoint, or as ✛, called a cell pointer in Excel. Hold down the left mouse button, and drag to the end of the text or cells to be selected. Release the mouse button. Summer vacation destinations I In some cases, a Mini toolbar displays when you release the mouse after selecting text. Summer vacation destinations Mini toolbar	Tap at the beginning of the text to be selected. A selection handle appears below the text (displays as an empty circle). Summer vacation destinations O — selection handle Touch the selection handle and slide your finger across the screen to the end of the text or cells to be selected. Summer vacation destinations O O A second selection handle appears at the end of the selected text when you remove your finger from the screen. Use the selection handles to redefine the area if necessary. To display the Mini toolbar, tap inside the selected text area. The toolbar displays already optimized for touch. Summer vacation destinations Mini toolbar	Tap or click the object. Selection handles appear at the ends, corners, and middle (depending on width and height) of each side of the object. A LAYOUT OPTIONS button also appears next to a selected object with options for aligning and moving the object with surrounding text. LAYOUT OPTIONS button for selected object

1. At a blank Word screen, type **Summer vacation destinations** and tap or press Enter.

2. Type **Explore the beaches of Florida and experience the Florida sunset with friends or family.** and tap or press Enter.

3. Select the title *Summer vacation destinations* and display the **Mini toolbar**. If using a touch-enabled device, tap inside the selection area to display the Mini toolbar.

The Mini toolbar that appears next to selected text or with the shortcut menu contains frequently used formatting commands.

If necessary, refer to the instructions in Table 3.3 for selecting text using the mouse or touch.

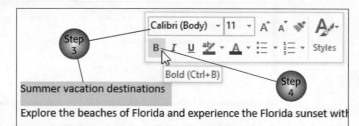

4. Tap or click the Bold button on the Mini toolbar.

5. Tap or click in the blank line below the sentence that begins with *Explore* to deselect the title.

6. Tap or click the INSERT tab in the ribbon.

7. Tap or click the Pictures button in the Illustrations group.

This opens the Insert Picture dialog box.

8. Slide or scroll down the Navigation pane and tap or click the Removable Disk for your USB flash drive.

9. Double-tap or double-click the *ComputerCourse, Student_Data_Files*, and *Ch3* folder names and then double-tap or double-click the image file named *FloridaSunset.*

The **FloridaSunset** image file is inserted in the document and is automatically selected.

10. Slide or drag the selection handle at the bottom right corner of the image until the picture is resized to the approximate height and width shown at the right.

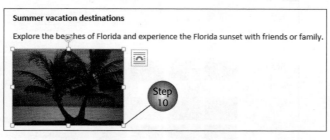

When using a mouse to resize, the pointer changes shape to a double-headed diagonal arrow (⬂) when you point at the bottom right corner of the image. Drag downward and to the right when you see this icon. The pointer changes shape to a crosshairs—a large, thin, black cross (✛)—while you drag the mouse. When you release the mouse, the selection handles reappear.

Quick **STEPS**

Select Text or an Object
Tap or click in word, paragraph, cell, or placeholder or tap or click the object OR tap or point at beginning of text and drag or slide selection handle to end of text.

Format Text Using the Mini Toolbar
1. Select text.
2. Click desired button on Mini toolbar OR tap inside selected text to display Mini toolbar and tap desired button.

App Tip

All of the buttons available on the Mini toolbar are also available in the ribbon.

oops!

No selection handles? If you tap or click away from the object, the selection handles disappear. Tap or click the picture to redisplay the selection handles.

The first time a document
is saved, the Save As tab
Backstage view appears.

11 Tap or click the Save button on the QAT.

12 Tap or click *Computer* and tap or click the *Ch3* folder within CompletedTopicsByChapter in the *Recent Folders* list.

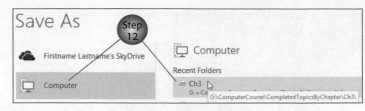

13 Type **3.4-VacationDestinations-Your Name** and then tap or press Enter or tap or click the Save button.

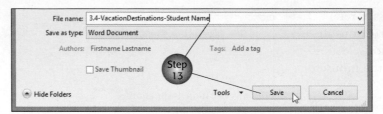

Live preview lets you see the effect of a change before applying the option. Watch the text or object change as you move the mouse over each option.

Working with Objects, Contextual Tabs, and Dialog Boxes

An **object** is a picture, shape, chart, or other item that can be manipulated separately from text or other objects around it. When an object is selected, a contextual ribbon tab appears. More than one contextual tab may appear. **Contextual tabs** contain commands or options related to the type of object that is currently selected.

Some buttons in the ribbon display a drop-down **gallery**. A gallery displays visual representations of options for the selected item in a drop-down list or grid. Pointing to an option in a gallery displays a **live preview** of the selected text or object if the option is applied.

14 Tap or click the Corrections button in the Adjust group of the PICTURE TOOLS FORMAT tab.

15 Point to the last option in the *Corrections* gallery.

Notice the picture brightens significantly when you point to the option.

16 Tap or click the last option in the *Corrections* gallery to apply the *Brightness +40% Contrast +40%* correction.

PICTURE TOOLS FORMAT tab not visible? This tab appears only when a picture is selected. Tap or click the picture to display the contextual tab.

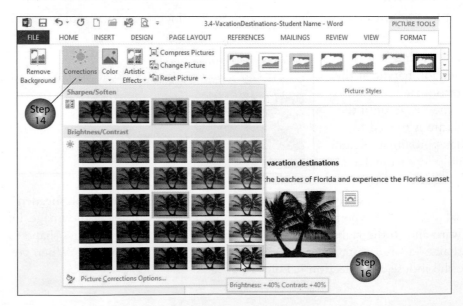

Some ribbon groups have a small button at the bottom right corner of the group that displays with a diagonal downward-pointing arrow ( ). This button is called a **dialog box launcher**. Tapping or clicking this button causes a task pane or a dialog box to appear. A **task pane** appears at the left or right side of the window, whereas a **dialog box** opens in a separate window above (or, from the viewer's perspective, in front of) the document. Task panes and dialog boxes contain more options related to the ribbon group as buttons, lists, sliders, check boxes, text boxes, and option buttons.

(17) Tap or click the dialog box launcher at the bottom right corner of the Picture Styles group.

Step 17

The Format Picture task pane opens at the right. You will work in a task pane in the next topic.

(18) Tap or click the Close button (×) at the top right corner of the Format Picture task pane.

Step 18

(19) Tap or click the dialog box launcher at the bottom right corner of the Size group.

(20) The Layout dialog box opens with the Size tab active.

(21) Select the current value in the *Absolute* text box in the *Width* section and type **3**.

(22) Tap or click the Text Wrapping tab and tap or click the *Square* option.

(23) Tap or click OK to close the Layout dialog box.

(24) With the picture still selected, slide the picture up to the top of the document, or position the pointer on top of the picture and drag the picture up to the top of the document. Release the picture when the green horizontal and vertical **alignment guides** show that the picture is aligned at the top and left margins.

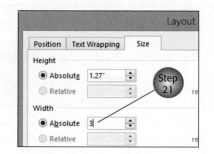

Step 21

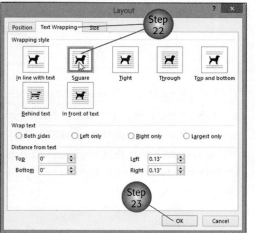

Step 22

Step 23

oops!

Measurement displays with cm (centimeters)? Change to inches at the Options dialog box from the FILE tab. Select Advanced pane and slide or scroll down to *Display* section.

App Tip

Vertical and horizontal lines called alignment guides are new in Office 2013. Guides help you place and align objects while the object is being manipulated.

Alignment guides show the picture is aligned at the top left margin.

Summer vacation destinations
Explore the beaches of Florida and experience the Florida sunset with friends or family.

Step 24

(25) Tap or click the Save button on the QAT. Leave the document open for the next topic.

Because the document has already been saved once, the Save button saves the changes using the existing file name and location.

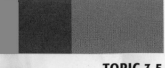

TOPIC 3.5

SKILLS

Copy and paste text and an object

Copy and paste formatting options using Format Painter

Use a task pane to format a selected object

 Tutorial

3.5   Cutting, Copying, Pasting, and Aligning Text

Using the Office Clipboard

The Clipboard group is standardized across all Microsoft Office programs. The buttons in the Clipboard group are Cut, Copy, Paste, and Format Painter. You used Cut, Copy, and Paste in Chapter 1 when you learned how to move and copy files and folders. Cut, Copy, and Paste are also used to move or copy text or objects.

Format Painter is used to copy formatting options from selected text or an object to other text or another object.

1 With the **3.4–VacationDestinations–Your Name** document still open, display the Windows Start screen, start PowerPoint 2013, and tap or click Blank Presentation.

2 Tap or click *Click to add title* in the placeholder on the blank slide and type **Florida Sunset**.

3 Switch back to Word.

4 Select the sentence that begins with *Explore* below the title and tap or click the Copy button in the Clipboard group of the HOME tab.

5 Switch to PowerPoint and tap or click *Click to add subtitle*.

6 Tap or click the top of the Paste button in the Clipboard group. (Do *not* tap or click the down-pointing arrow on the button.)

The selected text that was copied from Word is pasted into the slide in PowerPoint. Notice also the Paste Options button that appears below the pasted text.

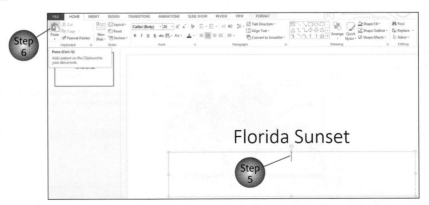

App Tip

Some buttons in the ribbon have two parts. Tapping or clicking the top or left of the button causes the default action to occur. Tapping or clicking the bottom or right of the button (down-pointing arrow) displays a list of options to modify the action that occurs.

7 Tap or click the Paste Options button to display the *Paste Options* gallery.

Paste Options vary depending on the pasted text or object. Buttons in the gallery allow you to change the appearance or behavior of the pasted text or object in the destination location.

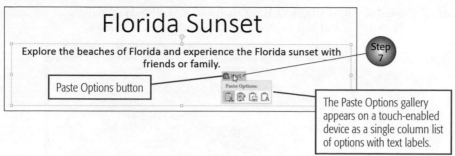

8 Switch back to Word.

9 Tap or click to select the picture, tap or click the Copy button, switch to PowerPoint, and then tap or click the Paste button. (Remember not to tap or click the down-pointing arrow on the Paste button.)

The pasted picture is dropped onto the slide over the text.

10 Tap or click the Paste Options button that appears below the pasted picture.

Notice that the Paste Options for a picture are different than the Paste Options for text.

11 Tap or click in the white space away from the picture to remove the *Paste Options* gallery.

12 If necessary, tap or click the picture to select the object.

13 Slide or drag the selected picture below the text. Release the picture when the orange guide shows the picture is aligned with the middle of the text placeholders.

14 Tap or click the Save button on the QAT.

Don't remember how to navigate to your USB flash drive or to folders or subfolders? Refer to Topic 3.2 for help navigating drives and folders.

15 At the Save As tab Backstage view, tap or click *Computer* and tap or click Browse.

16 Navigate to the Ch3 subfolder in the CompletedTopicsByChapter folder on your USB flash drive.

17 Select the current text in the *File name* text box, type **3.5-FloridaSunset-Your Name**, and tap or press Enter, or tap or click Save.

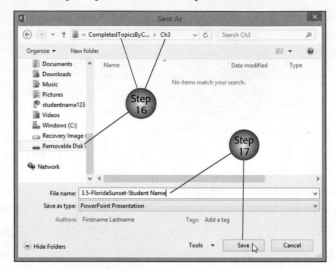

Using Format Painter to Copy Formatting Options

Sometimes instead of copying text or an object, you want to copy formatting options. Format Painter copies to the clipboard the formatting attributes for selected text or an object.

Tap once or single-click the Format Painter button to do a one-time copy of formatting options. Double-tap or double-click the Format Painter button if you want to paste the formatting options multiple times. Double-tapping or double-clicking the Format Painter button turns the feature on. The feature stays on until you tap or click the button again to turn the feature off. Buttons that operate as on or off are called **toggle buttons**.

18 Select the first occurrence of the word *Florida* in the subtitle on the slide.

19 Tap or click the Font Color button arrow (down-pointing arrow at right of Font Color button) in the Font group of the HOME tab.

20 Tap or click the *Purple* color square (last option in *Standard Colors* section).

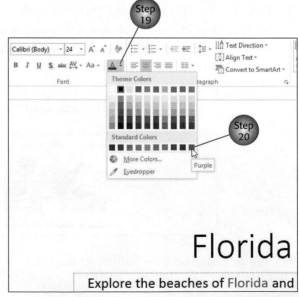

21 With the text still selected, tap or click the Italic button in the Font group.

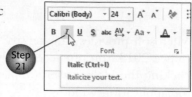

Step 21

22 With the text still selected, tap or click the Format Painter button (displays as a paint brush) in the Clipboard group.

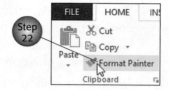

Step 22

23 Slide or drag across the second occurrence of the word *Florida* in the subtitle.

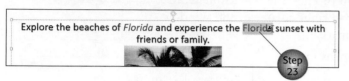

Explore the beaches of *Florida* and experience the *Florida* sunset with friends or family.

Step 23

24 Tap or click in white space away from the selected text to deselect the text.

25 Tap or click the Save button on the QAT.

26 Tap or click to select the picture and display the contextual tab.

27 If necessary, tap or click the PICTURE TOOLS FORMAT tab.

28 Tap or click the *Drop Shadow Rectangle* option in the *Picture Styles* gallery (fourth picture style option).

Step 27

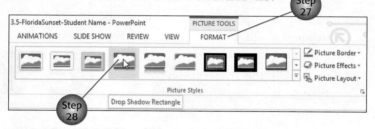

Step 28

Drop Shadow Rectangle

29 With the picture still selected, tap or click the HOME tab, tap or click the Format Painter button, and tap or click the title text *Florida Sunset* at the top of the slide.

30 With the Florida Sunset placeholder selected, tap or click the dialog box launcher in the Drawing group of the HOME tab.

31 Tap or click the Size & Properties button (last button) in the Format Shape task pane.

32 Tap or click TEXT BOX to expand the options in the task pane.

33 Tap or click the Vertical alignment button arrow (down-pointing arrow next to *Bottom*) and tap or click *Middle* at the drop-down list.

34 Close the Format Shape task pane.

Step 31

Title aligned in the middle of the placeholder vertically at Steps 31 to 34.

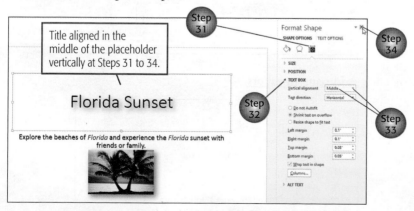

Florida Sunset

Explore the beaches of *Florida* and experience the *Florida* sunset with friends or family.

Step 32

Step 33

Step 34

35 Save, then close PowerPoint. Leave the Word document open for the next topic.

SKILLS

Use the Help
feature to browse
help topics
and search for
information on
Office.com

 **Tutorial**

3.6 Using the Word
Help Feature

oops!

Word Help window is mostly
empty and displays Can't
connect message? When the
device is not connected to the
Internet you are using offline
help. Proceed to Step 6. Be
aware your search results will
differ and you will need to
substitute a different link at
Step 7. After Step 8, proceed
to Step 12.

oops!

Word Help window looks different than the screens shown
here? Help is updated often
and may not appear exactly as
shown. If necessary, explore
other links.

 **Check
This Out**

office.microsoft.com

Go here to find help by product. At the Support link, you
can search for help articles or
browse links to training videos
and tutorials.

Finding Help in an Office Program

Microsoft provides an extensive set of online resources to assist you as you learn
Office 2013. You can access Help within any Office application by tapping or
clicking the Help button (displays as a question mark) near the top right corner of
the application window.

1 With the **3.4-VacationDestinations–Your Name**
document still open, tap or click the Microsoft Word
Help button near the top right corner of the window
(displays as a question mark ?).

A Word Help window opens inside
the Word window.

2 Tap or click <u>See what's new</u> in the
Getting Started section.

3 Slide or scroll down and review the
headings in the *What's new
in Word 2013* article.

4 Read a paragraph below
a heading about a new
feature that interests you.

5 Tap or click the Back button to
return to the main Word Help
window.

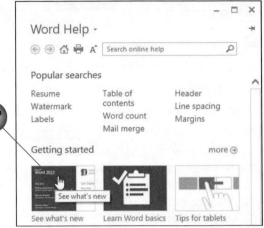

6 Tap or click in the *Search online help* text box, type **add page numbers**,
and then tap or press Enter or tap or click the Search button (displays as a
magnifying glass).

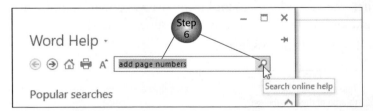

7 Tap or click <u>Add page numbers</u>.

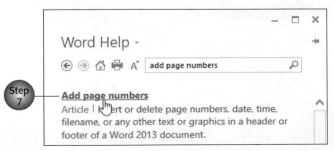

8 Slide or scroll down to review the Add page numbers article.

9 Tap or click the Home button near the top of the Word Help window to return to the main page.

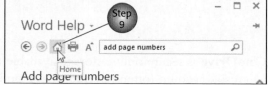

10 Tap or click <u>Tips for tablets</u>.

11 Explore the diagrams and instructions in the *Office Touch Guide* if you are using Office with a touch-enabled device.

This guide contains information on how to use touch gestures to work with Office.

12 Close the Internet Explorer window to return to the main Word Help page.

You can find help for an Office application by tapping or clicking a link in the *Popular searches* section, an article in the *Getting Started* section, or by typing a keyword or phrase in the *Search online help* text box. Microsoft also includes links to free online training modules at <u>Office.com</u>.

13 Close the Word Help window.

14 Close the **3.4-VacationDestinations-Your Name** document. Tap or click the Save button if prompted to save changes to the document.

15 Close Microsoft Word. Tap or click the No button when prompted to keep the last item you copied.

Figure 3.4 The Office page on Facebook. The page is frequently updated and may not appear exactly as shown here.

Microsoft Office Resources on Facebook

Microsoft has a Facebook page for Office (Figure 3.4). Go to <u>facebook.com/office</u> and check out the links to resources such as the Microsoft Community, where you can post questions, search answers, view videos, read blogs, and more.

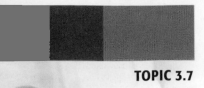

Using OneDrive for Storage, Scrolling in Documents, and Using Undo

SKILLS

Save and open files to and from OneDrive

Navigate in longer documents

Use Undo

Nothing happening yet? A short delay as OneDrive accesses your storage on Microsoft servers may occur.

You can access the file you will save to OneDrive from any device even if the device does not have a local copy of PowerPoint. You will learn about the Office web apps in Chapter 15.

The Save button on the QAT displays with an Internet Explorer icon when you are working with a document saved to OneDrive.

OneDrive is secure online storage available to individuals signed in with a Microsoft account (often referred to as cloud storage). You can save files to and open files from OneDrive, meaning you have access to the files from any device as long as you have an Internet connection. You may prefer to use OneDrive as the place to store your completed work. OneDrive can also be used if you forget your USB flash drive one day and need to save a file worked on at school or at home.

When working with longer documents, you will need to scroll the display or change the zoom settings to see more or less text within the window. The Zoom feature is explored in the next topic. Undo restores the document if you make a mistake.

Note: To complete this activity you need to be signed in with a Microsoft account. If you do not have a Microsoft account, skip the OneDrive section in Steps 2 to 19 and proceed to Step 20 after opening the presentation.

1. Start PowerPoint 2013 and open the presentation named **SpeechTechniques** from the Ch3 subfolder within the Student_Data_Files folder on your USB flash drive.

2. Tap or click the FILE tab and tap or click Save As.

3. Tap or click *Your Name's OneDrive* (where *Your Name* is your first and last name) at the top left of the Save As tab Backstage view.

4. Tap or click the *Documents* folder name in the *Recent Folders* section of the *Your Name's OneDrive* folder list, or tap or click the Browse button and then double-tap or double-click the *Documents* folder name.

5. Type **3.7-SpeechTechniques–Your Name** in the *File name* text box at the Save As dialog box and then tap or press Enter or tap or click Save.

The file will be uploaded to your online storage space at OneDrive.

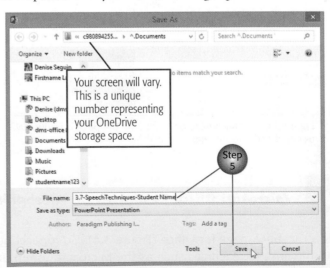

A progress message displays in the Status bar as the file is uploaded.

Progress message displays as file is uploaded

Quick STEPS

Save a File to OneDrive

1. If necessary, sign in with your Microsoft account.
2. Tap or click FILE tab.
3. Tap or click Save As.
4. Tap or click OneDrive account name.
5. Tap or click Browse or choose folder in Recent folders list.
6. If necessary, navigate to desired folder.
7. If necessary, type name for file in *File name* text box.
8. Tap or click Save.

If you decided to use OneDrive for all completed work, you should use folders on OneDrive to keep each chapter's completed files together. In the next steps, you will save the presentation to OneDrive a second time by creating a folder as you save the file.

6 Tap or click the FILE tab and tap or click Save As.

7 With your OneDrive account already selected at the Save As tab Backstage view, tap or click the Browse button.

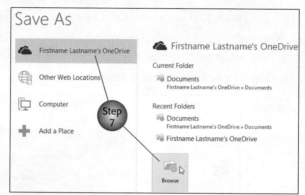

8 At the Save As dialog box, tap or click the New folder button in the Command bar.

Notice that the file saved at Step 5 appears in the Content pane.

9 Type **CompletedTopicsByChapter** and then tap or press Enter.

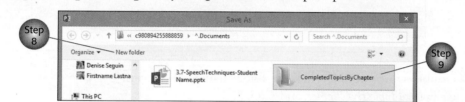

10 Double-tap or double-click the *CompletedTopicsByChapter* folder name to open the folder.

11 Tap or click the New folder button in the Command bar, type **Ch3**, and tap or press Enter.

12 Double-tap or double-click the *Ch3* folder name.

13 Tap or click the Save button to save the presentation using the same name as before.

You now have two copies of the presentation saved on OneDrive.

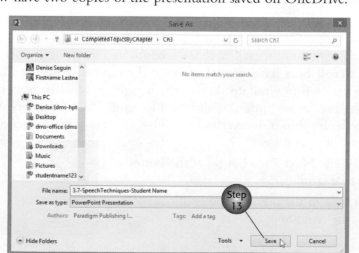

App Tip

You may notice a one- or two-second delay when navigating folders in the Open or Save As dialog box when working on OneDrive. If necessary, wait a few seconds for the screen to update.

14 Tap or click the FILE tab and then tap or click Close.

15 Tap or click the Open button on the QAT.

Because you just closed the **SpeechTechniques** presentation, you will notice the presentation appears twice in the *Recent Presentations* list. Notice that your OneDrive account is associated with each of these entries. You could reopen the presentation from OneDrive using the *Recent Presentations* list; however, in the next steps, you will use Browse to practice opening a file from OneDrive in case a file you need is not in the *Recent* list for the Office application.

16 Tap or click *Your Name's OneDrive* at the top left of the Open tab Backstage view.

You will notice the folder you need is in the *Recent Folders* list; however, you will practice navigating in case you ever need a file that has not been recently opened.

17 Tap or click the Browse button.

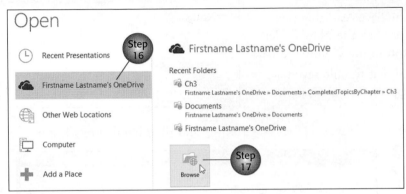

18 Double-tap or double-click the folder names *Documents*, *CompletedTopicsByChapter*, and *Ch3*.

19 Double-tap or double-click the **3.7-SpeechTechniques-Your Name** file name in the Content pane.

Navigating folders on OneDrive is the same as navigating folders on your USB flash drive.

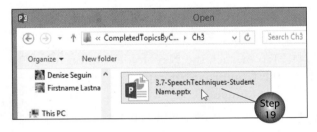

App Tip

Horizontal and vertical scroll bars appear when the file exceeds the viewing area.

Using the Scroll Bars

Until now, the files you have used in this chapter were small and able to be seen in one window. Larger files display with a horizontal and/or vertical scroll bar that allows you to navigate to other pages, slides, sections of a worksheet, or part of an Access object. **Scroll bars** have arrow buttons at the top and bottom or left and right ends that are used to scroll up, down, left, or right. A **scroll box** in the scroll bar between the two arrow buttons is also used to scroll. PowerPoint and Word have two buttons at the bottom of the vertical scroll bar that are used to navigate to the next or previous slide or page.

20 Tap or click the Next Slide button at the bottom of the vertical scroll bar.

The second slide in the presentation is the slide now shown in the window.

21. Tap or click the Next Slide button two more times to move to Slide 4.

22. Tap or click the up arrow button at the top of the vertical scroll bar repeatedly until you are returned to the first slide.

23. Slide or drag the scroll box at the top of the vertical scroll bar downward until you reach the end of the slides.

Notice that as you slide or drag the scroll box downward, a ScreenTip displays the slide numbers and titles for the slides so you know when to release your finger or the mouse.

24. Press the Ctrl + Home keys on your keyboard.

Ctrl + Home is the universal keyboard shortcut for returning to the beginning of a file.

25. Press the Ctrl + End keys on your keyboard.

Ctrl + End is the universal keyboard shortcut for navigating to the end of a file.

Using Undo

The **Undo** command in all Office applications can be used to restore a document, presentation, worksheet, or Access object to its state before the last action that was performed. This can be a real life saver if you make a change to a file and do not like the results. Note that not all actions (such as Save) can be reversed with Undo.

26. Navigate to the first slide in the presentation.

27. Select the title text *Speech Techniques*.

28. Tap or click the Bold button on the Mini toolbar or in the Font group of the HOME tab.

29. With the text still selected, tap or click the Underline button on the Mini toolbar or in the Font group of the HOME tab.

30. Tap or click in any part of the slide away from the selected text to deselect the title text.

31. Tap or click the Undo button on the QAT. Do *not* tap or click the down-pointing arrow on the button.

The underline is removed from the title text and the text is selected.

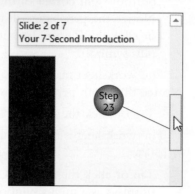

Speech Techniques
Making a Powerful Presentation

Undo Underline (Ctrl+Z)

32. Tap or click the Undo button a second time to remove the bold formatting.

33. Deselect the text and tap or click the Save button on the QAT.

34. Close the presentation and close PowerPoint.

SKILLS

Change the Zoom setting

Change the screen resolution to match textbook illustrations

oops!

Having trouble using the Zoom slider on a touch device? Tap the buttons or the percentage number to open the Zoom dialog box (steps 7 to 8), or use the Zoom buttons in the VIEW tab.

App Tip

The VIEW tab in Word, PowerPoint, and Excel contains a Zoom group with buttons to change zoom magnification. Access does not include the Zoom feature.

Changing Display Options

Word, Excel, and PowerPoint display a **Zoom slider** bar near the bottom right corner of the window. Using the slider, you can zoom out or zoom in to view more or less of a document, worksheet, slide, or presentation.

1. Start Excel 2013 and open the workbook named **CutRateRentals** from the Ch3 folder in Student_Data_Files.

2. Look at the Zoom slider bar near the bottom right corner of the Excel window. Notice the percentage displayed is 100%. Tap or click the **Zoom In** button (displays as a plus symbol).

The worksheet magnification increases by 10%. Notice the zoom percentage is now 110%.

3. Tap or click the Zoom In button two more times.

The worksheet is now much larger in the display area and the zoom percentage is 130%.

4. Tap or click the **Zoom Out** button (displays as a minus symbol).

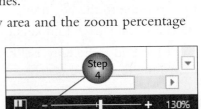

Zoom Out decreases the magnification by 10% each time the button is used.

5. Slide or drag the Zoom slider left or right and watch magnification of the worksheet decrease or increase as you move the slider.

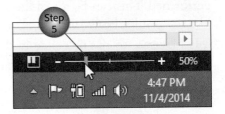

6. Slide or drag the Zoom slider to the middle of the slider bar to return the zoom to 100%.

7. Tap or click *100%* at the right of the Zoom In button.

This opens the Zoom dialog box in which you can choose a predefined magnification, type a custom percentage value, or choose the *Fit selection* option to fit a group of selected cells to the window.

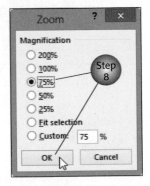

8. Tap or click *75%* and tap or click OK or press Enter.

9. Return the zoom magnification to 100% by dragging the Zoom slider to the middle of the slider bar.

Zoom In, Zoom Out, the Zoom slider, and the Zoom dialog box function the same in Word and PowerPoint.

Viewing and Changing Screen Resolution

You may have noticed that your ribbon has fewer or more buttons than the ones shown in this textbook or that, in some cases, buttons show icons only (no labels). The appearance of the ribbon is affected by the screen resolution, as shown in Figure 3.5 on the next page.

Screen resolution refers to the number of picture elements, called pixels, that make up the image shown on the display. A pixel is a square with color values. Thousands of pixels are used to render the images you see on your display. Resolution is expressed as the number of horizontal pixels by the number of vertical pixels.

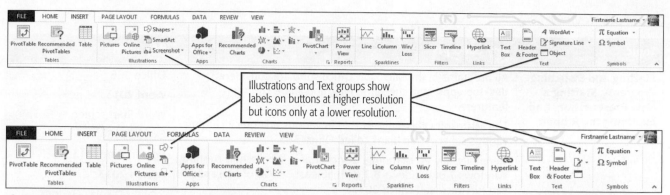

Illustrations and Text groups show labels on buttons at higher resolution but icons only at a lower resolution.

Figure 3.5 Excel's INSERT tab shown at 1440 x 900 (above) and at 1280 x 800 (below). The ribbon shows more or fewer buttons and/or displays buttons with or without labels at varying resolution settings. The lower resolution shown above is the setting from a tablet.

Note: Check with your instructor before proceeding. Some schools do not allow the display properties to be changed. If necessary, perform these steps on your personal PC or mobile device.

(10) Minimize the Excel window to display the desktop.

(11) Press and hold or right-click an unused area of the desktop to display the shortcut menu and then tap or click *Screen resolution*.

(12) If the current setting for *Resolution* is *1440 x 900*, skip to Step 15; otherwise, tap or click the *Resolution* button and slide or drag the slider up or down as needed until the resolution is *1440 x 900*. (Use the highest setting possible if your device cannot display 1440 x 900.)

(13) Tap or click the Apply button.

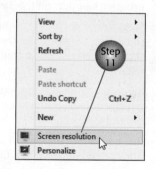

(14) Tap or click the Keep changes button.

(15) Tap or click OK to close the Screen Resolution window.

(16) Tap or click the Excel button on the Taskbar to restore the Excel window.

If you changed your screen resolution, examine the ribbon to see if there was a change in the quantity and/or display of the buttons (Figure 3.5).

(17) Close the **CutRateRentals** worksheet and close Excel.

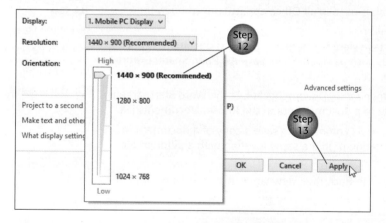

Quick
STEPS

Change Zoom Magnification
Tap or click Zoom In or Zoom Out button or drag Zoom slider to desired setting OR

1. Tap or click zoom percentage.
2. Select desired zoom option.
3. Tap or click OK.

App Tip

Screen resolution is an operating system setting. A higher resolution uses more pixels and means the image quality is sharper or clearer. It also means more content can be displayed in the viewing area.

oops!

Screen resolution won't go to 1440 x 900 or you cannot change the resolution? Choose a setting close to 1440 x 900 OR close the Screen Resolution dialog box. You do not need to change the screen resolution to successfully use this textbook. Just be aware that some illustrations won't match exactly what you see on your display.

Concepts Review

Topic	Key Concepts	Key Terms
Starting and Switching Programs, Starting a New Presentation, and Exploring the Ribbon Interface	All programs in the Microsoft Office suite are considered desktop apps, start the same way, and share common features.	Office 365
	The Microsoft Office suite is sold in various editions including various subscription plans called Office 365.	Word 2013
		Word Start screen
	Generally, any PC or mobile device that is successfully running Windows 7 or Windows 8.1 with at least 3.0 GB of free space can run Microsoft Office 2013.	Excel 2013
		PowerPoint 2013
	To start a program in the Microsoft Office suite, tap or click the program's tile at the Start screen or search for the tile in the Apps list.	Access 2013
		Ribbon Display Options button
	An Office program starts with the application's Start screen, which shows a list of recently opened files and a Templates gallery.	
	Switch between applications by tapping or clicking the desired program's button on the Taskbar in the desktop.	
	Start a new document, workbook, or presentation by tapping or clicking the button in the Templates gallery of the Start screen for a new document, workbook, presentation, or database.	
	All programs display the ribbon along the top of the window, which contains buttons for commands and features within the program.	
	Buttons within the ribbon are divided into tabs and groups to organize related features together.	
Using the Backstage View to Manage Documents	The FILE tab is used in all Office applications to open the Backstage view.	FILE tab
	The Backstage view is where you perform document-level commands such as Open, Save, Save As, Print, Share, Export, and Close.	Backstage view
		Print tab Backstage view
	Use the Open Other Documents link at the Word Start screen to navigate to a document not in the Recent Documents list.	Print Preview
		PDF document
	Use the Save As command to save a copy of a document in another location or in the same location with a different file name.	
	At the Print tab Backstage view you can preview a document and change the printer and/or print settings before printing.	
	A PDF document is an open standard created by Adobe systems for exchanging electronic documents.	
	Use the Export command to publish a Word document in PDF format.	
Customizing the Quick Access Toolbar	The Quick Access toolbar (QAT) is at the top left of each Office application window.	Quick Access Toolbar
	Add or remove buttons to/from the QAT by tapping or clicking the Customize Quick Access Toolbar button and tapping or clicking the desired option at the drop-down list.	
	The QAT can be customized individually for each Office application.	

Topic	Key Concepts	Key Terms
Selecting Text or Objects, Using the Ribbon and Mini Toolbar, and Selecting Objects in Dialog Boxes	Before choosing an option from the ribbon, a task pane, or a dialog box, you often first select text or an object.	Selection handle
	Selected objects display with circle or square icons around the perimeter called selection handles, which are used to resize or otherwise manipulate the object.	Mini toolbar
		Object
	The Mini toolbar contains the same buttons as the ribbon and appears near selected text or with shortcut menus.	Contextual tabs
		Gallery
	Sliding or dragging a selection handle resizes a picture, shape, chart, or other item referred to as an object.	Live preview
		Dialog box launcher
	Contextual tabs are tabs that appear with buttons related to the selected object.	Task pane
		Dialog box
	A gallery is a drop-down list or grid with visual representations of options that display a live preview of each option with the selected text or object.	Alignment guides
	The dialog box launcher causes a task pane or dialog box to appear.	
	Task panes and dialog boxes provide additional options for the related ribbon group as buttons, lists, sliders, check boxes, text boxes, and option buttons.	
	Horizontal and vertical alignment guides appear when moving an object to help you place and align the object with text or margins.	
Using the Office Clipboard	The Clipboard group in the ribbon is standardized across all Office applications.	Format Painter
		Toggle buttons
	Use Cut, Copy, and Paste buttons to move or copy text or objects.	
	A Paste Options button appears when you paste text or an object with options for modifying the paste action.	
	Use the Format Painter button to copy formatting options.	
	A button that operates in an on or off state is called a toggle button.	
Finding Help in an Office Program	Access Help within any Office application by tapping or clicking the Help button that displays as a question mark near the top right corner of the window.	
	Find help by following links to popular searches or articles, or by typing a search keyword or phrase.	
	Go to facebook.com/office to find help at Microsoft Office's Facebook page.	
Using OneDrive for Storage, Scrolling Documents, and Using Undo	OneDrive is cloud storage where you can save files that can be accessed from any other device using your Microsoft account.	OneDrive
		Scroll bars
	Select your OneDrive account at the Open and Save As tab Backstage view.	Scroll box
		Undo
	Saving and navigating folders on OneDrive is similar to saving and navigating folders on a USB flash drive.	
	Horizontal and vertical scroll bars with arrow buttons and a scroll box are used to navigate larger documents.	
	The Undo feature is used to reverse an action performed to restore a document to its previous state.	

continued....

Topic	Key Concepts	Key Terms
Changing Display Options	Use the Zoom In, Zoom Out, Zoom slider, and Zoom dialog box in Word, Excel, and PowerPoint to increase or decrease the magnification setting. Screen resolution refers to the number of horizontal and vertical pixels used to render an image on the display. The screen resolution setting for your PC or mobile device affects the display of the ribbon. Screen resolution is set at the desktop by opening the operating system's Screen Resolution window.	Zoom slider Zoom In Zoom Out Screen resolution

Multiple Choice

1. Which of the following is *not* an application within the Microsoft Office 2013 suite?
   a. Word
   b. Excel
   c. Internet Explorer
   d. Access

2. To switch to another open Office application, tap or click the button for the application in the
   _____.
   a. Title bar
   b. Taskbar
   c. ribbon
   d. templates gallery

3. This tab opens the Backstage view.
   a. INSERT
   b. HOME
   c. VIEW
   d. FILE

4. Export a document in this file format that is a common standard used for exchanging documents electronically.
   a. PDF
   b. RDF
   c. DOC
   d. PUB

5. This toolbar is located at the top left corner of each Office application window.
   a. New
   b. Quick Print
   c. File
   d. Quick Access

6. If you customize the toolbar at the top left corner in Word, the revised toolbar also appears automatically updated in Excel and PowerPoint.
   a. True
   b. False

7. The circles or squares that appear around a selected object are called _____.
   a. object handles
   b. zoom handles
   c. format handles
   d. selection handles

8. This term refers to a tab that appears with buttons related to a selected object.
   a. object tab
   b. contextual tab
   c. format tab
   d. quick access tab

9. A drop-down list that displays a live preview of options is called a _____.
   a. task pane
   b. dialog box
   c. gallery
   d. guide

10. Tap or click this button to open a task pane or dialog box.
    a. dialog box launcher
    b. task pane launcher
    c. object launcher
    d. selection launcher

11. Cut, Copy, and Paste buttons are found in this group in the HOME tab.
    a. Alignment
    b. Clipboard
    c. Editing
    d. Insert

12. Use this button to copy formatting options.
    a. Format Painter
    b. Copy Formats
    c. Paste Formats
    d. Cut Formats

13. The Help button displays as this symbol.
    a. Exclamation mark (!)
    b. Plus symbol (+)
    c. Question mark (?)
    d. Hyphen (-)

14. OneDrive is referred to as this type of storage.
    a. backup
    b. cloud
    c. extra
    d. redundant

15. This feature will reverse an action.
    a. Undo
    b. Redo
    c. Cut
    d. Restore

16. This slider is used to increase or decrease the magnification of the screen.
    a. Zoom
    b. Magnify
    c. Display
    d. Personalize

Crossword Puzzle

ACROSS

1 Name of toolbar at top left of Office apps
6 Name of toolbar that appears with selected text
8 Shows gallery option applied to selection in advance
10 Dialog box to change magnification setting
12 Opening window for all Office apps
13 Name for buttons that have an on and off state
14 Tab that opens Backstage view
15 Name of pane that opens at left or right side of window

DOWN

2 Reverse last action
3 Guides that help you place objects when moving
4 Save a copy of a file in another location
5 Navigational element in scroll bar between arrows
7 Picture, shape, or chart
9 Tab in Backstage view used to create a PDF
11 Online file storage

Matching

Match the term with the statement or definition.

_____ 1. Ribbon
_____ 2. Backstage view
_____ 3. Quick Access toolbar
_____ 4. Gallery
_____ 5. Format Painter
_____ 6. OneDrive
_____ 7. Scroll bars
_____ 8. Zoom In

a. Frequently used buttons
b. Cloud storage
c. Copy formats
d. FILE tab
e. Navigate long documents
f. Interface to access commands
g. Increase magnification
h. Live preview

Project 1 Start a New Presentation and Copy Object to Slide from Excel

Individual

Deliverable: PowerPoint Presentation

1. Start Excel 2013 and open the student data file named **CutRateRentals**.
2. Start a new blank presentation in PowerPoint 2013.
3. Type **CutRate Car Rentals** as the slide title text.
4. Use the Layout button in the Slides group of the HOME tab to change the slide layout option to *Title Only*.
5. Select the title text, apply formatting options of your choice, and then deselect the text.
6. Switch to Excel, select and copy the pie chart, switch to PowerPoint, and then paste the chart on the slide.
7. Save the presentation as **C3-Project1-CutRateRentals-Your Name** in a new folder named Ch3 in the ChapterProjectsWork folder on your USB flash drive.
8. Close the presentation, close PowerPoint, and then close Excel.
9. Submit the presentation to your instructor in the manner she or he has requested.

Project 2 Modifying a Presentation and Copying to Word

Individual

Deliverable: Word Document and PDF Document

1. Start PowerPoint and open the **C3-Project1-CutRateRentals-Your Name** presentation.
2. Use Save As to save a copy of the file as **C3-Project2-CutRateRentals-Your Name**.
3. Select and resize the chart so that the chart fills most of the slide below the title.
4. With the chart still selected, move the chart as needed so that it is centered below the title.
5. With the chart still selected, use the Change Colors gallery in the Chart Styles group of the CHART TOOLS DESIGN tab to change the color scheme for the pie chart to another color of your choosing.
6. With the chart still selected, use the Shape Styles gallery in the CHART TOOLS FORMAT tab to apply a shape style option of your choosing. ***Hint: Tap or click the More button (bottom button that displays with a bar and down-pointing arrow below it at right end of gallery) to view more options in a drop-down grid.***
7. Select the title text and change the font color to a color of your choosing.
8. Save the revised presentation using the same name.
9. Start a new blank document in Word 2013.
10. Copy the slide title text from the PowerPoint presentation and paste the text into the Word document. After the text is pasted, use the Paste Options button to apply the *Keep Source Formatting* option if the text is not pasted with source formatting already applied.
11. If necessary, press Enter to create a new blank line after the title text.
12. Copy the chart from the PowerPoint presentation and paste it below the title in the Word document.
13. Save the Word document as **C3-Project2-CutRateRentals-Your Name** in the Ch3 folder in ChapterProjectsWork.
14. Export the Word document as a PDF with the same name and save in the same location.
15. Close the Reader app if necessary.
16. Close the document in Word, close Word, and close PowerPoint.

Project 3 Florida Vacation Flyer

Individual or Pairs

Deliverable: Flyer as document or PDF

1. Research a Florida destination that you would like to travel to during the next school break, including the approximate cost for one week. Include in the cost estimate travel, lodging, food, visitor attractions, and souvenirs.
2. Make a list of five to 10 points to include in the flyer based on the research you conducted. For example, provide a list of tourist attractions or events that make the destination inviting.
3. Create a flyer in Word named **C3–Project3–FloridaFlyer–Your Name** and saved in the Ch3 folder in ChapterProjectsWork similar to the one shown in Figure 3.6, substituting your information where noted. Use your best judgment to determine options to apply to the text. Apply the following options to the picture: +40% Brightness and Contrast correction, width of 2.5 inches, Top and Bottom Text Wrapping, and Reflected Rounded Rectangle Picture Style.
4. Export the flyer as a PDF with the same name and saved in the same location, and close Word.
5. Submit the flyer to your instructor in the manner she or he has requested.

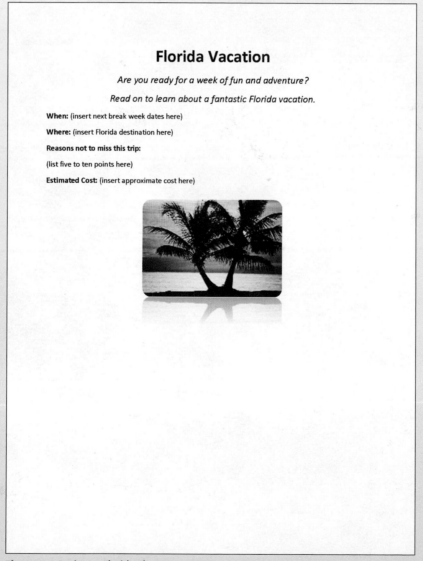

Figure 3.6 Project 3 Florida Flyer Document

Chapter 4

Organizing and Managing Class Notes Using OneNote

After successfully completing this chapter, you will be able to:

- Open and close an existing notebook
- Add and edit content
- Add sections and pages to a notebook
- Link external content to a notebook
- Tag notes
- Search notes
- Create a new notebook
- Share a notebook

OneNote is a note-taking software application referred to as a digital notebook. Think of OneNote as the electronic equivalent of a binder with notes written on loose leaf paper organized by dividers. Note-taking software can store, organize, search, and share notes of any type, including typed notes, handwritten notes on a tablet, web pages, pictures, documents, presentations, worksheets, emails, appointments, contacts, and more. A OneNote notebook can collect everything you want to keep track of for a subject or topic in one place.

OneNote notebooks can be stored on OneDrive so that you can access the notes from any device with an Internet connection. Another advantage to storing the notebook on OneDrive is that you can share the notebook with others. More than one person can edit a page at the same time. For group projects, OneNote is a useful tool for collaborating and sharing ideas, research, and content.

In this chapter you will learn how to open an existing notebook; create a new OneNote notebook; add sections, pages, and content; tag and search notes; and share a notebook with others.

Topic 4.1

SKILLS

Open an existing notebook

Create and move a note

Apply color to note text

Add a section and page

Opening a Notebook and Adding Notes, Sections, and Pages

A **OneNote notebook** is organized into sections, which are accessed by tabs across the top of the notebook. Think of sections as the dividers you would use in a binder to organize notes by subject, topic, or category. Within each section you add pages. Notes or other content are added to a page. You can add as many sections and pages as you like to organize a notebook. Notes can be typed or content added anywhere on a page.

① From the Windows Start screen, start **OneNote 2013**.

The first time OneNote is started, a Start screen appears with information on how to use OneNote (Figure 4.1). The default notebook called *Your Name's Notebook*, which is automatically saved to OneDrive opens. You can store everything in this notebook or create separate notebooks for keeping notes organized. For example, you may want to create one notebook for school-related content and another for personal content.

Note: The Start screen shown in Figure 4.1 may not appear depending on the configuration for the computer you are using.

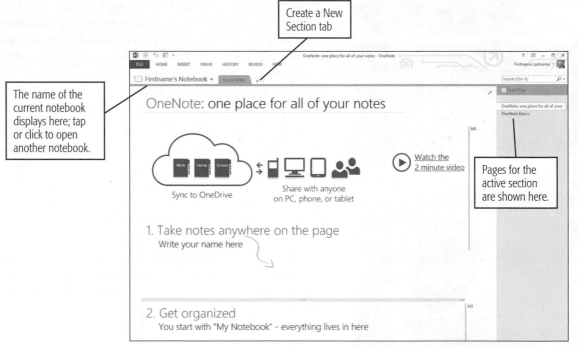

Figure 4.1 The OneNote Start screen opens with your OneDrive notebook and the Quick Notes tab active. You can learn about using OneNote from the Start screen by reading the content and following links to videos.

② Tap or click Your Name's Notebook (or other notebook name) near the top left corner of the OneNote window (below the ribbon) and tap or click *Open Other Notebooks* at the drop-down list.

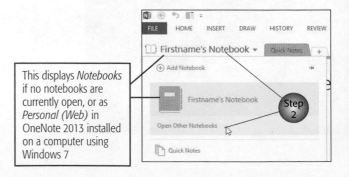

(3) At the Open Notebook Backstage view, tap or click Computer in the *Open from other locations* section, and then tap or click the Browse button.

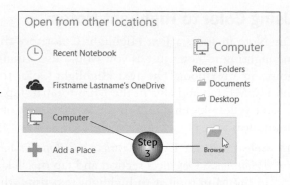

(4) Navigate to the Removable Disk for your USB flash drive in the Navigation pane, and double-tap or double-click the *ComputerCourse, Student_Data_Files*, and *Ch4* folder names in the Open Notebook dialog box.

(5) Double-tap or double-click the *BusTechnologyCourse* folder name.

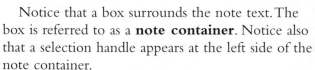

Folders navigated at Step 4

(6) Double-tap or double-click the file named **Open Notebook**.

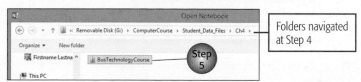

By default, OneNote creates a table of contents file named Open Notebook within a folder named for each notebook created. The table of contents file is similar to a table of contents for a book in that it stores the name of each section added to the notebook. OneNote saves each section in a separate file within the notebook folder.

(7) Review the information on the Business Technology page in the *CourseInformation* section. If necessary, slide or scroll down to view all information.

(8) Tap or click anywhere within the text *Prof. J. Wickham*.

Selection handle

Notice that a box surrounds the note text. The box is referred to as a **note container**. Notice also that a selection handle appears at the left side of the note container.

(9) Tap or click the selection handle at the left of the note container to select the text *Prof. J. Wickham*.

(10) Tap or click the Bold button on the Mini toolbar.

(11) Tap or click in the blank white space at the right of the Prof. J. Wickham note container and type **Office hours every Tuesday from 12:00 to 1:00**.

(12) Slide or drag the gray bar at the top of the note container to move the note next to *Prof. J. Wickham* in the approximate location shown.

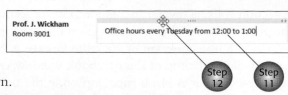

When using a mouse, a four-headed white arrow pointer appears when you point to the top gray bar on the note container. Drag the note container when you see this pointer.

oops!

Can't see the Browse button? You may need to slide or scroll down the *Computer* pane to see the button.

App Tip

OneNote differs from other Office apps in that the name that appears as the notebook name is the name of a *folder* (not an individual file). Each OneNote section is a *separate file saved within the notebook folder*.

oops!

Using touch? Remember to tap inside a selection to display the Mini toolbar.

App Tip

To delete a note, select the note text using the selection handle or the gray bar at the top of the note container and press the Delete key on the keyboard or choose Cut in the HOME tab.

Using Color to Highlight Notes

OneNote includes a Text Highlight Color tool that is used to apply color highlighting to notes just as you would use a highlighter to highlight important points in a textbook. The Text Highlight Color tool is in the Basic Text group of the HOME tab and also in the Mini toolbar. Tap or click the button to apply the default yellow highlighting to the selected text or use the down-pointing arrow on the button to apply a different highlight color.

13 Select the text *Examine various social media and communications applications* in the *Performance Objectives* section and tap or click the Text Highlight Color button in the Mini toolbar to highlight text using the default color.

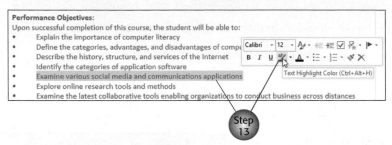

oops!

Ribbon is not pinned? Tap or click the HOME tab and tap or click the push pin icon at the bottom right corner of the ribbon to keep the buttons visible while you work.

14 Select the text *conducting work online and across distances via collaborative tools* in the *Course Description* section, tap or click the Text Highlight Color button arrow in the HOME tab, and then tap or click Green (second color option).

Adding Sections and Pages

A section is like a divider in a binder. Create sections to organize the notebook by category, topic, or subject. Each section can have multiple pages. To create a new section in a notebook, tap or click the **Create a New Section tab** (displays as a plus symbol) along the top of the notebook window, type a name for the section, and then tap or press Enter. A blank page displays in the new section with an insertion point in the page title section. Type a title for the page and tap or press Enter.

Tap or click the **Add Page icon** in the Pages pane to add another new page to the section. Type a title for the page and tap or press Enter.

(15) Tap or click the Create a New Section tab (displays as a plus symbol) next to the CourseInformation tab.

(16) Type **WebPages** and tap or press Enter.

(17) With the insertion point blinking in the page title placeholder, type **Technology Web Pages** and tap or press Enter.

(18) Tap or click the Create a New Section tab, type **TechnologyImages**, and then tap or press Enter.

(19) Type **Pictures for Technology Topics** as the page title and tap or press Enter.

(20) Tap or click the WebPages tab to display the section.

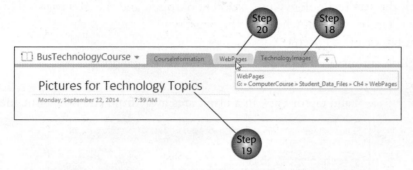

(21) Tap or click the Add Page icon (displays as a plus symbol inside a circle) in the Pages pane.

(22) Type **Technology Web Links** as the page title and tap or press Enter. Leave OneNote open for the next topic.

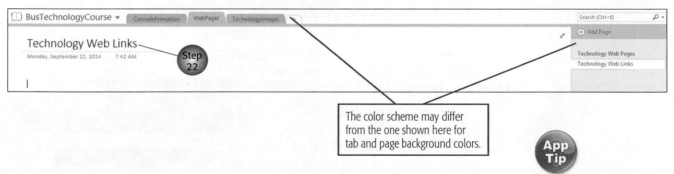

The color scheme may differ from the one shown here for tab and page background colors.

Quick STEPS

Open a Notebook
1. Tap or click notebook name left of section tabs.
2. Tap or click *Open Other Notebooks*.
3. Navigate to drive and/or notebook folder name.
4. Double-tap or double-click *Open Notebook*.

Add a Note to a Page
1. Tap or click at desired location on page.
2. Type note text.
3. Tap or click in blank space outside note container.

Add a Section and Page to a Notebook
1. Tap or click Create a New Section tab.
2. Type section title.
3. Tap or press Enter.
4. Type page title.
5. Tap or press Enter.

Add a Page to a Section
1. Make active desired section tab.
2. Tap or click Add Page icon.
3. Type page title.
4. Tap or press Enter.

App Tip

Notice that a Save button is not provided in OneNote; changes are saved automatically.

Beyond Basics    ## Tips for Typing Notes

OneNote automatically formats text into a table when you type some text and then press the Tab key. Each time you press Tab, a new column is inserted into the table. Press Enter to add a new row. You can also perform a calculation in OneNote by typing an expression. When you press the spacebar after an equals sign, OneNote calculates the expression. For example, typing *15*12=* and then pressing the spacebar causes OneNote to calculate the result and show *15*12=180* in the note container.

Topic 4.2

SKILLS

Insert a link to a web page

Insert a copy of a web page

Insert a screen clipping

Inserting Web Content into a Notebook

Web content can be inserted into a notebook as a link, as a web page, or as a screen clipping. The method you use will vary depending on the content and the frequency of updates to the content. For example, you may want to use a link if a web page updates frequently. Embed a copy of the web page directly into OneNote if you are not concerned with updates occurring in the content you are capturing. A screen clipping is useful if you want to embed only a portion of a web page.

You can also use the standard copy and paste tools to copy text from a web page and paste it into a notebook. When you paste text copied from a web page, OneNote automatically includes the source URL with the pasted text.

1 With the BusTechnologyCourse notebook open and the *WebPages* section active, tap or click anywhere on the page, type **www.techmeme.com**, and then tap or press Enter.

OneNote automatically formats web addresses as hyperlinks.

2 Type **Techmeme provides daily summaries of leading technology stories on the web.** and tap or click in a blank area away from the note container.

3 Tap or click www.techmeme.com to view the web page in the Internet Explorer or other browser window.

4 Select the web address in the Internet Explorer Address bar, type **wikipedia. org/wiki/tim_berners-lee**, and then tap or press Enter.

To embed a copy of a web page into a OneNote notebook, use the **Send to OneNote button** (OneNote button with scissors) in the Windows Taskbar.

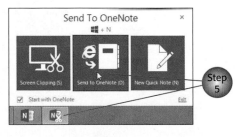

5 Tap or click the Send to OneNote button in the Taskbar and tap or click *Send to OneNote* at the pop-up menu.

6 At the Select Location in OneNote dialog box, tap or click *WebPages* in the *BusTechnologyCourse* section list and tap or click OK. **Hint: *You may need to tap or click the OneNote button in the Taskbar to display the Select Location in OneNote dialog box.***

OneNote inserts the web page as it would appear if the page had been printed, with the first page of the web page as a new page in the selected section and a subpage below the web page for each additional printed page (Figure 4.2).

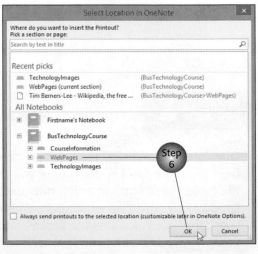

oops!

Web page not found? Check that you typed the web address as shown. As an alternative, find an article on Tim Berners-Lee that you can embed into OneNote.

oops!

Send to OneNote button not in Taskbar? Display the Search charm, type *Send to OneNote* in the *Search* box, and launch the app from the Search results.

App Tip

From Internet Explorer or any Office app, you can also send a copy of the current document to OneNote by printing the document using the Send to OneNote 2013 printer.

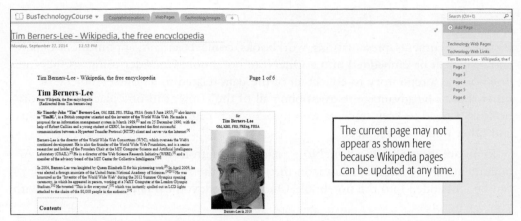

Figure 4.2 A web page copied into OneNote. OneNote embeds the page as it would appear if printed. The page title is a hyperlink to the source URL.

⑦ Switch back to the browser window, select the web address in the Address bar, type **wikipedia.org/wiki/3d_printer**, and then tap or press Enter.

Assume you want to save the picture of the 3D printer shown in the Wikipedia article on 3D printing.

⑧ Tap or click the Send to OneNote button in the Taskbar and then tap or click *Screen Clipping* at the pop-up menu.

The screen dims and a crosshairs pointer (✛) displays.

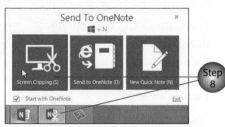

⑨ Slide or drag the crosshairs from the top left to the bottom right of the 3D printer image located at the right side of the Wikipedia page as shown.

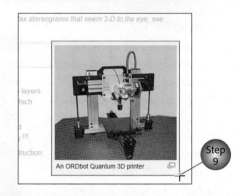

⑩ Tap or click the expand button (displays as a plus symbol) next to BusTechnologyCourse in the *All Notebooks* section of the Select Location in OneNote dialog box.

⑪ Tap or click *TechnologyImages* in the expanded list of sections and then tap or click the Send to Selected Location button.

⑫ Close the browser window.

⑬ If necessary, tap or click the TechnologyImages section tab and tap or click the 3D printing page in the Pages pane. Leave OneNote open for the next topic.

Expand button (plus symbol) changes to collapse button (minus symbol) when the list is expanded.

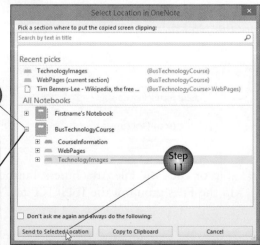

oops!

Picture shown not on the web page? Capture an image of another picture from the page if the one shown is no longer available.

App Tip

The Send to OneNote button also includes *New Quick Note*. Quick Notes are short reminders for things you might write on a sticky note. Each Quick Note is a page in the *Quick Notes* section, which can be viewed by selecting *Quick Notes* at the Notebooks drop-down list.

Topic 4.3

SKILLS

Insert a picture

Insert a document

Embed a copy of a presentation

App Tip

You can also drag and drop a picture onto a OneNote page from a Libraries or Pictures window.

Inserting Files into a Notebook

Pictures, documents, presentations, workbooks, contacts, emails, appointment details, and more can be embedded into a OneNote notebook. Consider using a OneNote notebook as a repository to collect all of the data related to a course, subject, or other topic. The advantage to assembling all of the content in one place is that you no longer need to keep track of web links or web pages separately from documents and other notes for a subject.

Items are inserted into a OneNote page using buttons from the INSERT tab. A document can be inserted as an icon that links to the source file, or the contents can be embedded into the notebook. Once inserted, you can annotate the files with your own notes.

1. With the BusTechnologyCourse notebook open and the 3D printing page active in the *TechnologyImages* section, tap or click the *Pictures for Technology Topics* page.

2. Tap or click the INSERT tab and tap or click the Pictures button in the Images group.

3. Navigate to the Ch4 folder in Student_Data_Files on the Removable Disk for your USB flash drive at the Insert Picture dialog box.

4. Double-tap or double-click the image named *AnalogCptr_1950s*.

5. With an insertion point positioned in the note container below the image, type **Analog computer from the 1950s** and then tap or click in a blank area outside the note container.

6. Tap or click the Create a New Section tab, type **Documents** as the section title, and then tap or press Enter.

7. Type **Course Documents** as the page title and tap or press Enter.

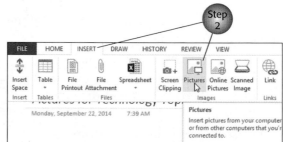

8. Tap or click the File Attachment button in the Files group of the INSERT tab.

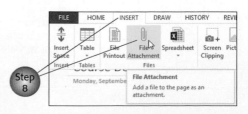

9. Navigate to the Ch4 folder in Student_Data_Files on your USB flash drive at the Choose a file or a set of files to insert dialog box.

10. Double-tap or double-click the Word document named *Tech_Wk1_SocialMedia*.

11. Tap or click Attach File at the Insert File dialog box.

12. With an insertion point positioned in the note container below the Word document icon and file name, type **Week 1 Assignment** and then tap or click in a blank area outside the note container.

A document inserted as a file displays an icon above the file name. The file is linked to the source location and can be launched from OneNote.

13. Double-tap or double-click the Word document icon, tap Open if using touch, and then tap or click OK at the Warning message that opening attachments could harm your computer or data.

14. Slide or scroll down and view the Word document and then close Word.

15. Create a new section titled *Presentations* with a page title *Course Presentations*.

16. With the Course Presentations page active, tap or click the File Printout button in the Files group of the INSERT tab.

17. Double-tap or double-click the PowerPoint presentation named *Tech_Wk1*.

18. Slide or scroll down and view the PowerPoint slides inserted into the OneNote page. Leave OneNote open for the next topic.

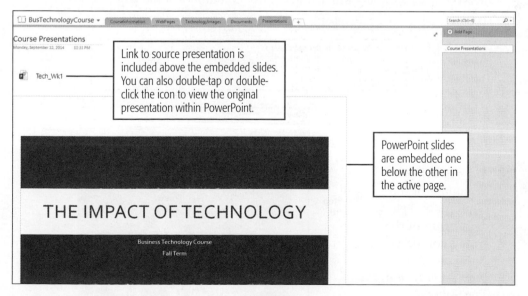

Link to source presentation is included above the embedded slides. You can also double-tap or double-click the icon to view the original presentation within PowerPoint.

PowerPoint slides are embedded one below the other in the active page.

THE IMPACT OF TECHNOLOGY

Business Technology Course
Fall Term

App Tip

Changes that occur in the file after the file has been inserted into OneNote as a printout are not updated. Be aware that the note container may not contain the most up-to-date content.

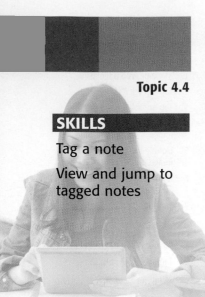

Tagging Notes, Viewing Tags, and Jumping to a Tagged Note

SKILLS

Tag a note

View and jump to tagged notes

A **tag** is a category assigned to a note that allows you to identify the note later as an item that you have flagged as important, as a question, as a definition, as an item for a to-do list, as an idea, or for some other purpose. OneNote includes a gallery of predefined tags in the Tags group of the HOME tab. You can customize tags by modifying a predefined OneNote tag or by creating a new tag of your own.

Once tags have been assigned to items in the notebook, you can display the **Tags Summary pane** and use the pane to navigate quickly to a tagged item.

1. With the BusTechnologyCourse notebook open and the Course Presentations page active in the *Presentations* section, tap or click the WebPages section tab.

2. Tap or click the Technology Web Links page.

3. Tap or click at the beginning of the note text *Techmeme provides daily summaries of leading technology stories on the web*, tap or click the HOME tab, and then tap or click *Important* in the Tags gallery.

OneNote inserts the tag icon for the Important tag (a gold star) next to the note text.

4. Tap or click the Tim Berners-Lee page.

5. Double-tap or double-click after the bolded title *Tim Berners-Lee* within the embedded web page to place an insertion point, and tap or click *Important* in the Tags gallery.

OneNote inserts the tag inside a new note container on the page.

6. Type **Use this information in Project 1**.

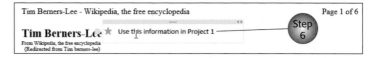

7. Tap or click the TechnologyImages section tab.

8. Tap or click at the beginning of the caption text below the picture of the analog computer, and then tap or click *? Question* in the Tags gallery.

9. Tap or click the Presentations section tab.

10 Slide or scroll down the page of embedded PowerPoint slides to the slide with the title *REFLECTION BLOG* and double-tap or double-click to place the insertion point at the right of the slide title.

11 Tap or click the More button (displays as a short bar with a down-pointing arrow below) at the bottom of the Tags gallery to display more predefined tag options.

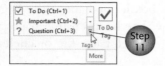

12 Tap or click *Remember for blog* in the drop-down gallery.

13 Type **Blog entry homework** in the note container next to the tag icon.

Once tags have been applied to notes, you can view all of the tagged notes and jump to a specific item that you need to review. Tap or click the Find Tags button in the Tags group of the HOME tab to display in a Tags Summary pane at the right side of the OneNote window a list of tagged items grouped by tag category.

14 Tap or click the Find Tags button in the Tags group.

The Tags Summary pane opens at the right side of the OneNote window.

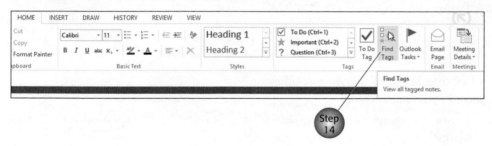

15 Tap or click <u>Techmeme provides daily summa…</u> in the Tags Summary pane.

OneNote jumps to the Technology Web Links page in the *WebPages* section of the notebook.

16 Tap or click each of the other tag links in the Tags Summary pane to jump to each tagged item in the notebook.

17 Tap or click the Close button at the top right of the Tags Summary pane. Leave OneNote open for the next topic.

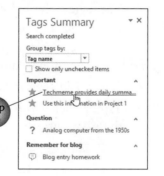

App Tip

Use the *Search* list box at the bottom of the Tags Summary pane to specify locations that should be searched for tags. For example, you can view tags from all open notebooks or from the active section only.

Beyond Basics   **Using the To-Do Tag**

You can use the Tags feature to create a to-do list by tagging items in your notebook with the To-Do tag. OneNote inserts a blank check box at the left of note text tagged with *To Do*. Tap or click the check box when a task has been completed to mark the item finished.

Topic 4.5

SKILLS

Search notes

Close a notebook

Searching Notes and Closing a Notebook

An advantage to using an electronic notebook instead of a paper-based notebook is the ability to search all of the pages in the notebook for a keyword or phrase and instantly locate each occurrence of the note text. The Search feature in OneNote searches all of the pages within all of the open notebooks. Type a search keyword or phrase in the *Search* text box located above the Pages pane at the right side of the OneNote window. OneNote begins listing pages with matches in a drop-down list and highlights matches on each page. Tap or click a page in the search results to view the matches.

When you close OneNote, the active notebook is left open so that you are returned to the place you left off when you start OneNote again. You may instead choose to close a notebook when you are finished working. One reason for closing a notebook is when you want to search for a keyword in another open notebook that you know also exists in the current notebook. Closing the current notebook will avoid pages showing up in search results that you are not interested in reviewing.

① With the BusTechnologyCourse notebook open, tap or click the CourseInformation section tab.

② Tap or click in the *Search* text box above the Pages pane that displays with the entry *Search (Ctrl + E)*, and type **Tim Berners-Lee**.

OneNote begins displaying matches as soon as you start typing.

③ Tap or click any entry in the search results list to navigate to the page and review the highlighted text entries on the page.

OneNote is able to provide search results from content embedded from external sources.

Your search results list may vary.

④ Select *Tim Berners-Lee* in the *Search* text box and type **analog**.

⑤ Tap or click *Pictures for Technology Topics* in the search results list to navigate to the page with the picture of the analog computer.

OneNote highlights matches to the search text on each page in the search results list.

⑥ Select *analog* in the *Search* text box and then type **blog**.

⑦ Tap or click each entry in the search results list to review each item.

(8) Tap or click the Close button at the right of the *Search* text box to close the search results list.

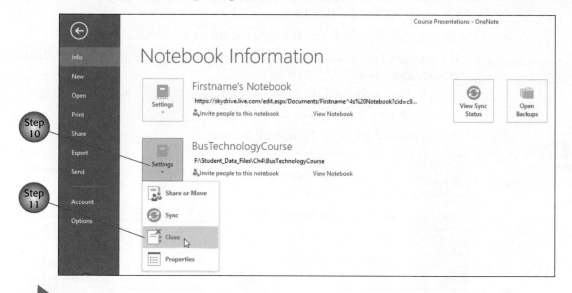

Because OneNote automatically saves changes to notebooks as you work, you can leave all of your notebooks open and be assured that changes are being updated. However, a notebook can be closed by selecting *Close* from the Settings drop-down list at the **Notebook Information Backstage view**.

(9) Tap or click the FILE tab.

(10) Tap or click the **Settings button** next to BusTechnologyCourse at the Notebook Information Backstage view.

(11) Tap or click *Close* at the Settings drop-down list to close the notebook.

Search Notes
1. Tap or click in *Search* text box.
2. Type search keyword or phrase.
3. Tap or click pages in search results list.

Close a Notebook
1. Tap or click FILE tab.
2. Tap or click Settings button.
3. Tap or click *Close*.

ALTERNATIVE method   To search for a keyword or phrase on the active page only, press Ctrl + F. OneNote displays *Find on page* in a yellow box next to the *Search* text box. Type the search keyword or phrase in the *Search* text box. OneNote displays an up and down arrow in the yellow box with the number of matches found. Tap or click the arrows to navigate to the matches on the current page.

Printing and Exporting Notebook Sections

Print a notebook section by making the desired section active, tapping or clicking the FILE tab, and then tapping or clicking Print. Use Print Preview at the Print tab Backstage view to view and modify print settings such as the print range, paper size, and page orientation. Consider exporting a page, section, or notebook as a PDF or XPS file instead of printing. Display the Export tab Backstage view, choose what you want to export and the export format, and then tap or click the Export button. OneNote displays the Save As dialog box in which you choose the drive, folder, and file name for the exported file.

Topic 4.6

SKILLS

Create a new
notebook

Share a notebook
using OneDrive

Creating a New Notebook and Sharing a Notebook

Some people may choose to organize all of their notes for all purposes within one notebook (the default notebook file), using sections and pages to create an organizational structure. Others may choose to create separate notebooks in which to organize notes. For example, you may want to have a separate notebook for home, work, and school items.

Another reason to create a separate notebook may be when you want to share a notebook with other people. For example, if you are working with a group on a project you can create a notebook that all members of the group can use to post research, links, ideas, or other notes. A shared notebook is stored on OneDrive.

Note: Check with your instructor for the name of the person with whom you will share the notebook created in this topic. At Step 13 you will need the Microsoft account email address for the classmate.

1. Tap or click the FILE tab. If necessary, tap or click New.

2. If necessary, tap or click your OneDrive account name at the **New Notebook Backstage view**.

3. Tap or click in the *Notebook Name* text box and type **MyElectives-xx**. Substitute your first and last initials for *xx*.

4. Tap or click the Create Notebook button.

oops!

OneDrive account name not shown? If you are signed in with a local account, your OneDrive account name does not appear; however, a Sign In button is available so that you can switch to your Microsoft account from within OneNote.

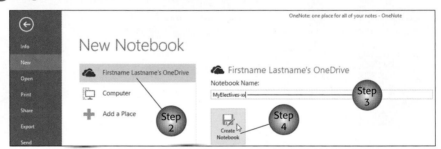

5. Tap or click Not now at the Microsoft OneNote message box asking if you would like to share the notebook with other people.

You will set up the sharing feature later in this topic. OneNote opens a new notebook with one section created titled *New Section 1*.

6. Press and hold or right-click the New Section 1 tab and tap or click *Rename* at the shortcut menu.

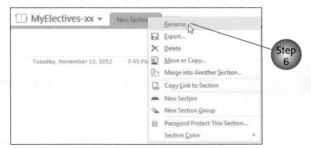

7. Type **ChildLit** and tap or press Enter.

8. Type **Children's Literature** as the page title and tap or press Enter.

oops!

Don't remember how to embed files? Refer to Topic 4.3, Step 16.

9. Embed a copy of the PowerPoint presentation file named ***ChildLitPres*** into the current page.

(10) Add a second section tab named *Film* with a page title of *Film Genres*, and embed a copy of the Word document named ***ApNowReflectionPaper***.

You decide to share the notebook with a classmate taking the same electives as you so that you can each add notes to the notebook.

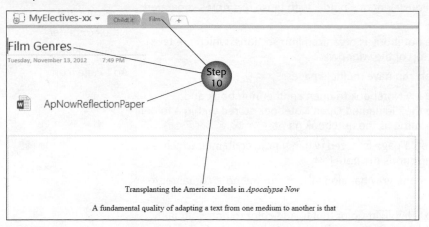

Create a New Notebook
1. Tap or click FILE tab.
2. Tap or click New.
3. If necessary, change notebook storage location.
4. Type name for new notebook.
5. Tap or click Create Notebook button.

Share a Notebook
1. Tap or click FILE tab.
2. Tap or click Settings button.
3. Tap or click *Share or Move*.
4. Type email address.
5. Type message text.
6. Tap or click Share button.
7. Tap or click Back button.

(11) Tap or click the FILE tab.

(12) Tap or click the Settings button and tap or click *Share or Move* at the drop-down list.

(13) At the **Share Notebook Backstage view**, tap or click in the *Type names or e-mail addresses* text box and type the classmate's Microsoft account email address.

(14) Tap or click in the message box and type **Here is a notebook I created that we can use to share notes for our electives.**

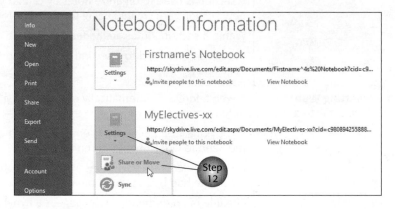

(15) Tap or click the Share button.

When sharing is completed, the student's name is shown in the *Shared with* section of the Backstage view.

(16) Tap or click the Back button.

(17) Close the MyElectives-xx notebook and close OneNote.

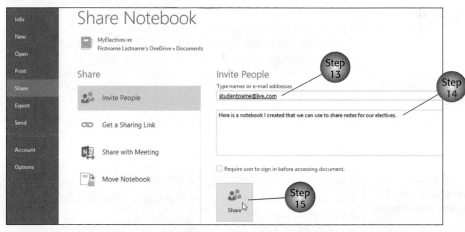

Optional

(18) Log in to OneDrive at <u>onedrive.live.com</u>.

(19) Open the shared notebook from the Shared folder and add a note to one of the pages. (You determine the note text.)

(20) Exit the OneNote Web app and then sign out and close OneDrive.

Concepts Review

Topic	Key Concepts	Key Terms
Opening a Notebook and Adding Notes, Sections, and Pages	OneNote 2013 is a note-taking software application that is the electronic equivalent of a binder with loose leaf notes separated by dividers. A OneNote notebook is organized into sections, which are tabs across the top of the window. Each section can have multiple pages. Tap or click My Notebook to open another notebook and navigate to the file named Open Notebook stored within a folder named the same as the notebook name. Each note on a page is stored within a note container, which is a box that surrounds the note text. Slide or drag the gray bar along the top of the note container to move a note. Use the Text Highlight Color tool to add color to notes similarly to using a highlighter to emphasize text in a textbook. A section is used to organize notes by category, topic, or subject; new sections are created using the Create a New Section tab. Within a section, notes are added to pages. Pages can be added to a section using the Add Page icon in the Pages pane.	OneNote notebook OneNote 2013 Note container Create a New Section tab Add Page icon
Inserting Web Content into a Notebook	A web address is automatically converted to a hyperlink in a note container. A copy of a web page can be embedded into a notebook using the Send to OneNote button on the Taskbar. An embedded web page is inserted into a notebook as if the web page had been printed on a printer. The title of an embedded web page is a hyperlink to the source website. A portion of a web page can be captured and inserted into a notebook using the Screen Clipping tool on the Send to OneNote button.	Send to OneNote button
Inserting Files into a Notebook	A OneNote notebook can be used as a repository to collect all of the files related to a course, subject, or other topic. From the INSERT tab you can insert pictures, a file as an icon linked to the source document, or a file as a printout, which embeds a copy of the file's contents into the notebook.	
Tagging Notes, Viewing Tags, and Jumping to a Tagged Note	A tag is a category assigned to a note. Tags are useful to identify notes that you want to flag for later review or follow up. OneNote includes a gallery of predefined tags such as *Important* or *Definition*. You can modify the predefined tags or create a new tag of your own. The Find Tags button in the HOME tab causes the Tags Summary pane to display with links to each tagged note.	Tag Tags Summary pane

Topic	Key Concepts	Key Terms
Searching Notes and Closing a Notebook	OneNote can search all pages in all open notebooks for a keyword or phrase typed in the *Search* text box. OneNote begins highlighting matches to the search keyword or phrase and displaying pages in the search results list as soon as you begin typing. Close a notebook using the Settings button at the Notebook Information Backstage view.	Notebook Information Backstage view Settings button
Creating a New Notebook and Sharing a Notebook	A new notebook can be created on OneDrive or in a drive connected to the PC or mobile device at the New Notebook Backstage view. Notebooks saved to OneDrive can be shared with other people. More than one person can edit a page at the same time when a notebook is shared. Use the Settings button at the Notebook Information Backstage view to share a notebook by typing the email address and a short message for each invitee.	New Notebook Backstage view Share Notebook Backstage view

Multiple Choice

1. Notes or other content are added inside a box called a _____.
   a. section
   b. page
   c. selection handle
   d. note container

2. The Create a New Section tab displays with this symbol.
   a. ×
   b. +
   c. –
   d. *

3. This option from the Send to OneNote button allows you to capture a portion of a web page to insert into a notebook.
   a. Screen Clipping
   b. Capture to OneNote
   c. Printout
   d. Embed to OneNote

4. A web address is automatically formatted by OneNote as a(n) _____.
   a. hyperlink
   b. embedded web page
   c. screen clipping
   d. Internet icon

5. Pictures or other files are added to a notebook using buttons in this tab in the ribbon.
   a. FILE
   b. INSERT
   c. VIEW
   d. HOME

6. Use this button to add a Word document as an icon in a notebook.
   a. File Printout
   b. File Attachment
   c. File Icon
   d. File Picture

7. This is the icon that appears next to a note tagged as Important.
   a. Red exclamation mark
   b. Orange check mark
   c. Gray question mark
   d. Gold star

8. This pane at the right side of the OneNote window is used to navigate to a tagged item in the notebook.
   a. Tags Summary
   b. View All Tags
   c. Tagged Items
   d. Tag Navigation

9. By default, the search feature in OneNote searches for a keyword or phrase in
_____.
   a. the current notebook only
   b. the current page only
   c. the current section only
   d. all pages in all open notebooks

10. A notebook is closed using this button at the Notebook Information Backstage view.
   a. Close
   b. Settings
   c. File
   d. Info

11. Display this view to share a notebook with other people.
   a. Notebook Information Backstage view
   b. Share Notebook Backstage view
   c. Multiple Notebooks Backstage view
   d. Settings Notebook Backstage view

12. A list of the people with whom a notebook has been shared is displayed in this section of the Backstage view.
   a. Notebook Information
   b. Shared with
   c. Invitees
   d. Settings

Crossword Puzzle

ACROSS

2 Button used to close a notebook
7 Button on Taskbar for embedding web content
8 Location where a shared notebook is stored
9 Button in Images group to insert a photograph
10 Gold star icon tag

DOWN

1 Option for capturing a portion of a web page
2 Tabs in a notebook
3 Button to display Tags Summary pane
4 Tab to access New Notebook Backstage view
5 Button in Files group to embed a copy of a file
6 Default notebook
7 Text box used to find all occurrences of a word

Matching

Match the term with the statement or definition.

_____ 1. Tabs
_____ 2. Text Highlight Color
_____ 3. Send to OneNote
_____ 4. File Icon
_____ 5. File Printout
_____ 6. Tag
_____ 7. Search
_____ 8. Share notebook

a. File Attachment
b. Important
c. View matches
d. Yellow background
e. SkyDrive
f. Embed web page
g. Copy of document
h. Sections

Project 1 Start a New Notebook and Create Notebook Structure

Individual

Deliverable: OneNote Notebook (continued in Project 2)

1. Create a new folder named *Ch4* in the ChapterProjectsWork folder on your USB flash drive.
2. Start OneNote 2013 and display the New Notebook Backstage view. Create a new notebook as follows:
   a. Select Computer as the storage place.
   b. Type **C4-Project1-NB-Your Name** as the Notebook Name.
   c. Tap or click <u>Create in a different folder</u>, navigate to the Ch4 folder in the ChapterProjectsWork folder on your USB flash drive, and then tap or click Create.
3. Rename the New Section 1 tab *Computer Research* and add the page title *Images*.
4. Add a new section titled *Law Course* with a page titled *Current Topics in Law*.
5. Add a new section titled *Tourism Course* with a page titled *Presentations*.
6. Add a new section titled *Volunteer Work* with a page titled *Medical Clinic Association Conference*.
7. Leave the notebook open if you are continuing on to Project 2; otherwise, close the notebook and submit the notebook to your instructor in the manner she or he has requested.

Project 2 Adding Notes and External Content to a Notebook

Individual

Deliverable: OneNote Notebook (continued in Project 3)

1. If necessary, open the notebook created in Project 1.
2. Embed a copy of the Excel file **MedClinicsFees** on the Medical Clinic Association Conference page in the *Volunteer Work* section. (Do *not* use the Spreadsheet button in the INSERT tab; use the button you learned about in Topic 4.3.)
3. Embed a copy of the PowerPoint file **WaikikiPres** on the Presentations page in the *Tourism Course* section.
4. Insert the Word document **FamilyAndLawAssgnt** as an icon on the Current Topics in Law page in the *Law Course* section and type **Assignment 1 due in week 5** as note text below the icon.
5. Insert the image file **IBMCptr_1961** on the Images page in the *Computer Research* section and type **IBM computer from 1961** as note text below the photograph.
6. Add a new page to the *Computer Research* section with the page title *History of Computers* and add a hyperlink to the web address <u>www.computerhistory.org/timeline</u>. Type **The timeline from the Computer History Museum provides the history of computing starting in 1939 and continuing to 1994.**
7. Leave the notebook open if you are continuing on to Project 3; otherwise, close the notebook and submit the notebook to your instructor in the manner she or he has requested.

Project 3 Tagging Notes and Adding a Copy of a Web Page

Individual

Deliverable: OneNote Notebook or PDF of Exported Notebook

1. If necessary, open the notebook created in Projects 1 and 2.
2. Assign the To Do tag at the beginning of the note text below the Word document icon on the Current Topics in Law page in the *Law Course* section.
3. Type **This is included in test 1** in a new note at the top of the PowerPoint slides embedded on the Presentations page in the *Tourism Course* section and assign the Important tag to the note.
4. Open a browser window and search for a recent article about 3D printing technology. Use the Screen Clipping tool to capture and copy the title and the first few paragraphs of an article that you find to a new page in the *Computer Research* section. Type **Article for project 1** in a new note above the embedded content and assign the note the Important tag.
5. Tap or click the FILE tab and tap or click Export. Select *Notebook* in the Export Current section and *PDF (*.pdf)* in the Select Format section at the Export tab Backstage view and tap or click the Export button. Save the PDF in the Ch4 folder in ChapterProjectsWork on your USB flash drive.
6. Close the notebook.
7. Submit the OneNote notebook or PDF file to your instructor in the manner she or he has requested.

Project 4 Creating a Notebook Repository for Projects

Individual

Deliverable: Shared Notebook on SkyDrive

Note: Check with your instructor for his or her Microsoft account email address for Step 7, or for alternative instructions if he or she prefers that you create the MyProjects notebook on your USB flash drive and not share the notebook.

1. Create a new notebook stored in your SkyDrive account with the name **MyProjects–Your Name**. Tap or click Not now when asked if you want to invite people to share the notebook.
2. Create the following sections and pages:

Sections	Pages
Windows	Chapter 1
Internet	Chapter 2
Office	Chapter 3
OneNote	Chapter 4
Outlook	Chapter 5
Word	Chapters 6 and 7
Excel	Chapters 8 and 9
PowerPoint	Chapters 10 and 11
Access	Chapters 12 and 13
Integrating	Chapter 14
CloudTech	Chapter 15

3. Make the Chapter 1 page in the *Windows* section active and insert a copy of the first project file that you completed for Chapter 1. Insert a copy of each remaining project file for Chapter 1, adding a new page for each file. Label each page with the project number from which you insert the copy.
4. Make the Chapter 2 page in the *Internet* section active and repeat the process you completed at Step 3 to insert a copy of each project file that you completed for Chapter 2.

5. Make the Chapter 3 page in the *Office* section active and repeat the process you completed at Step 3 to insert a copy of each project file that you completed for Chapter 3. Note that you can insert a copy of more than one file one below the other on the same page.

6. Make the Chapter 4 page in the *OneNote* section active and insert a copy of the PDF created for Project 3.

Note: If you receive any error messages when OneNote attempts the File Printout command, open the file in the source application (such as Paint or the Reader app) and use the Send to OneNote button on the Taskbar or print from the source application using the Send to OneNote 2013 printer. If you experience other technical difficulties with the Send to OneNote button or printer command, perform the Send to OneNote steps in a computer lab at your school where you can ask for technical assistance.

7. Share the notebook with your instructor, typing an appropriate message after entering your instructor's Microsoft account email address.

8. Close the notebook and then close OneNote.

Note: Closing the notebook may take a few moments while the notebook's changes are synced to SkyDrive.

Chapter 5

Communicating and Scheduling Using Outlook

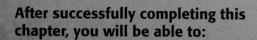

After successfully completing this chapter, you will be able to:

- Create, send, read, reply to, and forward email messages
- Attach a file to a message
- Delete a message and empty the Deleted Items folder
- Use file attachment tools to manage file attachments
- Schedule and edit appointments and an event
- Schedule and accept a meeting request
- Add and edit contacts
- Create, update, and delete tasks
- Search Outlook messages, appointments, contacts, or tasks

Microsoft Outlook is a software application often referred to as a **personal information management (PIM) program**. PIM programs organize items such as email messages, appointments or meetings, events, contacts, to-do lists, and notes. Reminders and flags help you remember and follow up on activities.

In the workplace Outlook is often used with an Exchange server, which allows employees within the organization to easily share calendars, schedule meetings, and assign tasks. Consider using Outlook on your home PC or mobile device to connect to your ISP's mail server and manage your messages. Outlook can also help you organize your time, activities, address book, and to-do list.

In this chapter you will learn how to use Outlook for email, scheduling, organizing contacts, and keeping a to-do list.

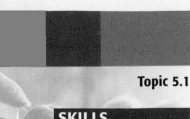

Topic 5.1

SKILLS

Create and send an email message

Reply to a message

Forward a message

Using Outlook to Send Email

Electronic mail (email) is communication between individuals by means of sending and receiving messages electronically. Email is the business standard for communication in today's workplaces. Individuals also use email to communicate with relatives and friends around the world. While text messaging is popular for brief messages between individuals, email is still used to send longer messages or file attachments.

Setting Up Outlook

The screen that you see when you start Outlook for the first time depends on whether a prior version of Outlook existed on the computer you are using. **Outlook 2013** can transfer information from an older version of Outlook to a new data file or, if no prior data file exists, will present a Welcome to Outlook 2013 screen at startup. Tap or click Next at the welcome screen and tap or click Next at the second screen to add a new account. At the Add Account dialog box shown in Figure 5.1, enter your name, email address, and email password and tap or click Next. Outlook automatically configures the email server settings displaying progress messages as each part is completed. Tap or click Finish when completed to start Outlook.

In instances where Outlook cannot automatically set up your email account, additional information will be required such as the incoming and outgoing mail server address. Contact your ISP if necessary for this information.

Note: The instructions in this chapter assume Outlook has already been set up and that you are connected to the Internet with an always-on connection (high-speed Internet service) at school or at home. If necessary, connect to the Internet and sign in to your email account before starting the topic activities. Check with your instructor for assistance if you are not sure how to proceed.

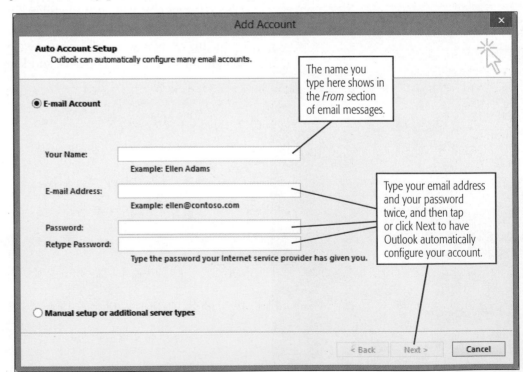

Figure 5.1 Outlook can automatically set up most email accounts with your name, email address, and password.

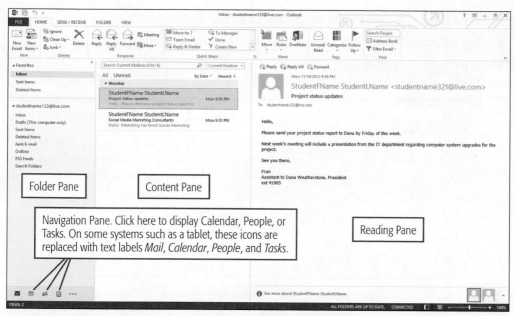

Figure 5.2 The Outlook window. By default, the Inbox folder is active and Outlook automatically connects to the mail server and checks for new messages when Outlook is started.

Once Outlook has been set up to send and receive email messages, the Outlook window appears similar to the one shown in Figure 5.2. By default, **Mail** is the active tool when Outlook is started with the **Inbox** folder shown. Messages in the Content pane are shown with the newest message received at the top of the message list. The left pane, called the Folder pane, is used to switch the display to another mail folder. At the bottom of the Folder pane is the Navigation pane, used to navigate to another Outlook item such as Calendar. The right pane, called the Reading pane, displays the contents of the selected message.

Creating and Sending a Message

Tap or click the **New Email button** in the New group of the HOME tab to start a new email message. Type the recipient's email address in the *To* text box, type a brief description in the *Subject* text box, and then type your message text in the white message text box. Tap or click the Send button when finished.

Note: Check with your instructor for instructions on whom you should exchange messages and meeting requests with for this chapter. Your instructor may designate an email partner to each person or allow you to choose your email partner. If necessary, you can send messages to yourself.

① From the Windows Start screen, start Outlook 2013.

② Tap or click the New Email button in the New group of the HOME tab.

oops!

Outlook window looks different than the one shown here? Turn on the Folder pane by tapping or clicking VIEW, Folder Pane, *Normal*. Turn on the Reading pane by tapping or clicking VIEW, Reading Pane, *Right*.

③ Type the email address for the recipient in the *To* text box.

④ Tap or press the Tab key twice, or tap or click in the *Subject* text box.

⑤ Type **Social Media Project**.

⑥ Tap or press Enter, or tap or click in the Message text window and type the following text:

Hi (type recipient's name), [tap or press Enter twice]

I think we should do our project on Pinterest.com. Pinterest is a virtual pinboard where people pin pictures of things they have seen on the Internet that they want to share with others. [tap or press Enter twice]

What do you think?

⑦ Tap or press Enter twice at the end of the message text and type your name as the sender.

⑧ Tap or click the Send button.

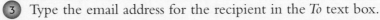
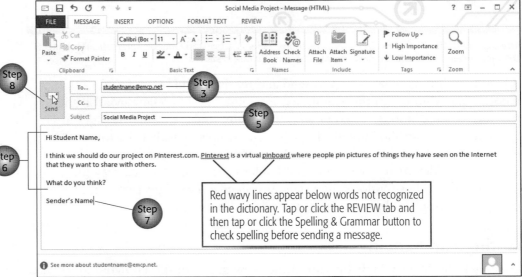

Replying to a Message

New messages appear at the top of the message list in the Content pane with message headers that show the sender, subject, time, and first line of message. Tap or click to select a message header and reply directly from the Reading pane using the **Reply button**. Replying from the Reading pane is called an **inline reply**.

As an alternative, double-tap or double-click the message header in the Content pane to open the message in a Message window from which you can choose to Reply or Forward the message.

⑨ Tap or click the SEND / RECEIVE tab and then tap or click the Send/ Receive All Folders button in the Send & Receive group to update the Content pane. (Skip this step if you can already see the message sent to you by a classmate or yourself from Step 8.)

⑩ If necessary, tap or click to select the message header and read the message text in the Reading pane.

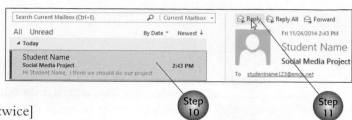

11 Tap or click the Reply button at the top of the message in the Reading pane.

12 Type the following reply message text and then tap or click the Send button.

(Type the name of the person from whom you received the message), [Enter twice]

I agree. I have a few pictures we can use to practice with if you want to set up a sample account at Pinterest.com. [Enter twice]

(Type your name)

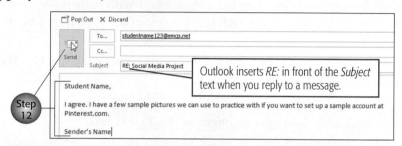

Outlook inserts *RE:* in front of the *Subject* text when you reply to a message.

Forwarding a Message

Forward a message if you want someone else to receive a copy of a message you have received. Choose the **Forward button**, type the email address for the person to whom you want to forward the message, and type a brief explanation if desired before sending the message.

Think carefully before forwarding a message to be certain that the original sender would not object to another person reading the message without his or her permission. If in doubt, do not forward the message.

13 With the message header for the message selected at Step 10 still active, tap or click the Forward button in the Reading pane.

14 Type the email address for the recipient in the *To* text box.

15 Tap or click in the message window above the original message text and type the following text:

Hi (type recipient's name), [Enter twice]

Do you want to join our group for the social media project? See message below discussing Pinterest. com. [Enter twice]

(Type your name)

16 Tap or click the Send button.

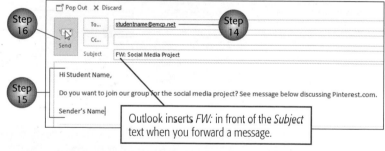

Outlook inserts *FW:* in front of the *Subject* text when you forward a message.

oops!

Reading pane off? Turn on the Reading pane by tapping or clicking VIEW, Reading Pane, *Right*.

App Tip

Use Reply All to send a reply in which more than one person was included in the initial message. Use good judgment with Reply All and be sure that all of the other recipients really need to see your response.

Quick **STEPS**

Forward a Message
1. Tap or click Forward button in Reading pane.
2. Type address in *To* text box.
3. Type message.
4. Tap or click Send.

 **Email Signatures**

A **signature** is a closing automatically inserted at the bottom of each sent message. Signatures usually include contact information for the sender such as name, title, department, company name, and contact telephone numbers.

To create a signature, open a message window, tap or click the Signature button in the MESSAGE tab, and tap or click *Signatures*.

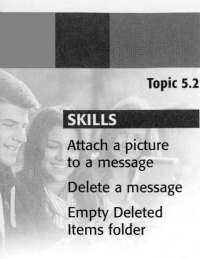

Attaching a File to a Message and Deleting Messages

Topic 5.2

SKILLS

Attach a picture to a message

Delete a message

Empty Deleted Items folder

Files are often exchanged between individuals via email. To attach a file to an email message, use the **Attach File** button in the Include group of the MESSAGE tab. The recipient of an email message with a file attachment can choose to open the file from the mail server or save it to a storage medium.

Messages that are no longer needed should be deleted to keep your mail folders to a manageable size. You can delete a message in the Inbox folder if you replied to the message because you can view the original text with your reply from Sent Items. Consider setting aside a time each week to clean up your Inbox by deleting messages.

1. With Outlook open and Inbox the active folder, tap or click the HOME tab if HOME is not the active tab.

2. Tap or click the New Email button in the New group.

3. Type the email address for the recipient in the *To* text box.

   Notice that as you begin typing an email address, Outlook provides email addresses that match what you are typing in a drop-down list. This feature is referred to as **AutoComplete**. Rather than type the entire email address, you can tap or click the correct recipient in the AutoComplete list.

4. Tap or press the Tab key twice, or tap or click in the *Subject* text box.

5. Type **Picture for Pinterest**.

6. Tap or press Enter, or tap or click in the Message text window and type the following text:

   Hi (type recipient's name), [Enter twice]

   Attached is a picture we can put on Pinterest.

7. Tap or press Enter twice at the end of the message text and type your name as the sender.

8. Tap or click the Attach File button in the Include group of the MESSAGE tab in the message window.

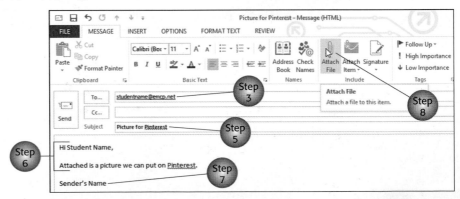

9. At the Insert File dialog box, navigate to the Student_Data_Files folder in the ComputerCourse folder on your USB flash drive.

10. Double-tap or double-click the *Ch5* folder name.

⑪ Double-tap or double-click the file named ***MurresOnFloatingIce***.

Outlook adds the file to an *Attached* field below the *Subject* text box.

⑫ Tap or click the Send button.

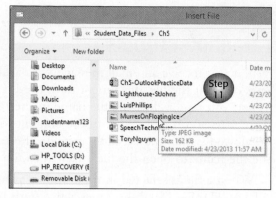

File attached at Step 11

Over time your mail folders (Inbox and Sent Items) can become filled with messages that are no longer needed. To delete messages, select the message headers and tap or click the Delete button in the Delete group of the HOME tab. Deleted messages are moved to the **Deleted Items** folder. Periodically, empty the Deleted Items folder to permanently delete the messages.

⑬ Tap or click the Send/Receive All Folders button on the Quick Access toolbar (second button from left) to update your Inbox folder. (Skip this step if you can already see the message sent to you by a classmate or yourself from Step 12.)

⑭ Tap or click *Sent Items* in the Folder pane.

⑮ If necessary, tap or click to select the message header for the message with the picture attached that you sent to a classmate or yourself in this topic.

⑯ Tap or click the Delete button in the Delete group of the HOME tab.

⑰ Tap or click *Deleted Items* in the Folder pane.

Notice the message you deleted appears in the Content pane.

⑱ Press and hold or right-click *Deleted Items* in the Folder pane and then tap or click *Empty Folder*.

⑲ Tap or click Yes at the Microsoft Outlook message box asking if you want to continue to permanently delete everything in the Deleted Items folder.

⑳ Tap or click *Inbox* in the Folder pane.

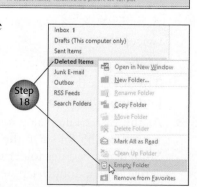

Previewing File Attachments and Using File Attachment Tools

Topic 5.3

SKILLS

Preview a file
attachment

Open a file
attachment

Save a file
attachment

When you receive an email message with a file attached, you can preview, open, save, or print the file attachment from the Reading pane or from a message window. When you tap or click the file name in the Reading pane, the message text disappears and is replaced with the contents of the attached file. Some files cannot be viewed within the Reading pane. In those instances, double-tap or double-click the file name to open the file attached to the message.

When a file is selected in the Reading pane or in a message window, the ATTACHMENTS tab becomes active with buttons to open, print, save, remove, select, or copy the file.

1. With Outlook open and Inbox the active folder, tap or click the message header for the message received in the previous topic with the file attachment. (Skip this step if the message header is already selected.)

2. Tap or click the file name *MurresOnFloatingIce.jpg* in the Reading pane.

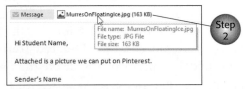

Outlook removes the message text and displays in the Reading pane the picture attached to the message. Notice also the ATTACHMENT TOOLS ATTACHMENTS tab becomes active in the ribbon.

3. Tap or click the Message icon in the Reading pane to return the display to the message text.

4. Tap or click the New Email button and type the email address for the recipient in the *To* text box.

5. Tap or click in the *Subject* text box and type **Presentation for Business class**.

6. Type the following text in the Message text window:

Hi (type recipient's name), [Enter twice]

Attached is the PowerPoint presentation for our group project. [Enter twice]

(Type your name)

7. Tap or click the Attach File button in the MESSAGE tab.

8. At the Insert File dialog box, with the Ch5 folder in the Student_Data_Files folder the active folder, double-tap or double-click the file named *SpeechTechniques*.

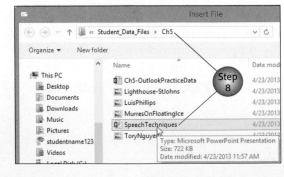

9 Tap or click the Send button.

10 Tap or click the Send/Receive All Folders button on the Quick Access toolbar to update your Inbox folder. (Skip this step if you can already see the message sent to you by a classmate or yourself from Step 9.)

11 Tap or click the message header for the message received with the subject *Presentation for Business Class.*

12 Tap or click the file name ***SpeechTechniques. pptx*** in the Reading pane.

13 Slide or scroll down the Reading pane to the last slide in the presentation.

14 Tap or click the Open button in the Actions group of the ATTACHMENT TOOLS ATTACHMENTS tab.

Microsoft PowerPoint starts with the **SpeechTechniques.pptx** file open. Notice the Title bar and Message bar displayed below the ribbon tabs indicate the presentation is open in **Protected view**. Protected view allows you to read the file's contents in the source application; however, editing the file is not permitted until you tap or click the Enable Editing button in the Message bar.

15 Close PowerPoint to return to Outlook.

16 Tap or click the Save As button in the ATTACHMENTS tab.

17 At the Save Attachment dialog box, navigate to the CompletedTopicsbyChapter folder on your USB flash drive, and create a new folder named *Ch5.*

18 Double-tap or double-click the *Ch5* folder and tap or click the Save button.

19 Tap or click the Show Message button in the Message group of the ATTACHMENTS tab.

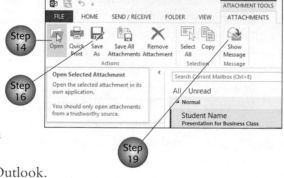

Step 14

Step 16

Step 19

Step 13

Quick STEPS

Preview a File Attached to a Message
Tap or click file name in Reading pane.

Open a File Attached to a Message
1. Tap or click file name in Reading pane.
2. Tap or click Open button.

Save a File Attached to a Message
1. Tap or click file name in Reading pane.
2. Tap or click Save As button.
3. Navigate to drive and/or folder.
4. Tap or click Save.

Be Cautious Opening File Attachments!

Outlook blocks certain file types attached to messages that are known to be the target for viruses and are considered unsafe. However, even with Outlook's protection you should exercise caution when opening a file received in an email message. Only open files received from people you know and trust and always make sure you have real-time, up-to-date virus protection turned on. When in doubt, delete the file or message without opening it.

Topic 5.4

SKILLS

Schedule an
appointment

Schedule an event

New to Outlook 2013 is the
current weather displayed
next to the current date or
month.

May 10 displayed instead of
October 5? Change the Region
Format in the Control Panel to
English (United States) and try
Step 3 again.

App Tip

A feature called *peek* works
with a mouse. Point to
Calendar, People, or Tasks
in the Navigation pane to
view current information in
a pop-up. For example, peek
at the day's appointments
without leaving Mail by simply
pointing to Calendar.

Scheduling Appointments and Events in Calendar

The **Calendar** tool in Outlook is used to schedule appointments and events such as meetings or conferences. An **appointment** is any activity where you want to track the day or time that the activity begins and ends in your schedule or that you want to be reminded to be somewhere. For example, an appointment can be a class, a meeting, a medical test, or a lunch date.

Note: In this topic and the next two topics, you will schedule appointments, an event, and a meeting in October 2015. Check with your instructor, if necessary, for alternate instructions that schedule these items in the current month or in October of the current year.

1. With Outlook open and Inbox the active folder, tap or click Calendar in the Navigation pane.

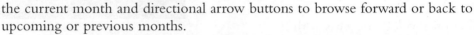

Outlook displays the current date or month in the Content pane in Day or Month view. A **Date Navigator** displays above the Folder pane with the current month and directional arrow buttons to browse forward or back to upcoming or previous months.

2. If necessary, tap or click the Day button in the Arrange group of the HOME tab, and then tap or click the Go to Date launcher button (downward-pointing diagonal arrow) at the bottom right of the Go To group.

3. At the **Go To Date** dialog box, type **10/5/2015** and then tap or press Enter, or tap or click OK.

4. Tap or click next to 9:00 a.m. in the Appointment area, type **Meet with program adviser**, and tap or press Enter, or tap or click in another time slot outside the appointment box.

By default, Outlook schedules the appointment for a half hour.

5. Drag the bottom boundary of the appointment box to 10:00 a.m. if you are using a mouse; otherwise, double-tap to open the appointment, tap the *End time* list arrow, tap *10:00 AM (1 hour)*, and then tap Save & Close.

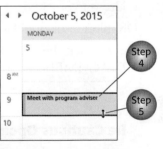

6. Tap or click next to 11:00 a.m. in the Appointment area.

7. Tap or click the **New Appointment button** in the New group of the HOME tab.

An Appointment window opens in which you can provide more details about the appointment.

8. Type **Intern Interview** in the *Subject* text box.

9. Tap or press Tab, or tap or click in the *Location* text box and type **Room 3001**.

10. Tap or click the *End time* list arrow and tap or click *12:00 PM (1 hour)* at the drop-down list.

11. Tap or click the Save & Close button in the Actions group of the APPOINTMENT tab in the Appointment window.

An **event** differs from an appointment in that it is an activity that lasts an entire day or longer. Examples of events include conferences, trade shows, or vacations. An event does not occupy a time slot in the Calendar. Event information appears in a banner along the top of the day in the Appointment area.

12. Double-tap or double-click in the white space with the date (*5*) at the top of the Appointment area below MONDAY and above the 8 a.m. time slot to open an Event window.

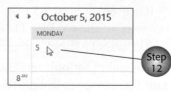

13. Type **Career Fair** in the *Subject* text box.

14. Tap or press Tab, or tap or click in the *Location* text box and type **Student Center**.

15. Tap or click the Save & Close button in the Actions group of the EVENT tab in the Event window.

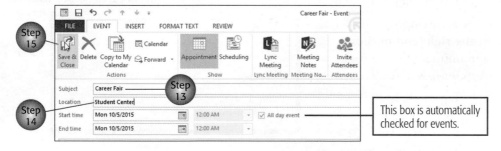

This box is automatically checked for events.

16. Tap or click next to a blank time slot in the Appointment area.

Quick STEPS

Schedule an Appointment
1. Display the Calendar.
2. Navigate to appointment date.
3. Tap or click next to appointment time.
4. Type appointment description.
5. Tap or press Enter.
OR
1. Display the Calendar.
2. Navigate to appointment date.
3. Tap or click next to appointment time.
4. Tap or click New Appointment button.
5. Enter appointment details in Appointment window.
6. Tap or click Save & Close.

Schedule an Event
1. Display the Calendar.
2. Navigate to event date.
3. Double-tap or double-click in white space next to date above Appointment area.
4. Enter event description.
5. Enter event location.
6. Tap or click Save & Close.

App Tip

Change the End time date if the event lasts more than one day.

Appointment Reminders and Tags

By default, new appointments have a reminder set at 15 minutes. Turn off the reminder or change the reminder time by selecting an appointment in the Appointment area and using the *Reminder* list box in the Options group of the CALENDAR TOOLS APPOINTMENT tab.

You can also assign tags to a selected appointment using the buttons in the Tags group. For example, assign the Private tag to a personal appointment so that no one with shared access to your calendar can see the appointment details.

Scheduling a Recurring Appointment and Editing an Appointment

Topic 5.5

Schedule a recurring appointment

Edit an appointment

An appointment that occurs on a regular basis at fixed intervals need only be entered once in Outlook and set up as a recurring appointment. Open the **Recurrence** dialog box to enter the recurrence pattern for a repeating appointment.

1. With Outlook open and Calendar active with October 5, 2015 displayed in the Appointment area, tap or click the Forward button to display October 6, 2015 in the Appointment area.

2. Tap or click next to 3:00 p.m. in the Appointment area, type **Math Extra Help Sessions**, and then tap or press Enter.

3. With the Math Extra Help Sessions appointment box selected in the Appointment area, tap or click the Recurrence button in the Options group of the CALENDAR TOOLS APPOINTMENT tab.

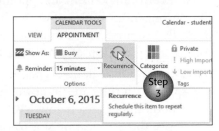

By default, Outlook sets the *Recurrence pattern* details for the appointment to recur *Weekly* at the same day and time as the appointment.

4. At the Appointment Recurrence dialog box, select *10* in the *End after* text box and type **5**.

5. Tap or click OK.

A recurring icon displays at the right end of the appointment box in the Appointment area.

6. Tap or click *13* in the October 2015 calendar in the *Date Navigator*

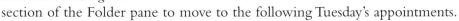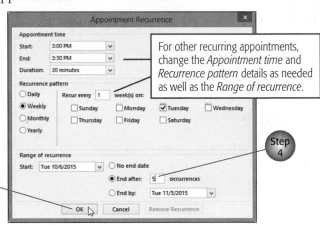

For other recurring appointments, change the *Appointment time* and *Recurrence pattern* details as needed as well as the *Range of recurrence*.

section of the Folder pane to move to the following Tuesday's appointments.

Notice the Math Extra Help Sessions appointment appears in the Appointment window.

7. Tap or click *20* in the October 2015 calendar in the Date Navigator.

Notice the Math Extra Help Sessions appointment appears in the Appointment window.

8. Tap or click the Go to Date launcher button in the Go To group, type **11/17/2015** in the Go To Date dialog box, and then tap or press Enter, or tap or click OK.

Notice the Math Extra Help Sessions appointment does not appear in the Appointment window because the range of recurrence has ended.

oops!

CALENDAR TOOLS APPOINTMENT tab not visible? Tap or click the appointment box to select the appointment and display the tab.

Consider entering your class schedule in the Outlook calendar for the current semester as recurring appointments.

Assign options or tags to an existing appointment by selecting the appointment and using the buttons in the CALENDAR TOOLS APPOINTMENT tab. Change the subject, location, day, or time of an appointment by opening the Appointment window.

9 Display October 5, 2015 in the Calendar.

10 Tap or click to select the appointment scheduled at 11:00 a.m.

A selected appointment box displays with a black outline. A pop-out opens at the left with the appointment details when you point at or tap an appointment.

11 Tap or click the Open button in the Actions group of the CALENDAR TOOLS APPOINTMENT tab.

Assume the intern interview has been rescheduled to Tuesday.

12 Tap or click the calendar icon in the *Start time* text box.

13 Tap or click *6* in the drop-down calendar.

14 Tap or click Save & Close.

15 Display October 6, 2015 in the Appointment area.

Notice the Intern Interview appointment appears next to 11:00 a.m.

Schedule a Recurring Appointment
1. Display Calendar.
2. Navigate to appointment date.
3. Tap or click next to appointment time.
4. Type appointment description.
5. Tap or press Enter.
6. Tap or click Recurrence button.
7. Enter recurrence pattern and/or range details.
8. Tap or click OK.

Edit an Appointment
1. Select appointment.
2. Tap or click Open button.
3. Change appointment details as needed.
4. Tap or click Save & Close.

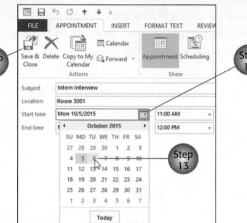

ALTERNATIVE method

Consider using the following keyboard shortcuts to work with appointments:

Ctrl + N to open a new Appointment window

Ctrl + O to open the Appointment window for the selected appointment

Ctrl + G to open the Go To Date dialog box

Ctrl + P to print the current day's appointments

Topic 5.6

SKILLS

Schedule a meeting

Respond to a meeting request

Scheduling a Meeting

Scheduling a **meeting** involves selecting the day and time and opening a Meeting window in which you enter the email addresses for the individuals you want to invite to the meeting, the meeting topic, location, and other details as needed. Meeting attendees receive a **meeting request** email message. Responses to the meeting request are sent back to the meeting organizer via buttons in the email message window or Reading pane.

1. With Outlook open and Calendar active with October 6, 2015 displayed in the Appointment area, tap or click next to 1:00 p.m. in the Appointment area.

2. Tap or click the **New Meeting button** in the New group.

3. Type the email address for the classmate with whom you have been exchanging emails in the *To* text box.

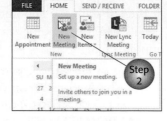

Note: If you have been sending email messages to yourself in this chapter, send the meeting request message to a friend or relative, or use an email address for yourself that is different from your Microsoft account address because you cannot send a meeting request to yourself. You will not be able to complete Step 8 to Step 16 if you do not receive a meeting request message from someone else.

4. Tap or press Tab, or tap or click in the *Subject* text box and type **Fundraising Planning Meeting**.

5. Tap or press Tab, or tap or click in the *Location* text box and type **Room 1010**.

6. Tap or click the *End time* list arrow and tap or click *2:30 PM (1.5 hours)* at the drop-down list.

7. Tap or click the Send button.

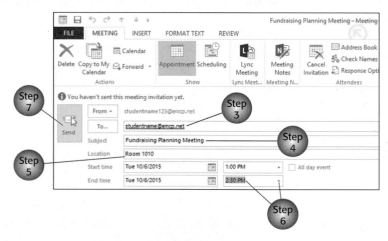

Consider using the space in the message window below *End time* to type a meeting agenda or other explanatory text to inform attendees about the purpose of the meeting.

8. Tap or click Mail in the Navigation pane.

9. Tap or click the Send/Receive All Folders button on the Quick Access toolbar to update your Inbox folder. (Skip this step if you can already see the meeting request message sent to you by a classmate at Step 7.)

10. Tap or click to select the message header for the meeting request to view the message details in the Reading pane.

The Accept, Tentative, Decline, Propose New Time, and Calendar buttons along the top of the Reading pane are used to respond to the meeting organizer. Outlook also displays your Calendar in the Reading pane so that you can see if you are available at the requested day and time.

11. Double-tap or double-click the message header to open the Meeting window.

12. Tap or click the **Accept button** in the Respond group of the MEETING tab.

13. Tap or click *Send the Response Now* at the drop-down list.

Notice that the meeting request email message is deleted from your Inbox once you have responded to the meeting invitation.

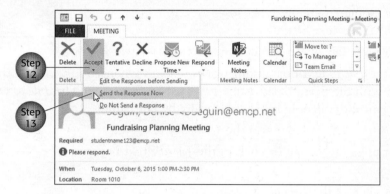

14. Tap or click *Sent Items* in the Folder pane.

15. Tap or click the message header for the message sent to the meeting organizer with your Accepted reply and read the message sent to the meeting organizer in the Reading pane.

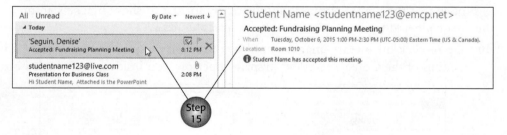

16. Tap or click *Inbox* in the Folder pane.

 **Updating and Canceling a Meeting**

If you need to reschedule a meeting, open the Meeting window, make the required changes to the day, time, or location, and tap or click the Send Update button. Outlook will send an email message to each attendee with the updated information. To delete a meeting, open the Meeting window and tap or click the Cancel Meeting button in the Actions group. Outlook sends an email message to each attendee informing each person that the meeting is canceled and removes the meeting from each person's calendar.

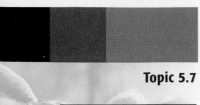

Topic 5.7

SKILLS

Add a Contact

Edit a Contact

Adding and Editing Contacts

The **People** tool in Outlook is used to store contact information such as email addresses, mailing addresses, telephone numbers, and other information about the people with whom you communicate. Think of People as an electronic address book. If you have a picture of an individual, you can display the person's picture with his or her contact information in the **People card**.

1. With Outlook open and Inbox the active folder, tap or click People in the Navigation pane.

2. Tap or click the **New Contact button** in the New group.

3. At the Contact window, type **Tory Nguyen** in the *Full Name* text box.

4. Tap or press Tab, or tap or click in the *Company* text box.

Notice the *File as* text box automatically updates when you move past the *Full Name* field with the person's last name followed by first name. The *File as* entry is used to organize the People list alphabetically by last names.

5. Type **NuWave Personnel** in the *Company* text box.

6. Tap or press Tab, or tap or click in the *Job title* text box and type **Recruitment Specialist**.

7. Tap or click in the *E-mail* text box and type **tory@emcp.net**.

8. Tap or click in the *Business* text box in the *Phone numbers* section and type **8885559840**.

9. Tap or click in the *Mobile* text box in the *Phone numbers* section and type **8885553256**.

Notice that the phone numbers automatically format to show brackets around the area code and hyphens when you move past the field.

10. Tap or click the picture image control box between the name and business card sections of the Contact window (displays a person icon inside a gray-shaded box).

App Tip

You can also add a picture using the Picture button in the Options group of the CONTACT tab.

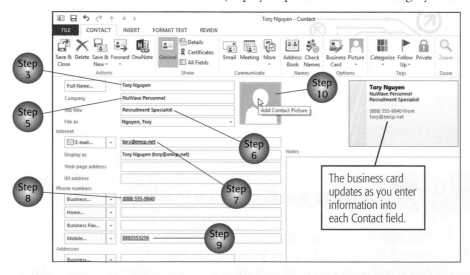

The business card updates as you enter information into each Contact field.

11. At the **Add Contact Picture** dialog box, navigate to the Ch5 folder in the Student_Data_Files folder and double-tap or double-click the file named *ToryNguyen*.

12. Tap or click the Save & Close button in the Actions group of the CONTACT tab.

A selected person's information displays in the Reading pane in a People card with links to schedule a meeting or send an email to that person. Tap or click *Edit* to open the People card fields for editing in the Reading pane, or double-tap or double-click the name in the People list to add or modify information in a People card window.

13　Tap or click Edit near the top right of the Reading pane with Tory Nguyen's information displayed.

14　Tap or click at the end of the *Work* telephone number *(888) 555-9840,* tap or press the spacebar and type **extension 3115**.

15　Tap or click the Save button at the bottom right of the Reading pane.

16　Double-tap or double-click in the white space at the bottom of the People list.

Double-tapping or double-clicking in blank space in the People list opens a new Contact window.

17　Enter your instructor's name, your school name, and your instructor's email address in the Contact window and tap or click Save & Close.

oops!

No Reading pane? Your Contact view may be set to Business Card or Card. Tap or click People in the Current View group of the HOME tab. If necessary, tap or click VIEW, Reading Pane, Right.

oops!

A Check Full Name dialog box may appear after you enter a name. This happens when Outlook cannot determine the first and last name. For example, typing errors or hyphenated names can cause the dialog box to open. Enter or edit the text as needed and tap or click OK.

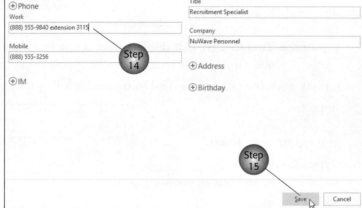

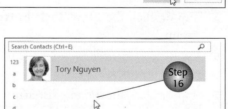

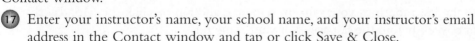

You can also edit a contact by opening the full Contact window. To do this, tap or click the <u>Outlook (Contacts)</u> link below *View Source* in the Reading pane for the selected person. This causes the same Contact window to open that you used to add the person. Use this method if you need to change a contact's picture or access the complete set of people fields or ribbon options.

Topic 5.8

SKILLS

Add a task

Edit a task

Delete a task

Mark a task complete

oops!

Tasks icon not visible? Slide or drag the right boundary for the Folder pane to the right OR tap or click the button with the three dots and tap or click *Tasks* at the pop-up list.

Adding and Editing Tasks

Working with **Tasks** in Outlook is similar to maintaining a to-do list. Outlook provides the ability to track information about a task such as how much of the task is completed, how much time has been spent on the task, the priority for the task, and the task's due date.

1. With Outlook open and People active, tap or click Tasks in the Navigation pane and then tap or click To-Do List in the Current View group if To-Do List is not active.

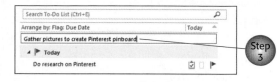

If the Tasks icon is not visible, tap or click here and then tap or click Tasks.

2. Tap or click in the text box at the top of the **To-Do List** that displays *Type a new task*, type **Do research on Pinterest**, and tap or press Enter.

Outlook adds the task to the To-Do list under a flag with the heading *Today*.

3. Type **Gather pictures to create Pinterest pinboard** and tap or press Enter.

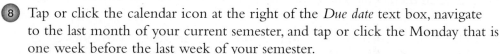

4. Type **Create resume for Career Fair** and tap or press Enter.

5. Tap or click the **New Task button** in the New group.

6. Type **Prepare study notes for exams** in the *Subject* text box.

7. Tap or click the *Priority* list arrow and tap or click *High* at the drop-down list.

8. Tap or click the calendar icon at the right of the *Due date* text box, navigate to the last month of your current semester, and tap or click the Monday that is one week before the last week of your semester.

9. Tap or click the Save & Close button in the Actions group of the TASK tab.

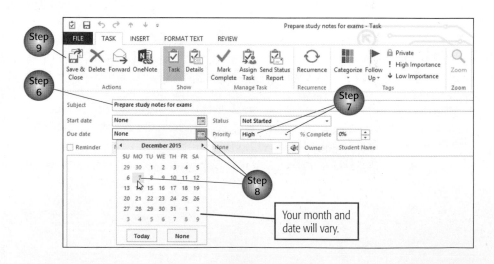

Your month and date will vary.

Editing or updating a task can include activities such as assigning or changing a due date, assigning a priority, entering the percentage of completion, or changing a task's status.

When a task is completed, use the Remove from List button in the Manage Task group or mark the task as complete in the Task window.

10. Tap or click the task entry *Do research on Pinterest*.

11. Tap or click the Remove from List button in the Manage Task group.

Notice the task is removed from the To-Do list. You can also use the Delete button in the Delete group of the HOME tab to remove a task.

12. Double-tap or double-click the task entry *Create resume for Career Fair* to open the Task window.

13. Tap or click the Mark Complete button in the Manage Task group of the TASK tab.

14. Double-tap or double-click the task entry *Gather pictures for Pinterest pinboard*.

15. Tap or click the *Status* list arrow and tap or click *Waiting on someone else* at the drop-down list.

16. Tap or click in the white space below the *Reminder* options and type **Waiting for Leslie to send me pictures from her renovation clients.**

17. Tap or click Save & Close.

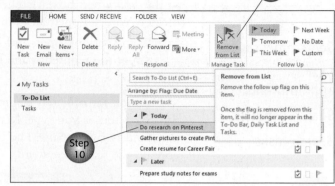

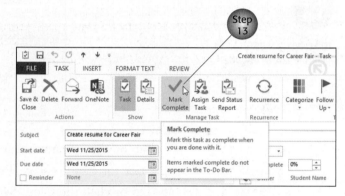

Notice the updated task details appear in the Reading pane for the selected task.

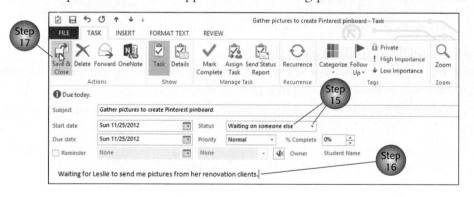

18. Display the Inbox.

Add a Task
1. Display Tasks.
2. Tap or click in *Type a new task* text box.
3. Type task description.
4. Tap or press Enter.

OR

1. Display Tasks.
2. Tap or click New Task button.
3. Enter task details.
4. Tap or click Save & Close.

Remove from List versus Mark Complete

Remove from List deletes the task while **Mark Complete** retains the task in the task list with a line drawn through the task and a gray check mark showing the task is finished. Mark Complete should be used if you need to retain task information for timekeeping or billing purposes. Display the complete Tasks list by tapping or clicking *Tasks* in the Folder pane.

Topic 5.9

SKILLS

Search messages

Search appointments

Search contacts

Search tasks

The keyboard shortcut Ctrl + E opens the *Search* text box.

Searching Outlook Items

Outlook's Search feature is a powerful tool used to quickly find a message, appointment, contact, or task. A *Search* text box located between the ribbon and content is used to find items. Outlook begins a search as soon as you start typing in the *Search* text box. Matched items are highlighted in the search results. Once located, you can open an item to view or edit the information.

1 With Outlook open and Inbox active, tap or click in the *Search* text box at the top of the Content pane (displays *Search Current Mailbox*).

2 Type **pinterest**.

Outlook immediately begins matching messages in the Content pane with the characters as you type. Matched words are highlighted in both the Content pane and Reading pane. The list that remains is filtered to display all messages that contain the search keyword.

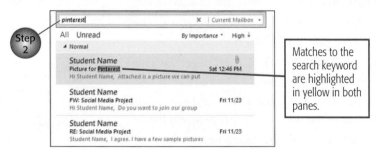

Matches to the search keyword are highlighted in yellow in both panes.

3 Tap or click each message in the search results list.

Notice for each message, Pinterest is highlighted in the Reading pane.

4 Tap or click the Close Search button in the *Search* text box to close the search results list and return to the Inbox.

5 Display the Calendar.

6 Tap or click in the *Search* text box at the top right of the Appointment area (displays *Search Calendar*) and type **career fair**.

Outlook displays the appointment found with the search keywords in a filtered list.

7 Double-tap or double-click the entry in the filtered list to view the details in the Event window and then tap or click Save & Close.

8 Tap or click the Close Search button to restore the Calendar to the current day's appointments.

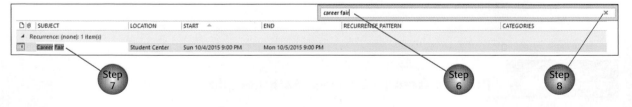

9 Display People.

10 Tap or click in the *Search* text box at the top of the People list (displays *Search Contacts*) and type **nuwave**.

Outlook displays the contact for Tory Nguyen who works at NuWave Personnel. You can use the Search feature to find any Outlook item by any field within the item. For example, you could find a contact by name, job title, company name, or even telephone number.

11 Tap or click the Close Search button to restore the People list.

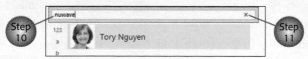

12 Display Tasks.

13 Tap or click in the *Search* text box at the top of the To-Do list (displays *Search To-Do List*) and type **ex**.

Outlook displays the task entry *Prepare study notes for exams*. Outlook can match items with only a partial entry for a word.

14 Tap or click the Close Search button to restore the To-Do list.

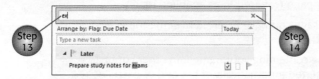

15 Display Mail with the Inbox folder.

16 Close Outlook.

 **Other Search and Filter Techniques**

The HOME tab in Mail, Calendar, People, and Tasks contains a *Search People* text box in the Find group. Use this text box to find a contact from any Outlook area. You can tap or click a person in the Search results list to view the contact information in a People card.

In Mail, the Find group also contains a Filter Email button. Use this button to filter the message list by categories such as *Unread, Has Attachments, Flagged,* or *Important*.

Concepts Review

Topic	Key Concepts	Key Terms
Using Outlook to Send Email	Microsoft Outlook 2013 is an application for organizing messages, appointments, contacts, and tasks and is referred to as a personal information management (PIM) program.	Personal information management program (PIM)
	Electronic mail (email) is the exchange of messages between individuals electronically.	Electronic mail (email)
	When you start Outlook for the first time, existing email account information is transferred to Outlook 2013 or you set up a new email account at the Add Account dialog box.	Outlook 2013
		Inbox
	When Outlook is started, Mail is the active application with the Inbox folder active.	New Email button
	The Inbox displays email messages with the newest message received at the top of the Content pane.	Reply button
		Inline reply
	Create and send a new email message using the New Email button.	Forward button
	Tap or click the message header for a new message received to read the message contents in the Reading pane.	Signature
	Reply directly to a message by tapping or clicking the Reply button in the Reading pane (referred to as an inline reply).	
	Send a copy of a message you have received to someone else using the Forward button.	
	A signature is a closing containing your name and other contact information that is inserted automatically at the end of each message.	
Attaching a File to a Message and Deleting Messages	Files are often exchanged between individuals via email messages.	Attach File button
	Attach a file to a message using the Attach File button in the Include group of the MESSAGE tab.	AutoComplete
		Deleted Items
	As you type an email address in the *To* text box, the AutoComplete feature shows email addresses in a drop-down list that match what you are typing.	
	Delete messages from mail folders that are no longer needed to keep folders to a manageable size.	
	Deleted messages are moved to the Deleted Items folder.	
	Empty the Deleted Items folder to permanently delete messages.	

Topic	Key Concepts	Key Terms
Previewing File Attachments and Using File Attachment Tools	Preview a file attached to a message by tapping or clicking the file name in the Reading pane.	Protected View
	While a file is being previewed, message text is temporarily removed from the Reading pane.	
	Some files cannot be viewed in the Reading pane and must be viewed by double-tapping or double-clicking the file name.	
	Open or Save a file using buttons in the Actions group of the ATTACHMENT TOOLS ATTACHMENTS tab.	
	A file opened from an email message is opened in Protected view.	
	Protected view allows you to read the contents, but you cannot edit the file until you tap or click the Enable Editing button in the Message bar.	
	Certain types of files known to contain viruses are automatically blocked by Outlook.	
Scheduling Appointments and Events in Calendar	The Calendar is used to schedule appointments and events.	Calendar
	An appointment is any activity for which you want to record the occurrence by day and time.	Appointment
	A Date Navigator at the top of the Folder pane displays the current month with directional arrows to browse to the previous or next month.	Date Navigator
	Use the Go To Date dialog box to display a specific date in the Appointment area of the Calendar.	Go To Date
	Tap or click next to the time in the Appointment area and type a description to enter a new appointment.	New Appointment button
	A new appointment can also be entered in an Appointment window by tapping or clicking the New Appointment button.	Event
	An event is an appointment that lasts an entire day or longer.	
	Events appear in a banner along the top of the date in the Appointment area.	
	Double-tap or double-click in the white space between the Appointment area and the date to enter a new event in an Event window.	
Scheduling a Recurring Appointment and Editing an Appointment	An appointment that occurs at fixed intervals on a regular basis can be entered once, and Outlook schedules the remaining appointments automatically.	Recurrence
	Tap or click the Recurrence button to set the recurrence pattern and range of recurrence details for a recurring appointment.	
	Select an appointment in the Appointment area to assign options or tags to the appointment in the CALENDAR TOOLS APPOINTMENT tab.	
	Open the Appointment window to make changes to the subject, location, day, or time.	

continued....

Topic	Key Concepts	Key Terms
Scheduling a Meeting	A meeting is an appointment in which you invite people that you want to attend the meeting. Information about a meeting is sent to people via a meeting request email message. Tap or click the New Meeting button to enter the email addresses for meeting attendees and the meeting particulars. A meeting attendee responds to a meeting request from the Reading pane or the message window by tapping or clicking respond buttons such as Accept. Meetings can be updated or canceled, and Outlook automatically informs all attendees via email messages.	Meeting Meeting request New Meeting button Accept button
Adding and Editing Contacts	Use the People tool to store and manage contact information for the people with whom you communicate in a People card. Tap or click the New Contact button or double-tap or double-click in a blank area of the People list to open a Contact window and add information to a People card. Tap or click the picture image control for a contact to select a picture of a contact in the Add Contact Picture dialog box. A contact's picture displays in the People card. The People card for a selected individual in the People list displays in the Reading pane. Tap or click *Edit* in the Reading pane or double-tap or double-click a person's name to edit the contact information in the People card.	People People Card New Contact button Add Contact Picture
Adding and Editing Tasks	Use Tasks in Outlook to maintain a To-Do list. Tap or click in the *Type a new task* text box to add a task to the To-Do list. Tap or click the New Task button to enter a new task in a Task window. Open a Task window to add a due date or to add other task information such as a priority or status. Select a task and use the Remove from List button when a task is completed. Open a task and use the Mark Complete button to indicate a task is completed; completed tasks are retained in the Task list but removed from the To-Do list.	Tasks To-Do List New Task button Remove from List Mark Complete
Searching Outlook Items	A *Search* text box appears at the top of Mail, Calendar, People, and Tasks in which you can quickly search for an item by typing a keyword or phrase. Outlook begins to match items as soon as you begin typing a search keyword. Matches to the search keyword are highlighted in the filtered lists. A *Search People* text box also appears in the Find group of the HOME tab in Mail, Calendar, People, and Tasks with which you can view the People card for an individual.	

Multiple Choice

1. This is the name of the default Mail folder that is active when Outlook is started.
   a. New Mail
   b. Inbox
   c. Sent Items
   d. Deleted Items

2. A reply typed directly from the Reading pane is referred to as a(n) _____ reply.
   a. direct
   b. instant
   c. inline
   d. quick

3. This button is used to send a copy of a presentation to someone via email.
   a. Attach PPT
   b. Attach Document
   c. Attachment
   d. Attach File

4. A deleted message is moved to this folder.
   a. Deleted Items
   b. Deleted Messages
   c. Deleted Mail
   d. Deletions

5. Preview a file sent by email in this pane.
   a. Folder pane
   b. Navigation pane
   c. Reading pane
   d. Content pane

6. Save a selected file received via email using the Save as button in this tab.
   a. ATTACHMENTS
   b. FILE
   c. VIEW
   d. MESSAGE

7. Open this dialog box to navigate to a specific date in the Calendar.
   a. Go To Date
   b. Go To Appointment
   c. Launch Date
   d. Date Navigator

8. An appointment that lasts an entire day is referred to as a(n) _____.
   a. event
   b. conference
   c. all-day appointment
   d. task

9. Use this button to set up an appointment that occurs on a regular basis at fixed intervals.
   a. Repeat
   b. Recurrence
   c. Manage Appointment
   d. Copy

10. Use buttons in this tab to add options or tags to a selected appointment.
    a. CALENDAR TOOLS OPTIONS
    b. CALENDAR TOOLS APPOINTMENT
    c. APPOINTMENT TOOLS OPTIONS
    d. APPOINTMENT TOOLS CALENDAR

11. An email message that invites you to an upcoming meeting is referred to as a(n) _____.
    a. attendance request
    b. meeting requirement
    c. meeting request
    d. meeting message

12. Tap or click this button to send a confirmation to the meeting organizer that you will attend a meeting.
    a. Tentative
    b. Accept
    c. Reply
    d. OK

13. Add a new contact to the People list using the New Contact button or by double-tapping or double-clicking in this pane.
    a. People list
    b. Reading pane
    c. Folder pane
    d. Navigation pane

14. Tap or click here to change a contact's telephone number in the Reading pane.
    a. Edit Source
    b. Edit
    c. Link Contacts
    d. What's New

15. A new task appears at the top of this list.
    a. Assignment list
    b. Job list
    c. Today list
    d. To-Do list

16. Use this button to indicate a task is completed but retain the task information in the Task list.
    a. Remove from List
    b. Mark Complete
    c. Delete
    d. Manage Task

17. This feature allows you to locate items in Outlook by typing a keyword.
    a. Find
    b. Search
    c. Filter
    d. Arrange

18. Tap or click this button to remove a filtered list after finding an item that matched your keyword.
    a. Close Arrange
    b. Close Filter
    c. Close Search
    d. Close Find

Crossword Puzzle

ACROSS

4 Button in Mail that starts source application to view attached file

5 Activity you want to track in Calendar

7 Button to set up a repeating activity in Calendar

9 Where deleted messages are moved

10 Tool to locate items in Outlook by keyword

13 Navigation pane option to maintain To-Do list

14 Button to respond to an email message

15 All-day activity entered in Calendar

DOWN

1 Attached files opened in the source application display in this view

2 Option to delete an item from the To-Do list

3 Send copy of email message to someone else

6 Button to schedule meeting

8 A file sent with an email message

11 Navigation pane option to view contacts

12 Where to find a meeting request

Matching

Match the term with the statement or definition.

_____ 1. Personal Information Management (PIM)

_____ 2. Signature

_____ 3. Empty Folder

_____ 4. Reading pane

_____ 5. Calendar

_____ 6. Meeting

_____ 7. People

_____ 8. Tasks

a. Option to permanently delete messages
b. Preview a file attachment
c. Appointment with email addresses
d. To-Do list
e. Contacts
f. Microsoft Outlook
g. Message closing text
h. Scheduling

Project 1 Open an Outlook Data File and Add and Edit Items

Individual

Deliverable: Updated Outlook Data File (continued in Project 2)

1. Create a new folder named *Ch5* in the ChapterProjectsWork folder on your USB flash drive.
2. Start Outlook 2013 and make sure the Folder pane and Reading pane are displayed.
3. Open an existing Outlook data file with Outlook items by completing the following steps:
   a. Tap or click FILE and then tap or click Open & Export.
   b. Tap or click Open Outlook Data File.
   c. At the Open Outlook Data File dialog box, navigate to the Ch5 folder in the Student_Data_Files folder on your USB flash drive and double-tap or double-click the file named **Ch5-OutlookPracticeData**. (A new entry appears in the Folder pane below your current mail folders with the title *Ch5-OutlookPracticeData*.)
4. Tap or click the white right-pointing arrow next to **Ch5-OutlookPracticeData** in the Folder pane to expand the folder list, and tap or click the black diagonal downward-pointing arrow next to your email address (or your Outlook user name) in the Folder pane to collapse the folder list. (The Folder pane now should show only the mail folders in the new data file opened at Step 3.)

Note: For the remaining steps in this project and the next project, complete all tasks using the folders in the expanded folder list for Ch5-OutlookPracticeData.

5. Make Inbox active to view the two messages and forward each message to yourself (use your email address) with the message text *Here is a copy of the message from (enter sender's name in the original message).*
6. Display all of the other folders in the data file by selecting the three dots in the Navigation pane and choosing *Folders* at the pop-up list. If necessary, collapse again the list of folders for your regular email account.
7. Tap or click Calendar in the Folder pane and display October 12, 2015 in the Appointment area. Make the following changes to appointments in the Calendar (respond Yes to any messages that appear about reminders):
   a. On Monday, October 12, add *Room A-109* as the appointment location.
   b. Change the lunch with Taylor Gorski from Tuesday, October 13 to Wednesday, October 14 at 1:00 p.m.
   c. Make the doctor appointment on Wednesday, October 14, 1.5 hours in duration.
   d. Make the Health and Safety Training on Thursday, October 15 a recurring appointment at the same day and time for three weeks.
8. Tap or click Contacts in the Folder pane, and make the following changes to the People list:
   a. Change the *Work* telephone number for Xavier Borman to *888-555-4523*.
   b. Change the *Title* for Taylor Gorski to *President & CEO*.
   c. Add a new person to the People list with the following contact information and add a picture using the file named **LuisPhillips** in the Ch5 folder in Student_Data_Files:
      Luis Phillips, NewAge Advertising, Sales Representative, luis@emcp.net
9. Tap or click Tasks in the Folder pane and make the following changes:
   a. Remove the task *Find volunteers to help at conference* from the To-Do list.
   b. Mark the task *Update project wiki pages* completed.
   c. Change the due date for the task *Research click marketing strategies* to October 22, 2015.
   d. Add the following new tasks:
      Compile report from volunteer survey
      Return equipment rented for conference
10. Leave Outlook open if you are continuing to Project 2; otherwise, press and hold or right-click **Ch5-OutlookPracticeData** and choose *Close "Ch5-OutlookPracticeData"* at the shortcut menu; then close Outlook and submit the project to your instructor in the manner she or he has instructed.

Project 2 Sending Outlook Items to a OneNote Notebook and Creating a PDF

Individual

Deliverable: Page in OneNote notebook and PDF with Outlook Items Completed in Project 1

Note: You must have completed Project 4 in Chapter 4 and Project 1 in this chapter before starting this project.

1. Start OneNote 2013 and open the MyProjects notebook created in Chapter 4, Project 4.
2. Switch to Outlook and make Calendar active. Display October 12, 2015 in the Appointment area and send the calendar to your OneNote notebook by completing the following steps:
    a. Tap or click the Month button in the Arrange group of the HOME tab.
    b. Display the Print tab Backstage view and change the Printer to *Send to OneNote 2013*.
    c. Tap or click the Print button.
    d. Switch to OneNote 2013 using the button on the Taskbar.
    e. At the Select Location in OneNote dialog box, tap or click the plus symbol next to *Outlook* in the section list for the MyProjects-YourName notebook and tap or click *Chapter 5*. Tap or click OK. (The Calendar will appear on the Chapter 5 page in OneNote.)
3. Switch to Outlook and display the Contacts folder. Send the People list to your OneNote notebook by completing steps similar to those in Steps 2b to 2e. Accept the default *Card Style* format for the print *Settings*.
4. Switch to Outlook and display the Tasks folder. Send the Task list to your OneNote notebook by completing steps similar to those in Steps 2b to 2e.
5. Switch to Outlook. Press and hold or right-click *Ch5-OutlookPracticeData* in the Folder pane and tap or click *Close "Ch5-OutlookPracticeData"*.
6. Tap or click the white right-pointing arrow next to your email address (or your Outlook user name) to expand the folder list.
7. Make Inbox active and tap or click Send/Receive All Folders if necessary to update the message list.
8. Open the first message window for the message you forwarded to yourself in Project 1, Step 5. Send a copy of the message to your OneNote notebook by completing steps similar to those in Steps 2b to 2e and then close the message window. Accept the default *Memo Style* format.
9. Switch to Outlook and repeat Step 8 for the second message you forwarded to yourself in Project 1, Step 5.
10. With OneNote open and the Chapter 5 page in the *Outlook* section active, display the Export tab Backstage view. With *Page* selected by default in the *Export Current* section, select *PDF (*.pdf)* in the *Select Format* section and choose *Export*. Navigate to the Ch5 folder in the ChapterProjectsWork folder on your USB flash drive. Type **C5-Project2-Your Name** in the *File name* text box and tap or click the Save button.
11. Leave OneNote open if you are continuing to Project 3; otherwise, close the notebook and close OneNote.
12. In Outlook, tap or click Mail in the Navigation pane to restore the Folder pane to the default folder list that displays mail folders only.
13. Leave Outlook open if you are continuing to Project 3; otherwise, close Outlook and submit the project to your instructor in the manner she or he has requested.

Project 3 Organizing Your School Activities in Outlook

Individual

Deliverable: Page in OneNote notebook and PDF with New Outlook Items

1. In OneNote, create a new page in the *Outlook* section with the title *Project 3*.

2. Switch to Outlook, make Calendar active, and make sure the current date is displayed. Create appointments for your class schedule for all of the courses you are currently taking as recurring appointments in the calendar for the remainder of the current semester.

3. Add other appointments to your Outlook calendar for any other school activities that you want to attend. For example, add an appointment or event for any extracurricular school activity.

4. Make People active and add your teacher's contact information to the People list.

5. Make Tasks active and create in the To-Do list a task entry for each upcoming project and assignment (including due dates) of which you are aware in each of the courses you are currently taking.

6. Send the calendar in Month view, the People list in Card Style, and the To-Do list to the Project 3 page in the *Outlook* section of your OneNote notebook.

7. Create a PDF of the Project 3 page in your OneNote notebook, saving the PDF in the Ch5 folder in the ChapterProjectsWork folder on your USB flash drive with the name **C5-Project3-Your Name**.

8. Close your MyProjects notebook in OneNote and close OneNote.

9. Close Outlook.

10. Submit the project to your instructor in the manner she or he has requested.

Chapter 6

Creating, Editing, and Formatting Documents Using Word

After successfully completing this chapter, you will be able to:

- Create and edit a new document
- Insert and delete text
- Insert symbols and special characters
- Check spelling and grammar
- Find and replace text
- Move text
- Insert bullets and numbering
- Format text using font options
- Change paragraph alignment, indent, and spacing
- Choose a Style Set and apply styles
- Create a new document from a template

Microsoft Word (referred to as Word) is a **word processing application** used to create documents that are composed mostly of text for personal, business, or school purposes. Word documents can also include pictures, charts, tables, or other visual elements to make the document more interesting and easier to understand. Examples of the types of documents you might create in Word are letters, essays, reports, invitations, recipes, agendas, contracts, and resumes. Any type of document that you need to create that is mostly text can easily be generated using Word.

Word automatically corrects some errors as you type and indicates other potential spelling and grammar errors for you to consider. Other features provide tools to format and enhance a document. In this chapter you will learn how to create, edit, and format documents. You will create new documents starting from a blank page and other documents by selecting from Word's template gallery.

Note: If you are using a tablet, consider completing this chapter using a USB or wireless keyboard because you will be typing longer passages of text.

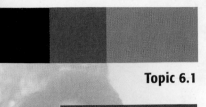

Creating and Editing a New Document

Recall from Chapter 3 that when Microsoft Word starts, you are presented with the Word Start screen from which you choose to open an existing document, create a new blank document, or search for and select a template to create a new document. Generally, creating a new blank document involves typing the document text, editing the text, and correcting errors. As you type, Word's AutoCorrect and AutoFormat features help you fix common typing errors and format common characters.

Topic 6.1

1. Start Word 2013.

2. At the Word Start screen, tap or click *Blank document* in the *Templates* gallery and compare your screen with the one shown in Figure 6.1.

If necessary, review the ribbon interface and QAT described in Chapter 3. Table 6.1 describes the elements shown in Figure 6.1.

3. Type **Social Bookmarking** and tap or press Enter.

Notice that extra space is automatically added below the text before the next line.

4. Type the text on the next page allowing the lines to end automatically; tap or press Enter only where indicated.

Word will move text to a new line automatically when you reach the end of the current line. This feature is called **wordwrap**. Word will also put a red wavy line

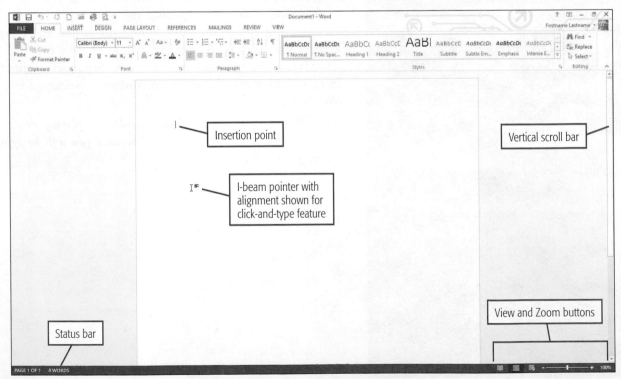

Figure 6.1 A new blank document screen. Word's default settings show a new document in Print Layout view and with rulers turned off; your display may vary if settings have been changed on the computer you are using. See Table 6.1 for a description of screen elements.

Table 6.1	Word Features
Feature	Description
Insertion point	Blinking vertical bar indicates where the next character typed will appear.
I-beam pointer	Pointer appearance for text entry or selection when you move the pointer using a mouse or trackpad.
	The I-beam pointer displays with a paragraph alignment option (left, center, or right) depending on the location of the I-beam within the current line. You can double-tap or double-click and type text anywhere on a page and the alignment option will be left-aligned, center-aligned, or right-aligned. This feature is called **click and type**.
Status bar	Displays page number with total number of pages and number of words in the current document. The right end of the Status bar has view and zoom options. The default view is Print Layout view, which shows how a page will look when printed with current print options.
Vertical scroll bar	Use the scroll bar to view parts of a document not shown in the current window.
View and Zoom buttons	By default, Word opens in Print Layout view. Other view buttons include Read Mode and Web Layout view. Read Mode is a new view in Word 2013 that maximizes reading space and removes editing tools, providing a more natural environment for reading.
	Zoom buttons, as you learned in Chapter 3, are used to enlarge or shrink the display.

below the word *bookmarklet*. Red wavy lines below words indicate words that are not found in Word's dictionary, indicating a possible spelling error. Correct typing mistakes as you go using the Backspace key to delete the character just typed and then retype the correct character. You will learn other editing methods later in this topic.

> **Social bookmarking websites are used to organize, save, and share web content. Links are called bookmarks and include tags, which are keywords you assign to the content when you create the bookmark.** [Tap or press Enter]
>
> **Many websites now include icons for popular social bookmarking sites that capture the page references for bookmarking. Another way to bookmark a page is to add the bookmarklet for the social bookmarking site you use to your browser's toolbar. Bookmarklets add a bookmark instantly when clicked.** [Tap or press Enter]

5 Type **teh** and tap or press the spacebar. Notice that Word changes the text to *The*.

A feature called **AutoCorrect** changes commonly misspelled words as soon as you press the spacebar.

App Tip

AutoCorrect also fixes common capitalization errors such as two initial capitals, no capital at the beginning of a sentence, and no capital in the name of a day. AutoCorrect also turns off the Caps Lock key and corrects text when a new sentence is started with the key left on. Use Undo if AutoCorrect changes text that you don't want changed.

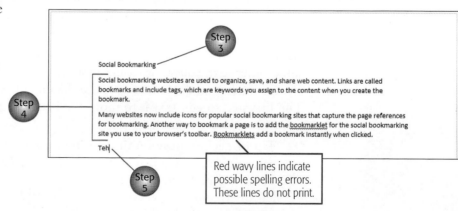

Red wavy lines indicate possible spelling errors. These lines do not print.

⑥ Type **popular social bookmarking site Pinterest.com is used to pin pictures found on the Web to virtual pinboards.** and tap or press Enter.

⑦ Type **a study by a marketing company found that 1/2 of frequent web surfers use a social bookmarking site, with Pinterest the 1st choice for most females.** and tap or press Enter.

Notice that Word automatically corrects the capitalization of the first word in the sentence, 1/2 is changed to a fraction character (½), and 1st is automatically formatted as an ordinal with the st shown as superscript text (superscript characters are smaller text placed at the top of the line). The **AutoFormat** feature automatically changes some fractions, ordinals, quotes, hyphens, and hyperlinks as you type. AutoFormat also converts straight apostrophes (') or quotation marks (") to smart quotes ('smart quotes'), also called curly quotes ("curly quotes").

App Tip

AutoFormat does not recognize all fractions. For example, typing 1/3 will not format to the one-third fraction character. You will learn about inserting symbols for these characters in the next topic.

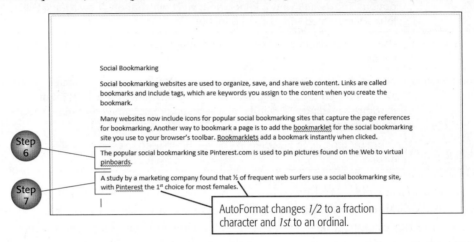

⑧ Tap or click the Save button on the QAT.

Because this is the first time the document has been saved, the Save As Backstage view appears.

⑨ Tap or click *Computer* and tap or click the Browse button.

⑩ At the Save As dialog box, navigate to the CompletedTopicsByChapter folder on your USB flash drive and create a new folder named *Ch6*.

⑪ Double-tap or double-click the *Ch6* folder name.

⑫ Select the current text in the *File name* text box, type **6.1-SocialMediaProject-Your Name**, and tap or press Enter or tap or click the Save button.

Many times when you are creating a new document, you need to make changes to the text after the text has been typed. In some cases, you need to correct typing errors you did not notice as you typed, you want to change a word or phrase to some other text, you want to add new text, or you want to remove some text. A change made to a document after the document has been typed is called **editing**. The first step to edit text is to move the insertion point to the location where you want to make a change.

⑬ Tap or click to position the insertion point at the beginning of the last paragraph that begins with the text *A study by a marketing company* (insertion point will be blinking just left of *A*), type **Experian Hitwise**, and press the spacebar.

Step 13

Experian Hitwise A study by a marketing company found that ½ of frequent web surfers use a social bookmarking site, with Pinterest the 1st choice for most females.

Word automatically inserts the new text and moves existing text to the right.

(14) With the insertion point still positioned at the left of *A* in *A study*, press the Delete key until you have removed *A study by*, type **(**, tap or click to position the insertion point just after the *y* in *company*, and then type **) conducted a survey of frequent web surfers and**.

(15) Position the insertion point just left of ½, press the Delete key until you have removed *½ of frequent web surfers*, and then type **one-half**.

(16) Position the insertion point at the left of *1ˢᵗ*, delete *1ˢᵗ*, and then type **first**.

(17) Position the insertion point below the last paragraph and type your first and last name.

(18) Check your text with the document shown in Figure 6.2. If necessary, make further corrections by moving the insertion point and inserting and deleting text as needed.

App Tip

You can also move the insertion point by pressing the Right arrow key on the keyboard. Use the Up, Down, Left, or Right arrow keys to move within a document. Hold down an arrow key to rapidly move the insertion point.

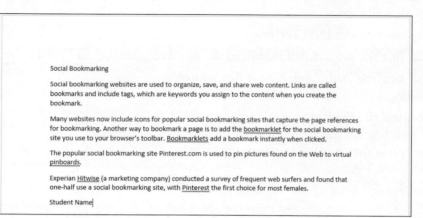

Figure 6.2 Document text for 6.1-SocialMediaProject-Student Name

(19) Tap or click the Save button on the QAT. Leave the document open for the next topic.

Because the document has already been assigned a file name at Step 12, the Save button saves the document's changes using the same name.

Quick **STEPS**

Create a New Document
1. Start Word 2013.
2. Tap or click *Blank document*.
3. Type text.

Save a New Document
1. Tap or click Save button on QAT.
2. Navigate to drive and/or folder.
3. Enter file name.
4. Tap or click Save.

Save a Document Using the Existing Name
Tap or click Save button on QAT.

Edit a Document
1. Position insertion point at location of change.
2. Type new text or delete text as needed.
3. Save changes.

 Beyond Basics   **Line Breaks versus New Paragraphs**

As you have learned in this topic, you press Enter only at the end of a short line of text (such as the title) or at the end of a paragraph. Pressing Enter is referred to as inserting a **hard return** and in Word creates a new paragraph. By default, line spacing in Word 2013 is set to 1.08, and 8 points of space is added after each paragraph. A point is a measurement system in which 1 point is equal to about 1/72 of an inch in height. Think of 8 points as approximately .11 of an inch of space added after each hard return.

If you want to end a short line of text and do not want an extra 8-point space added after the line, use the **Line Break** command Shift + Enter (hold down the Shift key while pressing Enter). A line break moves to the next line without creating a new paragraph. For example, use Shift + Enter when typing an address in a letter.

Inserting Symbols and Completing a Spelling and Grammar Check

Topic 6.2

SKILLS

Insert symbols and special characters

Check spelling and grammar

Tutorials

6.2.1 Inserting Symbols and Special Characters

6.2.2 Checking the Spelling and Grammar in a Document

oops!

Different font and/or subset? Use the *Font* or *Subset* list arrow to change the option to *(normal text)* and *Basic Latin* if the Symbol dialog box has different settings.

In some documents you need to insert a symbol or special character such as a copyright symbol (©), registered trademark (™), or a fraction character for a fraction that AutoCorrect does not recognize such as one-third (⅓). Symbols and special characters are inserted using the **Symbol gallery** or the Symbol dialog box.

The **Spelling & Grammar** button in the REVIEW tab starts Word's Spelling and Grammar feature, which is used to review a document and correct spelling and grammar errors.

1. With the **6.1-SocialMediaProject-Your Name** document open, position the insertion point after *n* in *Experian* in the last paragraph.

Experian is a registered trademark, so you will add the registered trademark symbol after the name.

2. Tap or click the INSERT tab.

3. Tap or click the Symbol button in the Symbols group.

4. Tap or click *Trade Mark Sign* at the *Symbol* gallery.

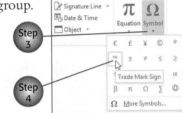

5. Position the insertion point after the period at the end of the paragraph that begins *Experian* and press the spacebar to insert a space.

6. Type **The survey sample size of 1,000 interviews provides a standard error at 95% confidence of** and press the spacebar.

7. Tap or click the Symbol button and tap or click *More Symbols* at the *Symbol* gallery.

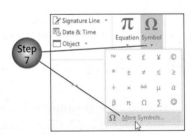

8. At the Symbol dialog box, with *Font* set to *(normal text)*, and *Subset* set to *Basic Latin*, scroll down the symbol list as needed, tap or click ±, and tap or click Insert.

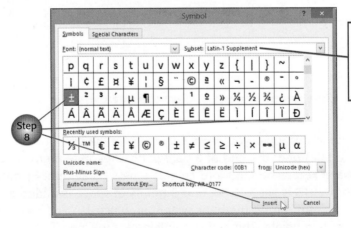

The *Subset* changes to *Latin-1 Supplement* when you select the plus-minus symbol in the symbol list.

9. Tap or click Close to return to the document and then type **3%.**.

You may have noticed the Plus–Minus Sign symbol is also available in the *Symbol* gallery. In Steps 7 to 9 you practiced using the Symbol dialog box so that you will know how to find a symbol that is not in the drop-down gallery.

The Spelling feature works by matching words in the document with words in a dictionary. Words that have no match are flagged as errors, and the Spelling task pane opens at the right side of the window with suggestions for the word not found and buttons to ignore, change, or add the word.

Word's Spelling feature also checks for duplicate words and presents the option to automatically remove the repeated word. Spelling and Grammar helps you correct many errors; however, you still need to proofread your documents. For example, the errors in the following sentence escaped detection: The plain fair was expensive!

10 Tap or click the REVIEW tab and then tap or click the Spelling & Grammar button in the Proofing group.

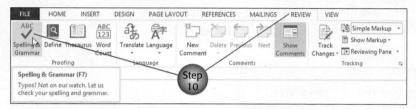

11 When the word *bookmarklet* is selected, tap or click the Ignore All button in the Spelling task pane.

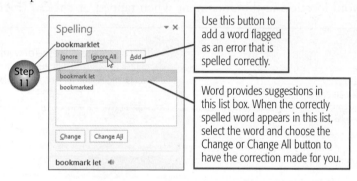

12 When the word *bookmarklets* is selected, tap or click the Ignore All button in the Spelling task pane.

13 Choose Ignore when *pinboards* is selected.

14 Choose Ignore when *Hitwise* is selected.

15 Choose Ignore when *Pinterest* is selected.

16 Tap or click OK at the message that the spelling and grammar check is complete.

17 Save the document using the same name. Leave the document open for the next topic.

ALTERNATIVE method

Consider using the following typing alternatives to insert a symbol:

Type *(c)* to have AutoCorrect insert the copyright symbol ©

Type *(r)* to have AutoCorrect insert the registered symbol ®

Type *(tm)* to have AutoCorrect insert the registered trademark symbol ™

To view the complete list of AutoCorrect entries, tap or click the FILE tab, then choose Options, *Proofing* (left pane of Word Options dialog box), and the AutoCorrect Options button.

App Tip

Press and hold or right-click a word with a red wavy line to view suggested replacements in a shortcut menu. You can also instruct Word to *Ignore All* or *Add to Dictionary* at the shortcut menu.

oops!

Spell check stopped at a different word? Respond to other errors as needed to correct variations that have occurred when you typed the document text in the previous topic.

Quick **STEPS**

Insert Symbol from Symbol Dialog Box
1. Position insertion point.
2. Tap or click INSERT tab.
3. Tap or click Symbol button.
4. Tap or click *More Symbols*.
5. If necessary, change font or subset.
6. Scroll down to locate symbol.
7. Tap or click symbol.
8. Tap or click Insert button.
9. Tap or click Close button.

Perform a Spelling and Grammar Check
1. Tap or click REVIEW tab.
2. Tap or click Spelling & Grammar button.
3. Ignore, Ignore All, Add, Change, or Change All as needed.
4. Tap or click OK.

Topic 6.3

SKILLS

Use Find command

Use Replace command

 **Tutorials**

6.3.1 Finding and Replacing Text

6.3.2 Using the Thesaurus

Finding and Replacing Text

The Find and Replace features move the insertion point to each occurrence of a word or phrase (**Find**), or automatically change each occurrence of a word or phrase to something else (**Replace**). Find is helpful if, for example, you think you have overused a particular term. Replace makes short work of editing a document if a word or phrase needs to be changed throughout.

1. With the **6.1-SocialMediaProject-Your Name** document open, position the insertion point at the beginning of the document.

2. Tap or click the HOME tab.

3. Tap or click the Find button in the Editing group.

This opens the Navigation pane at the left side of the Word document window.

4. Type **social bookmarking** in the *Search* box.

When you finish typing, Word highlights in the document all of the occurrences of the search word or phrase and displays the search results below the *Search* box. The total number of occurrences appears at the top of the RESULTS list. Each entry in the search results list is a link that moves to the search word location in the document when tapped or clicked (Figure 6.3).

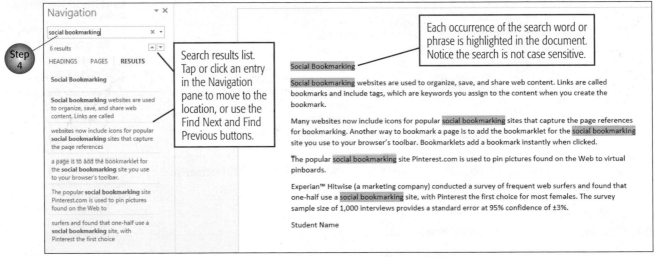

Figure 6.3 Search results for *social bookmarking* in 6.1-SocialMediaProject-Your Name document

Ctrl + Home is the keyboard shortcut to move the insertion point to the beginning of a document.

You can find text using a partial word search. For example, entering *exp* would find *Experian*, *expert*, and *experience*. Use partial word searches if you are not sure of correct spelling.

5. Tap or click each entry one at a time in the RESULTS list in the Navigation pane.

Notice that each occurrence of the search word is selected as you move to the phrase location.

6. Tap or click the Close button at the top right of the Navigation pane to close the pane.

(7) Position the insertion point at the beginning of the document.

(8) Tap or click the Replace button in the Editing group of the HOME tab.

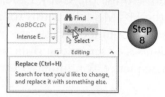

App Tip

Find and Replace searches start from the location of the insertion point.

(9) At the Find and Replace dialog box, with *social bookmarking* selected in the *Find what* text box, type **bookmarklet**.

(10) Tap or press Tab, or tap or click in the *Replace with* text box and type **bookmark button**.

(11) Tap or click the Replace All button.

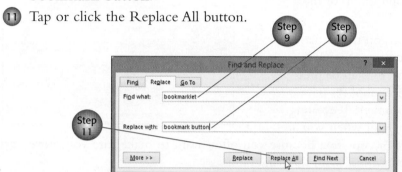

(12) Tap or click OK at the message that 2 replacements were made.

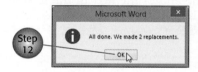

(13) Tap or click the Close button to close the Find and Replace dialog box.

Notice that Word matches the correct case of a word when the word is replaced at the beginning of a sentence, as seen in the last sentence of the paragraph that begins with *Many websites now include.*

(14) Save the document using the same name. Leave the document open for the next topic.

oops!

No replacements made? Tap or click OK and check your spelling in the *Find what* text box. Correct the text and try Replace All again. Still have 0 replacements? Cancel the Replace command and check the spelling of *bookmarklet* within your document. Correct the text in the document and repeat Steps 8 to 12.

Quick **STEPS**

Find Text
1. Position insertion point at beginning of document.
2. Tap or click Find button.
3. Type search text.

Replace Text
1. Position insertion point at beginning of document.
2. Tap or click Replace button.
3. Type *Find what* text.
4. Tap or press Tab, or tap or click in *Replace with* text box.
5. Type replacement text.
6. Tap or click Replace All.
7. Tap or click OK.
8. Tap or click Close button.

Beyond Basics — Using the Thesaurus to Replace a Word

Sometimes when you find yourself overusing a word, you are stuck for an alternative word to use in its place in one or two occurrences. Consider using the **Thesaurus** to help you find a word with a similar meaning. Thesaurus is located in the Proofing group of the REVIEW tab. Position the insertion point anywhere within a word you want to change and start the Thesaurus. Point to a word in the results list in the Thesaurus task pane and use the down-pointing arrow that appears at the end of a highlighted word to choose *Insert.*

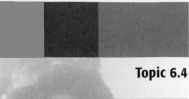

Topic 6.4

SKILLS

Move text

Insert a bulleted list

Insert a numbered list

 Tutorials

6.4.1 Cutting, Copying, and Pasting Text

6.4.2 Creating Bulleted and Numbered Lists

The dot that appears between words with hidden formatting symbols displayed indicates you pressed the spacebar.

oops!

Forgot how to select text? Refer to Topic 3.4 in Chapter 3 for help with selecting text and objects.

Moving Text and Inserting Bullets and Numbering

In Chapter 3 you learned how to use the Copy, Paste, and Format Painter buttons in the Clipboard group of the HOME tab. In this topic you will use the Cut button to move a selection. Bulleted and numbered lists are used to set apart information that is structured in short phrases or sentences. Bullets set apart a list of items that are entered in no particular sequence. A numbered list is used for a sequential list of tasks, items, or other text.

1 With the **6.1-SocialMediaProject-Your Name** document open, position the insertion point at the beginning of the paragraph that begins with *The popular social bookmarking site*.

2 Tap or click the Show/Hide button in the Paragraph group of the HOME tab.

Show/Hide turns on the display of hidden formatting symbols. For example, each time you tap or press Enter, a paragraph symbol (¶) is inserted in the document. Revealing these symbols is helpful when you are preparing to move or copy text because you often want to make sure you move or copy the paragraph symbol with the paragraph.

3 Select the paragraph *The popular social bookmarking site Pinterest.com is used to pin pictures found on the Web to virtual pinboards.* Make sure to include the paragraph formatting symbol at the end of the text in the selection.

4 Tap or click the Cut button in the Clipboard group of the HOME tab.

The text is removed from the current location and placed in the Clipboard.

5 Position the insertion point at the beginning of the paragraph that begins with *Many websites now include.*

6 Tap or click the top of the Paste button in the Clipboard group (do *not* tap or click the down-pointing arrow on the button).

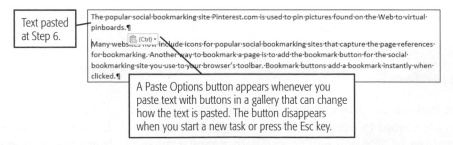

Text pasted at Step 6.

A Paste Options button appears whenever you paste text with buttons in a gallery that can change how the text is pasted. The button disappears when you start a new task or press the Esc key.

7 Tap or click the Show/Hide button to turn off the display of hidden formatting symbols.

8 Position the insertion point after the period that ends the sentence *The popular social networking site Pinterest.com is used to pin pictures found on the Web to virtual pinboards*, press the spacebar, type **Other social bookmarking sites include:**, and then tap or press Enter.

9 Tap or click the left part of the **Bullets button** in the Paragraph group of the HOME tab (do *not* tap or click the down-pointing arrow on the button).

Step 9

This indents and inserts the default bullet character, which is a solid round bullet.

10 Type **StumbleUpon.com** and tap or press Enter.

11 Type **Delicious.com** and tap or press Enter.

12 Type **Digg.com** and tap or press Enter.

13 Type **Reddit.com**.

Steps 10-13

> The popular social bookmarking site Pinterest.com is used pinboards. Other social bookmarking sites include:
> - StumbleUpon.com
> - Delicious.com
> - Digg.com
> - Reddit.com
>
> Many websites now include icons for popular social bookm

14 Position the insertion point after the period that ends the sentence *Bookmark buttons add a bookmark instantly when clicked*, press the spacebar, type **To add a bookmark button:**, and then tap or press Enter.

15 Tap or click the left part of the **Numbering button** in the Paragraph group of the HOME tab (do *not* tap or click the down-pointing arrow on the button).

This indents and inserts 1.

16 Type **Display the browser's Favorites toolbar.** and then tap or press Enter.

17 Type **Right-click the bookmark button and choose Add to favorites.** and then tap or press Enter.

18 Type **Choose Add button at dialog box that appears.**

> Many websites now include icons for popular social bookmarking sites that capture the page references for bookmarking. Another way to bookmark a page is to add the bookmark button for the social bookmarking site you use to your browser's toolbar. Bookmark buttons add a bookmark instantly when clicked. To add a bookmark button:
>
> 1. Display the browser's Favorites toolbar.
> 2. Right-click the bookmark button and choose Add to favorites.
> 3. Choose Add button at dialog box that appears.

Steps 16-18

19 Save the document using the same name. Leave the document open for the next topic.

ALTERNATIVE method

The **AutoFormat as You Type** feature creates automatic bulleted and numbered lists when you do the following:

Type *****, **>**, or **–**, press the spacebar, type text, and then tap or press Enter (bulleted list)

Type **1.**, press the spacebar, type text, and tap or press Enter (numbered list)

Immediately use Undo if an automatic list appears and you do not want to create a list. An AutoCorrect Options button will appear with which you can turn off automatic lists.

App Tip

The Bullets button arrow is used to choose a different bullet character from the Bullet Library.

App Tip

Similarly to the Bullets button, the Numbering button arrow is used to choose a different number format from the Numbering Library.

Quick **STEPS**

Move Text
1. Select text.
2. Tap or click Cut button.
3. Position insertion point.
4. Tap or click Paste button.

Create a Bulleted List
1. Tap or click Bullets button.
2. Type first list item.
3. Tap or press Enter.
4. Type second list item.
5. Tap or press Enter.
6. Continue typing until finished.

Create a Numbered List
1. Tap or click Numbering button.
2. Type first numbered item.
3. Tap or press Enter.
4. Type second numbered item.
5. Tap or press Enter.
6. Continue typing until finished.

Formatting Text with Font and Paragraph Alignment Options

Topic 6.5

SKILLS

Change font and font options

Change paragraph alignment

 Tutorials

6.5.1 Modifying the Font Using the Font Group

6.5.2 Formatting with the Mini Toolbar

6.5.3 Highlighting Text

6.5.4 Applying Formatting Using the Font Dialog Box

6.5.5 Aligning Text in Paragraphs

oops!

Mini toolbar disappeared? The Mini toolbar disappears if you move away from it after selecting text. Use the Font button arrow in the Font group of the HOME tab instead.

 App Tip

Make several font changes at once in the Font dialog box. Tap or click the Dialog Box Launcher button at the bottom right of the Font group.

 App Tip

Use the Font Color button arrow to choose a color other than red. Once the color is changed, the new color can be applied to the next selection without using the button arrow. The color on the button resets to red after Word is closed.

Generally, you enter and edit text in a new document and then turn your attention to the document's appearance. The process of changing the appearance of the text is referred to as **formatting**. Changing the appearance of characters is called **character formatting**. Changing the appearance of a paragraph is called **paragraph formatting**. In some cases, the first step in formatting is to select the characters or paragraphs to be changed.

Some people prefer to format as they type. In that case, you can change the character or paragraph options before typing.

Applying Font Formatting

The Font group in the HOME tab contains the buttons used to change character formatting. A **font** is also referred to as a typeface and includes the design and shape of the letters, numbers, and special characters. A large collection of fonts is available from simple to artistic to suit a variety of documents. The font size is set in points. As you learned in Topic 6.1, one point is approximately 1/72 of an inch in height. The default font and font size in a new document is 11-point Calibri.

The Font group also includes buttons to increase or decrease the font size, change the case, change the font style (bold, italic, or underline) or font color, highlight text, and add font effects (outline, shadow, glow, reflection, and accents).

1. With the **6.1-SocialMediaProject-Your Name** document open, select the title text at the top of the document *Social Bookmarking*.

2. Tap or click the Font button arrow in the Mini toolbar.

3. Slide or scroll down and tap or click *Century Gothic* in the *Font* gallery.

4. With the title text still selected, tap twice or click twice the Increase Font Size button in the Mini toolbar or in the Font group of the HOME tab.

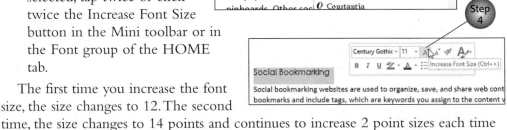

The first time you increase the font size, the size changes to 12. The second time, the size changes to 14 points and continues to increase 2 point sizes each time until you reach 28. After 28 points, the size changes to 36, 48, and then 72.

5. With the title text still selected, tap or click the Bold button in the Mini toolbar or in the Font group of the HOME tab.

6. With the title text still selected, tap or click the Font Color button (do *not* tap or click the Font Color button arrow) in the Mini toolbar or in the Font group of the HOME tab.

The default Font Color is Red.

7. Tap or click in the document away from the selected title to deselect the text.

Applying Paragraph Formatting

The Paragraph group in the HOME tab contains the buttons used to change paragraph formatting. You have already used the Bullets and Numbering buttons in this group. The bottom row of buttons in the group contains the buttons for changing the alignment of paragraphs from the default **Align Left** to **Center**, **Align Right**, or **Justify**. Justified text adds space within a line so that the text is distributed evenly between the left and right margins. You will explore other buttons in this group in the next topic.

⑧ Tap or click the insertion point anywhere within the title text *Social Bookmarking.*

To format a single paragraph, you do not need to select the paragraph text because paragraph formatting applies to all text within the paragraph to the point where a hard return was inserted.

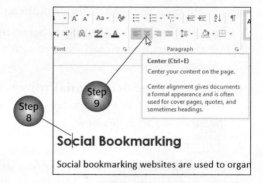

⑨ Tap or click the Center button in the Paragraph group of the HOME tab.

⑩ Tap or click the insertion point anywhere within the first paragraph of text and tap or click the Justify button in the Paragraph group of the HOME tab.

Justified text spreads the lines out so that the text ends evenly at the right margin.

App Tip

Select more than one paragraph first if you want to apply the same alignment option to multiple paragraphs.

⑪ With the insertion point still positioned in the first paragraph, tap or click the Align Left button in the Paragraph group of the HOME tab.

⑫ Save the document using the same name. Leave the document open for the next topic.

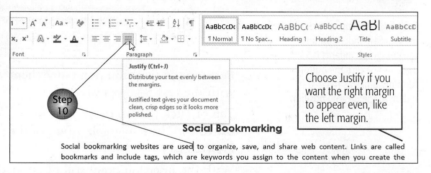

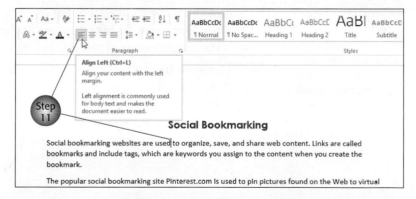

The following keyboard shortcuts change paragraph alignment:

Ctrl + L   Align Left   Ctrl + R   Align Right

Ctrl + E   Center   Ctrl + J   Justify

App Tip

Use the Clear All Formatting button in the Font group to remove all formatting from selected text.

Indenting Text and Changing Line and Paragraph Spacing

Topic 6.6

SKILLS

Indent text

Change line spacing

Change spacing after paragraphs

Tutorials

6.6.1 Changing Text Indentation

6.6.2 Setting Line and Paragraph Spacing

App Tip

Each time you tap or click the Increase Indent button, the paragraph indents 0.5 inch. Tap or click the button as many times as needed to indent to the desired position.

App Tip

When a paragraph has been indented more than one position, decrease indent moves the paragraph left toward the margin one position (0.5 inch) each time the button is tapped or clicked.

Paragraphs are indented to set the paragraph apart from the rest of the document. In reports, essays, or research papers, long quotes are indented. A paragraph can be indented for the first line only, or for all lines in the paragraph. Paragraphs can also be indented from the right margin. A paragraph where the first line remains at the left margin but subsequent lines are indented is called a **hanging indent**. Hanging indents are used in bulleted lists, numbered lists, bibliographies, and works cited pages.

Use the **Line and Paragraph Spacing button** in the Paragraph group to change the spacing between lines of text within a paragraph and to change the spacing before and after paragraphs.

1. With the **6.1-SocialMediaProject–Your Name** document open, position the insertion point at the left margin of the first paragraph (begins with the text *Social bookmarking websites*).

2. Tap or press the Tab key.

   Pressing the Tab key indents the first line only 0.5 inch. The AutoCorrect Options button also appears. Use the button if you want to change the first line indent back to a Tab, stop setting indents when you press Tab, or change other AutoFormat options.

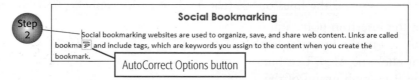

3. Position the insertion point anywhere within the second paragraph (begins with the text *The popular*).

4. Tap or click the **Increase Indent button** in the Paragraph group of the HOME tab.

5. With the insertion point still positioned in the second paragraph, tap or click the **Decrease Indent button** in the Paragraph group of the HOME tab.

   Decrease Indent moves the paragraph back to the left margin.

6. Position the insertion point anywhere within the third paragraph (begins with the text *Many websites now include*).

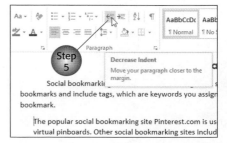

7. Tap or click the Line and Paragraph Spacing button in the Paragraph group of the HOME tab and then tap or click *Line Spacing Options* at the drop-down list.

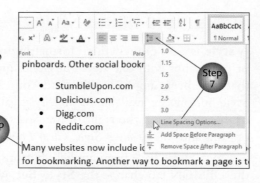

8. Select the current entry in the *Left* text box and type **0.5**.

9. Select the current entry in the *Right* text box and type **0.5**.

10. Tap or click OK.

The paragraph is indented from both margins by 0.5 inch.

11. With the insertion point still positioned in the paragraph that begins with the text *Many websites*, tap or click the Line and Paragraph Spacing button and then tap or click *Line Spacing Options*.

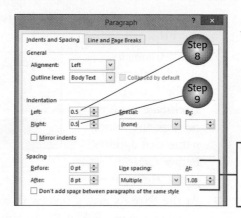

12. Change the entry in the *Left* and *Right* text boxes to *0*.

13. Tap or click the *Special* list arrow and tap or click *First line*.

14. Tap or click OK.

15. Format the second paragraph that begins with the text *The popular* and the last paragraph that begins with the text *Experian* with a first line indent.

16. Tap or click the Select button in the Editing group of the HOME tab and tap or click *Select All* at the drop-down list.

17. Tap or click the Line and Paragraph Spacing button and tap or click *1.5* at the drop-down gallery.

The line spacing is changed to 1.5 lines for the entire document. Notice the other line spacing options are *1.0*, *1.15*, *2.0*, *2.5*, and *3.0*.

18. With the entire document still selected, tap or click the Line and Paragraph Spacing button and then tap or click *Remove Space After Paragraph* at the drop-down gallery.

19. Tap or click in any section of the document to deselect the text.

20. Save the document using the same name. Leave the document open for the next topic.

Quick STEPS

Indent a Paragraph from Both Margins
1. Position insertion point in paragraph.
2. Tap or click Line and Paragraph Spacing button.
3. Tap or click *Line Spacing Options*.
4. Change *Left* value.
5. Change *Right* value.
6. Tap or click OK.

Change Spacing Before and After Paragraphs
1. Position insertion point or select paragraphs.
2. Tap or click Line and Paragraph Spacing button.
3. Tap or click *Add Space Before Paragraph* or *Remove Space After Paragraph*.

You can also adjust the spacing before or after paragraphs or change line spacing in this section of the dialog box.

Ctrl + A is the keyboard shortcut to Select All.

ALTERNATIVE method

The PAGE LAYOUT tab also contains a Paragraph group with the same Indent and Spacing options you used in this topic. Use the *Left* and *Right* text boxes to indent paragraphs or the *Before* and *After* text boxes to change the spacing inserted before and after paragraphs.

In the DESIGN tab, use the Paragraph Spacing button in the Document Formatting group to set line and paragraph spacing options for the entire document, including new paragraphs.

Topic 6.7

SKILLS

Apply Styles

Change Style Set

SNAP Tutorial

6.7   Applying Styles, Style Sets, and Themes

Formatting Using Styles

A **style** is a set of predefined formatting options that can be applied to selected text or paragraphs with one step. The Styles group in the HOME tab shows the styles that have been supplied with Word. You can also create your own styles. Two rows of Style buttons are available in the *Styles* gallery. Use the More button at the bottom of the scroll bar at the right of the *Styles* gallery to show the second row of Style options and the *Create a Style, Clear Formatting,* and *Apply Styles* options.

Once Styles have been applied, buttons in the Document Formatting group of the DESIGN tab change the **Style Set**, which changes the look of a document. Each Style Set has different formatting options associated with each style.

1. With the **6.1-SocialMediaProject–Your Name** document open, tap or click the FILE tab and tap or click Save As.

2. With *Computer* already selected in the Save As Backstage view, tap or click the folder name that appears below *Current Folder* in the right pane.

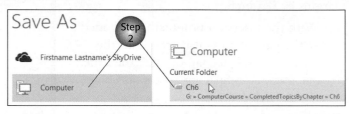

3. At the Save As dialog box, with the text in the *File name* text box already selected, tap or click at the beginning of the file name or press the Home key on the keyboard.

4. Change *6.1* at the beginning of the file name to *6.7* by moving the insertion point and inserting and deleting text.

5. Tap or press Enter, or tap or click the Save button.

6. Position the insertion point anywhere within the title text *Social Bookmarking*.

7. Tap or click the *Title* style in the *Styles* gallery in the HOME tab.

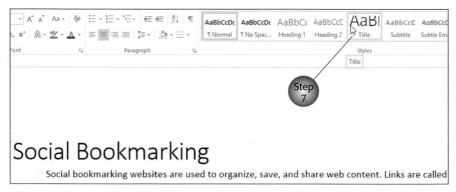

8. Position the insertion point anywhere within the first paragraph of text below the title.

9. Tap or click the More button in the *Styles* gallery. The button displays with a bar above a down-pointing arrow.

10. Tap or click the *Quote* style in the second row of the *Styles* gallery.

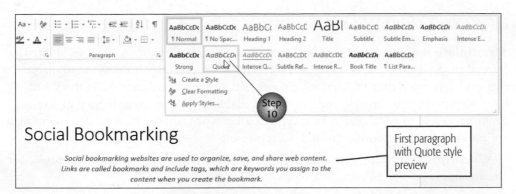

Quick STEPS

Format Using Styles
1. Select text or position insertion point.
2. Tap or click desired Styles button.

Change Style Set
1. Tap or click DESIGN tab.
2. Tap or click desired Style Set.

First paragraph with Quote style preview

11. Select *Pinterest.com* in the second paragraph and tap or click the *Intense Reference* style in the *Styles* gallery.

12. Deselect *Pinterest.com*.

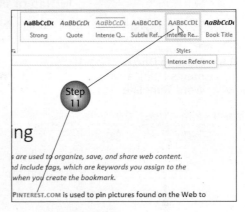

Once styles have been applied to text, you can experiment with various Style Sets in the Document Formatting group of the DESIGN tab. Changing the Style Set changes font and paragraph formatting options. Two rows of Style Sets are in the *Document Formatting* gallery.

13. Tap or click the DESIGN tab.

14. Tap or click the *Basic (Stylish)* Style Set in the *Document Formatting* gallery (fourth option from left).

The Basic (Stylish) Style Set causes the look of the document to change.

15. Position the insertion point anywhere within the title text *Social Bookmarking*.

16. Tap or click the HOME tab and tap or click *Heading 1* in the Styles group.

App Tip

Change the theme at the DESIGN tab.

The title text formats to the options stored in the Heading 1 style in the new Style Set. The formatting is also affected by the document **Theme** (set of colors and fonts).

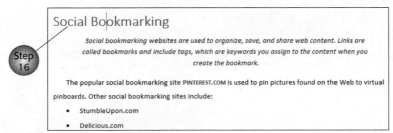

17. Save the document using the same name (**6.7-SocialMediaProject-Your Name**).

18. Close the document. Leave Word open for the next topic.

Topic 6.8

SKILLS

Create a new
document from
a template

SNAP **Tutorial**

6.8 Creating Docu-
ments Using a
Word Template

Creating a New Document from a Template

A **template** is a document that has been created with formatting options applied.
Several professional-quality templates for various types of documents are available
that you can use rather than creating a new document from scratch. At the Word
Start screen you can browse and preview available templates by category, or in the
Search for online template search box, type in a keyword for the type of document you
are looking for and browse through search results.

When Word is already opened, the New tab Backstage view is used to browse for
a template.

1. Tap or click the FILE tab and then tap or click New.
2. At the New tab Backstage view, tap or click <u>Letters</u> in the *Suggested searches* section.

3. Slide or scroll down and review the various types of letter templates available,
then tap or click Home at the top of the New tab Backstage view.

4. Tap or click in the *Search for online templates* search box, type **time sheet**,
and tap or press Enter, or tap or click the Start searching button (displays as a
magnifying glass at end of the search box).

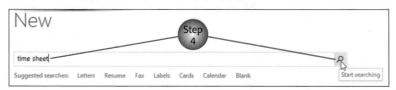

oops!

Your Time Sheet template
looks different? Available
templates are changed often.
If the first template looks different, close the preview and
look for one that is closest to
the one shown. If necessary,
adjust the remaining instructions to suit the available
templates.

5. Tap or click the
first *Time Sheet*
template in the
Templates gallery.

A preview of the
template opens with
a description that
provides information
on the template
design.

6. Tap or click the
Create button.

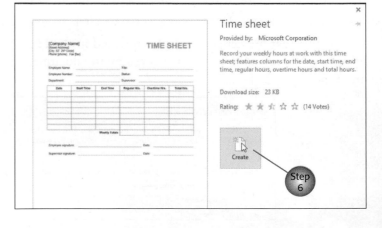

(7) Tap or click *[Company Name]* and type **A+ Tutoring Advantage**.

(8) Tap or click *[Street Address]* and type **1015 Montreal Way**.

(9) Tap or click *[City, ST ZIP Code]* and type **St. Paul, MN 55102**.

(10) Tap or click *[phone]* and type **888-555-3125**.

(11) Tap or click *[fax]* and type **888-555-3445**.

A+ Tutoring Advantage
1015 Montreal Way
St. Paul, MN 55102
Phone 888-555-3125 Fax 888-555-3445

Steps 7-11

TIME SHEET

(12) Tap or click next to *Employee Name* and type your name.

(13) Complete the remainder of the time sheet document using the text shown in Figure 6.4 by completing steps similar to Step 12.

A+ Tutoring Advantage
1015 Montreal Way
St. Paul, MN 55102
Phone 888-555-3125 Fax 888-555-3445

Step 12

TIME SHEET

Employee Name:	Student Name	Title:	Computer Tutor
Employee Number:	101	Status:	Part-time
Department:	Computers	Supervisor:	Dayna Summerton

Date	Start Time	End Time	Regular Hrs.	Overtime Hrs.	Total Hrs.
Oct. 13	9:00 am	12:00 pm	3.0		3.0
Oct. 14	1:00 pm	4:30 pm	3.5		3.5
Oct. 15	7:00 pm	9:30 pm	2.5		2.5
Oct. 16	10:00 am	1:00 pm	3.0		3.0
	Weekly Totals		12.0		12.0

Employee signature: _____ Date: _____

Supervisor signature: _____ Date: _____

Figure 6.4 Completed time sheet for 6.8-Oct13to16Timesheet-Your Name.

(14) Save the completed time sheet in the Ch6 folder in the CompletedTopicsByChapter folder on your USB flash drive as **6.8-Oct13to16TimeSheet-Your Name**. Choose OK when a message displays that the document will be upgraded to the newest file format.

(15) Close the document.

Template Designs

Templates are available for any type of document. The next time you need to type a letter, memo, report, invitation, announcement, flyer, or labels, look for a template design.

Concepts Review

Topic	Key Concepts	Key Terms
Creating and Editing a New Document	A word processing application is software used to create documents that are composed mostly of text.	Word processing application
	Start a new blank document from the Word Start screen.	Click and type
	Creating a new document generally involves typing text, editing text, and correcting errors.	Wordwrap
	Double-tapping or double-clicking on the page in blank space and typing is referred to as click and type. Text is automatically aligned left, center, or right depending on the location in the line at which click and type occurs.	AutoCorrect AutoFormat Editing Hard return Line Break
	Wordwrap is the term that describes Word moving text to the next line automatically when you reach the right margin.	
	As you type new text, AutoCorrect fixes common misspellings, and AutoFormat automatically converts some text to fractions, ordinals, quotes, hyphens, and hyperlinks.	
	Pressing the Enter key creates a new paragraph and is called a hard return.	
	A change made to text that has already been typed is referred to as editing and involves inserting, deleting, and replacing characters.	
	The first step in editing is to position the insertion point at the location of the change.	
	Press Shift + Enter to insert a Line Break command, which moves to the next line without adding extra spacing.	
Inserting Symbols and Completing a Spelling and Grammar Check	Symbols or special characters such as a copyright symbol or registered trademark are entered using the *Symbol* gallery or Symbol dialog box.	*Symbol* gallery Spelling & Grammar
	AutoCorrect recognizes some special characters and symbols and converts them automatically.	
	The Spelling & Grammar button is used to match words in the document with words in the dictionary; words not found are flagged as potential errors.	
	During a spell check, a word not found in the dictionary is highlighted and suggestions for replacement appear in the Spelling task pane.	
	Ignore, Ignore All, Add, Change, or Change All are buttons in the Spelling task pane used to respond to each potential error.	
Finding and Replacing Text	The Find feature highlights all occurrences of a keyword or phrase and provides in the Navigation pane a link to each location in the document.	Find Replace Thesaurus
	Use Replace if you want Word to automatically change each occurrence of a keyword or phrase with another word or phrase.	
	Find a word with a similar meaning in the Thesaurus.	

Topic	Key Concepts	Key Terms
Moving Text and Inserting Bullets and Numbering	Turn on the display of hidden formatting symbols using the Show/Hide button in the Paragraph group.	Bullets button
	Hidden formatting symbols such as the paragraph symbol are inserted in a document whenever the Enter key is pressed.	Numbering button
	Displaying formatting symbols is helpful when moving text to make sure the paragraph symbol is selected before cutting the text.	AutoFormat as You Type
	Bullets are items in a list that are entered in no particular sequence.	
	The default bullet symbol is a solid round bullet.	
	Additional bullet options are available using the Bullets button arrow.	
	A numbered list is a sequential series of tasks or other items that are each preceded by a number.	
	AutoFormat as You Type creates a bulleted list when you start a new line with *, >, or – and then press the spacebar.	
	AutoFormat as You Type creates a numbered list when you start a new line by typing 1. and then press the spacebar.	
Formatting Text with Font and Paragraph Alignment Options	Changing the appearance of text is called formatting.	Formatting
	Character formatting involves applying changes to the appearance of characters, whereas paragraph formatting changes the appearance of an entire paragraph.	Character formatting
		Paragraph formatting
	Use buttons in the Font group of the HOME tab to change character formatting.	Font
	A font is also called a typeface and refers to the design and shape of letters, numbers, and special characters.	Align Left
		Center
	Change a font, font size, case, font style, font color; highlight text; and add font effects to change character formats.	Align Right
	Change a paragraph's alignment from the default Align Left to Center, Align Right, or Justify using the buttons in the bottom row of the Paragraph group in the HOME tab.	Justify
	Justified text has extra space within a line so that the left and right margins are even.	

continued....

Topic	Key Concepts	Key Terms
Indenting Text and Changing Line and Paragraph Spacing	Indent a paragraph such as a long quote to set the paragraph apart from others in the document. Press Tab at the beginning of a paragraph to indent only the first line or change *Special* to *First line* at the Paragraph dialog box. A paragraph in which all lines are indented except the first line is called a hanging indent. Indent all lines of a paragraph using the Increase Indent button or change the *Left* text box entry at the Paragraph dialog box. A paragraph indents 0.5 inch each time the Increase Indent button is tapped or clicked. Use the Decrease Indent button to move a paragraph closer to the left margin; the paragraph moves left 0.5 inch each time the button is tapped or clicked. Indent a paragraph from both margins using the *Left* and *Right* text boxes in the Paragraph dialog box. Change line spacing by selecting the desired spacing option from the Line and Paragraph Spacing button. Extra space can be added or removed before or after paragraphs using options from the Line and Paragraph Spacing button or the Paragraph dialog box. Indents and paragraph spacing can also be set using text boxes in the Paragraph group of the PAGE LAYOUT tab.	Hanging indent Line and Paragraph Spacing button Increase Indent button Decrease Indent button
Formatting Using Styles	Format text by applying a style, which is a set of predefined formatting options. Two rows of styles are available in the *Styles* gallery of the HOME tab. Change the Style Set using buttons in the Document Formatting group of the DESIGN tab. Each Style Set applies a different set of formatting options for the styles in the HOME tab, meaning you can change a document's appearance by changing the Style Set. A Theme is a set of colors, fonts, and font effects that alter the appearance of a document.	Style Style Set Theme
Creating a New Document from a Template	A template is a document that is already set up with text and/or formatting options. Browse available templates in the template gallery at the Word Start screen or at the New tab Backstage view. Find a template by browsing the gallery by a category or by typing a keyword in the *Search for online templates* search box. Tap or click a template design to preview the template and create a new document based upon the template. Within a template, text placeholders or instructional text is included to help you personalize the document.	Template

Multiple Choice

1. This feature fixes common misspellings as you type.
   a. AutoFormat
   b. AutoCorrect
   c. AutoSpell
   d. Click and Type

2. This feature automatically converts text such as 1/2 to a fraction character.
   a. AutoFormat
   b. AutoCorrect
   c. AutoSpell
   d. Click and Type

3. Insert a trademark sign using this gallery.
   a. Styles
   b. Document Formatting
   c. Spelling
   d. Symbol

4. In this task pane you can instruct Word to ignore a word that is spelled correctly but that Word has highlighted as a potential error.
   a. Spelling
   b. Styles
   c. Navigation
   d. Replace

5. Use this feature to locate all occurrences of a word in the current document.
   a. Replace
   b. Navigate
   c. Find
   d. Search

6. A word or phrase can be automatically changed to another word or phrase throughout the entire document using this feature.
   a. Replace
   b. Navigate
   c. Find
   d. Search

7. This button in the Clipboard group is used to remove selected text from its current location and paste it at another location.
   a. Move
   b. Cut
   c. Copy
   d. Select All

8. Set apart a list of items that is in no particular sequence with this button in the Paragraph group of the HOME tab.
   a. Numbering
   b. Decrease Indent
   c. Bullets
   d. Justify

9. Changing the appearance of text is referred to as _____.
   a. formatting
   b. editing
   c. justifying
   d. organizing

10. Apply a different font to selected text using this toolbar.
    a. Formatting
    b. Editing
    c. Mini
    d. Styles

11. Pressing the Tab key at the beginning of a paragraph creates this type of indent.
    a. Hanging
    b. First line
    c. Left
    d. Special

12. Open this dialog box to indent a paragraph from both margins.
    a. Indent
    b. Paragraph
    c. Alignment
    d. Format

13. This button in the Paragraph group moves text closer to the left margin.
    a. Increase Indent
    b. Align Left
    c. Decrease Indent
    d. Align Right

14. Buttons in this gallery allow you to apply a set of predefined formatting options in one step.
    a. Styles
    b. Font
    c. AutoFormat
    d. AutoCorrect Options

15. Browse available templates at the Word Start screen or this Backstage view.
    a. Info
    b. New
    c. Open
    d. Options

Crossword Puzzle

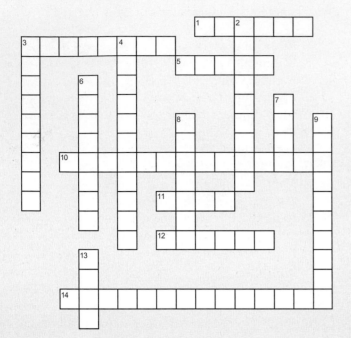

ACROSS

1 Button to use when flagged error is not a misspelling
3 Use to create a document from one already formatted
5 A set of colors, fonts, and font effects
10 Move all lines of a paragraph left 0.5 inch
11 Feature that causes Navigation pane to open
12 Dialog box to insert a special character
14 Move all lines of a paragraph right 0.5 inch

DOWN

2 Button to format a sequential list of steps
3 Feature that shows words with a similar meaning
4 Fixes spelling of *teh* after you press spacebar
6 Document Formatting buttons change this
7 Do this with Cut and Paste
8 Option that makes left and right margins appear even
9 Feature that converts *1st* to an ordinal
13 Group for character formatting options

Matching

Match the term with the statement or definition.

_____ 1. Word
_____ 2. Symbol
_____ 3. Thesaurus
_____ 4. Move text
_____ 5. AutoFormat as You Type
_____ 6. Character formatting
_____ 7. Hanging
_____ 8. Style
_____ 9. Template

a. Clipboard group
b. Indent used in lists
c. Font group
d. Synonyms
e. Title
f. Word processing
g. New tab Backstage view
h. Plus–Minus sign
i. Automatic lists

Project 1 Creating and Editing a New Document

Individual

Deliverable: Word document (continued in Project 2)

1. At a new blank document, type the following text, pressing Enter only where indicated.

   Social Media Popularity, Profitability, and Privacy [Tap or press Enter]

   Ninety-six percent of Americans and Canadians between the ages of 16 and 24 are Internet users. For most people, a majority of time spent on the Internet involves the use of social communication websites such as Facebook. All ages prefer the convenience and accessibility of social media websites to connect with family, friends, and acquaintances. [Tap or press Enter]

   Social media websites such as Facebook make money using a traditional model of selling advertisements such as banner and pop-up ads. Facebook games such as Farmville also provide a source of income for Facebook. In 2012 Facebook launched a service called Facebook Gifts, which lets Facebook users send presents to one another. [Tap or press Enter]

   Users of social media websites such as Facebook need to be wary of privacy issues and security threats. The risk of identity theft, clickjacking, and phishing scams is rising due to the popularity of social media. Review privacy options and keep personal information that could identify you to a stranger to a minimum at each social network. Consider asking your family and friends not to tag you in pictures without your knowledge. [Tap or press Enter]

   Your Name [Tap or press Enter]

2. Save the document as **C6-Project1-SocialMedia-Your Name** in a new folder named *Ch6* within the ChapterProjectsWork folder on your USB flash drive.

3. Edit the document as follows:

   a. In the first sentence change *16 and 24 are Internet users* to *10 and 34 are social media users*.

   b. In the second sentence change *social communication websites* to *social networking websites*.

   c. Add the following sentence to the end of the second paragraph.

   Also in 2012, Facebook reported over $150 million from mobile ads, which represent their fastest growing revenue source.

   d. Delete the last sentence in the first paragraph that begins with *All ages prefer*.

   e. Delete the second sentence in the second paragraph that begins with *Facebook games*.

   f. Move the last sentence that begins with *Consider asking* to the beginning of the last paragraph (before the sentence that begins *Users of social media websites*).

   g. Type the following new paragraph after the third paragraph and before your name.

   When posting content at a social media website, be mindful not to violate copyright by copying pictures that belong to someone else. Look for a copyright symbol © or refer to terms of use before downloading content. Be careful also not to misrepresent or misuse a registered trademark of a company. Look for the ® or ™ symbol to identify a company's trademark.

   h. Replace all occurrences of *social media* with *social networking*. When finished, change *networking* in the title to *Networking*.

4. Complete a spelling and grammar check of the document.

5. Proofread the document carefully to make sure the document is error-free.

6. Save the revised document using the same name (**C6-Project1-SocialMedia-Your Name**).

7. Leave the document open if you are continuing to Project 2; otherwise, close the document and submit the project to your instructor in the manner she or he has requested.

Project 2 Editing and Formatting a Document

Individual

Deliverable: Word document

Note: You must have completed Project 1 before starting this project.

1. If necessary, open **C6-Project1-SocialMedia-Your Name**.
2. Use Save As to change the file name to **C6-Project2-SocialMediaFormatted-Your Name**, saving in the same folder.
3. Type the following new paragraph and bulleted list between the second and third paragraphs.
   Facebook's $1 billion revenue from last year is segmented as follows:
   - **85 percent from ads (including mobile ads)**
   - **14 percent from games (such as Farmville)**
   - **1 percent from other sources (such as Facebook Gifts)**
4. Format the document as follows:
   a. Change the title to 12-point Verdana bold red font and center-aligned.
   b. Indent the first line of each paragraph.
   c. Justify the first two and the last two paragraphs.
   d. Select the entire document, change the line spacing to 1.5, and remove the space after paragraphs.
5. Depending on the method used to format a paragraph with a first line indent, the indent position for the last three paragraphs may be at 0.25 inch instead of the 0.5 inch in the first two paragraphs. This occurs because the bullet list formatting carries over to the paragraphs before and after. If necessary, change the first line indent position to 0.5 inch for the last three paragraphs by positioning the insertion point within the paragraph and opening the Paragraph dialog box.
6. Save the revised document using the same name (**C6-Project2-SocialMediaFormatted-Your Name**).
7. Submit the project to your instructor in the manner she or he has requested.
8. Close the document.

Project 3 Formatting with Styles

Individual

Deliverable: Word document

Note: You must have completed Project 1 before starting this project.

1. Open **C6-Project1-SocialMedia-Your Name**.
2. Use Save As to change the file name to **C6-Project3-SocialMediaStyles-Your Name**, saving in the same folder.
3. Apply the Heading 1 style to the document title.
4. Select all of the text below the title except for your name at the bottom of the document and apply the Emphasis style.
5. Select your name at the bottom of the document and apply the Intense Reference style.
6. Change the Style Set to *Black & White (Classic)*.
7. Save the revised document using the same name (**C6-Project3-SocialMediaStyles-Your Name**).
8. Submit the project to your instructor in the manner she or he has requested.
9. Close the document.

Project 4 Creating an Invoice from a Template

Individual

Deliverable: Invoice document from template

1. Search for and select a service invoice template of your choosing to create a new document.
2. Personalize the template by adding your name as the company name and your school's address, city, state, ZIP Code, and phone as the company information. Fill in other company information with fictitious information if necessary.
3. Using today's date, create invoice 136 to:

> Leslie Taylor
> HBC Enterprises
> 1240 7th Street West
> St. Paul, MN 55102
> 888-555-6954
> Customer ID: CA6-3312

   a. Type the body of the invoice as follows:

Qty	Description	Unit Price	Total
5 hours	**Social media consulting**	**65.00**	**325.00**

   b. Add appropriate sales tax for your area. Check with your instructor if necessary for sales tax rates in your state or province.

   c. Make sure the total at the bottom of the invoice is 325.00 plus tax.

   d. Add or delete other information as needed so that the invoice is of mailable quality.

4. Save the document in the Ch6 folder within the ChapterProjectsWork folder on your USB flash drive as **C6-Project4-InvoiceTemplate-Your Name**.
5. Submit the project to your instructor in the manner she or he has requested.
6. Close the document.

Project 5 Campus Flyer from Template

 Grade It

Individual

Deliverable: Campus Flyer

1. Create a flyer for your school campus similar to the one shown in Figure 6.5. Use a current date and a location suitable for concerts on or near your campus. Add current popular band names to the *FEATURING* section. Enter a fictitious web address and sponsor information. Make any other changes you think are necessary.

   Note: Search for the template shown using the keywords* student flyer *at the New tab Backstage view.

2. Save the flyer in the Ch6 folder within the ChapterProjectsWork folder on your USB flash drive as **C6-Project5-CampusBandBattleFlyer-Your Name**.

3. Submit the project to your instructor in the manner she or he has requested.

4. Close the document.

CAMPUS BAND BATTLE

WHEN
June 8th, 2012
8pm – 12pm

WHERE
Student Union Auditorium
1234 Academic Circle, Berkeley, CA

FEATURING · Your Band Name · Your Band Name · Your Band Name · Your Band Name · Your Band Name · Your Band Name

WEB ADDRESS

ALL AGES EVENT

ADVANCE TICKETS
$18 General
$36 VIP
Group rates available on site

AT THE DOOR
$20 General
$40 VIP
Group rates available on site

SPONSORS
Adventure Works
Alpine Ski House
Contoso, Ltd.
Fourth Coffee
Margie's Travel
School of Fine Art
The Phone Company
Wingtip Toys

BENEFITING
The School of Music and the University Arts and Entertainment Council

Figure 6.5 Project 5 Campus Flyer

Project 6 Internet Research and Composing a New Document

Individual or Pairs

Deliverable: Word document

1. Listen to the audio file named ***Project6_Instructions***. The file is located in the Ch6 folder in the Student_Data_Files folder on your USB flash drive.
2. Complete the research and compose the document as instructed.
3. Save the document in the Ch6 folder within the ChapterProjectsWork folder on your USB flash drive as **C6-Project6-SocialMediaResearch-Your Name**.
4. Submit the project to your instructor in the manner she or he has requested.
5. Close the document.

Project 7 Sending Project Work to OneNote Notebook

Individual

Deliverable: New Page in Shared OneNote notebook

1. Start OneNote and open the MyProjects notebook created in Chapter 4, Project 4.
2. Make Word the active section and add a new page titled *Chapter 6 Projects*.
3. Switch to Word. For each project that you completed, open the document, send the project to OneNote 2013 selecting the Chapter 6 Projects page in the Word section in the MyProjects notebook, and then close the document.
4. Close your MyProjects notebook in OneNote and close OneNote.
5. Close Word.
6. Submit the project to your instructor in the manner she or he has requested.

Chapter 7

Enhancing a Document with Special Features

S everal features in Word allow you to add visual appeal, organize information, or format a document for a special purpose such as a research paper. Word provides different views in which to work and navigate a document and includes collaborative tools such as comments for working on a document with other people. Several resume and cover letter templates are available in Word to help you build these important job search documents.

In this chapter, you will enhance documents already typed and finalize an academic research paper by adding formatting, citations, and a works cited page. Lastly, you will create a resume and cover letter using templates.

After successfully completing this chapter, you will be able to:

- Insert images into a document
- Add borders and shading to text
- Insert a text box into a document
- Create and format a table
- Change page layout options
- Format a research paper with a header and page numbers
- Insert citations and a works cited page
- Display a document in different views in Word
- Insert comments
- Create a resume and cover letter

Inserting, Editing, and Labeling Images in a Document

SKILLS

Insert clip art

Insert a picture

Edit a picture

Insert a caption

 **Tutorials**

7.1.1 Inserting, Sizing, and Moving Images

7.1.2 Inserting and Formatting a Picture Image

7.1.3 Creating and Customizing Captions

7.1.4 Inserting and Modifying WordArt

7.1.5 Inserting and Formatting a Shape

7.1.6 Creating SmartArt

Graphic elements such as pictures, clip art, shapes, SmartArt, charts, or other types of images help a reader understand content or add visual appeal to a document. Office.com provides a large selection of royalty-free photos and illustrations. If you have a picture stored at an online service such as Flickr, Facebook, or OneDrive, you can insert the image directly from the Web. Pictures saved to your PC or mobile device can also be inserted into a document. Once inserted, images can be edited and labeled with a caption.

Inserting Pictures from Online Sources

You can search for a suitable image for a document in the Microsoft Office **clip art gallery** or on the Web using Bing without leaving the Word document. You can also choose to insert a photo you have saved at an online service without leaving the Word document.

① Start Word 2013 and open the document **InsulaSummary_AddictionsCourse**.

This document is located in the Ch7 folder in the Student_Data_Files folder on your USB flash drive.

② Using Save As, navigate to the CompletedTopicsByChapter folder on your USB flash drive, create a new folder named *Ch7*, and save a copy of the document within the Ch7 folder as **7.1-InsulaSummary-Your Name**.

③ Position the insertion point at the beginning of the first paragraph of text.

④ Tap or click the INSERT tab and then tap or click the **Online Pictures button** in the Illustrations group.

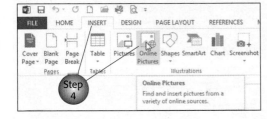

⑤ At the Insert Pictures dialog box with the insertion point positioned in the *Office.com Clip Art* search text box, type **scientist** and then tap or press Enter, or tap or click the Search button (displays as a magnifying glass).

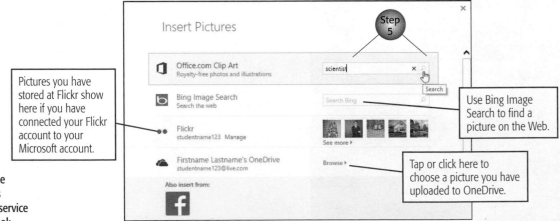

Pictures you have stored at Flickr show here if you have connected your Flickr account to your Microsoft account.

Use Bing Image Search to find a picture on the Web.

Tap or click here to choose a picture you have uploaded to OneDrive.

 App Tip

New to Word 2013 is the ability to choose photos directly from an online service such as Flickr or Facebook. Another new feature is the Online Video button in the Media group used to add and play videos within a Word document.

⑥ Slide or scroll down the search results list to the image shown at the right, tap or click to select the image, and then tap or click the Insert button.

⑦ Tap or click the **Layout Options button** that appears to the right of the inserted image.

⑧ Tap or click *Square*, the first option in the *With Text Wrapping* section of the *LAYOUT OPTIONS* palette, and then tap or click the Close button.

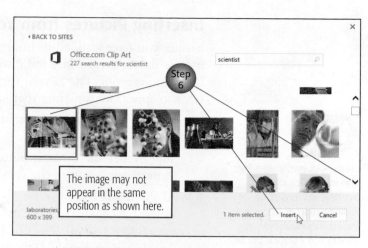

The *LAYOUT OPTIONS* gallery provides choices to control how text wraps around the picture object and whether the picture should remain fixed at its current position or move with the text. Notice also that the PICTURE TOOLS FORMAT tab becomes active when a picture is selected. You will work with buttons in this tab later in this topic.

⑨ Slide or drag the picture right until the right edge of the picture is aligned at the right margin.

As you move the picture, green alignment guides help you position the image at the top of the paragraph and at the right margin.

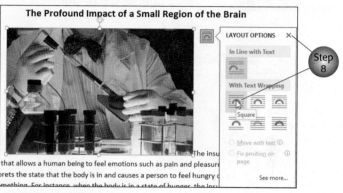

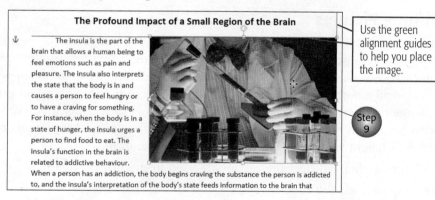

oops!

Image shown not in search results? Choose another suitable image if the one shown is not available.

App Tip

Live layout and alignment guides (also called smart guides) are new to Word 2013.

⑩ Slide or drag the selection handle at the bottom left of the image up and toward the right until the picture is resized to the approximate size shown.

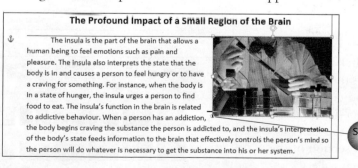

⑪ Save the revised document using the same name (**7.1-InsulaSummary-Your Name**).

Inserting Pictures from Your Computer

Images you have scanned or imported from your digital camera to your PC or mobile device can be inserted into the document using the **Pictures button** in the Illustrations group. The Layout Options button and PICTURE TOOLS FORMAT tab also appear for a picture that has been inserted from your PC.

App Tip

Create your own images by drawing Shapes, creating SmartArt or WordArt, or adding a chart or screenshot. Explore these features if you want to add a graphic but do not have a picture available.

12. Position the insertion point at the beginning of the second paragraph in the document.

13. Tap or click the Pictures button in the Illustrations group of the INSERT tab.

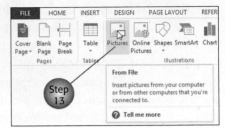

14. At the Insert Picture dialog box, navigate to the Ch7 folder in the Student_Data_Files folder on your USB flash drive and double-tap or double-click the image named *USCPhoto*.

15. Tap or click the Layout Options button, tap or click *Square*, and then close the *LAYOUT OPTIONS* palette.

16. Resize the picture to the approximate size shown in the image at right and position the photo at the left margin.

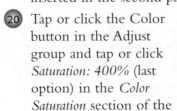

the person will do whatever is necessary to get the substance into his or her system.

If scientists could alter how the insula works in living people, the insula could be used to treat or cure drug addictive behaviour by focusing on regions that are involved in one's decision making. If the insula could be altered to focus on decision making in areas that involve habits, addiction could be controlled. Scientists could weaken some social functions in the insula that give a person the temptation toward a habit such as drugs or alcohol.

Editing Pictures

Buttons in the PICTURE TOOLS FORMAT tab are used to edit an image inserted into a document. Use options in the Adjust group to modify a picture's appearance such as the sharpness, contrast, or color tone, or to apply an artistic effect. Add a border or picture effect with options in the Picture Styles group. Change the picture's position, text wrapping option, order, alignment, or rotation with buttons in the Arrange group. Crop or specify exact measurements for the picture's height and width with buttons in the Size group.

17. Tap or click to select the picture inserted in the first paragraph.

18. Tap or click *Soft Edge Rectangle* (sixth option) in the Picture Styles group of the PICTURE TOOLS FORMAT tab.

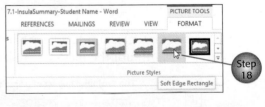

19. Tap or click to select the picture inserted in the second paragraph.

20. Tap or click the Color button in the Adjust group and tap or click *Saturation: 400%* (last option) in the *Color Saturation* section of the drop-down gallery.

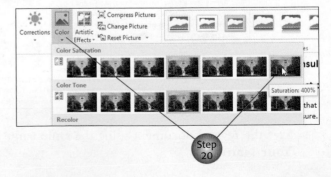

You will notice the picture appears brighter than it did before. Saturation refers to the purity of colors in a photo. Some digital cameras use a low saturation level, making pictures' color seem dull; increasing the saturation level brightens a picture.

Inserting a Caption with a Picture

Adding a caption below a photograph can help a reader understand the picture's context, or you can use captions to number figures in a report. With the **Insert Caption** feature, Word will automatically number pictures, inserting the number after the label Figure.

21 With the picture in the second paragraph still selected, tap or click the REFERENCES tab.

22 Tap or click the Insert Caption button in the Captions group.

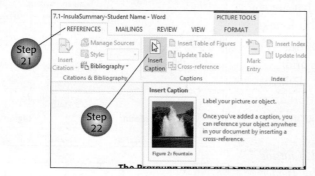

23 At the Caption dialog box, with the insertion point positioned in the *Caption* text box, press the spacebar and type **Insula research is being done at the University of Southern California**.

24 Tap or press Enter or tap or click OK.

25 Tap or click in the document outside the caption box to deselect the caption.

26 Save the revised document using the same name (**7.1-InsulaSummary-Your Name**). Leave the document open for the next topic.

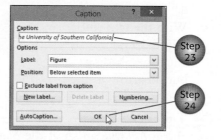

 **Cropping and Removing a Picture's Background**

You can remove unwanted portions of a picture with the Crop tool in the Size group of the PICTURE TOOLS FORMAT tab. Tap or click the Crop button and then use the crop handles to modify the picture. The portion of the image that will remain appears normal, while the cropped area becomes dark gray. Tap or click outside the image to complete the crop action.

The Remove Background button in the PICTURE TOOLS FORMAT tab is another tool you can use to remove portions of a photo. With this button, you can focus on an object in the foreground of a picture and remove the background. For example, with a photo of an airplane in the sky, you can select the airplane and have Word remove the sky in the background.

Adding Borders and Shading and Inserting a Text Box

Topic 7.2

SKILLS

Add a paragraph border

Add shading within a paragraph

Add a border to a page

Insert a text box

 Tutorials

7.2.1 Adding a Border and Shading to Selected Text

7.2.2 Inserting a Watermark, Page Color, and Page Border

7.2.3 Creating a Drop Cap and Inserting a Text Box

Use *Borders and Shading* from the *Borders* gallery to create a custom border in the Borders and Shading dialog box in which you change the border style, color, and width.

oops!

Orange, Accent 6, Lighter 80% not in color gallery? Choose a color similar to light orange, or pick another color of your choice.

Add a border and/or add color behind text (called **shading**) to make text stand out from the rest of a document. You can add borders and shading to a single paragraph, to a group of selected paragraphs, or choose to add a page border to the entire page. You can also add a line that spans the entire page width by choosing *Horizontal Line* at the *Borders* gallery.

A text box is used to set a short passage of text apart from the rest of a document. Word includes several built-in text box styles that can be used for this purpose.

1. With the **7.1-InsulaSummary–Your Name** document open, select the first two lines of the document that are the title and subtitle text.

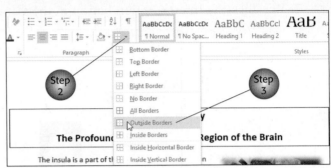

2. Tap or click the HOME tab and then tap or click the Borders button arrow in the Paragraph group.

3. Tap or click *Outside Borders* at the *Borders* gallery.

4. With the text still selected, tap or click the Shading button arrow in the Paragraph group.

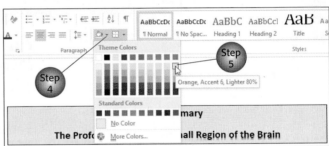

5. Tap or click *Orange, Accent 6, Lighter 80%* at the *Shading* color gallery (last color in second row of *Theme Colors* section).

6. Tap or click in any paragraph to deselect the text.

7. Tap or click the DESIGN tab.

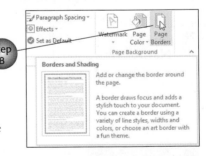

8. Tap or click the **Page Borders button** in the Page Background group.

9. At the Borders and Shading dialog box with the Page Border tab selected, tap or click *Shadow* in the *Setting* section.

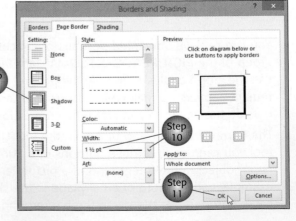

10. Tap or click the *Width* list arrow and then tap or click *1 ½ pt* at the drop-down list.

11. Tap or click OK.

Inserting text inside a box is a way to draw the reader's attention to an important quote or point in a document. A quote inside a text box is called a **pull quote**.

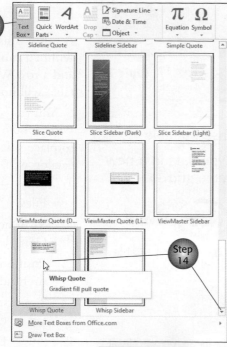

(12) Position the insertion point at the end of the document and tap or click the INSERT tab.

(13) Tap or click the **Text Box button** in the Text group.

(14) Slide or scroll down and then tap or click *Whisp Quote* at the drop-down list.

Word adds the text box with default text already selected inside the text box.

(15) Type **Some people with damage to the insula were able to quit smoking instantly!**

(16) Press and hold or right-click *[Cite your source here]* and choose *Remove Content Control* at the shortcut menu.

(17) Slide or drag the text box (point to the border of the box if using a mouse) to the bottom of the page to the approximate location shown.

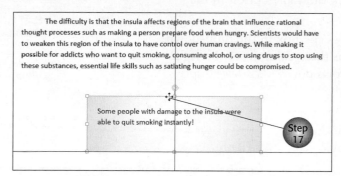

(18) Slide or drag the bottom middle selection handle up to reduce the height of the text box as shown.

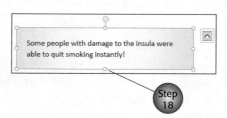

(19) Tap or click in any paragraph to deselect the text box and save the revised document using the same name (**7.1-InsulaSummary-Your Name**).

(20) Close the document.

Quick STEPS

Add a Paragraph Border
1. Select paragraph(s).
2. Tap or click Borders button arrow.
3. Tap or click desired border style.

Add Shading to a Paragraph
1. Select paragraph(s).
2. Tap or click Shading button arrow.
3. Tap or click desired color.

Add a Page Border
1. Tap or click DESIGN tab.
2. Tap or click Page Borders button.
3. Select desired *Setting* and *Style, Color, Width,* or *Art* options.
4. Tap or click OK.

Insert a Text Box
1. Tap or click INSERT tab.
2. Tap or click Text Box button.
3. Tap or click desired text box style.
4. Type text.
5. Move and/or resize box as needed.

Formatting Tools to Edit a Text Box

Use buttons in the DRAWING TOOLS FORMAT tab to edit a text box. You can change the text box shape style, fill, or outline and add shape effects. Edit the appearance of the text inside the box by applying a WordArt style, changing the text fill or outline, adding text effects, or changing the alignment or direction of the text.

Topic 7.3

SKILLS

Insert a table

Type data in a new table grid

7.3   Creating a Table

Use the *Recent Folders* list at the Open tab Backstage view with *Computer* selected to return to the Student_Data_ Files folder with just one tap or click.

The advantage to using a table versus typing information in tabbed columns is that information can wrap around within a table cell.

oops!

Added a new row by mistake? Tap or click the Undo button to remove the extra row.

Inserting a Table

A **table** is used to organize and present data in columns and rows. Text is typed within a **table cell**, which is a rectangular box that is the intersection of a column and a row. When you create a table, you specify the number of columns and rows the table will hold and Word creates a blank grid within which you type the table data.

You can also create a new table using **Quick Tables**, which are predefined tables with sample data that you can replace with your own text. Text that you want to place side-by-side, or in rows, is ideal for a table. For example, a price list or a catalog with items and descriptions is ideal for a table.

1. Open the document **RezMealPlans** from the Ch7 folder in Student_Data_ Files.

2. Save the document as **7.3-RezMealPlans-Your Name** in the Ch7 folder in CompletedTopicsByChapter.

3. Position the insertion point at the left margin in the blank line below the subheading *Meal Plans with Descriptions*.

4. Tap or click the INSERT tab and then tap or click the Table button in the Tables group.

5. Tap or click the box in the drop-down grid that is three columns to the right and two rows down (*3x2 Table* displays above grid).

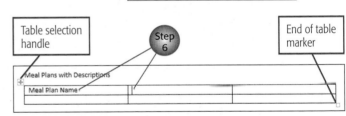

6. With the insertion point positioned in the first table cell, type **Meal Plan Name** and then tap or press Tab, or tap or click in the next cell.

7. Type **Cost** and then tap or press Tab, or tap or click in the next cell.

8. Type **Description** and then tap or press Tab, or tap or click in the first cell in the second row.

9. Type the second row of data as follows. When you finish typing the text in the last column, tap or press Tab to add a new row to the table automatically.

   Minimum $1,900   Suitable for students with small appetites who plan to be away from residence most weekends.

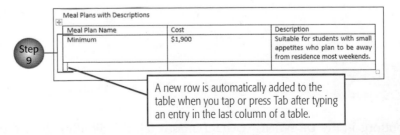

A new row is automatically added to the table when you tap or press Tab after typing an entry in the last column of a table.

10. Type the remainder of the table as shown in Figure 7.1 by completing steps similar to those in Steps 6 to 9, except do not tap or press Tab after typing the last table cell entry.

Meal Plans with Descriptions

Meal Plan Name	Cost	Description
Minimum	$1,900	Suitable for students with small appetites who plan to be away from residence most weekends.
Light	$2,100	Best plan for students with a lighter appetite who spend occasional weekends on campus.
Full	$2,200	Full is the most popular plan. This plan is for students with an average appetite who will stay on campus most weekends.
Plus	$2,300	Students with a hearty appetite who will stay on campus most weekends choose the Plus plan.

The column alignment is Justified because of the document's style set. Generally, cells are aligned left in new tables.

Figure 7.1 Table data for first table in Topic 7.3 with the default design and layout options shown

11 Position the insertion point at the left margin in the blank line below the subheading *Meal Plan Fund Allocations*.

12 Tap or click the Table button in the INSERT tab and then tap or click *Insert Table* at the drop-down list.

You can also insert a new table using a dialog box in which you specify the number of columns and rows.

13 At the Insert Table dialog box, with the value in the *Number of columns* text box already selected, type **5** and then tap or press Tab, or select the value in the *Number of rows* text box.

14 Type **5** and then tap or press Enter, or tap or click OK.

15 Type the data in the new table as shown in Figure 7.2. Tap or click in the paragraph below the table after typing the text in the last table cell.

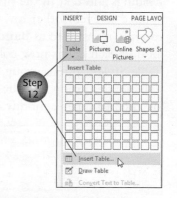
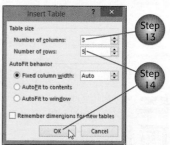

Quick STEPS

Insert a Table
1. Tap or click INSERT tab.
2. Tap or click Table button.
3. Tap or click box in drop-down grid for desired columns and rows.
4. Type table text.
OR
1. Tap or click INSERT tab.
2. Tap or click Table button.
3. Tap or click *Insert Table*.
4. Type number of columns.
5. Change *Number of rows* to desired value.
6. Tap or click OK.
7. Type table text.

Meal Plan Fund Allocations

Meal Plan Name	Total Cost	Operating Fund	Basic Fund	Flex Fund
Minimum	$1,900	$100	$1,575	$225
Light	$2,100	$100	$1,725	$275
Full	$2,200	$100	$1,775	$325
Plus	$2,300	$100	$1,850	$350

Note that the Basic fund is tax exempt and is designed for use at all on-campus restaurants. Flex fund purchases are taxable.

Tap or click outside the table grid after typing the last table cell entry to avoid adding a new row to the table.

Figure 7.2 Table data for second table in Topic 7.3

16 Save the document using the same name (**7.3-RezMealPlans-Your Name**). Leave the document open for the next topic.

Formatting and Modifying a Table

Topic 7.4

Once a table has been inserted into the document, use buttons in the TABLE TOOLS DESIGN and LAYOUT tabs to format the table's appearance and add or delete rows and columns. Choose a predesigned collection of formatting options that add borders, shading, and color to a table from the **Table Styles** gallery.

SKILLS

Apply and customize a table style

Insert and delete rows and columns

Change column width

Change cell alignment

Merge cells

 **Tutorials**

7.4.1 Changing the Table Design

7.4.2 Changing the Table Layout

7.4.3 Merging and Splitting Cells and Tables

① With the **7.3-RezMealPlans-Your Name** document open, position the insertion point in any table cell within the first table.

② Tap or click the TABLE TOOLS DESIGN tab.

③ Tap or click the More button (displays with a bar and down-pointing arrow) in the *Table Styles* gallery.

④ Tap or click *Grid Table 4 – Accent 2* (third option in fourth row in *Grid Tables* section).

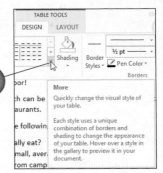

Notice the formatting applied to the column headings and text in the first column. Shading applied to every other row makes the table data easier to read (referred to as **banded rows**) and the border around each cell is now colored. The check boxes in the Table Style Options group, the Shading button in the Table Styles group, and the buttons in the Borders group are used to further modify the table formatting.

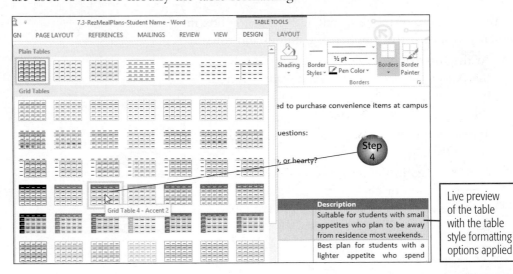

Live preview of the table with the table style formatting options applied

⑤ Tap or click the *First Column* check box in the Table Style Options group to remove the check mark.

Notice the bold formatting is removed from the text in the first column.

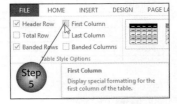

6 Select the column headings in the first row of the table, tap or click the Shading button arrow in the Mini toolbar or in the Table Styles group of the TABLE TOOLS DESIGN tab, and then tap or click *Orange, Accent 2, Darker 50%* (sixth option in last row of *Theme Colors* section).

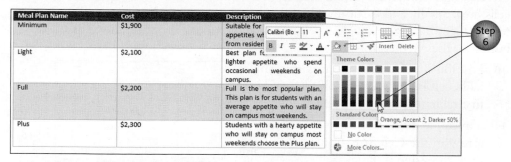

Inserting and Deleting Columns and Rows

Buttons in the Rows & Columns group of the TABLE TOOLS LAYOUT tab are used to insert or delete columns or rows. Position the insertion point within a table row and tap or click the Insert Above or Insert Below button to add a new row to the table. The Insert Left and Insert Right buttons are used to add a new column to the table.

Position the insertion point within a table cell, select multiple rows or columns or select the entire table, and then tap or click the Delete button to delete cells, a column, a row, or the table.

7 Position the insertion point within any table cell in the third row of the first table (begins with *Light*).

8 Tap or click the TABLE TOOLS LAYOUT tab.

9 Tap or click the Delete button in the Rows & Columns group.

10 Tap or click *Delete Rows* at the drop-down list.

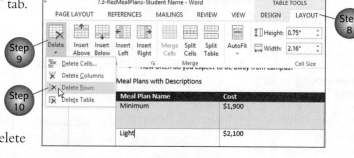

11 Position the insertion point within any table cell in the third row of the second table (begins with *Light*), tap or click the Delete button, and tap or click *Delete Rows*.

12 Position the insertion point within any table cell in the last column of the first table.

13 Tap or click the Insert Left button in the Rows & Columns group.

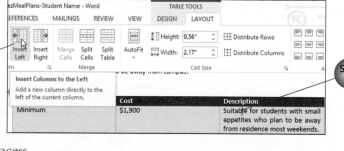

A new column is created between the *Cost* and *Description* columns. Notice that Word adjusts each column to be the same width. New rows are inserted by following a similar process.

14 Position the insertion point within the table cell in the first row of the new column (between *Cost* and *Description*) and type **Daily Spending**.

15 Type the values below the column heading in rows 2, 3, and 4 as follows:

$17.38

$20.23

$21.12

Modifying Column Width and Alignment and Merging Cells

Adjust the width of a column by dragging the border line between columns left or right. You can also enter precise width measurements in the *Width* text box in the Cell Size group. Use the buttons in the Alignment group to align text within cells horizontally and vertically. Combine two or more cells into one cell using the Merge Cells button or divide a cell into two or more cells using the Split Cells button in the Merge group.

16 Position the insertion point within any table cell in the second column of the first table (column heading is *Cost*).

17 Tap or click the *Width* down-pointing arrow in the Cell Size group until the value is 1".

You can also drag the right column border left or right to resize a column width or select the value in the text box and type a measurement value.

18 Position the insertion point within any table cell in the last column of the first table (column heading is *Description*) and tap or click the *Width* up-pointing arrow until the value is 2.3".

19 With the insertion point still positioned within the last column of the first table, tap or click the Select button in the Table group and then tap or click *Select Column* at the drop-down list.

20 Tap or click the Align Top Left button in the Alignment group (first button).

21 Select the first column in the first table (column heading is *Meal Plan Name*) and tap or click the Align Center button in the Alignment group (second button in second row).

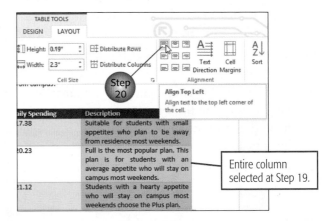

Entire column selected at Step 19.

22 Repeat step 21 to Align Center the second and third columns in the first table.

Steps 21-22

Meal Plans with Descriptions			
Meal Plan Name	Cost	Daily Spending	Description
Minimum	$1,900	$17.38	Suitable for students with small appetites who plan to be away from residence most weekends.
Full	$2,200	$20.23	Full is the most popular plan. This plan is for students with an average appetite who will stay on campus most weekends.
Plus	$2,300	$21.12	Students with a hearty appetite who will stay on campus most weekends choose the Plus plan.

23. Position the insertion point within any table cell in the first row of the second table and tap or click the Insert Above button in the Rows & Columns group.

24. With the new row already selected, tap or click the Merge Cells button in the Merge group.

25. With the new row still selected, type **Breakdown of Meal Plan Cost by Fund** and then tap or click the Align Top Center button in the Alignment group (second button in first row).

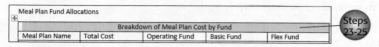

Steps 23-25

oops!

Merged row selected too? Select the cells by sliding or dragging with a mouse—do not use the Select button because *Select Column* will include the merged cell.

26. Select the column headings and all of the values in columns 2, 3, 4, and 5 in the second table and then tap or click the Align Center button.

27. With the insertion point positioned within any table cell in the second table, tap or click the Select button and then tap or click *Select Table*.

28. Tap or click the TABLE TOOLS DESIGN tab.

29. Tap or click the Borders button in the Borders group and then tap or click *No Border* at the drop-down list.

App Tip

You can also select the table with a mouse by clicking the Table selection handle at the top left corner of the table.

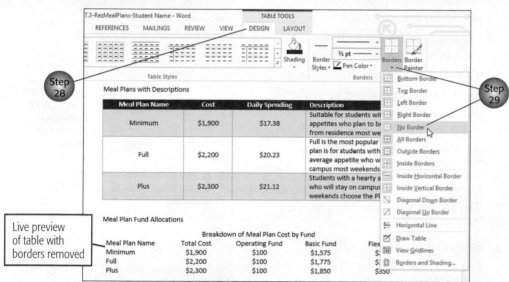

Step 28

Step 29

Live preview of table with borders removed

30. Tap or click in the paragraph below the table to deselect the table.

31. Apply the Heading 2 style to the text *Meal Plans with Descriptions* and *Meal Plan Fund Allocations* above the first and second tables.

32. Save the document using the same name (**7.3-RezMealPlans-Your Name**) and then close the document.

App Tip

Create a table for any type of columnar text instead of setting tabs—tables are simpler to create and have more formatting options.

ALTERNATIVE method

In this topic you used buttons in the TABLE TOOLS DESIGN and LAYOUT tabs to format and modify tables. Press and hold or right-click within a table cell or with table cells selected to display a context-sensitive shortcut menu and Mini toolbar. Use options from the shortcut menu or Mini toolbar to insert or delete cells, columns, or rows, merge or split cells, change a border style, or modify table properties.

Topic 7.5

SKILLS

Change page orientation

Change margins

Insert a page break

 Tutorials

7.5.1 Changing Margins, Page Orientation, and Paper Size

7.5.2 Inserting Page Numbers and Page Breaks

7.5.3 Inserting Section Breaks

7.5.4 Creating Newspaper Columns

Use the Size button in the Page Setup group to change the paper size to legal (8.5 x 14), envelope, or several other predefined photo or index card sizes.

App Tip

The Columns button in the Page Setup group formats a document into two or more newspaper-style columns of text.

Changing Page Layout Options

By default, new documents in Word are set up for a letter-sized page (8.5 x 11 inches) in portrait orientation with one-inch margins at the left, right, top, and bottom. **Portrait** orientation means that the text on the page is vertically oriented with a 6.5-inch line length (8.5 inches minus two inches for the left and right margins). This is the orientation commonly used for most documents and books. You can change to **landscape** orientation, where the text is rotated to the wider side of the page with a 9-inch line length.

1. Open the document **ChildLitBookRpt** from the Ch7 folder in Student_Data_Files.

2. Save the document as **7.5-ChildLitBookRpt-Your Name** in the Ch7 folder in CompletedTopicsByChapter.

3. Tap or click the PAGE LAYOUT tab.

4. Tap or click the Orientation button in the Page Setup group and then tap or click *Landscape*.

Notice the width of the page is extended, and the page is now wider than it is tall.

5. Slide or scroll down to view the document in landscape orientation.

6. With the insertion point positioned at the top of the document, tap or click the Margins button in the Page Setup group.

7. Tap or click *Custom Margins* at the drop-down list.

8. With the insertion point positioned in the *Top* text box in the *Margins* section of the Page Setup dialog box, tap or press Tab twice, or select the current value in the *Left* text box and type **1.2**.

9. Tap or press Tab, or select the current value in the *Right* text box, type **1.2**, and tap or press Enter, or tap or click OK.

10. Slide or scroll down to view the document with the new left and right margin settings.

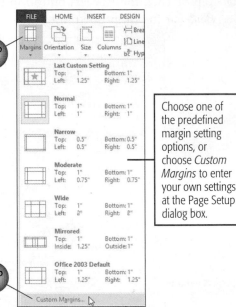

Choose one of the predefined margin setting options, or choose *Custom Margins* to enter your own settings at the Page Setup dialog box.

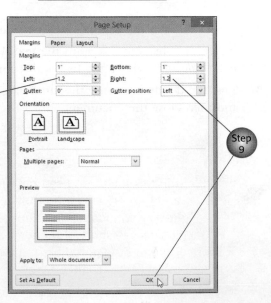

Sometimes you want to end a page before the point at which Word ends a page automatically and starts a new page (referred to as a **soft page break**). Soft page breaks occur when the maximum number of lines that can fit within the current page size and margins has been reached. A page break that you insert at a different location is called a **hard page break**.

11 Position the insertion point at the left margin next to the subtitle *The Allegories* near the bottom of page 1.

12 Tap or click the INSERT tab.

13 Tap or click the Page Break button in the Pages group.

Notice that all of the text from the insertion point onward is moved to page 2.

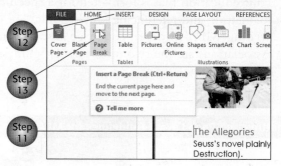

14 Slide or scroll up and down to view the book report with the new page break.

15 Save the document using the same name (**7.5-ChildLitBookRpt-Your Name**) and then close the document.

ALTERNATIVE method You can also insert a Page Break using the Breaks button in the Page Setup group of the PAGE LAYOUT tab or by using the keyboard command Ctrl + Enter.

App Tip

Insert hard page breaks as your last step in preparing a document because hard page breaks do not adjust if you add or delete text.

oops!

Page break at wrong location? Press Backspace until the page break is deleted or use Undo to remove the page break. Position the insertion point at the correct location and try Step 13 again.

Quick **STEPS**

Change to Landscape Orientation
1. Tap or click PAGE LAYOUT tab.
2. Tap or click Orientation button.
3. Tap or click *Landscape*.

Change Margins
1. Tap or click PAGE LAYOUT tab.
2. Tap or click Margins button.
3. Tap or click predefined margin option.

OR

1. Tap or click PAGE LAYOUT tab.
2. Tap or click Margins button.
3. Tap or click *Custom Margins*.
4. Set custom measurements.
5. Tap or click OK.

Insert a Hard Page Break
1. Position insertion point.
2. Tap or click INSERT tab.
3. Tap or click Page Break button.

 **Beyond Basics** **Changing Page Layout for a Section of a Document**

By default, changes such as margins or orientation affect the entire document. A **section break** is inserted to change page layout options for a portion of a document. The Breaks button in the Page Setup group of the PAGE LAYOUT tab is used to insert a section break. Choose *Next Page* to insert a section break that also starts a new page or choose *Continuous* to have the section break start at the insertion point position without starting a new page. For example, use section breaks if you want one page in a document to be landscape while the other pages are portrait. To do this, insert a section break where you want a landscape page, change the orientation to landscape, then insert another section break after the landscape page and return the orientation to portrait.

Formatting a Research Paper with a Header and Page Numbers

Topic 7.6

SKILLS

Insert a header

Insert page numbers

Chances are you will have to submit a research paper or essay during the course of your education that is formatted for a specific **style guide** (a set of rules for paper formatting and referencing). Style guides are used in academic and professional writing; MLA (Modern Language Association) and APA (American Psychological Association) are the two most popular guides. See Table 7.1 for general MLA and APA guidelines.

Table 7.1	Formatting and Page Layout Guidelines for MLA and APA	
Item	**MLA**	**APA**
Paper size and margins	8.5 x 11 with one-inch margins	8.5 x 11 with one-inch margins
Font size	12-point; typeface is not specified other than that it should be easily readable	12-point, with Times New Roman the preferred typeface
Line and paragraph spacing	2.0 with no spacing between paragraphs	2.0 with no spacing between paragraphs
Paragraph indent	Indent first line one-half inch	Indent first line one-half inch
Page numbering	Top right of each page one space after your last name	Top right of each page with paper's title all uppercase at the left margin on the same line
Title page	No (unless specifically requested by your instructor)	Yes Running Head: title of the paper at left margin all uppercase with page number at right margin one-inch from the top. In the upper half of the page centered horizontally include: Title of the paper Your name School name
First page	Top left corner (double-spaced): Your name Instructor's name Course title Date A double-space below the above headings center the title (title case) and then begin the paper.	Center the word *Abstract* at the top of the page. Type a brief summary of the paper in a single paragraph in block format (no indents). Limit yourself to approximately 150 words. Start paper on a new page after the Abstract with the paper's title centered (title case) at the top of the page.
Bibliography	Create separate Works Cited page at end of document organized alphabetically by author.	Create separate References page at end of document organized alphabetically by author.

Check This Out

owl.english.purdue.edu/owl/ resource/747/01

Go here for a comprehensive MLA guide.

A **header** is text that appears at the top of each page and a **footer** is text that appears at the bottom of each page. Word provides several predefined headers and footers or you can create your own. Page numbers are added to a document within a header or footer.

1. Open the document **CohabitationEssay** from the Ch7 folder in Student_ Data_Files.

2. Save the document as **7.6–CohabitationEssay–Your Name** in the Ch7 folder in CompletedTopicsByChapter.

3. Slide or scroll down and review the formatting in the essay. Notice the paper size, font, margins, line and paragraph spacing, and first line indents are already formatted.

4. Position the insertion point at the beginning of the document and replace the text *Toni McBride* with your first and last name.

   The first four lines of this report are set up in MLA format for a first page; however, you need to add the page numbering for an MLA report.

5. Tap or click the INSERT tab and tap or click the Header button in the Header & Footer group.

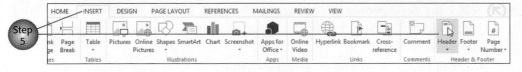

6. Tap or click *Edit Header* at the drop-down list.

7. Tap or press Tab twice to move the insertion point to the right margin, type your last name, and then press the spacebar.

8. Tap or click the **Page Number button** in the Header & Footer group of the HEADER & FOOTER TOOLS DESIGN tab.

9. Tap or point to *Current Position* and then tap or click *Plain Number*.

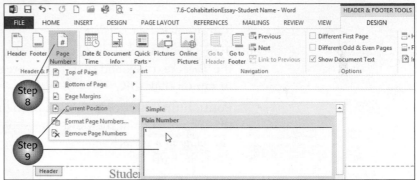

10. Select your last name and the page number in the Header pane.

11. Tap or click the Font button arrow in the Mini toolbar, slide or scroll down the font list, and then tap or click *Times New Roman*.

12. Tap or click the Font Size button arrow in the Mini toolbar and then tap or click *12*.

13. Tap or click within the Header pane to deselect the text.

14. Tap or click the Close Header and Footer button in the Close group of the HEADER & FOOTER TOOLS DESIGN tab.

15. Slide or scroll down through the document to view your last name and the page number at the top of each page.

16. Save the document using the same name (**7.6-CohabitationEssay-Your Name**). Leave the document open for the next topic.

Quick STEPS

Insert a Header or Footer
1. Tap or click INSERT tab.
2. Tap or click Header or Footer button.
3. Tap or click built-in option or choose *Edit Header* or *Edit Footer*.
4. Type text and/or add options as needed.
5. Tap or click Close Header and Footer button.

Insert Page Numbering
1. Within Header or Footer pane, tap or click Page Number button.
2. Tap or point to *Current Position*.
3. Tap or click page number option.
4. Tap or click Close Header and Footer button.

oops!

Mini toolbar not visible? Tap or click the HOME tab and change the font and font size using the buttons in the Font group. Tap or click the HEADER & FOOTER TOOLS DESIGN tab at Step 13.

 **Check This Out**

owl.english.purdue.edu/owl/resource/560/01

Go here for a comprehensive APA guide.

 **Beyond Basics**

Removing Page Number from First Page

In many reports or books, a header and/or page number is suppressed on the first page. Tap or click the *Different First Page* check box in the HEADER & FOOTER TOOLS DESIGN tab to create a First Page header that you can leave blank.

Topic 7.7

SKILLS

Edit a citation

Insert a citation

SNAP Tutorial

7.7 Inserting and Modifying Sources and Citations

Inserting and Editing Citations

Direct quotations copied from sources or material you have written in an academic paper that is paraphrased from a source needs to be referenced in a **citation** (source of the information used). Word provides tools to manage sources, insert citations, and edit citations.

① With the **7.6-CohabitationEssay-Your Name** document open, tap or click the REFERENCES tab.

② Look at the *Style* option in the Citations & Bibliography group. If the *Style* is not *MLA*, tap or click the *Style* arrow and then tap or click *MLA* at the drop-down list. (You may need to slide or scroll down the list.)

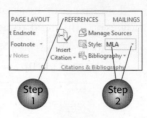

You will begin by editing an existing citation.

③ Position the insertion point within the *(Jay par. 12)* citation at the end of the indented quotation after the first paragraph (begins with *Cohabitation in the. . .*) to display the citation placeholder.

④ Tap or click the Citation Options arrow that appears.

⑤ Tap or click *Edit Citation*.

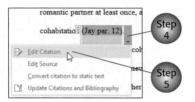

⑥ Type **par. 9** at the Edit Citation dialog box in the *Pages* text box and then tap or press Enter, or tap or click OK.

⑦ Position the insertion point left of the period that ends the last sentence in the third paragraph that begins *According to a research study done at Ohio . . ,* and press the spacebar.

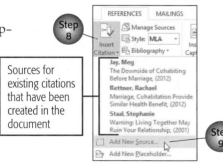

⑧ Tap or click the Insert Citation button in the Citations & Bibliography group.

⑨ Tap or click *Add New Source* at the drop-down list.

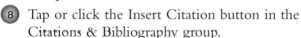

Sources for existing citations that have been created in the document

⑩ At the Create Source dialog box, tap or click the *Type of Source* list arrow and then tap or click *Document From Web site* at the drop-down list. (You may need to slide or scroll down the list.)

⑪ Tap or click in the *Author* text box and type **Grabmeier, J.**.

⑫ Tap or click in the *Name of Web Page* text box and type **Couples Live Together for Convenience, Not to Test Marriage**.

⑬ Tap or press Tab, or tap or click in the *Name of Web Site* text box and type **Ohio State University**.

⑭ Continue tapping or pressing Tab, or tapping or clicking in the designated text boxes and typing the information as shown below:

Year	**2004**	*Month Accessed*	**November**
Month	**July**	*Day Accessed*	**15**
Day	**28**	*Medium*	**Web**
Year Accessed	**2015**		

Did You Know

In the seventh edition of the MLA handbook, URLs are no longer required. MLA advises writers to include URLs only if a reader is unlikely to find the source without the web address.

15. Tap or click OK.

16. Tap or click in the *(Grabmeier)* citation, tap or click the Citation Options arrow, and then tap or click *Edit Citation*.

17. Type **2-3** in the *Pages* text box at the Edit Citation dialog box and then tap or click OK.

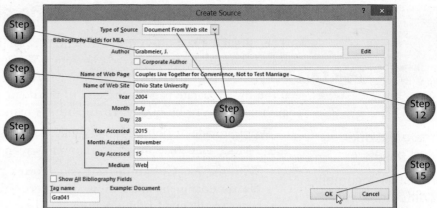

18. Position the insertion point left of the period at the end of the indented quotation on page 2 (third paragraph that begins *In the past 25 years. . .*), press the spacebar, tap or click the Insert Citation button, and then tap or click *Add New Source*.

19. Change the *Type of Source* to *Journal Article* and then tap or click to insert a check mark in the *Show All Bibliography Fields* check box near the bottom left of the dialog box.

20. Enter the information in the designated text boxes as follows. (You will have to slide or scroll down to find the *Volume* and *Issue* text boxes):

Author	**Popenoe, D.**
Title	**Cohabitation, Marriage, and Child Wellbeing: A Cross-National Perspective**
Journal Name	**Society**
Year	**2009**
Month	**July**
Day	**9**
Pages	**429–486**
Volume	**46**
Issue	**5**
Medium	**Print**

21. Edit the citation to add *432* as the page number by completing steps similar to Steps 16 to 17.

22. Position the insertion point left of the period at the end of the quotation in the third paragraph on page 3 that reads *"More than 40% of . . . convert to marriage"* and press the spacebar.

23. Tap or click the Insert Citation button and tap or click *Popenoe, D.* at the drop-down list.

24. Edit the citation to add *480* as the page number.

25. Save the document using the same name (**7.6-CohabitationEssay-Your Name**). Leave the document open for the next topic.

Insert a Citation with a New Source
1. Position insertion point.
2. Tap or click REFERENCES tab.
3. Tap or click Insert Citation button.
4. Tap or click *Add New Source*.
5. If necessary, change *Type of Source*.
6. Enter information as needed.
7. Tap or click OK.

Insert a Citation with an Existing Source
1. Position insertion point.
2. Tap or click REFERENCES tab.
3. Tap or click Insert Citation button.
4. Tap or click source.

Edit a Citation
1. Position insertion point in citation.
2. Tap or click Citation Options button.
3. Tap or click *Edit Citation*.
4. Type page reference.
5. Tap or click OK.

Did You Know ?

MLA recommends the abbreviations n. pag. for a source without page numbers, n.d. for a source without a date, and N.p. for a source without a publisher.

 **Editing a Source**

To change the source information for a citation, position the insertion point within the citation, tap or click the Citation Options arrow, and then tap or click *Edit Source*. This opens the Edit Source dialog box where you can make changes to the bibliography fields for the reference.

Creating a Works Cited Page and Using Word Views

The Bibliography button in the Citations & Bibliography group of the REFERENCES tab is used to generate a **Works Cited** page for MLA papers or a References page for APA papers. The MLA style guide requires a Works Cited page to be on a separate page at the end of the document organized alphabetically by author's name, or by title when an author's name is absent.

Word provides various views in which to review a document, including a new Read Mode view that provides maximum screen space for reading longer documents.

Topic 7.8

SKILLS

Create a Works Cited page

Browse a document in different views

 Tutorials

7.8.1 Inserting a Works Cited Page

7.8.2 Changing Document Views

1. With the **7.6-CohabitationEssay-Your Name** document open, move the insertion point to the end of the document and tap or press Enter to move to a new blank line.

2. Tap or click the INSERT tab and then tap or click the Page Break button to start a new page.

3. Tap or click the REFERENCES tab.

4. Tap or click the **Bibliography button** in the Citations & Bibliography group.

5. Tap or click *Works Cited* in the drop-down list.

Word automatically generates the Works Cited page. In the next steps you will format the text to match the font, size, and spacing of the rest of the document.

6. Select all of the text in the Works Cited page.

Word surrounds the entire text on the page with a border and displays a Bibliographies button and an Update Citations and Bibliography button along the top of the placeholder.

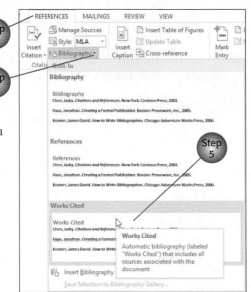

App Tip

Do not change formatting until you are sure your Works Cited page is complete because the page will revert to predefined formats if you make changes to sources and update the Works Cited page.

7. Tap or click the HOME tab and make the following changes to the selected text:

   a. Change the font to 12-point Times New Roman.

   b. Change the line spacing to 2.0 and remove space after paragraphs.

8. Select the title text *Works Cited*, change the font color to Automatic (black), and center the title.

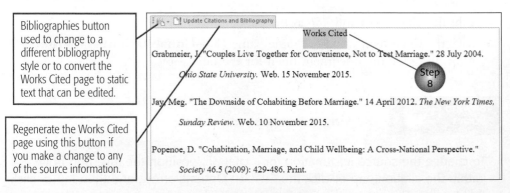

Bibliographies button used to change to a different bibliography style or to convert the Works Cited page to static text that can be edited.

Regenerate the Works Cited page using this button if you make a change to any of the source information.

Did You Know?

The seventh edition of the MLA guide now requires all entries in a reference list to include the medium in which the reference has been published; for example: Film, Print, or Web.

The default view for new documents is **Print Layout view**, which displays the document as it will appear when printed. **Read Mode view** displays a document full screen in columns, allowing you to read longer documents more easily without screen elements such as the QAT and ribbon. **Draft view** hides print elements such as headers and footers. **Web Layout view** displays a document as it would appear as a web page, and **Outline view** displays content as bulleted points.

9 Position the insertion point at the beginning of the document.

10 Tap or click the VIEW tab and then tap or click the Read Mode button in the Views group.

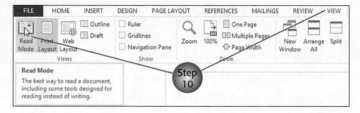

Use Read Mode to view a document without editing.

11 Tap or click the Next Screen button (right-pointing arrow inside circle at the middle right side of the screen) to move to the next screen until you have reached the end of the document.

12 Tap or click the VIEW tab, tap or point to *Layout*, and then tap or click *Paper Layout* at the drop-down list to display the document as single pages instead of screens in columns.

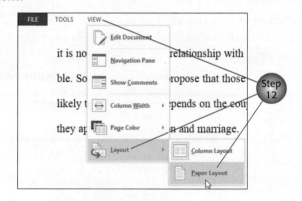

13 Browse the document.

14 Tap or click the VIEW tab and then tap or click *Edit Document* to return to Print Layout view.

15 Tap or click the Draft button in the Views group of the VIEW tab to view just the text in the document and then browse the document.

16 Tap or click the Print Layout view button near the right end of the Status bar.

17 Save the document using the same name (**7.6-CohabitationEssay-Your Name**). Leave the document open for the next topic.

New to Word 2013 is the *Welcome back!* balloon that appears near the lower right corner of the screen when you reopen a document. Tap or click the balloon to scroll to where you left the document when you closed it.

Turn on the Navigation pane (VIEW tab, Navigation Pane) and tap or click PAGES to move through a document by tapping or clicking miniature page thumbnails.

Quick STEPS

Generate a Works Cited Page
1. Position insertion point at end of document.
2. Insert page break.
3. Tap or click REFERENCES tab.
4. Tap or click Bibliography button.
5. Tap or click *Works Cited*.
6. Format as required.

Change Document View
1. Tap or click VIEW tab.
2. Tap or click desired view button.

Footnotes and Endnotes

In some academic papers, you need to insert footnotes or endnotes. **Footnotes** are explanatory comments or source information placed at the bottom of a page. **Endnotes** are explanatory comments or source information that appear at the end of a section or document. Position the insertion point and use the Insert Footnote or Insert Endnote button in the REFERENCES tab to add these elements.

Topic 7.9

SKILLS

Insert comments

Change the markup view

Reply to a comment

Mark a comment done

 **Tutorial**

7.9 Inserting and Editing Comments

 App Tip

If necessary, open the Word Options dialog box from the FILE tab to change the user name to another name.

Inserting and Replying to Comments

Comments is a collaborative tool in Word that is useful when working on a document with another person or team. A **comment** is a short note associated with text that provides explanatory information to a reader. A comment can also be used to pose a question to document reviewers. New to Word 2013 is the ability to reply to a comment and mark a comment as done.

When working in teams or on group projects, consider using comments in documents to explain portions of your text, ask questions of your teammates, or add general feedback.

1. With the **7.6-CohabitationEssay-Your Name** document open, position the insertion point at the beginning of the document.

2. Select the word *Canada* at the end of the first paragraph in the document.

3. Tap or click the REVIEW tab.

4. Tap or click the New Comment button in the Comments group.

Word opens a new comment box (referred to as a comment balloon) in the **Markup Area** at the right side of the screen.

5. Type **Consider looking for research specific to Europe?** and then tap or click in the document outside the comment box.

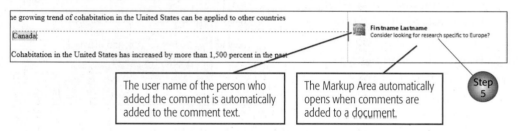

The user name of the person who added the comment is automatically added to the comment text.

The Markup Area automatically opens when comments are added to a document.

6. Select *In the 1960s* in the second sentence of the third paragraph.

7. Tap or click the New Comment button.

8. Type **Change the final copy to: Until the 1990s** and then tap or click in the document.

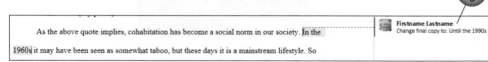

9. Position the insertion point at the beginning of the subheading *Advantages of Cohabitation* near the bottom of the first page and insert a page break.

10. Position the insertion point at the beginning of the subheading *Disadvantages of Cohabitation* near the bottom of the second page and insert a page break.

11. Position the insertion point at the beginning of the document.

12. If necessary, tap or click the REVIEW tab.

13 Tap or click the Display for Review button arrow in the Tracking group (currently displays *All Markup* or *Simple Markup*), and tap or click *No Markup* at the drop-down list.

Notice the two comments on page 1 are removed from the document display.

14 Tap or click the Display for Review button arrow and tap or click *Simple Markup* at the drop-down list.

15 Tap or point to the first comment box on page 1.

Notice Word shows a callout line pointing to the text with which the comment is associated. The comment box also displays a Reply button.

16 Tap or click the Reply button (displays as a small white page with a left-pointing arrow) in the first comment box.

17 Type **Asked Prof Williamson and she said it was not necessary** and then tap or click in the document.

Notice the reply comment text is indented below the original comment in a conversation-style dialogue.

18 Edit the second sentence in the third paragraph from *In the 1960s* to *Until the 1990s* by tapping or clicking after *In* (and *60*), using Backspace to remove text, and then typing the new text. (You are editing using this method so that the comment is not deleted.)

19 Press and hold or right-click the second comment box on page 1 and then tap or click *Mark Comment Done* at the shortcut menu.

20 Tap or click in the document outside the comment box.

Notice the comment text is dimmed for the comment marked as done.

Comment marked as done is displayed as dimmed text.

21 Save the document using the same name (**7.6-CohabitationEssay-Your Name**) and then close the document.

App Tip

Simple Markup revision view is a new view for Word 2013 that sports a less cluttered look at a document's changes and comments.

App Tip

You can also delete a comment instead of marking the comment done.

Quick STEPS

Insert a Comment
1. Position insertion point or select text.
2. Tap or click REVIEW tab.
3. Tap or click New Comment button.
4. Type comment text.
5. Tap or click in document.

Reply to a Comment
1. Tap or point to comment box.
2. Tap or click Reply button.
3. Type reply text.
4. Tap or click in document.

Mark a Comment Done
1. Press and hold or right-click comment.
2. Tap or click *Mark Comment Done*.

Change Display for Review
1. Tap or click REVIEW tab.
2. Tap or click Display for Review button arrow.
3. Tap or click desired markup view.

Tracking Changes made to a Document

In situations in which a document will be circulated to multiple readers for revisions, turning on track changes is a good idea. Track changes (REVIEW tab) logs each person's insertions, deletions, and formatting changes. Changes can be reviewed, accepted, and rejected in the Revisions pane.

Creating a Resume and Cover Letter from Templates

Topic 7.10

SKILLS

Create a resume

Create a cover letter

 Tutorials

7.10.1 Using Vertical Alignment

7.10.2 Creating and Printing Envelopes

7.10.3 Preparing Mailing Labels

Word provides more than 40 professionally designed and formatted resume and cover letter templates that take the work out of designing and formatting these two crucial documents, letting you focus your efforts on writing documents that will win you a job interview!

1. Tap or click the FILE tab and then tap or click New.

2. At the New tab Backstage view, tap or click <u>Resume</u> below the *Search for online templates* search box.

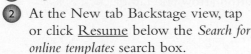

3. Tap or click *Entry Level* in the *Category* list.

4. Tap or click *Resume for recent college graduate* in the *Templates* gallery.

5. Tap or click the Create button.

6. Select your name in the *Author* placeholder and type **Dana Jelic**.

7. Select and delete the *Street Address* and *City, ST ZIP Code* placeholders.

8. Select the *Phone Number* placeholder and type **800-555-4577**.

9. Select the *E-mail Address* placeholder and type **jelic@domain.net**.

This is the number of available templates in the gallery for the category and will vary as templates are frequently updated.

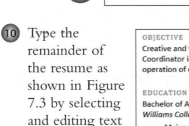

Print multiple copies of a resume by changing the *Copies* value at the Print tab Backstage view.

Check This Out

career-advice.monster.com

Go here for articles and examples on how to write effective resumes and cover letters.

Did You Know?

Most recruiters advise job seekers to begin a job search with a reverse chronological resume style which lists your work experience from most to least recent.

10. Type the remainder of the resume as shown in Figure 7.3 by selecting and editing text in placeholders, or by deleting placeholders or text.

OBJECTIVE
Creative and team-oriented liberal arts graduate seeking an entry-level position as a Conference Coordinator in order to leverage planning and communication skills to organize and ensure seamless operation of conferences in a topnotch facility.

EDUCATION
Bachelor of Arts degree   June 2015
Williams College, MA
- Major: English
- Minor: Sociology
- Overall GPA 3.91; Honors in each semester
- Completed a semester in Helsingor, Denmark, January 2014

SKILLS & ABILITIES
Organization and Communication
- Campus Editor at *The Williams Record*, independent student newspaper for Williams College. Wrote and edited columns for regular features and assisted Editor-in-chief with other newspaper organization tasks.
- Community and Diversity Rep for College Council, 2013 to 2015

EXPERIENCE
Library Assistant   2013 to Present
Sawyer Library, Williams College
- Check in and out library materials at circulation desk
- Sort and shelve books

English Peer Tutor   2013 to 2014
Williams College
- Tutored English students
- Organized English peer study group

Figure 7.3 Resume text for Topic 7.10

⑪ Save the document as **7.10-JelicResume-Your Name** in the Ch7 folder in CompletedTopicsByChapter. Tap or click OK if a message appears about upgrading to the newest file format.

⑫ Close the resume document and display the New tab Backstage view.

⑬ Tap or click <u>Letters</u> below the *Search for online templates* search box and then tap or click *Cover Letter* in the *Category* list.

⑭ Tap or click the *Sample resume cover letter in response to a technical position advertisement* and then tap or click the Create button.

⑮ Create the letter as shown in Figure 7.4 by selecting and editing text in placeholders, or by deleting placeholders or text.

Use the Envelopes or Labels button in the Create group of the MAILINGS tab to generate an envelope or label for a letter.

Create a Resume
1. Tap or click FILE tab.
2. Tap or click New.
3. Tap or click <u>Resume</u>.
4. Tap or click category if desired.
5. Tap or click desired template.
6. Tap or click Create button.
7. Edit as required.

Create a Cover Letter
1. Tap or click FILE tab.
2. Tap or click New.
3. Tap or click <u>Letters</u>.
4. Tap or click *Cover Letter* category.
5. Tap or click desired template.
6. Tap or click Create button.
7. Edit as required.

Dana Jelic
880 Main Street
Williamstown, MA 01267

May 12, 2015

Ms. Patel
Conference Manager
Williams College
39 Chapin Hall Drive
Williamstown, MA 01267

Dear Ms. Patel:

I am writing in response to your advertisement in The Williams Record for a Conference Coordinator. After reading your job description, I am confident that my planning and organizational skills and my passion for representing Williams College are a perfect match for this position. As a graduate of Williams College I am very familiar with the college venues and local area attractions.

I would bring to Williams College a broad range of skills, including:

- Excellent time management skills
- Ability to organize complex tasks
- Experienced communicator

I would welcome the opportunity to further discuss this position with you. If you have questions or would like to schedule an interview, please contact me by phone at 800-555-4577 or by email at jelic@domain.net. I have enclosed my resume for your review, and I look forward to hearing from you.

Figure 7.4 Cover letter text for Topic 7.10

⑯ Tap or click the PAGE LAYOUT tab and then tap or click the Page Setup dialog box launcher.

⑰ If necessary, tap or click the Layout tab in the Page Setup dialog box.

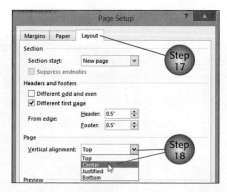

⑱ Tap or click the *Vertical alignment* list arrow, tap or click *Center* at the drop-down list, and then tap or click OK.

⑲ Save the document as **7.10-JelicCoverLetter-Your Name** in the Ch7 folder in CompletedTopicsByChapter and then close the document.

Vertically center a letter to make sure the letter has a professional appearance. For short letters, add extra space between letter elements to balance the content on the page.

Concepts Review

Topic	Key Concepts	Key Terms
Inserting, Editing, and Labeling Images in a Document	Graphic elements assist with comprehension and/or add visual appeal to documents. Insert a picture from the clip art gallery, the Web, or an online service such as Flickr using the Online Pictures button in the Illustrations group of the INSERT tab. Buttons in the *Layout Options* palette are used to control how text wraps around the picture and the picture's position on the page. The Pictures button in the INSERT tab is used to insert pictures stored on your computer. Edit an image's appearance and/or add special effects using buttons in the PICTURE TOOLS FORMAT tab. A caption is explanatory text above or below a picture that is added using the Insert Caption button in the REFERENCES tab. Word automatically numbers pictures as Figures.	Clip art gallery Online Pictures button Layout Options button Pictures button Insert Caption
Adding Borders and Shading, and Inserting a Text Box	Add a border or shading to paragraphs to make text stand out on a page. Shading is color applied to the page behind the text. Apply a border to selected text using the *Borders* gallery from the Borders button arrow in the Paragraph group of the HOME tab. Add shading using the Shading button arrow in the Paragraph group of the HOME tab. A page border surrounds the entire page and is added from the Page Borders button in the Page Background group of the DESIGN tab. A pull quote is a quote inside a text box. Insert text inside a box using the Text Box button in the Text group of the INSERT tab.	Shading Borders gallery Page Borders button Pull quote Text Box button
Inserting a Table	A table is a grid of columns and rows in which you type text and is used when you want to arrange text side-by-side or in rows. A table cell is a rectangular-shaped box in the table grid that is the intersection of a column and a row into which you type text. Create a table by tapping or clicking a box in a drop-down grid or by entering the number of columns and rows in the Insert Table dialog box. Tapping or pressing Tab in the last table cell automatically adds a new row to the table. Quick Tables are predesigned tables with sample data such as calendars and tabular lists.	Table Table cell Quick Tables

Topic	Key Concepts	Key Terms
Formatting and Modifying a Table	Apply a predesigned collection of borders, shading, and color to a table using an option from the *Table Styles* gallery.	Table Styles
	Shading or other formatting applied to every other row to make the table data easier to read is called banded rows.	Banded rows
	Check boxes in the Table Style Options group are used to customize the formatting applied from a Table Styles option.	
	Apply shading or borders using buttons in the Table Styles and Borders group of the TABLE TOOLS DESIGN tab.	
	New rows and columns are inserted above, below, left, or right of the active table cell using buttons in the Rows & Columns group of the TABLE TOOLS LAYOUT tab.	
	Remove selected table cells, rows, columns, or the entire table using options from the Delete button in the Rows & Columns group.	
	Adjust the width of a column by changing the *Width* text box value in the Cell Size group of the TABLE TOOLS LAYOUT tab or by dragging the column border.	
	Buttons to change alignment options for selected table cells are found in the Alignment group of the TABLE TOOLS LAYOUT tab.	
	Cells in a table can be merged or split using buttons in the Merge group of the TABLE TOOLS LAYOUT tab.	
Changing Page Layout Options	New Word documents are automatically formatted for a letter-sized page with one-inch margins in portrait orientation.	Portrait
	Portrait orientation means the text on the page is oriented to the taller side (8.5-inch width) while landscape orientation rotates the text to the wider side of the page (11-inch measurement becomes the page width).	Landscape
	Change the margins by choosing one of the predefined margin options or by entering measurements for the top, bottom, left, and right margins at the Page Setup dialog box.	Soft page break
	A soft page break is a page break that Word inserts automatically when the maximum number of lines that can fit on a page has been reached.	Hard page break
	A hard page break is a page break inserted by you in a different location than the soft page break occurred.	Section break
	A section break is inserted from the Breaks button in the Page Setup group of the PAGE LAYOUT tab and is used to format a portion of a document with different page layout options.	
Formatting a Research Paper with a Header and Page Numbers	A style guide is a set of rules for formatting and referencing academic papers.	Style guide
	MLA and APA are the two most popular style guides used for academic writing.	Header
	A header is text that appears at the top of each page, while a footer is text that appears at the bottom of each page.	Footer
	Tap or click the INSERT tab and choose the Header or Footer button to create a header or footer in the Header or Footer pane.	Page Number button
	Page numbers are added to a document at the top or bottom of a page within a Header or Footer pane using the Page Number button in the HEADER & FOOTER TOOLS DESIGN tab.	

continued....

Topic	Key Concepts	Key Terms
Inserting and Editing Citations	A citation provides a reader with the reference for information that is quoted or paraphrased within an academic paper. Position the insertion point where a citation is needed and use the Insert Citation button in the REFERENCES tab to create a reference. Select an existing source for a citation or choose *Add New Source* to create a new reference. At the Create Source dialog box, begin by choosing the *Type of Source* for the reference, and then fill in the bibliography fields as needed. Edit a citation to add a page number or paragraph number to the reference.	Citation
Creating a Works Cited Page and Using Word Views	The MLA style guide requires a Works Cited page as a separate page at the end of the document with the references used for the paper. Use the Bibliography button in the Citations & Bibliography group of the REFERENCES tab to generate a Works Cited page formatted for the MLA style guide. Print Layout view displays the document as it will appear when printed. Read Mode view displays a document full screen in columns or pages without editing tools. Draft view hides print elements such as headers, footers, and page numbering. Web Layout view displays the document as a web page. Outline view displays content as bullet points. Footnotes are sources or explanatory comments placed at the bottom of a page in an academic paper. Endnotes are sources or explanatory comments placed at the end of a section or document in an academic paper.	Works Cited Bibliography button Print Layout view Read Mode view Draft view Web Layout view Outline view Footnotes Endnotes
Inserting and Replying to Comments	A comment is a short note associated with text that provides explanatory information or poses a question to a reader. Select text that you want to associate with a comment and type the comment text inside a comment box by tapping or clicking the New Comment button in the REVIEW tab. Comments display in the Markup Area, which is a pane that opens at the right side of the document when comments are added. A document with comments can be shown with *No Markup*, *Simple Markup*, or *All Markup*, which refers to the way in which comment boxes are displayed. Tap or point inside a comment box and use the Reply button to enter reply text that responds to a comment. Mark a comment as done to retain the comment text but display the comment dimmed in the Markup Area.	Comment Markup Area
Creating a Resume and Cover Letter from Templates	More than 40 professionally designed resume and cover letter templates are available in Word. At the New tab Backstage view, select the <u>Resume</u> hyperlink to browse templates for resumes in various styles, themes, and purposes by category. At the New tab Backstage view, select the <u>Letters</u> hyperlink and the *Cover Letter* category to locate a cover letter template.	

Multiple Choice

1. Search for images in the Clip Art gallery from this button in the INSERT tab.
   a. Pictures
   b. Online Pictures
   c. Shapes
   d. SmartArt

2. Label a picture using this Insert option.
   a. Text box
   b. SmartArt
   c. Caption
   d. Citation

3. Color added to the background of a paragraph is applied using this button in the Paragraph group.
   a. Borders
   b. Text Highlight Color
   c. Page Background
   d. Shading

4. A short passage of text inside a box is created with this button in the INSERT tab.
   a. Pictures
   b. Text Box
   c. Quick Parts
   d. WordArt

5. Tables are used to type text arranged in columns and rows within rectangular-shaped boxes called _____.
   a. table cells
   b. spreadsheets
   c. text boxes
   d. headers

6. Use this option from the *Table* drop-down list to create a table by typing a value for the number of columns and rows.
   a. Insert Table
   b. Create Table
   c. Draw Table
   d. Make Table

7. New rows and columns are added to an existing table using buttons in the Rows & Columns group of the TABLE TOOLS _____ tab.
   a. DESIGN
   b. LAYOUT
   c. FORMAT
   d. DRAWING

8. Adjust the width of a column in a table by changing the *Width* value in this group of buttons.
   a. Cell Layout
   b. Cell Design
   c. Cell Alignment
   d. Cell Size

9. A document's orientation can be changed to landscape using the Orientation button in this tab.
   a. HOME
   b. PAGE LAYOUT
   c. DESIGN
   d. INSERT

10. A page break inserted automatically by Word is called a _____ page break.
    a. hard
    b. soft
    c. manual
    d. section

11. Text that appears at the top of each page is called a _____.
    a. header
    b. footer
    c. quick part
    d. section

12. Page numbers are added to the top of each page inside this pane.
    a. Header
    b. Footer
    c. Quick Part
    d. Section

13. Add a page number reference to an existing citation by selecting this option from the Citation Options arrow list.
    a. New source
    b. Edit source
    c. New citation
    d. Edit citation

14. When creating a new source for a citation, this option is usually changed first at the Create Source dialog box.
    a. Type of Source
    b. Author
    c. Name of Web Page
    d. Medium

15. Use this button in the REFERENCES tab to create a Works Cited page.
    a. Bibliography
    b. Insert Citation
    c. Manage Sources
    d. Style

16. This Word view displays documents full screen without editing tools.
    a. Draft
    b. Print Layout
    c. Outline
    d. Read Mode

17. Comments are displayed in this area.
    a. Markup
    b. Revisions
    c. Print Layout
    d. Review

18. A comment displayed as dimmed text has had this option applied.
    a. Mark Comment Complete
    b. Mark Comment Finished
    c. Mark Comment Replied
    d. Mark Comment Done

19. Browse for a resume or cover letter template in this Backstage view.
    a. Info tab
    b. New tab
    c. Open tab
    d. Share tab

20. Vertically center a letter on the page in this dialog box.
    a. Page Layout
    b. Page Alignment
    c. Page Setup
    d. Page Options

Crossword Puzzle

ACROSS

1 Default view for Word documents
5 Text that appears at the bottom of each page
7 Display option to remove display of comments
12 Button to insert photo stored on computer
13 Predesigned resumes or cover letters
14 Option to type your own margin measurements
15 Text orientated to the wider side of the page
16 Rules for formatting and referencing academic papers

DOWN

1 Quote inside a text box
2 Button to change text wrapping option for a picture
3 References page for MLA papers
4 Combine two or more cells into one
6 Button to draw a border around the entire page
8 Collection of predesigned table formatting options
9 Short note associated with text
10 Reference in academic paper that credits source
11 Predesigned table with sample data

Matching

Match the term with the statement or definition.

_____ 1. Adds border or effect to photo
_____ 2. Graphic with short passage of text
_____ 3. Ideal for typing a price list
_____ 4. Every other row is shaded
_____ 5. Start a new page
_____ 6. Style guide
_____ 7. Add source of information
_____ 8. New view in Word 2013
_____ 9. Respond to a comment
_____ 10. Document to send with resume

a. Banded rows
b. MLA or APA
c. Read Mode
d. Text Box
e. Cover letter
f. Picture Styles
g. Reply button
h. Page Break
i. Table
j. Insert Citation

Project 1 Enhancing a Document with Visual Elements

Individual

Deliverable: National Park Trip Planner document (continued in Project 2)

1. Open **GrandCanyonHikingPlanner**.
2. Save the document as **C7-Project1-GrandCanyonTripPlanner-Your Name** in a new folder named *Ch7* within the ChapterProjectsWork folder on your USB flash drive.
3. Insert, label, and edit pictures as follows:
   a. Insert the picture named ***ScorpionRidge*** at the right margin aligned with the first line of text in the first paragraph and with the *Square* text wrapping option. You determine an appropriate size for the picture with the paragraph.
   b. Insert the picture named ***BrightAngelPoint*** at the left margin aligned with the first line of text in the last paragraph and with the *Square* text wrapping option. Do not resize the picture.
   c. Add a caption below the picture inserted at Step 3a with the label text *Scorpion Ridge, North Rim*. Accept all default caption options.
   d. Add a caption below the picture inserted at Step 3b with the label text *Bright Angel Point, North Rim*. Accept all default caption options.
   e. Apply a Picture Style of your choosing to both pictures.
   f. Apply Color Saturation at 200% to both pictures.
4. Add borders, shading, and a text box as follows:
   a. Select the sentence in the second paragraph below the subtitle *Park Entrance Fees* (begins *Admission to the park. . .*), center the text, and add an outside border.
   b. Add *Blue, Accent 1, Lighter 80%* shading to the same sentence selected in Step 4a.
   c. Add a *Blue, Accent 1*, 1 ½ point, Shadow page border to the document.
   d. Insert an *Austin Quote* text box and type the following text inside the box:
      Grand Canyon National Park is a World Heritage Site
   e. Move the text box inserted at Step 4d so that the bottom of the text box aligns at the center of the page and bottom margin.
5. Save the revised document using the same name (**C7-Project1-GrandCanyonTripPlanner-Your Name**).
6. Leave the document open if you are continuing to Project 2; otherwise, close the document and submit the project to your instructor in the manner she or he has requested.

Project 2 Inserting, Formatting, and Modifying a Table into a Document

Individual

Deliverable: National Park Trip Planner document

Note: You must have completed Project 1 before starting this project.

1. If necessary, open **C7-Project1-GrandCanyonTripPlanner-Your Name**.
2. Use Save As to change the file name to **C7-Project2-GrandCanyonTripPlanner-Your Name**, saving in the same folder.
3. Position the insertion point at the end of the document text and tap or press Enter until you create a new blank line at the left margin below the picture of Bright Angel Point.

4. Insert a 5 x 5 table and type the following text in the table grid at the default table cell options:

Rim	Trail Name	Round Trip Distance	Round Trip Estimated Time	Elevation Change
South	Rim Trail	13 miles (21 km)	All day depending on desired distance	200 feet (60 m)
South	Bright Angel Trail	3 miles (4.8 km) to 9.2 miles (14.8 km)	From 2 to 9 hours depending on desired distance	2,112 feet (644 m) to 3,060 feet (933 m)
North	Bright Angel Point	0.5 miles (0.8 km)	30 minutes	200 feet (60 m)
North	Widforss Trail	10 miles (16 km)	6 hours	200 feet (60 m)

5. Format the table as follows:
   a. Apply a table style of your choosing.
   b. Deselect the *First Column* table style option if it is selected.
   c. Change the font size to 10 for all of the text in the table cells.
6. Modify the layout of the table as follows:
   a. Set the width of the first column to 0.6 inches, and the third, fourth, and fifth columns to 1.5 inches.
   b. Align all table cells at the center horizontally and vertically.
   c. Insert a new row above row 4 and type the following text in the new table cells:

South	Kaibab Trail	1.8 miles (2.9 km) to 6 miles (9.7 km)	From 1 to 6 hours depending on desired distance	600 feet (180 m) to 2,040 feet (622 m)

   d. Insert a new row at the bottom of the table and type the following text in the table cells:

North	Kaibab Trail	1.4 miles (2.3 km) to 4 miles (6.4 km)	From 1 to 4 hours depending on desired distance	800 feet (245 m) to 1,450 feet (445 m)

7. If necessary, delete extra space above or below the table to make sure the text box remains at the bottom center of the page.
8. Save the revised document using the same name (**C7-Project2-GrandCanyonHikingPlanner-Your Name**).
9. Submit the project to your instructor in the manner she or he has requested.
10. Close the document.

Project 3 Completing a Research Report with Formatting, Citations, and Works Cited

Individual

Deliverable: Academic Paper in MLA Format

1. Open **EtanerceptEssay**.
2. Use Save As to change the file name to **C7-Project3-EtanerceptEssay-Your Name**, saving in the Ch7 folder within ChapterProjectsWork.
3. Select the entire document and change the font, line and paragraph spacing, and paragraph indents to conform to MLA guidelines (see Table 7.1 in Topic 7.6). *Hint: Turn on the display of nonprinting symbols to determine where paragraphs end to correctly complete the first line indent formatting.*
4. Insert your name, your instructor's name, the title of your course, and the current date at the top of the first page as per MLA guidelines (see Table 7.1 in Topic 7.6).
5. Add page numbering one space after your last name at the right margin in a header and format the header text to the same font and font size as the rest of the document.

6. Edit existing citations in the document as follows:
   a. Edit the source for Bradley and Desmeules in the first paragraph to change the second author's first name from *Marie* to *Mary*, and the page from *215* to *225*.
   b. Change the page from *61* to *65* for the Hashkes and Laxer citation at the end of the indented quotation on page 2.
7. Position the insertion point at the end of the quotation that reads "*The Etanercept injection is used to reduce signs and symptoms of active arthritis . . . This medicine may also slow the progression of damage to the body from active arthritis or rheumatoid arthritis*" and insert a new citation referencing *par. 14* from the following new source:

Type of Source	Document from Web site		
Author	**Jarvis, B.; Faulds, D.**		
Name of Web Page	**Etanercept: a review of its use in rheumatoid arthritis**		
Name of Web Site	**PubMed, US National Library of Medicine**		
Year	**1999**	*Month Accessed*	**March**
Month	**June**	*Day Accessed*	**15**
Year Accessed	**2015**	*Medium*	**Web**

8. Position the insertion point at the end of the quotation that reads "*When Etanercept is administered alone or in combination with methotrexate in patients with refractory rheumatoid arthritis, significant reductions in disease activity occur within two weeks and are sustained for at least 6 months*" and cite *par. 20* from the Jarvis and Faulds source.
9. Position the insertion point at the end of the sentence that reads *Missed doses will mean that the TNF protein is no longer being effectively controlled and inflammation, pain, and disease progression will quickly return within a month from stopping treatment* and insert a new citation referencing *par. 12* from the following new source:

Type of Source	Document from Web site		
Author	(leave blank)		
Name of Web Page	**Medication Guide: Enbrel (Etanercept)**		
Name of Web Site	**Immunex Corporation**		
Year	**2011**	*Month Accessed*	**March**
Month	**December**	*Day Accessed*	**25**
Year Accessed	**2015**	*Medium*	**Web**

10. Create and format a Works Cited page on a separate page at the end of the document.
11. Save the revised document using the same name (**C7-Project3-EtanerceptEssay-Your Name**).
12. Submit the project to your instructor in the manner she or he has requested and then close the document.

Project 4 Resume and Cover Letter with Comments

Individual

Deliverable: Personal Resume and Cover Letter Targeted to a Specific Job Ad

1. Find a recent job ad for a position in your field of study.
2. Choose a resume template that you like and create a new resume for yourself that could be used as an application for the job ad.
3. Insert at least two comments in the resume. Each comment should be associated with an entry in your resume and pose a specific question to your instructor asking him or her for tips on how to improve the entry, or provide additional explanation as to the writing style or tone that you used.
4. Choose a cover letter template that you like and write a cover letter to enclose with the resume written specifically for the requirements in the job ad.
5. Add the URL or other source for the job ad that you used for this project in a comment associated with the current date text in the cover letter.
6. Save the resume as **C7-Project4-Resume-Your Name** and save the cover letter as **C7-Project4-CoverLetter-Your Name**.
7. Submit the resume and cover letter to your instructor in the manner she or he has requested.

Project 5 Enhance and Format a Tourist Information Document

Individual

Deliverable: Travel Information Flyer

1. Open **HangzhouTravelInfo**.
2. Format the document as shown in Figure 7.5 using the following information:
   a. The font used is 11-point Book Antiqua for the body of the document and 16-point Antiqua for the title and subtitle.
   b. The subheadings are 14-point with the Subtitle style and *Dark Blue* font color applied.
   c. Substitute your name in the footer in place of *Student Name*.
   d. The image is a picture named **Hangzhou** with the *Simple Frame, Black* picture style; locate the clip art shown or a similar clip art image by searching using the keyword *pagoda*; the text box is the *Grid Quote* with the font formatting changed to 12-point Book Antiqua and the case changed.
   e. Use your best judgment to match other formatting shown.
3. Save the revised document as **C7-Project5-HangzhouTravelInfo–Your Name** in the Ch7 folder within ChapterProjectsWork.
4. Submit the project to your instructor in the manner she or he has requested.
5. Close the document.

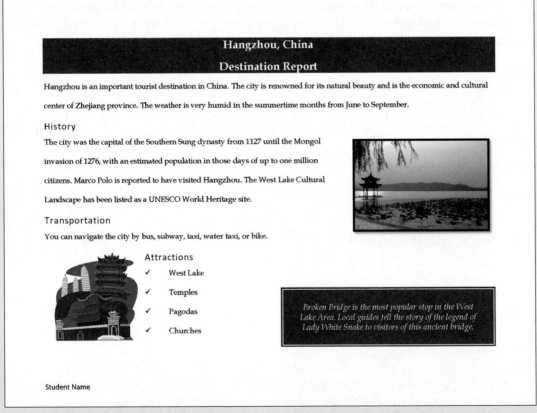

Figure 7.5 Project 5 Hangzhou Informational Flyer

Project 6 Composing a New Flyer

Individual or Pairs

Deliverable: Food Drive Flyer

1. Listen to the audio file named ***Project6_Instructions***. The file is located in the Ch7 folder in the Student_Data_ Files folder on your USB flash drive.
2. Create the flyer as instructed.
3. Save the flyer in the Ch7 folder within the ChapterProjectsWork folder on your USB flash drive as **C7-Project6-FoodDriveFlyer-Your Name**.
4. Submit the project to your instructor in the manner she or he has requested.
5. Close the document.

Project 7 Sending Project Work to OneNote Notebook

Individual

Deliverable: New Page in Shared OneNote notebook

1. Start OneNote and open the MyProjects notebook created in Chapter 4, Project 4.
2. Make Word the active section and add a new page titled *Chapter 7 Projects*.
3. Switch to Word. For each project that you completed, open the document, send the project to OneNote 2013 selecting the Chapter 7 Projects page in the Word section in the MyProjects notebook, and then close the document.
4. Close your MyProjects notebook in OneNote and close OneNote.
5. Close Word.
6. Submit the project to your instructor in the manner she or he has requested.

Chapter 8

Creating, Editing, and Formatting Worksheets Using Excel

After successfully completing this chapter, you will be able to:

- Create and edit a worksheet
- Format cells with font, alignment, number, and style options
- Adjust column widths and row heights
- Use the Fill feature to enter data
- Add a column or row of values with AutoSum
- Insert and delete columns and rows
- Sort data
- Change print options
- Display formulas in cells
- Insert and rename worksheets
- Copy cells between worksheets
- Use Go To and Freeze Panes

Microsoft Excel (referred to as Excel) is a **spreadsheet application** used to create, analyze, and present information that is organized into a grid of columns and rows. Data is calculated, analyzed, and can be graphed in a chart. The ability to do "what-if" analysis during which one or more values are changed to view the effect on other values is a popular feature of Excel. Examples of the type of data for which Excel is used include budgets, income, expenses, investments, loans, schedules, grade books, attendance, inventory, and research data. Any information that can be set up in a grid-like structure is suited to Excel.

Files that you save in Excel are called **workbooks**. A workbook contains a collection of **worksheets**; a worksheet is the structure into which you enter, edit, and manipulate data. Think of a workbook as a binder and a worksheet as a page within the binder. Initially, a workbook has only one worksheet (page), but you can add more as needed.

Many of the features that you learned about in Word operate the same or similarly in Excel, which will make learning Excel faster and easier. You will begin by creating new worksheets in a blank workbook and then open other worksheets in which to practice navigating, editing, sorting, and formatting tasks.

Note: If you are using a tablet, consider using a USB or wireless keyboard because parts of this chapter involve a fair amount of typing.

Creating and Editing a New Worksheet

Topic 8.1

SKILLS

Enter text and values

Create formulas

Edit cells

When you start a new blank workbook, you begin at a worksheet that is divided into columns and rows. The intersection of a column and a row is called a **cell** into which you type text, a value, or a formula. The cell with the green border around its edges is called the **active cell**. Each cell is identified with the letter of the column and the number of the row that intersect to form the cell. For example, A1 refers to the cell in column A, row 1.

A new workbook starts with one worksheet labeled *Sheet1* that has columns labeled A to Z, AA to AZ, BA to BZ, and so on to the last column, which is labeled XFD. Rows are numbered 1, 2, 3, up to 1,048,576.

Method for Creating a New Worksheet

Generally you begin a new worksheet by entering titles and column and row headings to give the worksheet an organizational layout and provide context for the reader. Next, you enter values in the columns and rows. Complete the worksheet by inserting formulas that perform calculations or otherwise summarize data.

1. Start Excel 2013.

2. At the Excel Start screen, tap or click *Blank workbook* in the *Templates* gallery and compare your screen with the one shown in Figure 8.1.

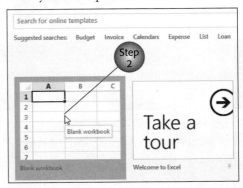

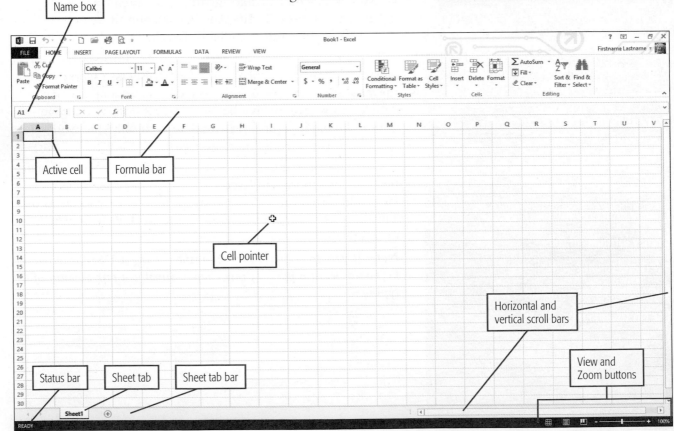

Figure 8.1 A new blank worksheet in Excel. The worksheet area below the ribbon is divided into columns and rows, which creates cells in which data is typed. See Table 8.1 for a description of screen elements.

Table 8.1	Excel Features
Feature	**Description**
Active cell	Location in the worksheet in which the next typed data will be stored or that will be affected by a command. Move the active cell position by tapping or clicking in another cell or by using the Arrow keys.
Cell pointer	Icon that displays when you are able to select cells with the mouse by clicking or dragging.
	On touch devices with no mouse attached, tap a cell to display selection handles (round circles) at the top left and bottom right corners.
Formula bar	Displays contents stored in the active cell and is also used to create formulas.
Horizontal and vertical scroll bars	Use the scroll bars to view parts of a worksheet not shown in the current viewing area.
Name box	Displays active cell address or name assigned to active cell.
Sheet tab	Displays the name of the active worksheet. By default, new sheets are named *Sheet#* where # is the number of the sheet in the workbook.
Sheet tab bar	Area with sheet tabs used to navigate between worksheets and New sheet button used to insert a new worksheet.
Status bar	Displays messages indicating the current mode of operation; READY indicates the worksheet is ready to accept new data.
View and Zoom buttons	Excel opens by default in Normal view. Other view buttons include Page Layout and Page Break Preview. Zoom buttons are used to enlarge or shrink the display.

SNAP Tutorials

8.1.1 Opening, Saving, and Closing an Excel Workbook

8.1.2 Entering Data in Cells and Saving a Workbook with a New Name

8.1.3 Performing Calculations Using Formulas

8.1.4 Editing Cells and Using Proofing Tools

When you start a new worksheet, the active cell is positioned in A1 at the top left corner of the worksheet area. Entries are created by moving the active cell and typing text, a value, or a formula.

3 With A1 the active cell, type **Car Purchase Cost** and then tap or press Enter, or tap or click in A2 to make A2 the active cell.

4 Type **Pre-owned Ford Focus Sedan** and then tap or press Enter twice, or tap or click in A4.

5 Type **Total Purchase Price** and then tap or click in A6.

6 Type **Loan Details:** and then tap or click in B7.

7 Type the remaining row headings by moving the active cell and typing the text shown in the image at right.

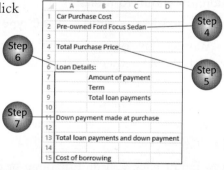

8 Tap or click in F4, type **16700.00**, and then tap or click in E7.

Notice Excel does not display the decimal place values that you typed. By default, zeros to the right of a decimal are not stored or shown. You will learn how to format the display of values in the next topic.

App Tip

You can use Arrow keys to move the active cell up, down, left, or right.

App Tip

Excel's AutoComplete matches an entry in the same column with the first few characters that you type. Accept an AutoComplete entry with Tab, Enter, or an Arrow key, or continue typing to ignore the suggestion.

App Tip

By default, text entries align at the left edge of a cell while numeric entries are right-aligned.

9 Type the remaining values by moving the active cell and typing the numbers shown below.

	A	B	C	D	E	F
1	Car Purchase Cost					
2	Pre-owned Ford Focus Sedan					
3						
4	Total Purchase Price					16700
5						
6	Loan Details:					
7		Amount of payment			470.05	
8		Term			36	
9		Total loan payments				
10						
11	Down payment made at purchase				1700	

Step 9

Creating Formulas to Perform Calculations

A **formula** is used to perform mathematical operations on values. A formula entry begins with the equals sign (=) to indicate to Excel the entry that follows is a calculation. Following the equals sign, type the first cell address that contains a value you want to use, type a mathematical operator such as a +, and then type the second cell address. Continue typing cell addresses with mathematical operators between each address until finished.

The mathematical operators are + (addition), - (subtraction), * (multiplication), / (division), and ^ (exponentiation).

10 Tap or click to make E9 the active cell and then type **=e7*e8**.

11 Tap or click the Enter button in the Formula bar.

Excel calculates the result and displays the value in E9. Notice that the worksheet area displays the formula results while the entry in the Formula bar displays the formula used to calculate the result. Notice also that Excel capitalizes column letters in cell addresses within formulas.

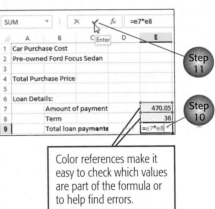

Step 11

Step 10

Color references make it easy to check which values are part of the formula or to help find errors.

12 Make F13 the active cell and type **=**.

Another way to enter a formula is to use the pointing method in which you tap or click the desired cells instead of typing their cell addresses.

13 Tap or click E9.

A moving dashed border surrounds E9, the cell is color coded, and the address *E9* is inserted in the formula cell.

14 Type **+**.

15 Tap or click E11 and then tap or click the Enter button in the Formula bar, or tap or press Enter.

16 Make F15 the active cell and type the formula **=f13-f4**, or enter the formula using the pointing method.

The result, *1921.8*, displays in the cell.

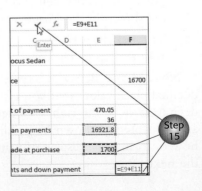

Step 15

oops!

Tapped or clicked the wrong cell? Simply tap or click the correct cell—the cell reference is not fixed in the formula until you type an operator. You can also press the Esc key to start over.

Editing Cells

A cell can be changed by making the cell active and typing a new entry to replace the existing contents. Double-tap or double-click to open a cell for editing in the worksheet area. You can also edit the active cell's contents by inserting or deleting text or values in the Formula bar.

Press the Delete key to delete the contents in the active cell, or tap or click the **Clear button** in the Editing group of the HOME tab and then tap or click *Clear All* at the drop-down list.

17 Make E7 the active cell, type **480.95**, and then tap or press Enter.

Notice the new payment amount caused the values in E9, F13, and F15 to update.

18 Double-tap or double-click cell F4, position the insertion point between *6* and *7*, tap or press Backspace to remove *6*, type **5**, and then tap or click any other cell.

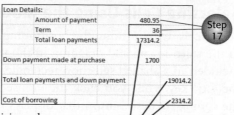

These values are updated automatically when the new loan payment is entered in E7.

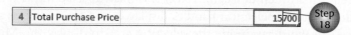

| 4 | Total Purchase Price | | | | 15700 | Step 18 |

App Tip

F2 is the keyboard command to edit a cell.

19 Make E11 the active cell, tap or click in the Formula bar, position the insertion point between *1* and *7*, press Backspace to remove *1*, and then tap or click any other cell.

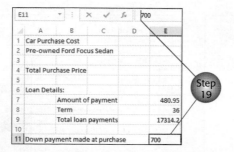

App Tip

AutoCorrect operates in Excel; however, red wavy lines do *not* appear below misspelled words. Consider using the Spelling feature in the Proofing group of the REVIEW tab to spell check all worksheets.

20 Save the new workbook as **8.1-CarCost-Your Name** in a new folder named *Ch8* in the CompletedTopicsByChapter folder on your USB flash drive. Leave the workbook open for the next topic.

Order of Operations in Formulas

Excel gives precedence to exponentiation, multiplication, and division before addition and subtraction when calculating a formula. Use parentheses around a part of the formula you want calculated first, such as addition, before multiplication or division. For example, in the formula *=(A1+A2)*A3*, Excel adds the values in A1 and A2 first and then multiplies the result by the value in A3.

Topic 8.2

SKILLS

Change the font

Apply bold

Format values

Add borders

Merge cells

 **Tutorials**

8.2.1 Applying Font Formatting

8.2.2 Applying Number Formatting

8.2.3 Adding Borders and Shading to Cells

Formatting Cells

Similarly to Word, the HOME tab in Excel contains the formatting options for changing the appearance of text, values, or formula results. The Font group contains buttons to change the font, font size, and font color, and to apply bold, italic, underline, borders, and shading. The alignment group contains buttons to align text or values within the cell's edges.

Selecting Cells Using the Mouse

Select cells with a mouse by positioning the cell pointer (large white cross icon ⊕) in the starting cell and dragging in the required direction until all cells have been included in a shaded selection rectangle. Select nonadjacent cells by holding down the Ctrl key while you click the mouse in each desired cell. New to Excel 2013 is the Quick Analysis button that displays when a group of cells has been selected. You will learn about the options available from this button in Chapter 9.

Selecting Cells Using Touch

Selecting cells on a touch device in Excel is similar to selecting text in Word with the exception that two selection handles display in the active cell, as shown in Figure 8.2. As in Word, tap inside the selection area to display the Mini toolbar.

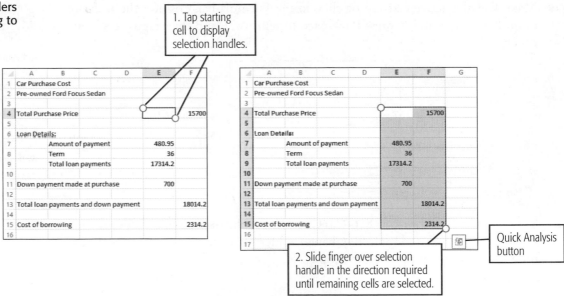

Figure 8.2 Selecting cells using a touch device

Select cells using the keyboard by holding down the Shift key while you press an arrow key (Up, Down, Left, or Right).

① With the **8.1-CarCost-Your Name** workbook open, starting at cell A1, select all of the cells down and right to F15.

A rectangular-shaped group of cells is referred to as a **range**. A range is referenced with the address of the cell at the top left corner, a colon (:), and the address of the cell at the bottom right corner. For example, the reference for the range selected in Step 1 is *A1:F15*.

(2) Tap or click the Font button arrow in the HOME tab, slide or scroll down the font gallery, and then tap or click *Century Gothic*.

(3) Tap or click in any cell to deselect the range.

(4) Select A1:A2 and then tap or click the Bold button in the Font group.

Notice the entire text in A1 and A2 is bold, including the characters that spill over the edge of column A into columns B, C, and D. This is because the entire text entry is stored in the cell that was active when the text was typed. Overflow text in adjacent columns is not problematic when the adjacent columns are empty. You will learn how to widen a column in the next topic.

(5) Select cell F15 and then tap or click the Bold button.

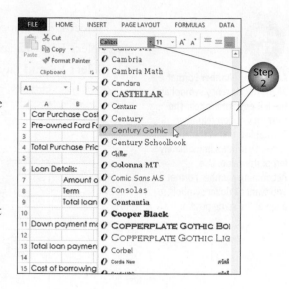

Formatting Values

By default, cells in a new worksheet are all in the General format, which has no specific appearance options. Buttons in the Number group of the HOME tab are used to format the appearance of numeric entries in a worksheet. Add a dollar symbol, a comma in the thousands, and/or adjust the number of decimal places to improve the appearance of values. Use the Percent Style format to convert decimal values to percentages and include the percent symbol.

Use the Number Format list arrow (next to *General*) to choose other formats for dates, times, fractions, or scientific values, or to open the Format Cells dialog box from the *More Number Formats* option.

(6) Select E4:F15.

(7) Tap or click the Comma Style button in the Number group.

Comma Style formats values with a comma in thousands and two decimal places.

(8) Select F4 and tap or click the Accounting Number Format button in the Number group. (Do not tap or click the down-pointing arrow on the button.)

Accounting Number Format adds a currency symbol ($ for United States and Canada), comma in thousands, and two decimal places. Use the Accounting Number Format button arrow to choose a currency symbol other than the dollar symbol (such as € for Euros).

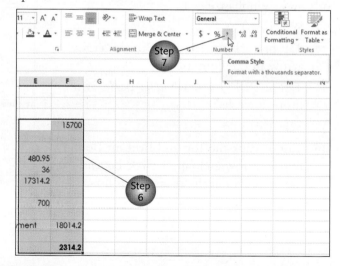

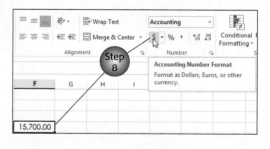

App Tip

Excel automatically widens columns as needed when you apply a format that adds more characters to a column such as Comma Style.

Accounting Number Format aligns the currency symbol at the left edge of the cell. The Currency option (Number Format list) places the currency symbol immediately left of the value. Use Accounting Number Format if you want all dollar symbols to align at the same position.

Apply the wrong format or select the wrong cell? Use the Undo command or simply apply the correct format to the cell or range.

(9) Select E7 and apply the Accounting Number Format.

(10) Select F13:F15 and apply the Accounting Number Format.

(11) Select E8 and tap twice or click twice the Decrease Decimal button.

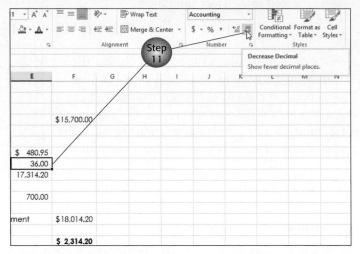

One decimal place is removed from the active cell or range each time you tap or click the **Decrease Decimal button.** Tap or click the **Increase Decimal button** to add one decimal place.

Adding Borders

Borders in various styles and colors can be added to the top, left, bottom, or right edge of a cell. Borders are used to underscore column headings or totals or to otherwise emphasize cells.

The Borders button updates to the most recently selected border style so that you can apply the same border to another cell or range by simply tapping or clicking the button (not the arrow).

(12) Select F13.

(13) Tap or click the Bottom Border button arrow in the Font group.

(14) Tap or click *Top and Bottom Border* at the drop-down list.

(15) Select F15.

(16) Tap or click the Top and Bottom Border button arrow and tap or click *Bottom Double Border* at the drop-down list.

(17) Tap or click in any other cell to view the border style applied to F15.

Merging Cells

A worksheet title is often centered across the columns used in the worksheet. The **Merge & Center button** in the Alignment group is used to combine a group of cells into one large cell and center its contents. Use the Merge & Center button arrow to choose to merge without centering or to unmerge a merged cell.

18 Select A1:F1.

19 Tap or click the Merge & Center button in the Alignment group.

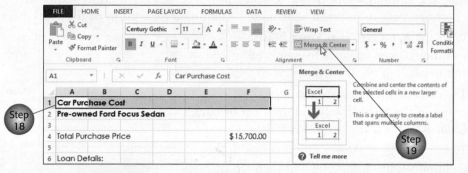

20 Select A2:F2 and tap or click the Merge & Center button.

21 Save the workbook using the same name (**8.1-CarCost-Your Name**). Leave the workbook open for the next topic.

Change a Font
1. Select cell(s).
2. Tap or click Font button arrow.
3. Tap or click desired font.

Change Numeric Format
1. Select cell(s).
2. Tap or click style button in Number group.

Adjust Decimal Places
1. Select cell(s).
2. Tap or click Increase Decimal or Decrease Decimal button.

Add Borders
1. Select cell(s).
2. Tap or click Borders button arrow.
3. Tap or click border style.

Merge Cells
1. Select cells.
2. Tap or click Merge & Center button.

Consider formatting using the Mini toolbar (tap or right-click inside selection area) or using these keyboard shortcuts:

Ctrl + B	Bold
Ctrl + I	Italic
Ctrl + 1 (one)	Opens the Format Cells dialog box
Ctrl + Shift + $	Currency Format
Ctrl + Shift + %	Percent Style

Beyond Basics

Format Cells Dialog Box

Tapping or clicking the dialog box launcher button at the bottom right of the Font, Alignment, or Number group opens the Format Cells dialog box. Use the dialog box to apply multiple formats in one operation, to further customize format options, or to apply font effect options such as strikethrough, superscript, or subscript.

Adjusting Column Width and Row Height, and Changing Alignment

Topic 8.3

SKILLS

Adjust column width

Adjust row height

Change cell alignment

 **Tutorials**

8.3.1 Adjusting Column Width and Row Height

8.3.2 Applying Alignment Formatting

In a new worksheet, each column width is 8.43 and each row height is 15. You can make cells larger by widening a column's width or increasing a row's height. In many instances, Excel automatically makes columns wider and rows taller to accommodate the cell entry, formula result, or format that you apply. Manually changing the column width or the row height is a technique used to add more space between cells to improve readability or emphasize a section of the worksheet.

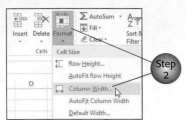

1. With the **8.1-CarCost-Your Name** workbook open, make active any cell in column E.

2. Tap or click the Format button in the Cells group in the HOME tab and then tap or click *Column Width* at the drop-down list.

3. Type **15** in the *Column width* text box at the Column Width dialog box and then tap or press Enter, or tap or click OK.

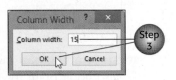

4. Make active any cell in column F, tap or click the Format button, and then tap or click *Column Width* at the drop-down list.

5. Type **10** at the Column Width dialog box and then tap or press Enter, or tap or click OK.

Notice the cells with values in column F have been replaced with a series of pound symbols (######). This occurs when the column's width has been made too narrow to show all of the characters.

6. Make active F4.

7. Tap or click the Format button and then tap or click *AutoFit Column Width* at the drop-down list.

AutoFit changes the width of the column to fit the contents of the active cell. F4 was made active at Step 6 because this cell has the largest number in the column. Notice the pound symbols have disappeared and the values are redisplayed now that the column is wide enough.

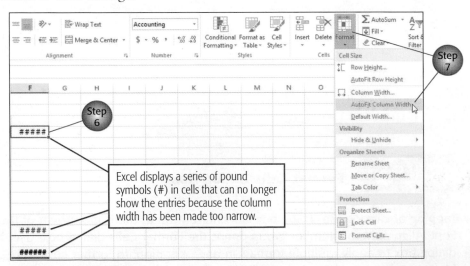

Excel displays a series of pound symbols (#) in cells that can no longer show the entries because the column width has been made too narrow.

8 Select A1:A2.

Select cells in multiple rows or columns to change the height or width of more than one row or column at the same time.

9 Tap or click the Format button and then tap or click *Row Height* at the drop-down list.

10 Type **26** in the *Row height* text box at the Row Height dialog box and then tap or press Enter, or tap or click OK.

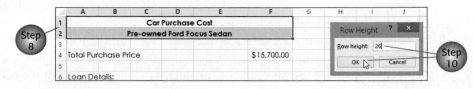

The Alignment group of the HOME tab contains buttons to align the entry of a cell horizontally and/or vertically. You can align at the left, center, or right horizontally, or at the top, middle, or bottom vertically.

11 With A1:A2 still selected, tap or click the **Middle Align button** in the Alignment group.

Middle Align centers text vertically within a cell.

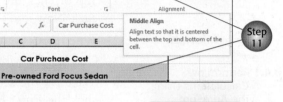

12 Make active any cell in row 15.

13 Tap or click the Format button, tap or click *Row Height*, type **26**, and then tap or press Enter, or tap or click OK.

14 Select A15:F15 and then tap or click the Middle Align button.

15 Tap or click in any cell to deselect the range.

16 Save the workbook using the same name (**8.1-CarCost-Your Name**) and then close the workbook.

Quick **STEPS**

Change Column Width
1. Activate cell within column.
2. Tap or click Format button.
3. Tap or click *Column Width*.
4. Type width.
5. Tap or click OK.

Change Row Height
1. Activate cell within row.
2. Tap or click Format button.
3. Tap or click *Row Height*.
4. Type height.
5. Tap or click OK.

AutoFit Column Width or Row Height
1. Activate cell.
2. Tap or click Format button.
3. Tap or click *AutoFit Row Height* or *AutoFit Column Width*.

ALTERNATIVE method Change column widths using a mouse by dragging the column boundary at the right of the column letter to the right to increase the width or left to decrease the width. Change row height using a mouse by dragging the row boundary below the row number up to decrease the height or down to increase the height. Double-click the right column boundary or the bottom row boundary to AutoFit the column width or row height.

Entering or Copying Data with the Fill Command and Using AutoSum

Topic 8.4

SKILLS

Use Auto Fill to enter a series

Use Fill Right to copy a value

Use the fill handle to enter data

Add a column with AutoSum

 **Tutorials**

8.4.1 Performing Calculations Using the AutoSum Button

8.4.2 Copying and Testing Formulas

The **Auto Fill** feature in Excel is used to enter data automatically based on a pattern or series that exists in an adjacent cell or range. For example, if *Monday* is entered into cell A1, Auto Fill can enter *Tuesday*, *Wednesday*, and so on automatically in the cells immediately right or below A1. Excel fills many common text or number series and also detects patterns for other data when you select the first few entries in a list. When no pattern or series applies, the fill feature can be used to copy an entry or formula across or down to other cells.

New to Excel 2013 is the **Flash Fill** feature that works to automatically fill data as soon as a pattern is recognized. When Flash Fill presents a suggested list in dimmed text, tap or press Enter to accept the suggestions, or ignore the suggestions and continue typing. A Flash Fill Options button appears when a list is presented with options to undo Flash Fill, accept the suggestions, or select changed cells.

1. Tap or click the New button in the QAT, or tap or click the FILE tab, tap or click New, and then tap or click *Blank workbook*.

2. Type the text entries in A2:A13 as shown in the image at right.

3. Change the width of column A to 18.

4. Make B1 the active cell, type **Sep**, and then tap or click the Enter button in the Formula bar.

5. Select B1:I1.

6. Tap or click the **Fill button** in the Editing group and then tap or click *Series* at the drop-down list.

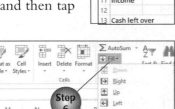

7. Tap or click *AutoFill* in the *Type* section of the Series dialog box and then tap or click OK.

AutoFill enters the column headings *Oct* through *Apr* in the selected range.

8. Make B3 the active cell, type **875**, and then tap or click the Enter button.

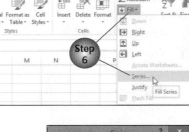

9. Select B3:I3, tap or click the Fill button, and then tap or click *Right* at the drop-down list.

Fill Right copies the entry in the first cell to the other cells within the selected range.

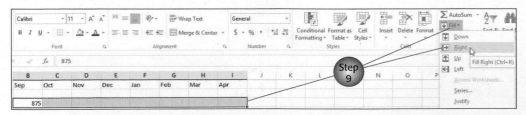

10 Enter the remaining values as shown in the image at right. In rows 5, 6, and 7, use Fill Right to enter the data by completing steps similar to those in Steps 8 and 9.

	A	B	C	D	E	F	G	H	I
1		Sep	Oct	Nov	Dec	Jan	Feb	Mar	Apr
2	Expenses								
3	Housing	875	875	875	875	875	875	875	875
4	Food	260	340	310	295	320	280	300	345
5	Transportation	88	88	88	88	88	88	88	88
6	Cell phone	48	48	48	48	48	48	48	48
7	Internet	42	42	42	42	42	42	42	42
8	Entertainment	150	110	95	175	100	85	95	120
9	Total Expenses								

Step 10

Using the Fill Handle to Copy Cells

A small, green square at the bottom right corner of the active cell (or selected range) is called the **fill handle**. When you point at the square with a mouse, the cell pointer changes appearance from the large white cross to the fill handle (✛). Drag right or down when you see the fill handle icon to copy data or a formula, or extend a series from the active cell or range to adjacent cells.

Using the Fill Handle on a Touch Device

Tapping a cell on a touch device displays the active cell with two selection handles instead of the fill handle. See Figure 8.3 for instructions on how to use the fill handle on a touch device.

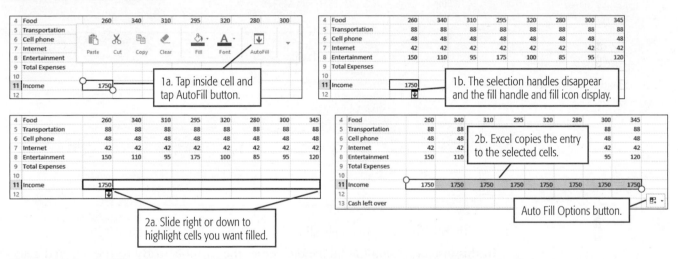

Figure 8.3 Using the fill handle on a touch device

11 Make B11 the active cell, type **1750**, and then tap or click the Enter button.

12 Slide or drag the fill handle right to I11.

The value *1750* is copied to the cells in the selected range. See Beyond Basics at the end of this topic for more information about using the versatile fill handle.

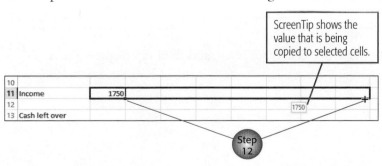

ScreenTip shows the value that is being copied to selected cells.

Step 12

oops!

Don't see fill handle? The fill handle may have been turned off. Open the Excel Options dialog box with Advanced tab (FILE, Options, *Advanced*) and then tap or click *Enable fill handle and cell drag-and-drop* to insert a check mark.

Using the SUM function

To add the expenses in B9, you could type the formula $=b3+b4+b5+b6+b7+b8$; however, Excel includes a built-in preprogrammed function called SUM that can be used to add a column or row of numbers. The SUM function is faster and easier to use. To add the expenses in B9 using SUM, you would type the formula $=SUM(b3:b8)$. Notice you need to provide only the range of cells to add within parentheses after $=SUM$ rather than each individual cell reference. Because the SUM function is used frequently, an **AutoSum button** is included in the HOME tab that automatically detects the range to be added.

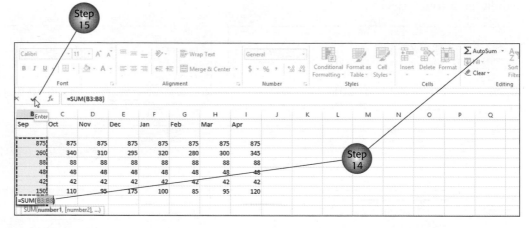

App Tip

In most cases the suggested range is correct; however, always check to make sure the included cells are the correct cells to be added. If necessary, drag to select a different range before completing the formula.

⑬ Make B9 the active cell.

⑭ Tap or click the AutoSum button in the Editing group of the HOME tab. (Do not tap or click the down-pointing arrow at the right of AutoSum.)

    Excel inserts the formula $=SUM(B3:B8)$ in B9 with the suggested range *B3:B8* selected.

⑮ Tap or click the Enter button, or tap or press Ctrl + Enter to complete the formula (Ctrl + Enter completes the entry and keeps the active cell in B9.)

⑯ With B9 still the active cell, slide or drag the fill handle right to I9.

    In this instance, using the fill handle copies the formula in B9 to the selected cells.

⑰ Make B13 the active cell, type **=b11-b9**, and then tap or click the Enter button or tap or press Ctrl + Enter.

⑱ With B13 the active cell, slide or drag the fill handle right to I13.

9	Total Expenses	1463	1503	1458	1523	1473	1418	1448	1518
10									
11	Income	1750	1750	1750	1750	1750	1750	1750	1750
12									
13	Cash left over	287	247	292	227	277	332	302	232
14									

⑲ Make J1 the active cell, type **Total**, and then tap or press Enter.

20 Make J3 the active cell and tap or click the AutoSum button.

In this instance, Excel suggests the range B3:I3 in the SUM function. Excel looks for values immediately above or left of the active cell. Because no value exists above J3, Excel correctly suggests adding the values to the left in the same row.

21 Tap or click the Enter button to accept the formula.

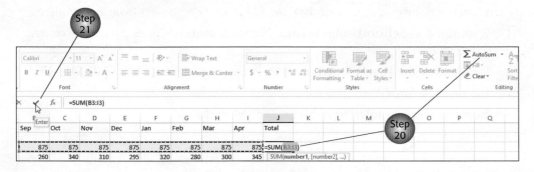

22 With J3 the active cell, slide or drag the fill handle down to J13.

23 Make J10 the active cell and press the Delete key, or tap or click the Clear button in the Editing group and then tap or click *Clear All* at the drop-down list.

24 Make J12 the active cell and repeat the instruction in Step 23.

	A	B	C	D	E	F	G	H	I	J
1		Sep	Oct	Nov	Dec	Jan	Feb	Mar	Apr	Total
2	Expenses									
3	Housing	875	875	875	875	875	875	875	875	7000
4	Food	260	340	310	295	320	280	300	345	2450
5	Transportation	88	88	88	88	88	88	88	88	704
6	Cell phone	48	48	48	48	48	48	48	48	384
7	Internet	42	42	42	42	42	42	42	42	336
8	Entertainment	150	110	95	175	100	85	95	120	930
9	Total Expenses	1463	1503	1458	1523	1473	1418	1448	1518	11804
10										
11	Income	1750	1750	1750	1750	1750	1750	1750	1750	14000
12										
13	Cash left over	287	247	292	227	277	332	302	232	2196

25 Save the new workbook as **8.4-SchoolBudget-Your Name** in the Ch8 folder in CompletedTopicsByChapter on your USB flash drive. Leave the workbook open for the next topic.

App Tip

With options from the Clear button drop-down list, you can clear only contents and leave formatting intact or vice versa.

Quick **STEPS**

AutoFill Series
1. Select range.
2. Tap or click Fill button.
3. Tap or click *Series*.
4. Tap or click *AutoFill*.
5. Tap or click OK.

Fill Right
1. Select range.
2. Tap or click Fill button.
3. Tap or click *Right*.

Copy Using Fill Handle
1. Make cell active.
2. Slide or drag fill handle in required direction.

Add with the SUM Function
1. Activate formula cell.
2. Tap or click AutoSum button.
3. Tap or click Enter button OR select correct range and tap or click Enter button.

 **More Examples of Using the Fill Command**

Excel's Fill command can detect patterns in values, dates, times, months, days, years, or other data. The pattern is detected based on the cells selected before dragging the fill handle. Following are some examples of series the fill handle can extend. In each example, you would select both cells in column A and column B and then drag the fill handle right to extend the data.

Column A	Column B	Extends this data when fill handle is dragged right
10	20	30, 40, 50, and so on
9:00	10:00	11:00, 12:00, 1:00 and so on
2014	2015	2016, 2017, 2018 and so on
Year 1	Year 2	Year 3, Year 4, Year 5 and so on

Topic 8.5

Inserting and Deleting Rows and Columns

New rows or columns are inserted or deleted using the Insert or Delete buttons in the Cells group of the HOME tab. New rows are inserted above the row in which the active cell is positioned, and new columns are inserted to the left.

Cell references within formulas and formula results are automatically updated when new rows or columns with data are added to or removed from a worksheet.

SKILLS

Insert a new row

Insert a new column

Delete a row

Tutorial

8.5   Inserting and Deleting Columns and Rows

1. With the **8.4-SchoolBudget-Your Name** workbook open, make active any cell in row 4.

2. Tap or click the **Insert button** arrow in the Cells group of the HOME tab.

3. Tap or click *Insert Sheet Rows* at the drop-down list.

A new blank row is inserted between *Housing* and *Food*.

oops!

Only one cell inserted instead of an entire row? Tapping or clicking the top part of the Insert button inserts a cell instead of an entire new row. Use Undo and then try again, making sure to tap or click the arrow on the bottom part of the Insert button to access the drop-down list.

4. Type the following entries in the cells indicated:

A4	**Utilities**	F4	**128**
B4	**110**	G4	**106**
C4	**115**	H4	**118**
D4	**132**	I4	**112**
E4	**147**		

5. Make J3 the active cell and slide or drag the fill handle down to J4 to copy the SUM formula to the new row.

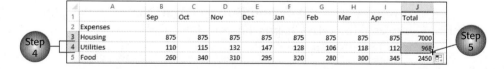

App Tip

With a mouse you can also insert multiple rows by selecting the row numbers along the left edge of the worksheet area, right-clicking, and then choosing *Insert*.

6. Select A1:A2, tap or click the Insert button arrow, and then tap or click *Insert Sheet Rows*.

Two rows are inserted above the worksheet.

7. Make A1 the active cell and type **Proposed School Budget**.

8. Make A2 the active cell and type **First Year of Program**.

9. Merge & Center A1 in columns A to J.

10. Merge & Center A2 in columns A to J.

⑪ Make any cell in column J active.

⑫ Tap or click the Insert button arrow and then tap or click *Insert Sheet Columns* at the drop-down list.

A new column is inserted between *Apr* and *Total*. Notice also an **Insert Options button** appears. Options from this button are used to format the new column with the same format options as those in the column at the left or the column at the right of the new column.

Insert Rows or Columns
1. Activate cell or select range.
2. Tap or click Insert button arrow.
3. Tap or click *Insert Sheet Rows* or *Insert Sheet Columns*.

Delete Rows or Columns
1. Activate cell or select range.
2. Tap or click Delete button arrow.
3. Tap or click *Delete Sheet Rows* or *Delete Sheet Columns*.

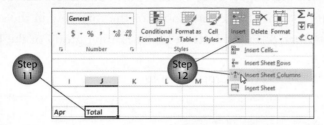

To delete a single row or column, position the active cell in any cell within the row or column to be removed and choose *Delete Sheet Rows* or *Delete Sheet Columns* from the **Delete button** arrow drop-down list. Remove multiple rows or columns from the worksheet by first selecting the range of rows or columns to be deleted.

⑬ Make any cell in row 10 active.

⑭ Tap or click the Delete button arrow and then tap or click *Delete Sheet Rows* at the drop-down list.

Row 10 is removed from the worksheet, and existing rows below are shifted up to fill in the space.

App Tip

Delete a column by performing similar steps except choose *Delete Sheet Columns* at the Delete button drop-down list.

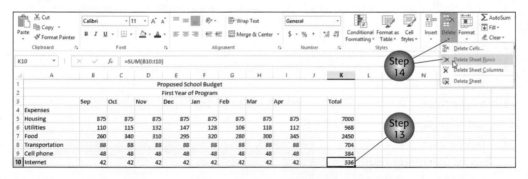

⑮ Save the workbook using the same name (**8.4-SchoolBudget-Your Name**). Leave the workbook open for the next topic.

Inserting and Deleting Cells

The Insert and Delete buttons are also used to insert or delete cells within a worksheet. Select the range of cells you need to add and choose *Insert Cells* from the Insert button drop-down list. At the Insert dialog box, choose whether you want to shift existing cells right or down.

Select the range of cells to delete, choose *Delete Cells* at the Delete button drop-down list, and then select whether to shift existing cells left or up to fill the space.

Sorting and Applying Cell Styles

A range in Excel can be rearranged by sorting in either ascending or descending order on one or more columns. For example, you can sort a list of names and cities first by the city and then by the last name. To sort by more than one column, select the range and open the Sort dialog box from the Sort & Filter button drop-down list.

① With the **8.4-SchoolBudget-Your Name** workbook open, select A5:K10.

Notice you do not include the heading in A4 or the total row in the sort range.

② Tap or click the **Sort & Filter button** in the Editing group of the HOME tab.

③ Tap or click *Sort A to Z* at the drop-down list.

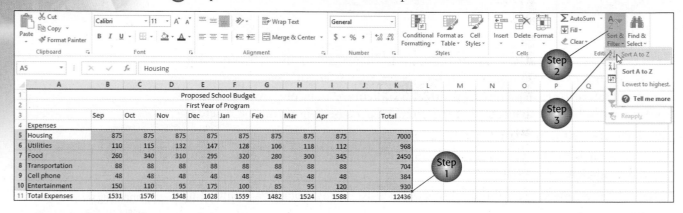

 **Tutorials**

8.6.1 Sorting Data

8.6.2 Applying Cell Styles and Themes

④ Tap or click in any cell to deselect the range and review the new order of the expenses.

⑤ Select A5:K10.

⑥ Tap or click the Sort & Filter button and then tap or click *Custom Sort* at the drop-down list.

⑦ At the Sort dialog box, tap or click the *Sort by* list arrow in the *Column* section and then tap or click *Column K*.

⑧ Tap or click the *Order* list arrow (currently displays *Smallest to Largest*) and then tap or click *Largest to Smallest*.

⑨ Tap or click OK.

The range is rearranged in descending order from highest expense total to lowest.

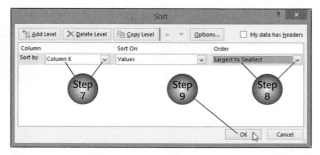

⑩ Tap or click in any cell to deselect the range and review the new order of expenses.

Similar to Word's Styles feature, **Cell Styles** in Excel are a set of predefined formatting options that can be applied to a single cell or a range. Using Cell Styles to format a worksheet is faster and promotes consistency in worksheets. The *Cell Styles* gallery groups styles by the sections *Good, Bad and Neutral, Data and Model, Titles and Headings, Themed Cell Styles,* and *Number format.*

⑪ Make A1 the active cell and then tap or click the **Cell Styles button** in the Styles group of the HOME tab.

⑫ Tap or click *Heading 1* in the *Titles and Headings* section of the *Cell Styles* gallery.

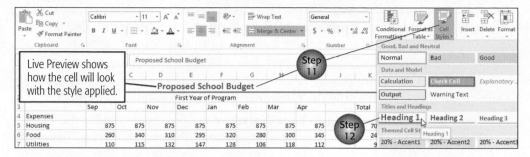

Live Preview shows how the cell will look with the style applied.

⑬ Make A2 the active cell, tap or click the Cell Styles button, and then tap or click *Heading 4* in the *Titles and Headings* section of the *Cell Styles* gallery.

⑭ Apply the Heading 4 Cell Style to A4, A13, and A15.

⑮ Select B3:K3, apply the *Accent1* style in the *Themed Cell Styles* section of the *Cell Styles* gallery, and then Center the cells.

⑯ Select B5:K15 and apply the *Comma [0]* style in the *Number Format* section of the *Cell Styles* gallery.

⑰ Select B15:K15 and apply the *Total* style in the *Titles and Headings* section of the *Cell Styles* gallery.

⑱ Tap or click in any cell to deselect the range, and compare your worksheet with the one shown in Figure 8.4.

	A	B	C	D	E	F	G	H	I	J	K
1					Proposed School Budget						
2					First Year of Program						
3		Sep	Oct	Nov	Dec	Jan	Feb	Mar	Apr		Total
4	Expenses										
5	Housing	875	875	875	875	875	875	875	875		7,000
6	Food	260	340	310	295	320	280	300	345		2,450
7	Utilities	110	115	132	147	128	106	118	112		968
8	Entertainment	150	110	95	175	100	85	95	120		930
9	Transportation	88	88	88	88	88	88	88	88		704
10	Cell phone	48	48	48	48	48	48	48	48		384
11	Total Expenses	1,531	1,576	1,548	1,628	1,559	1,482	1,524	1,588		12,436
12											
13	Income	1,750	1,750	1,750	1,750	1,750	1,750	1,750	1,750		14,000
14											
15	Cash left over	219	174	202	122	191	268	226	162		1,564

Figure 8.4 Sorted worksheet with cell styles applied

⑲ Save the workbook using the same name (**8.4–SchoolBudget–Your Name**). Leave the workbook open for the next topic.

Workbook Themes

Options in the *Titles and Headings* and *Themed Cell Styles* sections change depending on the active theme (set of colors, fonts, and effects). Change the theme for a workbook using the *Themes* gallery in the PAGE LAYOUT tab.

oops!

No Cell Styles button? On larger displays the Cell Styles gallery displays in place of the Cell Styles button. Tap or click the More button to view the Cell Styles gallery.

App Tip

If you are using a mouse, hold down the Ctrl key and click A4, A13, and A15 to format all three cells in one operation.

Quick **STEPS**

Sort a Range by the First Column
1. Select range.
2. Tap or click Sort & Filter button.
3. Tap or click *Sort A to Z* or *Sort Z to A*.

Custom Sort
1. Select range.
2. Tap or click Sort & Filter button.
3. Tap or click *Custom Sort*.
4. Change options and/or add levels as needed.
5. Tap or click OK.

Apply Cell Styles
1. Select cell or range.
2. Tap or click Cell Styles button.
3. Tap or click desired cell style.

Changing Orientation and Scaling and Displaying Cell Formulas

Topic 8.7

SKILLS

Preview a worksheet

Change orientation

Display cell formulas

Change scaling

By default, new Excel workbooks have print options set to print the active worksheet on a letter-sized page (8.5 x 11 inches), in portrait orientation, and with 0.75-inch top and bottom margins and 0.7-inch left and right margins. Preview a new worksheet before printing to make sure these print options are appropriate.

Workbooks are often distributed as PDF files and circulated electronically. Always preview the worksheet and change print options as needed before exporting as PDF because PDF files are essentially the electronic view of the printed worksheet.

1. With the **8.4-SchoolBudget-Your Name** workbook open, display the Print tab Backstage view and compare your screen with the one shown in Figure 8.5.

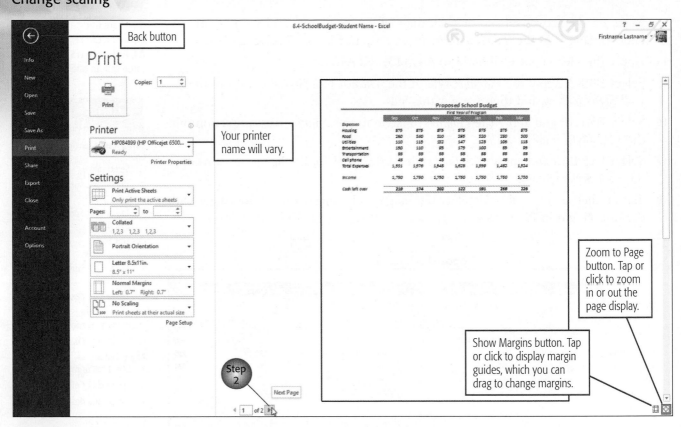

Figure 8.5 Print tab Backstage view with first page displayed for the **8.4-SchoolBudget-Student Name** worksheet

2. Tap or click the Next Page button at the bottom of the preview area to view the second page of the worksheet.

3. Tap or click the Orientation button (displays *Portrait Orientation*) and then tap or click *Landscape Orientation* at the drop-down list.

Change the Orientation
1. Display Print tab Backstage view.
2. Tap or click Orientation button.
3. Tap or click *Landscape Orientation*.

Notice the worksheet now fits on one page. Landscape is a common layout used for wide worksheets.

4. Tap or click the Back button to return to the worksheet and then save the revised workbook using the same name (**8.4-SchoolBudget-Your Name**).

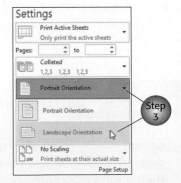

Formula results display in the worksheet area with the formula used to generate the result visible in the Formula bar when a cell is active. On a printed copy of the worksheet only the formula result is printed. You may want to print a second copy of the worksheet with the formulas displayed in the cell as a backup or documentation strategy for a complex or otherwise important worksheet.

Ctrl + ` (called grave accent usually located above the Tab key) is the keyboard command to turn on or off the display of formulas.

5 Tap or click the FILE tab and then tap or click Options.

6 Tap or click *Advanced* in the left pane of the Excel Options dialog box.

7 Slide or scroll down the Advanced options for working with Excel until you reach the section titled *Display options for this worksheet*.

8 Tap or click to insert a check mark in the *Show formulas in cells instead of their calculated results* check box.

9 Tap or click OK.

10 Slide or scroll right if necessary to review the worksheet with formulas displayed.

11 Display the Print tab Backstage view.

12 Tap or click the Scaling button (displays *No Scaling*) and then tap or click *Fit Sheet on One Page*.

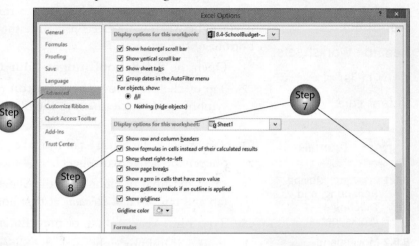

Fit Sheet on One Page shrinks the size of text on the printout to fit all columns and rows on one page.

13 Tap or click the Back button to return to the worksheet.

14 Use Save As to save a copy of the worksheet with the formulas displayed in the Ch8 folder in CompletedTopicsByChapter as **8.4-School BudgetWithFormulasDisplayed-Your Name**.

15 Close the workbook.

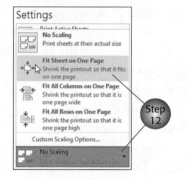

Other methods used to print wide worksheets are decreasing the margins and changing the scaling percentage.

Quick
STEPS

Display Cell Formulas
1. Tap or click FILE tab.
2. Tap or click Options.
3. Tap or click *Advanced*.
4. Slide or scroll down dialog box.
5. Tap or click *Show formulas in cells instead of their calculated results*.
6. Tap or click OK.

Scale a Worksheet
1. Display Print tab Backstage view.
2. Tap or click Scaling button.
3. Tap or click scaling option.

ALTERNATIVE method

Tap or click PAGE LAYOUT and use the Margins and Orientation buttons in the Page Setup group, the *Width* and *Height* lists, and the *Scale* text box options in the Scale to Fit group to change print options.

Beyond Basics   **More Scaling Options**

The scaling option **Fit All Columns on One Page** shrinks the size of text until all of the columns fit the page width; more than one page may print if there are many rows. **Fit All Rows on One Page** shrinks the size of text until all of the rows fit the page height; more than one page may print if there are many columns.

Inserting and Renaming a Worksheet, Copying Cells, and Indenting Cells

A workbook can contain more than one worksheet. Use multiple worksheets as a method to organize or group data into manageable units. For example, a homeowner might have one household finance workbook in which he or she keeps track of bills and loans in one worksheet, savings and investments in a second worksheet, and a household budget in a third worksheet. Insert, rename, and navigate between worksheets using the sheet tabs in the **Sheet tab bar** near the bottom of the window.

SKILLS

Insert a new worksheet

Rename worksheets

Copy cells

Indent cells

 **Tutorials**

8.8.1 Inserting, Moving, Renaming, and Deleting a Worksheet

8.8.2 Moving and Copying Cells

8.8.3 Using Format Painter

 App Tip

Other options on the sheet tab shortcut menu are used to delete, move, copy, hide, or protect entire sheets, and to change the color of the background in the sheet tab.

oops!

Pasted to the wrong starting cell? Slide or drag the border of the selected range to the correct starting point or use Cut and Paste to move cells.

1. Open the **8.4-SchoolBudget-Your Name** workbook.

2. Tap or click the **New sheet button** (plus symbol inside circle) next to the Sheet1 tab in the Sheet tab bar.

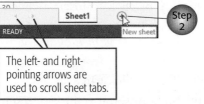

The left- and right-pointing arrows are used to scroll sheet tabs.

3. Tap or click the Sheet1 tab to make Sheet1 the active worksheet.

4. Press and hold or right-click the Sheet1 tab and tap or click *Rename* at the shortcut menu.

5. Type **First Year** and tap or press Enter.

6. Press and hold or right-click the Sheet2 tab, tap or click *Rename*, type **Second Year**, and then tap or press Enter.

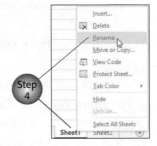

7. Tap or click the First Year tab to make First Year the active worksheet.

8. Select A4:A15 and tap or click the Copy button in the Clipboard group of the HOME tab.

9. Make Second Year the active worksheet, make A4 the active cell, and then tap or click the top portion of the Paste button (not the down-pointing arrow) in the Clipboard group.

10. Tap or click the Paste Options button and then tap or click *Keep Source Column Widths*.

11. Make First Year the active worksheet, select A1:K3, and then tap or click the Copy button.

12. Make Second Year the active worksheet, make A1 the active cell, and then tap or click the Paste button.

13. Edit A2 in the Second Year worksheet to change *First* to *Second*.

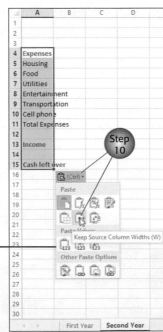

This menu displays differently on a tablet or other touch device with the options optimized for touch in a single column with text labels next to each button.

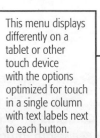

14 Enter the data, complete the formulas, and format the cells in the Second Year worksheet, as shown in Figure 8.6.

	A	B	C	D	E	F	G	H	I	J	K
1					Proposed School Budget						
2					Second Year of Program						
3		Sep	Oct	Nov	Dec	Jan	Feb	Mar	Apr		Total
4	Expenses										
5	Housing	910	910	910	910	910	910	910	910		7,280
6	Food	245	330	298	285	308	275	295	355		2,391
7	Utilities	112	118	140	151	131	118	122	124		1,016
8	Entertainment	160	95	100	185	110	95	90	125		960
9	Transportation	90	90	90	90	90	90	90	90		720
10	Cell phone	50	50	50	50	50	50	50	50		400
11	Total Expenses	1,567	1,593	1,588	1,671	1,599	1,538	1,557	1,654		12,767
12											
13	Income	1,800	1,800	1,800	1,800	1,800	1,800	1,800	1,800		14,400
14											
15	Cash left over	233	207	212	129	201	262	243	146		1,633

Figure 8.6 Completed Second Year worksheet

The Increase Indent button in the Alignment group of the HOME tab moves an entry approximately one character width inward from the left edge of a cell each time the button is tapped or clicked. Use this feature to indent entries in a list below a subheading. The Decrease Indent button moves an entry approximately one character width closer to the left edge of the cell each time the button is tapped or clicked.

15 With Second Year still the active worksheet, select A5:A10 and then tap or click the Increase Indent button in the Alignment group of the HOME tab.

16 Make A11 the active cell and tap twice or click twice the Increase Indent button.

17 Change the orientation to landscape for the Second Year worksheet.

18 Make First Year the active worksheet, indent once A5:A10, and indent twice A11.

19 Save the workbook using the same name (**8.4–SchoolBudget–Your Name**) and then close the workbook.

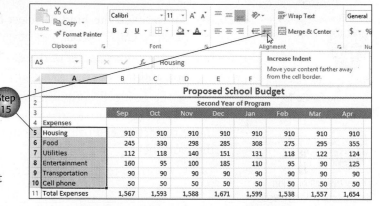

ALTERNATIVE method Another way to rename a worksheet is to double-tap or double-click the sheet tab, type a new name, and then tap or press Enter.

App Tip

Use the fill handle, copy formulas from the First Year sheet to the Second Year sheet, and/or use the Format Painter feature to copy data, formulas, and formatting whenever possible.

Quick STEPS

Insert a Worksheet
Tap or click New sheet button.

Rename a Worksheet
1. Press and hold or right-click sheet tab.
2. Tap or click *Rename*.
3. Type new name.
4. Tap or press Enter.

Indent Cells
1. Activate cell or select range.
2. Tap or click Increase Indent button.

App Tip

Each worksheet has its own page layout/print options.

Beyond Basics **Scrolling Sheet Tabs in the Sheet tab bar**

Use the left- and right-pointing arrows to the left of the first sheet tab to scroll to sheet tabs not currently visible, or press and hold or right-click an arrow to open the Activate dialog box, tap or click the sheet to make active, and then tap or click OK.

Using Go To, Freezing Panes, and Shading, Wrapping, and Rotating Cell Entries

Topic 8.9

SKILLS

Use Go To

Freeze panes

Add fill color

Wrap text

Rotate text

 **Tutorials**

8.9.1 Navigating and Scrolling in a Worksheet

8.9.2 Freezing Panes and Changing the Zoom

Ctrl + G is the keyboard command for Go To.

The active cell position determines which rows and columns are fixed—all rows above and all columns left of the active cell are frozen.

Once cells have been frozen, *Freeze Panes* from the Freeze Panes button changes to *Unfreeze Panes*.

In large worksheets where you cannot see all cells at once, use the **Go To** and **Go To Special** commands to move the active cell to a specific location in a worksheet. Column or row headings are not visible when you scroll right or down beyond the viewing area, making it difficult to relate text or values. The **Freeze Panes** option fixes column and/or row headings in place for scrolling large worksheets.

1. Open the **NSCSuppliesInventory** workbook from the Ch8 folder in Student_Data_Files.

2. Save the workbook as **8.9-NSCSuppliesInventory-Your Name** in the Ch8 folder in CompletedTopicsByChapter.

3. Slide or scroll down the worksheet area until the titles and column headings are no longer visible.

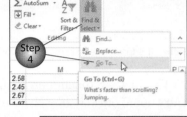

4. Tap or click the **Find & Select button** in the Editing group of the HOME tab and then tap or click *Go To* at the drop-down list.

5. At the Go To dialog box, type **a4** in the *Reference* text box, and then tap or press Enter, or tap or click OK.

6. Tap or click the Find & Select button and then tap or click *Go To Special*.

7. Tap or click *Last cell* in the Go To Special dialog box and tap or click OK.

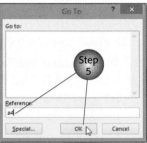

Use the Last cell option in the Go To Special dialog box in a large worksheet to move the active cell to the bottom right of the worksheet.

8. Use Go To to move the active cell back to A4.

9. If necessary, slide or scroll up until you can see the first three rows of titles and column headings.

10. With A4 the active cell, tap or click the VIEW tab and then tap or click the Freeze Panes button in the Window group.

11. Tap or click *Freeze Panes* at the drop-down list.

12. Slide or scroll down past all data. Notice that rows 1 to 3 do not scroll out of the viewing area.

Column headings can be formatted to stand out from the rest of the worksheet by shading the background of the cell or rotating the cell entries. Cells with long entries can still be housed in narrower columns by formatting the text to automatically wrap within the width of the cell.

13 Slide or scroll to the top of the worksheet and select A1.

14 Tap or click the HOME tab, tap or click the **Fill Color button** arrow in the Font group, and then tap or click *Orange, Accent 6* (last color in first row of *Theme Colors* section) at the drop-down gallery.

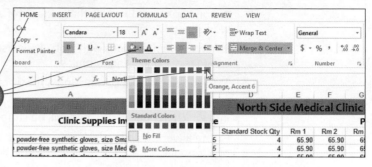

15 Select A2:M2 and apply *Orange, Accent 6, Lighter 60%* fill color (last option in third row of *Theme Colors* section).

16 Select A3:M3 and apply *Orange, Accent 6, Lighter 80%* fill color (last option in second row of *Theme Colors* section).

17 Make M3 the active cell, change the row height to 30, and change the column width to 10.

18 With M3 still the active cell, tap or click the **Wrap Text button** in the Alignment group.

Notice the entire column heading is visible again with the text wrapping within the cell.

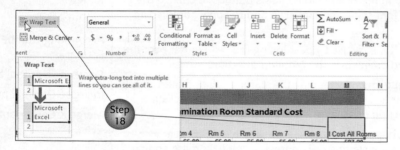

19 Make D3 the active cell, change the column width to 9, and then tap or click the Wrap Text button.

20 Select E3:L3, tap or click the Orientation button in the Alignment group, and then tap or click *Angle Counterclockwise* at the drop-down list.

Angle Counterclockwise rotates the text within the cell boundaries 45 degrees.

21 Tap or click any cell to deselect the range and then display the Print tab Backstage view.

22 Change settings to *Landscape Orientation* and *Fit All Columns on One Page* and then go back to the worksheet display.

23 Save the workbook using the same name (**8.9-NSCSuppliesInventory-Your Name**) and then close the workbook.

oops!

Forgot how to change row height and column width? Refer to Topic 8.3.

Quick **STEPS**

Freeze Panes
1. Activate cell below and right of cells to freeze.
2. Tap or click VIEW tab.
3. Tap or click Freeze Panes button.
4. Tap or click *Freeze Panes*.

Shade Cell Background
1. Select cell or range.
2. Tap or click Fill Color button arrow.
3. Tap or click desired color.

Rotate Cells
1. Select cell or range.
2. Tap or click Orientation button in Alignment group.
3. Tap or click rotate option.

App Tip

Rotate column headings diagonally or vertically in narrow columns.

Concepts Review

Topic	Key Concepts	Key Terms
Creating and Editing a New Worksheet	A spreadsheet is an application in which data is created, analyzed, and presented in a grid-like structure of columns and rows.	Spreadsheet application
	A workbook is an Excel file that consists of a collection of individual worksheets.	Workbooks
	A new workbook opens with a blank worksheet into which you create text, values, and formulas.	Worksheets
	The intersection of a column and a row is called a cell.	Cell
	The active cell is indicated with a green border and is the location into which the next data typed will be stored.	Active cell
	Create a worksheet by making a cell active and typing text, a value, or a formula.	Formula
	A formula is used to perform mathematical operations on values.	Clear button
	Formula entries begin with an equals sign and are followed by cell references with operators between the references.	
	Edit a cell by typing new data to overwrite existing data, by double-tapping or double-clicking to open the cell for editing, or by inserting or deleting characters in the Formula bar.	
	Press Delete or use the Clear button to delete the contents in the active cell.	
Formatting Cells	The Font group in the HOME tab contains buttons to change the font, font size, font color, and font style and to apply borders and shading.	Range
	Select cells with the mouse by positioning the cell pointer over the starting cell and dragging in the required direction.	Comma Style
	Select cells using touch by tapping the starting cell and then sliding your finger over a selection handle until the remaining cells are inside the selection rectangle.	Accounting Number Format
	A rectangular-shaped group of cells is called a range and is referenced with the starting cell address, a colon, and the ending cell address (e.g., A1:F15).	Decrease Decimal button
	By default, cells in a new worksheet have the General format, which has no specific formatting options.	Increase Decimal button
	Comma Style adds a comma in thousands and two decimal places.	Merge & Center button
	Accounting Number Format adds a dollar symbol, comma in thousands, and two decimal places.	
	The Decrease Decimal button and Increase Decimal button remove or add one decimal place each time the button is tapped or clicked.	
	Borders in various styles and colors can be added to the edges of a cell.	
	The Merge & Center button in the Alignment group is often used to center a worksheet title over multiple columns.	

Topic	Key Concepts	Key Terms
Adjusting Column Width and Row Height, and Changing Alignment	A technique to add more space between cells to improve readability or emphasize a section is to widen a column or increase the height of a row. Open the Column Width dialog box to enter a new value for the width of the column in which the active cell is positioned. Excel displays a series of pound symbols when a column width has been made too narrow to display all of the cell contents. AutoFit changes the width of a column to fit the contents of the active cell. Open the Row Height dialog box to enter a new value for the height of the row in which the active cell is positioned. Align a cell at the left, center, or right horizontally, or top, middle, or bottom vertically using buttons in the Alignment group. The Middle Align button centers a cell's contents vertically.	AutoFit Middle Align button
Entering or Copying Data with the Fill Command and Using AutoSum	Auto Fill can be used to automatically enter data in a series or pattern based upon an entry in an adjacent cell. A new feature in Excel 2013 is Flash Fill, which automatically suggests entries when a pattern is detected. Select a range and use the Fill button to open the Series dialog box or copy an entry down, right, up, or left. The small, green square at the bottom right of an active cell is the fill handle and can be used to copy data and formulas or to enter a series. Excel includes the AutoSum button in the HOME tab that is used to enter a SUM function to add a column or row of numbers.	Auto Fill Flash Fill Fill button Fill handle AutoSum button
Inserting and Deleting Columns and Rows	A new row is inserted above the active cell or selected range. A new column is inserted left of the active cell or selected range. Use the Insert button in the Cells group to insert new rows or columns. Options for formatting new rows or columns are available from the Insert Options button that appears when rows or columns are inserted. Delete rows or columns from the Delete button in the Cells group. The Insert and Delete buttons can also be used to insert or delete cells within the worksheet.	Insert button Insert Options button Delete button
Sorting and Applying Cell Styles	A range can be sorted in ascending or descending order by one or more columns. Select a range and choose the sort order option from the Sort & Filter button in the Editing group to arrange the rows by the entries in the first column. Open the Sort dialog box to sort by more than one column or to choose a different column in the range by which to sort. Cell Styles are a set of predefined formatting options. Use Cell Styles to format faster and/or promote consistency among worksheets. Select cells and use the Cell Styles button to choose a set of formatting options.	Sort & Filter button Cell Styles Cell Styles button

continued....

Topic	Key Concepts	Key Terms
Changing Orientation and Scaling, and Displaying Cell Formulas	New workbooks print on a letter-size page, in portrait orientation, with top and bottom margins of 0.75-inch and left and right margins of 0.7-inch.	Fit Sheet on One Page
	Change print options even if you are only exporting the workbook as a PDF because PDFs are generated using the print settings.	Fit All Columns on One Page
	Change to landscape orientation using the Orientation button at the Print tab Backstage view or in the Page Setup group of the PAGE LAYOUT tab.	Fit All Rows on One Page
	Landscape is a common layout used for wide worksheets.	
	Open the Excel Options dialog box with the *Advanced* pane active to turn on or turn off the display of formulas in cells.	
	Fit Sheet on One Page scales text on a printout so that all columns and rows print on one page.	
	Fit All Columns on One Page is a scaling option that shrinks text to fit all columns in one page width.	
	Fit All Rows on One Page is a scaling option that shrinks text to fit all rows in one page height.	
Inserting and Renaming a Worksheet, Copying Cells, and Indenting Cells	The Sheet tab bar near the bottom left of the window is used to insert, rename, and navigate among sheets in a workbook.	Sheet tab bar
	Tap or click the New sheet button in the Sheet tab bar to insert a new worksheet.	New sheet button
	Press and hold or right-click a sheet tab and choose *Rename* to type a new name for a worksheet.	
	Copy and paste cells between worksheets using the Copy and Paste buttons in the Clipboard group.	
	Keep Source Column Widths from the Paste Options button lets you paste new cells with the same column width as the source cell.	
Using Go To, Freezing Panes, and Shading, Wrapping, and Rotating Cell Entries	Go To and Go To Special are options from the Find & Select button used to move to a specific cell in a large worksheet.	Go To
	Freeze Panes fixes rows and/or columns in place for scrolling in large worksheets so that column and row headings do not scroll out of the viewing area.	Go To Special
		Freeze Panes
	All rows above and all columns left of the active cell are frozen when Freeze Panes is turned on.	Find & Select button
	Cells are shaded with color using the Fill Color button in the Font group.	Fill Color button
	Long text entries in cells can be displayed in narrow columns by wrapping text within the cell's column width using the Wrap Text button in the Alignment group.	Wrap Text button
	Angle Counterclockwise is an option from the Orientation button in the Alignment group that rotates text within a cell 45 degrees.	Angle Counterclockwise

Multiple Choice

1. Which of the following is *not* a valid cell or range reference?
   a. Z1
   b. 3Z
   c. Z1:Z100
   d. AA1

2. Which of the following is *not* a valid operator for a formula?
   a. *
   b. +
   c. -
   d. @

3. By default, cells in a new worksheet have this format.
   a. General
   b. Comma Style
   c. Accounting Number Format
   d. Number

4. This feature is often used to center titles in a worksheet.
   a. Orientation
   b. Wrap Text
   c. Merge & Center
   d. Merge Columns

5. This symbol displays across a cell in a column in which the width is too narrow.
   a. @
   b. $
   c. *
   d. #

6. This option from the Format button sets the width of the column to fit the contents of the active cell.
   a. AutoFit
   b. AutoWidth
   c. AutoAlign
   d. AutoSize

7. This feature is used to enter data automatically into a range based upon a pattern or series.
   a. Auto Fit
   b. Auto Enter
   c. Auto Complete
   d. Auto Fill

8. The button creates a SUM function in the active cell.
   a. AutoSum
   b. AutoAdd
   c. AutoFunction
   d. AutoFormula

9. The Insert button to add a new row or column is found in this group in the HOME tab.
   a. Cells
   b. Alignment
   c. Styles
   d. Editing

10. This button appears when a new column has been inserted with options to apply formatting to the new column from the column at the left or the column at the right.
    a. Insert Options
    b. Column Options
    c. Auto Options
    d. Fill Options

11. Choose this option from the Sort & Filter button drop-down list to sort a range by a column other than the first column.
    a. Sort
    b. Custom Sort
    c. Sort Columns
    d. Sort Order

12. Buttons in this gallery are used to apply a predefined collection of formatting options to the selected cell or range.
    a. Cell Formats
    b. Cell Styles
    c. Cell Formatting
    d. Format Painter

13. Open this dialog box to turn on the display of cell formulas.
    a. Formula Options
    b. Format Cells
    c. Excel Options
    d. Sheet Options

14. This setting at the Print tab Backstage view will fit a two-page worksheet on one page.
    a. Shrink to Fit
    b Scale to Fit
    c. Fit All Text on One Page
    d. Fit Sheet on One Page

15. Use this area to navigate to a different worksheet in the workbook.
    a. Sheets bar
    b. Sheet tab bar
    c. Navigation bar
    d. Scroll bar

16. This button will move text within the active cell approximately one character width away from the left edge of the cell.
    a. Left Indent
    b. Increase Indent
    c. Indent
    d. Decrease Indent

17. This option fixes in place for scrolling purposes all rows above the active cell.
    a. Fix Rows
    b. Freeze Rows
    c. Freeze Top Row
    d. Freeze Panes

18. This option is used to rotate text within the cell 45 degrees.
    a. Angle Counterclockwise
    b. Rotate 45
    c. Rotate Up
    d. Angle Right

Crossword Puzzle

ACROSS
3 Button to vertically center a cell
4 Dialog box to move active cell to specific address
5 Layout often used for wide worksheets
7 Format that displays 1000.5 as 1,000.50
10 =E7*E8
15 Rectangular block of cells
16 Predefined set of formats for a cell
17 Button that creates SUM function

DOWN
1 Button to insert a new worksheet
2 Excel file
6 Small square at bottom right of active cell
8 Cell with green border
9 Button to display a long cell entry in a narrow column
11 Button to open Column Width dialog box
12 Option from shortcut menu to type new name for worksheet
13 Button to shrink text for printing large worksheet
14 Rearrange order of rows in range

Matching

Match the term with the statement or definition.

_____ 1. Intersection of a column and a row
_____ 2. Displays contents stored in active cell
_____ 3. Group of cells
_____ 4. Adds dollar symbol to values
_____ 5. Copies first cell to remaining cells in range
_____ 6. Heading 1
_____ 7. Wide worksheet setting
_____ 8. Plus symbol inside circle button
_____ 9. Move to last cell
_____ 10. Applies color to background of cell

a. Accounting Number Format
b. Cell Styles
c. Landscape Orientation
d. Fill Color
e. New sheet
f. Cell
g. Go To Special
h. Range
i. Formula bar
j. Fill

Project 1 Creating and Editing a New Workbook

Individual

Deliverable: Excel worksheet with Auction Fee Calculations (continued in Project 2)

1. Start a new blank workbook and enter the text and values in the worksheet as shown in Figure 8.7.

	A	B	C	D	E	F	G	H	I	J
1	Fees Paid for Video Game Online Auctions									
2	Auctions ended in January									
3										
4	AuctionID	Game			Platform	Sale Price	Fee	Shipping	Fee	Total Fee
5	25687	Ghost Recon Future Soldier			Xbox 360	40.99		4.99		
6	31452	Far Cry 3			Xbox 360	39.99		4.99		
7	98563	Call of Duty Black Ops II			Xbox 360	37.99		4.99		
8	17586	Halo 4			Xbox 360	35.99		4.99		
9	32586	Call of Duty Black Ops II			PS 3	33		7.99		
10	45862	Legends of Troy			PS 3	50		6.5		
11	13485	Skyrim			Windows	37		5		
12	65985	Grand Theft Auto V			Windows	58.99		5		

Figure 8.7 Project 1 worksheet

2. Save the workbook as **C8-Project1-AuctionFees-Your Name** in a new folder named *Ch8* within the ChapterProjectsWork folder on your USB flash drive.
3. Enter the following formulas by typing the formula in the active cell or by using the pointing method:

    G5   =F5*.10   J5   =G5+I5

    I5   =H5*.10

4. Use the fill handle to copy each formula to the remaining rows in columns G, I, and J.
5. Type **Total Fees Paid for January Auctions** in B13.
6. Use the AutoSum button to calculate the totals in G13 and I13.

Note: Flash Fill should automatically calculate the total in J13; however, if no total appears in J13, calculate the total yourself.

7. Edit the worksheet as follows:
    a. Change the sale price of Halo 4 from *35.99* to *43.99*.
    b. Change the platform for Skyrim from *Windows* to *PS 3*.
    c. Change the shipping for Skyrim from *5.00* to *6.50*.
    d. Type the current year one space after January in A2 so that the entry reads *Auctions ended in January 2015*. (Your year will vary.)
8. Proofread carefully to make sure the worksheet is error-free.
9. Change the scaling option to fit all columns on one page.
10. Save the revised workbook using the same name (**C8-Project1-AuctionFees-Your Name**).
11. Leave the workbook open if you are continuing to Project 2; otherwise, close the workbook and submit the project to your instructor in the manner she or he has requested.

Project 2 Editing and Formatting a Worksheet

Individual

Deliverable: Excel worksheet with Auction Fee Calculations

Note: You must have completed Project 1 before starting this project.

1. If necessary, open **C8-Project1-AuctionFees-Your Name**.
2. Use Save As to change the file name to **C8-Project2-AuctionFeesFormatted-Your Name**, saving in the same folder.
3. Insert a new row above row 12 and type the following auction item information in the appropriate cells:

   57834   Angry Birds Trilogy   PS 3   29.99 (sale price)   **6.50** (shipping)

Note: The formulas in fees cells should be automatically created; however, if no fees are calculated, enter the required formulas yourself.

4. Insert a blank column between columns I and J so that the *Total Fee* column is set apart from the rest of the data.
5. Change the width of column B to *25* and then delete columns C and D.
6. Change the height of row 4 to *25* and middle-align the column headings.
7. Format the worksheet as follows:
   a. Merge and center the titles in row 1 and row 2 over columns A through I.
   b. Left-align A5:A13 and center-align E4 and G4.
   c. Apply Comma Style to D5:I14.
   d. Add a *Thick Bottom Border* to A4:I4 and a *Top and Double Bottom Border* to E14, G14, and I14.
   e. Select A1:A2 and change the font to *Cambria*, the font size to *16*, the font color to *Dark Blue*, and apply bold.
   f. Select A4:I4, apply bold, and add *Gold, Accent 4* shading.
   g. Bold B14, E14, G14, and I14.
8. Select A5:I13 and sort the range by the *Game* column in ascending order.
9. Change the worksheet to landscape orientation.
10. Save the revised workbook using the same name (**C8-Project2-AuctionFeesFormatted-Your Name**).
11. Turn on the display of cell formulas.
12. Use Save As to save a copy of the worksheet with the formulas displayed as **C8-Project2-AuctionFeesWithCellFormulas-Your Name**.
13. Submit the project to your instructor in the manner she or he has requested.
14. Close the workbook.

Project 3 Formatting with Styles and Inserting a New Worksheet

Individual

Deliverable: Excel workbook with Cancer Patient Statistics in two worksheets

1. Open **CancerStatsReport**.
2. Use Save As to change the file name to **C8-Project3-CancerStatsReport-Your Name**, saving in the Ch8 folder in ChapterProjectsWork.
3. Merge and center the titles in row 1 and row 2 over columns A through G.
4. Wrap the text in A3:G3.
5. Change column widths as follows:

   | Column B to *10* | Column E to *10* |
   | Column C to *9* | Column F to *20* |

6. Apply cell styles of your choosing to A1, A2, and A3:G3 to improve the appearance of the worksheet.
7. Insert a new worksheet in the workbook and change the name to **Quarter 2**.
8. Rename the ReportData worksheet to **Quarter 1**.
9. Copy A1:G3 from the Quarter 1 sheet and paste it to A1 in the Quarter 2 sheet, keeping the source column widths.

10. Copy A4:G30 from the Quarter 1 sheet and paste it to A4 in the Quarter 2 sheet.
11. In the Quarter 2 sheet, clear the contents of A4:A30 and G4:G30.
12. Set the print settings for each worksheet to *Fit All Columns on One Page*.
13. Freeze the first three rows in each worksheet.
14. Save the revised workbook using the same name (**C8-Project3-CancerStatsReport–Your Name**).
15. Submit the project to your instructor in the manner she or he has requested.
16. Close the workbook.

Project 4 Creating a Weekly Schedule from a Template

Individual

Deliverable: Worksheet with a schedule for the current week

1. You learned about creating new documents from templates in Word in Chapter 6. Excel also has many templates available for creating new workbooks that are grouped into the categories *Budget, Invoice, Calendars, Expense, List, Loan,* and *Schedule*. Search for and select a template of your choosing to create a weekly schedule using the *Schedule* category.
2. Enter your schedule for the current week into the new worksheet. Make sure the schedule is complete with all of your classes and other activities.
3. Save the workbook in the Ch8 folder within ChapterProjectsWork as **C8-Project4-WeeklySchedule–Your Name**.
4. Submit the project to your instructor in the manner she or he has requested.
5. Close the workbook.

Project 5 Creating a Party Expense Worksheet

Individual

Deliverable: 25th Anniversary Party Expense Worksheet

1. Create a worksheet similar to Figure 8.8 with the following information:
   a. The amounts in the *Difference* column are formulas that calculate the actual expenses minus the estimated expenses, and the values shown in row 12 are formulas.
   b. The width of column A is 42, and columns B, C, and D is 12. The height of row 1 is 36 and row 2 is 24.
   c. The font and size used in A1 is 16-point Bradley Hand ITC. The font for the rest of the cells in the worksheet is Book Antiqua.
   d. A2:D2 have the Accent6 cell style applied and A12:D12 have the Total cell style applied.
   e. Use your best judgment for any other format options such as shading.
2. Save the worksheet in the Ch8 folder within the ChapterProjectsWork folder as **C8-Project5-PartyExpenses–Your Name**.
3. Submit the project to your instructor in the manner she or he has requested.
4. Close the workbook.

	A	B	C	D
1	Mom and Dad's 25th Anniversary Party Budget			
2		Estimated	Actual	Difference
3	Decorations	$ 225.00	$ 240.00	$ 15.00
4	Flowers	450.00	335.00	(115.00)
5	Disc jockey service	350.00	475.00	125.00
6	Photographer and prints	625.00	585.00	(40.00)
7	Rental of reception room	150.00	150.00	-
8	Rental of tables, chairs, plates, and cutlery	90.00	110.00	20.00
9	Food and drinks	1,750.00	1,855.00	105.00
10	Invitations	55.00	48.00	(7.00)
11	Miscellaneous supplies	100.00	115.00	15.00
12	Total Expenses	$ 3,795.00	$ 3,913.00	$ 118.00

Figure 8.8 Project 5 worksheet

Project 6 Internet Research and Composing a New Workbook

Individual or Pairs

Deliverable: Excel workbook with costs for a spring break trip

1. Listen to the audio file named *Project6_Instructions*. The file is located in the Ch8 folder in the Student_Data_Files folder.
2. Complete the research and compose the worksheet as instructed.
3. Save the workbook in the Ch8 folder within ChapterProjectsWork as **C8-Project6-SpringBreakContest-Your Name**.
4. Submit the project to your instructor in the manner she or he has requested.
5. Close the workbook.

Project 7 Sending Project Work to OneNote Notebook

Individual

Deliverable: New Page in Shared OneNote notebook

1. Start OneNote and open the MyProjects notebook created in Chapter 4, Project 4.
2. Make Excel the active section and add a new page titled *Chapter 8 Projects*.
3. Switch to Excel. For each project that you completed, open the document, send the project to OneNote 2013 selecting the Chapter 8 Projects page in the Excel section in the MyProjects notebook, and then close the workbook. Make sure to include all worksheets in workbooks with more than one sheet tab.
4. Close your MyProjects notebook in OneNote and close OneNote.
5. Close Excel.
6. Submit the project to your instructor in the manner she or he has requested.

Chapter 9

Working with Functions, Charts, Tables, and Page Layout Options in Excel

E xcel's function library is updated and expanded with each new release of the software. Several hundred pre-programmed formulas grouped by category in the function library are used to perform data analysis, decision making, or data modeling. Charts are widely used to present data or results of analysis in a visual snapshot. Excel provides Page Layout view for previewing page layout and print options. Collaborative tools such as Comments allow individuals to add notes or other feedback into a worksheet. Data organized in a list format is best suited for the Table feature, which allows you to easily format, sort, and filter large blocks of data.

In this chapter, you continue working with formulas by learning about the various types of references used in formulas and how to use functions to perform basic statistical, date, financial, and logical analysis. Next, you explore strategies for presenting data with the inclusion of charts, comments, and tables as well as formatting a worksheet with page layout options and print options.

After successfully completing this chapter, you will be able to:

- Create formulas with absolute addresses and range names
- Create statistical and date functions
- Perform decision making using the logical IF function
- Use the PMT function to calculate a loan payment
- Insert and modify charts and Sparklines
- Use Page Layout view
- Change margins, add a header, and center a worksheet
- Insert comments
- Format cells as a table
- Sort and filter data in a table

Using Absolute Addressing and Range Names in Formulas

Topic 9.1

SKILLS

Create a formula with an absolute address

Create a range name

Create a formula with a range name

 **Tutorials**

9.1.1 Creating Formulas and Absolute Addressing

9.1.2 Naming and Using a Range

The formulas in the previous chapter used cell references considered **relative addresses**, where column letters and row numbers change relative to the destination when a formula is copied. For example, the formula *=SUM(A4:A10)* becomes *=SUM(B4:B10)* when copied from a cell in column A to a cell in column B. Relative addressing is the most common addressing method.

Sometimes you need a formula in which one or more addresses should not change when the formula is copied. In these formulas, use cell references that are **absolute addresses**. A dollar symbol precedes a column letter and/or row number in an absolute address, for example, *=$A$10*. Some formulas have both a relative and an absolute reference; these are referred to as **mixed addresses**. See Table 9.1 for formula addressing examples.

Table 9.1	Cell Addressing and Copying Examples	
Formula	**Type of Reference**	**Action If Formula Is Copied**
=B4*B2	Relative	Both addresses will update.
=$B$4*$B$2	Absolute	Neither address will update.
=B4*$B$2	Mixed	The address B4 will update; the address $B$2 will not update.
=B4*$B2	Mixed	The address B4 will update; the row number in the second address will update but the column letter will not.
=B4*B$2	Mixed	The address B4 will update; the column letter in the second address will update but the row number will not.

1. Start Excel 2013 and open the workbook named *FinancialPlanner* from the Ch9 folder in Student_Data_Files.

2. Use Save As to save a copy of the workbook as **9.1-FinancialPlanner–Your Name** in a new folder named *Ch9* in the CompletedTopicsByChapter folder.

3. Review the worksheet noticing the three rates in row 2; these rates will be used to calculate gross pay, payroll deductions, and savings amounts.

4. Make C4 the active cell, type **=b4*b2**, and then tap or click the Enter button in the Formula bar or tap or press Ctrl + Enter.

5. Use the fill handle in C4 to copy the formula to C5:C30.

6. Make C5 the active cell and look at the formula in the Formula bar.

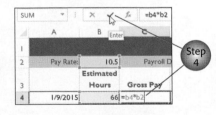

The #VALUE! error occurs because B3 is a label and has no mathematical value.

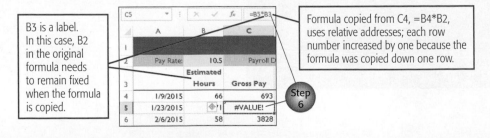

B3 is a label. In this case, B2 in the original formula needs to remain fixed when the formula is copied.

Formula copied from C4, =B4*B2, uses relative addresses; each row number increased by one because the formula was copied down one row.

7. Select C5:C30 and press the Delete key, or tap or click the Clear button in the Editing group and then tap or click *Clear All*.

8. Make C4 the active cell and edit the formula so that it reads *=B4*$B$2*.

9. Use the fill handle in C4 to copy the formula to C5:C30.

10. Make D4 the active cell and enter the formula **=c4*e2**.

11. Make E4 the active cell and enter the formula **=c4-d4**.

12. Select D4:E4 and use the fill handle to copy the formulas to D5:E30.

A cell or a range can be referenced by a descriptive label, which makes a formula easier to understand. For example, the formula *=Hours*PayRate* is readily understood. Names are also used when a formula needs an absolute reference because a cell or range name is automatically absolute. Cell or range names are assigned using the *Name* box at the left end of the Formula bar. Use the Name Manager button in the FORMULAS tab to manage cell names after they are created.

13. Make G2 the active cell, tap or click in the *Name* text box at the left end of the Formula bar, type **SaveRate**, and then tap or press Enter.

A range name can use letters, numbers, and some symbols. Spaces are not valid in a range name, and the first character in a name must be a letter, an underscore, or a backward slash (\).

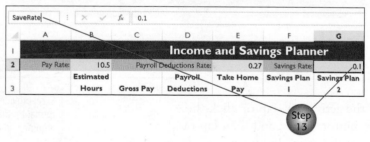

14. Make F4 the active cell, type **=e4*SaveRate**, and then tap or press Ctrl + Enter or tap or click the Enter button.

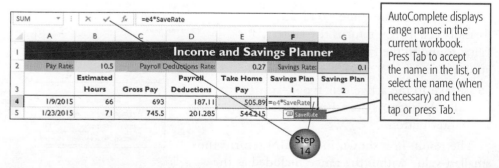

AutoComplete displays range names in the current workbook. Press Tab to accept the name in the list, or select the name (when necessary) and then tap or press Tab.

15. Use the fill handle in F4 to copy the formula to F5:F30.

16. Save the revised workbook using the same name (**9.1-FinancialPlanner-Your Name**). Leave the workbook open for the next topic.

App Tip

Press function key F4 to make an address absolute. F4 cycles though variations of absolute and mixed addresses for the reference in which the insertion point is positioned.

Quick **STEPS**

Make Cell Reference Absolute
Type dollar symbol before column letter and/or row number OR press F4 to cycle through variations of addressing.

Name a Cell or Range
1. Select cell or range.
2. Type name in *Name* text box.
3. Tap or press Enter.

App Tip

A range name can also be used in the Go To dialog box to move the active cell.

App Tip

Upper and lowercase letters separate words in a range name; however, range names are not case sensitive—*SaveRate* and *saverate* are considered the same name.

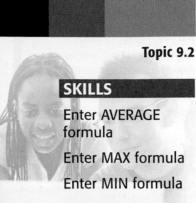

Topic 9.2

SKILLS

Enter AVERAGE formula

Enter MAX formula

Enter MIN formula

SNAP Tutorial

9.2   Using Statistical Functions

Entering Formulas Using Statistical Functions

Excel's function library contains more than 400 preprogrammed formulas grouped into 13 categories. All formulas that are based on functions begin with the name of the function followed by the function's parameters within parentheses. The parameters for a function (referred to as an **argument**) will vary depending on the formula chosen and can include a value, a cell reference, a range, multiple ranges, or a combination of values with references.

1 With the **9.1-FinancialPlanner-Your Name** workbook open, make I4 the active cell.

2 Tap or click the AutoSum button arrow in the Editing group of the HOME tab and then tap or click *Average* at the drop-down list.

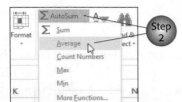

Excel enters *=AVERAGE(B4:H4)* in the formula cell with the range *B4:H4* selected. In this instance, Excel suggests the wrong range.

3 With the range B4:H4 highlighted in the formula cell, select B4:B30 and then tap or click the Enter button or tap or press Enter.

Excel returns the result *68.962963* in the formula cell, which is the arithmetic mean of the hours in column B. If empty cells or cells containing text are included in the formula's argument, they are ignored.

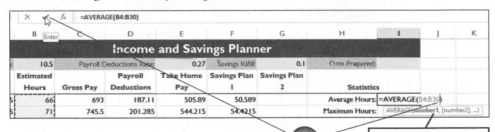

4 Make I5 the active cell, tap or click the AutoSum button arrow, and then tap or click *Max* at the drop-down list.

Excel provides the format for the function's argument in a ScreenTip.

5 Type **b4:b30** and then tap or press Enter or tap or click the Enter button.

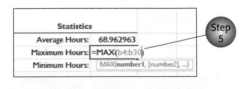

Excel returns the value *80* in the formula cell. MAX returns the largest value found in the range included in the argument.

6 Make I6 the active cell, type **=min(b4:b30)**, and then tap or press Enter or tap or click the Enter button.

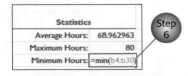

The result *48* is shown in I6. MIN returns the smallest value within the range included as the argument.

Excel's Insert Function dialog box assists with finding and entering functions and their arguments into a formula cell. A variety of methods can be used to open the Insert Function dialog box, including tapping or clicking the Insert Function button in the Formula bar.

7. Make I8 the active cell and then tap or click the Insert Function button in the Formula bar (button right of Enter button).

8. Tap or click the *Or select a category* list arrow and then tap or click *Statistical* at the drop-down list.

9. Tap or click *AVERAGE* in the *Select a function* list box and then tap or click OK.

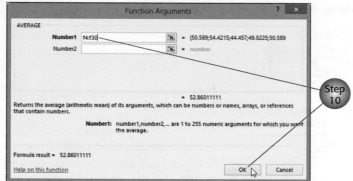

10. Type **f4:f30** in the *Number1* text box at the Function Arguments dialog box and then tap or press Enter or tap or click OK.

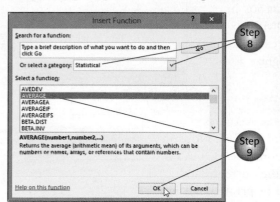

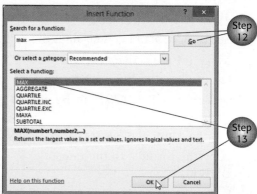

11. Make I9 the active cell, tap or click the AutoSum button arrow, and then tap or click *More Functions* at the drop-down list.

12. With the text already selected in the *Search for a function* text box, type **max** and then tap or press Enter or tap or click the Go button.

13. With MAX selected in the *Select a function* list box, tap or click OK.

14. Type **f4:f30** in the *Number1* text box at the Function Arguments dialog box and then tap or press Enter or tap or click OK.

15. Make I10 the active cell, tap or click the AutoSum button arrow, and then tap or click *Min* at the drop-down list.

16. Type **f4:f30** and then tap or press Enter or tap or click the Enter button.

17. Save the revised workbook using the same name (**9.1-FinancialPlanner-Your Name**). Leave the workbook open for the next topic.

Quick **STEPS**

AVERAGE, MAX, or MIN Functions
1. Activate formula cell.
2. Tap or click AutoSum button arrow.
3. Tap or click required function.
4. Type or select argument range.
5. Tap or press Enter.

 **COUNT Function**

The *Count Numbers* option from the AutoSum button arrow inserts the COUNT function, which returns the number of cells from the range included in the argument that have values. Use the function COUNTA if you want to count all of the non-empty cells within a range.

Topic 9.3

SKILLS

Enter a valid date

Enter the current date using a function

Create a formula using a date

Format dates

  Tutorial

9.3   Writing Formulas with Date Functions and Dates

The function *=NOW()* returns the current date and time in the active cell.

oops!

General instead of *Date* appears? Excel did not recognize your entry as a valid date. Generally, this is because of a typing error. Try Step 2 again. Still *General?* You may need to check the Region in the Control Panel.

Entering, Formatting, and Calculating Dates

A date typed into a cell in normal date format such as *May 1, 2015* or *5/1/2015* is stored as a numerical value. Times are stored as decimal values representing fractions of a day. Because dates and times are stored as values, calculations can be performed using the cells, and various date and time formats can be applied to the results.

Consider using Excel to calculate elapsed time for scheduling, payroll, membership, or other purposes that involve analysis of date or time.

1   With the **9.1-FinancialPlanner-Your Name** workbook open, make I2 the active cell.

2   Type **12/20/2014** and then tap or press Enter.

3   Make I2 the active cell and notice that *Date* appears in the *Number Format* list box in the Number group on the HOME tab. See Table 9.2 on the next page for examples of cell entries that Excel will recognize as a valid date.

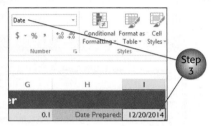

Step 3

4   Clear the contents of I2, type **=today()**, and then tap or press Enter.

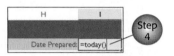

Step 4

Excel enters the current date into the cell. No argument is required for this function. The TODAY function updates the cell entry to the current date whenever the worksheet is opened or printed. Do not use *=TODAY()* if you want the date to stay the same.

5   Make B3 the active cell and insert a new column.

6   Type **Pay Date** in B3 and then tap or click A3.

7   Type **End Date** in A3 and then tap or click the Enter button.

8   Select A3:B3 and center-align the cells.

9   Make B4 the active cell, type **=a4+7**, and then tap or click the Enter button.

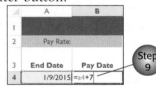

Step 9

Excel returns *1/16/2015* in B4, which is 7 days from January 9, 2015.

10   Use the fill handle in B4 to copy the formula to the range B5:B30.

11   Select A4:B30, tap or click the *Number Format* list arrow (down-pointing arrow next to *Date*), and then tap or click *More Number Formats* at the drop-down list.

12   At the Format Cells dialog box with *Date* selected in the *Category* list box, tap or click *14-Mar-12* in the *Type* list box and then tap or click OK.

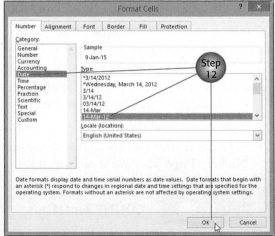

Step 12

13 Tap or click any cell to deselect the range.

14 Save the revised workbook using the same name (**9.1-FinancialPlanner-Your Name**). Leave the workbook open for the next topic.

	A	B
3	**End Date**	**Pay Date**
4	9-Jan-15	16-Jan-15
5	23-Jan-15	30-Jan-15
6	6-Feb-15	13-Feb-15
7	20-Feb-15	27-Feb-15
8	6-Mar-15	13-Mar-15
9	20-Mar-15	27-Mar-15
10	3-Apr-15	10-Apr-15
11	17-Apr-15	24-Apr-15
12	1-May-15	8-May-15
13	15-May-15	22-May-15
14	29-May-15	5-Jun-15
15	5-Jun-15	12-Jun-15
16	19-Jun-15	26-Jun-15
17	3-Jul-15	10-Jul-15
18	17-Jul-15	24-Jul-15
19	31-Jul-15	7-Aug-15
20	7-Aug-15	14-Aug-15
21	21-Aug-15	28-Aug-15
22	4-Sep-15	11-Sep-15
23	18-Sep-15	25-Sep-15
24	2-Oct-15	9-Oct-15
25	16-Oct-15	23-Oct-15
26	30-Oct-15	6-Nov-15
27	6-Nov-15	13-Nov-15
28	20-Nov-15	27-Nov-15
29	4-Dec-15	11-Dec-15
30	18-Dec-15	25-Dec-15

Formatted dates in A4:B30

TODAY Function
1. Activate formula cell.
2. Type **=today()**.
3. Tap or press Enter.

Did You Know?

Many businesses that operate globally have adopted the International Standards Organization (ISO) date format YYYY-MM-DD to avoid confusion with a date written as 02/04/03 which could mean February 4, 2003 (US) or April 2, 2003 (UK). Another strategy is to format a date with the month spelled out like the format used at Step 12.

Table 9.2	**Entries Excel Recognizes as Valid Dates or Times**
Dates	**Times**
12/20/15; 12-20-15	4:45 (stored as 4:45:00 AM)
Dec 20, 2015	4:45 PM (stored as 4:45:00 PM)
20-Dec-15 or 20 Dec 15 or 20/Dec/15	16:45 (stored as 4:45:00 PM)
Note that the year can be entered as two digits or four digits and the month as three characters or spelled in full. Times are generally entered as hh:mm, but in situations that require a higher level of accuracy, they are entered as hh:mm:ss.	

ALTERNATIVE method You can also enter dates into cells as DATE functions. A DATE function is typed as *=DATE(Year,Month,Day)*. For example *=DATE(2014,12,20)*.

Beyond Basics **Region Setting and Dates**

The Region setting in the Control Panel affects the format that Excel 2013 will recognize as a valid date. Following are examples of date format by region:

English (United States)   *m/d/yy*

English (Canada)   *yy/m/d* (Windows 8) or *d/m/yy* (Windows 7)

English (United Kingdom)   *d/m/yy*

To change the Region, open the Control Panel from the Desktop and select the Region icon or the Clock, Language, and Region category.

Topic 9.4

SKILLS

Enter IF function

   **Tutorial**

9.4   Using the Logical IF Function

Using the IF Function

Logical functions are used when you need a formula to perform a calculation based upon a condition or comparison of a cell with a value or the contents of another cell. For example, in column G of the Income and Savings Planner worksheet, you calculated a savings value based on the take-home pay amounts in column F. Suppose you decide that you cannot afford to contribute to your savings plan unless your take home pay is more than $500. The formula in column G does not accommodate this scenario; however, an IF formula can analyze the take-home pay and calculate the savings for those values that are over your minimum.

1. With the **9.1-FinancialPlanner-Your Name** workbook open, make H4 the active cell.

2. Tap or click the FORMULAS tab.

The category drop-down lists in the Function Library group are another way that you can find an Excel function to insert into a cell.

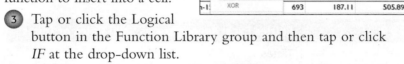

3. Tap or click the Logical button in the Function Library group and then tap or click IF at the drop-down list.

4. With the insertion point positioned in the *Logical_test* text box at the Function Arguments dialog box, type **f4>500** and tap or press Tab, or tap or click in the *Value_if_true* text box.

A logical test is a statement to evaluate a comparison so that one of two actions can be performed. In this case, the statement *f4>500* tells Excel to determine if the value that resides in F4 is greater than 500. All logical tests result in either a true or a false response—either the value is greater than 500 (true) or the value is not greater than 500 (false). See Table 9.3 on the next page for more examples of logical tests.

5. Type **f4*SaveRate** and then tap or press Tab or tap or click in the *Value_if_false* text box.

The statement in the *Value_if_true* text box is the formula you want Excel to calculate when the logical test proves true. In other words, if the value in F4 is greater than 500, you want Excel to multiply the value in F4 times the value in the cell named SaveRate (.10).

6. Type **0** and then tap or click OK.

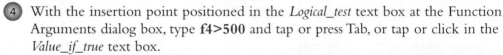

oops!

Cannot locate > on touch keyboard? With the &123 keyboard active, tap the button with the right-pointing arrow inside a circle above &123 to display the next symbol palette where > is located.

    App Tip

Formulas, values, or text are all valid entries for the *Value_ if_true* and *Value_if_false* text boxes.

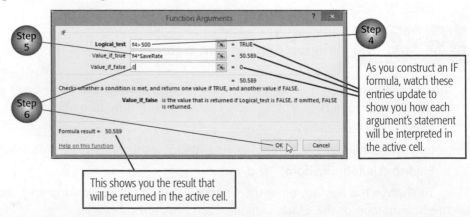

As you construct an IF formula, watch these entries update to show you how each argument's statement will be interpreted in the active cell.

This shows you the result that will be returned in the active cell.

The *Value_if_false* statement is the formula you want Excel to calculate when the logical test proves false. In other words, if the value in F4 is 500 or less, you want zero placed in the cell because you have decided that you cannot afford to contribute to your savings plan.

7 Look in the Formula bar at the IF statement entered into the active cell =IF(F4>500,F4*SaveRate,0).

Using the Function Arguments dialog box to build an IF statement is a good idea because the commas and parentheses are inserted automatically in the correct positions within the formula.

8 Use the fill handle in H4 to copy the formula to the range H5:H30.

9 Review the results in H5:H30. Notice the cells that have 0 appear in a row where the take-home pay value in column F is 500 or less.

10 Select C4:H30, tap or click the Quick Analysis button that appears below the selection, tap or click TOTALS, and then tap or click the Sum button in the *TOTALS* gallery (first button).

Excel creates SUM functions in each column in the range in row 31.

11 Select D4:H31, tap or click the HOME tab, and then tap or click the Comma Style button.

12 Apply the Comma Style format to C2 and J4:J10.

13 Apply the Percent Style format to F2 and H2.

Step 10

61.32

Step 7

H4	▼	:	×	✓	*fx*	=IF(F4>500,F4*SaveRate,0)			
	A	B	C	D	E	F	G	H	I	J
1					**Income and Savings Planner**					
2	Pay Rate:		10.50		Payroll Deductions Rate:	27%	Savings Rate:	10%	Date Prepared:	1/23/2013
3	**End Date**	**Pay Date**	**Estimated Hours**	**Gross Pay**	**Payroll Deductions**	**Take Home Pay**	**Savings Plan 1**	**Savings Plan 2**	**Statistics**	
4	9-Jan-15	16-Jan-15	66	693.00	187.11	505.89	50.59	50.59	Average Hours:	68.96
5	23-Jan-15	30-Jan-15	71	745.50	201.29	544.22	54.42	54.42	Maximum Hours:	80.00
6	6-Feb-15	13-Feb-15	58	609.00	164.43	444.57	44.46	-	Minimum Hours:	48.00
7	20-Feb-15	27-Feb-15	65	682.50	184.28	498.23	49.82	-		
8	6-Mar-15	13-Mar-15	66	693.00	187.11	505.89	50.59	50.59	Average Savings:	52.86
9	20-Mar-15	27-Mar-15	60	630.00	170.10	459.90	45.99	-	Maximum Savings:	61.32
10	3-Apr-15	10-Apr-15	63	661.50	178.61	482.90	48.29	-	Minimum Savings:	36.79

First 10 rows showing formatting applied at Steps 11 to 13

14 Select C31:H31 and add a Top and Double Bottom Border.

15 Save the revised workbook using the same name (**9.1-FinancialPlanner-Your Name**). Leave the workbook open for the next topic.

App Tip

Percent Style multiplies the value in the cell by 100 and adds a percent symbol (%) to the cell.

Table 9.3	IF Statement Logical Test Examples	
Logical Test	**Condition Evaluated**	**IF Statement Example**
F4>=500	Is the value in F4 greater than or equal to 500?	=IF(F4>=500,F4*SaveRate,0)
F4<500	Is the value in F4 less than 500?	=IF(F4<500,0,F4*SaveRate)
F4<=500	Is the value in F4 less than or equal to 500?	=IF(F4<=500,0,F4*SaveRate)
F4=$K$2	Is the value in F4 equal to the value in K2? Assume value in K2 is the take-home pay value for which you will set aside savings.	=IF(F4=$K$2,F4*SaveRate,0)
Hours<>0	Is the value in the cell named Hours not equal to 0?	=IF(Hours<>0,Hours*PayRate,0) Calculates Gross Pay when hours have been logged

Topic 9.5

SKILLS

Enter PMT function

SNAP Tutorial

9.5 Using Financial Functions

Using the PMT Function

Financial functions in Excel can be used for a variety of tasks that involve saving or borrowing money, such as calculating the future value of an investment, the present value of an investment, or borrowing criteria such as interest rates, terms, or payments. If you are considering a loan or mortgage, use Excel's PMT function to determine an estimated loan payment. The PMT function uses a specified interest rate, number of payments, and loan amount to calculate a regular payment. Once a payment is shown, you can manipulate the interest rate, term, or loan amount to find a payment with which you are comfortable.

1. With the **9.1-FinancialPlanner-Your Name** workbook open, tap or click the LoanPlanner sheet tab.

2. Make B7 the active cell.

3. Tap or click the FORMULAS tab, tap or click the Financial button, slide or scroll down the drop-down list, and then tap or click *PMT*.

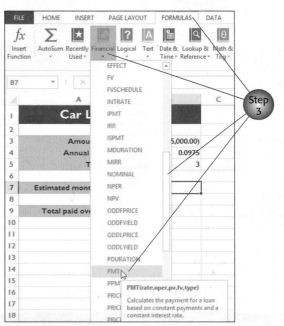

oops!

Can't see B4? Slide or drag the Function Arguments title bar right until the dialog box is no longer obscuring your view of columns A and B.

4. With the insertion point positioned in the *Rate* text box at the Function Arguments dialog box, tap or click B4 and then type **/12**.

The interest rate in B4 is expressed as the interest rate per year. Typing /12 after B4 causes Excel to divide the interest rate in B4 by 12 to calculate the monthly interest rate. To use the PMT function correctly, you need to ensure that the time periods are all the same. In other words, if you want to find a monthly payment, you need to make sure the rate and terms are also in monthly units. Most lending institutions express interest with the annual rate (not monthly) but compound the interest monthly.

5. Tap or click in the *Nper* text box, tap or click B5, and then type ***12**.

The value in B5 is the number of years you will take to pay back the loan. Multiplying the value times 12 will convert the value to the number of months to repay the loan. Most lending institutions express the repayment term in years (not months).

6 Tap or click in the *Pv* text box and then tap or click B3.

Pv stands for present value and represents the amount you want to borrow (referred to as the principal). Notice the amount borrowed is entered as a negative value in this worksheet. By default, Excel considers payments as negative values because money is subtracted from your bank balance when you make a loan payment. By entering a negative number for the amount borrowed, the PMT formula will return a positive value for the calculated loan payment. Whether you prefer to show a negative value for the amount borrowed or for the estimated monthly loan payment is a matter of personal preference; both options are acceptable.

7 Tap or click OK.

Excel returns the payment *$482.25* in B7.

8 Look in the Formula bar at the PMT statement entered into the active cell *=PMT(B4/12,B5*12,B3)*.

9 Make B9 the active cell and enter the formula **=b7*b5*12**.

Excel calculates the total cost for the loan to be $17,360.97.

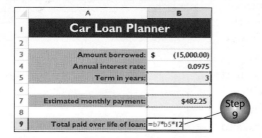

10 Change the value in B5 from *3* to *4*.

Notice that increasing the term one more year reduces your monthly payment; however, the total cost of the loan increases because you are making more payments.

11 Save the revised workbook using the same name (**9.1-FinancialPlanner-Your Name**) and close the workbook.

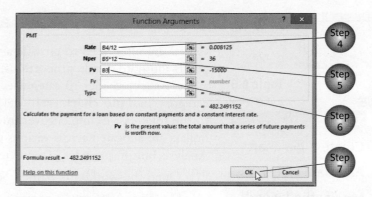

Quick STEPS

PMT Function
1. Activate formula cell.
2. Tap or click FORMULAS tab.
3. Tap or click Financial button.
4. Slide or scroll down list.
5. Tap or click *PMT*.
6. Enter *Rate* particulars.
7. Enter *Nper* particulars.
8. Enter *Pv* value or reference.
9. Tap or click OK.

App Tip

PMT assumes a constant payment and a constant interest rate; this function cannot be used to estimate loan payments where the payment or interest rate is variable.

App Tip

Type a negative symbol in front of PMT if the amount borrowed is a positive value and you want the payment to be a positive value. For example, *=-PMT(B4/12,B5*12,B3)*.

Beyond Basics

Using FV to Calculate the Future Value of an Investment

Another useful financial function is FV, which is used to calculate the future value of a series of regular payments that earn a constant interest rate. For example, if you deposit $100 each month for 10 years into an investment account that earns 9.75% per year (compounded monthly), the FV function *=FV(9.75%/12,10*12,100)* calculates the value of the account after the 10-year period to be $20,193.76.

Topic 9.6

Creating and Modifying a Pie Chart

Charts are often used to provide a visual snapshot of data. Many readers find that charts illustrate trends, proportions, and comparisons more distinctly than numbers alone. Excel provides 10 categories of charts with multiple styles within each category. In a **pie chart**, each data point (pie slice) is sized to show its proportion to the total. For example, governments often use a pie chart to illustrate how tax dollars are allocated across various programs and services. Excel 2013's new Quick Analysis button provides live previews of popular chart styles with selected data.

1. Open the workbook named *SocialMediaStats*.

2. Use Save As to save a copy of the workbook as **9.6-SocialMediaStats-Your Name** in the Ch9 folder in CompletedTopicsByChapter.

3. Select A5:B10.

Before you can insert a chart you first need to select the data that you want Excel to represent in a chart.

4. Tap or click the Quick Analysis button that appears below the selection area and then tap or click the CHARTS tab.

5. Tap or click *Pie* at the *Charts* gallery.

Excel graphs the data in a pie chart and places the chart overlapping the worksheet's cells within a chart object window. Notice also that the chart object is selected with selection handles, three chart editing buttons, and

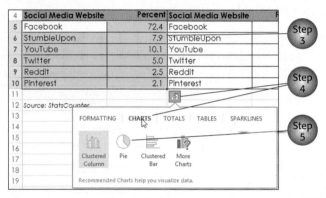

the CHART TOOLS DESIGN and FORMAT tabs in the ribbon.

6. With the chart selected, slide or drag the chart with your finger or mouse over any white unused area inside the chart's borders to the approximate location shown below.

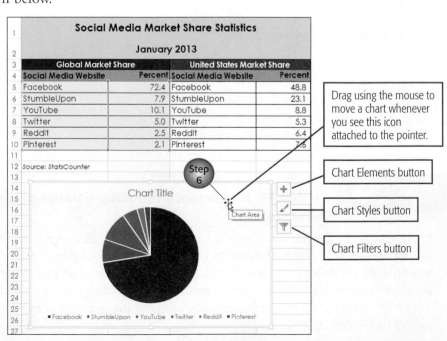

⑦ Tap or click the Chart Elements button (displays as a plus symbol next to the chart).

⑧ Tap or click the *Data Labels* check box to insert a check mark, tap or point at the right end of the *Data Labels* option when the right-pointing arrow appears, and then tap or click *Outside End*.

Although pie charts show proportions well, adding data labels allows a reader to include context with the size of each pie slice.

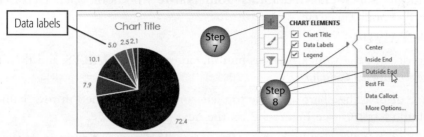

⑨ With CHART ELEMENTS still displayed, tap or click at the right end of *Legend* when the right-pointing arrow appears and then tap or click *Right*.

⑩ Tap or click to select the *Chart Title* object inside the chart window, slide or drag to select *Chart Title*, type **Global Market Share**, and then tap or click in any white unused area within the chart to deselect the title.

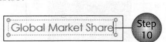

⑪ Select C5:D10 and insert a pie chart, as shown in Figure 9.1, by completing steps similar to those in Steps 4 to 10.

⑫ Save the revised workbook using the same name (**9.6–SocialMediaStats–Your Name**). Leave the workbook open for the next topic.

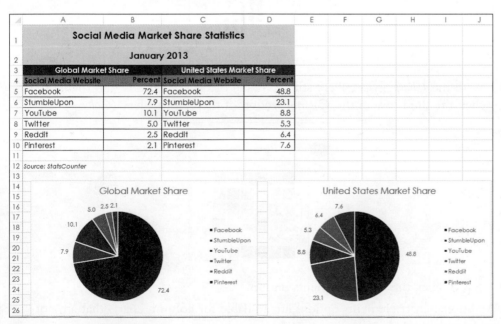

Figure 9.1 Side-by-side pie charts

oops!

Selecting with touch? Tap *Chart Title* to display selection handles, tap inside the selected object, and then tap the Edit Text button in the Mini toolbar.

App Tip

A popular technique to emphasize a pie slice is to move the slice away from the rest of the pie (called a *point explosion*). To do this, tap or click to select the pie slices, then tap or click to isolate the individual slice and slide or drag it away from the pie.

Topic 9.7

SKILLS

Create a column chart

Change the chart style

Change the chart color scheme

Add axis titles

Creating and Modifying a Column Chart

In a **column chart**, each data point is a colored bar that extends up from the **category axis** (horizontal axis, also called x-axis) with the bar height representing the data point's value on the **value axis** (vertical axis, also called y- or z-axis). Use a column chart to compare one or more series of data side by side. Column charts are often used to identify trends or illustrate comparisons over time or categories.

1. With the **9.6-SocialMediaStats–Your Name** workbook open, tap or click the Facebook sheet tab.

2. Select A7:B14.

3. Tap or click the Quick Analysis button, tap or click CHARTS, and then tap or click *Clustered Column*.

4. Slide or drag the chart until the top left corner is positioned in row 1 under column letter C (see Figure 9.2 on the next page).

5. Slide or drag the bottom right selection handle down and right to resize the chart until the bottom right corner is at approximately the bottom right border of J16 (see Figure 9.2 on the next page).

6. With the chart selected, tap or click the Chart Styles button (displays as a paintbrush next to the chart).

7. Slide or scroll down to the bottom of the STYLE list and then tap or click the last option in the gallery (*Style 16*).

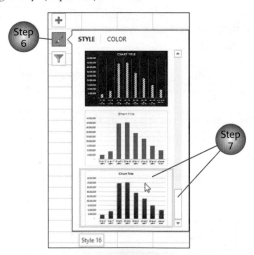

8. With the *Chart Styles* gallery still open, tap or click COLOR and then tap or click the third row in the *Colorful* section of the color gallery (*Color 3*).

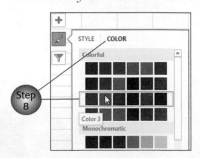

9. Tap or click the Chart Elements button.

Additional chart elements options are available for column charts that are not possible with a pie chart.

⑩ Tap or click the *Axis Titles* check box to insert a check mark.

Excel adds an Axis Title object to the vertical axis and to the horizontal axis.

⑪ With the *Axis Title* object along the vertical axis already selected, select the title text and type **Millions**.

⑫ Tap or click to select the *Axis Title* object along the horizontal axis and tap or press Delete to remove the object.

⑬ Edit the *Chart Title* to **Facebook Audience by Age Group**.

⑭ Compare your chart to the one shown in Figure 9.2. If necessary, redo an action in Steps 4 to 13.

⑮ Save the revised workbook using the same name (**9.6–SocialMediaStats–Your Name**). Leave the workbook open for the next topic.

CHART ELEMENTS
- ☑ Axes
- ☑ Axis Titles ▶
- ☐ Chart Title
- ☐ Data Labels
- ☐ Data Table
- ☐ Error Bars
- ☑ Gridlines
- ☐ Legend
- ☐ Trendline

Step 9
Step 10

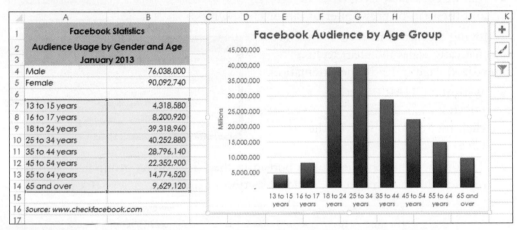

Figure 9.2 Column chart

Charts can also be created using the buttons in the Charts group of the INSERT tab. Select the data range, tap or click the INSERT tab, and then tap or click the button for the desired chart type in the Charts group.

Once a chart has been inserted, the CHART TOOLS DESIGN and FORMAT tabs contain the same options to modify the chart as those found in the *Chart Elements* and *Chart Styles* galleries.

Beyond Basics **Recommended Charts**

Not sure which chart type best represents your data? New to Excel 2013 is the **Recommended Charts** feature. Select the data you want to graph, and Excel will show a series of customized charts that best suit the selection. Use the *More Charts* option from the Quick Analysis button or tap or click the INSERT tab and then tap or click the Recommended Charts button in the Charts group.

Topic 9.8

SKILLS

Create a line chart

Move a chart to a new sheet

Format an axis

Format data labels

Creating and Modifying a Line Chart

Line charts are best suited for data where you want to illustrate trends and changes in values over a period of time. With a **line chart**, a reader can easily spot a trend, or identify growth spurts, dips, or unusual points in the series. Line charts are also often used to help predict future values based on the direction of the line.

1. With the **9.6–SocialMediaStats–Your Name** workbook open, tap or click the FacebookUserTimeline sheet tab.

2. Select A4:B12.

3. Tap or click the Quick Analysis button, tap or click CHARTS, and then tap or click *Line*.

4. With the chart selected, tap or click the **Move Chart button** in the Location group of the CHART TOOLS DESIGN tab.

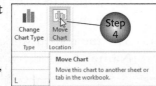

5. Tap or click *New sheet*, type **FBUserTimelineChart**, and then tap or press Enter or tap or click OK.

Moving a chart to its own chart sheet automatically scales the chart to fit a letter-sized page in landscape orientation.

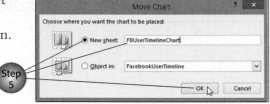

6. With the CHART TOOLS DESIGN tab active, tap or click the second option in the *Chart Styles* gallery (*Style 2*).

7. Tap or click the Change Colors button in the Chart Styles group and then tap or click the third row in the *Colorful* section of the color gallery (*Color 3*).

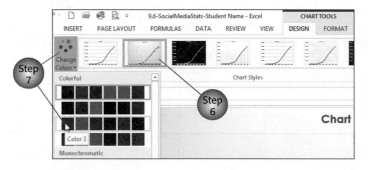

8. Edit the *Chart Title* to **Facebook User Timeline**.

In the next step you will correct the axis labels. Excel incorrectly converted the dates that were in column A, changing *Dec* to *Jan*.

9. Tap or click to select the dates in the category axis along the bottom of the chart. Make sure you see a border and selection handles around the axis labels.

10. Double-tap or double-click inside the selected axis labels to open the Format Axis task pane at the right side of the window.

11. Tap or click *Text axis* in the *AXIS OPTIONS* section of the task pane.

Notice the axis labels change to show the December dates as they appeared in the worksheet.

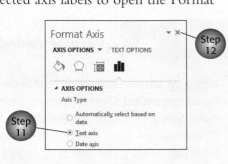

12. Close the Format Axis task pane.

oops!

No border around dates? Tap or click the axis labels a second time. Sometimes the chart is selected the first time you tap or click.

(13) Tap or click any data value on a data point in the line chart to select the entire series of data labels.

(14) Tap or click the CHART TOOLS FORMAT tab and then tap or click the Format Selection button in the Current Selection group.

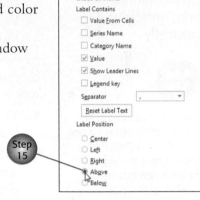

This opens the Format Data Labels task pane.

(15) Tap or click *Above* in the *Label Position* section of the Format Data Labels task pane with the LABEL OPTIONS tab active.

(16) Tap or click TEXT OPTIONS, and then tap or click *TEXT FILL* to expand the options list.

(17) Tap or click the Color button and then tap or click *Black, Text 1* (second color in first row).

(18) Close the Format Data Labels task pane and then tap or click in the window outside the chart to deselect the data labels.

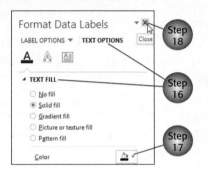

(19) Compare your chart with the chart shown in Figure 9.3 and make corrections if necessary.

(20) Save the revised workbook using the same name (**9.6-SocialMediaStats-Your Name**). Leave the workbook open for the next topic.

Create a Line Chart
1. Select range.
2. Tap or click Quick Analysis button.
3. Tap or click CHARTS.
4. Tap or click *Line*.
5. Move and/or modify chart elements as required.

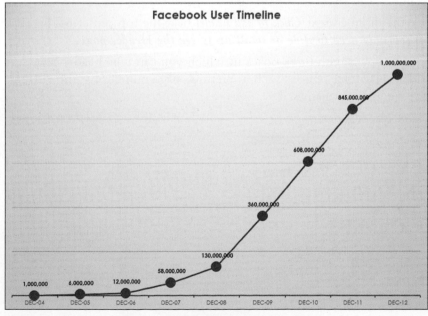

Figure 9.3 Line chart created in new chart sheet

Using Page Layout View, Adding a Header, and Changing Margins

In **Page Layout view** you can preview page layout options similarly to Print Preview; however, you also have the advantage of being able to edit the worksheet. The worksheet is divided into pages with white space around the edges of each page showing the size of the margins and a ruler along the top and left of the column letters and row numbers. Pages and cells outside the active worksheet are grayed out; however, you can click any page or cell and add new data.

Topic 9.9

SKILLS

Work in Page Layout view

Add a header

Change margins

Center worksheet horizontally and vertically

View buttons are also at the right end of the Status bar next to the Zoom buttons. Page Layout view is the middle of the three view buttons.

oops!

Can't see the full width of the page? If you're using a tablet or device with a small screen, decrease the Zoom to less than 100% until you can view the page width.

Tap or click the Go to Footer button in the Navigation group of the HEADER & FOOTER TOOLS DESIGN tab to move to the Footer sections.

1. With the **9.6-SocialMediaStats-Your Name** workbook open, tap or click the SocialMediaWebsites sheet tab, and then tap or click E1.

2. Tap or click the VIEW tab and then tap or click the Page Layout button in the Workbook Views group.

Notice in Page Layout view you can see that the right pie chart is split over two pages.

3. Tap or click the PAGE LAYOUT tab, tap or click the Orientation button in the Page Setup group, and then tap or click *Landscape* at the drop-down list.

4. Tap or click the *Width* list arrow in the Scale to Fit group (displays *Automatic*) and then tap or click *1 page* at the drop-down list.

Inserting a Header or Footer

As with Word, a header prints at the top of each page and a footer prints at the bottom of each page. Headers and footers are divided into three sections with the left section left-aligned, the center section centered, and the right section right-aligned by default.

5. Tap or click the dimmed text *Click to add header* near the top center of the page. **Hint: You may need to slide or scroll up to see the Header pane.**

The Header pane opens with three boxes in which you can type header text and/or add header and footer options such as pictures, page numbering, the current date or time, and file or sheet names.

6. Type your first and last names.

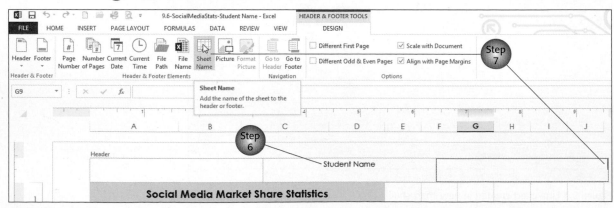

7. Tap or click at the right of the center section text box in the Header pane to open the right section text box and then tap or click the Sheet Name button in the Header & Footer Elements group of the HEADER & FOOTER TOOLS DESIGN tab.

Excel inserts the code *&[Tab]*, which is replaced with the sheet tab name when you tap or click outside the Header section.

8. Tap or click at the left of the Header pane to open the left section text box and then tap or click the File Name button in the Header & Footer Elements group.

Excel inserts the code *&[File]*, which is replaced with the file name when you tap or click in the worksheet area.

9. Tap or click in any cell in the worksheet area.

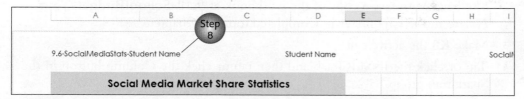

Changing Margins

Worksheet margins are 0.75 inch top and bottom and 0.7 inch left and right with the header or footer printing 0.3 inch from the top or bottom of the page. Adjust margins to add more space around the edges of a page or between the header and footer text and the worksheet. Center a smaller worksheet horizontally and/or vertically to improve the page's appearance.

10. Tap or click the PAGE LAYOUT tab, tap or click the Margins button in the Page Setup group, and tap or click *Wide*.

The *Wide* preset margin option changes the top, bottom, left, and right margins to 1 inch and the header and footer margins to 0.5 inch.

11. Tap or click the Margins button and tap or click *Custom Margins*.

12. Tap or click the *Horizontally* and the *Vertically* check boxes in the *Center on page* section to insert a check mark in each box and then tap or click OK.

13. Tap or click the Facebook sheet tab, tap or click A6, change to Page Layout view, and modify print options by completing steps similar to those in Steps 3 to 12 to improve the appearance of the printed worksheet.

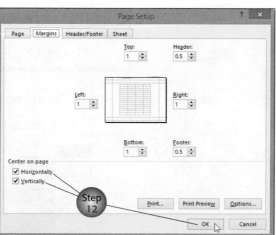

14. Save the revised workbook using the same name (**9.6-SocialMediaStats-Your Name**) and then close the workbook.

Quick **STEPS**

Add a Header
1. Switch to Page Layout view.
2. Tap or click *Click to add header*.
3. Type header text in center section or tap or click left or right section.
4. Add header elements as required.
5. Tap or click in worksheet area.

Change Margins
1. Tap or click PAGE LAYOUT tab.
2. Tap or click Margins button.
3. Tap or click preset option OR tap or click *Custom Margins* and change margins at Page Setup dialog box.

Center the Worksheet
1. Tap or click PAGE LAYOUT tab.
2. Tap or click Margins button.
3. Tap or click *Custom Margins*.
4. Tap or click *Horizontally* and/ or *Vertically* check boxes.
5. Tap or click OK.

Page Layout view is not available for chart sheets; however, you can add a header or change margins in Print Preview by using the Margins button or Page Setup link.

Creating and Modifying Sparklines and Inserting Comments

Topic 9.10

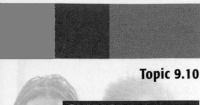

SKILLS

Insert Sparkline charts

Insert comments

Edit a comment

SNAP Tutorials

9.10.1 Summarizing Data with Sparklines

9.10.2 Inserting and Editing Comments

Increase the row height and/or column width to enlarge Sparkline charts.

Sparklines are miniature charts inserted into individual cells within a range in the worksheet. Sparklines are used to draw attention to trends or variations in data on a smaller scale than a column or line chart. Excel offers three types of Sparkline charts: Line, Column, or Win/Loss.

A comment attached to a cell pops up when the reader points or clicks the cell. Comments are used to add explanatory information, pose questions, or provide other feedback to readers when a workbook is shared.

1. Open the workbook named **SchoolBudget**.

2. Use Save As to save a copy of the workbook as **9.10–SchoolBudget–Your Name** in the Ch9 folder in CompletedTopicsByChapter.

3. Make K3 the active cell.

4. Tap or click the INSERT tab and then tap or click the Column button in the Sparklines group.

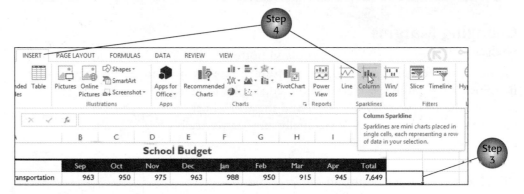

5. Type **b3:i3** in the *Data Range* text box at the Create Sparklines dialog box and then tap or press Enter or tap or click OK.

Excel embeds a column chart within the cell.

6. Use the fill handle to copy the Sparklines column chart from K3 to K4:K11.

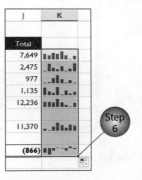

⑦ Tap or click the *High Point* check box in the Show group of the SPARKLINE TOOLS DESIGN tab to insert a check mark.

Excel colors red the bar in the column chart with the highest value. Other options in the tab are used to change the type or style, emphasize other points, show markers, or edit the data source.

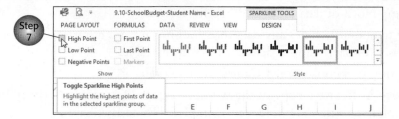

⑧ Make K2 the active cell, type **Trend**, and then tap or click E9.

⑨ Tap or click the REVIEW tab and then tap or click the New Comment button in the Comments group.

⑩ Type **Assuming extra hours during Christmas break.** and tap or click I3.

Excel inserts a diagonal red triangle in the upper right corner of a cell to indicate a comment exists for the cell.

⑪ Tap or click the New Comment button, type **May be able to use last month's rent.**, and tap or click any cell.

⑫ Tap I3 and tap the Show/Hide Comment button in the Comments group, or point to I3 with the mouse to display the comment in a pop-up box.

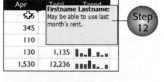

⑬ If necessary, tap or click I3 to activate the cell.

⑭ Tap or click the Edit Comment button in the Comments group and edit the comment text to *May be able to use last month's rent, which lowers this value to 55.*

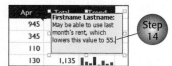

⑮ Tap or click any cell to finish editing the Comment box

⑯ Tap or click the Show All Comments button in the Comments group to display both comment boxes in the worksheet.

⑰ Tap or click the Show All Comments button to turn off the display of comment boxes.

⑱ Save the revised workbook using the same name (**9.10-SchoolBudget–Your Name**) and close the workbook.

 **Beyond Basics**   **Printing Comments**

By default, comments do not print with a worksheet. You can choose to print a list of comments on a separate page after the worksheet prints, or you can turn on the display of the comment boxes and print the worksheet with the comments as shown in the worksheet. Use the *Comments* option in the *Print* section of the Page Setup dialog box with the Sheet tab active to specify the print option.

Topic 9.11

SKILLS

Format a range
as a table

Sort a table

Filter a table

 **Tutorials**

9.11.1 Formatting Data
as a Table

9.11.2 Using the Sort
Feature in Tables

9.11.3 Filtering a Table

**App
Tip**

Recall from Chapter 7 that
different formatting applied to
every other row is referred to
as *banded rows* and is used
to improve readability. The fill
color, border style, and other
options vary by table style.

Working with Tables

Format a range of cells as a table to analyze, sort, and filter data as an independent unit. A worksheet can have more than one table, which means you can isolate and analyze data in groups. A table also allows you to choose from a variety of preformatted table styles, which is faster than manually formatting a range. Use tables for any block of data organized in a list format.

A **filter** temporarily hides any data that does not meet a criterion. Use filters to look at subsets of data without deleting rows in the table.

1. Open the workbook named *CalorieActivityTable*.

2. Use Save As to save a copy of the workbook as **9.11-CalorieActivityTable-Your Name** in the Ch9 folder in CompletedTopicsByChapter.

3. Select A3:D23.

4. Tap or click the Quick Analysis button, tap or click the TABLES tab, and then tap or click the Table button.

5. Select A1:A2 and apply *White, Background 1, Darker 5%* fill color (first color in second row).

6. Make A4 the active cell.

7. Tap or click the TABLE TOOLS DESIGN tab and then tap or click the *Table Style Medium 1* option in the *Table Styles* gallery (option to the left of the active style).

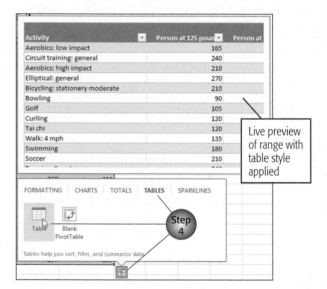

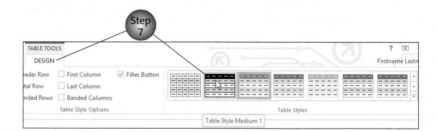

8. Tap or click the Filter button at the top of the *Activity* column in the table (displays as down-pointing arrow).

9. Tap or click *Sort A to Z* at the drop-down list.

The table rows are sorted in ascending order by the activity descriptions.

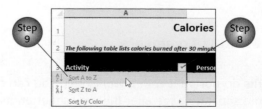

10 Tap or click the Filter button at the top of the *Person at 155 pounds* column.

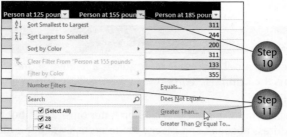

A check box is included for each unique value within the column. Filter a table by clearing check boxes for values or items you do not want to see in the filtered list, or use the *Filter by Color* and *Number Filters* options to specify a filter condition.

11 Tap or point to *Number Filters* and then tap or click *Greater Than*.

12 Type **200** at the Custom AutoFilter dialog box with the insertion point positioned in the text box at the right of *is greater than* and then tap or click OK.

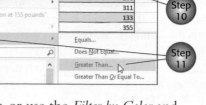

Excel filters the table and displays only those activities in which the calories burned are more than 200 for a person at 155 pounds.

13 Tap or click the Filter button at the top of the *Person at 155 pounds* column and tap or click *Clear Filter from "Person at 155 pounds"*.

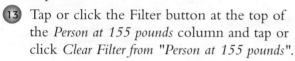

Clearing a filter redisplays the entire table.

14 Change the orientation to landscape and center the worksheet horizontally.

15 Save the revised workbook using the same name (**9.11-CalorieActivityTable-Your Name**) and close the workbook.

New to Excel 2013 is the ability to add Filter Slicer panes to filter a table. A Slicer pane contains all of the unique values for a column within the table. Tap or click a value within the pane to filter the table. Use the Insert Slicer button in the Tools group of the TABLE TOOLS DESIGN tab and insert a check mark for each column heading for which a Slicer pane is needed.

Quick STEPS

Format a Table
1. Select range.
2. Tap or click Quick Analysis button.
3. Tap or click TABLES.
4. Tap or click Table button.

Sort a Table
1. Tap or click Filter button at top of column by which to sort.
2. Tap or click *Sort A to Z* or *Sort Z to A*.

Filter a Table
1. Tap or click Filter button at top of column by which to filter.
2. Clear check boxes for items you want to hide OR tap or point to *Text Filters* or *Number Filters* and specify criterion.

A funnel icon appears in the Filter button in the column being used to filter a table, and the row numbers display in blue.

You can filter a table by one column and then filter again by another column to further drill down to the data you want to analyze.

Beyond Basics — Conditional Formatting

Another tool that is used to highlight or review cells is **conditional formatting**. Conditional formatting applies formatting options only to cells that meet a specified criterion. Select a range, tap or click the Quick Analysis button, and then tap or click the desired conditional formatting button in the FORMATTING tab. More conditional formatting options are available from the Conditional Formatting button in the Styles group of the HOME tab.

Concepts Review

Topic	Key Concepts	Key Terms
Using Absolute Addresses and Range Names in Formulas	By default, a cell address in a formula is a relative address, which means the column letter or row number will update as the formula is copied. A dollar symbol in front of a column letter or row number makes an address absolute and means the reference will not update when the formula is copied. A formula that has both relative and absolute addresses is referred to as a mixed address. A descriptive label can be assigned to a cell or range and used in a formula. A name is assigned to a cell by typing the label in the *Name* text box. A cell or range name is automatically an absolute address.	Relative addresses Absolute addresses Mixed addresses
Entering Formulas Using Statistical Functions	A formula that uses a function begins with the function name followed by the parameters for the formula (called the argument) within parentheses. The AVERAGE function returns the arithmetic mean from the range used in the formula. The MAX function returns the largest value from the range. The MIN function returns the smallest value from the range. The Insert Function dialog box accessed from the Insert Function button provides tools to find and enter a function and argument. The Count numbers option from the AutoSum drop-down list returns the number of cells with values in the range.	Argument
Entering, Formatting, and Calculating Dates	A valid date or time entered into a cell is stored as a numerical value and can be used in formulas. The TODAY function enters the current date into the cell and updates the date whenever the worksheet is opened or printed. Date and time cells can be formatted to a variety of month, day, and year combinations at the Format Cells dialog box with the *Date* category selected. The format in which Excel expects a date to be entered is dependent on the Region setting in the Control Panel. In the United States, the date is expected to be in the format m/d/y.	
Using the IF Function	The IF function performs a comparison of a cell with a value of another cell and performs one of two calculations depending on whether the comparison proves true or false. Use the Insert Function dialog box to assist with entering an IF statement's arguments. The *logical_test* argument is the statement you want Excel to evaluate to determine which calculation to perform. The *value_if_true* argument is the value or formula if the logical test proves true. The *value_if_false* argument is the value or formula if the logical test proves false.	

Topic	Key Concepts	Key Terms
Using the PMT Function	Financial functions can be used for a variety of financial calculations that involve saving or borrowing money. The PMT function calculates a regular loan payment from a specified interest rate, term, and amount borrowed. Make sure the interest rate and terms are in the same units as the payment you want calculated. For example, divide the interest rate by 12 and/or multiply the term times 12 to calculate a monthly payment from an annual rate or terms. In the PMT argument, *Rate* means the interest rate, *Nper* means the term, and *Pv* means the amount borrowed. The FV function calculates the future value of a regular series of payments that earn a constant interest rate.	
Creating and Modifying a Pie Chart	Charts are often used to portray a visual snapshot of data. A pie chart shows each data point as a pie slice. The size of each pie slice in the chart represents the value of the data point in proportion to the total of all of the values. Use the CHARTS tab in the *Quick Analysis* gallery to create a pie chart from a selected range. The Chart Elements button is used to add or modify a chart title, data labels, or legend.	Pie chart
Creating and Modifying a Column Chart	A column chart shows one bar for each data point extending upward from a horizontal axis with the height of the bar representing its value. The horizontal axis in a column chart is the category axis, also called the x-axis, and shows the labels for each bar. The vertical axis in a column chart is called the value axis, also known as the y- or z-axis, and is scaled to the values of the bars graphed. A column chart is used to show trends or comparisons over time. The Chart Styles button is used to choose a style for a column chart or change the color scheme. The *Axis Titles* option from the Chart Elements button is used to add titles to each axis in a column chart. The Recommended Charts feature is new to Excel 2013 and provides a set of customized charts recommended for the data you have selected.	Column chart Category axis Value axis Recommended Charts
Creating and Modifying a Line Chart	A line chart helps a reader identify trends, growth spurts, dips, or unusual points in a data series. Use the Move Chart button in the Location group of the CHART TOOLS DESIGN tab to move a chart from the worksheet into a chart sheet. A chart in a chart sheet is automatically scaled to fill a letter-sized page in landscape orientation. Change axis options in the Format Axis task pane or data label options in the Format Data Labels task pane.	Line chart Move Chart button

continued....

Topic	Key Concepts	Key Terms
Using Page Layout View, Adding a Header, and Changing Margins	In Page Layout view the worksheet is divided into pages with white space depicting the size of the margins and a ruler along the top and left edges.	Page Layout view
	You can see page layout and print options in Page Layout view while viewing and editing the worksheet.	
	Add a header in Page Layout view by tapping or clicking the dimmed text *Click to add header*.	
	Use buttons in the HEADER & FOOTER TOOLS DESIGN tab to add options to a header or footer such as a picture, page numbering, date or time, or file or sheet names.	
	Change to a preset set of margins from the Margins button in the PAGE LAYOUT tab, or choose *Custom Margins* to enter your own margin settings.	
	Open the Page Setup dialog box with the Margins tab to center a worksheet horizontally and/or vertically.	
Creating and Modifying Sparklines and Inserting Comments	Miniature charts embedded into a cell are called Sparklines.	Sparklines
	Sparkline charts emphasize trends or variations in data on a smaller scale.	
	Activate a cell and choose a Sparkline chart type from the INSERT tab.	
	Once created, add or modify Sparkline options using buttons in the SPARKLINE TOOLS DESIGN tab.	
	Comments appear in pop-up boxes when you point or click a cell with an attached comment.	
	Excel displays a diagonal red triangle in a cell with a comment.	
	Use the New Comment button in the REVIEW tab to add a comment.	
Working with Tables	A block of data set up in list format can be formatted as a table for formatting, analyzing, sorting, or filtering purposes.	Filter
	A filter temporarily hides data that does not meet a criterion.	Conditional formatting
	Use a filter to review subsets of data without deleting rows.	
	Use the Filter button at the top of a column to sort or filter a table.	
	Conditional formatting applies formatting options to cells within a range that meet a criterion.	

Multiple Choice

1. This symbol in an address makes the reference absolute.
   a. #
   b. !
   c. :
   d. $

2. A range name automatically uses this type of referencing.
   a. Relative
   b. Absolute
   c. Mixed
   d. Auto

3. This statistical function returns the arithmetic mean from the range.
   a. MEDIAN
   b. COUNT
   c. AVERAGE
   d. MAX

4. This is the term for a function's parameters within parentheses.
   a. Arguments
   b. Criteria
   c. Range
   d. Logical test

5. This function enters the current date into the cell and updates the entry each time the worksheet is opened.
   a. =DATE()
   b. =TODAY()
   c. =TODAY(now)
   d. =NOW(today)

6. This setting in the Control Panel affects the format that Excel recognizes as valid for a date.
   a. Date and Time
   b. Region
   c. PC Settings
   d. System

7. The IF function is located in this category button in the Function Library group.
   a. Logical
   b. Statistical
   c. Financial
   d. Text

8. Enter the formula to evaluate a condition or comparison for an IF statement in this text box in the Function Arguments dialog box.
   a. Value_if_true
   b. Value_if_false
   c. Logical test
   d. Formula result

9. This is the financial function that calculates a regular payment for a loan.
   a. PYT
   b. PMT
   c. FV
   d. RATE

10. This is the financial function that calculates the value of an investment at the end of a series of regular payments that earned a constant interest rate.
    a. PMT
    b. FV
    c. PYT
    d. RATE

11. In this type of chart, each data point is sized to show its value as a proportion to the total.
    a. Column
    b. Line
    c. Sparklines
    d. Pie

12. This button is *not* one of the three buttons that appear next to a chart used for modifying the chart.
    a. Chart Elements
    b. Chart Styles
    c. Chart Filters
    d. Chart Analysis

13. This feature presents a series of customized charts that is best suited to portray the data in the selected range.
    a. Sparklines
    b. Recommended Charts
    c. Chart Series
    d. PivotCharts

14. In a column chart, each data point is a colored bar that extends upward from this axis.
    a. Value axis
    b. Category axis
    c. Z-axis
    d. Legend axis

15. Use this button to have a chart object placed in its own chart sheet.
    a. Move Chart
    b. Graph Chart
    c. Chart Sheet
    d. Chart Styles

16. Open this task pane to make changes to the way Excel has generated the axis labels in a chart.
    a. Format Labels
    b. Format Axis
    c. Format Chart
    d. Format Title

17. This view allows you to add a header to a worksheet by tapping or clicking in the Header pane.
    a. Print Preview
    b. Page Break Preview
    c. Normal view
    d. Page Layout

18. Use this option from the Margins drop-down list to open a dialog box in which you can center a worksheet horizontally or vertically on the printed page.
    a. Custom Margins
    b. Preset Margins
    c. Page Layout
    d. Wide

19. This type of chart is embedded within a single cell.
    a. Pie
    b. Line
    c. Column
    d. Sparklines

20. This indicator in a cell appears when a comment is attached to the cell.
    a. Diagonal green triangle
    b. Diagonal red triangle
    c. Green bullet
    d. Red bullet

21. This feature temporarily hides rows in a table that do not meet a specified criterion.
   a. Quick Analysis
   b. Table Styles
   c. Filter
   d. Sort

22. Tap or click this button to restore the full table after viewing a subset of data.
   a. Sort
   b. Quick Analysis
   c. Table Styles
   d. Filter

Crossword Puzzle

ACROSS

5 Function that uses an interest rate, term, and amount borrowed
6 Address with both relative and absolute reference
9 Function that finds the smallest number in the range
10 Format for a large block of data that can be sorted independently
11 Function that finds the largest number in the range
12 Type of chart often used to predict future values
13 View in which you can adjust print options and still edit worksheet
14 Function that can evaluate two alternatives
16 Miniature charts in cells
17 Format for a cell entry such as 12/20/2016

DOWN

1 Text that appears in a pop-up box when cell is activated
2 Preset margin option that changes top, bottom, left, and right margins to 1 inch
3 Name for horizontal axis in a column chart
4 Button that appears below selected range used to create a chart
7 Term for chart element added to a pie slice to show its value
8 Name for vertical axis in a column chart
15 Box where you type a label to assign to a cell

Matching

Match the term with the statement or definition.

_____ 1. Default type of cell addressing
_____ 2. Fixed address not updated during copy
_____ 3. Function parameters
_____ 4. A date is stored as this
_____ 5. *F4>500* is an example of this
_____ 6. One of the arguments in PMT
_____ 7. Chart that shows proportions to whole
_____ 8. Chart for identifying a trend
_____ 9. Print sheet name at top of each page
_____ 10. Miniature charts
_____ 11. Filter buttons appear at top of columns

a. Argument
b. Logical test
c. Pie
d. Header
e. Table
f. Relative
g. Sparklines
h. Nper
i. Absolute
j. Value
k. Column

Project 1 Adding Statistical, Date, Financial, and Logical Functions to a Workbook

Individual

Deliverable: Worksheet with Auction Fee Financial Analysis and Mortgage Options

1. Open **AuctionFeesandMortgagePlanner**.
2. Use Save As to change the file name to **C9-Project1-AuctionFeesandMortgagePlanner-Your Name** in a new folder named *Ch9* within the ChapterProjectsWork folder on your USB flash drive.
3. In J2 enter a formula that will insert the current date and update the date each time the workbook is opened or printed.
4. Assign the following names to the cells indicated:
    C2   AuctionFee   G2   PaymentFee
5. Complete the formulas required in the worksheet using the following information:
    a. In column B, calculate the payment due dates as 5 days following the auction end date.
    b. In column D, calculate the auction fees as the sale price times the auction fee percentage. Use the range name created in Step 4 in the formula.
    c. In column E, calculate the payment processing fees as the sale price times the payment fee percentage. Use the range name created in Step 4 in the formula.
    d. In column F, calculate the net auction earnings as the sale price minus the auction fee and payment processing fee.
    e. In column G, calculate the amount to transfer to the checking account as the value that resides in net auction earnings for those instances in which the net auction earnings are less than or equal to $20.00; otherwise, calculate the amount as 50 percent of the net auction earnings.
    f. In column H, calculate the amount to transfer to the investment account as 50 percent of the net auction earnings for those instances in which the net auction earnings are more than $20.00; otherwise, show zero in the cell.
    g. In column J, calculate the three sets of required statistics. Use the labels to help you determine the functions and arguments required.
    h. In row 27, calculate totals for columns C through H.
6. Format C2 and G2 to Percent Style, format the dates in columns A and B to the style *14-Mar*, and format all other values to Comma Style.
7. Make MortgageAnalysis the active worksheet and complete the formulas required in the worksheet using the following information:
    a. In B7 and D7, calculate the estimated monthly payments.
    b. In B9 and D9, calculate the total paid over the life of each mortgage.
8. For each worksheet, change page layout options as necessary to make sure the worksheet will fit on one page centered horizontally and with your name centered in a header, the file name at the left margin in a footer, and the sheet name at the right margin in a footer.
9. Save the revised workbook using the same name (**C9-Project1-AuctionFeesandMortgagePlanner-Your Name**).
10. Submit the project to your instructor in the manner she or he has requested.
11. Close the workbook.

Project 2 Creating and Modifying Charts

Individual

Deliverable: Worksheet with Charts Illustrating Vacation Destination Statistics

1. Open **VacDestinations**.
2. Use Save As to change the file name to **C9-Project2-VacDestinations-Your Name**, saving in the Ch9 folder within ChapterProjectsWork.
3. With the TopVacDestinations sheet active, create a pie chart at the bottom left of the worksheet area that graphs the Worldwide destinations and percentages. Create a second pie chart at the bottom right of the worksheet area that graphs the United States and Canada destinations and percentages. Add and/or modify chart elements you think are appropriate to make sure the charts are easy to read and understand.
4. With the NationalParks worksheet active, create a clustered column chart that graphs the national parks and visitors. Position the chart where you think the chart looks good and add and/or modify chart elements you think are appropriate to make sure the chart is easy to read and understand.
5. With the InternationalTravel worksheet active, select A3:D15 and create a line chart in a chart sheet named *InternationalTravelChart*. Add and/or modify chart elements you think are appropriate to make sure the chart is easy to read and understand.
6. For the three worksheets with charts, change page layout options as necessary to make sure the worksheet will fit on one page centered vertically and with your name centered in a header, the file name at the left margin in a footer, and the sheet name at the right margin in a footer. *Hint: Add the header and footer in the InternationalTravelChart sheet using the Page Setup link in Print Preview*.
7. Save the revised workbook using the same name (**C9-Project2-VacDestinations-Your Name**).
8. Submit the project to your instructor in the manner she or he has requested.
9. Close the workbook.

Project 3 Adding Sparklines and Comments

Individual

Deliverable: Worksheet with Comments and Sparklines Illustrating School Newspaper Budget Values

1. Open **SchoolPaperBudget**.
2. Use Save As to change the file name to **C9-Project3-SchoolPaperBudget-Your Name**, saving in the Ch9 folder within ChapterProjectsWork.
3. Create line Sparklines in column K that graph the budget values for September through April. Show the high and low points. Add and/or modify any other Sparkline elements you think are appropriate.
4. Add the following comments to the cells indicated:
   E9   Christmas ads expected to increase 10% this year.
   I5   New ISP contract takes effect in April.
   I9   Consider end-of-year special pricing to raise ad revenue.
5. Display the worksheet in Print Preview and use the Page Setup link to open the Page Setup dialog box. Change the *Comments* option to *At end of sheet* in the Sheet tab.
6. Save the revised workbook using the same name (**C9-Project3-SchoolPaperBudget-Your Name**).
7. Submit the project to your instructor in the manner she or he has requested.
8. Close the workbook.

Project 4 Working with Tables

Individual

Deliverable: Worksheet with Model Home Pricing Table

1. Open **ModelHomes**.
2. Use Save As to change the file name to **C9-Project4-ModelHomes-Your Name**, saving in the Ch9 folder within ChapterProjectsWork.

3. Format A5:E20 as a table.
4. Change to a table style of your choosing.
5. Sort in ascending order by the *Description* column.
6. Add totals below each model home that sum the total cost of the upgrades.
7. In A23 enter the text **TOTAL MODEL HOME PRICE WITH UPGRADES**.
8. Create formulas in B23:E23 that show the total price of each model home with the base price and total upgrade costs.
9. Change the worksheet to landscape orientation, centered vertically, and with your name centered in a header and the file name centered in a footer.
10. Save the revised workbook using the same name (**C9-Project4-ModelHomes-Your Name**).
11. Submit the project to your instructor in the manner she or he has requested.
12. Close the workbook.

Project 5 Creating a Worksheet and Charts to Show Food Drive Results

Individual

Deliverable: Worksheet with Food Drive Results and Charts

1. Create a worksheet similar to the one shown in Figure 9.4 with the following additional information:
   a. The workbook theme is *Frame*.
   b. The charts are clustered bar charts using *Style 13*.
   c. Set the height for row 1 to *28.50* and row 2 to *21.00*. Set the width of column A to *16.50*.
   d. The font size for row 1 is 18 points and row 2 is 12 points.
   e. Use your best judgment for any other format options such as shading.
2. Save the worksheet in the Ch9 folder within the ChapterProjectsWork folder as **C9-Project5-FoodDrive-Your Name**.

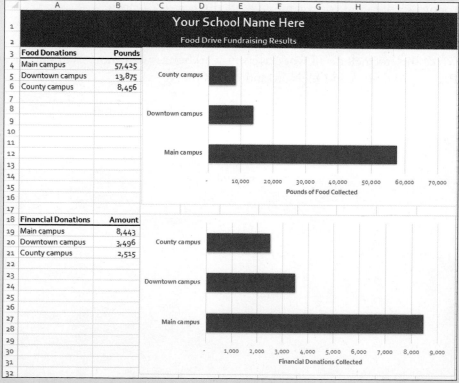

Figure 9.4 Project 5 Food Drive Worksheet and Charts

3. Change the top margin to 1.5 inches. Make sure the worksheet will fit on one page in portrait orientation with your name centered in a header and the file name centered in a footer.

4. Save the workbook again using the same name (**C9-Project4-FoodDrive-Your Name**).

5. Submit the project to your instructor in the manner she or he has requested.

6. Close the workbook.

Project 6 Internet Research and Composing a New Workbook

Individual or Pairs

Deliverable: Worksheet with Membership Statistical Data and Line Chart

1. Listen to the audio file named *Project6_Instructions*. The file is located in the Ch9 folder in the Student_Data_Files folder.

2. Complete the research and compose the worksheet and chart as instructed.

3. Save the workbook in the Ch9 folder within ChapterProjectsWork as **C9-Project6-Instagram-Your Name**.

4. Submit the project to your instructor in the manner she or he has requested.

5. Close the document.

Project 7 Sending Project Work to OneNote Notebook

Individual

Deliverable: New Page in Shared OneNote notebook

1. Start OneNote and open the MyProjects notebook created in Chapter 4, Project 4.

2. Make Excel the active section and add a new page titled *Chapter 9 Projects*.

3. Switch to Excel. For each project that you completed, open the workbook, send the project to OneNote 2013 selecting the Chapter 9 Projects page in the Excel section in the MyProjects notebook, then close the workbook. Make sure to include all worksheets in workbooks with more than one sheet tab.

4. Close your MyProjects notebook in OneNote and close OneNote.

5. Close Excel.

6. Submit the project to your instructor in the manner she or he has requested.

Chapter 10

Creating, Editing, and Formatting a Presentation Using PowerPoint

After successfully completing this chapter, you will be able to:

- Create a new presentation based on a theme
- Insert slides and add content
- Change the design theme and variants to the theme
- Insert a table on a slide
- Format slides using font and paragraph options
- Select, resize, align, and move slide placeholders
- Use Slide Sorter view
- Duplicate, move, and delete slides
- Modify the slide master
- Add notes and comments
- Run a presentation in Slide Show view and Presenter view
- Prepare slides for audience handouts or speaker notes

Presentations occur in a variety of meetings, seminars, classrooms, or other events for a variety of purposes. Some presentations are informational, while others are designed to deliver news or persuade you to buy a product or service. Some people use presentations at events such as weddings, anniversaries, or family reunions to entertain an audience. Often, a collection of slides that includes text and multimedia is displayed on a large screen to support a speaker's presentation. Other types of presentations are used to provide information to an individual at a self-running kiosk. You may have used a presentation as a study guide to prepare for an exam.

Microsoft PowerPoint is the **presentation application** in the Microsoft Office suite. The program is widely used to create a set of slides that incorporates text and multimedia. In this chapter you will learn how to create, edit, and format a presentation. You will create a presentation with a variety of text-based slide layouts; edit content and placeholders; move, duplicate, and delete slides; format slides using a variety of techniques; add notes and comments; and preview the presentation as a slide show. Lastly, you will preview options for audience and speaker handouts.

Note: If you are using a tablet, consider using a USB or wireless keyboard because you will be typing text in several slides for new presentations in this chapter.

TOPIC 10.1

SKILLS

Create a new presentation

Choose a theme and variant

Insert slides

Edit text on slides

Double-tap or double-click a theme to start a new presentation using the theme's default style and color scheme.

SNAP Tutorials

10.1.1 Creating and Saving a Presentation

10.1.2 Navigating and Inserting Slides in a Presentation

10.1.3 Using the Spelling and Thesaurus Features

Creating a New Presentation and Inserting Slides

A new presentation can be created at the PowerPoint Start screen by choosing a template, a theme and variant on a theme, or by starting with a blank presentation. The first slide in a presentation is a **title slide** with a text **placeholder** for a title and a subtitle. A placeholder is a rectangular container on a slide that can hold text or other content. Each placeholder on a slide can be manipulated independently.

PowerPoint starts a new presentation with a title slide displayed in Normal view. In Normal view, the current slide displays in widescreen format in the **slide pane**. Numbered slide thumbnails display in the **Slide Thumbnail pane** at the left of the current slide. A Notes pane at the bottom and a Comments pane at the right can be opened as needed.

1. Start PowerPoint 2013.

2. At the PowerPoint Start screen, tap or click the *Ion* theme.

PowerPoint 2013 starts with a gallery of newly designed themes. Tap or click to preview a theme along with the theme's variants. **Variants** are a collection of different style and color schemes included in the theme family.

3. Tap or click the last variant (orange color scheme) and then tap or click the right-pointing arrow below the preview slide next to *More Images*.

When previewing variants, browse through the *More Images* slides to view the color scheme with a variety of content. This allows you to get a better perspective of the theme's or variant's style and colors before making your selection.

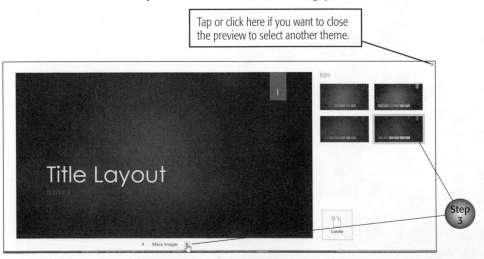

4. Tap or click the second variant (blue color scheme) and then tap or click the right-pointing arrow below the preview slide to view the blue color scheme with a Title and Content layout depicting a chart.

⑤ Tap or click the right-pointing arrow below the preview slide two more times to view other types of content with the blue color scheme.

⑥ With the Photo Layout in the preview, tap or click the Create button.

⑦ Compare your screen with the one shown in Figure 10.1.

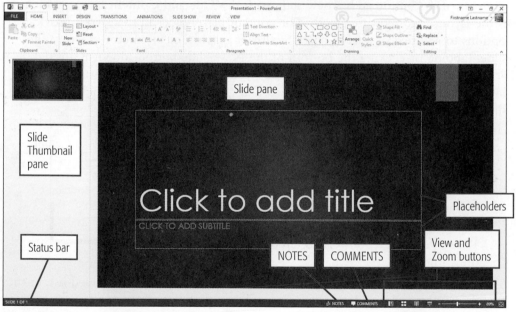

Figure 10.1 A new PowerPoint presentation with Ion theme and color variant in the default Normal view. See Table 10.1 for a description of screen elements.

Quick STEPS

Start a New Presentation
1. Start PowerPoint 2013.
2. Tap or click theme.
3. Tap or click variant.
4. Tap or click Create button.

Insert a Slide
Tap or click New Slide button in Slides group.
OR
1. Tap or click down-pointing arrow on New Slide button.
2. Tap or click required slide layout.

Edit Text
1. Activate slide.
2. Select text or tap or click in placeholder.
3. Type new text or change text as required.

Table 10.1	PowerPoint Features
Feature	**Description**
COMMENTS	Turn on or off Comments pane at the right side of the Slide pane.
NOTES	Turn on or off the Notes pane at the bottom of the Slide pane.
Placeholders	Containers in which you type or edit text or place other content.
Slide pane	Displays the active slide. Add or edit content on slides in this area.
Slide Thumbnail pane	Displays numbered thumbnails of the slides in the presentation. Navigate, insert, or manage slides in this pane.
Status bar	Displays active slide number with total number of slides in presentation and messages with the progress of some actions.
View and Zoom buttons	By default, PowerPoint opens in Normal view. Other view buttons in order are Slide Sorter, Reading View, and Slide Show. Zoom buttons are used to enlarge or shrink the display of the active slide.

8 Tap or click *Click to add title* and type **Car Maintenance**.

9 Tap or click *CLICK TO ADD SUBTITLE* and type **Tips for all seasons**.

The subtitle text displays in all capital letters regardless of how you type the text because the Ion theme uses the All Caps font effect.

10 Tap or click in an unused area of the slide to close the placeholder.

Inserting New Slides

The **New Slide button** in the Slides group of the HOME tab is used to insert a new slide after the active slide. The button has two parts. Tapping or clicking the top part of the button adds a new slide with the Title and Content layout, which is the layout used most frequently. The content placeholder in this layout provides options to add text or a table, chart, SmartArt graphic, or picture or video to the slide. Tapping or clicking the bottom of the New Slide button (down-pointing arrow) provides a drop-down list of slide layouts and other new slide options. **Slide layouts** determine the number, position, and type of content placeholders for a slide.

11 Tap or click the top part of the New Slide button in the Slides group of the HOME tab.

12 Tap or click *Click to add title* and type **Why maintain a car?**.

13 Tap or click *Click to add text*, type **Preserve vehicle value**, and tap or press Enter.

Typing text in the content placeholder automatically creates a bulleted list. In the Ion theme, the bullet character is a green, right-pointing arrow.

14 Type the remaining bulleted list items, tapping or pressing Enter after each item except the last.

Prolong vehicle life

Improve driver safety

Spend less for repairs

Lower operating costs

Improved vehicle appearance

Reduced likelihood of breakdowns

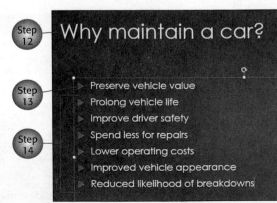

15 Tap or click the top part of the New Slide button in the Slides group.

16 Type the text in the third slide as shown in the image below.

Step 16

Editing Text on Slides

Activate the slide you want to edit by tapping or clicking the slide in the Slide Thumbnail pane. Select the text you want to change or delete, or tap or click in the placeholder to place an insertion point at the location where you want to edit text, and then type new text, change text, or delete text as needed.

17 Tap or click to select Slide 1 in the Slide Thumbnail pane.

18 Select ALL SEASONS in the subtitle text placeholder and type **car owners** so that the subtitle text now reads TIPS FOR CAR OWNERS.

Step 17

Step 18

19 Select Slide 2 in the Slide Thumbnail pane.

20 Tap or click at the beginning of the text in the third bulleted list item, delete *Improve*, and type **Sustain**.

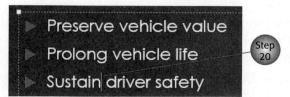

Step 20

21 Tap or click to place an insertion point within the title placeholder and edit the title so that *m* in *maintain* and *c* in *car* are capital letters. The title should now read *Why Maintain a Car?*

22 Tap or click in an unused area of the slide to deactivate the placeholder.

23 Save the presentation as **10.1-CarMaintenance-Your Name** in a new folder named *Ch10* in the CompletedTopicsByChapter folder on your USB flash drive. Leave the presentation open for the next topic.

Changing the Theme and Inserting and Modifying a Table

TOPIC 10.2

The presentation's theme and/or variant can be changed after a presentation has been created. To do this, tap or click the DESIGN tab and browse the themes and theme families in the *Themes* and *Variants* galleries.

SKILLS

Change theme

Change variant

Insert a table on a slide

Modify table layout

Tutorials

10.2.1 Changing Slide Size, Design Themes, and Background Styles

10.2.2 Creating a Table in a Slide

1. With the **10.1-CarMaintenance-Your Name** presentation open, tap or click Slide 1 in the Slide Thumbnail pane.

2. Tap or click the DESIGN tab.

3. Tap or click the *Facet* theme in the *Themes* gallery (third option).

   If you are using a mouse you can roll the mouse over the various theme options to view the active slide with a live preview of the theme.

4. Tap or click the More button at the bottom right of the *Variants* gallery.

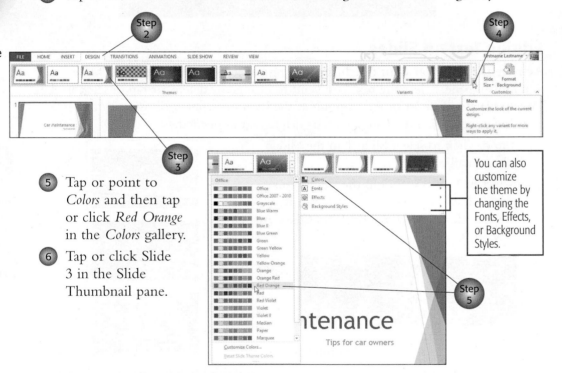

5. Tap or point to *Colors* and then tap or click *Red Orange* in the *Colors* gallery.

6. Tap or click Slide 3 in the Slide Thumbnail pane.

> You can also customize the theme by changing the Fonts, Effects, or Background Styles.

Inserting a Table on a Slide

PowerPoint includes a Table feature for organizing text on a slide in columns and rows similar to the Table feature in Word. To insert a table on a slide, tap or click the Insert Table button in the Content Placeholder.

7. Tap or click the HOME tab and then tap or click the top part of the New Slide button to insert a new slide with the Title and Content layout.

8. Tap or click *Click to add title* and type **Typical Annual Maintenance Costs**.

9. Tap or click the Insert Table button in the content placeholder.

10. Select *5* in the *Number of columns* text box and type **2**.

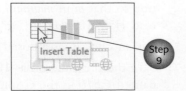

(11) Select *2* in the *Number of rows* text box, type **6**, and then tap or click OK.

    PowerPoint inserts a table in the slide with the colors in the theme family.

(12) With the insertion point positioned in the first cell in the table, type **Type of Car** and then tap or press Tab or tap or click in the second cell.

(13) Type **Cost**.

(14) Type the remaining entries in the table as follows:

Small size	**$600**
Medium size	**$675**
Large family sedan	**$750**
Minivan	**$775**
SUV	**$825**

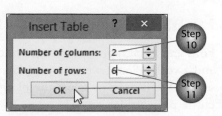

Quick STEPS

Change Theme
1. Tap or click DESIGN tab.
2. Tap or click option in *Themes* gallery.
3. If desired, tap or click variant option.

Insert a Table on a Slide
1. Insert new slide.
2. Tap or click Insert Table button in content placeholder.
3. Enter number of columns.
4. Enter number of rows.
5. Tap or click OK.

Modifying a Table

The TABLE TOOLS DESIGN and LAYOUT tabs provide options for modifying and customizing a table with the same tools you learned about in Word. Use the sizing handles to enlarge or shrink the table size. Slide or drag the border of a table to move the table's position on the slide.

(15) Slide or drag the right middle sizing handle left until the right border of the table ends below the first *e* in *Maintenance* in the title text.

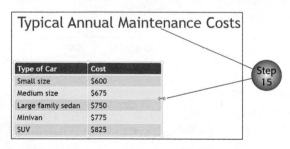

(16) Tap or click in any cell in the second column.

(17) Tap or click the TABLE TOOLS LAYOUT tab, tap or click the Select button in the Table group, and then tap or click *Select Column* at the drop-down list.

(18) Tap or click the Center button in the Alignment group.

(19) Tap or click in any cell in the first column, select the current entry in the *Width* text box in the Cell Size group of the TABLE TOOLS LAYOUT tab, type **3.5**, and then tap or press Enter.

(20) Slide or drag the top border of the table to move the table until it is positioned at the approximate location shown in the image at right.

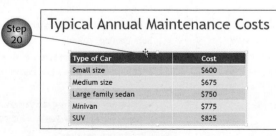

(21) Save the revised presentation using the same name (**10.1-CarMaintenance-Your Name**). Leave the presentation open for the next topic.

oops!

Table appears too small with first column wrapping text? You probably changed the width using the *Width* text box in the Table Size group instead of the Cell Size group. Use Undo and try Step 19 again.

TOPIC 10.3

SKILLS

Create multilevel bulleted list

Change font color

Center text in a placeholder

 Tutorials

10.3.1 Applying Fonts Using the Font Group

10.3.2 Changing Paragraph Formatting

A bulleted list can have up to eight levels.

You can also press Tab to increase the list level and Shift + Tab to decrease the list level.

Formatting Text with Font and Paragraph Options

Font and paragraph formatting options in PowerPoint are the same as those in Word and Excel. Select text within a placeholder and apply formatting changes to the selected text only, or select the placeholder and apply a formatting option to the entire placeholder.

1. With the **10.1-CarMaintenance-Your Name** presentation open, tap or click Slide 3 in the Slide Thumbnail pane.

2. Insert a new slide with the Title and Content layout.

   New slides are inserted after the active slide. The new slide should be positioned between the Fall and Winter Maintenance slide and the Typical Annual Maintenance Costs slide.

3. Type **Spring and Summer Maintenance** as the slide title.

4. Type **Thoroughly clean vehicle** as the first bulleted list item in the content placeholder and then tap or press Enter.

5. With the insertion point positioned at the beginning of the second bulleted list item, tap or click the **Increase List Level button** in the Paragraph group of the HOME tab.

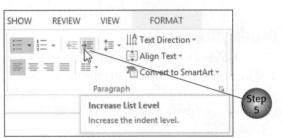

6. Type **Prevents rust by removing sand and salt accumulated from winter driving** and then tap or press Enter.

7. Tap or click the **Decrease List Level button** in the Paragraph group to move the bullet for the new item back to the previous level in the slide, type **Check cooling system**, and then tap or press Enter.

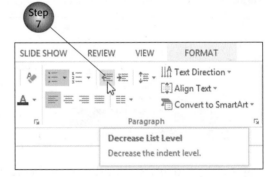

8. Type the remaining text on the slide as shown in the image below using the Increase List Level and Decrease List Level buttons as needed.

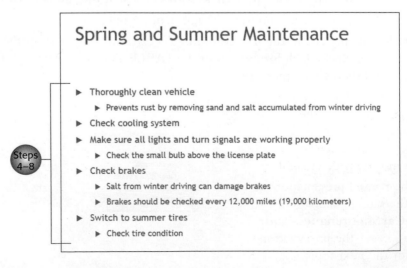

9 Select *12,000* in the content placeholder, tap or click the Font Color button arrow in the Mini toolbar or in the Font group of the HOME tab, and then tap or click *Red, Accent 1* (fifth option in first row of *Theme Colors* section).

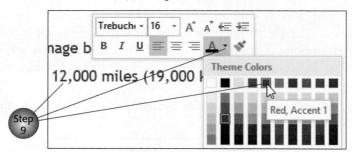

Quick STEPS

Change Font Options
1. Select text.
2. Tap or click font option in Mini toolbar or Font group of HOME tab.

Change Paragraph Options
1. Activate placeholder or select text.
2. Tap or click paragraph option in Mini toolbar or Paragraph group of HOME tab.

10 Tap or click the Bold button in the Font group.

11 Tap or click in the title text to activate the title placeholder.

12 Tap or click the Center button in the Paragraph group.

13 Tap or click the Align Left button in the Paragraph group to return the title placeholder to the default paragraph alignment.

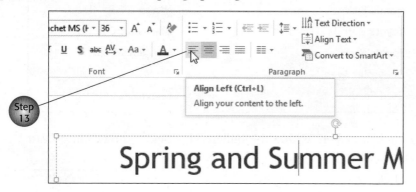

The default paragraph spacing is single line spacing with 10 points of space before and 0 points of space after each paragraph. Use the Line Spacing button or open the Paragraph dialog box to make changes to these settings.

14 Save the revised presentation using the same name (**10.1-CarMaintenance-Your Name**). Leave the presentation open for the next topic.

Changing the Bullet Symbol

The bullet symbols vary with each theme; however, you can change the bullet character to another symbol from the Bullets button arrow for an individual list item or a selected list. Tap or click *Bullets and Numbering* at the Bullets drop-down list to open the Bullets and Numbering dialog box. Choose the Picture button to select a bullet image, or the Customize button to select a bullet character from the Symbol dialog box. You can also change the size and color of the bullet character in the dialog box.

Selecting, Resizing, Aligning, and Moving Placeholders

TOPIC 10.4

SKILLS

Insert a slide with comparison layout

Change bulleted list to numbered list

Resize a placeholder

Align placeholders

Move a placeholder

 Tutorial

10.4   Modifying Placeholders

The active placeholder displays with a border and selection handles, which are used to resize or move the placeholder. Paragraph or font options apply to the text in which the insertion point is positioned or to selected text. To apply a font or paragraph change to all of the text in a placeholder, tap or click the placeholder's border to remove the insertion point or deselect text.

① With the **10.1-CarMaintenance–Your Name** presentation open, tap or click Slide 5 in the Slide Thumbnail pane.

② Tap or click the down-pointing arrow on the New Slide button and tap or click *Comparison* at the drop-down list.

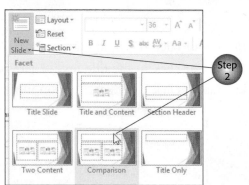

③ Type **Top 5 Cars Rated by Maintenance Costs** as the slide title.

④ Type the title and bulleted list text in the left and right content placeholders as shown in the image below.

Least Expensive	Most Expensive
▶ Honda Fit	▶ Nissan GT-R
▶ Toyota Corolla	▶ Chevrolet Corvette
▶ Toyota Yaris	▶ Mercedes-Benz SL-Class
▶ Chevrolet Aveo	▶ BMW Z4
▶ Ford Focus	▶ Chevrolet Camaro

⑤ Tap or click anywhere within the bulleted list below the heading *Least Expensive* to activate the placeholder.

⑥ Tap or click anywhere along the border of the active placeholder to remove the insertion point from within the bulleted list text, selecting the entire placeholder.

   The next action will affect all of the text within the placeholder. You can change font options or paragraph options for the entire bulleted list.

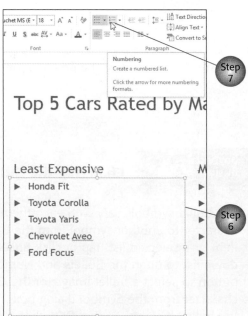

⑦ Tap or click the Numbering button in the Paragraph group to change the bulleted list to a numbered list. (Do *not* tap or click the down-pointing arrow on the button.)

oops!

Only one bullet changed to a number? This occurs if you have an insertion point within the placeholder; only the item in the list at which the insertion point was positioned is changed. Go back to Step 6 and try again.

8 Tap or click anywhere in the bulleted list below *Most Expensive*, tap or click along the border of the placeholder to select the entire placeholder text, and then tap or click the Numbering button.

9 Select the numbered list placeholder below the title *Least Expensive*.

10 Slide or drag the right middle sizing handle left until the right border of the placeholder is at the approximate location shown in the image below.

11 Select the *Least Expensive* title placeholder and slide or drag the right middle sizing handle left to resize the placeholder until the smart guide appears, indicating the title placeholder is the same width as the content placeholder below it.

Smart guides, also called alignment guides, appear automatically to help you align, space, or size placeholders or objects evenly.

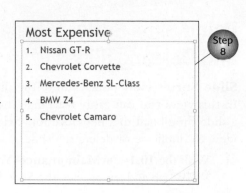

Step 8

Step 10

Step 11

Smart guide helps resize close objects to the same width.

12 With the *Least Expensive* placeholder still selected, slide or drag the border of the placeholder right to move the placeholder until the smart guides appear as shown in the image at right.

13 Select the numbered list placeholder below *Least Expensive* and slide or drag right until left, right, top, and bottom smart guides appear, indicating the placeholder is aligned evenly with the placeholders above and right.

14 Save the revised presentation using the same name (**10.1-CarMaintenance-Your Name**). Leave the presentation open for the next topic.

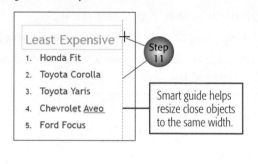
Step 12

Smart guides help align and evenly space close objects.

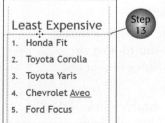
Step 13

Using Slide Sorter View and Moving, Duplicating, and Deleting Slides

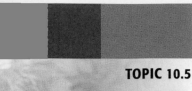

TOPIC 10.5

SKILLS

Use Slide Sorter view

Move a slide

Duplicate a slide

Delete a slide

 Tutorials

10.5 Rearranging, Deleting, and Hiding Slides

Using Touch? Slide right first and then upward to move the slide to the first row.

Slide Sorter view displays all of the slides in a presentation as slide thumbnails. In this view, you can easily rearrange the order of the slides by sliding or dragging a slide thumbnail to a new location. Select a slide in Slide Sorter view or Normal view to duplicate or delete the slide.

1. With the **10.1-CarMaintenance-Your Name** presentation open, tap or click the VIEW tab and tap or click the Slide Sorter button in the Presentation Views group.

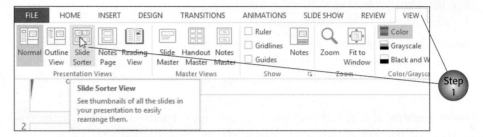

Step 1

2. Tap or click Slide 5 to select the slide.

3. Slide or drag Slide 5 to the top row, placing it to the right of Slide 2.

As you slide or drag to move a slide in Slide Sorter view, the existing slides rearrange around the slide.

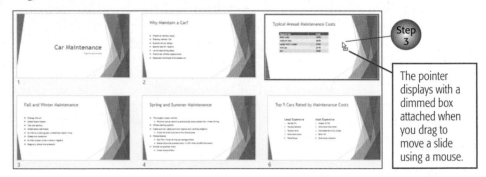

Step 3

The pointer displays with a dimmed box attached when you drag to move a slide using a mouse.

Duplicating a Slide

When you need to create a new slide with the same layout as an existing slide and with the placeholders sized, aligned, and positioned the same, make a duplicate copy of the existing slide. Once the slide is duplicated, all you have to do is change the text inside the placeholders. A duplicated slide is inserted in the presentation immediately after the slide selected to duplicate.

4. Tap or click to select Slide 6.

5. Press and hold to display the Mini toolbar, or right-click to display the shortcut menu.

6. Tap or click the Duplicate button on the touch Mini toolbar or the *Duplicate Slide* option at the shortcut menu.

7. Double-tap or double-click Slide 7 to return to Normal view.

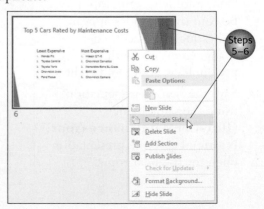

Steps 5–6

Deleting a Slide

Slides can be deleted in Slide Sorter view or Normal view by selecting the slide and displaying the Mini toolbar on touch devices or the shortcut menu on devices operated with a mouse.

(8) Press and hold or right-click Slide 7 in the Slide Thumbnail pane to display the Mini toolbar or shortcut menu.

(9) Tap or click the Delete button on the Mini toolbar or *Delete Slide* at the shortcut menu.

(10) Save the revised presentation using the same name (**10.1-CarMaintenance-Your Name**). Leave the presentation open for the next topic.

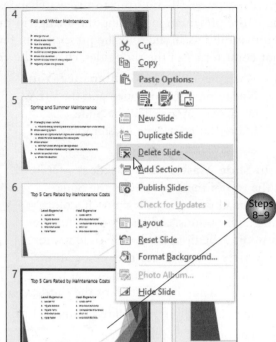

Select more than one slide to delete by holding down the Ctrl key while you click other slides, then right-click any selected slide and choose *Delete Slide*.

Slide Sorter View
Tap or click Slide Sorter button in Status bar.
OR
1. Tap or click VIEW tab.
2. Tap or click Slide Sorter button.

Move a Slide
Slide or drag slide in Slide Sorter view to required location.

Duplicate a Slide
1. Select slide.
2. Display Mini toolbar or shortcut menu.
3. Tap Duplicate button or click *Duplicate Slide*.

Delete a Slide
1. Select slide.
2. Display Mini toolbar or shortcut menu.
3. Tap Delete button or click *Delete Slide*.

Consider using these alternative methods for moving and duplicating slides:

Move slide   In Normal view, slide or drag slide up or down in Slide Thumbnail pane.

Duplicate slide   Select slide, tap or click down-pointing arrow on New Slide button, and then tap or click *Duplicate Selected Slides*.

Beyond Basics — **Hiding a Slide**

You may have a slide in a presentation that you want to hide during a particular slide show because the slide does not apply to the current audience or provides more detail than you have time to explain. In Slide Sorter view or Normal view, press and hold or right-click the slide to be hidden and choose the Hide button on the Mini toolbar (touch devices) or *Hide Slide* (shortcut menu).

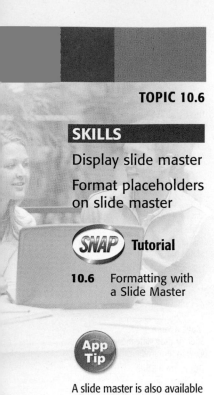

TOPIC 10.6

SKILLS

Display slide master

Format placeholders
on slide master

SNAP **Tutorial**

10.6   Formatting with
a Slide Master

App Tip

A slide master is also available
for formatting handouts and
notes.

Modifying the Slide Master

Each presentation that you create includes a slide master. A **slide master** determines the default formatting and paragraph options for placeholders when you insert new slides. If you want to make a change to a font or paragraph option for the entire presentation, making the change in the slide master will apply the change automatically to all slides in the presentation. For example, if you want a different font color for all of the slide titles, change the color on the slide master.

① With the **10.1-CarMaintenance-Your Name** presentation open and the VIEW tab active, tap or click the Slide Master button in the Master Views group.

In **Slide Master view**, a slide master at the top of the hierarchy in the Slide Thumbnail pane controls the font, colors, paragraph options, and background for the entire presentation. Below the slide master is a variety of layouts for the presentation. Changes made to the slide master at the top of the hierarchy affect all of the slide layouts below it except the title slide.

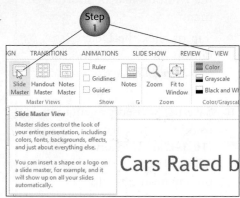

② Slide or scroll up the Slide Thumbnail pane to the first slide.

③ Tap or click to select Slide 1.

④ Tap or click the border of the title text placeholder on the slide master to select the placeholder.

⑤ Tap or click the HOME tab, tap or click the Font Color button arrow, and then tap or click *Dark Red, Accent 6* (last color in first row of *Theme Colors* section).

App Tip

Formatting changes made on
individual slides override the
slide master. Presentations
should have a consistent look;
therefore, limit individual slide
formatting changes to only
when necessary such as to
indicate a change in topic or
speaker.

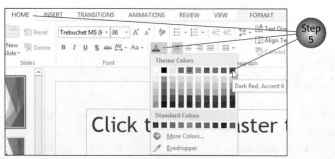

⑥ Tap or click the border of the content placeholder to select the placeholder and then tap or click the Bullets button arrow in the Paragraph group.

7 Tap or click *Bullets and Numbering* at the drop-down list.

8 Tap or click the Color button in the Bullets and Numbering dialog box and then tap or click *Dark Red, Accent 6*.

9 Tap or click the *Hollow Square Bullets* option (first option in second row).

10 Tap or click OK.

Slide Master View
1. Tap or click VIEW tab.
2. Tap or click Slide Master button.

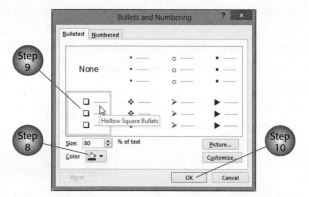

11 Tap or click the SLIDE MASTER tab.

12 Tap or click the Close Master View button in the Close group.

13 Tap or click the Previous Slide or Next Slide buttons at the bottom of the vertical scroll bar or tap or click each slide in the Slide Thumbnail pane to scroll through and view each slide in the presentation.

Notice that the font color for the title text and the bullet character are changed on each slide *after* the title slide. A title slide has its own slide master and is the first layout below slide 1 in the slide master hierarchy.

14 Save the revised presentation using the same name (**10.1-CarMaintenance-Your Name**). Leave the presentation open for the next topic.

Page Up and Page Down also display the previous or next slide in the presentation.

 **Adding Text to the Bottom of Each Slide**

Add text to the bottom of each slide in a footer placeholder by selecting the *Footer* check box and typing footer text at the Header and Footer dialog box with the Slides tab active (INSERT tab, Header & Footer button). Use the Slide Master to format the footer text to a different font, font size, or color as required. For example, many speakers use the Footer placeholder to add a company name or presentation title at the bottom of each slide.

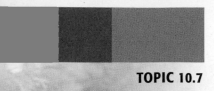

TOPIC 10.7

SKILLS

Display the Notes
and Comments
panes

Add speaker notes

Add comments

SNAP **Tutorial**

10.7 Comparing
and Combining
Presentations;
Inserting
and Deleting
Comments

Text in the Notes pane is
visible to the presenter but not
the audience during a slide
show.

Adding Notes and Comments

Notes, generally referred to as speaker notes, are text typed in the **Notes pane**
below the Slide pane in Normal view. Use notes to type reminders for the
presenter, or use this pane to add more details about the slide content for the person
giving the presentation.

Comments can be added to slides and will appear in the **Comments pane**
at the right of the Slide pane. If you are creating a presentation with a group of
people, use comments to provide feedback or pose questions to others in the group.

1. With the **10.1-CarMaintenance-Your Name** presentation open, display
Slide 1 in the Slide pane.

2. Tap or click the NOTES button in the
Status bar to turn on the display of the
Notes pane at the bottom of the Slide
pane. Skip this step if the Notes pane is
already visible.

3. Tap or click *Click to add notes* in the Notes pane and then type **Begin this
slide with the statistic that approximately 5.2% of motor vehicle
accidents are caused by vehicle neglect.**.

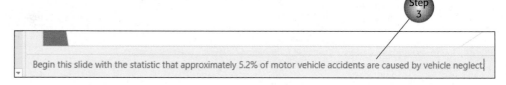

4. Display Slide 3 in the Slide pane.

5. Slide or drag the top border of the
Notes pane upward to increase the
height of the pane by approximately
one-half inch.

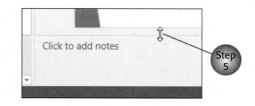

6. Tap or click in the Notes pane and
type **Mention that these costs
are estimated for a driving
distance of 12,000 miles (19,000
kilometers) per year.**.

7. Tap or press Enter twice and type **Ask the audience if anyone wants to
share the total amount paid each year to maintain his or her vehicle.**.

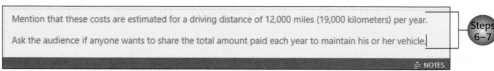

8. Tap or click the NOTES button to turn off the Notes pane.

9. Tap or click the COMMENTS button in the Status bar to
turn on the Comments pane.

10. Tap or click the New button near the top of
the Comments pane.

PowerPoint opens a comment box in the
Comments pane with your account name
associated with the comment.

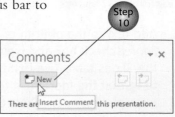

11 Type **Consider adding the source of these statistics to the slide.**.

12 Tap or click Slide 4 in the Slide Thumbnail pane, tap or click the New button in the Comments pane, and then type **Add more information for any of these points?**.

13 Tap or click in the Comments pane outside the Comment box to close the comment.

14 Close the Comments pane.

A comment balloon appears in the top left corner of a slide for which a comment has been added.

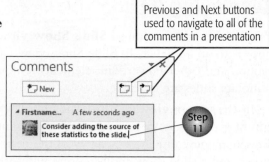

Previous and Next buttons used to navigate to all of the comments in a presentation

Step 11

Step 12

New to PowerPoint 2013 is the ability to reply to a comment.

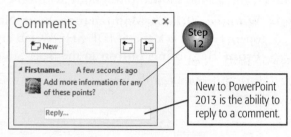

Comment balloon displays on slides with comments. Tap or click the balloon to open the Comments pane and view the comments and replies.

Fall and Winter Maintenance

15 Save the revised presentation using the same name (**10.1-CarMaintenance-Your Name**). Leave the presentation open for the next topic.

ALTERNATIVE method
A comment can also be added to selected text on a slide. The comment balloon displays at the end of the selected text. To do this, select the text and reveal the Comments pane, or tap or click the New Comment button in the REVIEW tab.

Deleting or Hiding Comments

Tapping a comment or pointing to a comment with the mouse in the Comments pane displays a Delete icon (black X) at the top right of the comment, which you can tap or click to delete the comment. Hide comment balloons with the Show Comments button in the Comments group of the REVIEW tab by removing the check mark next to *Show Markup* at the drop-down list.

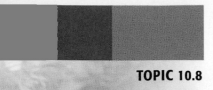

TOPIC 10.8

SKILLS

Display a presentation in Slide Show view

Display a presentation in Presenter view

 **Tutorial**

10.8   Running a Presentation

Press F5 to start a slide show from Slide 1.

oops!

Using Touch? Tap the slide to display the Slide Show toolbar.

Displaying a Slide Show

Display the presentation in **Slide Show view** to preview the slides as they will appear to an audience. In Slide Show view, each slide fills the screen with the ribbon and other PowerPoint elements removed; however, tools to navigate and annotate slides are available.

In **Presenter view**, the slide show displays full screen on one monitor (the monitor the audience will see), and in Presenter view on a second monitor. Presenter view displays a preview of the next slide, notes from the Notes pane, a timer, and a slide show toolbar along with other options.

1 With the **10.1-CarMaintenance-Your Name** presentation open, tap or click the SLIDE SHOW tab and then tap or click the **From Beginning button** in the Start Slide Show group.

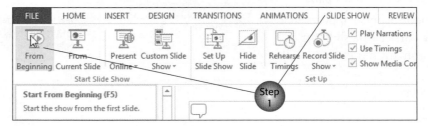

2 Tap or click the right-pointing arrow that appears in the Slide Show toolbar near the bottom left corner of the screen to move to Slide 2 (see Figure 10.2).

If you are using a mouse or keyboard, you can also click anywhere on a slide or press the Page Down key to move to the next slide.

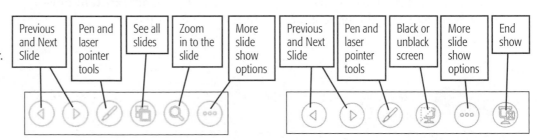

Figure 10.2 The Slide Show toolbar for a mouse-enabled device (left) and for a touch-enabled device (right). See Table 10.2 for a description of each button.

Table 10.2	Slide Show Toolbar Buttons
Button	**Description**
Previous Slide and Next Slide	Display the previous or next slide in the presentation.
Pen and laser pointer tools	Point, write on the slides, or highlight text during a presentation.
See all slides	View all slides in the presentation similarly to Slide Sorter view. Use this to jump to a slide out of sequence during a presentation.
Zoom in to the slide	Use this button to slide or click on a portion of a slide that you want to enlarge to temporarily fill the screen for a closer look. Tap or click the button again or right-click to restore the slide.
More slide show options	Displays a pop-up menu with more options. On mouse-enabled devices, use this button to end the show or black/unblack the screen during a presentation.
Black or Unblack screen	On a touch-enabled device, this button blacks the screen or unblacks the screen.
End show	On a touch-enabled device, use this button to end the show.

③ Continue tapping or clicking the Next Slide arrow to navigate through the remaining slides in the presentation until the black screen appears.

After the last slide is viewed, a black screen is shown with the message *End of slide show, click to exit*. Many presenters leave the screen black when their presentation is ended until the audience has left because tapping or clicking to exit displays the presentation in Normal view on the screen.

④ At the black screen that appears, tap the screen and then tap the End show button (see Figure 10.2 on the previous page), or click anywhere on the screen to return to Normal view.

⑤ Display Slide 1 in the Slide pane and then tap or click the **Slide Show button** in the Status bar.

The Slide Show button in the Status bar starts the slide show at the active slide.

⑥ Tap or click the More slide show options button (button with three dots) in the Slide Show toolbar and then tap or click *Show Presenter View* at the pop-up list.

You can use Presenter view on a system with only one monitor to preview or rehearse a presentation. At a presentation venue, PowerPoint automatically detects the computer setup and chooses the correct monitor on which to show Presenter view.

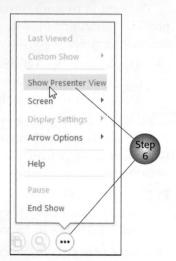

⑦ Tap or click the Next Slide button in the slide navigator near the bottom of Presenter view until you have navigated to Slide 3 (see Figure 10.3).

⑧ Compare your screen with the one shown in Figure 10.3.

⑨ Continue tapping or clicking the Next Slide button until you reach Slide 6 and then tap or click End Slide Show at the top of the screen.

⑩ Leave the presentation open for the next topic.

Quick STEPS

Display a Slide Show
1. Tap or click SLIDE SHOW tab.
2. Tap or click From Beginning button.
OR
1. Display Slide 1.
2. Tap or click Slide Show button in Status bar.

Display Presenter View
1. Display presentation as Slide Show.
2. Tap or click More slide show options button.
3. Tap or click *Show Presenter View*.

Did You Know ?

Many speakers include a closing slide as the last slide in a presentation that is left on the screen until the audience has left. The closing slide contains the speaker's contact information, a favorite or memorable quote related to the topic, or a thank-you message.

App Tip

You can also preview a slide show in Reading view where each slide fills the screen. A Title bar, Status bar, and Taskbar remain visible with buttons to navigate slides in the Status bar.

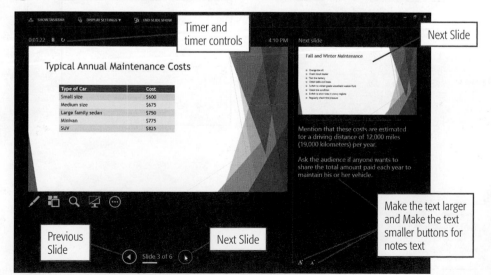

Figure 10.3 Slide 3 in Presenter View

Preparing Audience Handouts and Speaker Notes

Some speakers provide audience members with a printout of their slides in a format that allows an individual to add his or her own handwritten notes during the presentation. PowerPoint provides several options for printing slides as handouts. Speakers who do not use Presenter view during a presentation may also print a copy of the slides with the notes included.

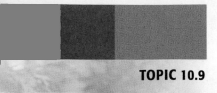

1. With the **10.1-CarMaintenance-Your Name** presentation open, tap or click the FILE tab and then tap or click Print.

2. At the Print tab Backstage view, tap or click the Full Page Slides list arrow in the *Settings* section.

3. Tap or click *3 Slides* in the *Handouts* section of the drop-down or pop-up list.

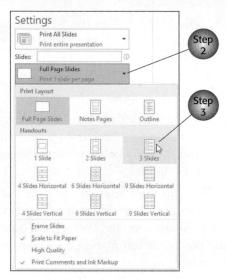

The option to print three slides per page provides horizontal lines next to each slide for writing notes.

4. Tap or click the 3 Slides list arrow and tap or click *6 Slides Horizontal* at the drop-down or pop-up list.

Notice that the printout requires two pages even though only six slides are in the presentation. By default, comments print with the presentation; the second page is for printing the comments.

5. Tap or click the 6 Slides Horizontal list arrow and tap or click *Print Comments and Ink Markup* to remove the check mark. The printout is now only one page.

6. Tap or click the 6 Slides Horizontal list arrow and tap or click *Notes Pages* in the *Print Layout* section of the drop-down or pop-up list.

Notes Pages prints one slide per page with the slide at the top half of the page and notes or blank space in the bottom half.

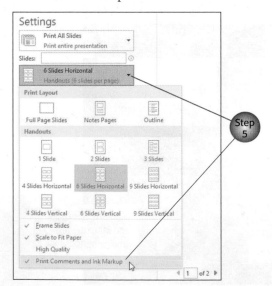

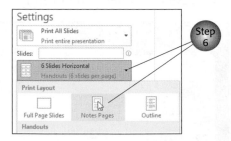

7. Tap or click the Next Page button to display Slide 2 in the *Preview* section.

8. Tap or click the Next Page button to display Slide 3.

Notice the notes text is displayed below the slide.

9. Tap or click the <u>Edit Header & Footer</u> link at the bottom of the *Settings* section.

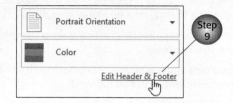

Step 9

10. At the Header and Footer dialog box with the Notes and Handouts tab active, tap or click the *Header* check box to insert a check mark, tap or click in the *Header* text box, and then type your first and last names.

11. Tap or click the *Footer* check box to insert a check mark, tap or click in the *Footer* text box, and then type your school name.

12. Tap or click the Apply to All button.

13. Preview the header and footer text by scrolling through the remaining slides.

Tap or click here to print the date at the top right of each page. By default, the date updates to the date the slides are printed; choose *Fixed* to enter a specific date.

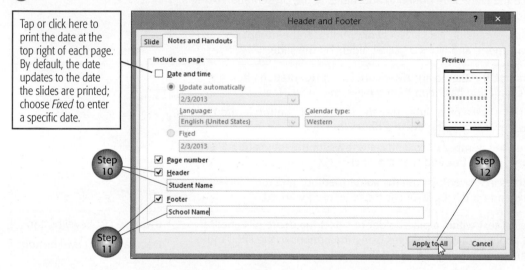

Step 10

Step 11

Step 12

14. Tap or click the Back button to exit the Print tab Backstage view.

15. Save the revised presentation using the same name (**10.1-CarMaintenance-Your Name**) and then close the presentation.

Did You Know?

To conserve paper and ink some presenters publish their presentations to a web service such as slideshare.net instead of printing handouts.

Slide Size and Orientation for Printing

By default, slides print in landscape orientation when printed as slides or in portrait orientation when printed as notes or handouts. Change the orientation with the orientation list arrow in the *Settings* section of the Print tab Backstage view or at the *Custom Slide Size* option from the Slide Size button in the Customize group of the DESIGN tab.

Concepts Review

Topic	Key Concepts	Key Terms
Creating a New Presentation and Inserting Slides	A new presentation is created from the Start screen by choosing a template, a theme, or a blank presentation.	Presentation application
	A placeholder is a rectangular container in which you type text or insert other content.	Title slide
	PowerPoint starts a new presentation with the title slide in widescreen format in Normal view.	Placeholder
	Normal view includes the Slide pane, which displays the active slide, and the Slide Thumbnail pane, which displays numbered thumbnails of all of the slides in a presentation.	Slide pane
	Variants of a theme family are based upon the same theme but with different colors, styles, and effects.	Slide Thumbnail pane
	Add or edit text on a slide by tapping or clicking inside the placeholder and typing or editing text.	Variants
	Use the New Slide button to add slides to the presentation using a slide layout.	New Slide button
	Slide layouts provide a variety of options for the number, placement, and types of placeholders on the slide.	Slide layouts
Changing the Theme and Inserting and Modifying a Table	Change the theme and/or variant for a presentation after the presentation has been started using the DESIGN tab.	
	Insert a table on a slide using the Insert Table button located within the content placeholder of a new slide.	
	Type the number of columns and rows for the table at the Insert Table dialog box and then tap or click OK.	
	Tables in PowerPoint use the same methods and tools for entering text and modifying layout as those learned in Word.	
Formatting Text with Font and Paragraph Options	Select text within a placeholder or select the entire placeholder to apply formatting changes using the options in the Font and Paragraph groups of the HOME tab.	Increase List Level button
	Create a multilevel bulleted list using the Increase List Level and Decrease List Level buttons in the Paragraph group.	Decrease List Level button
	Bullet symbols vary for each theme.	
	You can change the bullet symbol character using the Bullets button arrow.	
Selecting, Resizing, Aligning, and Moving Placeholders	The active placeholder displays with sizing handles and a border with which you can resize or move the placeholder.	Smart guides
	Smart guides are colored lines that appear on the slide as you resize or move placeholders to assist in aligning the placeholders or evenly spacing placeholders with other close objects.	

Topic	Key Concepts	Key Terms
Using Slide Sorter View and Moving, Duplicating, and Deleting Slides	Slide Sorter view displays all slides as slide thumbnails and is used to rearrange the order of slides.	Slide Sorter view
	Slide or drag a slide in Slide Sorter view to move the slide to a new location in the presentation.	
	Duplicating a slide makes a copy of an existing slide with the placeholders sized, aligned, and positioned the same as the original slide.	
	Delete a slide you no longer need in a presentation by selecting the slide or slides and using the Delete option from the Mini toolbar (touch) or shortcut menu (mouse).	
	A slide can be hidden in the presentation if you do not want the slide to display in a slide show.	
Using Slide Master View	Each presentation has a slide master that determines the formatting and paragraph options for placeholders in new slides.	Slide Master
	Display the slide master to make formatting changes that you want to apply to all slides in the presentation automatically.	Slide Master view
	Change to Slide Master view from the VIEW tab to modify the slide master.	
	In Slide Master view, the Slide Thumbnail pane displays the slide master at the top of the hierarchy.	
	Below the slide master, individual slide layouts are included for formatting.	
	Add text to the bottom of each slide in a footer placeholder by typing footer text in the Header and Footer dialog box (INSERT tab, Header & Footer button).	
	Use the footer placeholder on the slide master to apply formatting options to the footer text.	
Adding Notes and Comments	The Notes pane appears below the Slide pane and is used to type speaker notes, reminders for the presenter, or more detailed information about the slide content for a reader.	Notes Pane
	Reveal the Notes pane with the NOTES button in the Status bar.	Comments Pane
	A comment is added to the active slide by displaying the Comments pane, tapping or clicking the New button, and then typing the comment text.	
	Reveal the Comments pane with the COMMENTS button in the Status bar.	
	Delete a comment using the Delete icon that appears when you tap or point to the comment text in the Comments pane.	
	Hide comments by removing the check mark next to *Show Markup* at the Show Comments drop-down list (REVIEW tab)	

continued....

Topic	Key Concepts	Key Terms
Displaying a Slide Show	Slide Show view previews each slide as the audience will see the slide with a full screen. Display a slide show starting at Slide 1 by tapping or clicking the From Beginning button in the SLIDE SHOW tab. The Slide Show toolbar provides buttons to navigate slides, annotate slides, zoom into a slide, or black/unblack the screen during the presentation. After the last slide is shown, a black screen displays indicating the end of the slide show. The Slide Show button in the Status bar starts the slide show from the active slide in the Slide pane. Display a slide show and tap or click the More slide show options button to switch the view to Presenter view. Presenter view works with two monitors, where one monitor displays the slide show as the audience will see it and the second monitor displays the slide show in Presenter view. Presenter view can also be seen on a computer with only one monitor so that you can rehearse a presentation. In Presenter view, the speaker's monitor displays a timer and timer controls, a preview of the next slide, notes, and a slide show toolbar along with other options.	Slide Show view Presenter view From Beginning button Slide Show button
Preparing Audience Handouts and Speaker Notes	Preview slides formatted as handouts at the Print tab Backstage view. The *3 Slides* option provides lines next to each slide for writing notes. Various other horizontal or vertical options are available for printing slide thumbnails. By default, comments print on a separate page after the slides; to prevent comments from printing, remove the check mark next to *Print Comments and Ink Markup* from the slides option list. Choose the *Notes Pages* option to print one slide per page with the notes from the Notes pane. Add header and/or footer text to a printout using the <u>Edit Header & Footer</u> link at the bottom of the *Settings* section. By default, slides printed as slides print in landscape orientation, while slides printed as handouts or notes pages print in portrait orientation.	Notes Pages

Multiple Choice

1. This is the first slide that is created in a new presentation.
   a. Bulleted list
   b. Title slide
   c. Presenter slide
   d. Title and Content slide

2. This is the view that is active when a new presentation is created.
   a. Notes view
   b. Slide Sorter view
   c. Normal view
   d. Reading view

3. Use this tab in the ribbon to change the theme after the presentation has been created.
   a. SLIDE SHOW
   b. INSERT
   c. VIEW
   d. DESIGN

4. Use this button in the content placeholder to type text in a grid of columns and rows.
   a. Insert Table
   b. Create Table
   c. Draw Table
   d. Make Table

5. Use this button to move to the next level (right) in a bulleted list.
   a. Next Level
   b. Increase Indent
   c. Next Bullet
   d. Increase List Level

6. A new slide is inserted _____.
   a. before the active slide
   b. after the active slide
   c. at the beginning of slides
   d. at the end of slides

7. Move a placeholder by sliding or dragging this part of the placeholder.
   a. any sizing handle
   b. guide line
   c. border
   d. move handle

8. These appear to help you align placeholders evenly as you resize or move a placeholder.
   a. smart lines
   b. smart tags
   c. smart tips
   d. smart guides

9. In this view, all of the slides in the presentation display as thumbnails so that you can easily rearrange the slide order.
   a. Slide view
   b. Slide Show view
   c. Slide Sorter view
   d. Slide Thumbnail view

10. Use this option to make an exact copy of the selected slide.
    a. Copy Slide
    b. Duplicate Slide
    c. Twin Slide
    d. Replica Slide

11. The formatting on this slide determines the default font and paragraph options for all new slides except title slides.
    a. Slide header
    b. Slide master
    c. Slide duplicate
    d. Slide control

12. This placeholder holds text that appears at the bottom of each slide.
    a. Footer
    b. Header
    c. Title
    d. Author

13. Type additional information about the content on the slide in this pane.
    a. Properties
    b. Notes
    c. Subject
    d. Text

14. This balloon appears on a slide when someone has typed feedback or posed a question about a slide.
    a. Comment
    b. Question
    c. Review
    d. Share

15. This view for a slide show shows a timer and a preview of the next slide.
    a. Slide Show view
    b. Slide Sorter view
    c. Set Up Show view
    d. Presenter view

16. This screen appears after the last slide in the presentation has been viewed.
    a. blue screen
    b. white screen
    c. black screen
    d. gray screen

17. Choose this handout option to have lines printed next to each slide.
    a. 6 Slides
    b. 6 Slides Vertical
    c. 9 Slides Vertical
    d. 3 Slides

18. Choose this Print Layout option to print one slide per page with each slide in the top half of the page.
    a. Outline
    b. Notes Pages
    c. Full Page Slides
    d. 1 Slide

Crossword Puzzle

ACROSS
1 Pane in which feedback for a slide is provided
5 Lines that help you align objects on a slide
7 View that displays all slides as thumbnails
8 Collections of color schemes for a theme
9 Container for text or other content

DOWN
2 View that displays when slide show is ended
3 Pane in which speaker reminders are typed
4 Option to print slides with speaker notes
5 View to preview slides as audience will see them
6 View to make global formatting changes

Matching

Match the term with the statement or definition.

_____ 1. Choose theme
_____ 2. Active slide
_____ 3. Default new slide layout
_____ 4. Change theme
_____ 5. Add subpoint below bullet text
_____ 6. Active placeholder
_____ 7. Remove slide
_____ 8. Change all slides
_____ 9. Status bar button
_____ 10. Display slide show
_____ 11. Handouts option

a. Title and Content
b. 3 Slides
c. Delete
d. Slide master
e. Start screen
f. NOTES
g. Presenter view
h. Slide pane
i. DESIGN tab
j. Selection handles
k. Increase List Level

Project 1 Creating and Editing a New Presentation

Individual

Deliverable: Presentation about world and U.S. landmarks (continued in Projects 2 and 3)

1. Start a new presentation, choosing a theme and variant that you like.
2. Save the presentation as **C10-Project1-Landmarks-Your Name** in a new folder named *Ch10* within the ChapterProjectsWork folder on your USB flash drive.
3. Create slides including multilevel lists, a table, and a comparison slide with the following information:

Slide 1	Title	Famous Landmarks
	Subtitle	Your Name

Slide 2	Title	World and National Landmarks
	List	Top 5 World Landmarks
		Top 5 U.S. Landmarks
		Survey Results
		Honorable Mentions

Slide 3   Title   Top 5 World Landmarks

Multilevel List   The Pyramid of Khufu
- Located in Giza, Egypt
- Largest pyramid ever built

The Great Wall of China
- Completed during the Ming dynasty (1368 to 1644)

Acropolis
- UNESCO World Heritage Site
- Parthenon Greek temple

Eiffel Tower
- 18,000 metallic parts joined by 2,500,000 rivets

Taj Mahal
- Agra, India

Slide 4   Title   Top 5 U.S. Landmarks

List   Statue of Liberty, New York
Grand Canyon, Arizona
Mount Rushmore, South Dakota
Independence Hall, Philadelphia
The National Mall, Washington, D.C.

Slide 5   Title   Survey Results

Table

Social Media Website	Votes Cast
Facebook	345,985
Twitter	420,870
Tumblr	155,329

Slide 6   Title   Honorable Mentions

Comparison Slide Layout

World Landmarks	U.S. Landmarks
Stonehenge, U.K.	Freedom Trail, Boston
Edinburgh Castle, Scotland	Fort Sumter, Charleston
Buckingham Palace, U.K.	The Alamo, San Antonio
Machu Picchu, Peru	Gateway Arch, St. Louis

4. Perform a spelling check and carefully proofread each slide, making corrections as needed.
5. Edit Slide 3 as follows:
   a. Delete the entry *Largest pyramid ever built*.
   b. Delete the entry *UNESCO World Heritage Site*.

   c. Insert the text *Tower located in Paris has* before the entry that begins *18,000 metallic parts.*

   d. Insert the text *Marble mausoleum located in* before *Agra, India.*

6. Edit Slide 5, changing the votes cast by Facebook from *345,985* to *543,589.*

7. Save the revised presentation using the same name (**C10-Project1-Landmarks-Your Name**).

8. Leave the presentation open if you are continuing to Project 2; otherwise close the presentation and submit the project to your instructor in the manner she or he has requested.

Project 2 Editing and Formatting a Presentation

Individual

Deliverable: Presentation about world and U.S. landmarks (continued in Project 3)

Note: You must have completed Project 1 before starting this project.

1. If necessary, open **C10-Project1-Landmarks-Your Name**.

2. Use Save As to change the file name to **C10-Project2-Landmarks-Your Name**, saving in the same folder.

3. Change the theme and variant to another design of your choosing. Check each slide after you change the theme for corrections that may be needed. For example, a theme that uses the All Caps font in a title or subtitle may cause changes in capitalization when the theme is changed to one that does not use the All Caps font.

4. Display the slide master and make the following changes to the top slide in the hierarchy:

   a. Change the font color for all of the titles to another color of your choosing.

   b. Change the bullet character to a different symbol and color than the one used in the theme.

5. Display Slide 5 and modify the table layout and design as follows:

   a. Change the width of the first column to 3.5 inches.

   b. Change the width of the second column to 1.75 inches.

   c. Center-align the entries in the second column.

   d. Change the table style to another style of your choosing.

   e. Move the table so that the table is positioned at the approximate center of the slide below the title.

6. Display Slide 6 and make the following changes:

   a. Change the bullet character to a different symbol for the two lists than the symbol that was used on the slide master.

   b. Resize the left list placeholder so that the placeholder's right border ends just after the longest entry in the list. Resize the left title placeholder to the same width as the list.

   c. Move the left title and list placeholders closer to the right title and list. Align the two titles and lists at the approximate center below the slide title.

7. Save the revised presentation using the same name (**C10-Project2-Landmarks-Your Name**).

8. Leave the presentation open if you are continuing to Project 3; otherwise, close the presentation and submit the project to your instructor in the manner she or he has requested.

Project 3 Rearranging Slides and Adding Notes and Comments

Individual

Deliverable: Presentation about world and U.S. landmarks

Note: You must have completed Projects 1 and 2 before starting this project.

1. If necessary, open **C10-Project2-Landmarks-Your Name**.

2. Use Save As to change the file name to **C10-Project3-Landmarks-Your Name**, saving in the same folder.

3. Move the *Survey Results* slide so that it becomes the third slide in the presentation.

4. Move the *Honorable Mentions* slide after the *Survey Results* slide.

5. Display Slide 2 and edit the bulleted list to reposition the bottom two bulleted list items so they become the top two bulleted list items.

6. Display the *Survey Results* slide and type the following text in the Notes pane:

   Our first survey using social media for reader voting was a phenomenal success. Plans for next year's survey are to expand voting to include other social media sites. Ask the audience for suggestions.

7. Display the *Honorable Mentions* slide and type the following text in the Notes pane:

   All honorable mentions had at least 20,000 votes.

8. Display the *Top 5 World Landmarks* slide, select the bulleted list text below *Eiffel Tower*, and type the following comment:

   Should I remove the number of parts and rivets?

9. Display the Top 5 U.S. Landmarks and type the following comment for the entire slide:

   Should I add the number of votes for each landmark?

10. Save the revised presentation using the same name (**C10-Project3-Landmarks-Your Name**).

11. Submit the project to your instructor in the manner she or he has requested.

12. Close the presentation.

Project 4 Internet Research and Creating a Presentation from a Template

Individual or Pairs

Deliverable: Presentation about inventions

1. Start a new presentation, browsing the *Education* category of templates and choosing a template that you like.

2. Create slides for a presentation about the inventions listed below. For each invention, research four to five interesting facts about the invention and add the information in a bulleted list on the slide.

Slide 1	(You determine an appropriate title and subtitle.)
Slide 2	(You determine an appropriate introductory slide for the presentation.)
Slide 3	The Telephone
Slide 4	The Television
Slide 5	The Automobile
Slide 6	The Light Bulb

3. Delete slides that were downloaded as part of the template that are not needed for this presentation.

4. Save the presentation in the Ch10 folder within ChapterProjectsWork as **C10-Project4-Inventions-Your Name**.

5. Submit the project to your instructor in the manner she or he has requested.

6. Close the presentation.

Project 5 Creating a Graduation Party Planning Presentation

Individual

Deliverable: Presentation on college graduation party planning

1. Create a presentation similar to the one shown in Figure 10.4 on the next page with the following additional information:

   a. The theme is *Integral* with one of the variants selected.

   b. On the slide master the first-level bullet character is removed and the second- and third-level bullet characters are changed.

   c. On the slide master, the font color for the title is changed from the default color. Use your best judgment to choose a similar color.

   d. Use your best judgment to determine other formatting, placeholder size, and alignment.

2. Save the presentation in the Ch10 folder within the ChapterProjectsWork folder as **C10-Project5-GradParty-Your Name**.

3. Submit the project to your instructor in the manner she or he has requested.

4. Close the presentation.

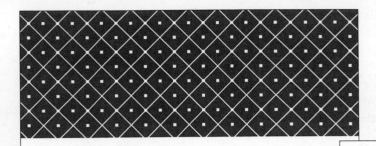

GRADUATION PARTY PLANNING | Student name

GRADUATION PARTY CHECKLIST

Date and venue
Budget
Invitations
Plan food, decorations, and entertainment

CHOOSE THE DATE AND VENUE

Survey close friends and family before setting the date
❑Find a date that conflicts the least with other events

Visit possible venues
❑Indoors
　○Restaurants, banquet or community halls
❑Outdoors
　○Local park, recreation area, or estate

BUDGET

Expense	Typical Budget
Location, Food, and Drinks	$500 to $750
Invitations	$100 to $150
Decorations	$100 to $150
Incidental Expenses	$100

INVITATIONS

Finalize the guest list
Send out invitations four to six weeks in advance
Set the RSVP date three weeks before party

Figure 10.4 Project 5 Graduation Party Planning Presentation

FOOD, DECORATIONS & ENTERTAINMENT

Choose caterer
❑Ask for recommendations from friends or family

Decorate around a theme
❑Choose a theme related to your program

Entertainment
❑Assemble your favorite music playlists
❑Plan to tell a few humorous stories from school

Project 6 Internet Research and Composing a New Presentation

Individual or Pairs

Deliverable: Presentation about favorite U.S. or Canadian historical figure

1. Listen to the audio file named *Project6_Instructions*. The file is located in the Ch10 folder in the Student_Data_Files folder.
2. Complete the research and compose the presentation as instructed.
3. Save the presentation in the Ch10 folder within ChapterProjectsWork as **C10-Project6-HistoricalFigure-Your Name**.
4. Submit the project to your instructor in the manner she or he has requested.
5. Close the presentation.

Project 7 Sending Project Work to OneNote Notebook

Individual

Deliverable: New page in Shared OneNote notebook

1. Start OneNote and open the MyProjects notebook created in Chapter 4, Project 4.
2. Make PowerPoint the active section and add a new page titled *Chapter 10 Projects*.
3. Switch to PowerPoint. For each project that you completed, open the presentation, send the slides formatted as handouts with six slides horizontal per page and with your name in a header to OneNote 2013, selecting the *Chapter 10 Projects page* in the *PowerPoint* section in the MyProjects notebook, then close the presentation.
4. Close your MyProjects notebook in OneNote and close OneNote.
5. Close PowerPoint.
6. Submit the project to your instructor in the manner she or he has requested.

Chapter 11

Enhancing a Presentation with Pictures, Sound, Video, and Animation Effects

After successfully completing this chapter, you will be able to:

- Insert and resize pictures and clip art
- Insert and modify a SmartArt object
- Insert and modify WordArt
- Insert and modify a chart
- Draw and modify shapes and text boxes
- Add video and sound
- Add transition and animation effects
- Set up a self-running presentation

A presentation is more interesting when multimedia is used to reinforce and help a speaker communicate his or her main points. Incorporating various types of graphics, sound, and video into a presentation can help an audience understand the content and remain engaged.

In this chapter you will learn how to add graphics to slides using clip art, pictures, SmartArt, WordArt, charts, and drawn shapes; add text in a text box; add sound and video; and complete the presentation by adding transitions and animation effects. Lastly, you will learn how to set up a slide show that advances through the slides automatically.

Inserting Graphics from Clip Art and Picture Collections

Topic 11.1

SKILLS

Add an image from your PC

Add an image from clip art

 **Tutorials**

11.1.1 Inserting and Formatting Images

11.1.2 Inserting and Formatting Clip Art Images

The addition of a picture, illustration, diagram, or chart on a slide is used to emphasize content, add visual interest to slides, and help an audience understand and make connections with the information more easily than with text alone. As you learned in Chapter 7, pictures can be inserted that are stored on your PC or at an online service such as Flickr, Facebook, or OneDrive. Microsoft's Office.com clip art collection contains thousands of clip art images, photos, and illustrations.

Inserting Pictures from Your Computer

Use the Pictures button in the Images group of the INSERT tab to add a picture that is stored as a file on your computer or a computer to which you are connected. Once inserted, move, resize, and/or modify the picture using buttons in the PICTURE TOOLS FORMAT tab. On a new slide, use the Pictures icon in the Content placeholder to add a picture to a slide.

1. Start PowerPoint and open the presentation named *PaintedBunting*.

2. Use Save As to save a copy of the presentation as **11.1-PaintedBunting-Your Name** in a new folder named *Ch11* in the CompletedTopicsByChapter folder.

3. Browse through the presentation and read the slides.

4. Make Slide 2 the active slide.

5. Tap or click the INSERT tab and then tap or click the Pictures button in the Images group.

6. At the Insert Picture dialog box, navigate to the Ch11 folder within Student_Data_Files and double-tap or double-click *PaintedBunting_NPS*.

7. Using one of the four corner selection handles, resize the image smaller to the approximate size shown in the image below.

8. Slide or drag the image to move the picture to the right side of the slide and align it with the horizontal and vertical smart guides that appear when the picture is even with the top of the text and the right margin on the slide.

Align picture with horizontal and vertical smart guides.

Steps 7-8

Painted Bunting Facts

- Passerina ciris
- Medium-sized finch
  - Male sports a colorful plumage
  - Female has distinctive green plumage
- Eastern and western populations
  - North and South Carolina, Georgia, Florida

9. Insert the picture named *PaintedBunting_Female* near the bottom right of the slide as shown on the next page by completing steps similar to Steps 5 to 8.

- Passerina ciris
- Medium-sized finch
  - Male sports a colorful plumage
  - Female has distinctive green plumage
- Eastern and western populations
  - North and South Carolina, Georgia, Florida
  - Kansas and Missouri south to Texas
- Habitat
  - Prefer thick vegetation next to open, grassy areas
- Winter migration to Cuba, Mexico, and South America

Step 9

Inserting Pictures from Office.com

The Online Pictures button is in the Images group of the INSERT tab or in a content placeholder. Use the Online Pictures button to find suitable images in the clip art collection at Office.com, by completing a web search, or from pictures you have stored at your Flickr, Facebook, or OneDrive account.

10 Make Slide 6 the active slide.

11 Tap or click the INSERT tab and then tap or click the Online Pictures button in the Images group.

12 With the insertion point positioned in the *Office.com Clip Art* search text box, type **bird watching** and then tap or press Enter, or tap or click the Search button (displays as a magnifying glass).

13 Double-tap or double-click the picture shown in the image below.

14 Resize and move the picture to the left side of the bulleted list and align it with the horizontal smart guide that appears when the center of the image is evenly positioned with the bulleted list.

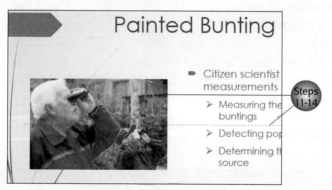

Painted Bunting

- Citizen scientist measurements
  - Measuring the buntings
  - Detecting pop
  - Determining th source

Steps 11-14

15 Save the revised presentation using the same name (**11.1-PaintedBunting-Your Name**). Leave the presentation open for the next topic.

 Beyond Basics

Editing Images

Edit an image with buttons in the PICTURE TOOLS FORMAT tab using techniques similar to those you learned in Chapter 7. For example, you can apply a picture style or artistic effect; adjust the brightness, contrast, or sharpness; or change the color properties. Use buttons in the Arrange and Size group to layer the image with other objects, specify the position of the image on the slide, crop unwanted portions of the picture, or specify measurements for height and width.

Topic 11.2

SKILLS

Add a SmartArt graphic

Modify a SmartArt graphic

 Tutorial

11.2   Inserting and Formatting SmartArt

Inserting a SmartArt Graphic

SmartArt uses graphics to visually communicate relationships in lists, processes, cycles, and hierarchies, or to create other diagrams. Begin creating a SmartArt graphic by choosing a predesigned layout and then adding text in the Text pane or by typing directly in the Text placeholders within the shapes. You can add and delete shapes to the graphic as needed and choose from a variety of color schemes and styles. See Table 11.1 for a description of layout category diagrams created using SmartArt.

Table 11.1	SmartArt Graphic Layout Categories
Layout Category	**Description**
List	Non-sequential tasks, processes, or other list items
Process	Illustrate a sequential series of steps to complete a process or task
Cycle	Show a sequence of steps or tasks in a circular or looped process
Hierarchy	Show an organizational chart or decision tree
Relationship	Show how parts or elements are related to each other
Matrix	Depict how individual parts or ideas relate to a whole or central idea
Pyramid	Show proportional or hierarchical relationships that build upward

① With the **11.1-PaintedBunting-Your Name** presentation open and Slide 6 the active slide, tap or click the INSERT tab if necessary.

② Tap or click the SmartArt button in the Illustrations group.

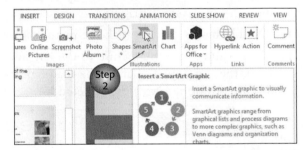

On a new slide with no other content, use the Insert a SmartArt Graphic icon in the Content placeholder to create a SmartArt object on a slide.

③ At the Choose a SmartArt Graphic dialog box, tap or click *Process* in the Category pane at the left, tap or click *Basic Chevron Process* in the layout pane in the center (second option in fifth row), and then tap or click OK.

PowerPoint places the SmartArt graphic in the center of the slide. Three shapes are automatically included in the *Basic Chevron Process* layout.

App Tip

Select a layout in the center pane to preview the layout and read a description with suggestions for the layout's usage in the right pane.

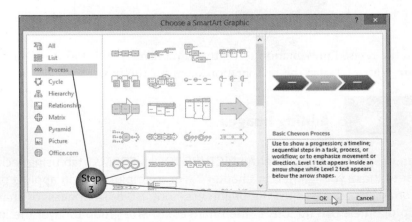

④ Tap or click the left-pointing arrow along the left border of the graphic if the Text pane is not visible; if the Text pane is already visible, proceed to Step 5.

⑤ With the insertion point in the Text pane next to the first bullet, type **Band**; tap or click next to the second bullet and type **Observe**; and then tap or click next to the third bullet and type **Analyze**.

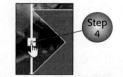

The SmartArt graphic updates as each word is typed in the Text pane to show the text in the shape. You can also add text to the shapes by typing text directly within the text placeholders inside each shape.

⑥ Tap or click the Close button to close the Text pane.

⑦ If necessary, tap or click the SMARTART TOOLS DESIGN tab.

⑧ Tap or click the More button at the bottom right of the *SmartArt Styles* gallery.

⑨ Tap or click *Polished* at the drop-down gallery (first option in *3-D* section).

⑩ Tap or click the Change Colors button in the SmartArt Styles group and then tap or click *Colorful – Accent Colors* at the drop-down gallery (first option in the *Colorful* section).

⑪ Slide or drag the border of the SmartArt graphic until the diagram is positioned near the bottom center of the slide, as shown in Figure 11.1.

⑫ Tap or click in an unused area of the slide to deselect the graphic.

⑬ Save the revised presentation using the same name (**11.1-PaintedBunting-Your Name**). Leave the presentation open for the next topic.

App Tip

Press the Down Arrow key to move to the next bullet in the Text pane.

Quick **STEPS**

Insert a SmartArt Graphic
1. Activate slide.
2. Tap or click INSERT tab.
3. Tap or click SmartArt button.
4. Select category in left pane.
5. Select layout in center pane.
6. Tap or click OK.
7. Add text in Text pane or shapes.
8. Format and/or move as required.

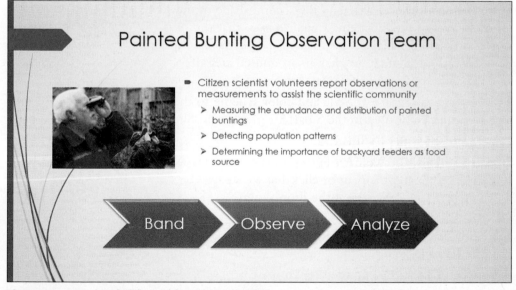

Figure 11.1 Completed Slide 6 with SmartArt graphic

Modifying a SmartArt Graphic

Use buttons in the Create Graphic group of the SMARTART TOOLS DESIGN tab to add shapes, change the direction of the layout (switch between *Right to Left* and *Left to Right*), and move shapes up or down the layout. Each shape in the layout can also be selected and moved or resized individually.

Topic 11.3

SKILLS

Convert text to a
SmartArt graphic

Insert and modify
WordArt

SNAP Tutorial

11.3 Inserting and
Formatting
WordArt

Converting Text to SmartArt and Inserting WordArt

An existing bulleted list on a slide can be converted to a SmartArt graphic using the **Convert to SmartArt button** in the Paragraph group of the HOME tab. **WordArt** is text that is created and formatted as a graphic object. With WordArt you can create decorative text on a slide with a variety of WordArt Styles and text effects. A WordArt object can also have the text formed around a variety of shapes.

1. With the **11.1-PaintedBunting-Your Name** presentation open, make Slide 5 the active slide.

2. Tap or click in the bulleted list to activate the placeholder.

3. Tap or click the Convert to SmartArt button in the Paragraph group of the HOME tab.

4. Tap or click *Hierarchy List* at the drop-down gallery (second option in second row).

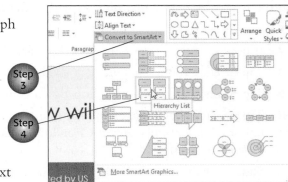

PowerPoint converts the text in the bulleted list into the selected SmartArt layout. Level 1 text from the bulleted list is placed inside shapes at the top level in the hierarchy diagram, with level 2 text in shapes below the corresponding level 1 box.

5. Close the Text pane if the Text pane is open.

6. Select and delete *Need to* in the second shape in the top level of the hierarchy, capitalize *m* so that the text inside the shape reads *Manage and preserve natural habitat*, and then tap or click in an unused area of the slide to deselect the SmartArt object.

7. Change the SmartArt Style and color scheme to the same style and color used in the SmartArt graphic on Slide 6.

8. Tap or click the INSERT tab.

9. Tap or click the WordArt button in the Text group and then tap or click *Fill – Green, Accent 1, Shadow* at the drop-down list (second option in first row).

10. Slide or drag the WordArt text box to the bottom center of the slide.

11. Select *Your text here* inside the WordArt text box and type **Help Save the Painted Bunting!**

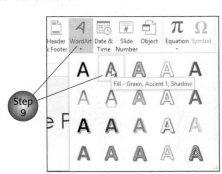

oops!

Other text is displayed inside the WordArt text box? This occurs if an insertion point is active inside another object with text when WordArt is created. Proceed to select whatever text is inside the box.

Help Save the Painted Bunting!

Step 11

(12) Tap or click the border of the WordArt text box to remove the insertion point and select the entire placeholder.

(13) Tap or click the Text Effects button in the WordArt Styles group of the DRAWING TOOLS FORMAT tab, tap or point to *Glow*, and then tap or click *Lime, 5 pt glow, Accent color 3* (third option in first row of *Glow Variations* section).

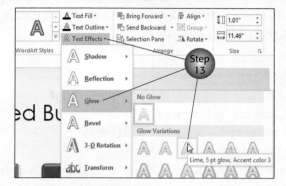

(14) Slide or drag the border of the WordArt text box until the smart guide appears, indicating the object is aligned with the center of the object above, as shown in Figure 11.2.

(15) Save the revised presentation using the same name (**11.1-PaintedBunting-Your Name**). Leave the presentation open for the next topic.

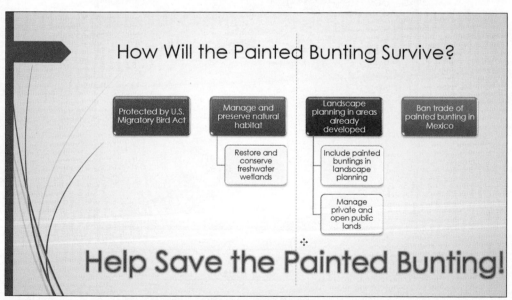

Figure 11.2 WordArt object aligned with center of SmartArt object

Transforming WordArt Text and Shape Styles

Use the *Transform* option from the Text Effects drop-down list to choose a shape around which WordArt text is formed. Text can be shaped to follow a circular or semi-circular path, slanted, or otherwise altered to create a distinctive effect. Experiment with options in the *Shape Styles* gallery to add a rectangular box around the WordArt.

Topic 11.4

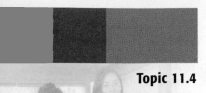

SKILLS

Create a chart

Modify the chart
style and color

SNAP **Tutorial**

11.4 Creating and
Formatting Charts

Creating a Chart on a Slide

Charts similar to the ones you learned to create in Chapter 9 with Excel can be added to a slide in PowerPoint. Add a chart using the Insert Chart icon in a content placeholder or with the Chart button in the Illustrations group of the INSERT tab. Charts are commonly used in presentations to show an audience dollar figures, targets, budgets, comparisons, patterns, trends, or variations in numerical data.

1. With the **11.1-PaintedBunting-Your Name** presentation open, make Slide 3 the active slide.

2. Tap or click the Insert Chart icon in the content placeholder.

3. At the Insert Chart dialog box with *Column* selected in the category list and *Clustered Column* selected as the chart type, tap or click OK.

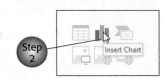

PowerPoint creates a sample chart on the slide and opens a chart data grid into which the data to be graphed is typed. As you enter labels and values into the chart data grid, the chart on the slide updates.

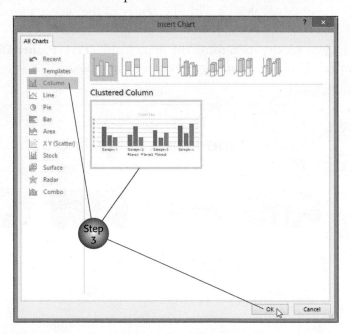

4. With B1 in the chart data grid the active cell, type **2011**.

5. Tap or click in C1 and type **2012**.

6. Type the remaining data in the cells in the chart data grid as shown in the image at right.

7. Select A5:D5, display the Mini toolbar (touch) or right-click, tap or click *Delete*, and then tap or click *Table Rows*.

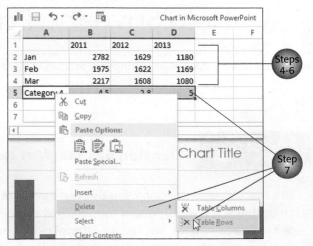

oops!

Using Touch? Tap the down-pointing arrow on the Mini toolbar to find *Delete* at the context menu.

8. Close the chart data grid.

9. Select *Chart Title* and type **Monthly Sightings in First Quarter**.

10. Select the chart so that the selection handles around the chart are displayed.

11. Change the Chart Style to *Style 4* (fourth option).

12. Change the chart colors to *Color 2* (second row in *Colorful* section).

13. Tap or click outside the chart to deselect the object and compare your slide with the one shown in Figure 11.3.

14. Save the revised presentation using the same name (**11.1-PaintedBunting-Your Name**). Leave the presentation open for the next topic.

oops!

Don't remember how to change the chart style or color? Refer to Topic 9.7 on page 270 and review Steps 7 and 8.

Quick **STEPS**

Insert a Chart
1. Activate slide.
2. Tap or click Insert Chart icon in content placeholder.
3. Choose category and chart type.
4. Tap or click OK.
5. Add data in chart data grid.
6. Format as required.

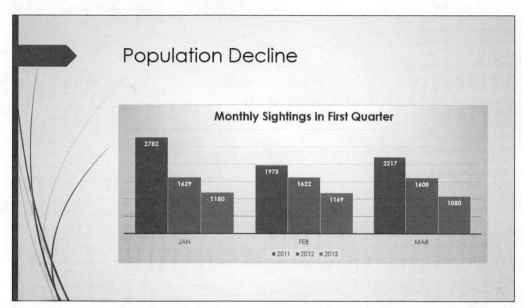

Figure 11.3 Completed Slide 3 with Clustered Column Chart

Sometimes the data needed to create a chart resides in an Excel worksheet. Rather than duplicate the data in PowerPoint, create the chart in Excel and paste a copy of the chart onto the PowerPoint slide. You will practice this method in Chapter 14.

Beyond Basics   **Formatting Charts and Editing Data**

Use the same tools you learned in Excel to modify and format charts in PowerPoint, such as the Chart Elements and Chart Styles button at the top right of the chart or with buttons in the CHART TOOLS DESIGN and CHART TOOLS FORMAT tabs.

To make a change to the source data for the chart, redisplay the chart data grid by tapping or clicking the top part of the Edit Data button in the Data group of the CHART TOOLS DESIGN tab.

Drawing Shapes and Adding Text Boxes

Topic 11.5

SKILLS

Draw and modify
a shape

Add text inside a
shape

Format a shape

Create a text box

 Tutorials

11.5.1 Drawing and
Customizing
Shapes

11.5.2 Displaying
Gridlines;
Inserting a Text
Box; Copying and
Rotating Shapes

11.5.3 Inserting Action
Buttons and
Hyperlinks

When drawing other shapes,
hold down the Shift key while
dragging the mouse to create
a perfect square, circle, or
straight line.

A graphic can be created by drawing a shape such as a line, rectangle, circle, arrow, star, banner, or other item. Once the shape is drawn, text can be added inside the shape and the shape can be formatted by changing the outline color or fill color or by adding an effect. A text box is text inside a rectangular object that can be manipulated independently from other objects on a slide.

1. With the **11.1-PaintedBunting-Your Name** presentation open and with Slide 3 the active slide, tap or click the INSERT tab if necessary.

2. Tap or click the **Shapes button** in the Illustrations group.

3. Tap or click the *Striped Right Arrow* shape (fifth option in second row of the *Block Arrows* section).

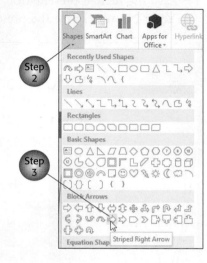

For touch users, a shape is placed in the center of the slide at the default shape size; for mouse users, the cross-hair pointer displays with which you click on the slide to place a shape at the default size. You may then drag to create the shape the required height and width.

4. If you are using a mouse, click on the slide inside the chart near the JAN bar for 2012 (with the value *1629*); if you are using touch, proceed to Step 5.

5. With the shape selected, type **A 41% decline!**

6. Slide or drag the middle right sizing handle to the right until the text fits on one line inside the arrow shape.

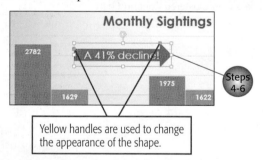

Yellow handles are used to change
the appearance of the shape.

7. Slide or drag the rotation handle (circled arrow above top center sizing handle) in an upward diagonal direction toward the left until the shape is at the approximate angle shown in the image below.

⑧ Slide or drag the arrow to the bottom left of the chart so that it points to the 2012 January bar, as shown in the image at right.

⑨ With the arrow shape still selected and the DRAWING TOOLS FORMAT tab active, tap or click the More button at the bottom right of the *Shape Styles* gallery and then tap or click *Intense Effect – Turquoise, Accent 6* (last option in gallery).

⑩ Tap or click the Text Box button in the Insert Shapes group of the DRAWING TOOLS FORMAT tab.

⑪ If you are using a mouse, click anywhere at the left side of the slide outside the chart to insert a text box with an insertion point; if you are using touch, proceed to Step 12.

⑫ Type **Source: Painted Bunting Observer Team, University of North Carolina Wilmington**.

⑬ Tap or click the border of the text box to remove the insertion point and select the entire placeholder, tap or click the HOME tab, and then tap or click the Italic button in the Font group.

⑭ Move and/or resize the text box, aligning the text box with the bottom of the chart as shown in the image below.

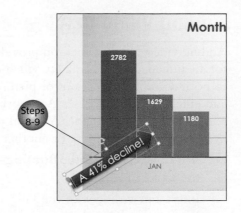

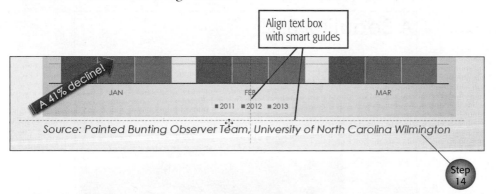

Align text box with smart guides

⑮ Save the revised presentation using the same name (**11.1–PaintedBunting-Your Name**). Leave the presentation open for the next topic.

Action Buttons

A category of shapes called *Action Buttons* contains a series of buttons with actions assigned that are used to create a navigation interface or launch other items during a slide show. For example, draw the *Action Button: Home* button on a slide to move to the first slide when the button is clicked during a slide show.

Topic 11.6

 **Tutorial**

11.6 Adding Audio and Video

Adding Video to a Presentation

Adding video to a presentation provides a more interesting multimedia experience for an audience. A high-quality video can show a process or task that is difficult to portray using descriptions or pictures. Video is widely used for instructional and entertainment purposes. Appropriately used, video provides a more enjoyable experience for the audience. You can play a video from a file stored on your PC or link to a video at YouTube or another online source.

1. With the **11.1-PaintedBunting-Your Name** presentation open, make Slide 6 the active slide.

2. Insert a new slide with the Title and Content layout and type **A Beautiful Bird** as the slide title.

3. Tap or click the Insert Video icon in the content placeholder.

4. At the Insert Video dialog box, tap or click the <u>Browse From a file</u> link in the *From a file* section.

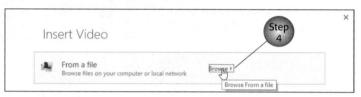

5. Navigate to the Ch11 folder in Student_Data_Files and double-tap or double-click the file named ***PaintedBuntingVideo***.

6. Tap or click the Play/Pause button below the video to preview the video clip.

   The video plays for approximately 52 seconds.

7. Tap or click the VIDEO TOOLS PLAYBACK tab.

8. Tap or click the **Trim Video button** in the Editing group.

Trimming a video allows you to show only a portion of a video file if the video is too long or if you do not wish to show parts at the beginning or end. Slide or drag the green or red slider to start playing at a later starting point and/or end before the video is finished, or enter the start and end times.

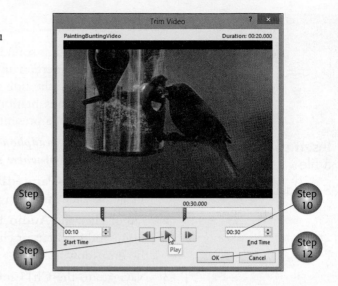

9. At the Trim Video dialog box, select the current entry in the *Start Time* text box and type **00:10**.

10. Select the current entry in the *End Time* text box and type **00:30**.

11. Tap or click the Play button to preview the shorter video clip.

12. Tap or click OK.

13. Tap or click the *Start* list arrow (displays *On Click*) in the Video Options group and then tap or click *Automatically*.

This option means the video will begin playing as soon as the slide is displayed in the slide show.

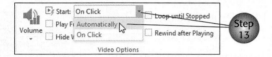

14. Slide or drag the video object left until the smart guide appears at the left, indicating the object is aligned with the slide title.

15. Tap or click the VIDEO TOOLS FORMAT tab and tap or click the *Soft Edge Rectangle* in the Video Styles group (third option).

16. Save the revised image using the same name (**11.1-PaintedBunting-Your Name**). Leave the presentation open for the next topic.

Add video to an existing slide by tapping or clicking the INSERT tab, tapping or clicking the Video button in the Media group, and then choosing *Online Video* or *Video on my PC* at the drop-down list.

Link to a video at YouTube by typing the name of the video in the *Search YouTube* text box at the Insert Video dialog box. Select the video in the search results list and choose Insert.

Add Video from a File on a PC
1. Tap or click Insert Video icon in placeholder.
2. Tap or click Browse From a file.
3. Navigate to drive and/or folder.
4. Double-tap or double-click video file.
5. Edit and/or format as required.

Other Video Playback Options

The video can be set to display full screen, to loop continuously so that the video repeats until the slide show has ended, and to fade in or out. Configure these settings in the Editing and Video Options group of the VIDEO TOOLS PLAYBACK tab.

Adding Sound to a Presentation

Adding music or other sound during a slide show is another method to add interest, communicate, or entertain an audience. For example, a speaker may choose to have music playing while the title slide is displayed, with the end of the music cueing the audience that the presentation is about to begin. Music can also be timed to play during a segment of a presentation during which a series of images is running.

Note: You will need headphones or earbuds if you are completing this topic in a computer lab at school where sound through the speakers is disabled.

1. With the **11.1-PaintedBunting-Your Name** presentation open, make Slide 1 the active slide and then tap or click the INSERT tab if necessary.

2. Tap or click the **Audio button** in the Media group and then tap or click *Audio on My PC* at the drop-down list.

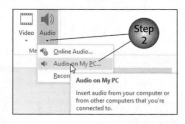

3. Navigate to the Ch11 folder in Student_Data_ Files and double-tap or double-click the file named *Allemande*.

4. Slide or drag the sound icon to the bottom right of the slide.

5. Tap or click the Play/Pause button and listen to the recording for a few seconds.

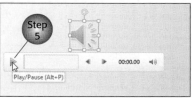

The entire music clip plays for approximately two and a half minutes.

6. With the AUDIO TOOLS PLAYBACK tab active, tap or click the *Hide During Show* check box in the Audio Options group to insert a check mark.

7. Tap or click the *Start* list arrow (displays *On Click*) and then tap or click *Automatically*.

This option will start the music as soon as the slide is displayed in the slide show.

8. Tap or click the *Loop until Stopped* check box to insert a check mark.

This option will cause the music to replay continuously until the slide is advanced during the slide show.

App Tip

Choose *Online Audio* to search for royalty-free sound clips at Office.com, or choose *Record Audio* to record a new sound clip.

App Tip

PowerPoint recognizes most audio file formats including MIDI files, MP3 and MP4 audio files, Windows audio files (.wav), and Window Media Audio files (.wma).

9. Make Slide 7 the active slide.

10 Insert the audio file named *PaintedBunting_Song* in the slide by completing steps similar to those in Steps 2 to 8.

The audio recording of the Painted Bunting bird song is slightly less than two seconds in length.

11 Insert a new slide after Slide 7 with the Title and Content layout and type **Photo, Video, and Audio Credits** as the slide title.

12 Insert a table, type the information shown in Figure 11.4, and then adjust the layout using your best judgment for column widths and position on the slide.

Always credit the source of images, audio, and video used in a presentation if you did not create the multimedia yourself. In this instance, the music from Slide 1 is not credited because the recording is in the public domain, and the picture on Slide 6 is not credited because you found the image using Office.com royalty-free clip art.

13 Save the revised presentation using the same name (**11.1–PaintedBunting-Your Name**). Leave the presentation open for the next topic.

Did You Know ?

Many websites offer copyright-free or public domain multimedia. Include the keywords copyright free or public domain in a search for a picture, audio, or video file. Check the terms of use at each site to be sure you credit sources appropriately because copyright-free allows free usage but requires attribution to the creator.

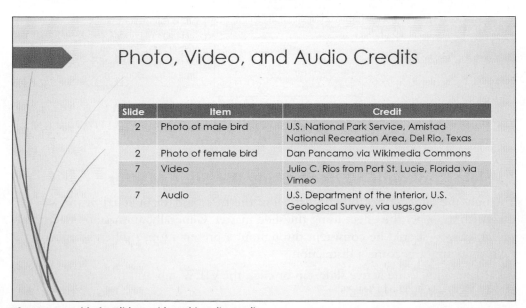

Slide	Item	Credit
2	Photo of male bird	U.S. National Park Service, Amistad National Recreation Area, Del Rio, Texas
2	Photo of female bird	Dan Pancamo via Wikimedia Commons
7	Video	Julio C. Rios from Port St. Lucie, Florida via Vimeo
7	Audio	U.S. Department of the Interior, U.S. Geological Survey, via usgs.gov

Figure 11.4 Table for Slide 8 with Multimedia Credits

Adding Transitions and Animation Effects to a Slide Show

SKILLS

Add transitions

Add animation on slide master

Add animation to individual objects

 **Tutorials**

11.8.1 Adding Transition Effects and Sound

11.8.2 Applying Animation to Objects and Text

oops!

Trouble finding *Blinds*? On smaller-screened devices such as tablets, the *Transitions* gallery displays fewer buttons per row. Look for *Blinds* further right or down.

App Tip

Use the Effect Options button in the Transition to This Slide group to choose a variation for the selected transition (such as the direction the blinds move).

A **transition** is a special effect that appears as one slide is removed from the screen and the next slide appears. Text and objects can be revealed using a variety of techniques that add interest to a slide show. **Animation** involves adding a special effect to an object on a slide that causes the object to move or change in some way. Animation is used to focus on or add emphasis to text or an object. Be mindful not to overdo transition and animation as too much movement can become a distraction.

1. With the **11.1-PaintedBunting-Your Name** presentation open, make Slide 1 the active slide.

2. Tap or click the TRANSITIONS tab and then tap or click the More button at the bottom right of the *Transition to This Slide* gallery.

3. Tap or click *Blinds* in the *Exciting* section of the gallery.

PowerPoint previews the effect with the current slide so that you can experiment with various transitions and effects before making your final selection.

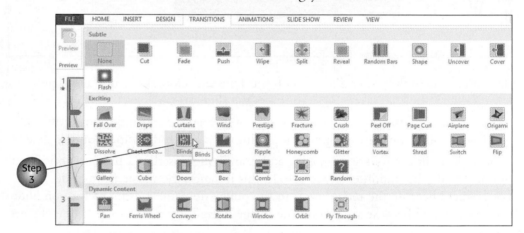

4. Tap or click the Apply To All button in the Timing group.

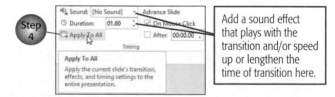

Add a sound effect that plays with the transition and/or speed up or lengthen the time of transition here.

5. Display the slide show, advance through the first three slides to view the transition effect, and then end the show to return to Normal view.

Applying Animation Effects Using the Slide Master

To apply the same animation effect to all of the titles and/or bulleted lists in a presentation, apply the effect using the slide master. Generally, animation effects for similar objects should be consistent throughout a presentation; a different effect on each slide might become a distraction.

6. Make Slide 2 the active slide, tap or click the VIEW tab, and then tap or click the Slide Master button.

7. Tap or click to select the border of the title placeholder on the slide master.

(8) Tap or click the ANIMATIONS tab.

(9) Tap or click *Split* in the *Animation* gallery.

See Table 11.2 for a description of Animation categories.

App Tip

The *Animation* gallery provides the most popular effects. View more effects by category using the options at the bottom of the gallery. For example, *More Entrance Effects* shows all 40 options.

This icon displays the animation's sequence; the slide title will animate first.

(10) Tap or click to select the border of the content placeholder and then tap or click the More button in the *Animation* gallery.

(11) Tap or click *Zoom* in the *Entrance* section.

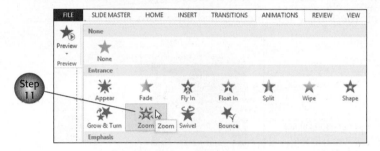

(12) Tap or click the *Start* list arrow (displays *On Click*) in the Timing group and then tap or click *After Previous*.

(13) Select the current entry in the *Duration* text box and type **1.5**.

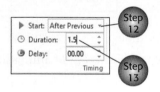

(14) Tap or click the SLIDE MASTER tab and then tap or click the Close Master View button.

(15) Make Slide 1 the active slide, run through the presentation in a slide show to view the transition and animation effects, and then return to Normal view.

Table 11.2	Animation Categories
Category	**Description**
Entrance	Most common animation effect in which the object animates as it appears on the slide
Emphasis	Animates text or object already in place by causing the object to move or to change in appearance; includes effects such as darkening, changing color, bolding, or underlining, to name a few
Exit	Animates the text or object after it has been revealed, such as by fading or flying off the slide
Motion Paths	An object moves along a linear path, an arc, or some other shape

Applying Animation Effects to Individual Objects

As you previewed the slide show, you probably noticed that images and other objects such as shapes or text boxes appeared on the slide before the title. You may want these items to remain hidden until the title and text have been revealed. To apply animation to an individual object, display the slide, select the object to be animated, and then apply the desired animation.

16 Make Slide 2 the active slide.

17 Select the male bird picture at the top right of the slide.

18 Tap or click the ANIMATIONS tab and then tap or click *Wipe* in the *Animation* gallery.

19 Tap or click the *Start* list arrow and then tap or click *After Previous*.

20 Tap or click to select the male bird picture and then tap or click the **Animation Painter button** in the Advanced Animation group.

Similar to the Format Painter button, the Animation Painter button is used to copy animation effects from one object to another.

21 Tap or click the female bird picture at the bottom right of the slide.

Animation Painter copies animation effects and options from one object to another.

Step 21

22 Make Slide 3 the active slide.

23 Select the arrow shape, apply the *Fly In* animation, and change the *Start* option to *After Previous*.

24 Copy the arrow shape's animation options to the text box object below the chart by completing steps similar to those in Steps 20 and 21.

25 Make Slide 5 the active slide.

26 Select the WordArt object at the bottom of the slide, apply the *Float In* animation, and change the *Start* option to *After Previous*.

27 Make Slide 6 the active slide.

28 Select the picture at the left side of the slide, apply the *Shape* animation, and change the *Start* option to *After Previous*.

29 Select the SmartArt graphic at the bottom of the slide. Make sure the entire graphic is selected and not an individual shape within the graphic.

30 Apply the *Fly-in* animation and change the *Start* option to *After Previous*.

31 Tap or click the Effect Options button and then tap or click *One by One* in the *Sequence* section of the drop-down list.

This option will cause each chevron in the graphic to animate on the slide one at a time, starting with the leftmost shape first.

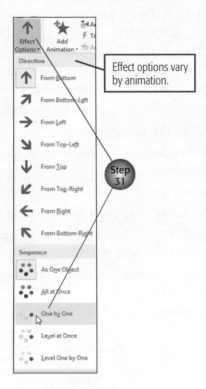

Effect options vary by animation.

Step 31

32 Run through the presentation in a slide show from the beginning to view the revised animation effects and then return to Normal view.

33 Save the revised presentation using the same name (**11.1-PaintedBunting-Your Name**). Leave the presentation open for the next topic.

Add a Transition
1. Tap or click TRANSITIONS tab.
2. Add transition effect.
3. Change effect options or timing options as required.
4. Tap or click Apply to All button.

Apply Animation to All Slides
1. Display slide master.
2. Tap or click ANIMATIONS tab.
3. Select placeholder.
4. Add animation effect.
5. Change effect options or timing options as required.
6. Close Slide Master view.

Apply Animation to an Individual Object
1. Activate slide.
2. Tap or click ANIMATIONS tab.
3. Select object.
4. Add animation effect.
5. Change effect options or timing options as required.

Did You Know?

You can deliver a presentation online using the free Office Presentation Service if you are signed in with a Microsoft account. Participants are able to view slides in a web browser. Access the service at the Share tab Backstage view.

Changing the Animation Sequence

To adjust the order in which objects are animated, display the required slide and open the Animation pane at the right side of the window. To do this, tap or click the Animation Pane button in the Advanced Animation group of the ANIMATIONS tab. Select the object that you want to move in the Animation pane and then use the Move Earlier or Move Later buttons in the Reorder Animation group.

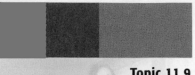

Topic 11.9

SKILLS

Add timings to slides

Change the show type to kiosk

SNAP Tutorial

11.9 Setting Timings for a Presentation

Setting Up a Self-Running Presentation

Some presentations are designed to be self-running, meaning that the slides are intended to be shown continuously at a kiosk or viewed at a PC by an individual. To create a presentation that advances through slides automatically, you need to set up a time for each slide to display and ensure that each slide's animation is set to start automatically for each object.

1. With the **11.1-PaintedBunting-Your Name** presentation open, use Save As to save a copy of the presentation in the current folder naming it **11.9-PaintingBuntingSelfRunning-Your Name**.

2. Make Slide 2 the active slide and display the slide master.

3. Select the border of the title placeholder.

4. Tap or click the ANIMATIONS tab and change the *Start* option in the *Timing* section to *After Previous*.

5. Close Slide Master view.

6. Make Slide 1 the active slide and select the sound icon.

7. Tap or click the AUDIO TOOLS PLAYBACK tab and then tap or click the *Play Across Slides* check box in the Audio Options group to insert a check mark.

This option will cause the music that starts at Slide 1 to continue playing through the remaining slides.

8. Tap or click the Volume button and then tap or click *Low* at the drop-down list.

9. Make Slide 7 the active slide and then select and delete the sound icon to remove the audio.

10. Make Slide 8 the active slide and then select and delete the last row in the table.

11. Tap or click the TRANSITIONS tab.

12. Tap or click the *After* check box in the *Timing* section to insert a check mark, select the current entry in the *After* text box, and then type **0:25**.

13. Tap or click the Apply To All button.

All of the slides will be advanced automatically after the same 25-second duration. To set individual times for slides, activate a slide and enter a different time in the *After* text box.

14. Make Slide 3 the active slide, select the entry in the *After* text box, and then type **0:10**.

15. Change the *After* time for Slide 5 and Slide 6 to **0:15** and for Slide 8 to **0:10**.

16 Tap or click the SLIDE SHOW tab and then tap or click the **Set Up Slide Show button** in the Set Up group.

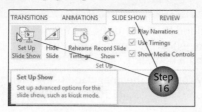

Step 16

17 At the Set Up Show dialog box, tap or click the *Browsed at a kiosk (full screen)* option in the *Show type* section.

18 Tap or click OK.

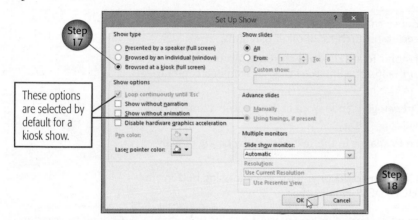

Step 17

These options are selected by default for a kiosk show.

Step 18

19 Start the slide show from the beginning and watch the presentation as it advances through all of the slides automatically. End the show when the presentation starts at Slide 1 again by pressing and holding to display the slide show toolbar and tapping the End Show button, or by pressing the ESC key.

20 Save the revised presentation using the same name (**11.9-PaintedBuntingSelf Running-Your Name**) and then close the presentation.

App Tip

You can create an MPEG 4 (MP4) movie file that you can burn to a disc or upload to a website using *Create a Video* at the Export tab Backstage view.

Beyond Basics

Using Rehearse Timings

The **Rehearse Timings** feature (SLIDE SHOW tab) lets you assign a time to each slide as you run through a slide show with a timer active and a Recording toolbar. Use the Next button on the Recording toolbar to advance each slide, and PowerPoint will enter the times for each slide transition. This method lets you time each slide for a typical audience member after a suitable time has elapsed in the slide show.

Concepts Review

Topic	Key Concepts	Key Terms
Inserting Graphics from Clip Art and Picture Collections	A picture from your PC can be added to a slide using the Pictures button in the Images group of the INSERT tab or with the Pictures icon in the content placeholder on a new slide.	
	Resize, move, or edit a picture by selecting the image and using the selection handles and/or buttons in the PICTURE TOOLS FORMAT tab.	
	Find a picture or other image from the Office.com clip art collection, the Web, or collections stored at your Flickr, Facebook, or OneDrive account using the Online Pictures button in the Images group of the INSERT tab.	
Inserting a SmartArt Graphic	SmartArt graphics use shapes with text to illustrate information in lists, processes, cycles, hierarchies, or other diagrams.	SmartArt
	Add a SmartArt graphic to a slide using the SmartArt button in the INSERT tab or the Insert a SmartArt Graphic icon in a content placeholder.	
	Choose a SmartArt category and layout at the Choose a SmartArt Graphic dialog box.	
	Text can be added to shapes in the Text pane or by typing directly inside a shape.	
	Modify SmartArt styles or colors or edit the graphic using buttons in the SMARTART TOOLS DESIGN tab.	
Converting Text to SmartArt and Inserting WordArt	A bulleted list can be converted into a SmartArt graphic using the Convert to SmartArt button in the Paragraph group of the HOME tab.	Convert to SmartArt button
	WordArt is decorative text inside an independent object on a slide.	WordArt
	Create WordArt using the WordArt button in the Text group of the INSERT tab.	
	Type the WordArt text inside the text box and then add text effects, move, and or otherwise edit the object using buttons in the DRAWING TOOLS FORMAT tab.	
Creating a Chart on a Slide	Charts similar to those learned in Excel can be added to a slide.	
	Insert a chart using the Insert Chart icon in the content placeholder or the Chart button in the Illustrations group of the INSERT tab.	
	Choose the chart category and chart type at the Insert Chart dialog box.	
	Type the data to be graphed in the chart data grid, which is a small Excel worksheet.	
	Modify the chart using the buttons in the CHART TOOLS DESIGN and CHART TOOLS FORMAT tabs.	
Drawing Shapes and Adding Text Boxes	Draw your own graphics on a slide using the Shapes button in the INSERT tab.	Shapes button
	Type text inside a selected shape and then resize, move, or otherwise modify the shape using buttons in the DRAWING TOOLS FORMAT tab.	
	A text box is a rectangular object in which you can type text and that can be moved, resized, or formatted independently.	
	Create a text box using the Text Box button in the INSERT tab or the DRAWING TOOLS FORMAT tab.	

Topic	Key Concepts	Key Terms
Adding Video to a Presentation	Add video to a slide using the Insert Video icon in a content placeholder or with the Video button in the Media group of the INSERT tab.	Trim Video button
	You can select a video clip from a file on your PC or by finding a video clip at YouTube or another website.	
	Use buttons in the VIDEO TOOLS PLAYBACK tab to edit a video or change the video options.	
	Use the Trim Video button to change the starting and/or ending position of the video if you do not want to play the entire clip.	
	Change the *Start* option if you want the video to start automatically when the slide is displayed in a slide show.	
	Options in the VIDEO TOOLS FORMAT tab are used to format the video object.	
Adding Sound to a Presentation	Add audio to a slide using the Audio button in the Media group of the INSERT tab.	Audio button
	Use buttons in the Audio Options group of the AUDIO TOOLS PLAYBACK tab to hide the sound icon during a slide show, start the audio automatically, play the sound in the background across all slides, or loop the audio continuously until the slide is advanced.	
	Always credit the sources of all multimedia used in a presentation that you did not create yourself unless the media was obtained from a public domain resource or Office.com royalty-free collection.	
Adding Transitions and Animation Effects to a Slide Show	A transition is a special effect that appears as one slide is removed from the screen and another is revealed during a slide show.	Transition
	Animation causes an object to move or transform in some way.	Animation
	Select a transition at the *Transition to This Slide* gallery in the TRANSITIONS tab.	Animation Painter button
	The Apply to All button in the Timing group of the TRANSITIONS tab sets the same transition effect to all slides.	
	Add an animation effect to a placeholder on the slide master to apply the effect to all slides in the presentation.	
	Animation effects are selected in the *Animation* gallery of the ANIMATIONS tab.	
	Specify how the animation will start and the animation's duration using options in the Timing group.	
	Animate an individual object on a slide by selecting the object and then adding an animation effect from the *Animation* gallery.	
	The Animation Painter button copies the animation effect and effect options from one object to another.	
	Animation effects are grouped into four categories: Entrance, Emphasis, Exit, and Motion Paths.	
	To change the sequence in which objects are animated, display the Animation pane, select the object to be reordered, and then use the Move Earlier or Move Later buttons in the Reorder Animation group.	

continued....

Topic	Key Concepts	Key Terms
Set Up a Self-Running Presentation	A self-running presentation is set up to run a slide show continuously. To create a self-running presentation, each slide needs to have a time entered in the *After* text box in the Timing group of the TRANSITIONS tab, and each animated object needs to be set to start automatically. Open the Set Up Show dialog box (SLIDE SHOW tab) and choose *Browsed at a kiosk (full screen)* to instruct PowerPoint to play the slide show continuously until stopped. Use the Rehearse Timings feature (SLIDE SHOW tab) to set a time for each slide to display while watching a slide show with a timer and Recording toolbar active.	Set Up Slide Show button Rehearse Timings

Multiple Choice

1. Use this button in the Images group to search for an image in the Office.com clip art collection.
   a. Pictures
   b. Online Pictures
   c. Clip Art
   d. Media

2. Use this button in the Images group to add an image to a slide from a file on your PC.
   a. Pictures
   b. Online Pictures
   c. Computer
   d. Images

3. Add text inside a SmartArt shape by typing directly within the shape or here.
   a. text box
   b. text placeholder
   c. Text pane
   d. text container

4. This SmartArt layout category is best suited for creating an organization chart.
   a. List
   b. Process
   c. Relationship
   d. Hierarchy

5. Use this button to change a bulleted list into a SmartArt graphic.
   a. SmartArt Graphic
   b. Convert to SmartArt
   c. Transform to SmartArt
   d. Switch to SmartArt

6. Text that is created and formatted as a graphic object is referred to as _____.
   a. SmartText
   b. WordArt
   c. TextArt
   d. TextPic

7. Use this icon in a content placeholder to add a clustered column chart to a slide.
   a. Insert Column Chart
   b. Insert Chart
   c. Insert Graph
   d. Insert Data

8. Data to be graphed in a chart is typed in this grid.
   a. table data
   b. bar data
   c. chart data
   d. graph data

9. Draw an arrow on a slide using this button from the INSERT tab.
   a. Block Arrows
   b. Shapes
   c. Illustration
   d. Draw

10. Type text inside this type of box to create an object that can be formatted independently of other objects.
    a. text box
    b. transition box
    c. graphic box
    d. animation box

11. Change the *Start* option to this setting to have video begin playing as soon as the slide is displayed in a slide show.
    a. After previous
    b. Before previous
    c. Automatically
    d. On start

12. Use this button in the Editing group of VIDEO TOOLS PLAYBACK to change the starting point at which a clip begins playing.
    a. On Start
    b. Edit Video
    c. Set Up Video
    d. Trim Video

13. Use this option from the Audio button to choose a sound clip stored on your computer.
    a. Audio on My PC
    b. Computer
    c. Local Disk
    d. PC Audio

14. This option in the AUDIO TOOLS PLAYBACK ribbon causes a sound clip to keep repeating until the slide is advanced in the slide show.
    a. Replay until Stopped
    b. AutoStart until Stopped
    c. Continuous until Stopped
    d. Loop until Stopped

15. This term refers to a special effect that occurs as the next slide in the slide show is revealed.
    a. animation
    b. transition
    c. conversion
    d. effect option

16. This term refers to a special effect added to an object on a slide that causes the object to move or change in some way.
    a. animation
    b. conversion
    c. transition
    d. effect option

17. The time that a slide should remain on screen during a self-running presentation is added in the *After* text box in this tab.
    a. ANIMATIONS
    b. SLIDE SHOW
    c. TRANSITIONS
    d. INSERT

18. Open this dialog box to specify that the show type is *Browsed at a kiosk (full screen)*.
    a. Show Type
    b. Set Up Show
    c. Animation Effects
    d. Slide Show

Crossword Puzzle

ACROSS

1 Object used to add text inside a rectangle
4 Graphic used to visually present a process
6 Ribbon tab for adding graphic elements to slides
7 Most common animation effect category
9 Graphic used to compare numbers
10 Media group button used to add sound
11 Button to access clip art

DOWN

1 Special effect as a new slide appears
2 Text box in which you type the time for a slide to display in a slide show
3 Button used to draw an arrow
4 Ribbon tab to find Set Up Slide Show button
5 Dialog box to edit ending point of video
8 Decorative text created as a graphic

Matching

Match the term with the statement or definition.

_____ 1. INSERT tab group for pictures
_____ 2. Basic Chevron Process layout
_____ 3. Add Glow special effect to WordArt
_____ 4. Present numerical data
_____ 5. Draw an arrow
_____ 6. Continuously play video clip
_____ 7. Hide sound icon
_____ 8. Transition option
_____ 9. Animation option
_____ 10. Copy animation
_____ 11. Self-running presentation

a. Video Options
b. Chart
c. Blinds
d. Animation Painter
e. Text Effects
f. Browsed at a kiosk (full screen)
g. Images
h. Shapes
i. Fly In
j. SmartArt
k. Audio Options

Project 1 Adding Graphics to a Presentation

Individual

Deliverable: Presentation about World War I (continued in Projects 2 and 3)

1. Open **WorldWarIPres**.
2. Use Save As to change the file name to **C11-Project1-WorldWarIPres-Your Name** in a new folder named *Ch11* within the ChapterProjectsWork folder on your USB flash drive.
3. Make Slide 2 the active slide and insert the picture named *MilitaryGroupWWI* near the bottom right of the slide, resizing the image as needed.
4. Make Slide 6 the active slide and insert the picture named *WeaponWWI* at the right side of the slide next to the bulleted list, resizing the image as needed.
5. Make Slide 3 the active slide and convert the bulleted list to a SmartArt graphic. You determine an appropriate SmartArt layout. Apply a SmartArt Style of your choosing. Resize and/or make other formatting changes you think are appropriate.
6. Make Slide 4 the active slide and convert the bulleted list to the same SmartArt layout you used on Slide 3. Apply the same design and formatting changes so that Slide 3 and Slide 4 are consistent.
7. Make Slide 5 the active slide and insert a chart using the following information:
   a. Choose the *Bar* category and the *Clustered Bar* chart type.
   b. Enter the following data in the chart data grid. Delete columns and rows with sample data that are not needed for the chart.
      A2 Allied Forces   B2 12.6
      A3 Central Forces   B3 8.4
   c. Delete the *Series 1* legend that appears below the chart.
   d. Edit the *Series 1* title that appears above the chart to read *Millions of Soldiers*.
   e. Apply a chart style of your choosing.
8. Draw a shape positioned near the top right of the chart on Slide 5 using the *Explosion 1* option in the *Stars and Banners* category with the following text inside: *Allies bear 4.2 million more injuries!* Resize the shape, allowing the shape to flow outside the chart's border if necessary. Apply a shape style of your choosing.
9. Draw a text box positioned below the picture on Slide 6 with the following text inside the box: *Canadian artillery loading a field gun*. Change the font size to 14 points and italicize the text.
10. Draw a text box positioned below the chart on Slide 5 and aligned at the left edge with the following text inside the box: *Source: Military Research, UK*. Italicize the text.
11. Insert a new slide after Slide 7 with a Title Only layout and type the following text as the slide title: **100 Year Anniversary**. Create a WordArt object with the following text: *2014 to 2018*. Change the font size to 72 points and format the text with WordArt styles and text effects of your choosing.
12. Save the revised presentation using the same name (**C11-Project1-WorldWarIPres-Your Name**).
13. Leave the presentation open if you are continuing to Project 2; otherwise, close the presentation and submit the project to your instructor in the manner she or he has requested.

Project 2 Adding Sound and Video

Individual

Deliverable: Presentation about World War I (continued in Project 3)

Note: You must have completed Project 1 before starting this project.

1. If necessary, open **C11-Project1-WorldWarIPres-Your Name**.
2. Use Save As to change the file name to **C11-Project2-WorldWarIPres-Your Name**, saving in the same folder.
3. Make Slide 7 with the title *American Forces in France* the active slide.

4. Insert the video clip named *AmericaGoesToWar* from the Ch11 folder in Student_Data_Files on the slide. Edit the video as follows:
    a. Change the *Start* option to *Automatically*.
    b. Trim the video to start at *0:48* and end at *2:35*.
    c. Apply a video style of your choosing to the video object.
5. Add the audio clip named *BulletsandBayonets* from the Ch11 folder in Student_Data_Files on Slide 1 with the following audio options:
    a. Change the *Start* option to *Automatically*.
    b. Change the volume to *Low*.
    c. Set the audio to play across all slides.
    d. Hide the sound icon during a slide show.
6. Type the following photo, video, and audio credits in a table on the last slide. You determine the table style, column widths, and other format options.

Slide	Item	Credit
1	Music	United States marine band at George Mason University
2	Photo	City of Toronto archives via Wikimedia Commons
6	Photo	Canadian Department of National Defence via Wikimedia Commons
7	Video	America Goes Over (Part I), U.S. Army, Signal Corps via Internet Archive

7. Save the revised presentation using the same name (**C11-Project2-WorldWarIPres-Your Name**).
8. Leave the presentation open if you are continuing to Project 3; otherwise, close the presentation and submit the project to your instructor in the manner she or he has requested.

Project 3 Adding Transition and Animation Effects and Setting Up a Slide Show

Individual

Deliverable: Self-Running Presentation about World War I

Note: You must have completed Projects 1 and 2 before starting this project.

1. If necessary, open **C11-Project2-WorldWarIPres-Your Name**.
2. Use Save As to change the file name to **C11-Project3-WorldWarIPres-Your Name**, saving in the same folder.
3. Apply a transition of your choosing to all slides.
4. With Slide 2 the active slide, display the slide master and add an animation effect of your choosing to the title placeholder and the content placeholder. For each animation, change the *Start* option to *After Previous*. Return to Normal view when finished.
5. Apply an animation effect of your choosing to the following objects with the *Start* option changed to *After Previous* for each object:
    Photo on Slide 2
    Explosion shape and text box on Slide 5
    Photo and text box on Slide 6
    WordArt on Slide 8
6. Set the time for all slides to remain on the screen during a slide show to *0:15* (15 seconds).
7. Change the times for three slides as follows: Slide 1 to *0:05*; Slide 5 to *0:08*; Slide 8 to *0:05*.
8. Change the *Show type* to *Browsed by an individual (window)* at the Set Up Show dialog box.
9. Preview the slide show.
10. Save the revised presentation using the same name (**C11-Project3-WorldWarIPres-Your Name**) and then close the presentation.
11. Submit the project to your instructor in the manner she or he has requested.

Project 4 Creating a Self-Running Multimedia Presentation

Individual or Pairs

Deliverable: Presentation with Money-Saving Strategies for College Students

1. Create a presentation with six to eight slides with your best money-saving tips you can give to college students to help students survive on limited income while in school. Incorporate graphics, sound, and video into the presentation to make the presentation interesting and communicate your ideas.
2. Apply transition and animation effects of your choosing, setting up the slide show as a self-running presentation with appropriate times assigned for each slide.
3. Save the presentation in the Ch11 folder within the ChapterProjectsWork folder as **C11–Project4–MoneyTips–Your Name** and then close the presentation.
4. Submit the project to your instructor in the manner she or he has requested.

Project 5 Creating a Self-Running Multimedia Presentation

Individual

Deliverable: Presentation about Yellowstone National Park

1. Create a presentation similar to the one shown in Figure 11.5 on the next page with the following additional information:
   a. Theme is *Wood Type*.
   b. Picture and video files are as follows:
Slide 2	**YellowstoneMap**
Slide 3	**OldFaithfulGeyser_NPS**
Slide 4	**GreatFountainGeyser**
Slide 5	**InsideYellowstoneVideo**
   c. Use your best judgment to determine other formatting and alignment.
2. Apply transition and animation effects of your choosing, setting up the slide show as a self-running presentation. You determine appropriate times for each slide.
3. Save the presentation in the Ch11 folder within the ChapterProjectsWork folder as **C11–Project5–YellowstoneNP–Your Name**.
4. Submit the project to your instructor in the manner she or he has requested.
5. Close the presentation.

YELLOWSTONE NATIONAL PARK

The World's First National Park

A designated World Heritage Site and designated Biosphere Reserve

PARK FACTS

❖ Established in 1872
  • 3,472 square miles or 8,987 square km
❖ Park extends into three states
  • Wyoming, Montana, Idaho
❖ Home to the world's largest collection of geysers
❖ Also known for wildlife
  • Grizzly bears
  • Wolves
  • Herds of bison and elk

WHERE THE WORLD'S GEYSERS ARE PRESERVED

❖ Approximately one-half of the world's hydrothermal features
  • Park has more than 300 geysers
    • Old Faithful, most famous geyser
❖ Yellowstone is home to two-thirds of all geysers on earth!

Old Faithful and Beehive Geysers

WHAT IS A GEYSER?

Great Fountain Geyser

❖ Hot spring
❖ Near surface, constrictions prevent water from moving freely
❖ As water rises, steam forms
❖ Steam expands as it nears surface and erupts
❖ Eruptions can last 1 to 5 minutes
❖ Average height of eruption is 145 feet or 44 meters

PREDICTING GEYSER ACTIVITY

Inside
Yellowstone

with

Park Ranger
George Heinz

Figure 11.5 Project 5 Yellowstone National Park Presentation

PHOTO AND VIDEO CREDITS

All photos and video courtesy of:

Yellowstone National Park, National Park Service, U.S. Department of the Interior

To view more multimedia from Yellowstone's Photo Collection, go to
http://www.nps.gov/features/yell/slidefile/index.htm

Project 6 Internet Research and Composing a New Multimedia Presentation

Individual or Pairs

Deliverable: Presentation about World War II

1. Listen to the audio file named ***Project6_Instructions***. The file is located in the Ch11 folder in the Student_Data_Files folder.
2. Complete the research, locate suitable images and video, and compose the presentation as instructed.
3. Save the presentation in the Ch11 folder within ChapterProjectsWork as **C11-Project6-WorldWarII-Your Name**.
4. Submit the project to your instructor in the manner she or he has requested.
5. Close the presentation.

Project 7 Sending Project Work to OneNote Notebook

Individual

Deliverable: New Page in Shared OneNote notebook

1. Start OneNote and open the MyProjects notebook created in Chapter 4, Project 4.
2. Make PowerPoint the active section and add a new page titled *Chapter 11 Projects*.
3. Switch to PowerPoint. For each project that you completed, open the presentation, send the slides formatted as handouts with six slides horizontal per page and with your name in a header to OneNote 2013, selecting the *Chapter 11 Projects* page in the *PowerPoint* section in the MyProjects notebook, then close the presentation.
4. Close your MyProjects notebook in OneNote and close OneNote.
5. Close PowerPoint.
6. Submit the project to your instructor in the manner she or he has requested.

Chapter 12

Using and Querying an Access Database

After successfully completing this chapter, you will be able to:

- Describe a database management system
- Define *field*, *field value*, and *record*
- Add, edit, and delete records using a datasheet
- Add, edit, and delete records using a form
- Find and replace data
- Sort and filter data
- Create queries
- Select records using criteria
- Perform calculations using a query
- Preview a database object

O rganizations and individuals rely on data to complete transactions, make decisions, and otherwise store and track information. Data that is stored in an organized manner to provide information to suit a variety of purposes is called a **database**. Microsoft Access is a software program designed to organize, store, and maintain large amounts of data in an application referred to as a **database management system (DBMS)**. You interact with a DBMS several times a day as you complete your daily activities. Examples of the types of transactions that involve a DBMS include withdrawing cash from your bank account, completing purchases, looking up a telephone number, or programming your GPS.

In this chapter you will learn database terminology and how to navigate a DBMS, including how to open and close objects; add and maintain records using a datasheet and form; find and replace data; sort and filter data; and use queries to look up information and perform calculations,

Topic 12.1

SKILLS

Open and close
a database

Identify objects
in a database

Open and close
objects

 Tutorial

12.1   Opening and
Closing an Access
Database and
Table

Understanding Database Objects and Terminology

An Access database is structured and organized with a specific purpose to keep track of large amounts of similar data. For example, a library database is organized so that information for each book in the library such as the title, author, publisher, and price is entered and maintained. Making sure that the data is entered and updated in the same manner for each item is important so that information that is retrieved is complete and accurate. For this reason, a database is created with a structure that defines the data that will be collected for each item. Examining and practicing working with data in an existing database will help you understand the various terms that are used and the method with which data is organized before you create your own database.

Identifying a Database Object

An Access database is a collection of related objects in which you enter, edit, and view data. Access opens with a Navigation pane along the left side of the window in which you select the object that you want to view. Objects are grouped by type. Most databases include tables, queries, forms, and reports. See Table 12.1 for a description of each type.

Table 12.1	Access Objects
Object	**Description**
Table	Data is organized into a collection of tables, each of which opens in a datasheet that displays data in columns and rows similarly to a spreadsheet. A table stores data about one topic or subject only. For example, in the LibraryFines database, one table contains data about each student and another table contains data about each fine.
Query	A query is used to extract information from one or more tables in a single datasheet and can show all of the data or only a subset of data that meets a specific condition. For example, a query could show all library fines that have been assessed or only those fines that are unpaid.
Form	A form provides a user-friendly interface with which data is entered or updated. The layout of a form can be customized to suit a variety of needs.
Report	Reports are used for viewing or printing data from a table or query. Reports can include summary totals and a customized layout.

App Tip

Opening a database displays the SECURITY WARNING message bar. Tap or click Enable Content only when you are sure the database has originated from a trusted source.

1. Start Access and open the database named *LibraryFines* from the Ch12 folder in Student_Data_Files.

2. Tap or click the Enable Content button in the SECURITY WARNING message bar that appears below the ribbon.

3. Compare your screen with the one shown in Figure 12.1.

(4) If necessary, slide or drag right the gray border along the right side of the Navigation pane to expand the width of the pane until the title *All Access Objects* is entirely visible.

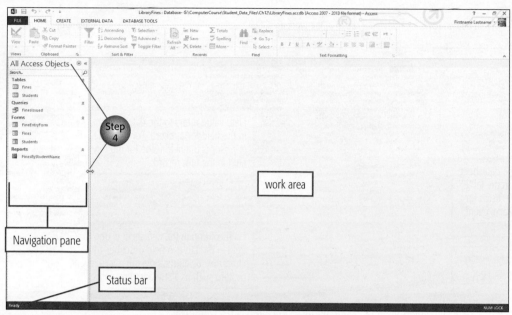

Figure 12.1 The LibraryFines Database opened in the Access window

Defining Database Terminology

Data in a database is organized by topic or subject about a person, place, event, item, or other category grouping in an object called a **table**. A database table is the first object that is created. The number of tables varies for each database depending on the information that needs to be stored. Tables are the building blocks for creating other objects such as a query, form, or report. In other words, you cannot create a query, form, or report without first creating a table.

(5) Double-tap or double-click *Fines* in the Tables group in the Navigation pane.

The table opens in Datasheet view within a tab in the work area.

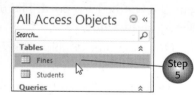

oops!

Trouble opening a table? Another way to open the table is to press and hold or right-click the object name and choose *Open.*

⑥ Double-tap or double-click *Students* in the Tables group in the Navigation pane and compare your screen with the one shown in Figure 12.2.

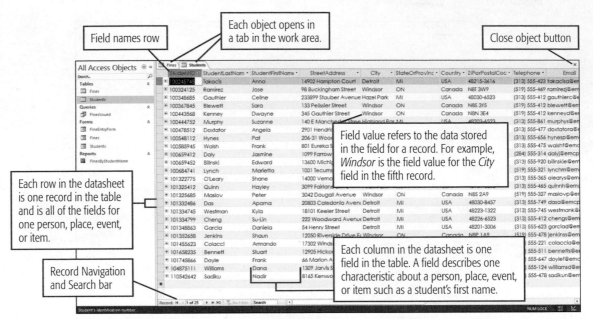

Figure 12.2 Datasheet View for Students Table in LibraryFines Database

A datasheet resembles a spreadsheet with the data organized in columns and rows. The information about the subject or topic of a table (such as students) is divided into columns, each of which is called a **field**. A field should store only one unit of information about a person, place, event, or item. For example, a mailing address is split into at least four fields so that the street address, city, state or province, and zip or postal code are separated. This allows the database to be sorted, filtered, or searched by any piece of information.

Each row in the datasheet shows all of the fields for one person, place, event, or item and is called a **record**. The data that is stored in one field within a record is called a **field value**.

⑦ Double-tap or double-click *FinesByStudentName* in the Reports group in the Navigation pane and review the report content and layout in the work area.

A **report** is designed to view or print data from one or more tables or queries in a customized layout and with summary totals. In this report, library fines are arranged and grouped by student name in alphabetical order.

⑧ Tap or click the Close button at the top right of the work area to close the report.

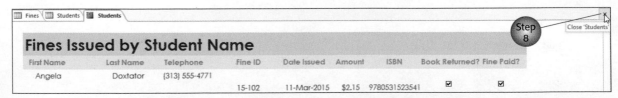

⑨ Double-tap or double-click *FineEntryForm* in the Forms group in the Navigation pane.

A **form** is used to enter, update, or view one record at a time.

App Tip

Forms can be created to resemble paper-based forms used within an organization.

10 Tap or click the Next record button (right-pointing arrow) in the Record Navigation and Search bar located at the bottom of the form.

Buttons in the Record Navigation and Search bar are used to move to the first record, previous record, next record, or last record. Use the *Search* box to navigate to a record by typing a field value.

11 Tap or click the Previous record button (left-pointing arrow).

12 Tap or click the Last record button (right-pointing arrow with vertical bar) to move to the last record in the form.

13 Tap or click the First record button (left-pointing arrow with vertical bar) to move to the first record in the form.

14 Tap or click the Close button at the top right of the work area to close the form.

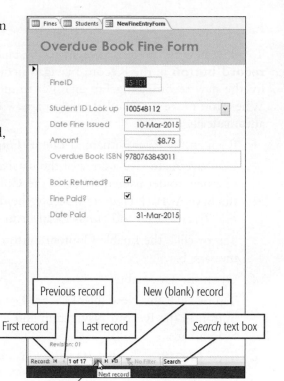

Quick STEPS

Open a Database Object
1. Open database file.
2. Double-tap or double-click object name in Navigation pane.

15 Double-tap or double-click *FinesIssued* in the Queries group in the Navigation pane.

A **query** opens in a datasheet similarly to a table. A query displays information from one or more tables and may show all of the records or only a subset of records that meet a specific condition.

FineID	DateIssued	StudentFirstName	StudentLastName	Telephone	Amount	OverdueBookISBN	BookReturned	FinePaid
15-101	10-Mar-2015	Pat	Hynes	(313) 555-6569	$8.75	9780763843011	✔	✔
15-102	11-Mar-2015	Angela	Doxtator	(313) 555-4771	$2.15	9780531523541	✔	✔
15-103	12-Mar-2015	Pat	Hynes	(313) 555-6569	$1.25	9780412533145	✔	☐
15-104	12-Mar-2015	Marietta	Lynch	(519) 555-3214	$1.40	9784123524158	✔	☐
15-105	13-Mar-2015	Edward	Bilinski	(313) 555-9200	$4.25	9784125312517	✔	✔
15-106	13-Mar-2015	Stuart	Bennett	(313) 555-5112	$3.25	8745125412352	✔	☐

A query can show data from more than one table and display the fields in any order.

16 Close the query and the two tables.

17 Tap or click the FILE tab and then tap or click Close at the Info tab Backstage view.

Always close a database file using the FILE tab before exiting Access so that all temporary files used by Access while you are viewing and updating records are properly closed.

Close objects as soon as you are finished viewing or updating data. Some Access commands will not run if an object is open in the background.

One Database at a Time

Unlike Word, Excel, or PowerPoint, Access allows only one file to be open at a time in the current window. If you open a second database in the current window, Access automatically closes the existing database before opening the new one.

Topic 12.2

SKILLS

Add a new record
in a datasheet

 Tutorial

12.2 Adding Records
in a Table

You can also move to the next
field by tapping or pressing
the Enter key or by tapping or
clicking in the next column.

Adding Records Using a Datasheet

To add a new record to a table, open the table and tap or click the **New (blank)
record button** in the Record Navigation and Search bar. Type the field values
for the new record, using Tab or Enter to move to the next field in the datasheet.
When you move past the last field in a new row in the datasheet, the record is
automatically saved.

1. Reopen the database named *LibraryFines*.

2. Use Save As to save a copy of the database as **12.2-LibraryFines-Your Name**
   in a new folder named *Ch12* in the CompletedTopicsbyChapter folder. At
   the Save As Backstage view, accept the default options *Save Database As* in the
   File Types section and *Access Database* in the *Save Database As* section.

3. Tap or click the Enable Content button in the SECURITY WARNING
   message bar.

4. Open the Fines table.

5. Tap or click the New (blank) record
   button in the Record Navigation and
   Search bar.

6. Type **15-118** in the *FineID* field and
   then tap or press Tab to move to the
   next field.

   The next field, *StudentID*, has been set up
   to look up names and ID numbers in the
   Students table. In this field a drop-down list is
   used to select the field value.

7. Tap or click the down-
   pointing arrow in the
   StudentID field, tap or
   click *100478512 Angela
   Doxtator* in the pop-
   up list, and then tap or
   press Tab.

   Pencil icon
   indicates
   the record is
   being edited.
   The pencil
   disappears when
   Access saves the
   changes.

   Access stores the student identification number
   as the field value once a selection is made in the
   list and the field value is connected to Angela Doxtator's record in the Students
   table.

8. Type **12apr2015** in the *DateIssued* field and tap or press Tab.

   The date field has been set up to
   display underscores and dashes as
   soon as you begin typing to help you
   enter the date in the correct format
   dd-mmm-yyyy. This configuration
   also ensures that all dates are entered
   consistently in the database.

oops!

Error message appears? This
occurs when a date has not
been typed in the pattern
that has been set for the field.
Tap or click OK, backspace to
delete the date entry, and try
Step 8 again.

9 Type **8.75** in the *Amount* field and then tap or press Tab.

10 Type **4348973098226** in the *OverdueBookISBN* field and then tap or press Tab.

11 Tap or press the spacebar to insert a check mark in the *BookReturned* field and then tap or press Tab.

BookReturned is a field that has been set up to store only one of two possible field values: *Yes* or *No*. Inserting a check mark stores *Yes*, while an empty check box stores *No*.

12 Tap or click the check box to insert a check mark in the *FinePaid* field and then tap or press Tab.

13 Type **15apr2015** in the *DatePaid* field and then tap or press Tab.

Moving to the next row in the datasheet automatically saves the record just typed and starts a new record.

Quick STEPS

Add New Record
1. Open table.
2. Tap or click New (blank) record button.
3. Type field values in new row in datasheet.
4. Close table.

App Tip

Saving in a database is not left to chance! As soon as you complete a new record, Access saves the data to disk.

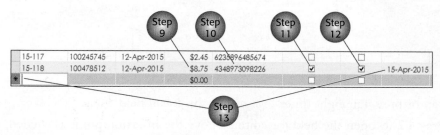

14 Add the following field values in the new row in the fields indicated:

FineID	**15–119**	*OverdueBookISBN*	**7349872345760**
StudentID	*101348863 Daniela Garcia*	*BookReturned*	Yes
DateIssued	**15apr2015**	*FinePaid*	No (leave blank)
Amount	**5.25**	*DatePaid*	(leave blank)

15-118	100478512	12-Apr-2015	$8.75	4348973098226	☑	☑	15-Apr-2015	
15-119	101348863	15-Apr-2015	$5.25	7349872345760	☑	☐		Step 14
*			$0.00		☐	☐		

15 With the insertion point positioned in the *FineID* field in a new row, close the Fines table. Leave the database open for the next topic.

ALTERNATIVE method New records can also be added to the table using any of these other methods to start a new blank row at the bottom of the datasheet:

- New button in the Records group of the HOME tab
- Keyboard shortcut Ctrl + + (hold down Ctrl key and press plus symbol)
- Tap or click in the last cell in the table and tap or press Tab

Topic 12.3

SKILLS

Edit a record
in a datasheet

Delete a record
in a datasheet

  Tutorial

12.3 Opening and
Closing an Access
Database and
Table

App Tip

As soon as you move to
another record in the
datasheet, the changes are
automatically saved.

oops!

Using Touch? Tap at the end
of murphy to place the insertion point in the field, tap
Backspace to delete the text,
and then type the new text.

Editing and Deleting Records in a Datasheet

Edit a field value in a datasheet by tapping or clicking in the table cell and inserting
or deleting text as required. Select a record for deletion by tapping or clicking in
the gray record selector bar along the left edge of the datasheet next to the record
and then tap or click the Delete button in the Records group of the HOME tab.
Access requires confirmation before deleting a record.

1. With the **12.2-LibraryFines-Your Name** database open, open the Students
   table.

2. Select the text *Murphy* in the *StudentLastName* column in the sixth row in the
   datasheet and type **Hall** as the new last name for Suzanne.

3. Tap or press Tab eight times to move to the *Email* field.

4. Press F2 to open the field for editing, move the insertion point as needed,
   delete *murphy* at the beginning of the email address, and then type **hall** so that
   the email address becomes *halls@emcp.net*.

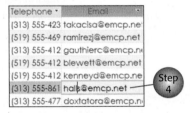

5. Tap or click at the end of *N8T 3W9* in the *ZIPorPostalCode* field in the second
   row in the datasheet to position the insertion point, tap or press Backspace to
   remove *3W9*, and then type **2E6**.

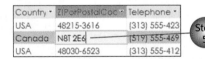
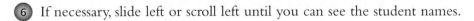

6. If necessary, slide left or scroll left until you can see the student names.

7 Tap or click in the record selector bar next to the record for the student *Das Aparna*.

The gray bar at the left edge of the datasheet is used to select a record. When using a mouse, the pointer displays as a black right-pointing arrow when positioned next to a record in the gray record selector bar.

Select all button

Record selector bar

Step 7

StudentID	StudentLastNam	StudentFirstName	StreetAddress	City	StateOrProvinc	Country	ZIParPostalCoc
100245745	Takacis	Anna	14902 Hampton Court	Detroit	MI	USA	48215-3616
100324125	Ramirez	Jose	98 Buckingham Street	Windsor	ON	Canada	N8T 2E6
100348685	Gauthier	Celine	233899 Stauber Avenue	Hazel Park	MI	USA	48030-6523
100367845	Blewett	Sara	133 Pelissier Street	Windsor	ON	Canada	N8S 3Y5
100443568	Kenney	Dwayne	345 Gauthier Street	Windsor	ON	Canada	N8N 3E4
100444752	Hall	Suzanne	140 E Manchester Stree	Highland Par	MI	USA	48203-6523
100478512	Doxtator	Angela	2901 Hendricks Street	Detroit	MI	USA	48207-2750
100548112	Hynes	Pat	206-31 Woodward Ave	Detroit	MI	USA	48202-1138
100585945	Walsh	Frank	801 Eureka Street	Lansing	MI	USA	48912-1423
100659412	Daly	Jasmine	1099 Farrow Avenue	Ferndale	MI	USA	48220-1234
100659452	Bilinski	Edward	13600 Michigan Avenu	Dearborn	MI	USA	48126-4224
100684741	Lynch	Marietta	1001 Tecumseh Road Ec	Windsor	ON	Canada	N8T 3W2
101322775	O'Leary	Shane	14000 Vernon Drive	Detroit	MI	USA	48237-1320
101325412	Quinn	Hayley	3099 Fairlane Drive	Allen Park	MI	USA	48101-3252
101325685	Maslov	Peter	3042 Dougall Avenue	Windsor	ON	Canada	N8S 2A9
101332486	Das	Aparna	20803 Caledonia Avent	Detroit	MI	USA	48030-8457
101334745	Westman	Kyla	18101 Keeler Street	Detroit	MI	USA	48223-1322

8 Tap or click the Delete button in the Records group of the HOME tab. Do *not* tap or click the down-pointing arrow on the button.

Step 8

9 Tap or click Yes at the message box that appears asking if you are sure you want to delete the record.

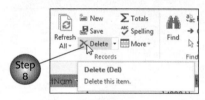

Microsoft Access

You are about to delete 1 record(s).

If you click Yes, you won't be able to undo this Delete operation.
Are you sure you want to delete these records?

Step 9

Yes   No

10 Close the Students table. Leave the database open for the next topic.

Quick STEPS

Edit a Record
1. Open table.
2. Tap or click in table cell.
3. Insert or delete text as required.

Delete a Record
1. Open table.
2. Select record.
3. Tap or click Delete button.
4. Tap or click Yes.

App Tip

Be cautious with the Delete command because Undo does not work to restore a record. Consider making a backup copy of a database before deleting records.

Best Practices for Deleting Records

Depending on the purpose of the database, deleting records is generally not performed until the records to be deleted are copied to an archive database and/or a backup copy of the database has been made. In most cases, records should be retained for historical data purposes.

SKILLS

Add a record
in a form

Edit a record
in a form

Delete a record
in a form

 **Tutorial**

12.4   Adding Records
in a Form

Adding, Editing, and Deleting Records in a Form

Recall from an earlier topic that a form is an interface that provides a different view for a table. Generally only one record at a time is displayed in a columnar layout. Forms are the preferred object for adding, editing, and deleting records.

1. With the **12.2-LibraryFines-Your Name** database open, open the form named *FineEntryForm*.

2. Tap or click the New (blank) record button in the Record Navigation and Search bar.

3. Add the field values as shown in the image below, using Tab to move to subsequent fields.

   A new blank form displays when you tap or press Tab after the last field in a form.

4. Tap or click the First record button in the Record Navigation and Search bar to display the first record in the form.

5. Select *8.75* in the *Amount* field and type **7.25**.

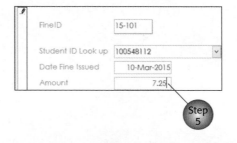

6 Tap or click the Next record button two times to display record 3 in the form.

7 Tap or click the Delete button arrow in the Records group of the HOME tab and then tap or click *Delete Record* at the drop-down list.

Delete a Record in a Form
1. Open form.
2. Display record.
3. Tap or click Delete button arrow.
4. Tap or click *Delete Record*.
5. Tap or click Yes.

oops!

Only the current field value is deleted? This occurs when you do not use the arrow on the button to select the option to delete the entire record. Try Step 7 again, making sure to choose *Delete Record*.

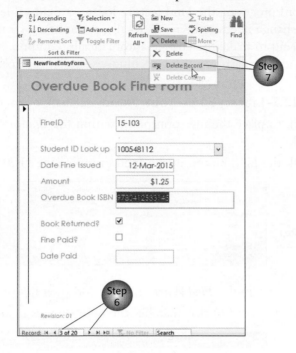

8 Tap or click Yes at the message box that appears asking if you are sure you want to delete the record.

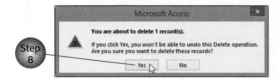

9 Close the form. Leave the database open for the next topic.

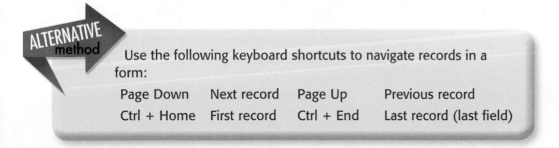

ALTERNATIVE method   Use the following keyboard shortcuts to navigate records in a form:

| Page Down | Next record | Page Up | Previous record |
| Ctrl + Home | First record | Ctrl + End | Last record (last field) |

Beyond Basics   Using Find to Move to a Record

As databases expand to store hundreds or thousands of records, using the navigation buttons at the bottom of the form to locate a record that needs to be changed or deleted is not feasible. The Find feature locates a record instantly when you search by a name or ID number. You will use Find in the next topic.

Finding and Replacing Data and Adjusting Column Widths

oops!

No records found? Tap or click OK and then check that you typed the ID number without errors.

Similar to a word processor, the Find feature locates a field value in a datasheet or form. When a change needs to be made to all occurrences of a field value, use the Replace command to make the change automatically. Column widths in a datasheet can be made wider or narrower using techniques similar to those you learned in Excel.

1. With the **12.2-LibraryFines-Your Name** database open, open the Fines table.

2. Tap or click to place the insertion point within the *StudentID* field value in the first record.

3. Tap or click the Find button in the Find group of the HOME tab.

4. Type **101348863** in the *Find What* text box and then tap or click Find Next.

   The first record (record 6) that matches the field value is made active.

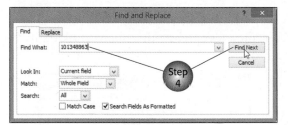

5. Continue tapping or clicking the Find Next button to review all occurrences of the matching field value.

6. Tap or click OK at the message that Microsoft Access has finished searching records.

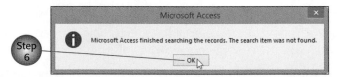

7. Tap or click Cancel to close the Find and Replace dialog box.

8. Tap or click to place the insertion point within the *FineID* field in the first record.

9. Tap or click the Replace button in the Find group.

10 Type **15-** in the *Find What* text box and then tap or press Tab.

11 Type **2015-** in the *Replace With* text box.

12 Tap or click the *Match* list arrow and then tap or click *Any Part of Field* at the drop-down list.

13 Tap or click the Replace All button.

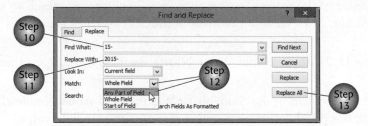

Step 10
Step 11
Step 12
Step 13

14 Tap or click Yes at the message asking if you want to continue and informing you that the Replace operation cannot be undone.

Step 14

15 Close the Find and Replace dialog box.

16 Tap or click to place the insertion point in any record within the *DateIssued* field.

17 Tap or click the More button in the Records group of the HOME tab and then tap or click *Field Width* at the drop-down list.

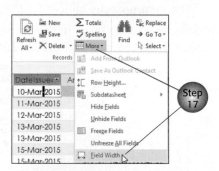

Step 17

18 Tap or click Best Fit at the Column Width dialog box.

   Best Fit is similar to AutoFit in Excel in that the column width is lengthened to accommodate the longest entry.

19 Close the Fines table. Tap or click Yes when prompted to save the changes to the layout of the table. Leave the database open for the next topic.

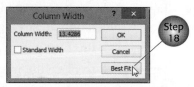

Step 18

   Saving changes to the layout of the table means that Access will retain the new column width for the *DateIssued* field when the table is reopened.

ALTERNATIVE method

You can also adjust column widths using the following methods:

- Slide or drag the right column boundary in the field names row right or left.
- Double-tap or double-click the right column boundary to best fit the width.
- Type a value in the *Column Width* text box at the Column Width dialog box.

Topic 12.6

SKILLS

Sort records

Filter records

 Tutorials

12.6.1 Sorting Records in a Table

12.6.2 Filtering Records

App Tip

When a datasheet is sorted by a field other than the primary key, an up-pointing arrow (ascending order) or down-pointing arrow (descending order) displays next to the name for the field used to sort.

Sorting and Filtering Records

Records are initially arranged in the datasheet alphanumerically by the field in the table that has been defined as the primary key. A **primary key** is a field that contains the data that uniquely identifies each record in the table. Generally, the primary key is an identification number such as *StudentID* in the Students table. To change the order of the records, tap or click in the column by which to sort and use the Ascending or Descending buttons in the Sort & Filter group of the HOME tab.

1. With the **12.2-LibraryFines–Your Name** database open, open the Students table.

    The primary key field in the Students table is the field named *StudentID*. Notice the records in the datasheet are arranged in order of the ID field values.

2. Tap or click to place the insertion point within any field value in the *StudentLastName* column.

3. Tap or click the Ascending button in the Sort & Filter group of the HOME tab.

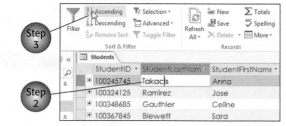

4. Close the Students table. Tap or click Yes when prompted to save the changes to the design of the table.

    Selecting Yes to save changes to the design of the table means that the table will remain sorted by the *StudentLastName* field when you reopen the table.

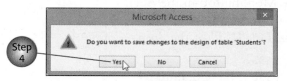

5. Open the Students form.

6. Tap or click the Next record button a few times to view the first few records. Notice the records are arranged by *StudentID*.

7. Tap or click the First record button to return the display to the first record.

8. Tap or click to place the insertion point in the *Student Last Name* field.

9. Tap or click the Ascending button in the Sort & Filter group.

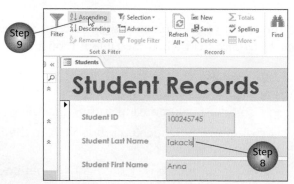

10. Scroll through the first 10 records in the form to view the sorted order and then close the form.

11 Open the Students table. Notice the records are arranged alphabetically by the student last names.

You can filter a datasheet in Access using the same techniques you learned for filtering a table in Excel in Chapter 9. Recall that a filter temporarily hides the rows that you do not want to view.

12 Tap or click the filter arrow (down-pointing arrow) next to *Country*.

13 Tap or click the check box next to *USA* to clear the check mark from the box at the Sort & Filter list box and then tap or click OK.

The datasheet is filtered to show records for students who reside in Canada only.

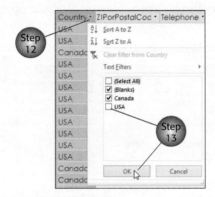

14 Tap or click the Toggle Filter button in the Sort & Filter group to clear the filter.

All records are now redisplayed.

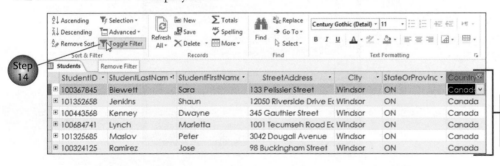

Filtered list of records after Step 13

15 Close the Students table. Tap or click No when prompted to save changes to the design of the table. Leave the database open for the next topic.

Quick STEPS

Sort a Datasheet or Form
1. Open table or form.
2. Tap or click in field by which to sort.
3. Tap or click Ascending or Descending button.

Filter a Datasheet
1. Open table.
2. Tap or click filter arrow next to field.
3. Clear check boxes as needed.
4. Tap or click OK.

App Tip

Access displays a funnel icon next to a field used to filter a datasheet and displays *Filtered* highlighted in orange in the Record Navigation and Search bar.

oops!

Toggle Filter button not active? Tap or click the filter arrow button next to *Country* and tap or click *Clear Filter from Country* to redisplay all records.

Beyond Basics

Sorting by More Than One Field

Sort by more than one field in a datasheet by sliding or dragging the field names at the top of the datasheet to select the columns by which to sort and then choose Ascending or Descending order. Access sorts left to right. For example, if *StudentLastName* and *StudentFirstName* columns are selected, Access sorts first by last names and then by first names when two or more records have the same last name. Move a column to change the sort order if necessary. To move a field for sorting purposes, slide or drag the field name to the left.

Topic 12.7

SKILLS

Create a query
using wizard

SNAP Tutorial

12.7 Creating Queries
Using the Simple
Query Wizard

Creating a Query Using the Simple Query Wizard

Queries are used to extract information from one or more tables in the database and display the results in a datasheet. Some queries are used to display fields from more than one table in the same datasheet. For example, in the LibraryFines database, the student names are in one table whereas the fines are in another table; a query can combine the names and fines in one datasheet. Other queries are designed to answer a question about the data; for example, *Which library fines are unpaid?*. The **Simple Query Wizard** assists with creating a query by making selections in a series of dialog boxes.

① With the **12.2-LibraryFines-Your Name** database open, tap or click the CREATE tab.

② Tap or click the Query Wizard button in the Queries group.

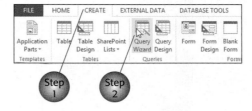

③ Tap or click OK at the New Query dialog box with *Simple Query Wizard* already selected.

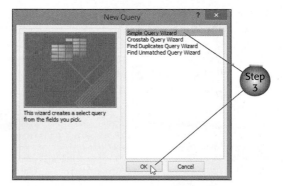

④ At the first Simple Query Wizard dialog box, tap or click the *Tables/Queries* list arrow and then tap or click *Table: Students* at the drop-down list. Skip this step if *Table: Students* is already displayed in the *Table/Queries* list box.

The first step in creating a query is to choose the tables or queries and the fields from each table or query that you want to display in a datasheet.

⑤ With *StudentID* already selected in the *Available Fields* list box, tap or click the Add Field button (displays as a right-pointing arrow) to move *StudentID* to the *Selected Fields* list box.

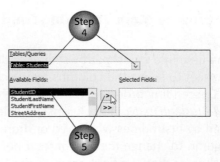

⑥ Double-tap or double-click *StudentFirstName* in the *Available Fields* list box to move the field to the *Selected Fields* list box.

Add fields to the *Selected Fields* list box in the order in which you want the fields displayed in the datasheet.

⑦ Double-tap or double-click the following fields in the *Available Fields* list box to move each field to the *Selected Fields* list box.

> *StudentLastName*
> *Telephone*
> *Email*

⑧ Tap or click the *Tables/Queries* list arrow and then tap or click *Table: Fines*.

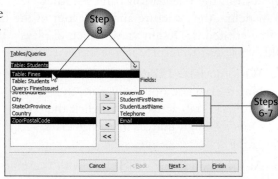

⑨ Double-tap or double-click the following fields in the *Available Fields* list box to move each field to the *Selected Fields* list box.

> *DateIssued*
> *Amount*
> *FinePaid*

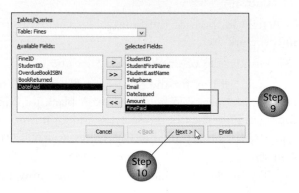

⑩ Tap or click Next.

⑪ Tap or click Next at the second Simple Query Wizard dialog to accept *Detail (shows every field of every record)* for the query results.

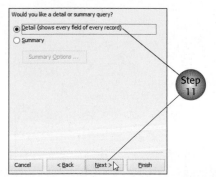

⑫ At the third Simple Query Wizard dialog box, select the current text in the *What title do you want for your query?* text box, type **StudentsWithFines**, and then tap or click Finish.

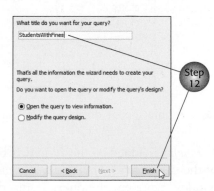

⑬ Review the query results datasheet. Notice the fields are displayed in the order selected at the first Simple Query Wizard dialog box.

⑭ Close the StudentsWithFines query. Leave the database open for the next topic.

Quick STEPS

Create a Query Using Simple Query Wizard

1. Tap or click CREATE tab.
2. Tap or click Query Wizard button.
3. Tap or click OK.
4. Choose each table and/or query and fields in required order.
5. Tap or click Next.
6. Tap or click Next.
7. Type title for query.
8. Tap or click Finish.

Topic 12.8

SKILLS

Create a query
using Design view

 Tutorials

12.8.1 Creating a Query
in Design View

12.8.2 Creating a Query
in Design View
Using Multiple
Tables

oops!

Closed the Show Table dialog
box by mistake? Reopen the
dialog box using the Show
Table button in the Query
Setup group of the QUERY
TOOLS DESIGN tab.

Creating a Query Using Design View

Every Access object has at least two views. In one view you browse the data in
the table, query, form, or report. This is the view that is active when you open the
object from the Navigation pane. Another view, called **Design view**, is used to set
up or define the structure and/or layout of the table, query, form, or report. A query
can be created in Design view, which displays a blank grid into which you add the
fields you want to display in the query results.

1. With the **12.2–LibraryFines–Your
   Name** database open and with the
   CREATE tab active, tap or click the
   Query Design button in the Queries
   group.

2. At the Show Table dialog box with the *Fines* table selected, tap or click the Add
   button.

   A field list box for the Fines table is added to the top of the *Query1* design grid
   in the work area.

3. Double-tap or double-click *Students*.

   A field list box for the Students table is added to the top of the design grid
   beside the *Fines* table field list box. A black join line connects the two tables
   together. The black line displays 1 and an infinity symbol (∞), which indicates the
   type of relationship for the two tables. You will learn about relationships in the next
   chapter.

4. Tap or click the Close button in the Show Table dialog box.

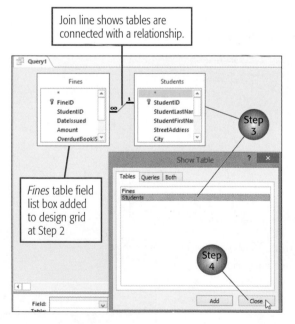

Join line shows tables are
connected with a relationship.

Fines table field
list box added
to design grid
at Step 2

FineID is added
here after you
perform Step 5.

5. Double-tap or double-click *FineID* in the *Fines* table field list
   box.

   FineID is added to the *Field* text box in the first column
   of the design grid. The blank columns in the bottom of the
   window represent the query results datasheet. You build the query
   by adding fields in the order you want them to appear in the
   datasheet by selecting fields from the table field list boxes in the
   top half of the window.

6 Double-tap or double-click the following fields in the *Fines* table field list box to add the fields to the query design grid.

> *DateIssued*
> *Amount*
> *BookReturned* (slide or scroll down the table field list box to the field)

7 Double-tap or double-click the following fields in the *Students* table field list box to add the fields to the query design grid.

> *StudentFirstName*
> *StudentLastName*

Quick STEPS

Create a Query Using Design View
1. Tap or click CREATE tab.
2. Tap or click Query Design button.
3. Add tables to design grid.
4. Close Show Table dialog box.
5. Double-tap or double-click field names in table field list boxes.
6. Tap or click Run button.
7. Tap or click Save button.
8. Type query name.
9. Tap or click OK.

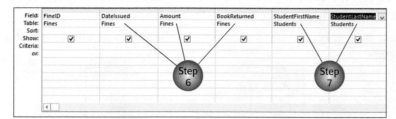

8 Tap or click the **Run button** in the Results group of the QUERY TOOLS DESIGN tab to view the query results datasheet.

A query is simply a set of instructions for which table names and field names display in a datasheet. The query results datasheet is not a duplicate copy of the data—each time a query is opened or run, the data is generated by extracting the field values from the tables.

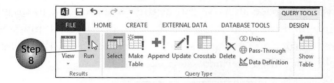

9 Tap or click the Save button in the Quick Access toolbar (QAT).

10 Type **BookReturnedList** at the Save As dialog box and tap or press Enter or tap or click OK.

11 Close the BookReturnedList query. Leave the database open for the next topic.

ALTERNATIVE method   Add fields to the design grid from the table field list boxes using these other methods:

- Slide or drag a field name from the table field list box to the Field text box in the desired column.
- Tap or click in a blank Field text box in the design grid, tap or click the down-pointing arrow that appears, and then tap or click the field name in the drop-down list.

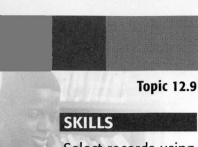

Topic 12.9

Entering Criteria to Select Records in a Query

Both of the query results datasheets for the queries you created using the Simple Query Wizard and Design view displayed all records in the tables. Often, queries are created to select records from the tables that meet one or more conditions. For example, in this topic you will add a criterion to show only those records in which the fines are unpaid.

SKILLS

Select records using criteria

 Tutorial

12.9 Extracting Records Using Criteria Statements

① With the **12.2-LibraryFines-Your Name** database open, open the StudentsWithFines query.

② Tap or click the View button in the Views group of the HOME tab. Do *not* tap or click the down-pointing arrow on the button.

The View button is used to switch between the query results datasheet and Design view.

③ Tap or click in the *Criteria* box in the *FinePaid* column in the design grid, type **No**, tap or press the spacebar, and then tap or press Enter.

Access displays functions in a drop-down list as you type text that matches the letters in a function name. As you type *No*, the function wizard displays *Now* in a drop-down list. Typing a space after *No* causes the *Now* function to disappear. *FinePaid* is a field in which the field value is either *Yes* or *No*. By typing *No* in the *Criteria* box, you are instructing Access to select the records from the *Fines* table in which *No* is the field value for *FinePaid*.

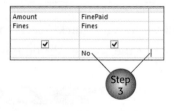

oops!

Empty datasheet? Use the View button to return to Design view and check that you typed *No* in the *FinePaid* column and/or that *No* is in the *Criteria* box of the column.

④ Tap or click the Run button.

Notice that 10 records are selected in the query results datasheet and that the check box in the *FinePaid* column for each record is empty.

StudentID	StudentFirstName	StudentLastName	Telephone	Email	DateIssued	Amount	FinePaid
100245745	Anna	Takacis	(313) 555-4235	takacisa@emcp.net	12-Apr-2015	$2.45	☐
100443568	Dwayne	Kenney	(519) 555-4125	kenneyd@emcp.net	15-Mar-2015	$12.50	☐
100443568	Dwayne	Kenney	(519) 555-4125	kenneyd@emcp.net	06-Apr-2015	$4.60	☐
100659412	Jasmine	Daly	(284) 555-3142	dalyj@emcp.net	30-Mar-2015	$2.40	☐
100684741	Marietta	Lynch	(519) 555-3214	lynchm@emcp.net	12-Mar-2015	$1.40	☐
101325685	Peter	Maslov	(519) 555-3276	maslovp@emcp.net	04-Apr-2015	$7.85	☐
101334799	Su-Lin	Cheng	(313) 555-3214	chengs@emcp.net	10-Apr-2015	$8.75	☐
101348863	Daniela	Garcia	(313) 555-6235	garciad@emcp.net	15-Mar-2015	$1.85	☐
101348863	Daniela	Garcia	(313) 555-6235	garciad@emcp.net	15-Apr-2015	$5.25	☐
101658235	Stuart	Bennett	(313) 555-5112	bennetts@emcp.net	13-Mar-2015	$3.25	☐

Query results datasheet showing unpaid fines only

⑤ Tap or click the FILE tab and then tap or click Save As.

⑥ At the Save As Backstage view, tap or click *Save Object As* and then tap or click the Save As button.

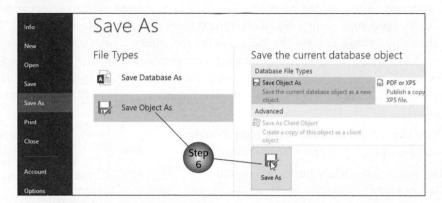

Quick STEPS

Select Records in a Query
1. Open query.
2. Tap or click View button.
3. Type criterion in *Criteria* box of field by which to select records.
4. Run query.
5. Save query or use Save As to save revised query using new name.

App Tip

A query that extracts records is referred to as a select query.

⑦ Type **UnpaidFines** in the *Save 'StudentsWithFines' to* text box at the Save As dialog box and then tap or press Enter or tap or click OK.

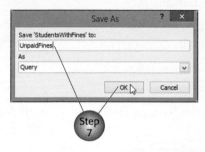

⑧ Close the UnpaidFines query. Leave the database open for the next topic.

See Table 12.2 for more criteria statement examples.

Table 12.2	Criteria Examples	
Field	**Entry Typed in Criteria Text Box**	**Records Selected**
Amount	<=5	Fines issued that were $5.00 or less
Amount	>5	Fines issued that were more than $5.00
DateIssued	March 15, 2015 (entry converts automatically to #3/15/2015#)	Fines issued on March 15, 2015
StudentLastName	Kenney (entry converts automatically to "Kenney")	Fines issued to student with the last name *Kenney*.

 **Selecting Records using a Range of Dates**

Table 12.2 provides the example that typing March 15, 2015 in the DateIssued field selects records of fines issued on March 15, 2015. What if one wanted to view a list of all of the fines issued in the month of March? To do this, type *Between March 1, 2015 and March 31, 2015* in the *Criteria* text box of the *DateIssued* column.

Entering Multiple Criteria to Select Records and Sorting a Query

Topic 12.10

More than one criterion can be entered in the query design grid to select records. For example, you may want a list of all unpaid fines that are more than $5.00. When more than one criterion is on the same row in the query design grid, it is referred to as an *AND* statement, meaning that each criterion must be met for a record to be selected. When more than one criterion is on different rows in the query design grid, it is referred to as an *OR* statement, meaning that any criterion can be met for a record to be selected.

1. With the **12.2-LibraryFines-Your Name** database open, open the UnpaidFines query.

2. Tap or click the View button to switch to Design view.

3. Tap or click in the *Criteria* box in the *Amount* column, type **>5**, and then tap or press Enter.

4. Tap or click the Run button.

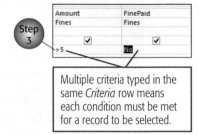

Multiple criteria typed in the same *Criteria* row means each condition must be met for a record to be selected.

StudentID	StudentFirstName	StudentLastName	Telephone	Email	DateIssued	Amount	FinePaid
100443568	Dwayne	Kenney	(519) 555-4125	kenneyd@emcp.net	15-Mar-2015	$12.50	☐
101325685	Peter	Maslov	(519) 555-3276	maslovp@emcp.net	04-Apr-2015	$7.85	☐
101334799	Su-Lin	Cheng	(313) 555-4125	chengs@emcp.net	10-Apr-2015	$8.75	☐
101348863	Daniela	Garcia	(313) 555-6235	garciad@emcp.net	15-Apr-2015	$5.25	☐

Query results datasheet showing unpaid fines over $5.00

SNAP Tutorials

12.10.1 Extracting Records Using AND Criteria; Sorting Query Results

12.10.2 Extracting Records Using OR Criteria

5. Use *Save Object As* at the Save As Backstage view to save the revised query as *UnpaidFinesOver$5*.

6. Close the UnpaidFinesOver$5 query.

7. Tap or click the CREATE tab and then tap or click the Query Design button.

8. Double-tap or double-click *Students* in the Show Table dialog box and then tap or click the Close button.

9. Double-tap or double-click the following fields in the *Students* table field list box to add the fields to the query design grid.

> *City*
> *StudentID*
> *StudentFirstName*
> *StudentLastName*
> *Telephone* (slide or scroll down the table field list box to the field)

10. Tap or click in the *Criteria* box in the *City* column, type **Detroit**, tap or click in the row below *Detroit* next to *or*, type **Windsor**, and then tap or press Enter.

Access inserts double quotation marks at the beginning and end of a criterion for a field that contains text such as a city, name, or other field that is not used for calculating values.

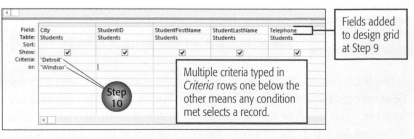

Fields added to design grid at Step 9

Multiple criteria typed in *Criteria* rows one below the other means any condition met selects a record.

11 Tap or click the Run button.

Only students who reside in Detroit or Windsor are shown in the query results datasheet.

12 Tap or click the View button to return to Design view.

A query is sorted by choosing *Ascending* or *Descending* in the *Sort* list box of the column by which you want to sort. At Step 9 *City* was placed first in the design grid because Access sorts query results by column left to right. To arrange the records alphabetically by student last name grouped by cities, the *City* field needs to be positioned left of the *StudentLastName* field.

13 Tap or click in the *Sort* list box in the *City* column to place the insertion point and display the list arrow, tap or click the *Sort* list arrow, and then tap or click *Ascending*.

14 Tap or click in the *Sort* list box in the *StudentLastName* column, tap or click the list arrow that appears, and then tap or click *Ascending*.

15 Tap or click the Run button.

The query results datasheet is sorted alphabetically by city and then by the student last name within each city.

Field:	City	StudentID	StudentFirstName	StudentLastName
Table:	Students	Students	Students	Students
Sort:	Ascending			Ascending
Show:	☑	☑	☑	Descending
Criteria:	"Detroit"			(not sorted)
or:	"Windsor"			

Step 13 / Step 14

DetroitAndWindsorStudents

City	StudentID	StudentFirstName	StudentLastNam	Telephone
Detroit	101658235	Stuart	Bennett	(313) 555-511
Detroit	101334799	Su-Lin	Cheng	(313) 555-412
Detroit	101455623	Armando	Colacci	(313) 555-221
Detroit	100478512	Angela	Doxtator	(313) 555-477
Detroit	101348863	Daniela	Garcia	(313) 555-623
Detroit	100548112	Pat	Hynes	(313) 555-656
Detroit	101322775	Shane	O'Leary	(313) 555-365
Detroit	110542642	Nadir	Sadiku	(313) 555-478
Detroit	100245745	Anna	Takacis	(313) 555-423
Detroit	101334745	Kyla	Westman	(313) 555-745
Detroit	104875111	Dana	Williams	(313) 555-124
Windsor	100367845	Sara	Blewett	(519) 555-412
Windsor	101352658	Shaun	Jenkins	(519) 555-478
Windsor	100443568	Dwayne	Kenney	(519) 555-412
Windsor	100684741	Marietta	Lynch	(519) 555-321
Windsor	101325685	Peter	Maslov	(519) 555-327
Windsor	100324125	Jose	Ramirez	(519) 555-469

Sorted query results datasheet showing students who reside in either Detroit or Windsor

16 Save the query and name it **DetroitAndWindsorStudents**.

17 Close the DetroitAndWindsorStudents query. Leave the database open for the next topic.

Beyond Basics

Selecting Using a Wildcard Character

A criterion can be entered that provides Access with a partial entry to match for selecting records. The asterisk is a wildcard character that can be inserted in a criterion in place of characters that you do not want to specify. For example, to select all students with the last name beginning with C, type *C** in the *Criteria* box in the *StudentLastName* column.

Creating a Calculated Field in a Query and Previewing a Datasheet

Topic 12.11

A calculated field can be created in a query that performs a mathematical operation on a numeric field. A database best practice is to avoid adding fields in a table with data that otherwise can be generated by performing calculations on other fields. For example, assume that in the LibraryFines database, each fine is also assessed a $2.50 administrative fee. Because the fee is a constant value, adding a field in the table to store the fee is not necessary. In this topic, you will use a query to calculate the total fine, including the administrative fee.

SKILLS

Delete and insert columns in a query

Create a calculated field

Format a field

Print Preview a datasheet

 Tutorials

12.11.1 Performing Calculations in a Query

12.11.2 Previewing and Printing a Table

oops!

Error message appears? Check your typing to make sure you typed a colon after *Fine with Admin Fee*, used square brackets, and that the entry has no other spelling errors.

1. With the **12.2-LibraryFines-Your Name** database open, open the FinesIssued query.

2. Switch to Design view.

3. Tap or click in any cell in the *Telephone* column in the query design grid.

4. Tap or click the Delete Columns button in the Query Setup group of the QUERY TOOLS DESIGN tab.

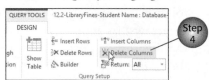

Use buttons in the Query Setup group to modify a query design by deleting columns or inserting new columns between existing fields.

5. Delete the *OverdueBookISBN* and *BookReturned* fields by completing steps similar to Steps 3 and 4.

6. With *FinePaid* the active field, tap or click the Insert Columns button in the Query Setup group.

7. With the insertion point positioned in the *Field* box in the new column between *Amount* and *FinePaid*, type **Fine with Admin Fee: [Amount]+2.50** and then tap or press Enter. Note that Access drops the zero at the end of the formula in the design grid.

8. Slide or drag the right column boundary line in the gray field selector bar at the top of the design grid to widen the column as shown in the image below.

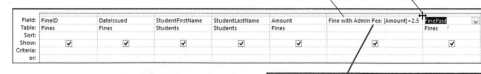

9. Tap or click the Run button.

Notice that the calculated field is not formatted the same as the *Amount* field, and the column needs to be widened to show the entire column heading.

> The text before the colon is the column heading for the calculated field *Fine with Admin Fee*. After the colon the mathematical expression *[Amount]+2.5* is typed. A field name to be used in a formula is typed within square brackets.

10. Tap or click in any cell in the *Fine with Admin Fee* column, tap or click the More button in the Records group, tap or click *Field Width*, and then tap or click Best Fit.

11. Switch to Design view.

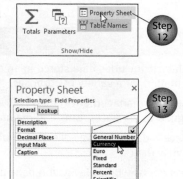

Create a Calculated Field in a Query
1. Open query in Design view.
2. Insert column if necessary.
3. Tap or click in *Field* box for calculated column.
4. Type formula.
5. Tap or press Enter.
6. Run query.
7. Save query.

⑫ Tap or click in any cell in the calculated column in the query design grid and then tap or click the Property Sheet button in the Show/Hide group of the QUERY TOOLS DESIGN tab.

⑬ Tap or click in the *Format* box in the Property Sheet task pane, tap or click the list arrow that appears, and then tap or click *Currency* at the drop-down list.

⑭ Close the Property Sheet task pane.

⑮ Tap or click the Run button.

⑯ Use *Save Object As* at the Save As Backstage view to save the revised query as *FinesWithAdminFee*.

A table datasheet or query results datasheet should be viewed in Print Preview before printing to make adjustments as necessary to the orientation and margins.

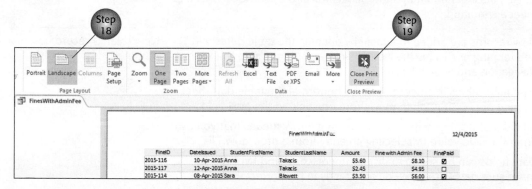

First five records in FinesWithAdminFee query showing calculated *Fine with Admin Fee* column

⑰ Tap or click the FILE tab, tap or click Print, and tap or click *Print Preview* at the Print tab Backstage view.

⑱ Tap or click the Landscape button in the Page Layout group of the PRINT PREVIEW tab.

Notice that by default, Access prints the query name and the current date at the top of the page and the page number at the bottom of the page.

⑲ Tap or click the Close Print Preview button in the Close Preview group.

⑳ Close the FinesWithAdminFee query and then close the LibraryFines database.

Exporting Data from Access

Buttons in the Data group of the PRINT PREVIEW tab are used to export the active table, query, form, or report shown in the work area. For example, tap or click the PDF or XPS button to save a copy of the query results datasheet shown above in a PDF file.

Concepts Review

Topic	Key Concepts	Key Terms
Understanding Database Objects and Terminology	A database includes data stored in an organized manner to provide information for a variety of purposes.	Database
	A database management system (DBMS) is a software program designed to organize, store, and maintain a database.	Database management system (DBMS)
	An Access database is a collection of objects used to enter, maintain, and view data.	Table
	Access opens with a Navigation pane along the left side of the window where you select the object in which you want to work.	Field
		Record
	A table stores data about a single topic or subject such as people, places, events, items, or other category.	Field value
	Each characteristic about the subject or topic of a table is called a field.	Report
		Form
	The data stored in a field is called a field value.	Query
	A set of fields for one person, place, event, item, or other subject of a table is called a record.	
	A table opens in a datasheet where the columns are fields and the rows are records.	
	A report is an object in which you view or print data from the tables in a customized layout and with summary totals.	
	A form is another interface with which you can view, enter, or edit data in a table that generally shows only one record at a time in a customized layout.	
	Use buttons in the Record Navigation and Search bar to scroll records in a form.	
	A query is used to combine fields from one or more tables in a single datasheet and may show all records or only some records that meet a condition.	
Adding Records Using a Datasheet	New records are added to a table by opening the table datasheet and tapping or clicking the New (blank) record button in the Record Navigation and Search bar.	New (blank) record button
	Type field values in a new row at the bottom of the table datasheet, tapping or pressing Tab to move from one field to the next field.	
	A field that displays with a down-pointing arrow means that you can enter the field value by selecting an entry from a drop-down list.	
	Date fields can be set up to display underscores and hyphens to make sure dates are entered consistently in the correct format.	
	A field that displays with a check box stores *Yes* if the box is checked and *No* if the box is left empty.	
	Access automatically saves a new record as soon as you tap or press Tab to move past the last field.	

Topic	Key Concepts	Key Terms
Editing and Deleting Records in a Datasheet	Edit a field value in a datasheet by tapping or clicking to place the insertion point within a field (cell) and inserting or deleting text as required. Function key F2 opens a field for editing. The gray bar along the left edge of a datasheet is used to select a record. Tap or click the Delete button in the Records group of the HOME tab to delete the selected record from the table. Access requires that you confirm a deletion before the record is removed. Generally, records are not deleted until data has been copied to an archive database and/or a backup copy of the database has been made.	
Adding, Editing, and Deleting Records in a Form	A form is the preferred object for adding, editing, and deleting records. A form displays one record at a time in a columnar layout. Add new records and edit field values in records using the same techniques as you used in a datasheet. To delete a record in a form, display the record, tap or click the Delete button arrow in the Records group of the HOME tab, and then tap or click *Delete Record* at the drop-down list. In a database with many records, navigating to a record using the Find feature is more efficient.	
Finding and Replacing Data and Adjusting Column Widths	Tap or click in the column in a datasheet that contains the field value you want to locate and use the Find command to move to all occurrences of the *Find What* text. Use the Replace command to find all occurrences of an entry and replace the field value with new text. Activate any cell in a column for which the width needs to be adjusted, tap or click the More button in the Records group, and then tap or click *Field Width*. The *Best Fit* button in the Column Width dialog box adjusts the width of the column to accommodate the longest entry.	Best Fit
Sorting and Filtering Records	Initially, a table is arranged alphanumerically by the primary key field values. A primary key is a field in the table that uniquely identifies each record such as *StudentID*. To sort by a field other than the primary key, tap or click in the field by which to sort and choose the Ascending or Descending button in the Sort & Filter group of the HOME tab. Filter a datasheet by clearing check boxes for items you do not want to view in the Sort & Filter list box accessed from the filter arrow next to the field name. Use the Toggle Filter button in the Sort & Filter group to redisplay all records. Sort by more than one field by selecting the columns before tapping or clicking the Ascending or Descending order button.	Primary key

continued....

Topic	Key Concepts	Key Terms
Creating a Query Using the Simple Query Wizard	Queries extract information from one or more tables in a single datasheet.	Simple Query Wizard
	The Simple Query Wizard helps you build a query by making selections in three dialog boxes.	
	At the first Simple Query Wizard dialog box, choose each table or query and the fields in the order that you want them in the query results datasheet.	
	At the second Simple Query Wizard dialog box, choose a detail or summary query.	
	Assign a name to the query at the third Simple Query Wizard dialog box.	
Creating a Query Using Design View	Every object in Access has at least two views.	Design view
	Opening an object from the Navigation pane opens the table, query, form, or report in Datasheet view.	Run button
	Design view is used to set up or define the structure or layout of an object.	
	Design view for a query presents a blank grid of columns in which you add the fields in the order you want them in the query results datasheet.	
	Add table field list boxes to the query design grid at the Show Table dialog box.	
	Double-tap or double-click field names in the table field list boxes in the order you want the columns in the query results datasheet.	
	The Run button is used after building a query in Design view to instruct Access to generate the query and show the query results datasheet.	
Entering Criteria to Select Records in a Query	Queries can be created that show only those records that meet one or more conditions.	
	Use the View button in the Views group of the HOME tab to switch between Datasheet view and Design view in a query.	
	Type the criterion by which you want records selected in the *Criteria* box of the column by which records are to be selected.	
	In a field that displays check boxes, the criterion is either *Yes* or *No*.	
Entering Multiple Criteria to Select Records and Sorting a Query	More than one criterion entered in the same *Criteria* row in the query design grid is an AND statement, which means each criterion must be met for the record to be selected.	
	More than one criterion entered in *Criteria* rows one below the other is an OR statement, which means that any condition can be met for the record to be selected.	
	Choose *Ascending* or *Descending* in the *Sort* box for the column by which to sort query results in Design view.	
	Access sorts a query by column left to right. If necessary, position the field to be sorted first to the left of another field that is to be sorted.	

Topic	Key Concepts	Key Terms
Creating a Calculated Field in a Query and Previewing a Datasheet	A calculated field can be created in a query that generates values using a mathematical expression.	
	Use the Delete Columns and Insert Columns buttons in the Query Setup group of the QUERY TOOLS DESIGN tab to remove or add new columns in a query.	
	A calculated column is created by typing in the *Field* box a column heading, a colon (:), and then the mathematical expression.	
	Type a field name in a mathematical expression within square brackets.	
	Open the Property Sheet task pane to format a calculated field.	
	A table or query results datasheet should be previewed before printing to make adjustments to page orientation and/or margins.	

Multiple Choice

1. A single characteristic about a person, place, event, or item is referred to as a _____.
   a. record
   b. field
   c. field value
   d. table

2. All of the data for a single topic or subject is stored in a _____.
   a. field value
   b. record
   c. table
   d. field

3. A new record can be added in a datasheet or in this other object.
   a. report
   b. form
   c. database
   d. Print Preview

4. Tap or press _____ to move from field to field in a new record.
   a. Backspace
   b. F2
   c. Ctrl + Enter
   d. Tab

5. This icon in a datasheet or form indicates the record is being edited.
   a. asterisk
   b. funnel
   c. down-pointing arrow
   d. pencil

6. The Delete button is found in this group in the HOME tab.
   a. Records
   b. Sort & Filter
   c. Cells
   d. Find

7. Preferred object for adding and editing records.
   a. Print Preview
   b. query
   c. report
   d. form

8. This button moves to record 1 in a datasheet or form.
   a. First record
   b. Previous record
   c. Go to 1
   d. Home

9. Use this feature to move quickly to a specific record in a datasheet.
   a. Go to
   b. Find
   c. Next record
   d. Move

10. Use this option to change all occurrences of a field value automatically.
    a. Find
    b. Go to
    c. Find All
    d. Replace

11. Tap or click this arrow in a datasheet to hide records you do not want to view.
    a. Filter
    b. Remove
    c. Sort
    d. Delete

12. Tap or click this button to rearrange records alphabetically by the contents in the active field.
    a. First field
    b. Search
    c. Ascending
    d. Filter

13. Fields to be displayed in a query are added to this list box in the Simple Query Wizard.
    a. Available fields
    b. Selected fields
    c. Detail fields
    d. Summary fields

14. Results of a query display in a query results _____.
    a. datasheet
    b. form
    c. report
    d. design grid

15. Add a field list box for a table to the query window at this dialog box.
    a. Add fields
    b. Selected fields
    c. Show fields
    d. Show table

16. Use this button after you define a new query to view the selected data.
    a. Show table
    b. Show records
    c. Run
    d. View query

17. Type text by which to select records in a query in this box.
    a. Field
    b. Sort
    c. Format
    d. Criteria

18. This button switches between Datasheet view and the query design grid.
    a. View
    b. Property Sheet
    c. Show Table
    d. Run

19. Multiple conditions all of which must be met to select records is this type of statement.
    a. OR
    b. AND
    c. Combo
    d. Wildcard

20. Multiple conditions any of which can be met to select records is this type of statement.
    a. Combo
    b. AND
    c. Wildcard
    d. OR

21. Which of the following entries is a valid formula for a calculated field?
    a. Fine with Admin Fee: (Amount)+2.50
    b. Fine with Admin Fee; [Amount]+2.50
    c. Fine with Admin Fee: [Amount]+2.50
    d. Fine with Admin Fee; (Amount)+2.50

22. Change to landscape orientation at this tab.
    a. PRINT PREVIEW
    b. PAGE SETUP
    c. PAGE LAYOUT
    d. CREATE

Crossword Puzzle

ACROSS

2 Datasheet with fields from more than one table
5 Displays fields in a columnar layout
6 All of the data for one person or item
9 View in which structure or layout of object is defined
10 Adjusts column width to longest entry
12 Statement where any condition can be met
13 All of the data about one topic or subject
14 Box in grid to enter condition to select records

DOWN

1 Field by which datasheet is initially sorted
3 Group with buttons to insert or delete columns in query
4 Item that indicates field values are either *Yes* or *No*
7 Statement in which all conditions must be met
8 Action in a datasheet or form that requires confirmation
11 Property to change a calculated field to Currency

Matching

Match the term with the statement or definition.

_____ 1. Datasheet
_____ 2. Last name
_____ 3. Add new record
_____ 4. Gray bar at left edge of datasheet
_____ 5. Scroll through records
_____ 6. Find any part of a field
_____ 7. Temporarily hide records
_____ 8. Assists with building a query
_____ 9. Create a query using a blank grid
_____ 10. Specify condition to select records
_____ 11. Multiple conditions in same row
_____ 12. Format a calculated field

a. New (blank) record
b. Property Sheet task pane
c. Design view
d. Filter
e. Simple Query Wizard
f. Criteria
g. Table
h. AND statement
i. Record selector
j. Match list arrow
k. Field
l. Record Navigation and Search bar

Project 1 Adding, Editing, and Deleting Records

Individual

Deliverable: Locker Rentals database (continued in all projects)

1. Open **LockerRentals** and tap or click Enable Content.
2. Use Save As to *Save Database As* and name the copy **C12-Projects-LockerRentals-Your Name** in a new folder named *Ch12* within the ChapterProjectsWork folder on your USB flash drive.
3. Enable content in the copy of the database.
4. Open the Students table. Add a new record using StudentID *999999999*. Type your first and last names in the appropriate fields and leave all of the other fields blank. Close the table.
5. Open the Rentals table. Add the following new record and then close the table when finished.

   RentalNumber   Tab past this field as the number is assigned automatically by Access
   LockerNumber   Select *A104* in the drop-down list
   StudentID   Select *999999999 Your Name* in the drop-down list
   DateRented   **15sep2015**
   RentalPaid   *Yes*
   DatePaid   **15sep2015**

6. Open the Lockers table and make the following changes to the data:
   a. Change all occurrences of *City Center* to *Downtown Campus*.
   b. Change the level number from *3* to *2* for locker numbers B108, B109, and B110.
   c. Change the locker type from *Box Size* to *Half Size* for locker numbers A101 and A102.
7. Delete the records for locker numbers A106 and C106.
8. Close the Lockers table.
9. Open the Rentals form and add the following new record:

   RentalNumber   Tab past this field as the number is assigned automatically by Access
   LockerNumber   Select *A102* in the drop-down list
   StudentID   Select *101334799 Su-Lin Cheng* in the drop-down list
   DateRented   **15sep2015**
   RentalPaid   *Yes*
   DatePaid   **15sep2015**

10. Use the Find feature to locate the record in the Locker Rentals form for locker number B100 and then delete the record.
11. Use the Find feature to locate the record in the Locker Rentals form for locker number B106 and then edit the record to show the rental paid on September 16, 2015.
12. Close the Rentals form.
13. Leave the database open if you are continuing to Project 2; otherwise, close the database and submit the project to your instructor in the manner she or he has requested.

Project 2 Sorting and Filtering Data

Individual

Deliverable: Locker Rentals database and PDF of filtered table (continued from Project 1)

1. If necessary, open **C12-Projects-LockerRentals-Your Name** and enable content.
2. Open the Rentals table and sort the table by *LockerNumber* in ascending order.
3. Close the Rentals table, saving the changes to the table design.
4. Open the Lockers table and filter the table to show only the Downtown Campus lockers.
5. *Optional:* With the filtered Lockers table active, create a PDF of the table by completing the following steps:
   a. Tap or click the EXTERNAL DATA tab.
   b. Tap or click the PDF or XPS button in the Export group.

   c. At the Publish as PDF or XPS dialog box, navigate to the Ch12 folder within ChapterProjectsWork, select the current entry in the *File name* text box, type **C12–Project2–FilteredLockersTable–Your Name**, and then tap or click the Publish button.

   d. If necessary, close the PDF window and return to Access.

   e. Close the Export – PDF dialog box that asks if you want to save the export steps.

6. Close the Lockers table. Click No when prompted to save changes to the table design.

7. Leave the database open if you are continuing to Project 3; otherwise, close the database and submit the project to your instructor in the manner she or he has requested.

Project 3 Creating and Editing Queries

Individual

Deliverable: Locker Rentals database (continued from Project 2)

1. If necessary, open **C12–Projects–LockerRentals–Your Name** and enable content.

2. Create a query using the Simple Query Wizard using the following information:

   a. Choose the tables and fields in this order:

     Table: Lockers   Add all fields

     Table: LockerTypesAndFees   *RentalFee*

   b. Choose a detail query.

   c. Change the title to *LockerListWithFees*.

3. Switch to Design view for the LockerListWithFees query and sort the query by the *LockerNumber* field in ascending order.

4. Run the query.

5. Save and close the query.

6. Open the LockerListWithFees query and switch to Design view.

7. Enter criteria to select the lockers in the Allen Park campus building. Run the query. Use Save Object As to save the revised query as *AllenParkLockers* and then close the query.

8. Open the LockerListWithFees query and switch to Design view.

9. Enter criteria to select the lockers in the first level only of the Borden Avenue campus building. Run the query. Use Save Object As to save the revised query as *BordenAveL1Lockers* and then close the query.

10. Open the LockerRentals2015 query, switch to Design view, and delete the *DateRented* column.

11. Insert a new column to the left of the *RentalPaid* column and type the following formula in the *Field* box: **Rental Fee with Tax: [RentalFee]*1.05**

12. Format the *Rental Fee with Tax* column to Currency.

13. Run the query. Adjust the column width of the calculated column to Best Fit.

14. Save and close the query.

15. Open the LockerRentals2015 query. Switch to Design view. Enter criteria to select only those records where the rental fee has been paid. Run the query. Use Save Object As to save the revised query as *PaidLockerRentals2015* and then close the query.

16. Leave the database open if you are continuing to Project 4; otherwise, close the database and submit the project to your instructor in the manner she or he has requested.

Project 4 Previewing and Creating PDFs of Database Objects

Individual

Deliverable: PDFs of tables and queries in Locker Rentals database (continued from Project 3)

1. If necessary, open **C12–Projects–LockerRentals–Your Name** and enable content.

2. Open the Lockers table and display the table in the Print Preview window.

3. Tap or click the PDF or XPS button in the Data group of the PRINT PREVIEW tab. At the Publish as PDF or XPS dialog box, navigate to the Ch12 folder within ChapterProjectsWork and publish a PDF of the table, naming it **C12–Project4–LockersTable–Your Name**. If necessary, close the PDF window and return to Access. Close the Export – PDF dialog box.

4. Close the Print Preview window and then close the Lockers table.
5. Complete steps similar to Steps 2 to 4 to create a PDF for each of the following objects, changing the file names as noted.
   *Note: Consider clearing the **Open file after publishing** check box in the **Publish as PDF or XPS** dialog box if the box is checked.*

Object Name	Name for PDF
Rentals table	C12-Project4-RentalsTable-Your Name
AllenParkLockers	C12-Project4-AllenParkLockers-Your Name
BordenAveL1Lockers	C12-Project4-BordenAveL1Lockers-Your Name
LockerListWithFees	C12-Project4-LockerListWithFees-Your Name

6. Create a PDF for each of the following queries by completing steps similar to Steps 2 to 4, changing the page layout to landscape orientation and the margins to *Normal*.

Object Name	Name for PDF
LockerRentals2015	C12-Project4-LockerRentals2015-Your Name
PaidLockerRentals2015	C12-Project4-PaidLockerRentals2015-Your Name

7. Leave the database open if you are continuing to Project 5; otherwise, close the database and submit the project to your instructor in the manner she or he has requested.

Project 5 Modifying a Query to Add Criteria and a Calculation

Individual

Deliverable: PDF of query with calculated field (continued from Project 4)

1. If necessary, open **C12-Projects-LockerRentals-Your Name** and enable content.
2. Open the LockerListWithFees query and modify the query to create the query results datasheet shown in Figure 12.3. You determine the required calculated column *Field* expression as well as the criteria used to generate the query results datasheet. **Hint: The rental fee is for eight months**.
3. Create a PDF of the query, naming it **C12-Project5-AllenParkAndBordenAveLockers-Your Name** and saving it in the Ch12 folder within ChapterProjectsWork. Make sure the datasheet fits on one page.
4. Use Save Object As to save the revised query as *AllenParkAndBordenAveLockers*, then close the query and close the LockerRentals database.
5. Submit the project to your instructor in the manner she or he has requested.

LockerNumber	LockerType	CampusBuilding	Level	RentalFee	Rental Fee Per Month
A101	Half size	Allen Park	1	$70.00	$8.75
A102	Half size	Allen Park	1	$70.00	$8.75
A103	Full Size Regular	Allen Park	1	$80.00	$10.00
A104	Full Size Regular	Allen Park	1	$80.00	$10.00
A105	Half size	Allen Park	1	$70.00	$8.75
A107	Full Size Regular	Allen Park	2	$80.00	$10.00
A108	Full Size Regular	Allen Park	2	$80.00	$10.00
A109	Full Size Wide	Allen Park	2	$95.00	$11.88
A110	Full Size Wide	Allen Park	2	$95.00	$11.88
A115	Full Size Regular	Allen Park	2	$80.00	$10.00
A120	Full Size Regular	Allen Park	2	$80.00	$10.00
B100	Full Size Regular	Borden Avenue	1	$80.00	$10.00
B101	Box Size	Borden Avenue	1	$65.00	$8.13
B102	Box Size	Borden Avenue	1	$65.00	$8.13
B103	Full Size Regular	Borden Avenue	1	$80.00	$10.00
B104	Full Size Wide	Borden Avenue	1	$95.00	$11.88
B105	Full Size Wide	Borden Avenue	1	$95.00	$11.88
B106	Full Size Regular	Borden Avenue	1	$80.00	$10.00
B107	Box Size	Borden Avenue	1	$65.00	$8.13
B108	Full Size Wide	Borden Avenue	2	$95.00	$11.88
B109	Full Size Wide	Borden Avenue	2	$95.00	$11.88
B110	Box Size	Borden Avenue	2	$65.00	$8.13

Figure 12.3 Project 5 Query with Criteria and Calculated Column

Project 6 Sending Project Work to OneNote Notebook

Individual

Deliverable: New page in Shared OneNote notebook

1. Start OneNote and open the MyProjects notebook created in Chapter 4, Project 4.
2. Make Access the active section and add a new page titled *Chapter 12 Projects*.
3. For each PDF you created in projects you completed in this chapter, send the PDF to OneNote 2013, selecting the Chapter 12 Projects page in the Access section in the MyProjects notebook.
4. Close your MyProjects notebook in OneNote and close OneNote.
5. Submit the project to your instructor in the manner she or he has requested.

Chapter 13

Creating a Table, Form, and Report in Access

After successfully completing this chapter, you will be able to:

- Create a new database
- List and describe guidelines for creating tables
- Create a new table
- Assign a primary key
- Add fields to a table
- Modify field properties
- Create a lookup list
- Identify relationship types
- Edit a relationship
- Create and edit a form
- Create and edit a report
- Compact and repair a database
- Back up a database

Creating a new database involves carefully planning the tables and other objects that will be needed by the individuals who will use the database. All of the data that need to be collected and stored are gathered and analyzed for the best possible way to define and group the elements into logical units. Tables are created first because they are the basis for all other objects. Tables that need to be connected for queries, forms, or reports are joined in a relationship. Objects such as queries, forms, and reports are created after the tables and relationships are defined.

In Chapter 12 you examined an existing database and added and edited data in a table and form. You also created queries to select records for a variety of purposes. Now that you have seen how Access data interacts with objects, you are ready to build a new database. In this chapter you will learn how to create a new database, create a new table, assign a primary key, modify field properties, edit relationships, create a form, create a report, compact and repair a database, and create a backup of a database.

Creating a New Database File and Understanding Table Design Guidelines

Topic 13.1

The first step in the process of creating a database is to assign a name and storage location for the new database file. Because Access saves records automatically as data is added to a table, the file name and storage location are required in advance. Once the file is created, Access displays a blank table. Before you create a new table, you must carefully plan the fields and field names and identify a primary key. Although the tables you will create in this chapter have already been planned, the guidelines in Table 13.1 provide you with an overview of the table design process.

Table 13.1	Guidelines for Planning a New Table
Guideline	**Description**
Divide data into the smallest possible units	A field should be segmented into the smallest units of information to facilitate sorting and filtering. For example, a person's name could be split into three fields: first name, middle name, and last name.
Assign each field a name	Up to 64 characters can be used in a field name with a combination of letters, numbers, spaces, and some symbols. Database programmers prefer short field names with no spaces. A field to store a person's last name could be assigned the name *LName*, *LastName*, or *Last_Name*. Access provides the ability to enter a longer descriptive title for column headings in datasheets, forms, and reports that is separate from the field name.
Assign each field a data type	Data type refers to the type of information that will be entered as field values. Look at examples of data to help you determine the data type. By assigning the most appropriate data type, Access can verify data as it is being entered for the correct format or type of characters. For example, a field defined as a Number field will cause Access to reject alphabetic letters typed into the field. The most common data types are Short text, Number, Currency, Date/Time, and Yes/No. Data types are described in Table 13.2 in the next topic.
Decide the field to be used as a primary key	Each table should have one field that uniquely identifies a record such as a student number, receipt number, or email address. Access creates an ID field automatically in a blank datasheet that can be used if the table data does not have a unique identifier. In some cases, a combination of two or more fields is used as a primary key.
Include a common identifier field in a table that will be joined to another table	Data should not be duplicated in a database. For example, a book title would not be stored in both the Books table and the Sales table. Instead, the book title is stored in the Books table only and a book ID field in the Sales table is used to join the two tables in a relationship. You will learn more about relationships in a later topic.

 **Tutorial**

13.1 Creating a New Database; Creating a Table in Datasheet View

1. Start Access.
2. Tap or click *Blank desktop database* at the Access Start screen.

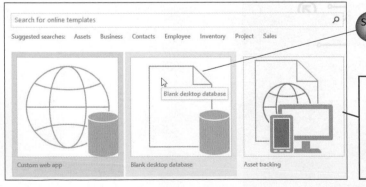

At the Access Start screen you can also choose to create a new database based on a template. Database templates have a set of predefined tables, queries, forms, and reports.

③ Type **13.1-UsedBooks-Your Name** in the *File Name* text box and then tap or click the Browse button (file folder icon).

④ At the File New Database dialog box, navigate to the CompletedTopicsByChapter folder on your USB flash drive, create a new folder named *Ch13*, double-tap or double-click to open the Ch13 folder, and then tap or click OK.

⑤ Tap or click the Create button.

Access creates the database file and opens a new table datasheet named *Table1* in the work area, as shown in Figure 13.1. You can create a new table using the blank datasheet.

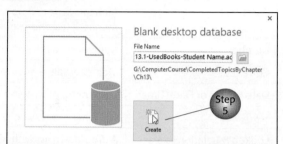

Quick
STEPS

Create a New Database
1. Start Access.
2. Tap or click *Blank desktop database*.
3. Type file name.
4. Tap or click Browse button.
5. Navigate to drive and/or folder location.
6. Tap or click OK.
7. Tap or click Create.

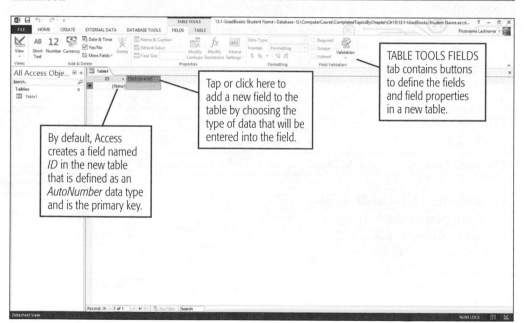

TABLE TOOLS FIELDS tab contains buttons to define the fields and field properties in a new table.

Tap or click here to add a new field to the table by choosing the type of data that will be entered into the field.

By default, Access creates a field named *ID* in the new table that is defined as an *AutoNumber* data type and is the primary key.

Figure 13.1 Blank table datasheet in new database file

⑥ Leave the blank table datasheet open for the next topic.

Each table in a database should contain information about one subject only. In this chapter you will create tables for a used textbook database that a student organization may use to keep track of students, textbooks, and sales. The three tables you will create in this chapter are described as follows:

Books: a table with the title, author, condition, and asking price for each book

Sales: a table that tracks each sale with the date, amount, and payment method

Students: a table with information about each student with textbooks for sale

App Tip

A database designer may use data models by creating sample forms and reports before creating tables to make sure all data elements are included in the table design.

SKILLS

Create a new table

Add a caption for
a field

Creating a New Table

A new table is created in a blank datasheet in Datasheet view by adding a column for each field. Begin by specifying the data type for a field and then typing the field name. Data types are described in Table 13.2. Once the fields have been defined, use the Save button on the QAT to assign the table a name.

Table 13.2	Field Data Types
Data Type	**Use for This Type of Field Value**
Short Text	Alphanumeric text up to 255 characters for names, identification numbers, telephone numbers, or other similar data
Number	Numeric data other than monetary values
Currency	Monetary values such as sales, costs, or wages
Date & Time or Date/Time	Dates or times that you want to verify, sort, select, or calculate
Yes/No	Data that can only be Yes or No or True or False
Lookup & Relationship or Lookup Wizard	A drop-down list with field values from another table or from a predefined list of items
Long Text or Rich Text	Alphanumeric text of more than 255 characters. Select Rich Text to enable formatting options such as font, font color, bold, and italic in the field values.
AutoNumber	A unique number generated by Access to be used as an identifier field
Hyperlink	Web addresses
Attachment	A file such as a picture attached to a field in a record
Calculated Field	A formula calculates the field value using data in other fields

① With the **13.1-UsedBooks-Your Name** database open and with the blank datasheet for *Table 1* open, tap or click the Date & Time button in the Add & Delete group of the TABLE TOOLS FIELDS tab.

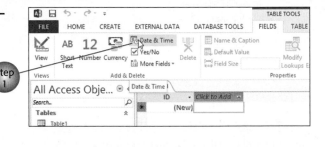

Choosing the most appropriate data type for a field is important for sorting, calculating, and verifying data. Access expects dates to be entered in the format m/d/y unless the region setting in the Control Panel is changed to another format.

② Type **SaleDate** and then tap or press Enter.

The *Click to Add* column opens the data type drop-down list for the next new field. Add a new field using either the *Click to Add* drop-down list or the buttons in the Add & Delete group of the TABLE TOOLS FIELDS tab.

③ Tap or click *Short Text* in the *Click to Add* drop-down list.

④ Type **BookID** and then tap or press Enter.

⑤ Tap or click *Currency*, type **Amount**, and then tap or press Enter.

App Tip

Access displays the field name as the column title in a datasheet unless an entry exists in the Caption property, in which case the caption text becomes the column title. (See Step 8.)

⑥ Tap or click *Short Text*, type **PayMethod**, and then tap or press Enter.

⑦ Tap or click *SaleDate* to select the field.

⑧ Tap or click the Name & Caption button in the Properties group of the TABLE TOOLS FIELDS tab.

The **Caption property** is used to type a descriptive title for a field that includes spaces between words or the full text of an abbreviated field name.

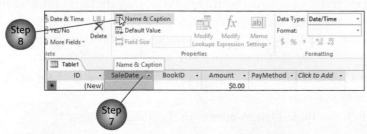

⑨ Tap or click in the *Caption* text box, type **Sale Date**, and then tap or click OK at the Enter Field Properties dialog box.

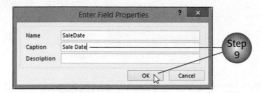

⑩ Tap or click to select the *Amount* field, tap or click the Name & Caption button, tap or click in the *Caption* text box, type **Sale Amount**, and then tap or click OK.

⑪ Slide or drag the right column boundary of the *Sale Amount* column until the entire column heading is visible.

⑫ Tap or click to select the *PayMethod* field, tap or click the Name & Caption button, tap or click in the *Caption* text box, type **Payment Method**, and then tap or click OK.

⑬ Slide or drag the right column boundary of the *Payment Method* column until the entire column heading is visible.

⑭ Tap or click the Save button on the QAT.

⑮ Type **Sales** in the *Table Name* text box in the Save As dialog box and then tap or press Enter or tap or click OK.

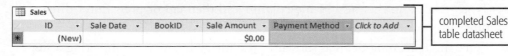

completed Sales table datasheet

⑯ Close the Sales table. Leave the database open for the next topic.

Topic 13.3

SKILLS

Create a new table in Design view

Assign a primary key

 Tutorial

13.3   Creating a Table in Design View

Creating a New Table in Design View and Assigning a Primary Key

A new table can be created in Design view in which fields are defined in rows in the top half of the work area. In the previous topic, the Sales table was created in Datasheet view, and Access automatically created the ID field and designated it as the primary key. In Design view, the *ID* field is not created for you. Recall that a primary key is a field that uniquely identifies each record in the table. Each new table should have a field assigned as the primary key. After creating the fields in the Design view window, assign the primary key and then save the table.

1. With the **13.1-UsedBooks-Your Name** database open, tap or click the CREATE tab.

2. Tap or click the Table Design button in the Tables group.

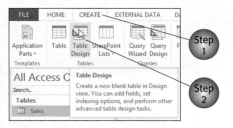

3. With the insertion point positioned in the first row of the *Field Name* column, type **StudentID** and then tap or press Enter.

4. With *Short Text* in the *Data Type* column, tap or press Enter to accept the default data type.

5. Tap or press Enter to move past the *Description* column and move down to the next row to start a new field.

Descriptions are optional entries. A description can be used to type additional information about a field or to enter instructions to end users who will see the description in the Status bar of a datasheet when the field is active.

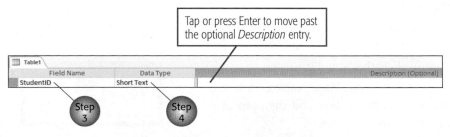

You can also use the Tab key to move to the next column in Design view.

6. Type **LName** in the *Field* Name column and then tap or press Enter three times to move to the next row.

7. Enter the remaining fields as shown in the image below by completing a step similar to Step 6.

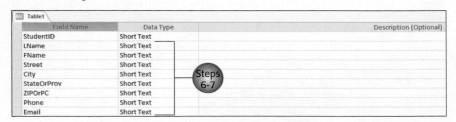

⑧ Tap or click to place the insertion point within the *StudentID* field name.

⑨ Tap or click the Primary Key button in the Tools group of the TABLE TOOLS DESIGN tab.

A key icon in the field selector bar (gray bar along left edge of *Field Name* column) indicates the field is designated as the primary key for the table.

⑩ Tap or click the Save button on the QAT, type **Students**, and then tap or press Enter or tap or click OK.

⑪ Close the Students table.

⑫ Tap or click the CREATE tab and then tap or click the Table Design button.

⑬ Create the first five fields in the new table using the default Short Text data type as follows:

> *BookID*
> *StudentID*
> *Title*
> *Author*
> *Condition*

⑭ Type **AskPrice** as the *Field Name* in the sixth row and then tap or press Enter.

⑮ Tap or click the *Data Type* list arrow and then tap or click *Currency* at the drop-down list.

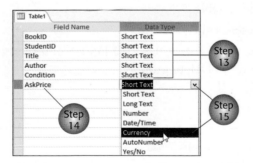

⑯ Tap or click to place an insertion point within the *BookID* field name and then tap or click the Primary Key button.

⑰ Tap or click the Save button on the QAT, type **Books**, and then tap or press Enter or tap or click OK.

⑱ Close the Books table. Leave the database open for the next topic.

Quick **STEPS**

Create a Table in Design View
1. Tap or click CREATE tab.
2. Tap or click Table Design button.
3. Type field name.
4. Tap or press Enter.
5. If necessary, change data type.
6. Tap or press Enter until new row is active.
7. Repeat Steps 3–6 until finished.
8. Assign primary key.
9. Save table.

Assign a Primary Key
1. If necessary, open table in Design view.
2. Tap or click in primary key field name.
3. Tap or click Primary Key button.
4. Save table.

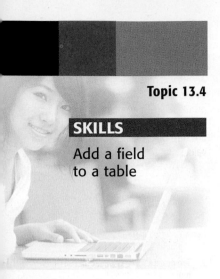

Adding Fields to an Existing Table

Open a table in Datasheet view and use the *Click to Add* column to add a new field, or make active a field in the datasheet and use the buttons in the TABLE TOOLS FIELDS tab to add a new field after the active field.

1. With the **13.1-UsedBooks-Your Name** database open, open the Books table.

2. Tap or click the *Click to Add* column heading and then tap or click *Currency* at the drop-down list.

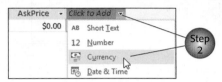

3. Type **StopPrice** and tap or press Enter.

4. Tap or click the top part of the View button in the Views group of the TABLE TOOLS FIELDS tab to switch to Design view.

5. Tap or click in the *Description* column in the *StopPrice* field row and type **Do not sell for lower than the student's stop price value**.

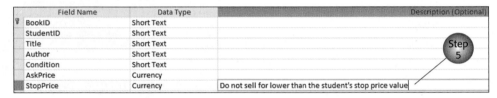

6. Save and close the Books table.

7. Open the Students table.

8. Tap or click to select the *Phone* field.

9. Tap or click the TABLE TOOLS FIELDS tab and then tap or click the Yes/No button in the Add & Delete group.

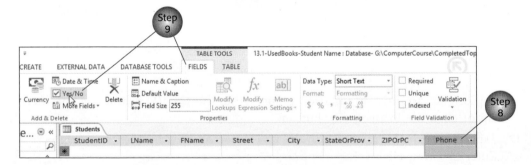

10. Type **DirectDeposit** and then tap or press Enter.

11. Slide or drag the right column boundary of the *DirectDeposit* field until the entire column heading is visible.

⑫ Save and close the Students table.

⑬ Open the Books table.

⑭ Tap or click to select the *StopPrice* field.

⑮ Look at the message that displays in the Status bar.

Notice that the text typed in the Description column for the field in Design view at Step 5 displays here. Description entries also display in the Status bar when a form is open that is based upon the same table.

Add a Field
1. Open table.
2. Tap or click *Click to Add* column.
3. Tap or click data type.
4. Type field name.
5. Tap or press Enter.
6. Save table.

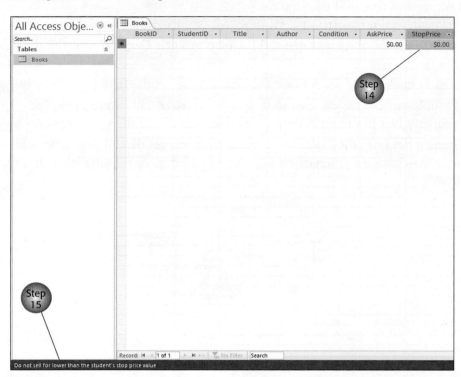

⑯ Close the Books table. Leave the database open for the next topic.

ALTERNATIVE method Open a table in Design view and type a new field name in the next available row, or make a field active and use the Insert Rows button in the Tools group of the TABLE TOOLS DESIGN tab to add a new field above the active field.

Beyond Basics

Deleting Fields

Generally, a field that contains data should not be deleted because deleting a field causes all field values to be removed from the database. However, if a field added to a table is considered unnecessary, remove the field by opening the table in either Datasheet view or Design view. In Datasheet view, make the field active and use the Delete button in the Add & Delete group of the TABLE TOOLS FIELDS tab. In Design view, make the field active and use the Delete Rows button in the TABLE TOOLS DESIGN tab.

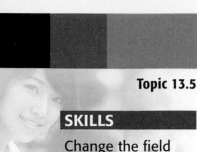

Topic 13.5

SKILLS

Change the field size

Add a default value

Add a caption in Design view

 **Tutorials**

13.5.1 Modifying Field Size, Caption, and Default Value Properties

13.5.2 Validating Field Entries

Options in the Field Properties pane vary by the field's data type. For example, a Date & Time field does not have the Field Size property.

Modifying Field Properties in Design View

Each field in a table has a set of field properties associated with the field. A **field property** is a single characteristic or attribute of a field. For example, the field name is a field property and the data type is another field property. Each field's properties can be modified to customize, format, or otherwise change the behavior of a field. The lower half of the work area of a table in Design view contains the **Field Properties pane** that is used to modify a field's properties other than the field name, data type, and description.

1. With the **13.1-UsedBooks-Your Name** database open, press and hold or right-click the Students table and then tap or click *Design view* at the shortcut menu.

2. Tap or click in the *StateOrProv* field name to select the field.

3. Double-tap, double-click, or slide or drag to select *255* in the *Field Size* property box in the Field Properties pane, type **2**, and then tap or press Enter.

Setting a field size for a state or province field ensures that all new field values use the two-character abbreviation for addressing letters or creating labels from the database.

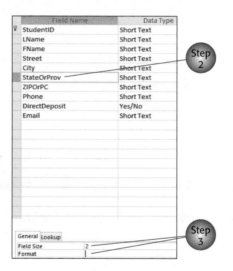

4. Tap or click in the *Default Value* property box, type **MI**, and then tap or press Enter.

Access automatically adds quotation marks to the text in a *Default Value* property box for a Short Text data type. Default value text is automatically entered in new records; the end user taps or presses Enter to accept the value, or types an alternative entry.

5. Tap or click in the *Caption* property box and then type **State or Province**.

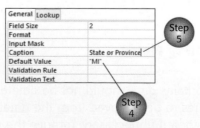

6. Tap or click in the *StudentID* field name to select the field, tap or click in the *Caption* property box, type **Student ID**, and then tap or press Enter.

7 Add the following caption properties by completing a step similar to Step 6.

Field Name	Caption
LName	**Last Name**
FName	**First Name**
Street	**Street Address**
ZIPOrPC	**ZIP or Postal Code**
Phone	**Telephone**
DirectDeposit	**Direct Deposit**
Email	**Email Address**

8 Save the table.

9 Tap or click the top part of the View button in the Views group to switch to Datasheet view.

10 Double-tap or double-click the right column boundary of column headings that are not entirely visible to best fit the column widths.

Notice that *MI* appears in the *State or Province* column by default.

11 Type your name and a fictitious student ID and address into a new record in the datasheet. If necessary, adjust column widths to show all data in all columns.

Modify a Field Property
1. Open table in Design view.
2. Tap or click in field name in top half of work area.
3. Tap, click, or select current value in field property box.
4. Type or select option from drop-down list.
5. Save table.

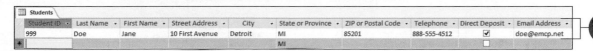

Students									
Student ID	Last Name	First Name	Street Address	City	State or Province	ZIP or Postal Code	Telephone	Direct Deposit	Email Address
999	Doe	Jane	10 First Avenue	Detroit	MI	85201	888-555-4512	☑	doe@emcp.net
*					MI			☐	

Steps 10-11

12 Close the table, saving the changes to the table layout. Leave the database open for the next topic.

ALTERNATIVE method

Field properties can also be changed for a table open in Datasheet view. Buttons in the Properties group of the TABLE TOOLS FIELDS tab can be used to enter a caption, default value, or field size. Modify or apply format, data validation, or required properties (see Beyond Basics) with buttons in the Formatting and Field Validation groups of the TABLE TOOLS FIELDS tab.

Beyond Basics

Formatting and Data Validation Field Properties

Other properties that are often changed for a field include:

- *Format.* Modifies the display of the field value. For example, a date can be formatted to display as a long date or medium date.

- *Validation.* Use a validation rule to enter an expression that is tested as each new field value is typed into a record. For example, the expression *>=5* in the *SaleAmount* field would ensure no amounts less than $5.00 are entered.

- *Required.* Select *Yes* to ensure that the field is not left blank in a new record. For example, a ZIP or Postal Code field should not be left blank.

Topic 13.6

SKILLS

Create a drop-down list for a field

SNAP Tutorial

13.6 Creating a Lookup Field

Creating a Lookup List

A **lookup list** is a drop-down list of field values that appears when a field is made active when new records are being added in a datasheet or form. The list entries can be a fixed list, or field values from another table can be shown in the list. A lookup list has many advantages, including consistency, accuracy, and efficiency when adding data in new records. Access provides the **Lookup Wizard** to assist with creating a lookup list's field properties.

1. With the **13.1-UsedBooks-Your Name** database open, press and hold or right-click the Books table and then tap or click *Design view* at the shortcut menu.

2. Tap or click in the *Condition* field name to select the field.

3. Tap or click the *Data Type* list arrow and then tap or click *Lookup Wizard* at the drop-down list.

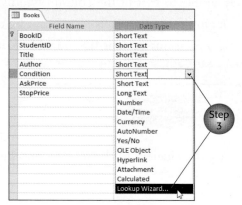

4. Tap or click *I will type in the values that I want* at the first Lookup Wizard dialog box and then tap or click Next.

5. Tap or click in the first blank row below *Col1* at the second Lookup Wizard dialog box and type **Excellent - Like new**.

6. Slide or drag the right column boundary approximately two inches to increase the column width.

7. Tap or click in the second row and type **Very Good - Minor wear to cover**.

8. Type the remaining entries in the list as shown in the image at right.

9. Tap or click Next.

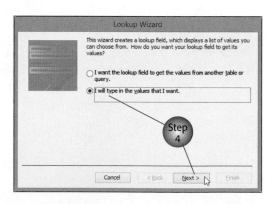

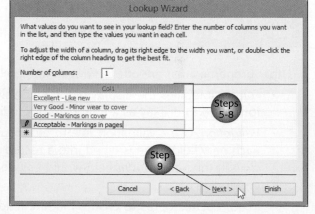

App Tip

You can also use the Tab or Down Arrow key to move to the next row in the column.

oops!

Tapped or pressed Enter by mistake? Tap or click the Back button to return to the list entries.

10. Tap or click Finish at the last Lookup Wizard dialog box.

11. Tap or click the Lookup tab in the Field Properties pane.

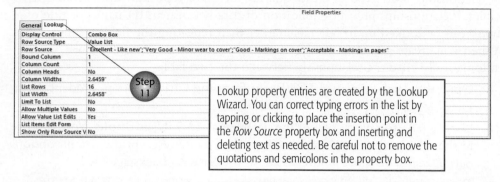

Field Properties

General Lookup

Display Control	Combo Box
Row Source Type	Value List
Row Source	"Excellent - Like new";"Very Good - Minor wear to cover";"Good - Markings on cover";"Acceptable - Markings in pages"
Bound Column	1
Column Count	1
Column Heads	No
Column Widths	2.6459"
List Rows	16
List Width	2.6458"
Limit To List	No
Allow Multiple Values	No
Allow Value List Edits	Yes
List Items Edit Form	
Show Only Row Source V	No

Step 11

> Lookup property entries are created by the Lookup Wizard. You can correct typing errors in the list by tapping or clicking to place the insertion point in the *Row Source* property box and inserting and deleting text as needed. Be careful not to remove the quotations and semicolons in the property box.

12. Save the table and then switch to Datasheet view.

13. Enter the following record as shown in the image below with the fictitious ID you created for yourself in the *StudentID* column. At the *Condition* field, tap or click the down-pointing arrow that appears and tap or click *Good - Markings on cover* in the drop-down list.

14. Adjust column widths as needed to show all data in each column.

Books

BookID	StudentID	Title	Author	Condition	AskPrice	StopPrice
DJ-1	999	Pride and Prejuidice	Austen	Good - Markings on cover	$15.00	$10.00
*					$0.00	$0.00

Steps 13-14

15. Close the table, saving the changes to the table layout.

16. Close the database.

App Tip

You can limit field values to only those items in the list by changing the *Limit To List* property to *Yes*.

Quick **STEPS**

Create a Lookup List
1. Open table in Design view.
2. Tap or click *Data Type* list arrow for field.
3. Tap or click *Lookup Wizard*.
4. Tap or click *I will type in the values that I want.*
5. Tap or click Next.
6. Type list entries in *Col1* column.
7. Adjust column width.
8. Tap or click Next.
9. Tap or click Finish.
10. Save table.

Beyond Basics

Creating a Lookup List with Field Values in Another Table

To create a lookup list in which the entries are field values from a field in another table, proceed through the dialog boxes in the Lookup Wizard as follows:

1. Select *I want the lookup field to get the values from another table or query.*

2. Select the table or query name that contains the field values you want to use in the list.

3. Move the fields you want displayed in the drop-down list from the *Available Fields* list box to the *Selected Fields* list box.

4. Select a field to sort the list entries, or leave empty for an unsorted list.

5. Adjust column widths as needed and/or uncheck *Hide key column*.

6. Select the field that contains the field value you want to store if more than one field was chosen at Step 3.

Topic 13.7

SKILLS

Identify a one-to-one relationship

Enforce referential integrity

Identify a one-to-many relationship

 **Tutorials**

13.7.1 Creating a Relationship between Two Tables

13.7.2 Editing a Relationship; Enforcing Referential Integrity; Viewing a Subdatasheet

13.7.3 Creating a One-to-One Relationship between Tables

13.7.4 Deleting a Relationship; Printing a Relationships Report

Displaying and Editing a Relationship

A relationship allows you to create queries, forms, or reports with fields from two tables. Relationships prevent duplication of data because an ID, name, or title of a book can be looked up in one table rather than repeating the field in other tables. When you create a lookup list that looks up field values in another table, Access automatically creates a relationship between the two tables.

1. Open the database named *UsedBooks* from the Ch13 folder in Student_Data_Files.

2. Use Save As to save a copy of the database as **13.7-UsedBooks-Your Name** in the Ch13 folder in CompletedTopicsbyChapter. Accept the default options *Save Database As* and *Access Database* at the Save As Backstage view.

3. Tap or click the Enable Content button in the SECURITY WARNING message bar.

This file is similar to the database you have been working on in this chapter but with the Books table modified, additional lookup lists, and with 10 records added to each table.

4. Open the Books table, review the datasheet, and then close the table.

5. Open the Sales table, review the datasheet, and then close the table.

6. Open the Students table and change *Doe* in the last record of the *Last Name* field to your last name.

7. Change *Jane* in the last record of the *First Name* field to your first name and then close the table.

8. Tap or click the DATABASE TOOLS tab and tap or click the Relationships button in the Relationships group.

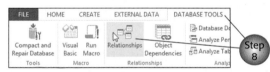

A field list box for each table is located in the Relationships window. A black join line connecting two table field list boxes indicates a relationship. Observe that each line connects a common field name.

9. Tap or click to select the black join line that connects the Books table field list box to the Sales table field list box, and then tap or click the Edit Relationships button in the Tools group of the RELATIONSHIP TOOLS DESIGN tab.

In the Edit Relationships dialog box that appears, *One-To-One* is shown in the *Relationship Type* section. A **one-to-one relationship** means that the two tables are joined on the primary key in each table. (*BookID* displays a key next to the field in each table field list box.) In this type of relationship, only one record can exist for the same *BookID* in each table.

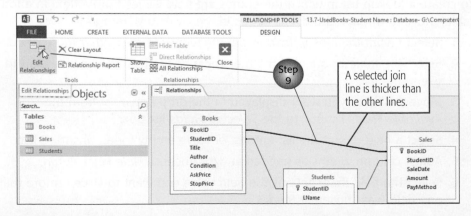

10 Tap or click to insert a check mark in the *Enforce Referential Integrity* check box and tap or click OK.

Turning on **Enforce Referential Integrity** means that a record in Books is entered first before a record with a matching *BookID* is entered in Sales. Books is the left table name below *Table/Query* and Sales is the right table name below *Related Table/Query*. The table below *Table/Query* is the one for which referential integrity is applied—the table in which new records are entered first. The table shown at the left is also referred to as the **primary table** (the table in which the joined field is the primary key and in which new records should be entered first).

11 Tap or click to select the black join line that connects the Books table field list box to the Students table field list box, and then tap or click the Edit Relationships button.

12 Tap or click to insert a check mark in the *Enforce Referential Integrity* check box and then tap or click OK.

A **one-to-many relationship** occurs when the common field used to join the two tables is the primary key in only one table (the primary table). *One* student can have *many* textbooks for sale. In this instance, a record must first be entered into Students (primary table) before a record with a matching student ID can be entered into Books (related table). A field added to a related table that is not a primary key and is included for the purpose of creating a relationship is called a **foreign key**.

13 Tap or click the Close button in the Relationships group. Leave the database open for the next topic.

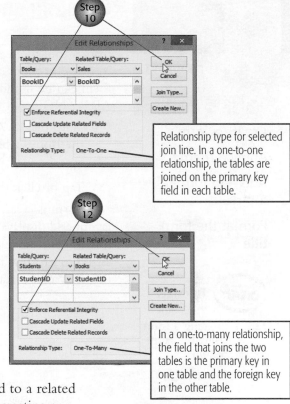

Step 10

Relationship type for selected join line. In a one-to-one relationship, the tables are joined on the primary key field in each table.

Step 12

In a one-to-many relationship, the field that joins the two tables is the primary key in one table and the foreign key in the other table.

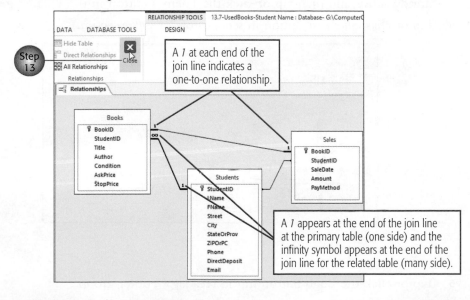

Step 13

A *1* at each end of the join line indicates a one-to-one relationship.

A *1* appears at the end of the join line at the primary table (one side) and the infinity symbol appears at the end of the join line for the related table (many side).

Quick
STEPS

Display Relationships
1. Tap or click DATABASE TOOLS tab.
2. Tap or click Relationships button.

Enforce Referential Integrity
1. Display Relationships.
2. Tap or click to select black join line.
3. Tap or click Edit Relationships button.
4. Tap or click *Enforce Referential Integrity* check box.
5. Tap or click OK.

App Tip

A one-to-many relationship is the most common type of relationship in databases.

Beyond Basics   **Creating Relationships**

To create a new relationship, slide or drag the common field name from the primary table field list box to the related table field list box. Always slide or drag starting from the primary table. If you need to add a table field list box to the window, use the Show Table button in the Relationships group.

Topic 13.8

SKILLS

Create a form

Apply a theme

Add and format
a picture

Format the form
title

 **Tutorials**

13.8.1 Creating a Form
Using the Form
Button

13.8.2 Formatting a
Form

**App
Tip**

Buttons to switch between
views are at the right end of
the Status bar.

Creating and Editing a Form

The Forms group of the CREATE tab includes buttons to create forms ranging from a tool to create a simple form that adds all of the fields in the selected table, to tools for more complex forms that work with multiple tables. Once created, a form can be modified using buttons in the FORM LAYOUT TOOLS DESIGN, ARRANGE, and FORMAT tabs.

1. With the **13.7-UsedBooks–Your Name** database open, tap or click to select the Books table name in the Navigation pane if Books is not already selected.

2. Tap or click the CREATE tab.

3. Tap or click the Form button in the Forms group.

A form is created with all of the fields in the selected table arranged in a vertical layout and displayed in Layout view. **Layout view** is the view in which you edit a form's structure and appearance using buttons in the FORM LAYOUT TOOLS tabs. **Form view** is the view in which data is viewed, entered, and updated and is the view that is active when a form is opened from the Navigation pane.

4. Tap or click the FORM LAYOUT TOOLS DESIGN tab if the tab is not already active, and then tap or click the Themes button in the Themes group.

5. Tap or click *Slice* (last option in second row of *Office* section).

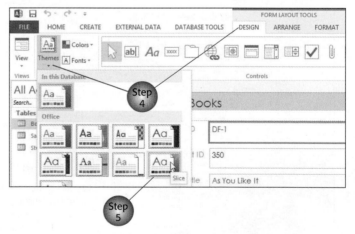

6. Tap or click the Logo button in the Header / Footer group.

7 At the Insert Picture dialog box, navigate to the Ch13 folder in Student_Data_Files and double-tap or double-click the file named *Textbooks*.

The picture is inserted into the selected logo **control object** near the top left of the form. A control object is a rectangular content placeholder in a form or report. Each control object can be selected and edited to modify the appearance of the content.

Control objects are placeholders for pictures, text, field names, and field values.

8 With the logo control object still selected, tap or click the Property Sheet button in the Tools group.

9 Tap or click in the *Size Mode* property box in the Property Sheet task pane with the Format tab active, tap or click the down-pointing arrow that appears, and then tap or click *Zoom*.

The Zoom *Size/Mode* property fits the picture to the control object size maintaining proportions.

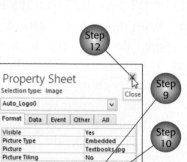

10 Select the current value in the *Width* property box and type **1.75**.

11 Select the current value in the *Height* property box and type **1.25**.

You can also slide or drag the orange border on a selected control object to resize the object.

12 Close the Property Sheet task pane.

13 Tap or click the *Books* title to select the control object.

An orange border around the control object indicates the object is selected.

14 Tap or click the FORM LAYOUT TOOLS FORMAT tab.

15 Tap or click the Font Size button arrow and then tap or click *48* at the drop-down list.

Quick STEPS

Create a Form
1. Tap or click to select table or query in Navigation pane.
2. Tap or click CREATE tab.
3. Tap or click Form button.
4. Modify as required.
5. Tap or click Save button.
6. Type form name.
7. Tap or click OK.

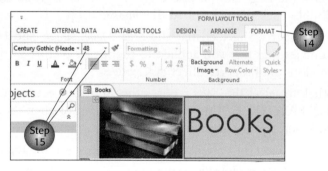

16 Tap or click the Save button in the QAT and then tap or click OK at the Save As dialog box to accept the default form name *Books*.

17 Close the Books form.

18 Double-tap or double-click the Books form in the Navigation pane to reopen the form, scroll through a few records, and then close the form. Leave the database open for the next topic.

Creating a Form Using the Form Wizard

Use the Form Wizard button in the Forms group of the CREATE tab to create a form in which you have control over the fields to include and over the form layout. Fields from related tables can be arranged in a columnar, tabular, datasheet, or justified layout.

Topic 13.9

SKILLS

Create a report

Resize control objects

 Tutorials

13.9.1 Creating and Editing a Report

13.9.2 Modifying a Report

App Tip

Reports use the same theme as forms so that all objects have a consistent look.

oops!

Textbooks image not shown? Access defaults to the last folder used at the Insert Picture dialog box. If necessary, navigate to the Ch13 folder in Student_Data_Files.

Creating, Editing, and Viewing a Report

A report is created using techniques similar to those used to create a form. The Reports group of the CREATE tab has a Report tool similar to the Form tool. Other buttons in the Reports group include options to design a report from a blank page, create a report using the Report Wizard, or generate mailing labels using the Label Wizard. Modify a report with buttons in the REPORT LAYOUT TOOLS tabs. Change the page layout options for printing purposes with buttons in the REPORT LAYOUT TOOLS PAGE SETUP tab.

1. With the **13.7-UsedBooks-Your Name** database open, tap or click to select the Sales table name in the Navigation pane.

2. Tap or click the CREATE tab and then tap or click the Report button in the Reports group.

A report is created with all of the fields in the Sales table arranged in a tabular layout. By default, Access includes the current date and time, page numbering, and totals for numeric fields.

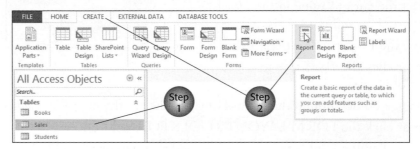

3. Tap or click the Logo button in the Header / Footer group and then double-tap or double-click the file named *Textbooks*.

4. Open the Property Sheet, change the *Size/Mode*, *Width*, and *Height* properties to the same settings that you applied to the form's picture in the previous topic, and then close the Property Sheet task pane.

5. Tap or click to select the *Sales* report title control object, tap or click the REPORT LAYOUT TOOLS FORMAT tab, tap or click the Font Size button arrow, and then tap or click *48*.

6. Tap or click to select the current date control object near the top right of the report.

7. Slide or drag the right border of the control object left until the control ends just left of the vertical dashed line that extends the height of the report.

The vertical dashed line indicates a page break. Resize control objects so that all objects are to the left of the vertical dashed line to fit on one page.

8. Tap or click to select the *Book ID* column heading control object.

9. Slide or drag the right border of the control object left approximately one-half inch to resize the object to the approximate width shown in the image at right.

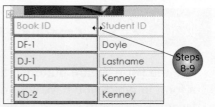

Notice that resizing a column heading control object resizes the entire column.

10 Select the *Page 1 of 1* control object and resize the control until the right border is just left of the vertical dashed line.

11 Select the control object with the total at the bottom of the *Sale Amount* column and slide or drag the bottom border of the control until the value is entirely visible within the object.

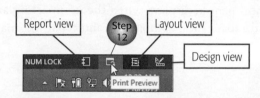

12 Tap or click the Print Preview button near the right end of the Status bar. Compare your report with the one shown in Figure 13.2. If necessary, switch to Layout view, resize control objects, and then switch back to Print Preview.

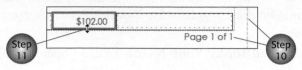

Figure 13.2 Sales report for Topic 13.9

13 Tap or click the Close Print Preview button in the Close Preview group.

14 Tap or click the Report View button near the right end of the Status bar.

Report view is the view in which a report is opened from the Navigation pane. Report view is used for viewing data on the screen; the report cannot be edited in Report view.

15 Close the Sales report, saving changes to the report design and accepting the default report name of *Sales*. Leave the database open for the next topic.

Grouping and Sorting a Report

The Group & Sort button in the Grouping & Totals group of the REPORT LAYOUT TOOLS DESIGN tab toggles on and off the Group, Sort, and Total pane at the bottom of the work area. Turn on the pane and use the Add a group and Add a sort buttons to change the arrangement of records in the report.

---

oops!

Having difficulty resizing controls using touch? Open the Property Sheet for a selected control and change the *Width* and *Height* values. Use *.25* for the *Height* of the column total control.

Create a Report

1. Tap or click to select table or query in Navigation pane.
2. Tap or click CREATE tab.
3. Tap or click Report button.
4. Modify as required.
5. Tap or click Save button.
6. Type report name.
7. Tap or click OK.

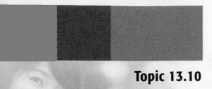

Topic 13.10

Compact and repair a database

Create a backup copy of a database

SNAP Tutorial

13.10 Compacting, Repairing, and Backing Up a Database

If a database is shared, make sure no one else is using the database before starting a compact and repair operation.

Compacting, Repairing, and Backing Up a Database

A database file becomes larger and fragmented over time as new records are added, edited, and deleted. The file size for the database may become larger than is necessary if the space previously used by records that have since been deleted is not compacted. The compacting process eliminates unused space in the file. Backing up a database file should be done regularly for historical record keeping and data loss prevention purposes.

1. With the **13.7-UsedBooks-Your Name** database open, tap or click the FILE tab.

2. At the Info tab Backstage view, tap or click the **Compact & Repair Database button**.

Access closes all objects and the Navigation pane during a compact and repair routine. The Navigation pane redisplays when the compacting and repairing is complete. For larger database files, compacting and repairing may take a few moments to process.

3. Tap or click the FILE tab and then tap or click Options.

At the Access Options dialog box, you can set the database file to compact and repair each time the file is closed.

4. Tap or click *Current Database* in the left pane of the Access Options dialog box.

5. Tap or click to insert a check mark in the *Compact on Close* check box in the *Application Options* section.

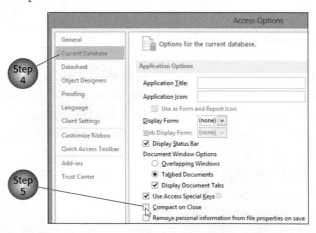

⑥ Tap or click OK to close the Access Options dialog box.

⑦ Tap or click OK at the message box that says the database must be closed and reopened for the option to take effect.

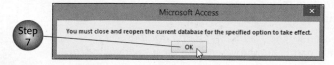

⑧ Tap or click the FILE tab and tap or click Save As.

⑨ At the Save As Backstage view, tap or click *Back Up Database* in the *Advanced* section of the Save Database As pane.

⑩ Tap or click the Save As button.

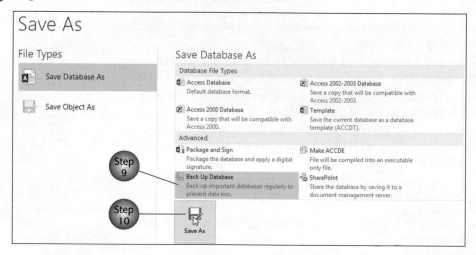

⑪ Tap or click the Save button at the Save As dialog box.

By default, the backup copy of the database is saved in the same folder as the current database and the file name is the same database file name with the current date added after an underscore at the end of the name, for example, 13.7-UsedBooks-Your Name_*currentdate*.

⑫ Close the database.

Encrypting a Database with a Password

Assign a password to a database to prevent unauthorized access to confidential data stored in a database. A database has to be opened in exclusive mode to assign a password. To do this, close the current database and then display the Open dialog box. Navigate to the location of the database, select the database file, and then use the down-pointing arrow on the Open button to choose *Open Exclusive*. Enable content and then display the Info tab Backstage view. Tap or click the Encrypt with Password button and then type the password twice in the Set Database Password dialog box.

Concepts Review

Topic	Key Concepts	Key Terms
Creating a New Database File and Understanding Table Design Guidelines	Access database files require that you provide the name and file storage location before creating data. To create a new database file, choose *Blank desktop database* at the Access Start screen, type the file name, and browse to the desired drive and/or folder. Access displays a blank table datasheet in a new database. Planning a new table involves several steps, some of which include: dividing the data into fields, assigning each field a name, assigning each field a data type, deciding the field that will be the primary key, and including a common field to join a table to another table if necessary.	
Creating a New Table	In a blank table datasheet, begin a new field by first selecting the data type and then typing the field name. Choose the data type from the *Click to Add* drop-down list or by choosing a data type button in the Add & Delete group of the TABLE TOOLS FIELDS tab. An entry in the Caption property is used as a descriptive title that becomes the column heading for a field in a datasheet. Several data types are available such as Short Text, Number, Currency, and Date & Time. A data type is selected based upon the type of field value that will be entered into records. Save a table by tapping or clicking the Save button on the QAT and then entering a name for the table.	Caption property
Creating a New Table in Design View and Assigning a Primary Key	In Design view, a new table is created by defining fields in rows in the top half of the work area. Type a field name in the first row in the *Field Name* column and then specify the data type using the data type drop-down list. An optional description can be added for a field with additional information about the purpose of the field or with instructions on what to type into the field. Once the fields are defined, assign the primary key by placing an insertion point anywhere within the field name and then tapping or clicking the Primary Key button in the Tools group of the TABLE TOOLS DESIGN tab.	
Adding Fields to an Existing Table	Open a table and use the *Click to Add* column to add a new field to the end of an existing table datasheet. Select a column in a datasheet and use the buttons in the Add & Delete group of the TABLE TOOLS FIELDS tab to add a new field to the right of the selected field.	
Modifying Field Properties in Design View	Each field in a table has a set of associated field properties. A field property is a single characteristic or attribute of a field that customizes, formats, or changes the behavior of the field. The lower half of the Design view window is the Field Properties pane in which properties for a selected field are modified. The Field Size property is used to limit the number of characters that can be entered into a field. The Default Value property is used to specify a field value that is automatically entered in the field in new records. Other field properties that are often modified are the *Format*, *Validation*, and *Required* field properties.	Field property Field Properties pane

Topic	Key Concepts	Key Terms
Creating a Lookup List	A lookup list is a drop-down list of items that displays when a field is made active in a datasheet or form.	Lookup list
	Items in the lookup list can be predefined or extracted from one or more fields in another table.	Lookup Wizard
	The Lookup Wizard presents a series of dialog boxes to help create the field properties for a lookup list field.	
	Create a predefined list of entries by choosing *I will type in the values that I want* at the first Lookup Wizard dialog box.	
	Type the list entries in the *Col1* column and adjust the column width as needed at the second Lookup Wizard dialog box.	
Displaying and Editing a Relationship	A relationship is when two tables are joined together on a common field.	One-to-one relationship
	Black join lines connecting a common field between two table field list boxes indicates a relationship has been created.	Enforce Referential Integrity
	A one-to-one relationship means that the two tables are joined on the primary key in each table.	Primary table
	Enforce Referential Integrity causes Access to check that new records are entered into the primary table first before records with a matching field value can be entered into the related table.	One-to-many relationship
	A primary table is the table in which the common field is the primary key and into which new records must first be entered. The primary table name is shown below *Table/Query* in the Edit Relationships dialog box.	Foreign key
	In a one-to-many relationship, the common field used to join the tables is the primary key in only one table (the primary table).	
	A field added to a table that is not a primary key and is added for the purpose of creating a relationship is called a foreign key.	
Creating and Editing a Form	The Form button in the Forms group of the CREATE tab creates a new form with all fields in the selected table or query arranged in a columnar layout.	Layout view
	Layout view is the view in which you modify the form's structure and appearance using buttons in the three FORM LAYOUT TOOLS tabs.	Form view
	Form view is the view in which a form is displayed when opened from the Navigation pane and is used to add, edit, and delete data.	Control object
	The Themes button is used to change the color scheme and fonts for a form.	
	Use the Logo button to choose a picture to display in the Logo control object near the top left of the form.	
	A control object is a rectangular placeholder for content.	
	Each control object can be selected and modified to change the appearance of the control's content.	
	Open the Property Sheet task pane to make changes to a selected picture's appearance.	
	Change the *Size Mode* property of a picture to *Zoom* to fit the content to the object size and with the height and width proportions maintained.	
	A control object can be resized by changing the values for the *Width* and *Height* in the Property Sheet task pane.	

continued....

Topic	Key Concepts	Key Terms
Creating, Editing, and Viewing a Report	The Report tool in the Reports group of the CREATE tab creates a report with all of the fields in the selected table or query in a tabular arrangement.	Report view
	Buttons in the REPORT LAYOUT TOOLS PAGE SETUP tab are used to change page layout options for printing purposes.	
	Access creates a current date and time control, a page number control, and a total control for each numeric column in a new report.	
	The vertical dashed line in a report indicates a page break.	
	Resizing a column heading control object resizes the entire column.	
	Report view is the view in which a report is displayed when opened from the Navigation pane and is the view that displays the data in the report.	
Compacting, Repairing, and Backing Up a Database	The compact and repair process eliminates unused space in the database file.	Compact & Repair Database button
	Use the Compact & Repair Database button at the Info tab Backstage view to perform a compact and repair operation.	
	During the compact and repair routine, Access closes all objects and the Navigation pane.	
	Turn on the *Compact on Close* option at the Access Options dialog box with *Current Database* selected.	
	Display the Save As Backstage view and choose *Back Up Database* in the *Advanced* section to create a backup copy of the current database.	
	Access adds the current date after an underscore character to the end of the current database file name when a backup is created.	

Multiple Choice

1. Choose this option from the Access Start screen to create a new database file.
   a. New database
   b. New blank database
   c. File New Database
   d. Blank desktop database
2. Which of the following is *not* a guideline for planning a new table?
   a. Divide data into the smallest unit
   b. Determine the number of records
   c. Assign each field a data type
   d. Decide the primary key
3. In a blank table datasheet, the data type can be selected from this drop-down list.
   a. Click to Add
   b. Data Type
   c. New Field
   d. Add & Delete
4. This property stores a descriptive title for a field that is used as the column heading in a datasheet.
   a. Long text
   b. Rich text
   c. Title
   d. Caption

5. An *ID* field that is assigned the primary key is *not* created automatically by Access when you create a table in this view.
   a. Datasheet view
   b. Design view
   c. Layout view
   d. New Table view
6. This icon appears in the field selector bar next to the field designated as the primary key.
   a. check mark
   b. asterisk
   c. key
   d. folder
7. New fields can be added to a table in this view.
   a. Datasheet view
   b. Layout view
   c. Report view
   d. New Table view
8. Assign a new field this data type to display a check box in the datasheet.
   a. Short Text
   b. Yes/No
   c. Rich Text
   d. Attachment

9. This field property is used to automatically insert a field value in new records.
   a. Format
   b. Field Size
   c. Required
   d. Default Value

10. Use this property to limit the number of characters in a field.
    a. Field Size
    b. Format
    c. Default Value
    d. Required

11. This is the name for a drop-down list that appears in a field in a datasheet or form.
    a. option list
    b. lookup list
    c. field list
    d. values list

12. This property contains the list entries and is used to correct typing errors after the list has been created.
    a. Row Source
    b. Bound Column
    c. Caption
    d. Display Control

13. In this relationship type, the common field that joins the tables is the primary key in each table.
    a. one-to-one relationship
    b. one-to-many relationship
    c. enforce referential integrity relationship
    d. foreign key relationship

14. In this type of relationship the common field that joins the tables is the primary key in only one of the two tables.
    a. foreign key relationship
    b. one-to-one relationship
    c. one-to-many relationship
    d. referential integrity relationship

15. This is the view in which a form is displayed after the form is generated with the Form button.
    a. Form view
    b. Datasheet view
    c. Layout view
    d. Design view

16. Use this button to insert a picture in the control object near the top left of a new form.
    a. Insert Picture
    b. Logo
    c. Insert Graphic
    d. Pictures

17. Which of the following is *not* a control object added to a report by Access for a report generated using the Report tool?
    a. Page numbering
    b. Current date and time
    c. Numeric column totals
    d. Table or query name

18. This is the view in which a report opens from the Navigation pane.
    a. Print Preview
    b. Design view
    c. Report view
    d. Layout view

19. Use this option to remove unused disk space from a database file.
    a. Back Up Database
    b. Compact & Repair Database
    c. Defragment Database
    d. Encrypt Database

20. This option at the Save As Backstage view saves a copy of the current database with the current date added to the end of the file name.
    a. Encrypt Database
    b. Defragment Database
    c. Back Up Database
    d. Compact & Repair Database

Crossword Puzzle

ACROSS

2 Rectangular placeholder for form or report content
3 Indicated by a black join line
4 Field property to limit *State* field to two characters
6 Field property for descriptive title for a field
12 Field property to add *MI* to *State* field in new records
13 Field that is not a primary key added to a table to create a relationship
14 REPORT LAYOUT TOOLS tab for changing page layout options

DOWN

1 Process that eliminates unused disk space
5 Property Sheet option to fit a picture to object size
7 Vertical dashed line in a report
8 Term for a drop-down list
9 Select data type for new field in this drop-down list
10 Button to assign the field that uniquely identifies each record
11 Backstage view to make a backup copy of file

Matching

Match the term with the statement or definition.

_____ 1. Create a new database file
_____ 2. Tab with data type buttons for new table
_____ 3. View in which fields are defined in rows
_____ 4. Column to tap or click to add a new field
_____ 5. Lower half of Design view
_____ 6. Single characteristic or attribute of a field
_____ 7. Assists with creating a drop-down list
_____ 8. Table in relationship in which records must be entered first
_____ 9. View in which data is entered and updated in a form
_____ 10. Button to add picture to a form or report
_____ 11. Removes unused disk space
_____ 12. Save copy of current database

a. Click to Add
b. Back Up Database
c. Primary table
d. Lookup Wizard
e. Logo
f. Form view
g. Blank desktop database
h. Field Properties pane
i. Compact on Close
j. TABLE TOOLS FIELDS tab
k. Field property
l. Design view

Project 1 Creating a New Database File and Creating Tables

Individual

Deliverable: Home listing database (continued in Project 2)

1. Create a new blank desktop database file named **C13-Project1-Listings-Your Name** in a new folder named *C13* in the ChapterProjectsWork folder on your USB flash drive.

2. Add the following fields in the blank *Table1* datasheet in addition to the default *ID* field:

Field Name	Data Type	Caption
SoldDate	Date & Time	Date Sold
SalePrice	Currency	Sale Price
Commission	Number	Commission Rate
SellingAgent	Short Text	Selling Agent

3. Adjust column widths so that all column headings are entirely visible.

4. Save the table as *Sales* and then close the table.

5. Create a new table in Design view using the following field names and data types:

Field Name	Data Type
ListingID	Short Text
AgentID	Short Text
StreetAdd	Short Text
ClientLName	Short Text
ClientFName	Short Text
ListDate	Date/Time
AskPrice	Currency
HomeType	Short Text

6. Assign *ListingID* as the primary key field.

7. Save the table naming it *Listings* and then close the table.

8. Create a third table in the database using the following field names. All of the fields are the Short Text data type. You decide the view in which to create the table.

   Field Name
   AgentID (assign this field as the primary key)
   LName
   FName

9. Save the table as *Agents* and then close the table.

10. Leave the database open if you are continuing to Project 2; otherwise, close the database and submit the project to your instructor in the manner she or he has requested.

Project 2 Adding Fields, Modifying Field Properties, and Creating a Lookup List

Individual

Deliverable: Home listing database and PDFs of tables (continued from Project 1)

1. If necessary, open **C13-Project1-Listings-Your Name** and enable content.

2. Open the Listings table, make *ClientFName* the active field, and add a new Short Text field named *ContactPhone*.

3. Switch to Design view and create a drop-down list for the *HomeType* field with the following list entries. Make *Single family home* the default value for the field.
   Single family home
   Condominium
   Townhouse
   Duplex
   Triplex
   Fourplex
   Other

4. Switch to Datasheet view, adjust the column widths as needed so that all column headings are entirely visible, and then close the table, savings changes to the layout.

5. Open the Sales table and then add a new Yes/No field named *SplitComm* to the end of the table. Add a caption to the field with the text *Split Commission?* and then adjust the column width to show the entire column heading.

6. Switch to Design view, make *Commission* the active field, and then change the following field properties:
   a. Type **.05** as the Default Value.
   b. Change the Field Size to *Double*.
   c. Change the Decimal Places to *2*.
   d. Change the Format to *Percent*.

7. Change the field name of the *ID* field to *ListingID* and then change the data type from *AutoNumber* to *Short Text*.

8. Save and close the Sales table.

9. Add the following captions to the fields in the Agents table and then adjust column widths in Datasheet view so that all column headings are entirely visible. Close the table, saving changes to the layout.

Field Name	Caption
AgentID	Agent ID
LName	Agent Last Name
FName	Agent First Name

10. Add a new record in the Agents table with your name and with *10* as the *AgentID*.

11. Add the following record in the Listings table:

ListingID	2015-1	*ContactPhone*	800-555-3225
AgentID	10	*ListDate*	03/15/2015
StreetAdd	98 First Street	*AskPrice*	87500
ClientLName	Jones	*HomeType*	Condominium
ClientFName	Marion		

12. Add the following new record to the Sales table:

ListingID	2015-1	*Commission Rate*	5.00%
Date Sold	03/22/2015	*SellingAgent*	10
Sale Price	82775	*Split Commission?*	Yes

13. Display each table datasheet in Print Preview and then create a PDF of the datasheet using the following file names and saving in the Ch13 folder in ChapterProjectsWork:

Table	Name for PDF
Agents	C13-Project2-Agents-Your Name
Listings (landscape; normal margins)	C13-Project2-Listings-Your Name
Sales (normal margins)	C13-Project2-Sales-Your Name

14. Close the **C13-Project1-Listings-Your Name** database.

15. Submit the project to your instructor in the manner she or he has requested.

Project 3 Editing Relationships, Creating a Form and a Report

Individual

Deliverable: Home listing database and PDFs of new objects (continued in Projects 4 and 5)

1. Open **HomeListings**.
2. Use Save As to *Save Database As*, naming the copy **C13-Project3-HomeListings-Your Name** in the Ch13 folder within ChapterProjectsWork.
3. Enable content in the copy of the database.
4. Display the relationships.
5. Edit each relationship to turn on *Enforce Referential Integrity*. With the relationships window active, tap or click the Relationship Report button in the Tools group. Create a PDF of the report, naming the PDF **C13-Project3-Relationships-Your Name** and saving in the Ch13 folder in ChapterProjectsWork. Close the report, saving the report using the default name, and then close the Relationships window.
6. Create a form using the Form tool for the Listings table and then modify the form as follows:
   a. Change to a theme of your choosing.
   b. Insert the picture named *ForSale*. Change the Size Mode property to *Zoom*, the *Width* to 1.5 inches, and the *Height* to 1 inch.
   c. Change the font size for the title text to a size of your choosing.
   d. Make any other changes you think improve the appearance of the form.
   e. Save the form using the default form name.
7. Display the form in Print Preview. Change the margins to *Normal*. Open the Page Setup dialog box with the Columns tab active and then change the *Width* in the *Column Size* section to 7.5 inches. Create a PDF of the <u>first page only</u> of the form, naming the PDF **C13-Project3-Form-Your Name** and saving in the Ch13 folder in ChapterProjectsWork. ***Hint: Use the Options button in the Publish as PDF or XPS dialog box to choose* Page(s) 1 to 1.** Close the form, saving changes.
8. Create a report using the Report tool for the Sales table and then modify the report as follows:
   a. Insert the **ForSale** picture, applying the same changes as those applied to the picture in the form.
   b. Change the title text to a font size of your choosing.
   c. Resize controls as needed so that all objects fit on one page.
   d. Select and delete the total and the line above the total at the bottom of the *Sale Price* column.
   e. Make any other changes you think improve the appearance of the report.
   f. Save the report using the default report name.
9. Create a PDF of the report, naming the PDF **C13-Project3-Report-Your Name** and saving in the Ch13 folder in ChapterProjectsWork. Close the report.
10. Leave the database open if you are continuing to Project 4; otherwise, close the database and submit the project to your instructor in the manner she or he has requested.

Project 4 Compacting on Close and Backing Up a Database

Individual

Deliverable: Home listing database (continued in Project 5)

1. If necessary, open **C13-Project3-HomeListings-Your Name** and enable content.
2. Turn on the *Compact on Close* option.
3. Create a backup copy of the database, accepting the default file name and saving in the default folder.
4. Leave the database open if you are continuing to Project 5; otherwise, close the database and submit the project to your instructor in the manner she or he has requested.

Project 5 Creating a Query and Report

Individual

Deliverable: PDF of Report (continued from Project 4)

1. If necessary, open **C13-Project3-HomeListings-Your Name** and enable content.
2. Create a query using all of the fields in the Sales table. Insert a calculated column titled *Amount* between *Commission Rate* and *Selling Agent* as shown in Figure 13.3. You determine the field expression and format. Save the query, naming it **SalesCommissions**.
3. Create a report similar to the one shown in Figure 13.3 based on the SalesCommissions query. Use your best judgment to determine the formatting options. Save the report using the default name.

Sales Commissions

ListingID	Date Sold	Sale Price	Commission Rate	Amount	Selling Agent	Split Commission?
2015-1	3/22/2015	$82,775.00	5.00%	$4,138.75	Student last name	☑
2015-3	3/31/2015	$59,000.00	4.00%	$2,360.00	Davidson	☑
2015-4	3/30/2015	$72,000.00	5.00%	$3,600.00	Polaski	☑
2015-7	3/31/2015	$74,500.00	5.00%	$3,725.00	Ungar	☑
2015-9	3/25/2015	$64,500.00	5.00%	$3,225.00	Antoine	☑

Figure 13.3 Project 5 Sales Commissions report

4. Open the Page Setup dialog box with the Columns tab active and change the *Width* in the *Column Size* section to 8 inches. Create a PDF of the report, saving it as **C13-Project5-SalesCommissions-Your Name** in the Ch13 folder within ChapterProjectsWork.
5. Close the report and close the database.
6. Submit the project to your instructor in the manner she or he has requested.

Project 6 Sending Project Work to OneNote Notebook

Individual

Deliverable: New Page in Shared OneNote notebook

1. Start OneNote and open the MyProjects notebook created in Chapter 4, Project 4.
2. Make Access the active section and add a new page titled *Chapter 13 Projects*.
3. For each PDF you created in projects you completed in this chapter, send the PDF to OneNote 2013, selecting the Chapter 13 Projects page in the Access section in the MyProjects notebook.
4. Close your MyProjects notebook in OneNote and close OneNote.
5. Submit the project to your instructor in the manner she or he has requested.

Chapter 14

Integrating Word, Excel, PowerPoint, and Access Components

After successfully completing this chapter, you will be able to:

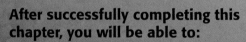

Import Excel data into Access

Export an Access query to Excel

Embed an Excel chart in a document

Embed Excel data in a presentation

Edit an embedded object

Link an Excel chart with a presentation

Update links

The Microsoft Office suite is designed to easily share and integrate data among the programs. For some tasks you may have portions of a project distributed across more than one application. For example, you may have a chart in Excel and a list in Access that you want to add into a report in Word. The ability to integrate data means that you can use the program that best fits each task and/or the expertise of each person, and assemble the portions into a complete product without duplicating individual efforts.

In Chapter 3 you used the Copy and Paste buttons in the Clipboard group to copy text, a picture, and a chart between Word, Excel, and PowerPoint. Copy and paste is the method of choice for situations in which the data to be shared is not large and is not likely to need updating. In this chapter you will learn other methods for integrating data that include importing, exporting, embedding, and linking.

Topic 14.1

SKILLS

Create a table by importing Excel data

Modify imported table design

Importing Excel Worksheet Data into Access

A new Access table can be created from data in an Excel worksheet, or Excel data can be appended to the bottom of an existing Access table. Because an Excel worksheet and an Access datasheet use the same column and row structure, the two programs are often used to interchange data. To facilitate the import, the Excel worksheet should be set up like an Access datasheet with the field names in the first row and with no blank rows or columns within the data. The **Import Spreadsheet Wizard** is used to perform an import operation.

① Start Access and open the **Parking** database from the Ch14 folder in Student_ Data_Files.

② Use Save As to save a copy of the database as **14.1-Parking-Your Name** in a new folder named *Ch14* within CompletedTopicsByChapter. Accept the default options *Save Database As* and *Access Database* at the Save As Backstage view.

③ Tap or click the Enable Content button in the SECURITY WARNING message bar.

④ Tap or click the EXTERNAL DATA tab.

⑤ Tap or click the Excel button in the Import & Link group.

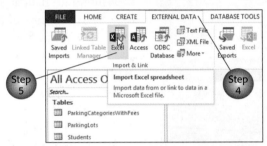

⑥ Tap or click the Browse button in the Get External Data – Excel Spreadsheet dialog box.

⑦ Navigate to the Ch14 folder in Student_Data_Files at the File Open dialog box and then double-tap or double-click *ParkingRecords*.

⑧ Tap or click OK to accept the default option *Import the source data into a new table in the current database*.

Use the Append option if the table already exists in the database and you want to add new records from an Excel worksheet to the end of the existing table.

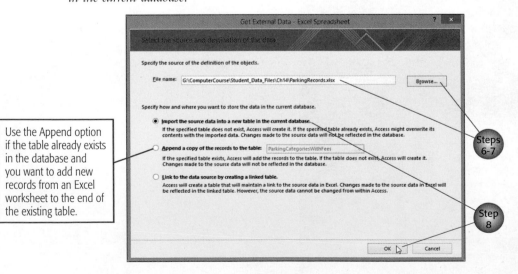

⑨ At the first Import Spreadsheet Wizard dialog box, tap or click Next to accept the worksheet labeled *Student Parking Records*.

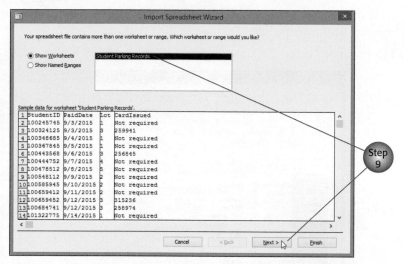

⑩ At the second Import Spreadsheet Wizard dialog box, tap or click Next with a check mark already inserted in the *First Row Contains Column Headings* check box.

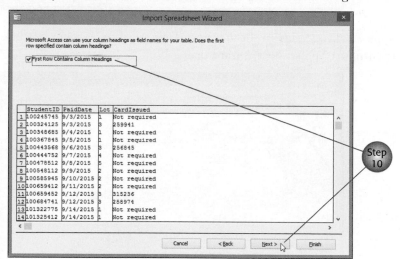

⑪ At the third Import Spreadsheet Wizard dialog box, tap or click the *PaidDate* column heading and look at the option selected in the *Data Type* list box.

Notice that Access has correctly identified the data as a Date field. At this dialog box, you can review each column and modify the options in the *Field Options* section as needed, or you can elect to make changes in Design view after the import is completed. If a column exists in the Excel worksheet that you do not wish to import into the table, select the column and insert a check mark in the *Do not import field (Skip)* check box.

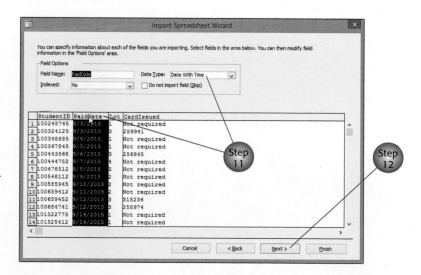

⑫ Tap or click Next.

13 At the fourth Import Spreadsheet Wizard dialog box, tap or click *Choose my own primary key*.

Access inserts the *StudentID* field name in the list box next to the option (the first column in the worksheet).

14 Tap or click Next.

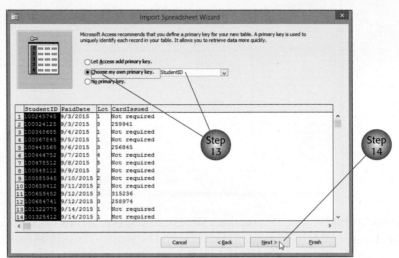

15 Type **ParkingSales** in the *Import to Table* text box and tap or click Finish at the last Import Spreadsheet Wizard dialog box.

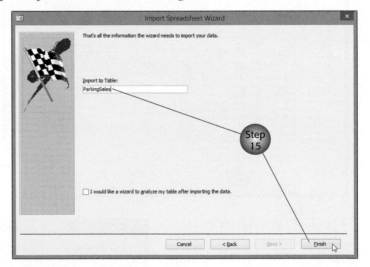

16 Tap or click Close to finish the import without saving the import steps at the Get External Data – Excel Spreadsheet dialog box.

For situations in which you frequently import from Excel to Access, you can save the import specifications so that you can repeat the import later using the same settings.

Import Worksheet Data into Access
1. Open destination database.
2. Tap or click EXTERNAL DATA tab.
3. Tap or click Excel button in Import & Link group.
4. Tap or click Browse button.
5. Navigate to and double-tap or double-click Excel file.
6. Tap or click OK.
7. Tap or click Next with worksheet selected.
8. Tap or click Next with *First Row Contains Column Headings* selected.
9. Change *Field Options* for columns if desired and tap or click Next.
10. Choose primary key field and tap or click Next.
11. Type table name and tap or click Finish.
12. Tap or click Close.

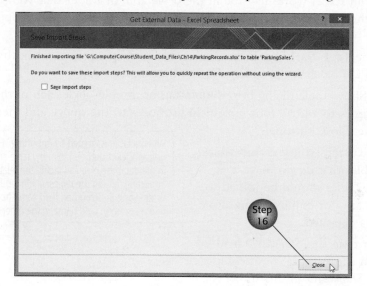

17 Open the ParkingSales table from the Navigation pane and review the datasheet.

18 Switch to Design view and review the field names and data types for the new table.

19 Tap or click the *Data Type* list arrow for the *Lot* field name and then tap or click *Short Text*.

In the Parking database, the Lot field should be defined as Short Text because lot numbers are not field values that you would add or subtract.

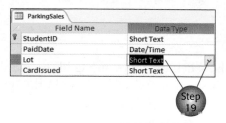

20 Save and then close the table. Leave the database open for the next topic.

Beyond Basics

Linking an Excel Worksheet to an Access Table

The option *Link to the data source by creating a linked table* at the Get External Data – Excel Spreadsheet dialog box is used when the data that is being imported is likely to be updated within Excel after the import is performed. Access will create a link between the source Excel worksheet and the Access table. Changes made to the Excel data will be automatically reflected in Access. Note that with this option the data cannot be changed from within Access.

Exporting an Access Query to Excel

Often, Access table data is exported to Excel to use the mathematical analysis tools available in a worksheet. Access creates a copy of the data within the selected table or query in an Excel worksheet file in the drive and/or folder that you specify. Buttons in the Export group of the EXTERNAL DATA tab provide options to send a copy of Access data in a variety of file formats.

1. With the **14.1-Parking-Your Name** database open, tap or click the CREATE tab and tap or click the Query Design button.

2. At the Show Table dialog box, double-tap or double-click each of the four table names to add all four table field list boxes to the query and then tap or click the Close button.

In the next steps you will join tables for those tables that do not have a relationship. Tables should be joined so that records are not duplicated in the query results datasheet.

> When a table is created by importing, a relationship does not exist between the new table and other tables in the database. You can create the relationships after importing, or join the tables within a query by sliding or dragging the common field name from one table to the common field name in the other table.

3. Slide or drag the *StudentID* field name in the ParkingSales field list box to *StudentID* in the Students field list box.

4. Slide or drag the *Lot* field name in the ParkingSales field list box to *LotNo* in the ParkingLots field list box.

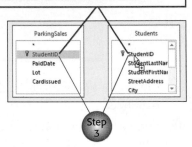

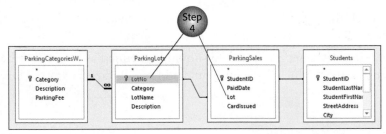

5. Double-tap or double-click the following fields to add the fields to the query design grid. (Note that you are selecting fields in the query from all four table field list boxes.)

Field Name	Table Name
StudentID	ParkingSales
StudentFirstName	Students
StudentLastName	Students
PaidDate	ParkingSales
Lot	Parking Sales
Description	ParkingLots
ParkingFee	ParkingCategoriesWithFees

6. Tap or click the Run button in the Results group.

7. Save the query as **ParkingSales2015** and then close the query.

8 Tap or click to select the *ParkingSales2015* query name in the Navigation pane.

9 Tap or click the EXTERNAL DATA tab and tap or click the Excel button in the Export group.

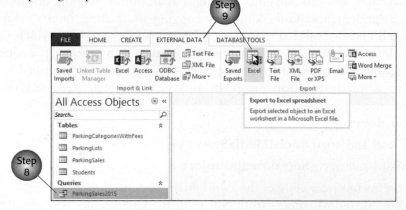

10 At the Export – Excel Spreadsheet dialog box, tap or click the Browse button, type **14.2-ParkingSales-Your Name** in the *File name* text box, navigate to the Ch14 folder in CompletedTopicsByChapter, and then tap or click Save.

11 Tap or click to insert a check mark in the *Export data with formatting and layout.* check box.

12 Tap or click to insert a check mark in the *Open the destination file after the export operation is complete.* check box, and then tap or click OK.

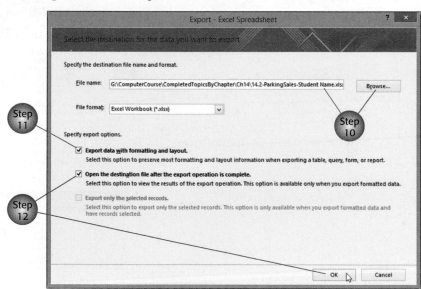

Excel is started automatically with the data from the query results datasheet shown in a worksheet. Notice the first row contains the field names from the query and the worksheet tab is renamed to the query name.

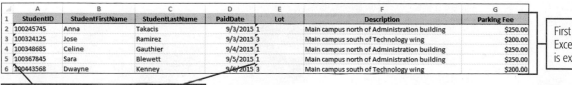

First six rows in Excel after query is exported.

Green triangles are shown in the *StudentID* and *Lot* columns because the data is numeric but was exported from Access as text. Green triangles flag data that is a potential error. You can ignore the error flags here.

13 Close Excel to return to Access.

14 Tap or click Close at the Export - Excel Spreadsheet dialog box to finish the export without saving the export steps.

15 Close the database and then close Access.

App Tip

Go to the Export tab Backstage view in Word, Excel, and PowerPoint to find options for sending data outside the source program.

Topic 14.3

SKILLS

Embed an Excel chart into a document

Embedding an Excel Chart into a Word Document

In Chapter 3 you used Copy and Paste features to duplicate text and a chart between programs. You can also embed content as an object within a document, worksheet, or presentation. Embedding, like copying and pasting, inserts a duplicate of the selected text or object at the desired location. The program in which the data originally resides is called the **source program**, and the data that is copied is referred to as the **source data**. The program in which the data is embedded is referred to as the **destination program**, and the document, worksheet, or presentation into which the embedded object is placed is referred to as the **destination document**.

1. Start Excel and open **SocialMediaStats**.

2. Start Word and open **SocialMediaProject**.

3. Use Save As to save a copy of the Word document as **14.3–SocialMediaProject–Your Name** in the Ch14 folder within CompletedTopicsByChapter.

4. Switch to Excel and tap or click to select the pie chart with the title *Global Market Share*.

5. If necessary, tap or click the HOME tab.

6. Tap or click the Copy button in the Clipboard group. (Do *not* tap or click the down-pointing arrow on the button.)

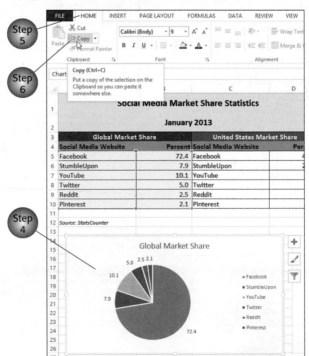

7. Switch to Word and tap or click to position the insertion point at the left margin on the blank line a double-space below the first table.

8 Tap or click the Paste button arrow and tap or click *Use Destination Theme & Embed Workbook* (first button in *Paste Options* section) at the drop-down list.

9 Tap or click to select the chart object and tap or click the Center button in the Paragraph group of the HOME tab.

The Chart feature is standardized in Word, Excel, and PowerPoint. A chart embedded within any of the three programs offers the CHART TOOLS tabs and three chart editing buttons with which the chart can be modified after being embedded.

10 Tap or click the CHART ELEMENTS button (button with plus symbol), tap or click at the right end of *Legend* (right-pointing arrow appears), and tap or click *Bottom*.

11 Switch to Excel and select and copy the pie chart with the title *United States Market Share*.

12 Switch to Word, position the insertion point at the bottom of the document, and then embed, center, and format the pie chart by completing steps similar to Steps 8 through 10.

13 Save the revised document using the same name (**14.3-SocialMediaProject-Your Name**) and then close Word. Leave Excel and the **SocialMediaStats** workbook open for the next topic.

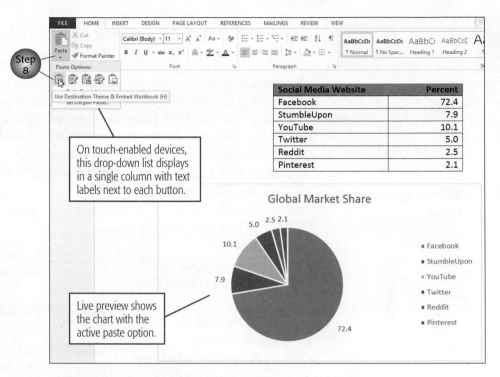

On touch-enabled devices, this drop-down list displays in a single column with text labels next to each button.

Live preview shows the chart with the active paste option.

Social Media Website	Percent
Facebook	72.4
StumbleUpon	7.9
YouTube	10.1
Twitter	5.0
Reddit	2.5
Pinterest	2.1

Global Market Share

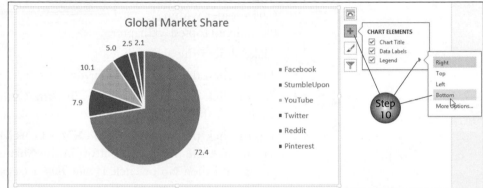

Step 8

Step 10

Quick **STEPS**

Embed an Excel Chart into Word
1. Open worksheet in Excel.
2. Open document in Word.
3. Make Excel active, select and copy chart.
4. Switch to Word.
5. Position insertion point.
6. Tap or click Paste button arrow.
7. Tap or click *Use Destination Theme & Embed Workbook.*

ALTERNATIVE method
Another way to embed copied data is to select *Paste Special* at the Paste button arrow drop-down list in the destination document. This opens the Paste Special dialog box in which you select the source object in the *As* list box and then tap or click OK.

Embedding Excel Data into and Editing the Data in a PowerPoint Presentation

Topic 14.4

SKILLS

Embed Excel data into a presentation

Edit an embedded table

Embedding text or worksheet data uses the same process as for embedding a chart. Double-tap or double-click an embedded object to edit text or worksheet data in the destination location. Embedded text or cell data is edited using the tools from the source program. Tap or click outside the embedded object to end editing and restore the destination program's ribbon.

1. With Excel active and the **SocialMediaStats** workbook open, select and copy A3:B10.

2. Start PowerPoint and open **SocialMediaPres**.

3. Use Save As to save a copy of the presentation as **14.4-SocialMediaPres-Your Name** in the Ch14 folder within CompletedTopicsByChapter.

4. Make slide 3 the active slide.

5. Tap or click the Paste button arrow.

6. Tap or click *Embed* (third button in *Paste Options* section) at the drop-down list.

7. Tap or click the DRAWING TOOLS FORMAT tab, tap or click the Shape Fill button in the Shape Styles group, and then tap or click *White, Text 1* (second option in *Theme Colors* section).

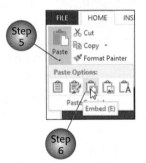

8. Resize and position the embedded object to the approximate size and position shown in the image below.

9. Double-tap or double-click the inserted cells to open the embedded object for editing.

Notice the embedded cells open in an Excel worksheet and the ribbon changes to Excel's ribbon.

10. Select B5:B10 and tap or click the Decrease Decimal button in the Number group of the HOME tab.

11. Tap or click the slide outside the embedded object to end editing and restore PowerPoint's ribbon.

12. Switch to Excel and select and copy C3:D10.

13. Switch to PowerPoint, make slide 4 the active slide, and embed, format, resize, and position the copied cells by completing steps similar to those in Steps 5 through 11.

Step 10

	A	B
3	Global Market Share	
4	Social Media Website	Percent
5	Facebook	72
6	StumbleUpon	8
7	YouTube	10
8	Twitter	5
9	Reddit	3
10	Pinterest	2

SocialMediaWebsites

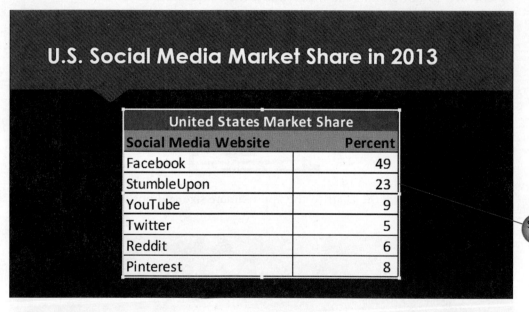

U.S. Social Media Market Share in 2013

United States Market Share	
Social Media Website	Percent
Facebook	49
StumbleUpon	23
YouTube	9
Twitter	5
Reddit	6
Pinterest	8

Step 13

Quick **STEPS**

Edit an Embedded Object
1. Double-tap or double-click embedded object.
2. Make desired changes.
3. Tap or click outside object.

14. Save the revised presentation using the same name (**14.4-SocialMediaPres-Your Name**) and then close PowerPoint. Leave Excel and the **SocialMediaStats** workbook open for the next topic.

Embedding an Entire File

Embed an entire document or worksheet using the Object button in the INSERT tab. At the Object dialog box, tap or click the Create from File tab and use the Browse button to navigate to the file name. Note that this method embeds the entire file's contents at the insertion point, active cell, or active slide.

Linking an Excel Chart with a Presentation and Updating Links

Topic 14.5

SKILLS

Link an Excel chart with a presentation

Turn on automatic link updates

Edit a linked chart

Update links

Did You Know?

Linking is not just for integrating data between two different programs; you can link two documents in Word, two worksheets in Excel, or two tables in Access.

If the data that you want to integrate between two programs is continuously updated, copy and link the data instead of copying and pasting or copying and embedding. When copied data is linked, changes made to the source data can be automatically updated in any other document, worksheet, or presentation to which the data was linked.

1. With Excel active and the **SocialMediaStats** workbook open, use Save As to save a copy of the workbook as **14.5-LinkedSocialMediaStats-Your Name** in the Ch14 folder within CompletedTopicsByChapter.

2. Start PowerPoint and open **SocialMediaPres**.

3. Use Save As to save a copy of the presentation as **14.5-LinkedSocialMediaPres-Your Name** in the Ch14 folder within CompletedTopicsByChapter.

4. Switch to Excel and select and copy the *Global Market Share* pie chart.

5. Switch to PowerPoint and make slide 3 the active slide.

6. Tap or click the Paste button arrow.

7. Tap or click *Use Destination Theme & Link Data* (third button in *Paste Options* section).

8. Resize and move the chart to the approximate size and position shown in the image below.

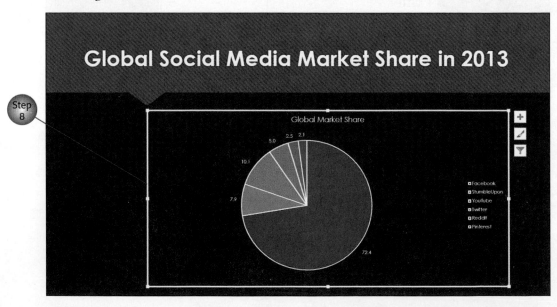

9. Switch to Excel and select and copy the *United States Market Share* pie chart.

⑩ Switch to PowerPoint, make slide 4 the active slide, and link, resize, and move the chart by completing steps similar to those in Steps 6 through 8.

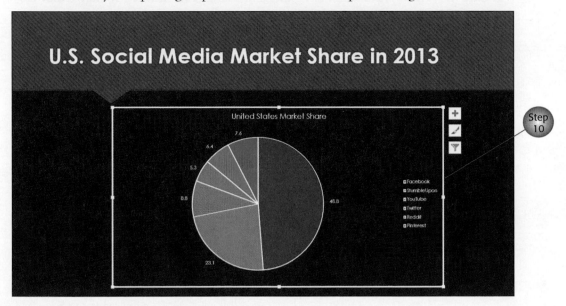

⑪ Tap or click the FILE tab and tap or click *Edit Links to Files* in the *Related Documents* section near the bottom right of the Info tab Backstage view.

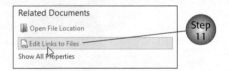

⑫ At the **Links dialog box**, tap or click to select the first link in the *Links* list box and then tap or click to insert a check mark in the *Automatic Update* check box.

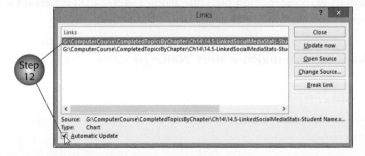

⑬ Tap or click to select the second link and then tap or click to insert a check mark in the *Automatic Update* check box.

⑭ Tap or click Close.

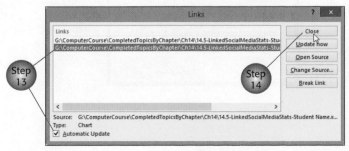

15 Tap or click the Back button at the Info tab Backstage view.

16 Save the revised presentation using the same name (**14.5-LinkedSocialMediaPres-Your Name**) and then close the presentation.

17 Switch to Excel.

18 Change the value in D6 from *23.1* to *5.1*.

19 Change the value in D7 from *8.8* to *18.8*.

20 Change the value in D10 from *7.6* to *15.6*.

Notice the pie chart updated after each change in value. The revised chart is noticeably different from the original pie chart.

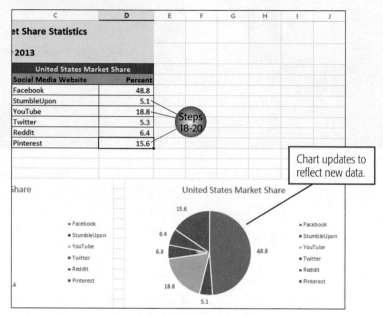

21 Save the revised worksheet using the same name (**14.5-LinkedSocialMediaStats-Your Name**) and then close Excel.

22 Switch to PowerPoint if PowerPoint is not already active and open **14.5-LinkedSocialMediaPres-Your Name**.

Because the presentation contains linked data that is set to automatically update, you are prompted to update links.

23 Tap or click the **Update Links button** at the Microsoft PowerPoint Security Notice dialog box.

If the source and destination files are both open at the same time, changes made to the source reflect in the destination file immediately.

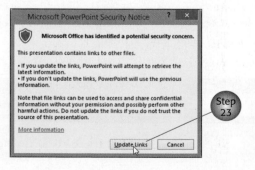

(24) Make slide 4 the active slide. Notice that the chart is updated to reflect the same data as the revised Excel chart.

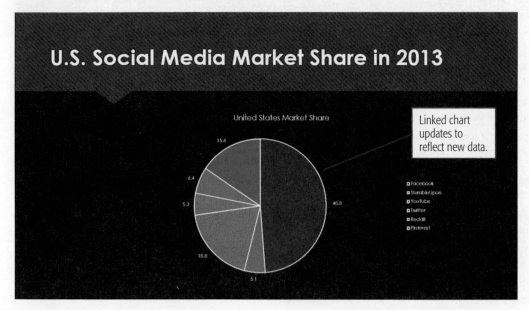

U.S. Social Media Market Share in 2013

United States Market Share

Linked chart updates to reflect new data.

□ Facebook
□ StumbleUpon
□ YouTube
□ Twitter
□ Reddit
□ Pinterest

Quick STEPS

Link Data
1. Open source program and file.
2. Open destination program and file.
3. With source program active, select and copy data.
4. Switch to destination program.
5. Activate destination location.
6. Tap or click Paste button arrow.
7. Tap or click *Use Destination Theme & Link Data*.

Turn on Automatic Link Updates
1. Make destination file active.
2. Tap or click FILE tab.
3. Tap or click *Edit Links to Files*.
4. Select link.
5. Tap or click *Automatic Update* check box.
6. Tap or click Close.

(25) Make slide 3 the active slide and delete the title inside the chart above the pie.

(26) Make slide 4 the active slide and delete the title inside the chart above the pie.

(27) Save the revised presentation using the same name (**14.5-LinkedSocialMediaPres-Your Name**) and then close PowerPoint.

ALTERNATIVE method

Another way to link copied data is to select *Paste Special* at the Paste button arrow drop-down list in the destination document. At the Paste Special dialog box, tap or click *Paste link*, make sure the correct source object is selected in the *As* list box, and then tap or click OK.

Beyond Basics   **Managing Links**

Open the Links dialog box (see Step 11) if the drive and/or folder for the source data in a linked file changes, or if you want to break a link to stop updating the destination data.

Concepts Review

Topic	Key Concepts	Key Terms
Importing Excel Worksheet Data into Access	The Import Spreadsheet Wizard starts when you tap or click the Excel button in the Import & Link group of the EXTERNAL DATA tab.	Import Spreadsheet Wizard
	Five dialog boxes in the Import Spreadsheet Wizard guide you through the steps to create a new table using data in an Excel worksheet.	
	You can save the Excel import settings to repeat the import later using the same settings.	
	Open an imported table in Design view to modify the table design after the import is complete.	
Exporting an Access Query to Excel	Export table or query data to Excel using the Excel button in the Export group of the EXTERNAL DATA tab.	
	Specify the file name, drive and/or folder, and export options at the Export – Excel Spreadsheet dialog box.	
	You can elect to export the data with formatting and layout options in the datasheet and to automatically open Excel with the worksheet displayed when the export is complete.	
	Export specifications can be saved to repeat the export later.	
Embedding an Excel Chart into a Word Document	Embedding inserts a copy of selected data as an object in a document, worksheet, or presentation.	Source program
	The program from which data is copied is called the source program.	Source data
	The data that is copied is referred to as the source data. The destination program is the program that receives the copied data.	Destination program
	The destination document refers to the document, worksheet, or presentation into which copied data is pasted as an object.	Destination document
	To embed copied data as an object, use the Paste button arrow in the destination document and choose the desired embed option from the drop-down list.	
Embedding Excel Data into and Editing the Data in a PowerPoint Presentation	Double-tap or double-click an embedded object to open the object data for editing using the source program's ribbon and tools.	
	Tap or click outside the embedded object to end editing and restore the source program's ribbon.	
	An entire document can be embedded using the Object button in the INSERT tab.	
Linking an Excel Chart with a Presentation and Updating Links	Link to source data that is continuously updated instead of copying and pasting or copying and embedding.	Links dialog box
	To link copied data, use the Paste button arrow in the destination document and choose the desired link option from the drop-down list.	Update Links button
	Tap or click *Edit Links to Files* at the Info tab Backstage view to open the Links dialog box in which you manage links to source data.	
	Select a link in the Links dialog box and insert a check mark in the *Automatic Update* check box to turn on automatic updates for the link.	
	Tap or click the Update Links button in the Security Warning dialog box that appears when you open a file with a linked object to update data from the source.	

Multiple Choice

1. This wizard is used to import Excel data into a new table.
   a. Import Excel Wizard
   b. Import Wizard
   c. Import Data Wizard
   d. Import Spreadsheet Wizard

2. Which of the following is *not* an option in the Get External Data – Excel Spreadsheet dialog box?
   a. Import source data into a new table
   b. Start Excel and open worksheet
   c. Append a copy of records to existing table
   d. Link to the data source

3. Do this action first before selecting the Excel button in the Export group to send a copy of Access data to an Excel worksheet.
   a. Select object to export in Navigation pane
   b. Start Excel
   c. Display the table in Design view
   d. Modify all data types to Short Text

4. Specify export options for Excel at this dialog box.
   a. File Open
   b. File Send to Excel
   c. Export – Excel Spreadsheet
   d. Save Export Options

5. This is the name of the program from which data is copied for embedding purposes.
   a. source
   b. destination
   c. embedded
   d. copied

6. This is the name of the program that receives the embedded data.
   a. copied
   b. destination
   c. embedded
   d. source

7. The ribbon from this program displays while an embedded object is being edited.
   a. source
   b. destination
   c. Windows Libraries
   d. embedded

8. Do this action to signal the end of editing an embedded object.
   a. Tap or click outside object
   b. Press Ctrl + Z
   c. Close the ribbon
   d. Tap or click inside object

9. Source data that is continuously updated should be inserted in a destination document using this integration method.
   a. Copy and paste
   b. Copy and embed
   c. Copy and link
   d. Copy and update

10. Open this dialog box to turn on automatic updates to source data.
    a. Embed
    b. Manage Links
    c. Paste Special
    d. Links

Crossword Puzzle

ACROSS

1 This program's ribbon is restored after editing embedded object

3 Ribbon tab to import and export in Access

5 Security warning button to use upon opening file with linked data

DOWN

2 Term for copied data for embedding or linking

3 Name for group of buttons for sending Access data to other programs

4 Dialog box to turn on automatic updates for linked data

Matching

Match the term with the statement or definition.

_____ 1. Create new Access table from worksheet

_____ 2. An option in Access dialog box to send copy of data to Excel

_____ 3. Button to use to embed copied data

_____ 4. Edit embedded object

_____ 5. Button that updates to most current source data

a. Paste button arrow

b. Double-tap or double-click object

c. Update Links

d. Export data with formatting and layout

e. Import & link group

Project 1 Importing and Exporting Data with Access and Excel

Individual

Deliverable: Database and worksheet with used books list

1. Start Access and open the **UsedBooks** database.
2. Use Save As to save a copy of the database as **C14-Project1-UsedBooks-Your Name** in a new folder named *Ch14* within ChapterProjectsWork.
3. Enable Content in the copy of the database.
4. Import the Excel workbook named ***BookList*** from the Ch14 folder in Student_Data_Files using the option *Append a copy of the records to the table* [Books] at the Get External Data – Excel Spreadsheet dialog box. Do not save the import steps.

Note: Only two dialog boxes are required in the Import Spreadsheet Wizard when you use the Append option.

5. Open the Books table when the import is complete, review the datasheet, and then close the table.
6. Create a query in Design view adding the Books table and the Students table to the query and with the following fields in order:

Field Name	Table Name
BookID	Books
FName	Students
LName	Students
Title	Books
Author	Books
Condition	Books
AskPrice	Books
StopPrice	Books

7. Save the query as **BookList** and then run the query.
8. Review the query results datasheet and then close the query.
9. Export the BookList query to Excel, saving the workbook as **C14-Project1-ExportedBookList-Your Name** in the Ch14 folder within ChapterProjectsWork. Select the options to export data with formatting and layout information and to open the destination when the export is complete. Do not save the export steps.
10. Make the following changes to the worksheet in Excel:
    a. Change each occurrence of *Jane Doe* to your first and last names in the *First Name* and *Last Name* columns.
    b. Change the orientation to *Landscape*.
    c. Make sure all columns will fit on one page.
    d. Create a header with the sheet tab name at the top center of the page and a footer with your name at the bottom center of the page.
11. Save the revised workbook using the same name (**C14-Project1-ExportedBookList-Your Name**) and then close Excel.
12. Close the database and then close Access.
13. Submit the project to your instructor in the manner she or he has requested.

Project 2 Embedding Data with Word and Excel

Individual

Deliverable: Document with embedded tables from Excel

1. Start Word and open **StatsCounterTables**.
2. Use Save As to change the file name to **C14-Project2-StatsCounterTables-Your Name**, saving in the Ch14 folder within ChapterProjectsWork.

3. Start Excel and open **SocialMediaStats**.
4. Select and copy A4:B10.
5. Switch to Word and position the insertion point at the left margin a double-space below the first paragraph. Use *Paste Special* from the Paste button arrow to open the Paste Special dialog box. Select *Microsoft Excel Worksheet Object* in the *As* list box and choose OK to embed the worksheet data.
6. Center the embedded worksheet cells.
7. Embed C4:D10 from the Excel worksheet, inserting the object a double-space below the last paragraph in the document.
8. Center the embedded worksheet cells.
9. Edit both embedded objects to display two decimal places after each percent value. ***Hint: Before ending editing of each embedded object, make sure the cells displayed in the editing window are only the cells that were copied.***
10. Add your name in a footer in the document.
11. Save the revised document using the same name (**C14-Project2-StatsCounterTables-Your Name**) and then close Word.
12. Close Excel. Tap or click No if prompted to save changes to the worksheet when closing Excel.
13. Submit the project to your instructor in the manner she or he has requested.

Project 3 Linking Data between Word and Excel

Individual

Deliverable: Document with linked Excel charts

1. Start Word and open **StatsCounterCharts**.
2. Use Save As to change the file name to **C14-Project3-LinkedStatsCounterCharts-Your Name**, saving in the Ch14 folder within ChapterProjectsWork.
3. Start Excel and open **SocialMediaStats**.
4. Use Save As to change the file name to **C14-Project3-LinkedSocialMediaStats-Your Name**, saving in the Ch14 folder within ChapterProjectsWork.
5. Select, copy, and link the *Global Market Share* pie chart to the Word document a double-space below the first paragraph. Select the option to link using the destination theme. Center the chart in the document.
6. Select, copy, and link the *United States Market Share* pie chart to the Word document a double-space below the last paragraph. Select the option to link using the destination theme. Center the chart in the document.
7. Turn on the option for each linked object to automatically update.
8. Add your name in a footer in the document.
9. Save the revised document using the same name (**C14-Project3-LinkedStatsCounterCharts-Your Name**) and then close the document.
10. Make the following changes to the data in the Excel worksheet:

Cell Address	Current Entry	New Entry
B5	72.4	64.4
D5	48.8	41.8
A6	StumbleUpon	Instagram
B6	7.9	15.9
C6	StumbleUpon	Instagram
D6	23.1	30.1

11. Save the revised workbook using the same name (**C14-Project3-LinkedSocialMediaStats-Your Name**) and then close Excel.
12. With Word active, open **C14-Project3-LinkedStatsCounterCharts-Your Name**, and choose Yes when prompted to update links. Save and close the document after updating links and exit Word.
13. Submit the project to your instructor in the manner she or he has requested.

Project 4 Embedding Excel Data in PowerPoint

Individual

Deliverable: PowerPoint presentation with embedded Excel data

1. Start PowerPoint and open **TopVacDestinations**.
2. Modify the presentation to resemble the one shown in Figure 14.1 using the following information:
   a. The tables on slide 2 and slide 3 are embedded from the Excel worksheet named *VacDestinations*.
   b. Edit the embedded objects to appear as shown in Figure 14.1.
   c. Add slide 4 as a new slide.
   d. Add the clip art image shown on the title slide. Substitute a suitable alternative image if the one shown is not available.
3. Save the revised presentation as **C14-Project4-TopVacDestinations-Your Name**.
4. Close PowerPoint and Excel.
5. Submit the project to your instructor in the manner she or he has requested.

Figure 14.1 Project 4 Vacation Destinations Survey Results presentation

Project 5 Sending Project Work to OneNote Notebook

Individual

Deliverable: New Page in Shared OneNote notebook

1. Start OneNote and open the MyProjects notebook created in Chapter 4, Project 4.
2. Make Integrating the active section and add a new page titled *Chapter 14 Projects*.
3. Send the following documents to OneNote selecting the Chapter 14 Projects page in the Integrating section in the MyProjects notebook. Skip any projects you were not assigned to complete.
   a. **C14-Project1-ExportedBookList-Your Name** from Excel.
   b. **C14-Project2-StatsCounterTables-Your Name** from Word.
   c. **C14-Project3-LinkedStatsCounterCharts-Your Name** from Word. Choose No when prompted to update links when you reopen this file.
   d. **C14-Project4-TopVacDestinations-Your Name** from PowerPoint. Send the slides formatted as handouts with four slides horizontal per page and with your name in a header. Save the changes when prompted when the file is closed.
4. Close your MyProjects notebook in OneNote and close OneNote.
5. Submit the project to your instructor in the manner she or he has requested.

Chapter 15

Using OneDrive and Other Cloud Computing Technologies

After successfully completing this chapter, you will be able to:

- Create a document in Word Online
- Create a worksheet in Excel Online
- Create a presentation in PowerPoint Online
- Edit a presentation in PowerPoint Online
- Upload and download files to and from OneDrive
- Share documents in OneDrive
- Create a document using Google Docs

Microsoft Office Online is the web-based version of Word, Excel, PowerPoint, and OneNote that are accessed from OneDrive. Web-based productivity software and storage technologies are called **cloud computing**. With cloud computing, all you need is a computer with a web browser to create and edit a document, worksheet, or presentation. With cloud computing technology such as Office Online, you do not need to install software on your PC or mobile device because all software and storage of documents is online. Google Docs is another popular web-based productivity suite. Both Microsoft and Google offer web-based productivity apps free to account holders.

In Chapter 3 you learned how to save a presentation to OneDrive within PowerPoint. In this chapter you will learn to create and edit files using Office Online; upload, download, and share files in OneDrive; and create a document using Google Docs from Google Drive.

Note: If you are using a tablet, consider completing this chapter using a USB or wireless keyboard because you will be typing longer passages of text. In this chapter, you will need to sign in with a Microsoft account and a Google account. If necessary, create a new account at each website. You may wish to check with your instructor before completing this chapter to confirm the required topics.

Topic 15.1

SKILLS

Create a document in Word Online

oops!

Don't know your Microsoft account? If you have a hot-mail.com or live.com email address, your email login is your Microsoft account; other-wise, tap or click the Sign up now link near the bottom right of the page and create a new account.

Creating a Document Using Word Online

With Word Online, you create and edit documents within a web browser. **Word Online** is similar to the desktop version of Microsoft Word that you used in Chapters 6 and 7; however, Word Online has fewer features than the desktop version. The program looks similar to the full-featured Microsoft Word, but you will notice that for some features, functionality within a browser environment is slightly different than the desktop version.

Note: Microsoft may update Office Online after publication of this textbook, in which case the information, steps, and/or screens shown here may vary.

1. Display the Desktop from the Windows 8.1 Start screen, or proceed to Step 2 if you are using Windows 7.

2. Tap or click the Internet Explorer icon in the Desktop taskbar.

3. Select the current text in the Address bar and then type **onedrive.com**.

4. If necessary, tap or click Sign in, type your Microsoft account user name and password, and then tap or click the Sign in button. Skip this step if you are already signed in to OneDrive.

Once signed in, the OneDrive window appears similar to the one shown in Figure 15.1.

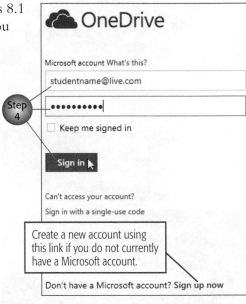

Create a new account using this link if you do not currently have a Microsoft account.

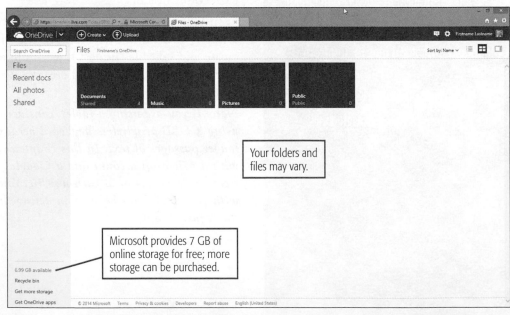

Your folders and files may vary.

Microsoft provides 7 GB of online storage for free; more storage can be purchased.

Figure 15.1 OneDrive window for signed-in user

⑤ Tap or click <u>Create</u> next to OneDrive near the top left of the window.

⑥ Tap or click <u>Word document</u> at the drop-down list.

⑦ Tap or click the Got it! button at the Welcome to your online Office message. Skip this step, if the message shown does not display and you are already at a document window.

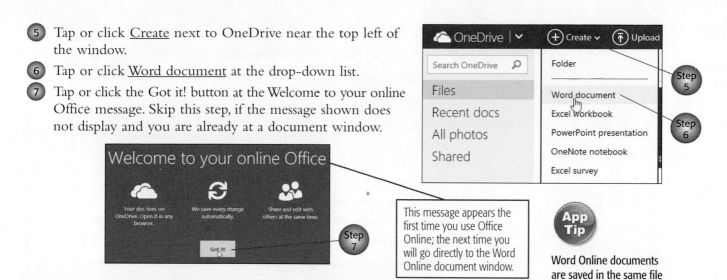

This message appears the first time you use Office Online; the next time you will go directly to the Word Online document window.

App Tip

Word Online documents are saved in the same file format as a desktop version of a Word document so that documents are transferable between editions.

Word Online launches, as shown in Figure 15.2.

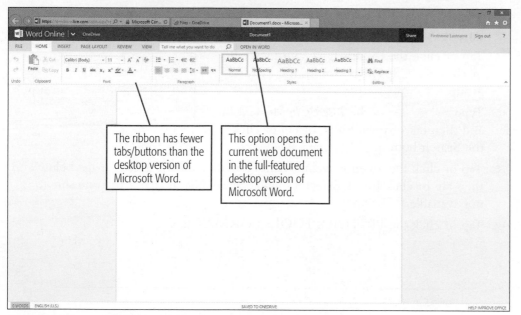

The ribbon has fewer tabs/buttons than the desktop version of Microsoft Word.

This option opens the current web document in the full-featured desktop version of Microsoft Word.

Figure 15.2 The Word Online window

⑧ Type the following text in the document window using all of the default settings:

What is Green Computing?

Green computing refers to the use of computers and other electronic devices in an environmentally responsible manner. Green computing can encompass new or modified computing practices, policies, and procedures. This trend is growing with more individuals and businesses adopting green computing strategies every year.

Strategies include the reduction of energy consumption of computers and other devices; reduction in use of paper, ink, and toner; and reuse, recycling, or proper disposal of electronic waste.

⑨ Proofread carefully and correct any typing errors that you find. If necessary, use the Spelling button in the Spelling group of the REVIEW tab to perform a spelling check of the document.

Use the same editing and formatting techniques in Word Online as you learned in the desktop edition of Microsoft Word.

10 Center the title *What is Green Computing?*

11 Select all of the text in the document and change the font size to 12.

12 Select the two paragraphs of text and change the line spacing to 1.5.

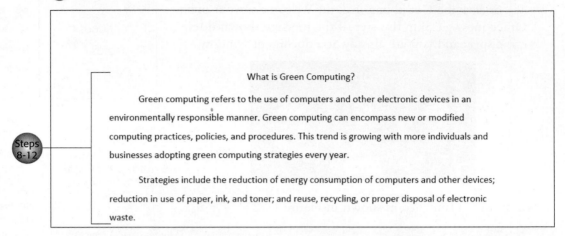

13 Position the insertion point at the end of the document on a new blank line.

14 Tap or click the INSERT tab and then tap or click the Clip Art button in the Pictures group.

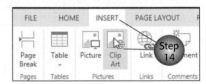

15 Type **recycling** in the *Insert Clip Art* text box and then tap or press Enter, or tap or click the Search button.

16 Tap or click the green recycling symbol picture shown in the image below and then tap or click Insert. Select a suitable alternative image if the one shown is not available.

17 Tap or click the PICTURE TOOLS FORMAT tab.

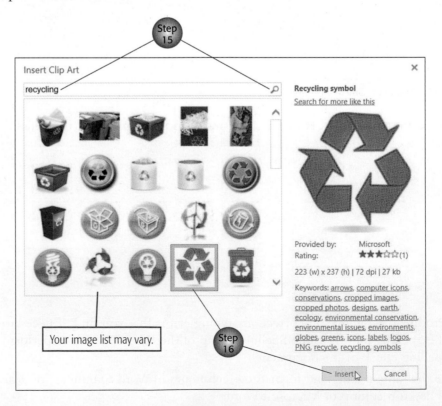

(18) Select the current value in the *Scale* text box, type **35**, and then tap or press Enter.

Notice that the clip art image does not have selection/resizing handles.

(19) With the image still selected, tap or click the HOME tab and then tap or click the Center button in the Paragraph group.

(20) Tap or click within the document text to deselect the image.

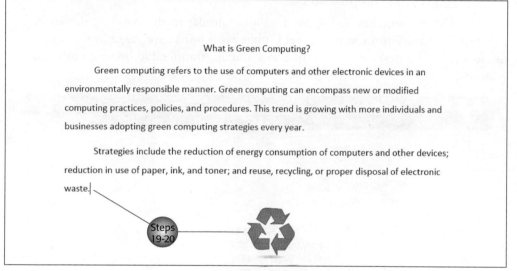

App Tip

Switch to the desktop version of Word if you need access to the full set of picture formatting and editing tools.

App Tip

Create a printable PDF of the document at the Print tab Backstage view.

(21) Tap or click Document# (where # is the document's number) in the middle of the blue bar along the top of the window.

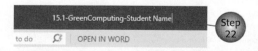

Word Online automatically saves documents as you work. This action allows you to assign a file name to the document.

(22) Type **15.1-GreenComputing-Your Name** and then tap or press Enter.

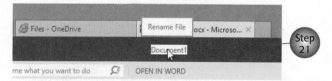

(23) Close the document's browser tab. Leave OneDrive open for the next topic.

A Word document thumbnail is added to the *Files* list in OneDrive. Additional options appear along the top of the OneDrive window when a document is selected. You will use some of these options in later topics.

Quick STEPS

Create a Document in Word Online
1. Open Internet Explorer.
2. Navigate to onedrive.com.
3. Sign in with Microsoft account.
4. Tap or click Create.
5. Tap or click Word document.
6. Type, edit, and format document.
7. Rename document.
8. Close document tab.

Topic 15.2

SKILLS

Create a worksheet
in Excel Online

Creating a Worksheet Using Excel Online

Excel Online looks the same as the full-featured desktop edition of Excel; however, the ribbon contains fewer options, and functionality for some features will vary. You can create a basic worksheet in the web-based version of Excel, but for worksheets that need advanced formulas or editing, the desktop version of Excel is preferred.

1. With OneDrive open, tap or click <u>Create</u> and then tap or click <u>Excel workbook</u> at the drop-down list.

Excel Online launches and opens a window similar to the window shown in Figure 15.3. Like Word Online, Excel Online workbooks are saved in the same file format as the desktop version of Excel and are transferable between software editions.

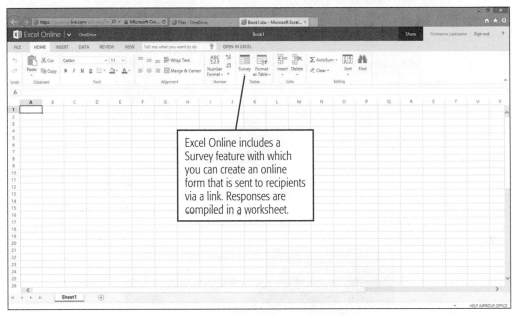

Excel Online includes a Survey feature with which you can create an online form that is sent to recipients via a link. Responses are compiled in a worksheet.

Figure 15.3 The Excel Online window. As with Word Online, Excel Online's ribbon has fewer tabs and buttons than the full-featured desktop version of Excel.

2. Type the labels and values in the cells as shown in the image below, substituting your first and last names for *Your Name* in A1.

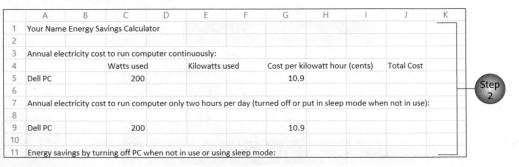

	A	B	C	D	E	F	G	H	I	J	K
1	Your Name Energy Savings Calculator										
2											
3	Annual electricity cost to run computer continuously:										
4			Watts used		Kilowatts used		Cost per kilowatt hour (cents)			Total Cost	
5	Dell PC		200				10.9				
6											
7	Annual electricity cost to run computer only two hours per day (turned off or put in sleep mode when not in use):										
8											
9	Dell PC		200				10.9				
10											
11	Energy savings by turning off PC when not in use or using sleep mode:										

Step 2

(3) Make E5 the active cell and type the formula **=(c5*24*365)/1000**.

The formula multiplies the watts used by a PC running continuously 24 hours per day, 365 days per year, and then divides the result by 1000 to convert watts to kilowatts.

(4) Make J5 the active cell and type the formula **=e5*(g5/100)**.

The cost per kilowatt hour in G5 is divided by 100 to convert 10.9 to a decimal value representing cents.

(5) Type the remaining formulas in the cells indicated:

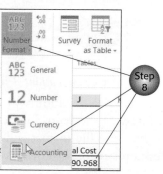

Kilowatts used	Cost per kilowatt hour (cents)	Total Cost
1752	10.9	190.968
two hours per day (turned off or put in sleep mode when not in use)		
146	10.9	15.914
use or using sleep mode:		175.054

Steps 3–5

E9 =(c9*2*365)/1000
J9 =e9*(g9/100)
J11 =j5-j9

(6) Select A1:J1 and merge and center the worksheet title.

(7) Bold the worksheet title and change the font size to 12.

(8) Select J5, tap or click the Number Format button in the Number group of the HOME tab, and then tap or click *Accounting* at the drop-down list.

Step 8

(9) Apply the Accounting Number format to J9 and J11.

(10) With J11 the active cell, tap or click the Borders button in the Font group and then tap or click *Outside Borders* at the drop-down list.

Notice that fewer border options exist in Excel Online.

(11) With J11 still the active cell, apply bold and the *Dark Green* font color (sixth color in *Standard Colors* section).

	A	B	C	D	E	F	G	H	I	J
1				Your Name Energy Savings Calculator						
2										
3	Annual electricity cost to run computer continuously:									
4			Watts used		Kilowatts used		Cost per kilowatt hour (cents)			Total Cost
5	Dell PC		200		1752		10.9			$ 190.97
6										
7	Annual electricity cost to run computer only two hours per day (turned off or put in sleep mode when not in use):									
8										
9	Dell PC		200		146		10.9			$ 15.91
10										
11	Energy savings by turning off PC when not in use or using sleep mode:									$ 175.05

Formatted worksheet after Steps 6 to 11 completed.

(12) Proofread carefully and correct any typing errors that you find.

(13) Rename the workbook **15.2-EnergySavings-Your Name** and then close the workbook tab by completing steps similar to Steps 21 to 23 in the previous topic. Leave OneDrive open for the next topic.

An Excel workbook thumbnail is added to the *Files* list in OneDrive.

Create a Workbook in Excel Online
1. Open Internet Explorer.
2. Navigate to onedrive.com.
3. Sign in with Microsoft account.
4. Tap or click Create.
5. Tap or click Excel workbook.
6. Type cell entries and format worksheet.
7. Rename workbook
8. Close workbook tab.

App Tip

Changes to the worksheet are saved automatically to the workbook in OneDrive.

App Tip

Display the worksheet in a printer-friendly format in a separate browser window from which you can print using the Print button at the Print tab Backstage view.

SKILLS

Create a presentation in PowerPoint Online

Creating a Presentation Using PowerPoint Online

A basic presentation that does not need to incorporate tables, charts, audio, or video can be created using **PowerPoint Online**. Other changes you will notice in PowerPoint Online is fewer animation and transition options, the inability to customize a slide show with timings or advanced animation options, and fewer views.

1 With OneDrive open, tap or click <u>Create</u> and then tap or click <u>PowerPoint presentation</u> at the drop-down list.

2 Tap or click the DESIGN tab, tap or click the More Themes button at the right of the Themes gallery, and then tap or click *Banded*.

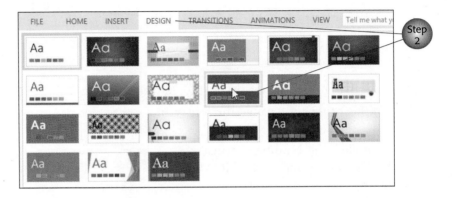

3 Tap or click *Variant 4* in the Variants gallery.

A new presentation with the selected theme is started in the PowerPoint Online window, as shown in Figure 15.4. As with Word and Excel, presentations are saved in the same file format and are transferable between PowerPoint Online and the desktop version of PowerPoint.

STEPS

Create a Presentation in PowerPoint Online
1. Open Internet Explorer.
2. Navigate to <u>onedrive.com</u>.
3. Sign in with Microsoft account.
4. Tap or click <u>Create</u>.
5. Tap or click <u>PowerPoint presentation</u>.
6. Enter and format slides.
7. Rename presentation.
8. Close presentation tab.

PowerPoint Online creates a printable PDF of full slides from the Print tab Backstage view.

Figure 15.4 The PowerPoint Online window. PowerPoint Online does not have the SLIDESHOW and REVIEW tabs found in the desktop version of PowerPoint.

④ Type **Green Computing** as the slide title and your name as the subtitle.

Note that the font for this theme converts titles to all uppercase text.

⑤ Tap or click the HOME tab and then tap or click the New Slide button in the Slides group.

⑥ At the New Slide dialog box, with the *Title and Content* layout selected, tap or click Add Slide.

Notice that content is limited to a SmartArt graphic, a picture, or clip art.

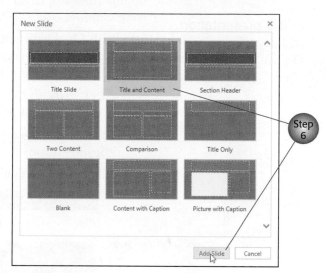

⑦ Type the text on Slide 2 as follows:

Slide title **What is Green Computing?**
Bulleted list **Use of computers and other electronic devices in an environmentally responsible manner including new or modified:**
        computing practices
        computing policies
        computing procedures

⑧ Add another new slide with the *Title and Content* layout and type the text on Slide 3 as follows:

Slide title **Green Computing Strategies**
Bulleted list **Reduction in energy consumption**
Reduction in use of paper, ink, and toner
Reuse or recycling of devices
Proper disposal of e-waste

⑨ Make Slide 2 the active slide, tap or click the INSERT tab, and then tap or click the Clip Art button in the Images group.

⑩ Type **computers** in the *Clip Art* text box and tap or press Enter, or tap or click the Search button.

⑪ Slide or scroll down to the image shown at right, tap or click to select the image, and then tap or click Insert. (Select another image if the one shown is not available.)

⑫ Move the image to the approximate position as shown in the image at right.

⑬ Make Slide 3 the active slide. Insert and position the clip art image at the approximate position as shown in the image at right. Search for the image by typing **recycling** in the *Clip Art* text box.

⑭ Rename the presentation **15.3-GreenComputingPres-Your Name** and then close the presentation tab. Leave OneDrive open for the next topic.

App Tip

A slight delay may occur after typing or clicking outside a placeholder as the screen refreshes.

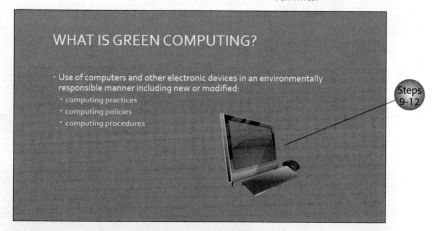

Steps 9-12

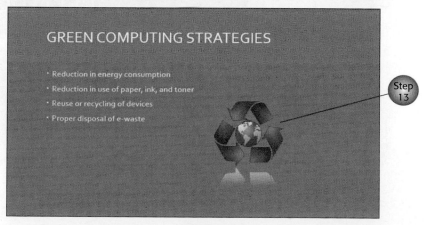

Step 13

Topic 15.4

Edit a presentation
in PowerPoint
Online

Editing a Presentation in PowerPoint Online

Open a presentation from OneDrive to view the slides in Reading view. Switch to editing mode by choosing the full-featured version of PowerPoint or PowerPoint Online from the EDIT PRESENTATION button near the top left of the Reading view window.

1. With OneDrive open, tap or click to insert a check mark in the check box at the top right corner of the **15.3-GreenComputingPres-Your Name** thumbnail, if the check box does not already have a check mark.

A check mark in the check box indicates the presentation is selected. Additional options display along the top of the OneDrive window when a presentation is selected.

2. Tap or click <u>Open</u> and then tap or click Open in PowerPoint Online at the drop-down list.

The presentation opens in Reading view, as shown in Figure 15.5.

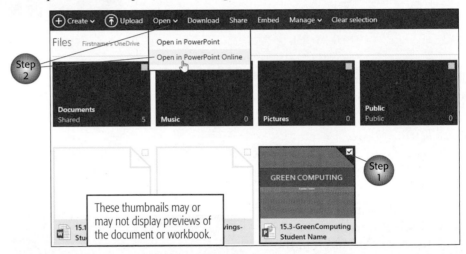

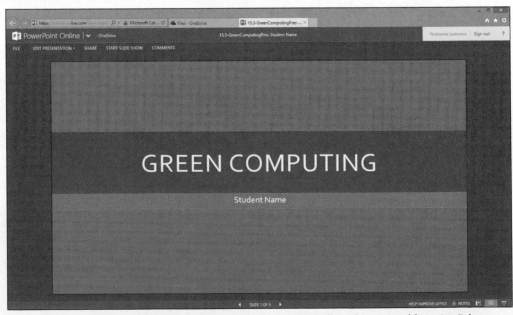

Figure 15.5 A presentation displays in Reading view in PowerPoint Online when opened from OneDrive.

③ Tap or click the Next Slide button (displays as right-pointing arrow) in the Status bar to view Slide 2 in the window.

④ Tap or click the Next Slide button again to view Slide 3.

⑤ Tap or click *EDIT PRESENTATION* and then tap or click *Edit in PowerPoint Online*.

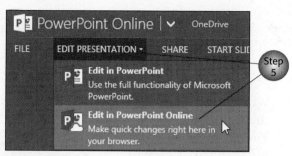

⑥ Make Slide 3 the active slide if necessary, and then type the following text on a new slide added to the end of the presentation using the *Title and Content* layout.

Slide title   **Green Computing Example**

Bulleted list **A desktop PC can use up to 1700 kilowatt hours per year if left on continuously**

Turning off or putting the PC in sleep mode when not in use can save over 1600 kilowatt hours per year for average use of 2 hours per day

This strategy can save $175 per year for electricity cost at 10.9 cents per kilowatt hour

⑦ Search for the image shown below using the keyword *power strip*. Insert and move the clip art to the approximate position as shown. Substitute another image if the one shown in the image below is not available.

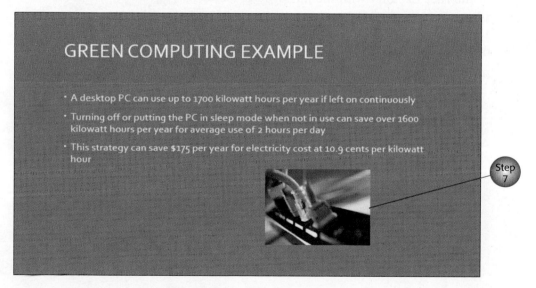

⑧ Close the presentation tab.

Quick STEPS

Edit a Presentation in PowerPoint Online
1. Open Internet Explorer.
2. Navigate to <u>onedrive.com</u>.
3. Sign in with Microsoft account.
4. Select presentation.
5. Tap or click <u>Open</u>.
6. Tap or click *Open in PowerPoint Online*.
7. View and/or edit as required.
8. Close presentation tab.

ALTERNATIVE method

Open a document, workbook, or presentation by tapping or clicking <u>Open</u> after selecting the thumbnail for the desired file and then choosing to open in the full-featured desktop version of Word, Excel, or PowerPoint.

Downloading and Uploading Files from and to OneDrive

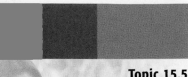

SKILLS

Download files from OneDrive

Upload files to OneDrive

Move files to a folder on OneDrive

oops!

No check box visible on thumbnail? Move the mouse over the thumbnail and a check box will appear.

You can copy files from your PC or mobile device to OneDrive for backup storage purposes; to access the files from another device instead of copying the files to a USB flash drive; or to share the files with other people. Conversely, you can download a file from OneDrive to your local PC or mobile device to view or edit the file offline.

1. With OneDrive open, tap or click to clear the check box for the **15.3-GreenComputingPres-Your Name** thumbnail, and then tap or click to insert a check mark in the check box for the **15.1-GreenComputing-Your Name** Word document.

2. Tap or click <u>Download</u> at the top of the OneDrive window.

3. Tap or click the down-pointing arrow on the Save button in the pop-up window at the bottom of Internet Explorer with the message asking if you want to open or save **15.1-GreenComputing-Your Name. docx** and then tap or click *Save as* at the pop-up list.

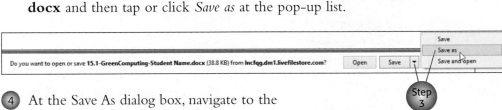

You can select and download multiple files in one operation. OneDrive creates a zipped folder when more than one file is downloaded.

4. At the Save As dialog box, navigate to the CompletedTopicsByChapter folder on your USB flash drive, create a new folder named *Ch15*, double-tap or double-click the *Ch15* folder, and then tap or click Save.

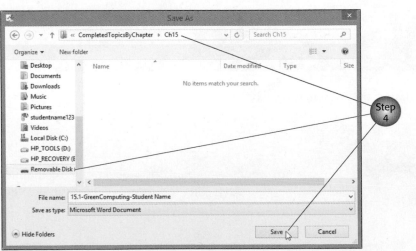

⑤ Close the pop-up window at the bottom of the Internet Explorer window.

⑥ Tap or click to clear the check mark in the check box for the **15.1-GreenComputing-Your Name** thumbnail to deselect the document.

⑦ Select and download the **15.2-EnergySavings-Your Name** workbook to the Ch15 folder by completing steps similar to those in Steps 1 through 6. Note that Ch15 will be the active folder at the Save As dialog box.

⑧ Select and download the **15.3-GreenComputingPres-Your Name** workbook to the Ch15 folder by completing steps similar to those in Steps 1 through 6. Note that Ch15 will be the active folder at the Save As dialog box.

In the next steps you will copy three pictures from your USB flash drive to your account storage at OneDrive.

⑨ Tap or click Upload at the top of the OneDrive window.

Step 9

⑩ At the Choose File to Upload dialog box, navigate to the Ch15 folder in Student_Data_Files, select the three files in the folder whose names begin with *PaintedBunting*, and then tap or click Open.

The three files are uploaded to your account storage in OneDrive. A progress message box appears in the window as the files are uploaded.

⑪ Select the three painted bunting picture thumbnails and deselect the thumbnail from Step 8 if the presentation is still selected.

⑫ Tap or click Manage and then tap or click Move to at the drop-down list.

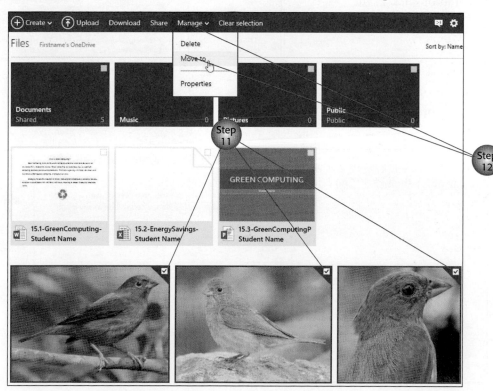

Step 11

Step 12

⑬ Tap or click *Pictures* in the folder list and then tap or click Move at the *The selected items will be moved to* dialog box. Leave OneDrive open for the next topic.

Sharing a File on OneDrive

OneDrive is an excellent tool for collaborating on documents when working with a team. A team leader can create or upload documents to OneDrive and then share the files with the team members who need them. An individual with shared access to a document receives an email with a link to the file. Changes to the file are made to the copy in OneDrive so that only one document, worksheet, or presentation has to be managed. Sharing a file on OneDrive is less cumbersome than sending a file as an email attachment and then trying to manage multiple versions of the same document.

Note: In this topic you will share a Word Online document with a classmate. Check with your instructor for instructions on with whom you should share the Word document. If necessary, share the document with yourself by using an email address other than your Microsoft account.

1. With OneDrive open, select the **15.1-GreenComputing-Your Name** document.

2. Tap or click <u>Share</u>.

3. Type the email address for a classmate in the *To* text box.

   More than one email address can be entered at the *To* text box. As with email messages, use a semicolon to separate email addresses.

4. Tap or click in the message box and then type **Please make your changes to the file accessed from this link.**.

5. Tap or click Share.

App Tip

You can share files with anyone with a valid email address—the recipient does not have to have a Microsoft account.

oops!

Security check requested? Sometimes a security check is required before sharing a file. If necessary, tap or click the link to the security check, type the characters you see in the box, and tap or click Continue. If necessary, close the Hotmail tab in Internet Explorer to return to OneDrive. You may need to re-enter the information in Steps 3 through 5 a second time including tapping or clicking Share again.

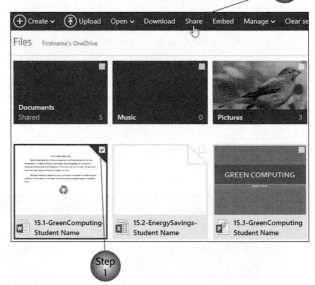

6   Tap or click Close when the classmate's name appears in the *Shared with* section.

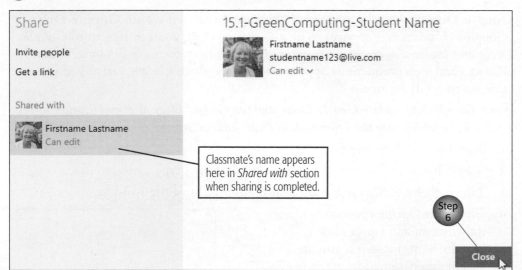

Share

Invite people

Get a link

Shared with

Firstname Lastname
Can edit

15.1-GreenComputing-Student Name

Firstname Lastname
studentname123@live.com
Can edit ⌄

Classmate's name appears here in *Shared with* section when sharing is completed.

Step 6

Close

Quick **STEPS**

Share a File on OneDrive

1. Sign in to OneDrive.
2. Select file.
3. Tap or click <u>Share</u>.
4. Type recipient's email address in *To* box.
5. Type message in message box.
6. Tap or click Share.
7. Tap or click Close.

7   Tap or click the down-pointing arrow next to OneDrive.

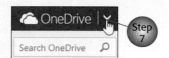

OneDrive | ⌄   Step 7

Search OneDrive 🔍

8   Tap or click the Outlook.com tile.

Step 8

Outlook.com   2   People   Calendar   OneDrive

9   With *Inbox* the active mail folder, open the message received from a classmate with the subject *Student Name has shared a document with you.*

10   If a security warning appears at the top of the message window saying that links in the message have been blocked for your safety, tap or click the <u>Show content</u> link.

11   Tap or click the link to the file in the message window.

The file opens in Word Online.

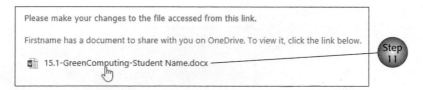

Please make your changes to the file accessed from this link.

Firstname has a document to share with you on OneDrive. To view it, click the link below.

📄 15.1-GreenComputing-Student Name.docx   Step 11

oops!

No message? Check the email address that the classmate used to make sure the correct address was typed. If an address other than hotmail or live was used, you need to go to another mail program to find the message with the link. In that case, sign out of OneDrive, launch your other mail program, and complete Steps 11 and 12. Note also that some mail programs may flag the message as Junk Mail. Check your Junk Mail folder if the message is not in your Inbox.

12   Close the document tab and close the Outlook.com tab.

13   Tap or click Shared in the left pane of OneDrive to view the file details of files shared by you and with you in the Content pane.

14   Sign out of OneDrive and close Internet Explorer.

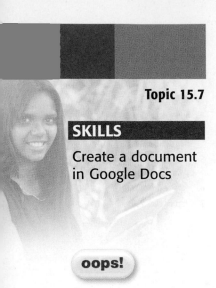

Topic 15.7

SKILLS

Create a document in Google Docs

oops!

Don't know your Google account? If you have a gmail.com email address, your email login is your Google account; otherwise, tap or click the Sign in with a different account link near the bottom of the sign in page to add a new account.

Creating a Document Using Google Docs

Google Docs is the web-based productivity suite offered within **Google Drive** (Google's cloud storage service). With a Gmail account, you can sign in to Google Drive and create a document, presentation, spreadsheet, form, or drawing. Gmail accounts and web productivity apps are free to use. With Google Drive you can store up to 5 GB for free.

Note: Google may update Google Drive and/or Google Docs after publication of this textbook, in which case the information, steps, and/or screens shown here may vary.

1. Start Internet Explorer from the Desktop.

2. Select the current text in the Address bar and then type **google.com**.

3. Tap or click the Sign in button near the top right of the window.

4. Type your Google account information and tap or click Sign in. Skip this step if you are automatically signed in when you go to the Google home page.

5. Tap or click the Apps button located near the top right of the screen (displays as a grid of black squares)

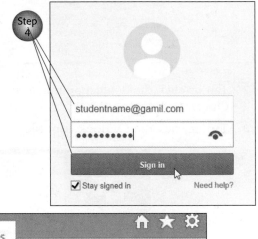

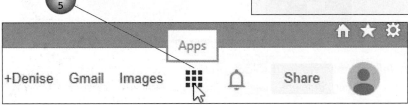

6. Tap or click *Drive* at the drop-down list.

7. Tap or click the Create button below *Drive* at the left side of the page and then tap or click Document at the drop-down list.

A document window opens similar to the one shown in Figure 15.6 on the next page.

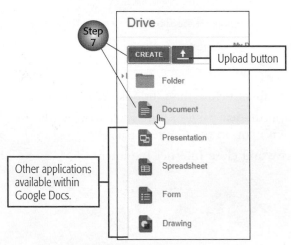

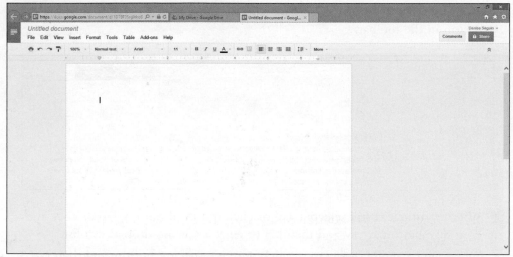

Figure 15.6 Google Docs document window. Google Docs automatically saves changes every few seconds to a document named *Untitled document*.

8 Type the following text in the document window using all of the default settings:

What is Cloud Computing?

   Cloud computing refers to a delivery model of software and file management using web-based service providers where all resources are online. Consumers of cloud computing services access software and files via a web browser. Some cloud-based services are free, with fees charged to access more storage or software features. (Tap or press Enter twice after the period.)

9 Tap or click the File menu and then tap or click <u>Rename</u> at the drop-down list.

You can upload and view a Word document in Google Docs.

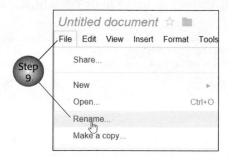

10 Type **15.7-CloudComputing-Your Name** in the *Enter a new document name* text box and then tap or click OK.

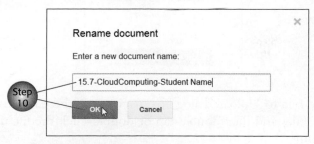

11 Select the title text *What is Cloud Computing?* and tap or click the Center align button in the toolbar.

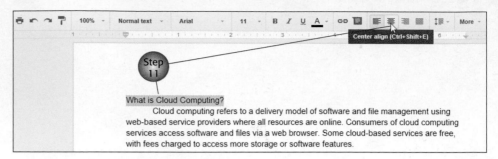

12 With the title text still selected, tap or click the Bold button, tap or click the Font Size button arrow, and then tap or click *14* at the drop-down list.

13 Select the paragraph text, tap or click the Line spacing button, and then tap or click *1.5* at the drop-down list.

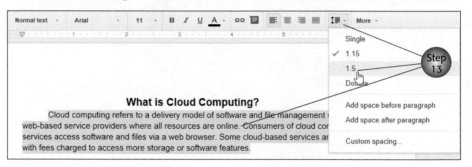

14 Deselect the text and position the insertion point on the blank line at the bottom of the document.

15 Tap or click the Insert menu and then tap or click <u>Image</u> at the drop-down list.

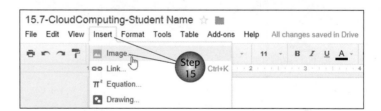

16 Tap or click the Choose an image to upload button in the middle of the Insert image dialog box.

17 At the Choose File to Upload dialog box, navigate to the Ch15 folder in Student_Data_Files and then double-tap or double-click the file named *Cloud-computing*.

18 Tap or click to select the image, resize the image using the resizing handles to approximately 2 inches wide by 1.5 inches tall, and then tap or click the Center align button.

19 With the image still selected, tap or click the Insert menu and tap or click Footnote at the drop-down list.

20 Type **Cloud computing image courtesy of Wikimedia Commons.** in the Footnote pane.

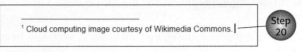

¹ Cloud computing image courtesy of Wikimedia Commons.

Step 20

21 Slide or scroll up to the top of the page.

22 If necessary, tap or click at the end of the paragraph to deselect the image.

23 Close the tabbed window for the document to return to Google Drive.

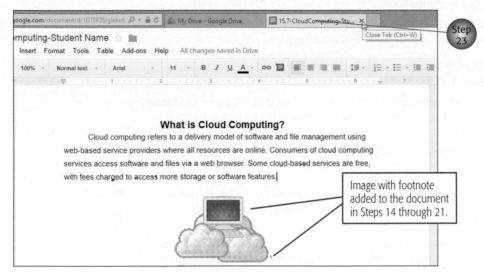

Close Tab (Ctrl+W)

Step 23

What is Cloud Computing?
Cloud computing refers to a delivery model of software and file management using web-based service providers where all resources are online. Consumers of cloud computing services access software and files via a web browser. Some cloud-based services are free, with fees charged to access more storage or software features.

Image with footnote added to the document in Steps 14 through 21.

Drive

CREATE

My Drive
Shared with me
Starred
Recent

My Drive

TITLE

☆ 15.7-CloudComputing-Student Name

Document in *My Drive* list.

24 Tap or click your account icon near the top right of the window and then tap or click Sign out.

25 Close the Internet Explorer window.

ALTERNATIVE method

You can also navigate to Google Drive by typing the URL **drive.google.com** or **docs.google.com**.

Quick **STEPS**

Create a Document in Google Drive
1. Open Internet Explorer.
2. Navigate to google.com.
3. Sign in with Google account.
4. Tap or click Apps button, then *Drive*.
5. Tap or click Create button, then Document.
6. Type, edit, and format document.
7. Tap or click File.
8. Tap or click Rename.
9. Type document name.
10. Tap or click OK.
11. Close window tab.

App Tip

Google Docs can be shared with others by selecting the file in the Google Drive list and using the Share button that appears above the file list.

 Check This Out

zoho.com

Go here to check out another popular web-based productivity suite. Register for a free account at Zoho to access several web-based applications including Writer (word processor), Show (presentation), and Sheet (spreadsheet).

Concepts Review

Topic	Key Concepts	Key Terms
Creating a Document Using Word Online	Cloud computing is a service provided by companies in which all software and storage resources are provided online. Cloud computing applications and files are accessed from a web browser. Word Online is the web-based version of Word accessed from OneDrive. Sign in to OneDrive with a Microsoft account and use Create to start a new document in Word Online. Documents created in Word Online are saved in the same file format as the desktop version of Word, meaning files can be transferred between editions. Word Online has fewer ribbon tabs and options than the desktop version of Word, and some features' functions will vary slightly.	Cloud computing Word Online
Creating a Worksheet Using Excel Online	Excel Online is suited for basic worksheets; use the desktop version of Excel for worksheets that need advanced formulas or editing. Worksheets created in Excel Online are saved in the same file format as the desktop version of Excel, meaning files can be transferred between editions. Like Word Online, Excel Online has fewer features than the desktop version and some functionality may vary.	Excel Online
Creating a Presentation Using PowerPoint Online	Use PowerPoint Online to create a presentation that does not need tables, charts, audio, video, or advanced animation or transition effects. Presentations created in PowerPoint Online are saved in the same file format as the desktop version of PowerPoint, meaning files can be transferred between editions. Graphic content in slides is limited to SmartArt graphics, pictures, or clip art.	PowerPoint Online
Editing a Presentation in PowerPoint Online	To open a presentation, select a presentation file's thumbnail and use Open from OneDrive. A presentation opens in Reading view from OneDrive. Use the EDIT PRESENTATION button and choose to open the presentation in either the desktop version of PowerPoint or PowerPoint Online.	
Downloading and Uploading Files from and to OneDrive	Select files that you want to download or manage in the Content pane. Use Download to copy a file from OneDrive to a folder on your local PC or mobile device. Use Upload to copy a file from your PC or device to your OneDrive storage. Manage provides options to move or delete selected files.	
Sharing a File on OneDrive	OneDrive can be used to collaborate with team members by sharing one copy of a file among several users. Select a file and choose Share to type the email address(es) for the individual(s) with whom you want to share a file. Individuals receive an email message with a link to the shared file on OneDrive.	

Topic	Key Concepts	Key Terms
Creating a Document Using Google Docs	The web-based productivity suite offered by Google is called Google Docs.	Google Docs
	Sign in to Google with a Gmail account, tap or click the Apps button, tap or click *Drive* in the drop-down list, and then tap or click the Create button to start a document, presentation, spreadsheet, form, or drawing.	Google Drive
	Google Drive is Google's online file storage service.	
	Google Docs saves changes automatically every few seconds to an untitled document.	
	Use the <u>Rename</u> option from the File menu to assign a name to the untitled document.	
	Use options from the Menu bar drop-down lists and toolbar to add elements, edit, and format a document.	

Multiple Choice

1. Tap or click this option at OneDrive to start a new document using Word Online.
   a. Files
   b. Create
   c. Document
   d. New

2. The ribbon in Word Online is exactly the same as the ribbon in the desktop version of Word.
   a. True
   b. False

3. Word Online and Excel Online documents and spreadsheets are transferable to the desktop versions of Word and Excel.
   a. True
   b. False

4. Excel Online is suited to a worksheet that needs advanced formulas and editing techniques.
   a. True
   b. False

5. Which of the following content can *not* be added to a slide using PowerPoint Online?
   a. Audio
   b. SmartArt
   c. Pictures
   d. Clip Art

6. PowerPoint Online contains the same set of transition options as the desktop version of PowerPoint.
   a. True
   b. False

7. Use this option in OneDrive to view a selected presentation.
   a. Create
   b. Preview
   c. View
   d. Open

8. A presentation opens in this view from OneDrive.
   a. Normal view
   b. Reading view
   c. Slide Show view
   d. Notes view

9. Use this option in OneDrive to create a copy of a document created in Word Online in a folder on your PC.
   a. Manage
   b. Upload
   c. Download
   d. New

10. Use this option to move a selected file to a folder in OneDrive.
    a. New
    b. Upload
    c. Download
    d. Manage

11. Use this option to send a link to someone else that lets him or her view a file you have stored on OneDrive.
    a. Move to
    b. Manage
    c. Share
    d. Create

12. A link to a file created by someone else is sent to you via this option.
    a. Instant message
    b. Facebook message
    c. Twitter message
    d. Email message

13. Google Docs are accessed from this Google tool.
    a. Google Mail
    b. Google Presentations
    c. Google Images
    d. Google Drive

14. A Google account mostly likely ends with this domain.
    a. gmail.com
    b. hotmail.com
    c. live.com
    d. gmail.net

Crossword Puzzle

ACROSS

3 Use this option to view slides in Reading view
5 Name for web-based version of Microsoft Word
8 Web-based productivity suite from Google
9 Sign in to this website to find Office Online apps

DOWN

1 Feature to let multiple people view or edit the same document
2 Create copy of file from PC to OneDrive
4 Workbook thumbnail displays in this OneDrive list
6 Create copy of file from OneDrive to PC
7 Selection you make at DESIGN tab in PowerPoint Online

Matching

Match the term with the statement or definition.

_____ 1. Where to find Word Online
_____ 2. Start new document, workbook, or presentation
_____ 3. Choose a theme
_____ 4. Check box at top right corner of file's thumbnail
_____ 5. Store a copy of a file from your PC at OneDrive
_____ 6. Collaboration tool
_____ 7. Gmail account

a. PowerPoint Online
b. Upload
c. OneDrive
d. Share
e. Create
f. Google Docs
g. Select document, workbook, or presentation

Project 1 Creating a Document with Word Online

Individual

Deliverable: Document in OneDrive

1. Start Internet Explorer and sign in to OneDrive.
2. Create a new Word document in Word Online with the file name **C15-Project1-Office365-Your Name**, and then type the following text in a new document using the default settings.

   What is Office 365?

   Office 365 is the subscription-based model for purchasing Office 2013. Office 365 Home Premium offers home users Office 2013 applications from the cloud for up to five PCs or Macs for $99 per year. At OneDrive, registered users have access to web-based editions for Word, Excel, PowerPoint, and OneNote. According to Microsoft, the additional benefits included with an Office 365 subscription are:
   - Web Apps for Outlook, Publisher, and Access
   - An extra 20 GB of storage at OneDrive for a total of 27 GB when added to the free 7 GB offered to all users
   - 60 Skype world minutes per month

   Because Office 365 is hosted by Microsoft as a cloud computing technology, the software will always be up to date and accessible from any device with an Internet connection. Office 365 is ideal for consumers with multiple devices who want to view or edit documents from any location at any time.

   Purchasing an Office 365 subscription is a new option that home users may want to consider. Keep in mind that to continue using the software, the subscription fee must be paid annually. Whether the annual fee will be less expensive over the long run depends on the number of traditional software licenses you would buy and whether you upgrade immediately to new releases. Finally, consider if you need the additional options that the subscription is offering. For example, if you do not use Access, Publisher, or Skype, the additional benefits are not meaningful to you.
3. Perform a spelling check and carefully proofread the document.
4. Apply formatting options of your choosing to improve the appearance of the document.
5. Search for and insert a suitable clip art image at the bottom center of the document.
6. Close the document tab.
7. Submit the project to your instructor in the manner she or he has requested.

Project 2 Creating a Worksheet in Excel Online

Individual

Deliverable: Workbook in OneDrive

1. With OneDrive open, create a new Excel workbook in Excel Online with the file name **C15-Project2-Office365CostComparison-Your Name**, and then set up the following information in a worksheet. You determine the worksheet layout.

Cost Comparison for Office 365 and Office 2013			
Subscription fee versus standard software license for each PC			
Office 365 Home Premium		Office 2013 Desktop PC	
Annual subscription fee	99	Office 2013 Home and Student license fee	139.99
Estimated years to subscribe	4	Number of licenses to buy	3
TOTAL COST FOR OFFICE 365		TOTAL COST FOR OFFICE 2013	
Difference in cost Office 365 versus Office 2013 Desktop licensing			

2. Create formulas to calculate the total cost of Office 365, the total cost of Office 2013, and the difference between the two models.
3. Apply formatting options of your choosing to improve the appearance of the worksheet.
4. Close the workbook tab.
5. Submit the project to your instructor in the manner she or he has requested.

Project 3 Creating a Presentation in PowerPoint Online

Individual

Deliverable: Presentation in OneDrive

1. With OneDrive open, create a new PowerPoint presentation in PowerPoint Online with the file name **C15-Project3-Office365Pres-Your Name**.
2. Select a theme and variant of your choosing.
3. On Slide 1 type **What is Office 365 Home Premium?** as the slide title and your name as the subtitle.
4. Add a minimum of two slides to the presentation with text that you compose that summarizes the main points from the text that you typed in Project 1. For example, in Slide 2 explain the cloud-based subscription model of purchasing Office 365, and in Slide 3 provide a list of what is included in Office 365 Home Premium.
5. Apply formatting options of your choosing to enhance the presentation.
6. Close the presentation tab.
7. Submit the project to your instructor in the manner she or he has requested.

Project 4 Download Project Files and File Management in OneDrive

Individual

Deliverable: Downloaded project files on USB; Word document with screen images of file lists in OneDrive

1. With OneDrive open, select and download **C15-Project1-Office365-Your Name** to a new folder named *Ch15* within ChapterProjectsWork on your USB flash drive.
2. Select and download **C15-Project2-Office365CostComparison-Your Name** to the Ch15 folder in ChapterProjectsWork.
3. Select and download **C15-Project3-Office365Pres-Your Name** to the Ch15 folder in ChapterProjectsWork.
4. Use Create to create a new folder named *C15-Projects*.
5. Select and move the files created from Projects 1, 2, and 3 to the C15-Projects folder.
6. With Files the active list displayed in OneDrive, create another new folder named *C15-Topics*.
7. Select and move the three files created from the topics in this chapter to the C15-Topics folder.
8. Capture an image of your desktop with *Files* active in your OneDrive account. Start a new Word document using the desktop edition of Microsoft Word (not Word Online) and paste the image.
9. Switch back to OneDrive, tap or click the C15-Projects folder tile and then capture an image of your desktop with the folder contents displayed. Paste the image into the Word document below the capture pasted at Step 8.
10. Switch back to OneDrive, tap or click *Files* to return to the previous list, tap or click the C15-Topics folder tile, and then capture an image of your desktop with the folder contents displayed. Paste the image into the Word document below the capture pasted at Step 9.
11. Save the Word document as **C15-Project4-OneDriveFiles-Your Name**.
12. Sign out of OneDrive and close Word.
13. Submit the project to your instructor in the manner she or he has requested.

Project 5 Creating a Spreadsheet in Google Docs

Individual

Deliverable: PDF of Google Docs document and spreadsheet

1. Sign in to Google Drive and create the spreadsheet shown in Figure 15.7.
2. Rename the spreadsheet as **C15–Project5–CloudStorage–Your Name**.
3. Use your best judgment to determine font size and shading color for cells.
4. When the spreadsheet is completed, complete the following steps to download a PDF copy of the Google Docs spreadsheet.
   a. At Google Drive, insert a check mark in the check box for the Project 5 file.
   b. Tap or click the More button located near the top of the Google Drive window (below Google search text box) and then tap or click <u>Download</u>.
   c. At the Convert and Download dialog box, tap or click <u>PDF</u> and then tap or click Download.
   d. Choose Save As at the pop-up window and save the PDF file in the Ch15 folder within ChapterProjectsWork. Close the pop-up window when completed.
   e. Deselect the file for Project 5 and select the file for the document created in Topic 15.7. Download a copy of the document as a PDF to the Ch15 folder within CompletedTopicsByChapter.
5. Sign out of Google Drive and close Internet Explorer.
6. Submit the project to your instructor in the manner she or he has requested.

	A	B	C	D	E
1	**Cloud Computing Storage Options**				
2	**Survey of Five Cloud Storage Service Providers**				
3	**Service Provider**	**Free storage (GB)**	**Upgrade storage (GB)**	**Annual upgrade fee**	**File size limit (GB)**
4	Microsoft SkyDrive	7	100	$50.00	2
5	Google Drive	5	100	$60.00	10
6	Dropbox	2	100	$120.00	
7	Box	5	Business users only	N/A	1
8	Mozy	2	50	$72.00	No limit

Figure 15.7 Project 5 Cloud Computing Storage Options Google Docs spreadsheet

Project 6 Sending Project Work to OneNote Notebook

Individual

Deliverable: New Page in shared OneNote notebook

1. Start OneNote and open the MyProjects notebook created in Chapter 4, Project 4.
2. Make CloudTech the active section and add a new page titled *Chapter 15 Projects*.
3. Send the following project documents to OneNote, selecting the Chapter 15 Projects page in the CloudTech section in the MyProjects notebook. For each project, open the file downloaded from OneDrive in the desktop version of the software to send the file to OneNote. Skip any projects you were not assigned to complete.
   a. **C15-Project1-Office365-Your Name** from Word.
   b. **C15-Project2-Office365CostComparison-Your Name** from Excel.
   c. **C15-Project3-Office365Pres-Your Name** from PowerPoint. Send the slides formatted as handouts with four slides horizontal per page and with your name in a header.
   d. **C15-Project4-OneDriveFiles-Your Name** from Word.
   e. **C15-Project5-CloudStorage-Your Name** from Adobe Reader or Microsoft Reader.
4. Close your MyProjects notebook in OneNote and close OneNote.
5. Submit the project to your instructor in the manner she or he has requested.

Glossary

A

absolute addresses addresses with a dollar symbol before the column letter and/or row number so that the address will not change when the formula is copied to another column or row

Accept button button used to send a message to a meeting organizer indicating acceptance of meeting request

Access 2013 database management application in Microsoft Office suite used to organize, store, and manage related data such as customers, vendors, employees, or products

Accounting Number Format a number format in Excel that adds a currency symbol, comma in thousands, and two decimal places

active cell the cell with the green border around its edges and in which the next entry will be stored or that will be affected by a command

Add Contact Picture control used in a Contact window to add a picture of a contact to display in the People card

Add Page icon in OneNote, the icon is used to add a new page in a section; pages organize note content within a section

Address bar the area in a web browser in which the web address (also called a URL) for a web page is viewed or typed

advanced search tools options provided by search engines that are used to narrow search results

Align Left paragraph alignment in which lines of text are aligned at the left margin; left edge of page appears even

Align Right paragraph alignment in which text is aligned at the right margin; right edge of page appears even

alignment guides colored vertical and horizontal lines that appear to help you align and place objects; also called smart guides

Angle Counterclockwise option from Orientation button in Excel that rotates text within the cell boundaries by 45 degrees

animation involves adding a special effect to an object on a slide that causes the object to move or change in some way during a slide show

Animation Painter button button used to copy animation effects from one object to another object

applications (apps) programs used on a PC by individuals to do tasks; also called apps

appointment any activity in your schedule that you want to keep track of, or be reminded of, including the day and time the activity begins and ends, the subject, and the location

argument parameters for a function formula that appear in parentheses

Attach File button button used to attach a file (such as a photo) to an email message in Outlook

Audio button button in Media group of INSERT tab used to add a sound clip to a slide in a presentation

Auto Fill Excel feature that enters data automatically based on a pattern or series that exists in an adjacent cell or range

Auto Sum button button in Excel used to enter SUM formula or access other functions

AutoComplete feature in software programs in which entries that match the first few characters that you type are displayed in a list so that you can enter text by accepting a suggestion; suggested entries are derived from prior entries that have been typed

AutoCorrect software feature that automatically corrects commonly misspelled words when you press the spacebar

AutoFit column width setting that adjusts the width of the column to accommodate the length of the active cell or longest entry in the column

AutoFormat software feature that automatically formats text or replaces text with symbols or special characters

AutoFormat as You Type feature that creates automatic bulleted or numbered lists depending on the character typed at the beginning of a line

B

Back button in web browser or other software that moves backward one page or screen

Backstage view view accessed from FILE tab used to perform file management; start a new document; display file information; manage document properties; and customize application options

banded rows shading applied to every other row to make it easier to read data organized in a table

Best Fit column width dialog box option in Access that adjusts column width to accommodate the length of the longest entry

Bibliography button button used to generate a Works Cited or References page in an academic paper

Bookmark this page in Google Chrome, the white star at the right end of the omnibox used to bookmark a frequently used web page

Bookmarks bar in Google Chrome, the bar below the omnibox that displays buttons for bookmarked web pages

Borders gallery feature that adds a border to a paragraph or cell

Bullets button button used to format text as a list with a bullet symbol at the beginning of each line; bullets are used for a list of items that are in no particular order

C

Calendar tool in Microsoft Outlook used to schedule, manage, and store appointments, meetings, and events

Calendar app Windows 8 app used to view your appointments and reminders stored in your Microsoft account calendar

Caption property Access field property used to store a descriptive title for a field; caption text displays as the column heading or control label in a datasheet or form

category axis horizontal axis in a column chart with the names or other labels associated with each bar; also called the x-axis

cell the intersection of a column with a row into which you type text, a value, or a formula in Excel

Cell Styles set of predefined formatting options that can be applied to selected cells in a worksheet

Cell Styles button button in Styles group of HOME tab in Excel used to apply a cell style to the active cell or range

Center paragraph alignment in which text is aligned centered between the left and right margins

Change PC settings Windows 8 option to customize Start screen

character formatting changing the appearance of characters

charms icons used to access system resources and commands

Charms bar five icons (called charms) that display when you swipe from the right edge of the screen or move the pointer to the top right or bottom right corner and slide up or down

citation reference to the source used for a quotation or for paraphrased text in an academic paper

Clear button button used in Excel to clear contents, formats, or both contents and formats in a cell or range

click and type feature in Word in which you can double-tap or double-click anywhere on a page and start typing

clip art gallery collection of royalty-free photos and illustrations provided by Microsoft for insertion into documents, workbooks, or presentations

Close button the red button with white X that displays at the top right of a desktop application window

Close Tab a control in a web browser that when tapped or clicked closes the tab for a web page

cloud computing software and computing services accessed entirely on the Internet

column chart a chart in which each data point is represented by a colored bar extending upward from the category axis with the bar height extending to its corresponding value on the value axis

Comma Style a number format option in Excel that inserts a comma in thousands and with two decimal places

comment a short note associated with text that provides explanatory information, poses a question, or provides feedback

Comments pane pane at right side of Slide pane in Normal view in which comments are added to a presentation in PowerPoint

Compact & Repair Database button button at Info tab Backstage view used to perform a compact and repair routine for the current database

Computer window window used to view devices attached to PC or mobile device

conditional formatting applies formatting options to cells only if the cells meet a specified criterion

Contextual tabs tabs that appear when an object is selected that contain commands or options related to the type of object

control object a rectangular content placeholder in a form or report

Convert to SmartArt button button used to convert existing text into a SmartArt graphic object

Copy button or menu option used to make a duplicate copy of a file or selected text

crawlers programs that read web pages and other information to generate index entries; also called spiders

Create a New Section tab the control used to add a new section to a OneNote notebook; sections are used to organize notes by category, topic, or subject

Customize and control Google Chrome in Google Chrome, the button at the end of the omnibox used to access the menu system

Cut button or menu option used to move a file or selected text to another location

D

database data stored in an organized manner to provide information to suit a variety of purposes

database management systems (DBMS) software that organizes and keeps track of large amounts of data

Date Navigator the calendars displayed above the Folder pane with which you can change the day that is displayed in the Appointment area in the Calendar

Decrease Decimal button button used in Excel to remove one decimal place from each value each time the button is tapped or clicked

Decrease Indent button button that moves a paragraph closer to the left margin in a document or left edge of a cell in a worksheet each time the button is tapped or clicked

Decrease List Level button button used to move text left to the previous indent position within a bullet list placeholder

Delete button or menu option used to remove a file, folder, selected text, or other object from storage or a document

Delete button button in the Cells group in the HOME tab of the Excel ribbon used for deleting cells, rows, or columns

Deleted Items Mail folder in which messages that have been deleted are moved; messages are not permanently deleted until Deleted Items folder is emptied

Design view Access view for an object in which the structure and/or layout of a table, form, query, or report is defined

Desktop the display with icons that launch programs and a taskbar used to switch between open programs

destination document document, worksheet, or presentation into which copied data is pasted, embedded, or linked

destination program program into which copied data is pasted, embedded, or linked

dialog box a box that opens in a separate window with additional options or commands for the related ribbon group as buttons, lists, sliders, check boxes, text boxes, and option buttons

Dialog box launcher diagonal downward-pointing button located at bottom right of a group in the ribbon that opens a task pane or dialog box

Display your bookmarks in Mozilla Firefox, the button used to access the bookmarks menu system

downloading the practice of copying content from a web page to your PC or mobile device

Draft view displays a document in Word without print elements such as headers or footers

E

editing the practice of making changes to a document after the document has been typed

electronic mail (email) the sending and receiving of digital messages, sometimes with documents or photos attached

endnotes explanatory text or source information for noted text placed at the end of a paper or report

Enforce Referential Integrity Access relationship option that verifies as a new record is added to a related table that a record with the matching field value in the joined field already exists in the primary table in the relationship

event an activity in the Calendar that lasts an entire day or longer

Excel 2013 spreadsheet application in Microsoft Office suite used to calculate, format, and analyze primarily numerical data

F

Favorites web pages you visit frequently that have been pinned to a list

field one characteristic about a person, place, event, or item in an Access table; for example, *Birthdate* is a field in a table about students

Field Properties pane lower half of Design view window for an Access table that contains field properties for the active field

field property a characteristic or attribute for a field that defines the field's data, format, behavior, or other feature

field value data that is stored within one field in a record; for example, *Jane* is the field value for a *FirstName* field in a record for Jane Smith

file a document, spreadsheet, presentation, picture, or any text and/or image that is saved as digital data

File Explorer window used to browse files and folders and perform file management routines

file name a series of characters you assign to a document, spreadsheet, presentation, picture, or other text or image that allows you to identify and retrieve the file later

FILE tab ribbon tab that opens the Backstage view in which file management commands and application options are located

Fill button button in Editing group of HOME tab in Excel used to access fill options

Fill Color button button used in Excel to add shading to the background of a cell

fill handle small green square at bottom right corner of active cell or range used to extend the pattern or series in adjacent cells

filter temporarily hides data that does not meet a criterion

Find feature that moves insertion point or cell to each occurrence of a word or phrase

Find & Select button button in Editing group in Excel's HOME tab with Find, Replace, and Go To options

Find bar in Google Chrome, the area used to locate words or phrases on a web page

Fit All Columns on One Page Excel Scaling option in Print tab Backstage view that shrinks the size of text until all columns fit in the page width

Fit All Rows on One Page Excel Scaling option in Print tab Backstage view that shrinks the size of text until all rows fit in the page height

Fit Sheet on One Page Excel Scaling option in Print tab Backstage view that shrinks the size of text to fit all columns and rows on one page

Flash Fill Excel feature that automatically fills data in adjacent cells as soon as a pattern is recognized

folder a name assigned to a placeholder or container in which you store a group of related files

font a typeface that includes the design and shape of the letters, numbers, and special characters

footer text that appears at the bottom of each page

footnotes explanatory text or source information at the bottom of the page in which the source is noted

foreign key a field added to a related table that is not the primary key and is included for the purpose of creating a relationship

form Access object used to enter, update, or view records generally one record at a time

Form view access view in which data is viewed, entered, and updated and is the view that is active when a form is opened

Format Painter clipboard option used to copy formatting options from selected text or an object to other text or another object

formatting changing the appearance of text

formula cell entry beginning with an equals sign (=) and followed by a statement that is calculated to determine the value displayed in the cell

Forward button in web browser or other software that moves forward or to the next screen

Forward button button used to send a copy of an email message to someone else

Freeze Panes Excel option that fixes column and/or row headings in place so that headings do not scroll off the screen

From Beginning button button in PowerPoint SLIDE SHOW tab used to start a slide show from slide 1

G

gallery in a drop-down list or grid, visual representations of options that can be applied to a selection

gestures actions or motions you perform with your finger, thumb, stylus, or mouse

Go To feature to move active cell to a specific location in the worksheet

Go To Date the dialog box used to type a date to display in the Appointment area of the Calendar

Go To Special dialog box with options for moving the active cell by various cell attributes

Google Chrome free web browser from Google that runs on PCs or Macs

Google Docs web-based free productivity suite offered by Google

Google Drive Google's cloud file storage service

H

hanging indent a paragraph in which the first line remains at the left margin but subsequent lines are indented

hard page break a page break that you insert before the maximum number of lines that can fit on the page has been reached

hard return creating a new paragraph in a document by tapping or pressing the Enter key

header text that appears at the top of each page

Help reference system used to look up information on Windows or Microsoft Office application features

hyperlinks addresses that when clicked or tapped on a touchscreen take you to a related Web page

I

Import Spreadsheet Wizard Access wizard used to perform an import of Excel data into a new table in Access

Inbox Mail folder into which received email messages are placed

Increase Decimal button button used in Excel to add one decimal place to each value each time the button is tapped or clicked

Increase Indent button button that moves a paragraph away from the left margin in a document or left edge of a cell in a worksheet each time the button is tapped or clicked

Increase List Level button button used to move text right to the next indent position within a bullet list placeholder

inline reply composing a reply to the sender of an email message from the Reading pane in Outlook

Insert button button in Cells group in HOME tab of Excel ribbon used to insert new cells, rows, or columns

Insert Caption feature used to add text above or below an image to label the image or add other descriptive text

Insert Options button button that appears in worksheet area after a new row or column has been inserted with options for formatting the new row or column

Internet (Net) a global network that links together other networks such as government departments, businesses, nonprofit organizations, educational and research institutions, and individuals

Internet Explorer (IE) the web browser included with Microsoft Windows

Internet Service Provider (ISP) a company that provides access to the Internet's infrastructure for a fee

J

Justify paragraph alignment in which extra space is added between words so that the text is evenly distributed between the left and right margins; both sides of the page appear even with this alignment

K

keyboard commands a key or combination of keys (such as Ctrl plus a letter) that performs a command

L

landscape page layout orientation in which the text is rotated to the wider side of the page with a 9-inch line length at the default margin setting

Layout Options button Gallery that provides options to control how an image and surrounding text interact with each other

Layout view Access view in which you edit the structure and appearance of a form or report

Libraries window window that displays when you tap or click File Explorer button that is used to view and or manage files

library name for a collection of places where files are stored that allows you to view all documents in one window

Line and Paragraph Spacing button button in Word's Paragraph group used to change the spacing of lines between text within a paragraph and the spacing before and after a paragraph

Line Break tapping or pressing Shift + Enter creates a new line in a document without creating a new paragraph (avoids the extra space created when Enter is used)

line chart a chart in which the values are graphed in a continuous line that allows a reader to easily spot trends, growth spurts, or dips in values by the line's shape and trajectory

links addresses that when clicked or tapped on a touchscreen take you to a related web page

Links dialog box dialog box opened from Info tab Backstage view in which linked objects can be updated or otherwise managed

live preview displays a preview of text or an object if the active option from a gallery is applied

local account user name and password used to sign in to Windows 8 that is stored on the local PC or device (not a Hotmail or live.com email address)

Location bar in Mozilla Firefox, the area in which you type or view a web address

Lock screen the screen that displays when a Windows 8 computer is locked to prevent other people from seeing programs or documents you have open

logging off action that closes all apps and files and displays the lock screen; also called signing out

lookup list a drop-down list in an Access field in which the list entries are field values from a field in another table or a fixed list of items

Lookup Wizard Access wizard used to assist with creating a lookup list

M

Mail tool within Microsoft Outlook used to send, receive, organize, and store email messages

Mark Complete option to retain a completed task in the To-Do list with a line drawn through the task entry indicating the task has been finished

Markup Area area at the right side of the screen in which comments and other changes made to a document are shown

meeting an appointment in your Calendar to which people have been invited to attend via email messages

meeting request email message sent to an invitee of a meeting that you have scheduled in Calendar

Merge & Center button button used in Excel that combines a group of cells into one and centers the content within the combined cell

Microsoft account email address from Hotmail.com or live.com used to sign in to Windows 8

Microsoft Excel Web App web-based version of Microsoft Excel accessed from SkyDrive that is similar to the desktop version of Excel but has fewer features; some functionality within features may also vary from the desktop version

Microsoft PowerPoint Web App web-based version of Microsoft PowerPoint accessed from SkyDrive that is similar to the desktop version of PowerPoint but has fewer features; some functionality within features may also vary from the desktop version

Microsoft Word Web App web-based version of Microsoft Word accessed from SkyDrive that is similar to the desktop version of Word but has fewer features; some functionality within features may also vary from the desktop version

Middle Align button alignment button in Excel that centers text vertically between the top and bottom edges of the cell

Mini toolbar toolbar that appears next to selected text or with the shortcut menu that contains frequently used formatting commands

mixed addresses cell addresses in a formula that have a combination of relative and absolute referencing

mouse pointing device that is used for computer input

Move Chart button button used to move a selected chart to a new chart sheet in a workbook

Mozilla Firefox free web browser from Mozilla foundation that runs on PCs or Macs

N

New (blank) record button button located in Record Navigation and Search bar used to add a new record in a table or form

New Appointment button button used to add a new activity into the appointment area in the Calendar

New Contact button button used to add a new contact to the People list

New Email button button used to create a new email message in Outlook

New folder button used to create a new folder on a device

New Meeting button button used to schedule a meeting in Calendar for which others are invited to attend

New Notebook Backstage view view used in OneNote to create a new notebook

New sheet button button that displays as a plus symbol inside a circle used to add a new worksheet to an Excel workbook

New Slide button button used to insert a new slide after the active slide in a presentation

New Tab a control in a web browser that is tapped or clicked to open a new tab in which a web page can be displayed

New Task button button used to create a new task in Outlook using the Task window

note container a box on a OneNote page that contains note content

Notebook Information Backstage view view that displays when the FILE tab is tapped or clicked with a OneNote notebook open

Notes pages handout option for printing slides in which one slide is printed per page with the slide printed in the top half of the page and the speaker notes or blank space when no notes are present in the bottom half of the page

Notes pane pane below Slide pane in Normal view in which speaker notes are typed and edited

Notification area area at right end of taskbar with icons to view or change system settings or resources such as the date and time or speaker volume

Numbering button button used to format text as a list with sequential numbers or letters used at the beginning of each line

O

object a picture, shape, chart, or other item that can be manipulated separately from text or other objects around it

Office 365 subscription-based edition of Microsoft Office 2013

omnibox in Google Chrome, the combined address bar and search bar

OneNote 2013 note-taking software application included in the Microsoft Office 2013 suite

OneNote notebook electronic notebook created in OneNote organized into sections and pages in which you store, organize, search, and share notes of various types

one-to-many relationship an Access relationship in which the common field used to join two tables is the primary key in only one table

one-to-one relationship an Access relationship in which two tables are joined on the primary key field in each table

Online Pictures button button used to search for an image to insert into a document from the clip art gallery, the Web, Flickr, or SkyDrive

Open a new tab in Mozilla Firefox, the button that displays with a plus symbol used to open a new tab for displaying a web page

Outline view displays content as bullet points

Outlook 2013 personal information management (PIM) software application included in the Microsoft Office suite

P

Page Borders button button used to choose a border that is drawn around the perimeter of a page

Page Layout view Excel view in which you can add or modify print options while also viewing the worksheet

Page Number button button used to insert page numbering in a header or footer

paragraph formatting changing the appearance of paragraphs

Paste button or menu option used to insert the copied or cut text or file

PDF document a document saved in Portable Document Format that is an open standard for exchanging electronic documents developed by Adobe systems

People tool in Microsoft Outlook used to add, maintain, organize, and store contact information for people with whom you communicate

People card contact information for an individual displays in a People card in the Reading pane

personal information management (PIM) program software programs that help you organize messages, schedules, contacts, and tasks

Photos app Windows 8 app used to view pictures from a local device and connected online services

Pictures button button used to insert an image stored on your PC or mobile device into a document, workbook, or presentation

pie chart a chart in which each data point is sized to show its proportion to the total in a pie shape

Pin site control in Internet Explorer that displays as a push pin used to add a web page to the Favorites list

Pin to Start Windows 8 option to add selected title to the Start screen

placeholder rectangular container on a slide in which text or other content is added

pointer the white arrow or other icon that moves on the screen as you move a pointing device

portrait page layout orientation in which the text on the page is vertically oriented with a 6.5-inch line length at the default margin setting

PowerPoint 2013 presentation application in Microsoft Office suite used to create multimedia slides for an oral or kiosk-style presentation

presentation application software used to create slides for an electronic slideshow that may be projected on a screen

Presenter view PowerPoint view for a second monitor in a slide show that displays the slide show along with a preview of the next slide, speaker notes, timer, and slide show toolbar

primary key the field that contains the data that uniquely identifies each record in the table

primary table table in an Access relationship in which the joined field is the primary key and in which new records should be added first

Print Layout view default view in Word that shows the document as it will appear when printed

Print Preview right pane in Print tab Backstage view that shows how a document will look when printed

private browsing a browsing option in which web pages visited do not appear in history list and cookies are automatically deleted when the private browsing window is closed

Protected view view in which a file is opened when the file is opened as an attachment from an email message or otherwise downloaded from an Internet source; file contents can be read but editing is prevented until Enable Editing is performed

pull quote a quote placed inside a text box in a document

Q

query Access object used to display information from one or more tables

Quick Access toolbar toolbar with frequently used commands located at the top left corner of each Office application window

Quick Tables predefined tables with sample data

R

range a rectangular group of cells referenced with the top left cell address, a colon, and the bottom right cell address (e.g., A1:B9)

Read Mode view displays a document full screen in columns or pages without editing tools such as the QAT and ribbon

Recommended Charts Excel 2013 feature that will show a series of customized charts that best suit a data selection; access Recommended Charts from the More Charts Quick Analysis option or from the INSERT tab

record all of the fields for one person, place, event, or item within an Access table

Recurrence dialog box in which you set up particulars of an appointment that repeats at the same day and time each week for a set period of time

Recycle Bin Window used to view and/or restore deleted files

Rehearse Timings feature in PowerPoint used to assign times to slides by running through a slide show with a timer and Recording toolbar active

relative addresses default addressing method used in formulas in which column letters and row numbers update when a formula is copied relative to the destination

Remove from List option to delete a task from the To-Do list

Rename button or menu option used to change the name of a file, folder, or tab

Replace feature that automatically changes each occurrence of a word or phrase to something else

Reply button button used to compose a reply to the sender of an email message

report Access object used to display or print data from one or more tables or queries in a customized layout and with summary totals

Report view Access view that displays a report's data without editing tools and is the view that is active when the report is opened

ribbon interface that displays buttons for commands organized within groups and tabs

Ribbon Display Options button button used to change the ribbon display to show tabs only or auto-hide the ribbon

Run button button in QUERY TOOLS DESIGN tab used to instruct Access to perform the query instructions and display the query results datasheet

S

Safely Remove Hardware and Eject Media option used to eject a USB flash drive from a PC or mobile device

Screen resolution display setting that refers to the number of picture elements, called pixels, that make up the image shown on a display device

scroll bars horizontal and/or vertical bars for navigating a larger file when a document exceeds the viewing space within the current window

scroll box a box between the two arrow buttons in a scroll bar that is used to navigate a larger file that cannot fit within the viewing area

Search bar in Mozilla Firefox, the area used to type search phrases to find web pages

search engine a company that searches Web pages to index the pages by keyword or subject and provides search tools to find pages

section break used to change page layout options for a section of a document instead of the entire document

Selection handle circle or square icons that appear around a selected object or at the beginning and end of text on touch-enabled devices that are used to manipulate the object or define a text selection area

Send to OneNote button button that appears on Taskbar with which you can embed a copy of content from a web page or other resource, capture a screen clipping, or create a new quick note in a OneNote notebook

Set Up Slide Show button button used in PowerPoint to configure options for a slide show such as setting up a self-running presentation

Settings button button used in OneNote to close an open notebook

shading color added behind text

Shapes button button used to select the type of shape to be drawn on a slide, in a document, or in a worksheet

Share Notebook Backstage view view used in OneNote to share the current notebook with another individual by providing an email address

Sheet tab bar bar above Status bar at bottom left of Excel window where sheet tabs are displayed

shut down process to turn off the PC or mobile device to ensure all Windows files are properly closed

sign out action that closes all apps and files and displays the lock screen; also called logging off

signature the closing containing your name and other contact information that is inserted automatically at the end of each email message

Simple Query Wizard Access wizard that assists with creating a new query by making selections in a series of dialog boxes

SkyDrive secure online storage provided by Microsoft that is available to users signed in with a Microsoft account

slide layouts content placeholders that determine the number, position, and type of content for a slide

slide master a slide master in PowerPoint is included for each presentation and slide layout and determines the default formatting of placeholders on each new slide

Slide Master view view in which global changes to the formatting options for slides in a presentation are made

slide pane the pane that displays the current slide in Normal view

Slide Show button button in PowerPoint Status bar used to start a slide show from the active slide

Slide Show view PowerPoint view in which you preview slides full screen as they will appear to an audience

Slide Sorter view PowerPoint view in which all of the slides in the presentation are displayed as slide thumbnails; view is often used to rearrange the order of slides

Slide Thumbnail pane pane at left side of Normal view in which numbered thumbnails of the slides are displayed

smart guides colored vertical and horizontal lines that appear to help you align and place objects; also called alignment guides

SmartArt graphics used to visually communicate relationships in lists, processes, cycles, and hierarchies, or to create other object diagrams

soft page break a page break inserted automatically by Word when the maximum number of lines for the page has been reached with the current page size and margins

Sort & Filter button button in Editing group of HOME tab in Excel used to sort and filter a worksheet

source data data that is selected for copying to be integrated into another program

source program program in which data resides that is being copied for integration into another program

Sparklines miniature charts embedded into a cell in an Excel worksheet

Spelling & Grammar feature in software applications that flags potential errors, displays suggestions for correction, as well as other options for responding to the potential error

spiders programs that read web pages and other information to generate index entries; also known as crawlers

spreadsheet application software in which you work primarily with numbers that you organize, calculate, and chart

Start screen Windows 8 user interface that displays tiles used to launch apps or other programs

Store app Windows 8 app used to download or buy new apps for your device

style set of predefined formatting options that can be applied to selected text with one step

style guide set of rules (such as MLA or APA) for formatting academic essays or research papers

Style Set a set of formatting options for each style based upon the document's theme, which is changed with options in the Document Formatting group of the DESIGN tab

subfolder a folder within a folder

Symbol gallery gallery used to insert a special character or symbol such as a copyright symbol or fraction character

T

tabbed browsing a feature in web browsers that allows you to view multiple web pages within the same browser window by displaying each page in a separate tab

table text organized within a grid of columns and rows

table in an Access database, all of the data for one topic or subject; for example, Customers is one table in a database that tracks invoices

table cell a box that is the intersection of a column with a row in which you type text in a table

Table Styles collection of predefined table formatting options that include borders, shading, and color

tag a short category or other label attached to an item such as a note in a OneNote page that allows you to categorize or otherwise identify the item

Tags Summary pane in OneNote, the pane opened from the Find Tags button that is used to navigate to the location of a tagged item

task pane a pane that opens at the right or left side of an application window with additional options or commands for the related ribbon group as buttons, lists, sliders, check boxes, text boxes, and option buttons

Taskbar bar along the bottom of the desktop used to switch between open programs

Tasks tool in Microsoft Outlook used to maintain a to-do list

template a document with formatting options already applied

Text Box button button used to create a text box in a document, workbook, or presentation

theme a set of colors, fonts, and font effects that alter the appearance of a document, spreadsheet, or presentation

thesaurus feature for looking up a word to find alternative words with a similar meaning; the word looked up can be changed to one in the results list

tiles square or rectangular icons on Windows 8 Start screen used to launch apps or programs

title slide first slide in a presentation that generally contains a title and subtitle

To-Do List list of tasks to be done that is maintained in Outlook

toggle buttons buttons that operate as on or off

touch keyboard onscreen keyboard that displays for touch-enabled devices

touchpad a flat surface on a laptop or notebook operated with your finger(s) as a pointing device

trackball a mouse in which the user manipulates a ball to move the on-screen pointer

transition a special effect that plays during a slide show as one slide is removed from the screen and the next slide appears

Trim Video button button used to modify a video clip to show only a portion of the clip by changing the start and/or end times in the Trim Video dialog box

Turn live tile off Windows 8 option to stop displaying headlines or other notifications from online services within a tile on the Start screen

U

Undo command that restores a document to its state before the last action was performed

uniform resource locator (URL) a text-based address used to navigate to a website; also called a web address

Unpin from Start Windows 8 option to remove selected tile from the Start screen

Update Links button button to tap or click to cause linked objects to be updated with new data; button appears inside Security Notice dialog box when destination document with linked objects set to automatically update is opened

user account the user name and password that you type to gain access to a PC or mobile device

user interface (UI) the icons, menus, and other means with which a person interacts with the OS, software application, or hardware device

V

value axis vertical axis in a column chart scaled for the values that are being charted; also called the y- or z-axis

variants a collection of style and color schemes in the PowerPoint theme family

W

web address a text-based address to navigate to a website; also called uniform resource locator (URL)

web browser a software program used to view web pages

Web Layout view displays document in Word as a web page

web page a document that contains text and multimedia content such as images, video, sound, and animation

Windows 8 Microsoft's Operating System for PCs released in October 2012

Word 2013 Word processing application in Microsoft Office suite used to create, edit, and format text-based documents

word processing application software used to create documents containing mostly text

Word Start screen the opening screen that displays when you start Microsoft Word 2013

WordArt text that is created and formatted as a graphic object

wordwrap feature in word processing applications in which text is automatically moved to the next line when the end of the current line is reached

workbooks spreadsheet files saved in Excel

Works Cited page at the end of an MLA paper or report that provides the references for the sources used in the paper

worksheets the grid-like structure of columns and rows into which you enter and edit text, values, and formulas in Excel

World Wide Web the global collection of electronic documents circulated on the Internet in the form of web pages; also called Web or WWW

Wrap Text button alignment option in Excel that wraps text within the cell's column width

Z

Zoom In button that displays as a plus symbol at bottom right corner of application window that increases magnification by 10 percent each time button is tapped or clicked

Zoom Out button that displays as a minus symbol at bottom right corner of application window that decreases magnification by 10 percent each time button is tapped or clicked

Zoom slider slider bar located near bottom right corner of an application window that is used to change the magnification option

Index

* Boldface page numbers indicate figures and tables.

A

Absolute addresses in Excel, 258, 259

Access 2013, 71, 353–377, 389–409
Best Fit in, 365
color scheme in, 74
column widths, adjusting, 364–365
control objects in, 405
database in
  compacting, repairing and backing up, 408–409
  encrypting, with password, 409
data in
  finding and replacing, 364–365
  importing Excel worksheet into, 420–423
datasheets in
  adding records using, 358–359
  editing and deleting records in, 360–361
  previewing, 376–377
data types in, **392**
Design view in, 370
  creating new tables in, 394–395
  creating queries using, 370–371
  modifying field properties in, 398–399
Enforce Referential Integrity in, 403
field properties in, 398
  formatting and data validation, 399
  modifying, in Design View, 398–399
Field Properties pane in, 398
fields in, 356
  adding, to existing tables, 396–397
  deleting, 397
  sorting by more than one, 367
field values in, 356

creating lookup list with, in another table, 400
files in, creating new, **390,** 390–391
finding and replacing data and adjusting column widths in, 364–365
foreign key in, 403
forms in, **354,** 356
  adding, editing and deleting records in, 362–363
  creating, using the Form Wizard, 405
  creating and editing, 404–405
Form view in, 404
Form Wizard in, creating forms using, 405
identifying database objects, **354,** 354–355
Layout View in, 404
lookup list in, 400
  creating, 400–401
Lookup Wizard in, 400
opening, 74
primary key in, 366
  assigning, 394–395
primary tables in, 403
queries in, **354,** 357
  calculated field in, 376–377
  Design view in creating, 370–371
  entering criteria to select records in, 372–373, **373**
  entering multiple to sort, 374–375
  exporting to Excel, 424–425
  Simple Query Wizard in creating, 368–369
records in, 356
  adding, editing, and deleting in a form, 362–363
  best practices for deleting, 361
  datasheets in adding, 358–359

editing and deleting using datasheets, 360–361
entering criteria to select, in queries, 372–373, **373**
entering multiple criteria to select, 374–375
sorting and filtering, 366–367
using find to move to, 363
relationships in
  creating, 403
  displaying and editing, 402–403
  one-to-many, 403
  one-to-one, 402
reports in, **354,** 356
  creating, editing, and viewing, 406–407
  grouping and sorting, 407
Simple Query Wizard in, creating queries using, 368–369
tables in, **354,** 355
  adding fields to existing, 396–397
  creating lookup list with field values in, 400
  creating new, 392
    in Design View, 394–395
  planning new, **390,** 390–391
  primary, 403
terminology in, 355–357
wildcard characters in, 375

Accounting number format in Excel, 229–230

Action Buttons, 331

Action Center flag, 20

Add Account dialog box, 128

Add Contact Picture dialog box, 142

Adding
in Access
  records in forms, 362–363
in Outlook
  contacts in, 142–143